W9-BEL-522

Computer Systems

FOURTH EDITION

J. Stanley Warford
Pepperdine University

JONES AND BARTLETT PUBLISHERS
Sudbury, Massachusetts
BOSTON   TORONTO   LONDON   SINGAPORE

World Headquarters

Jones and Bartlett Publishers
40 Tall Pine Drive
Sudbury, MA 01776
978-443-5000
info@jbpub.com
www.jbpub.com

Jones and Bartlett Publishers
Canada
6339 Ormindale Way
Mississauga, Ontario L5V 1J2
Canada

Jones and Bartlett Publishers
International
Barb House, Barb Mews
London W6 7PA
United Kingdom

Jones and Bartlett's books and products are available through most bookstores and online booksellers. To contact Jones and Bartlett Publishers directly, call 800-832-0034, fax 978-443-8000, or visit our website www.jbpub.com.

Substantial discounts on bulk quantities of Jones and Bartlett's publications are available to corporations, professional associations, and other qualified organizations. For details and specific discount information, contact the special sales department at Jones and Bartlett via the above contact information or send an email to specialsales@jbpub.com.

Production Credits

Acquisitions Editor: Timothy Anderson
Editorial Assistant: Melissa Potter
Production Director: Amy Rose
Production Assistant: Ashlee Hazeltine
Senior Marketing Manager: Andrea DeFronzo
V.P., Manufacturing and Inventory Control: Therese Connell
Composition: ATLIS Graphics
Cover Design: Kristin E. Parker
Assistant Photo Researcher: Bridget Kane
Cover and Title Page Image: © Styve Relneck/ShutterStock, Inc.
Printing and Binding: Malloy, Inc.
Cover Printing: Malloy, Inc.

Library of Congress Cataloging-in-Publication Data

Warford, J. Stanley, 1944-
    Computer systems / J. Stanley Warford.—4th ed.
        p. cm.
    ISBN-13: 978-0-7637-7144-7 (hardcover)
    ISBN-10: 0-7637-7144-9 (ibid.)
    1. Computer systems. I. Title.

QA76.W2372 2009
004—dc22   2009000461

6048

Printed in the United States of America
13 12 11 10 09   10 9 8 7 6 5 4 3 2 1

This book is dedicated to the memory of
my mother, Susan Warford.

Photo Credits

Preface

The fourth edition of *Computer Systems* offers a clear, detailed, step-by-step exposition of the central ideas in computer organization, assembly language, and computer architecture. The book is based in large part on a virtual computer, Pep/8, which is designed to teach the basic concepts of the classic von Neumann machine. The strength of this approach is that the central concepts of computer science are taught without getting entangled in the many irrelevant details that often accompany such courses. This approach also provides a foundation that encourages students to think about the underlying themes of computer science. Breadth is achieved by emphasizing computer science topics that are related to, but not usually included in, the treatment of hardware and its associated software.

Summary of Contents

Computers operate at several levels of abstraction; programming at a high level of abstraction is only part of the story. This book presents a unified concept of computer systems based on the level structure of Figure P.1.

The book is divided into seven parts corresponding to the seven levels of Figure P.1:

Level App7	Applications
Level HOL6	High-order languages
Level ISA3	Instruction set architecture
Level Asmb5	Assembly
Level OS4	Operating system
Level LG1	Logic gate
Level Mc2	Microcode

The text generally presents the levels top-down, from the highest to the lowest. Level ISA3 is discussed before Level Asmb5 and Level LG1 is discussed before

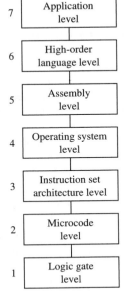

Figure **P.1**

The level structure of a typical computer system.

v

Level Mc2 for pedagogical reasons. In these two instances, it is more natural to revert temporarily to a bottom-up approach so that the building blocks of the lower level will be in hand for construction of the higher level.

Level App7   Level App7 is a single chapter on application programs. It presents the idea of levels of abstraction and establishes the framework for the remainder of the book. A few concepts of relational databases are presented as an example of a typical computer application. It is assumed that students have experience with text editors or word processors.

Level HOL6   Level HOL6 consists of one chapter, which reviews the C++ programming language. The chapter assumes that the student has experience in some imperative language, such as Java™ or C, not necessarily C++. Advanced features of C++, including object-oriented concepts, are avoided. The instructor can readily translate the C++ examples to other common Level HOL6 languages if necessary.

This chapter emphasizes the C++ memory model, including global versus local variables, function parameters, and dynamically allocated variables. The topic of recursion is treated because it depends on the mechanism of memory allocation on the run-time stack. A fairly detailed explanation is given on the details of the memory allocation process for function calls, as this mechanism is revisited at a lower level of abstraction later in the book.

Level ISA3   Level ISA3 is the instruction set architecture level. Its two chapters describe Pep/8, a virtual computer designed to illustrate computer concepts. The Pep/8 computer is a classical von Neumann machine. The CPU contains an accumulator, an index register, a program counter, a stack pointer, and an instruction register. It has eight addressing modes: immediate, direct, indirect, stack-relative, stack-relative deferred, indexed, stack-indexed, and stack-indexed deferred. The Pep/8 operating system, in simulated read-only memory (ROM), can load and execute programs in hexadecimal format from students' text files. Students run short programs on the Pep/8 simulator and learn that executing a store instruction to ROM does not change the memory value.

Students learn the fundamentals of information representation and computer organization at the bit level. Because a central theme of this book is the relationship of the levels to one another, the Pep/8 chapters show the relationship between the ASCII representation (Level ISA3) and C++ variables of type char (Level HOL6). They also show the relationship between two's complement representation (Level ISA3) and C++ variables of type int (Level HOL6).

Level Asmb5   Level Asmb5 is the assembly level. The text presents the concept of the assembler as a translator between two levels—assembly and machine. It introduces Level Asmb5 symbols and the symbol table.

The unified approach really comes into play here. Chapters 5 and 6 present the compiler as a translator from a high-order language to assembly language. Previously, students learned a specific Level HOL6 language, C++, and a specific von

Neumann machine, Pep/8. These chapters continue the theme of relationships between the levels by showing the correspondence between (a) assignment statements at Level HOL6 and load/store instructions at Level Asmb5, (b) loops and if statements at Level HOL6 and branching instructions at Level Asmb5, (c) arrays at Level HOL6 and indexed addressing at Level Asmb5, (d) procedure calls at Level HOL6 and the run-time stack at Level Asmb5, (e) function and procedure parameters at Level HOL6 and stack-relative addressing at Level Asmb5, (f) switch statements at Level HOL6 and jump tables at Level Asmb5, and (g) pointers at Level HOL6 and addresses at Level Asmb5.

The beauty of the unified approach is that the text can implement the examples from the C++ chapter at this lower level. For example, the run-time stack illustrated in the recursive examples of Chapter 2 corresponds directly to the hardware stack in Pep/8 main memory. Students gain an understanding of the compilation process by translating manually between the two levels.

This approach provides a natural setting for the discussion of central issues in computer science. For example, the book presents structured programming at Level HOL6 versus the possibility of unstructured programming at Level Asmb5. It discusses the goto controversy and the structured programming/efficiency tradeoff, giving concrete examples from languages at the two levels.

Chapter 7, Language Translation Principles, introduces students to computer science theory. Now that students know intuitively how to translate from a high-level language to assembly language, we pose the fundamental question underlying all of computing: What can be automated? The theory naturally fits in here because students now know what a compiler (an automated translator) must do. They learn about parsing and finite state machines—deterministic and nondeterministic—in the context of recognizing C++ and Pep/8 assembly language tokens. This chapter includes an automatic translator between two small languages, which illustrates lexical analysis, parsing, and code generation. The lexical analyzer is an implementation of a finite state machine. What could be a more natural setting for the theory?

Level OS4   Level OS4 consists of two chapters on operating systems. Chapter 8 is a description of process management. Two sections, one on loaders and another on trap handlers, illustrate the concepts with the Pep/8 operating system. Five instructions have unimplemented opcodes that generate software traps. The operating system stores the process control block of the user's running process on the system stack, and the interrupt service routine interprets the instruction. The classic state transition diagram for running and waiting processes in an operating system is thus reinforced with a specific implementation of a suspended process. The chapter concludes with a description of concurrent processes and deadlocks. Chapter 9 describes storage management, both main memory and disk memory.

Level LG1   Level LG1 uses two chapters to present combinational and sequential circuits. Chapter 10 emphasizes the importance of the mathematical foundation of computer science by starting with the axioms of Boolean algebra. It shows the relationship between Boolean algebra and logic gates, and then describes some common

SSI and MSI logic devices, including a complete logic design of the Pep/8 ALU. Chapter 11 illustrates the fundamental concept of a finite state machine through the state transition diagrams of sequential circuits. It concludes with a description of common computer subsystems such as bidirectional buses, memory chips, and two-port memory banks.

Level Mc2   Chapter 12 describes the microprogrammed control section of the Pep/8 CPU. It gives the control sequences for a few sample instructions and addressing modes and provides a large set of exercises for the others. It also presents concepts of load/store architectures contrasting the MIPS RISC machine with the Pep/8 CISC machine. It concludes with performance issues by describing cache memories, pipelining, dynamic branch prediction, and superscalar machines.

Use in a Course

This book offers such broad coverage that instructors may wish to omit some of the material when designing the course. Chapters 1–5 should be considered core. Selections can be made from Chapters 6 through 12.

In the book, Chapters 1–5 must be covered sequentially. Chapters 6 (Compiling to the Assembly Level) and 7 (Language Translation Principles) can be covered in either order. I often skip ahead to Chapter 7 to initiate a large software project, writing an assembler for a subset of Pep/8 assembly language, so students will have sufficient time to complete it during the semester. Chapter 11 (Sequential Circuits) is obviously dependent on Chapter 10 (Combinational Circuits), but neither depends on Chapter 9 (Storage Management), which may be omitted. Figure P.2, a chapter dependency graph, summarizes the possible chapter omissions.

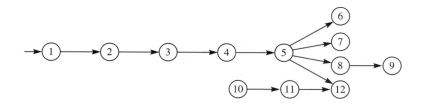

Figure **P.2**

A chapter dependency graph.

Support Materials

The support material listed below is available from the publisher's website

http://www.jbpub.com/catalog/9780763771447/ and in CD-ROM format.

Pep/8 Assembler and Simulator   The Pep/8 machine is available for MS Windows, Mac OS X, and Unix/Linux systems. The assembler features

- an integrated text editor;

- error messages in red type that are inserted within the source code at the place where the error is detected;

- student-friendly machine language object code in hexadecimal format;

- the ability to code directly in machine language, bypassing the assembler; and

- the ability to redefine the mnemonics for the unimplemented opcodes that trigger synchronous traps.

The simulator features

- simulated ROM that is not altered by load instructions;

- a small operating system burned into simulated ROM that includes a loader and a trap handler system;

- an integrated debugger that allows for break points, single-step execution, CPU tracing, and memory tracing;

- the option to trace an application, the loader, or the operating system in any combination;

- a user-defined upper limit on the statement execution count to recover from endless loops; and

- the ability to modify the operating system by designing new trap handlers for the unimplemented opcodes.

Pep/8 CPU Simulator   A CPU simulator, also available for MS Windows, Mac OS X, and Unix/Linux systems, is available for use in the computer organization course. The CPU simulator features

- color-coded display paths that trace the data flow depending on control signals to the multiplexers,

- a single-cycle mode of operation with GUI inputs for each control signal and instant visual display of the effects of the signal, and

- a multi-cycle mode of operation with an integrated text editor for the student to write Mc2 microcode sequences and execute them to implement ISA3 instructions.

Lecture Slides   A complete set of about 50 to 125 lecture slides per chapter is available in Keynote and PDF format. The slides include every figure from the text as well as summary information, often in bullet point format. They do not, however, include many examples and leave room for instructor presentation of examples and instructor-led discussions.

Exam Handouts   A set of exam handouts, including reference information such as the ASCII table, instruction set tables, etc., are provided for reference during exams and study sessions. These are available to instructors who adopt the book.

Digital Circuit Labs   A set of six digital circuit labs provides hands-on experience with physical breadboards. The labs illustrate the combinational and sequential devices from Chapters 10 and 11 with many circuits that are not in the book. Students learn practical digital design and implementation concepts that are beyond the scope of the text itself. They follow the sequence of topics from the text, beginning with combinational circuits and progressing through sequential circuits and ALUs.

Solutions Manual   Solutions to selected exercises are provided in an appendix. Solutions to the remaining exercises are available to instructors who adopt the book. For security reasons, the solutions are available directly from the publisher. For information please contact your Jones and Bartlett Publishers Representative at 1-800-832-0034.

Changes to the Fourth Edition

The changes to the third edition were extensive, including the use of Pep/8, which was a complete redesign of the Pep/7 architecture. The pedagogical features of Pep/8 have been well received by users of the previous editions, and the Pep/8 architecture is retained in the fourth edition. Improvements are in every chapter of this edition, and while they are too numerous to list the major ones are as follows:

- *Improved C++ review*—The C++ memory model introduced in the third edition is expanded and presented more systematically from the beginning. The memory allocation figures are more realistic and consistent for the main function, showing allocation for its return address and returned value. A major irritant is removed by renaming all variables previously named i. The confusion arises when programs are translated to Pep/8 assembly language, which uses the letter i to indicate immediate addressing.

- *Improved character code coverage*—A description of the Unicode character set replaces the treatment of EBCDIC.

- *Trace tags*—The Pep/8 assembler and simulator includes a new symbolic trace feature that displays global variables and the run-time stack in real time as the user single steps through the program. Use of the new feature requires the programmer to place trace tags in the comment field of certain assembly language statements that are ignored by the translator but used by the debugger. A big, serendipitous advantage of trace tags is the documentation they force on the programmer. To use the debugger, the student must specify in the comment field precisely which variables are allocated on the run-time stack and in which order. The assembler verifies that the number of bytes allocated matches the number of bytes required by the list of variables. The documentation advantage of trace tags is so great that the text now describes the trace tag syntax and includes trace tags in every assembly language program in the book and in the solutions manual.

- *Improved language translation coverage*—Chapter 7 on Language Translation Principles in the previous edition assumes no object-oriented knowledge. This edition assumes students have learned basic object-oriented design principles and presents the lexical analysis programs using class composition, inheritance, and polymorphic dispatch complete with UML diagrams.

- *New project problems*—This edition has two project problems, a new one in Chapter 6 to write a Pep/8 machine simulator and a revised one in Chapter 7 to write a Pep/8 assembler. The projects require the development of programs with hundreds of lines of code. Both problems have many parts, each one a milestone as more functionality is added to the application. They serve the dual purpose of (a) giving students experience in writing nontrivial programs and (b) reinforcing the computer systems concepts that is the problem domain of the course.

- *Improved RAID coverage*—This edition has more extensive coverage of RAID disk systems. The difference between RAID levels 01 and 10 is expanded with new figures and a new quantitative analysis exercise.

- *Improved MIPS coverage*—The MIPS coverage is expanded and has a more systematic comparison of Pep/8 as a CISC architecture versus MIPS as a RISC architecture. The new MIPS section describes all five addressing modes with a new instruction set table. Figures of the data section of the MIPS machine now include the data paths and multiplexers required for the pseudodirect addressing mode. Explicitly named control signals using the same syntax as the control signals for Pep/8 provide a more concise and detailed description of the implementation of MIPS instructions.

Unique Features

Computer Systems has several unique features that differentiate it from other computer systems, assembly language, and computer organization texts.

- *Conceptual approach*—Many textbooks attempt to stay abreast of the field by including the latest technological developments; for example, communication protocol specifications for the newest peripheral devices. They typically have how-this-device-works narrative explanations throughout. This text eschews such material in favor of selecting only those computing concepts that are fundamental, the mastery of which provides a basis for understanding both current and future technology. For instance, it is more important for students to master the concept of the space/time tradeoff by experiencing it with digital circuit design problems rather than simply reading about it in general. As another example, the concept of hardware parallelism is mastered best by learning how to combine cycles in a microcode implementation of an ISA instruction.

- *Problem solving emphasis*—Students retain less when they only hear about or read about a subject. They retain more when they experience the subject. *Computer Systems* reflects this emphasis by the nearly four hundred problem-solving exercises at the end of the chapters, many with multiple parts. Rather than ask the student to repeat verbiage from the text, the exercises require quantitative answers, or the analysis or design of a program or digital circuit at one of the levels of abstraction of the system.

- *Consistent machine model*—The Pep/8 machine, a small CISC computer, is the vehicle for describing all the levels of the system. Students clearly see the relation between the levels of abstraction because they either program or design digital circuits for that machine at *all* the levels. For example, when they design an ALU component at the LG1 level, they know where the ALU fits in the implementation of the ISA3 level. They learn the difference between an optimizing and nonoptimizing compiler by translating C++ programs to assembly language as a compiler would. Using the same machine model for these learning activities at the different levels is a huge productivity advantage because the model is consistent from top to bottom. However, *Computer Systems* also presents the MIPS machine to contrast RISC design principles with microprogrammed CISC designs.

- *Complete program examples*—Many computer organization and assembly language texts suffer from the code fragment syndrome. The memory model, addressing modes, and input/output features of Pep/8 enable students to write complete programs that can be easily executed and tested without resorting just to code fragments. Real machines, and especially RISC machines, have complex function calling protocols involving issues like register allocation, register spillover, and memory alignment constraints. Pep/8 is one of the few pedagogic machines—perhaps the only one—that permits students to write complete programs with input and output using: global and local variables, global and local arrays, call by value and by reference, array parameters, switch statements with jump tables, recursion, linked structures with pointers and the heap. Assignments to write complete programs further the goal of learning by doing, as opposed to learning by reading code fragments.

- *Integration of theory and practice*—Some readers observe that Chapter 7 on language translation principles is unusual in a computer systems book. This observation is a sad commentary on the gulf between theory and practice in computer science curricula and perhaps in the field of computer science itself. Because the text presents the C++ language at Level HOL6, assembly language at Level Asmb5, and machine language at Level ISA3, and has as one goal understanding the relationship between the levels, a better question is, "How could a chapter on language translation principles *not* be included?" *Computer Systems* incorporates theory whenever possible to bolster practice. For example, it presents Boolean algebra as an axiomatic system with exercises for proving theorems.

- *Breadth and depth*—The material in Chapters 1–6 is typical for books on computer systems or assembly language programming, and that in Chapters 8–12 for computer organization. Combining this breadth of material into one volume is unique and permits a consistent machine model to be used throughout the levels of abstraction of the complete system. Also unique is the depth of coverage at the digital circuit LG1 level, which takes the mystery out of the component parts of the CPU. For example, *Computer Systems* describes the implementations of the multiplexers, adders, ALUs, registers, memory subsystems, and bidirectional busses for the Pep/8 CPU. Students learn the implementation down to the logic gate level, with no conceptual holes in the grand narrative that would otherwise have to be taken on faith without complete understanding.

Computer Systems answers the question, "What is the place of assembly language programming and computer organization in the computer science curriculum?" It is to provide a depth of understanding about the architecture of the ubiquitous von Neumann machine. This text retains its unique goal to provide a balanced overview of all the main areas of the field, including the integration of software and hardware and the integration of theory and practice.

Computing Curricula 2001

The ACM and IEEE Computer Society have established Curriculum 2001 guidelines for Computer Science. The guidelines present a taxonomy of bodies of knowledge with a specified core. *Computer Systems* applies to the category Architecture and Organization (AR) and covers practically all of the core topics from the AR body of knowledge. The AR core areas from the preliminary report, together with the chapters from this text that cover each area, are:

AR1. Digital logic and digital systems, Chapters 10, 11, 12

AR2. Machine level representation of data, Chapter 3

AR3. Assembly level machine organization, Chapters 4, 5, 6

AR4. Memory system organization and architecture, Chapters 9, 11

AR5. Interfacing and communication, Chapters 8, 9

AR6. Functional organization, Chapters 11, 12

AR7. Multiprocessing and alternative architectures, Chapter 8

Acknowledgments

Pep/1 had 16 instructions, one accumulator, and one addressing mode. Pep/2 added indexed addressing. John Vannoy wrote both simulators in ALGOL W. Pep/3 had 32 instructions and was written in Pascal as a student software project by Steve Dimse, Russ Hughes, Kazuo Ishikawa, Nancy Brunet, and Yvonne Smith. In an early review, Harold Stone suggested many improvements to the Pep/3 architecture that were incorporated into Pep/4 and carried into later machines. Pep/4 had special stack instructions, simulated ROM, and software traps. Pep/5 was a more orthogonal design, allowing any instruction to use any addressing mode. John Rooker wrote the Pep/4 system and an early version of Pep/5. Gerry St. Romain implemented a MacOS version and an MS-DOS version. Pep/6 simplified indexed addressing and included the complete set of conditional branch instructions. John Webb wrote the trace facility using the BlackBox development system. Pep/7 increased the installed memory from 4 MBytes to 32 MBytes. Pep/8 increased the number of addressing modes from four to eight, and the installed memory to 64 KBytes. The GUI version of the Pep/8 assembler and simulator is implemented in C++ and maintained by teams of students using the Qt development system. The teams included Deacon Bradley, Jeff Cook, Nathan Counts, Stuartt Fox, Dave Grue, Justin Haight, Paul Harvey, Hermi Heimgartner, Matt Highfield, Trent Kyono, Malcolm Lipscomb, Brady Lockhart, Adrian Lomas, Ryan Okelberry, Thomas Rampelberg, Mike Spandrio, Jack Thomason, Daniel Walton, Di Wang, Peter Warford, and Matt Wells. Ryan Okelberry also wrote the Pep/8 CPU simulator. Luciano d'Ilori wrote the command line version of the assembler.

More than any other book, Tanenbaum's *Structured Computer Organization* has influenced this text. This text extends the level structure of Tanenbaum's book by adding the high-order programming level and the applications level at the top.

The following reviewers of the manuscript and users of the previous edition shaped the final product significantly: Wayne P. Bailey, Jim Bilitski, Fadi Deek, William Decker, Peter Drexel, Gerald S. Eisman, Victoria Evans, David Garnick, Ephraim P. Glinert, Dave Hanscom, Michael Hennessy, Michael Johnson, Andrew Malton, Robert Martin, Richard H. Mercer, Randy Molmen, John Motil, Peter Ng, Bernard Nudel, Carolyn Oberlink, Wolfgang Pelz, James F. Peters III, James C. Pleasant, Eleanor Quinlan, Glenn A. Richard, David Rosser, Gerry St. Romain, Harold S. Stone, J. Peter Weston, and Norman E. Wright. Joe Piasentin provided artistic consultation. Two people who influenced the design of Pep/8 significantly are Myers Foreman, who was a source of many ideas for the instruction set, and

Douglas Harms, who suggested among other improvements the MOVSPA instruction that makes possible the passing of local variables by reference.

At Jones and Bartlett Publishers, Acquisitions Editor Tim Anderson, Production Director Amy Rose, and Editorial Assistant Melissa Potter provided valuable support and were a true joy to work with. Kristin Parker captured the flavor of the book with her striking cover design.

I am fortunate to be at an institution that is committed to excellence in undergraduate education. Pepperdine University, in the person of Ken Perrin, provided the creative environment and the professional support in which the idea behind this project was able to evolve. My wife, Ann, provided endless personal support. To her I owe an apology for the time this project has taken, and my greatest thanks.

Stan Warford
Malibu, California

Contents

Preface   **v**

LEVEL 7   APPLICATION   1

Chapter 1   Computer Systems   3

1.1   Levels of Abstraction   3
Abstraction in Art   4
Abstraction in Documents   6
Abstraction in Organizations   7
Abstraction in Machines   8
Abstraction in Computer Systems   8

1.2   Hardware   10
Input Devices   12
Output Devices   15
Main Memory   16
Central Processing Unit   16

1.3   Software   17
Operating Systems   19
Software Analysis and Design   20

1.4   Database Systems   22
Relations   22
Queries   23
Structure of the Language   26

Summary   27
Exercises   28

LEVEL 6   HIGH-ORDER LANGUAGE   31

Chapter 2   C++   33

2.1   Variables   33
The C++ Compiler   33

Machine Independence   34
The C++ Memory Model   35
Global Variables and Assignment Statements   36
Local Variables   39

2.2   Flow of Control   41
The If/Else Statement   41
The Switch Statement   43
The While Loop   44
The Do Loop   45
Arrays and the For Loop   46

2.3   Functions   48
Void Functions and Call-By-Value Parameters   48
Functions   50
Call-By-Reference Parameters   51

2.4   Recursion   55
A Factorial Function   56
Thinking Recursively   59
Recursive Addition   60
A Binomial Coefficient Function   61
Reversing the Elements of an Array   68
Towers of Hanoi   68
Mutual Recursion   72
The Cost of Recursion   73

2.5   Dynamic Memory Allocation   74
Pointers   74
Structures   76
Linked Data Structures   77

Summary   80
Exercises   81

LEVEL 3   INSTRUCTION SET ARCHITECTURE   87

Chapter 3   Information Representation   89

3.1   Unsigned Binary Representation   89
Binary Storage   90
Integers   91
Base Conversions   93
Range for Unsigned Integers   94
Unsigned Addition   95
The Carry Bit   96

3.2   Two's Complement Binary Representation   97
    Two's Complement Range   99
    Base Conversions   101
    The Number Line   102
    The Overflow Bit   105
    The Negative and Zero Bits   106

3.3   Operations in Binary   107
    Logical Operators   107
    Register Transfer Language   108
    Arithmetic Operators   109
    Rotate Operators   111

3.4   Hexadecimal and Character Representations   112
    Hexadecimal   112
    Base Conversions   113
    Characters   115

3.5   Floating Point Representation   118
    Binary Fractions   118
    Excess Representations   120
    The Hidden Bit   121
    Special Values   122
    The IEEE 754 Floating Point Standard   127

3.6   Representations Across Levels   130
    Alternative Representations   134
    Models   135

Summary   138

Exercises   139

Chapter 4   **Computer Architecture**   **149**

4.1   Hardware   150
    Central Processing Unit (CPU)   150
    Main Memory   151
    Input Device   153
    Output Device   153
    Data and Control   153
    Instruction Format   154

4.2   Direct Addressing   157
    The Stop Instruction   158
    The Load Instruction   158
    The Store Instruction   159

The Add Instruction   160
The Subtract Instruction   161
The And and Or Instructions   162
The Invert and Negate Instructions   164
The Load Byte and Store Byte Instructions   165
The Character Input and Ouput Instructions   166

4.3   von Neumann Machines   168
The von Neumann Execution Cycle   168
A Character Output Program   170
von Neumann Bugs   174
A Character Input Program   175
Converting Decimal to ASCII   176
A Self-Modifying Program   177

4.4   Programming at Level ISA3   179
Read-Only Memory   181
The Pep/8 Operating System   182
Using the Pep/8 System   183

Summary   185

Exercises   185

LEVEL 5   ASSEMBLY   189

Chapter 5   Assembly Language   191

5.1   Assemblers   191
Instruction Mnemonics   192
Pseudo-Operations   194
The .ASCII and .END Pseudo-ops   195
Assemblers   196
The .BLOCK Pseudo-op   197
The .WORD and .BYTE Pseudo-ops   198
Using the Pep/8 Assembler   200
Cross Assemblers   201

5.2   Immediate Addressing and the Trap Instructions   202
Immediate Addressing   202
The DECI, DECO, and BR Instructions   203
The STRO Instruction   206
Interpreting Bit Patterns   207
Disassemblers   209

5.3   Symbols   211
A Program with Symbols   211
A von Neumann Illustration   213

5.4   Translating from Level HOL6   214
      The cout Statement   215
      Variables and Types   217
      Global Variables and Assignment Statements   218
      Type Compatibility   221
      Pep/8 Symbol Tracer   223
      The Shift and Rotate Instructions   224
      Constants and .EQUATE   226
      Placement of Instructions and Data   228

      Summary   229
      Exercises   230

Chapter 6   Compiling to the Assembly Level   237

6.1   Stack Addressing and Local Variables   237
      Stack-Relative Addressing   238
      Accessing the Run-Time Stack   239
      Local Variables   241

6.2   Branching Instructions and Flow of Control   244
      Translating the If Statement   245
      Optimizing Compilers   246
      Translating the If/Else Statement   247
      Translating the While Loop   249
      Translating the Do Loop   250
      Translating the For Loop   252
      Spaghetti Code   253
      Flow of Control in Early Languages   256
      The Structured Programming Theorem   257
      The Goto Controversy   257

6.3   Function Calls and Parameters   260
      Translating a Function Call   260
      Translating Call-By-Value Parameters with
         Global Variables   263
      Translating Call-By-Value Parameters with
         Local Variables   267
      Translating Non-Void Function Calls   269
      Translating Call-By-Reference Parameters with
         Global Variables   273
      Translating Call-By-Reference Parameters with
         Local Variables   277
      Translating Boolean Types   281

6.4   Indexed Addressing and Arrays   284
      Translating Global Arrays   285

Translating Local Arrays   288
Translating Arrays Passed as Parameters   291
Translating the Switch Statement   297

6.5   Dynamic Memory Allocation   300
Translating Global Pointers   300
Translating Local Pointers   306
Translating Structures   310
Translating Linked Data Structures   314

Summary   319

Exercises   320

Chapter 7   **Language Translation Principles   331**

7.1   Languages, Grammars, and Parsing   332
Concatenation   333
Languages   333
Grammars   335
A Grammar for C++ Identifiers   336
A Grammar for Signed Integers   337
A Context-Sensitive Grammar   338
The Parsing Problem   339
A Grammar for Expressions   340
A C++ Subset Grammar   341
Context Sensitivity of C++   346

7.2   Finite State Machines   346
An FSM to Parse an Identifier   347
Simplified Finite State Machines   347
Nondeterministic Finite State Machines   348
Machines with Empty Transitions   349
Multiple Token Recognizers   351

7.3   Implementing Finite State Machines   354
A Table-Lookup Parser   355
A Direct-Code Parser   357
An Input Buffer Class   360
A Multiple-Token Parser   361

7.4   Code Generation   368
A Language Translator   368
Parser Characteristics   381

Summary   382

Exercises   382

LEVEL 4   OPERATING SYSTEM   389

Chapter 8   Process Management   391

8.1   Loaders   392
The Pep/8 Operating System   392
The Pep/8 Loader   393
Program Termination   395

8.2   Traps   396
The Trap Mechanism   396
The RETTR Instruction   397
The Trap Handlers   398
Trap Addressing Mode Assertion   401
Trap Operand Address Computation   403
The No-Operation Trap Handlers   406
The DECI Trap Handler   408
The DECO Trap Handler   414
The STRO Trap Handler and OS Vectors   417

8.3   Concurrent Processes   419
Asynchronous Interrupts   420
Processes in the Operating System   421
Multiprocessing   423
A Concurrent Processing Program   424
Critical Sections   426
A First Attempt at Mutual Exclusion   427
A Second Attempt at Mutual Exclusions   428
Peterson's Algorithm for Mutual Exclusion   429
Semaphores   431
Critical Sections with Semaphores   433

8.4   Deadlocks   435
Resource Allocation Graphs   435
Deadlock Policy   437

Summary   437
Exercises   438

Chapter 9   Storage Management   447

9.1   Memory Allocation   447
Uniprogramming   448
Fixed-Partition Multiprogramming   448
Logical Addresses   449

Variable-Partition Multiprogramming   452
Paging   455

9.2   Virtual Memory   457
Large Program Behavior   457
Virtual Memory   458
Demand Paging   459
Page Replacement   461
Page-Replacement Algorithms   462

9.3   File Management   465
Disk Drives   465
File Abstraction   466
Allocation Techniques   467

9.4   Error Detecting and Correcting Codes   470
Error-Detecting Codes   470
Code Requirements   471
Single-Error-Correcting Codes   474

9.5   RAID Storage Systems   476
RAID Level 0: Nonredundant Striped   477
RAID Level 1: Mirrored   478
RAID Levels 01 and 10: Striped and Mirrored   478
RAID Level 2: Memory-Style ECC   480
RAID Level 3: Bit-Interleaved Parity   481
RAID Level 4: Block-Interleaved Parity   482
RAID Level 5: Block-Interleaved Distributed Parity   483

Summary   483

Exercises   484

LEVEL 1   LOGIC GATE   487

Chapter 10   Combinational Circuits   489

10.1   Boolean Algebra and Logic Gates   490
Combinational Circuits   490
Truth Tables   491
Boolean Algebra   491
Boolean Algebra Theorems   493
Proving Complements   495
Logic Diagrams   497
Alternate Representations   499

10.2   Combinational Analysis   500
Boolean Expressions and Logic Diagrams   501
Truth Tables and Boolean Expressions   503

Two-Level Circuits   506
The Ubiquitous NAND   508

10.3 Combinational Design   510
Canonical Expressions   510
Three-Variable Karnaugh Maps   512
Four-Variable Karnaugh Maps   518
Dual Karnaugh Maps   521
Don't-Care Conditions   522

10.4 Combinational Devices   523
Viewpoints   523
Multiplexer   525
Binary Decoder   526
Demultiplexer   527
Adder   528
Adder/Subtracter   531
Arithmetic Logic Unit   532
Abstraction at Level LG1   540

Summary   540
Exercises   541

Chapter 11   Sequential Circuits   549

11.1 Latches and Clocked Flip-Flops   549
The SR Latch   550
The Clocked SR Flip-Flop   552
The Master–Slave SR Flip-Flop   554
The Basic Flip-Flops   559
The JK Flip-Flop   560
The D Flip-Flop   562
The T Flip-Flop   563
Excitation Tables   564

11.2 Sequential Analysis and Design   564
A Sequential Analysis Problem   565
Preset and Clear   569
Sequential Design   569
A Sequential Design Problem   570

11.3 Computer Subsystems   574
Registers   574
Buses   575
Memory Subsystems   577
Address Decoding   582
A Two-Port Register Bank   588

Summary   590

Exercises   591

LEVEL 2   MICROCODE   595

Chapter 12   Computer Organization   597

12.1   Constructing a Level-ISA3 Machine   597
The Central Processing Unit   597
Implementing the Store Byte Instruction   606
Implementing the Add Instruction   607
Implementing the Load Instruction   608
Implementing the Arithmetic Shift Right Instruction   611

12.2   Performance Issues   612
The Bus Width   613
Specialized Hardware Units   615
Three Areas of Optimization   619
Microcode   621

12.3   The MIPS Machine   624
Load/Store Architectures   625
The Instruction Set   627
Cache Memories   634
MIPS Computer Organization   642
Pipelining   646

12.4   Conclusion   655
Simplifications in the Model   655
The Big Picture   656

Summary   658

Exercises   659

Appendix   Pep/8 Architecture   A1

Solutions to Selected Exercises   A9

Index   A29

Alan M. Turing

Alan M. Turing is one of the most enigmatic figures of twentieth-century science. Born in London in 1912, he attended Sherborne, an exclusive boarding school, and then studied at King's College in Cambridge. His doctoral dissertation *On the Gaussian Error Function* earned him a fellowship at Cambridge in 1935.

After leaving Cambridge, Turing crossed the Atlantic and studied at Princeton University with mathematician Alonzo Church and computer scientist John von Neumann. In 1937, Turing wrote what is considered his most significant contribution to mathematical logic, "On Computable Numbers, with an Application to the Entscheidungsproblem [decidability problem]." In this work, he developed the theoretical universal computing machine that is now called the Turing machine.

The Turing machine is an abstract mathematical conception of a computer that gives theoreticians the power to explore advanced questions in computability theory without being inhibited by the bounds of present technology. The simplicity of the Turing machine makes it possible to construct elegant mathematical proofs about what can and cannot be computed.

In 1939, at the onset of World War II, Turing returned to England, where he was hired by the Foreign Office and British Intelligence to work on breaking Germany's secret Enigma Code. The resulting machine, the Colossus (also nicknamed the Eastern Goddess), succeeded in breaking the code and enabled the British to keep up with Germany's military plans. For Turing's contribution to the war effort, King George VI awarded him the Order of the British Empire.

After the war, Turing worked at the National Physical Laboratory in London, where he directed the design, construction, and use of the Automatic Computing Engine (ACE), a large electronic digital computer. In 1948, he moved to the University of Manchester, where he was the assistant director of the Manchester Automatic Digital Machine (MADAM).

During this period of his research the burning question in Turing's mind was, Can machines think? In 1950, he published "Computing Machinery and Intelligence," an article that earned him the title of father of modern-day artificial intelligence.

Turing proposed that computers could be capable of thought. In the article, he described the Turing test, a behavioral test that has an impartial person pose a series of questions to both a computer and a human. The questions would be given to a computer in one room or a human in another, without the questioner knowing to which room the conversation was directed. Turing proposed that we acknowledge the machine or program as intelligent if, after a number of blind trials in which there were conversations with both the machine and the human, the questioner could not clearly identify which conversant was the machine.

In the early 1950s, homosexual relations were a felony in Britain. Turing was always frank about his sexual orientation, and he reported a homosexual affair to the police in 1952 after having been threatened with blackmail. He was convicted of gross indecency and was sentenced to a twelve-month period of hormone therapy.

Turing died at his home in Wiltshire, England, on June 7, 1954, at the age of 42. A spoon and a half-eaten apple, both covered with potassium cyanide, were found near his body. His mother believed his death to be an accident. Others, including the official coroner's report, concluded it was suicide. Some suspect that Turing had contrived his death to look accidental for his mother's benefit.

In recognition of Alan Turing's groundbreaking work in computer science, the Association for Computing Machinery instituted the annual A. M. Turing Award beginning in 1966. The award is the highest technical honor in the computing profession, a kind of "Nobel Prize for computer science." The chapters in this book contain biographical sketches of people whose professional accomplishments contributed to the subjects of the chapters. Most of them are recipients of the Turing Award.

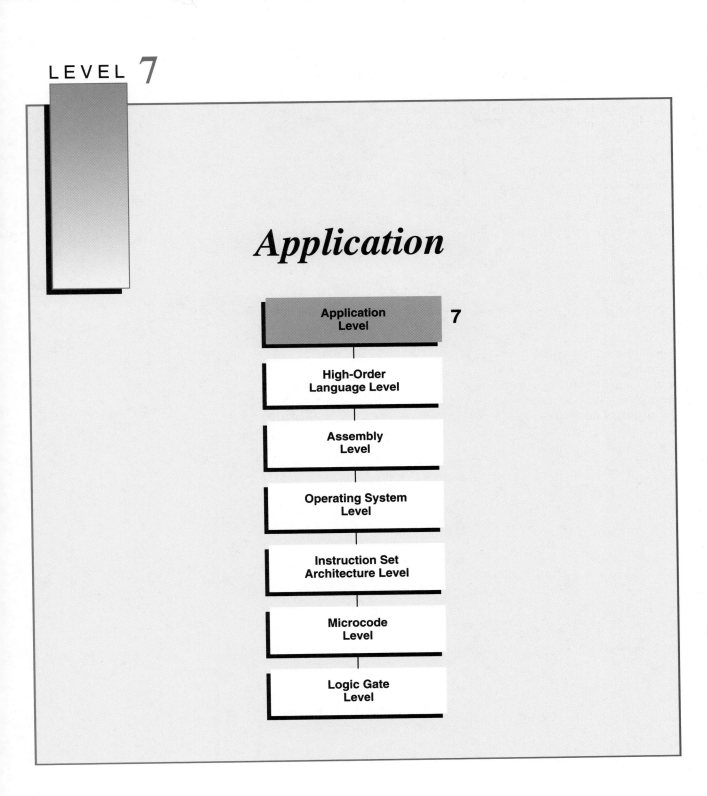

Application

Chapter

1

Computer Systems

The fundamental question of computer science is: What can be automated? Just as the machines developed during the Industrial Revolution automated manual labor, computers automate the processing of information. When electronic computers were developed in the 1940s, their designers built them to automate the solution of mathematical problems. Since then, however, computers have been applied to problems as diverse as financial accounting, airline reservations, word processing, and graphics. The spread of computers is so relentless that new areas of computer automation appear almost daily.

The fundamental question of computer science

The purpose of this book is to show how the computer automates the processing of information. Everything the computer does, you could do in principle. The major difference between computer and human execution of a job is that the computer can perform its tasks blindingly fast. However, to harness its speed, people must instruct, or program, the computer.

The nature of computers is best understood by learning how to program the machine. Programming requires that you learn a programming language. Before plunging into the details of studying a programming language, this chapter introduces the concept of abstraction, the theme on which this book is based. It then describes the hardware and software components of a computer system and concludes with a description of a database system as a typical application.

Programming languages

1.1   Levels of Abstraction

The concept of levels of abstraction is pervasive in the arts as well as in the natural and applied sciences. A complete definition of abstraction is multifaceted and for our purposes includes the following parts:

- Suppression of detail to show the essence of the matter

Definition of abstraction

- An outline structure

- Division of responsibility through a chain of command

- Subdivision of a system into smaller subsystems

The theme of this book is the application of abstraction to computer science. We begin, however, by considering levels of abstraction in areas other than computer science. The analogies drawn from these areas will expand on the four parts of our definition of abstraction and apply to computer systems as well.

Three common graphic representations of levels of abstraction are (a) level diagrams, (b) nesting diagrams, and (c) hierarchy, or tree, diagrams. We will now consider each of these representations of abstraction and show how they relate to the analogies. The three diagrams will also apply to levels of abstraction in computer systems throughout this book.

A *level diagram*, shown in Figure 1.1(a), is a set of boxes arranged vertically. The top box represents the highest level of abstraction, and the bottom box represents the lowest. The number of levels of abstraction depends on the system to be described. This figure would represent a system with three levels of abstraction.

Figure 1.1(b) shows a *nesting diagram*. Like the level diagram, a nesting diagram is a set of boxes. It always consists of one large outer box with the rest of the boxes nested inside it. In the figure, two boxes are nested immediately inside the one large outer box. The lower of these two boxes has one box nested, in turn, inside it. The outermost box of a nesting diagram corresponds to the top box of a level diagram. The nested boxes correspond to the lower boxes of a level diagram.

In a nesting diagram, none of the boxes overlaps. That is, nesting diagrams never contain boxes whose boundaries intersect the boundaries of other boxes. A box is always completely enclosed within another box.

The third graphic representation of levels of abstraction is a *hierarchy*, or *tree*, *diagram*, as shown in Figure 1.1(c). In a tree, the big limbs branch off the trunk, the smaller limbs branch off the big limbs, and so on. The leaves are at the end of the chain, attached to the smallest branches. Tree diagrams such as Figure 1.1(c) have the trunk at the top instead of the bottom. Each box is called a *node*, with the single node at the top called the *root*. A node with no connections to a lower level is a *leaf*. This figure is a tree with one root node and three leaves. The top node in a hierarchy diagram corresponds to the top box of a level diagram.

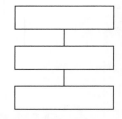

(a) A level diagram.

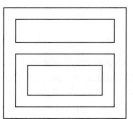

(b) A nesting diagram.

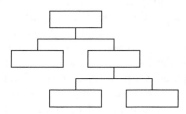

(c) A hierarchy, or tree, diagram.

Figure **1.1**

The three graphic representations of levels of abstraction.

Abstraction in Art

Henri Matisse was a major figure in the history of modern art. In 1909, he produced a bronze sculpture of a woman's back titled *The Back I*. Four years later, he created a work of the same subject but with a simpler rendering of the form, titled *The Back II*. After 4 more years, he created *The Back III*, followed by *The Back IV* 13 years later. The four sculptures are shown in Figure 1.2.

A striking feature of the works is the elimination of detail as the artist progressed from one piece to the next. The contours of the back become less distinct in the second sculpture. The fingers of the right hand are hidden in the third. The hips are barely discernible in the fourth, which is the most abstract.

The Back I
1909

The Back II
1913

The Back III
1917

The Back IV
1930

Matisse strove for expression. He deliberately suppressed visual detail in order to express the essence of the subject. In 1908, he wrote:[1]

> In a picture, every part will be visible and will play the role conferred upon it, be it principal or secondary. All that is not useful in the picture is detrimental. A work of art must be harmonious in its entirety; for superfluous details would, in the mind of the beholder, encroach upon the essential elements.

Suppression of detail is an integral part of the concept of levels of abstraction and carries over directly to computer science. In computer science terminology, *The Back IV* is at the highest level of abstraction and *The Back I* is at the lowest level. Figure 1.3 is a level diagram that shows the relationship of these levels.

Like the artist, the computer scientist must appreciate the distinction between the essentials and the details. The chronological progression of Matisse in the *The Back* series was from the most detailed to the most abstract. In computer science, however, the progression for problem solving should be from the most abstract to the most detailed. One goal of this book is to teach you how to think abstractly, to suppress irrelevant detail when formulating a solution to a problem. Not that detail is unimportant in computer science! Detail is most important. However, in computing problems there is a natural tendency to be overly concerned with too much detail in the beginning stages of the progression. In solving problems in computer science, the essentials should come before the details.

Figure **1.2**

Bronze sculptures by Henri Matisse. Each rendering is successively more abstract.

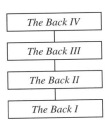

Figure **1.3**

The levels of abstraction in the Matisse sculptures. *The Back IV* is at the highest level of abstraction.

1. Alfred H. Barr, Jr., *Matisse: His Art and His Public* (New York: The Museum of Modern Art, 1951).

Abstraction in Documents

Levels of abstraction are also evident in the outline organization of written documents. An example is the United States Constitution, which consists of seven articles, each of which is subdivided into sections. The article and section headings shown in the following outline are not part of the Constitution itself.[2] They merely summarize the contents of the divisions.

Outline structure

United States Constitution

Article I.	Legislative Department
Section 1.	Congress
Section 2.	House of Representatives
Section 3.	Senate
Section 4.	Elections of Senators and Representatives—Meetings of Congress
Section 5.	Powers and Duties of Each House of Congress
Section 6.	Compensation, Privileges, and Disabilities of Senators and Representatives
Section 7.	Mode of Passing Laws
Section 8.	Powers Granted to Congress
Section 9.	Limitations on Powers Granted to the United States
Section 10.	Powers Prohibited to the States
Article II.	Executive Department
Section 1.	The President
Section 2.	Powers of the President
Section 3.	Duties of the President
Section 4.	Removal of Executive and Civil Officers
Article III.	Judicial Department
Section 1.	Judicial Powers Vested in Federal Courts
Section 2.	Jurisdiction of United States Courts
Section 3.	Treason
Article IV.	The States and the Federal Government
Section 1.	Official Acts of the States
Section 2.	Citizens of the States
Section 3.	New States
Section 4.	Protection of States Guaranteed
Article V.	Amendments
Article VI.	General Provisions
Article VII.	Ratification of the Constitution

2. California State Senate, J. A. Beak, Secretary of the Senate, *Constitution of the State of California, the Constitution of the United States, and Related Documents* (Sacramento, 1967).

The Constitution as a whole is at the highest level of abstraction. A particular article, such as Article III, Judicial Department, deals with part of the whole. A section within that article, Section 2, Jurisdiction of United States Courts, deals with a specific topic and is at the lowest level of abstraction. The outline organizes the topics logically.

Figure 1.4 shows the outline structure of the Constitution in a nesting diagram. The big outer box is the entire Constitution. Nested inside it are seven smaller boxes, which represent the articles. Inside the articles are the section boxes.

This outline method of organizing a document is also important in computer science. The technique of organizing programs and information in outline form is called *structured programming*. In much the same way that English composition teachers instruct you to organize a report in outline form before writing the details, software designers organize their programs in outline form before filling in the programming details.

Abstraction in Organizations

Corporate organization is another area that uses the concept of levels of abstraction. For example, Figure 1.5 is a partial organization chart in the form of a hierarchy diagram for a hypothetical textbook publishing company. The president of the company is at the highest level and is responsible for the successful operation of the entire organization. The four vice presidents report to the president. Each vice president is responsible for just one major part of the operation. There are more levels, not shown in the figure, under each of the managers and vice presidents.

Levels in an organization chart correspond to responsibility and authority in the organization. The president acts in the best interest of the entire company. She delegates responsibility and authority to those who report to her. They in turn use their authority to manage their part of the organization and may delegate responsibilities

Figure **1.4**

A nesting diagram of the United States Constitution.

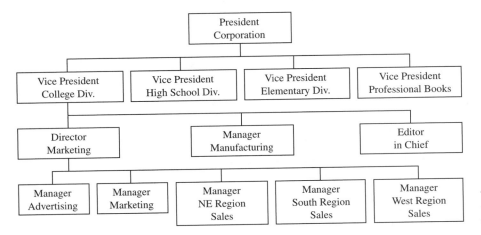

Figure **1.5**

A simplified organization chart for a hypothetical publishing company.

to their employees. In businesses, the actual power held by individuals may not be directly reflected by their positions on the official chart. Other organizations, such as the United States Army, have a rigid chain of command. Figure 1.6 is a level diagram that shows the line of authority in the U.S. Army and the units for which each officer is responsible.

There is a direct relationship between the way an organization functions, as reflected by its organization chart, and the way a computer system functions. Like a large organization, a large computer system is typically organized as a hierarchy. Any given part of a computer system takes orders from the part immediately above it in the hierarchy diagram. In turn, it issues orders to be carried out by those parts immediately below it in the hierarchy.

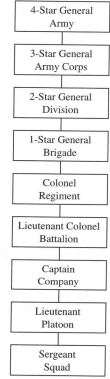

Abstraction in Machines

Another example of levels of abstraction that is closely analogous to computer systems is the automobile. Like a computer system, the automobile is a man-made machine. It consists of an engine, a transmission, an electrical system, a cooling system, and a chassis. Each part of an automobile is subdivided. The electrical system has, among other things, a battery, headlights, and a voltage regulator.

People relate to automobiles at different levels of abstraction. At the highest level of abstraction are the drivers. Drivers perform their tasks by knowing how to operate the car: how to start it, how to use the accelerator, and how to apply the brakes, for example.

At the next lower level of abstraction are the backyard mechanics. They understand more of the details under the hood than the casual drivers do. They know how to change the oil and the spark plugs. They do not need this detailed knowledge to drive the automobile.

At the next lower level of abstraction are the master mechanics. They can completely remove the engine, take it apart, fix it, and put it back together again. They do not need this detailed knowledge to simply change the oil.

In a similar vein, people relate to computer systems at many different levels of abstraction. A complete understanding at every level is not necessary to use a computer. You do not need to be a mechanic to drive a car. Similarly, you do not need to be an experienced programmer to use a word processor.

Figure **1.6**

The chain of command in the United States Army. The 4-Star General is at the highest level of abstraction. (**Source:** Henry Mintzberg, *The Structuring of Organizations*, © 1979, p. 27. Adapted by permission of Prentice Hall, Inc., Englewood Cliffs, NJ.)

Abstraction in Computer Systems

Figure 1.7 shows the level structure of a typical computer system. Each of the seven levels shown in the diagram has its own language:

Level 7 (App7):   Language dependent on applications program

Level 6 (HOL6):   Machine-independent programming language

Level 5 (Asmb5):   Assembly language

Level 4 (OS4):   Operating system calls

Level 3 (ISA3):   Machine language

Level 2 (Mc2):   Microinstructions and register transfer

Level 1 (LG1):   Boolean algebra and truth tables

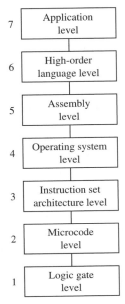

Figure **1.7**

The level structure of a typical computer system. Some systems do not have Level 2.

Programs written in these languages instruct the computer to perform certain operations. A program to perform a specific task can be written at any one of the levels of Figure 1.7. As with the automobile, a person writing a program in a language at one level does not need to know the language at any of the lower levels.

When computers were invented, only Levels LG1 and ISA3 were present. A human communicated with these machines by programming them in *machine language* at the instruction set architecture level. Machine language is great for machines but is tedious and inconvenient for a human programmer. *Assembly language*, at Level Asmb5, was invented to help the human programmer.

The first computers were large and expensive. Much time was wasted when one programmer monopolized the computer while the other users waited in line for their turn. Gradually, *operating systems* at Level OS4 were developed so many users could access the computer simultaneously. With today's personal computers, operating systems are still necessary to manage programs and data, even if the system services only one user.

In the early days, every time a company introduced a new computer model, the programmers had to learn the assembly language for that model. All their programs written for the old machine would not work on the new machine. *High-order languages* at Level HOL6 were invented so programs could be transferred from one computer to another with little modification and because programming in a high-order language is easier than programming at a lower level. Some of the more popular Level HOL6 languages that you may be familiar with are

- *FORTRAN*   Formula Translator
- *BASIC*   Beginner's All-purpose Symbolic Instruction Code
- *C++*   A popular general-purpose language
- *LISP*   List processing
- *Java*   For World Wide Web browsers

The widespread availability of computer systems spurred the development of many applications programs at Level App7. An *applications program* is one written to solve a specific type of problem, such as printing payroll checks, typing documents, or statistically analyzing data. It allows you to use the computer as a tool without knowing the operational details at the lower levels.

Level LG1, the lowest level, consists of electrical components called *logic gates*. Along the way in the development toward higher levels, it was discovered that a level just above the logic gate level could be useful in helping designers build the Level ISA3 machine. *Microprogramming* at Level Mc2 is used on some computer systems today to implement the Level ISA3 machine. Level Mc2 was an important tool in the invention of the hand-held calculator.

Your goal in studying this book is to communicate effectively with computers. To do so, you must learn the language. Languages at the higher levels are more human-oriented and easier to understand than languages at the lower levels. That is precisely why they were invented.

One goal of this book

Most people first learn about computers at Level App7 by using programs written by others. Office workers who prepare input for the company payroll program fall into this category, as do video game fans. Descriptions of applications programs at Level App7 are generally found in user's manuals, which describe how to operate the specific program.

As you study this book, you will gain some insight into the inner workings of a computer system by examining successively lower levels of abstraction. The lower you go in the hierarchy, the more details will come to light that were hidden at the higher levels. As you progress in your study, keep Figure 1.7 in mind. You must master a host of seemingly trivial details; it is the nature of the beast. Remember, however, that the beauty of computer science lies not in the diversity of its details but in the unity of its concepts.

1.2   Hardware

We build computers to solve problems. Early computers solved mathematical and engineering problems, and later computers emphasized information processing for business applications. Today, computers also control machines as diverse as automobile engines, robots, and microwave ovens. A computer system solves a problem from any of these domains by accepting input, processing it, and producing output. Figure 1.8 illustrates the function of a computer system.

Computer systems consist of hardware and software. *Hardware* is the physical part of the system. Once designed, hardware is difficult and expensive to change. *Software* is the set of programs that instruct the hardware and is easier to modify than hardware. Computers are valuable because they are general-purpose machines that can solve many different kinds of problems, as opposed to special-purpose machines that can each solve only one kind of problem. Different problems can be solved with the same hardware by supplying the system with a different set of instructions, that is, with different software.

Figure 1.8

The three activities of a computer system.

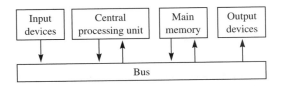

Figure **1.9**

Block diagram of the four components of a computer system.

Every computer has four basic hardware components:

- Input devices
- Output devices
- Main memory
- Central processing unit (CPU)

Components of hardware

Figure 1.9 shows these components in a block diagram. The lines between the blocks represent the flow of information. The information flows from one component to another on the *bus*, which is simply a group of wires connecting the components. Processing occurs in the CPU and main memory. The organization in Figure 1.9, with the components connected to each other by the bus, is common. However, other configurations are possible as well.

Computer hardware is often classified by its relative physical size:

- *Small*   personal computer
- *Medium* workstation
- *Large*   mainframe

Just the CPU of a mainframe often occupies an entire cabinet. Its input/output (I/O) devices and memory might fill an entire room. Personal computers can be small enough to fit on a desk or in a briefcase. As technology advances, the amount of processing previously possible only on large machines becomes possible on smaller machines. Personal computers now can do much of the work that only workstations or mainframes could do in the past.

The classification just described is based on physical size as opposed to storage size. A computer system user is generally more concerned with storage size, because that is a more direct indication of the amount of useful work that the hardware can perform. Speed of computation is another characteristic that is important to the user. Generally speaking, users want a fast CPU and large amounts of storage, but a physically small machine for the I/O devices and main memory.

When computer scientists study problems, therefore, they are concerned with space and time—the space necessary inside a computer system to store a problem and the time required to solve it. They commonly use the metric prefixes of Figure 1.10(a) to express large or small quantities of space or time.

Multiple	Prefix	Abbrev.
10^{15}	peta-	P
10^{12}	tera-	T
10^{9}	giga-	G
10^{6}	mega-	M
10^{3}	kilo-	K
10^{-3}	milli-	m
10^{-6}	micro-	μ
10^{-9}	nano-	n
10^{-12}	pico-	p

(a) Prefixes for powers of 10.

Prefix	Computer science value
peta-	$2^{50} = 1{,}125{,}899{,}906{,}842{,}624$
tera-	$2^{40} = 1{,}099{,}511{,}627{,}776$
giga-	$2^{30} = 1{,}073{,}741{,}824$
mega-	$2^{20} = 1{,}048{,}576$
kilo-	$2^{10} = 1{,}024$

(b) Computer science values of the large prefixes.

Figure 1.10

Prefixes for scientific notation.

Example 1.1   Suppose it takes 4.5 microseconds, also written 4.5 μs, to transfer some information across the bus from one component to another in Figure 1.9. (a) How many seconds are required for the transfer? (b) How many transfers can take place during one minute?

(a) A time of 4.5 μs is 4.5×10^{-6} from Figure 1.10(a), or 0.0000045 s. (b) Because there are 60 seconds in 1 minute, the number of times the transfer can occur is (60 s)/(0.0000045 s/transfer) or 13,300,000 transfers. Note that since the original value was given with two significant figures, the result should not be given to more than two or three significant figures. ■

Figure 1.10(a) shows that in the metric system the prefix kilo- is 1,000 and mega- is 1,000,000. But in computer science, a kilo- is 2^{10} or 1,024. The difference between 1,000 and 1,024 is less than 3%, so you can think of a computer science kilo- as being about 1,000, even though it is a little more. The same applies to mega- and giga-, as in Figure 1.10(b). This time, the approximation is a little worse, but for mega- it is still within 5%. The reason for these seemingly strange conventions has to do with information representation at the instruction set architecture level (Level ISA3).

Input Devices

Input devices transmit information from the outside world into the memory of the computer. Figure 1.11 shows the path the data takes from an input device to the memory via the bus. There are many different types of input devices, including

- Keyboards
- Disk drives

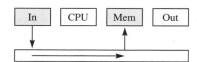

In	input devices
CPU	central processing unit
Mem	main memory
Out	output devices

Figure 1.11

The data path for input. Information flows from the input device on the bus to main memory.

- USB flash drives
- Mouse devices
- Bar code readers

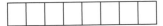

(a) Storage for an eight-bit byte.

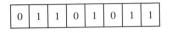

(b) The bit pattern for the character 'k.'

Figure **1.12**

A byte of information. When you press 'k' on the keyboard, the signal 01101011 goes on the bus to main memory for storage.

When you press a key on a computer keyboard, you send a character to main memory. The character is stored in memory as a sequence of eight electrical signals. Each signal in the sequence is called a *binary digit* (bit). A signal can have a high value, represented by the symbol 1, or a low value, represented by 0. The sequence of eight signals that make up the character is called a *byte* (pronounced bite), as shown in Figure 1.12.

Office workers typing on a computer keyboard are at the applications level (Level App7), the highest level of abstraction in the organization of a computer system. They do not need to know the bit pattern for each character they type. Programmers at the instruction set architecture level (Level ISA3) do need to know about bit patterns. For now, you should just remember that a byte of data corresponds to one keyboard character.

Example 1.2 A typist is entering some text on a computer keyboard at the rate of 35 words per minute. If each word is 7 characters long on average, how many bits per second are being sent to main memory? A space is a character. Assume that each word is followed by one space on average.

Including the spaces, there are 8 characters per word. The number of characters per second is (35 words/min) × (8 characters/word) × (1 min/60 s) = 4.67 characters/s. Because it takes one byte to store a character, and there are eight bits in a byte, the bit rate is (4.67 characters/s) × (1 byte/character) × (8 bits/byte) = 37.4 bits/s. ∎

Abbreviations for byte and bit

The abbreviation for a byte is the upper-case letter B. The abbreviation for a bit is the lower-case letter b. Hence you can write the final value in Example 1.2 as 37.4 b/s. As another example, you can write twelve thousand bytes as 12 KB.

Disk drive

A *disk drive* is the part of a computer that extracts data from or writes it onto a disk. The drive includes a motor that makes the disk spin, a spindle or hub clamp that secures the disk to the motor, and one or more read/write heads that detect individual bits on the surface of the disk itself.

Hard disks are rigid and are permanently sealed inside the disk drive. Typically, storage capacities range from 250 GB to 1 TB for personal computers, 1 TB to 100 TB for workstations, and more than 100 TB for mainframes. One way hard disk drives achieve their high capacity is by stacking several disk platters on a single spindle. A separate read/write head is dedicated to each disk surface.

Optical disks were first popular as audio compact discs but soon were adapted to store data for computers. The recording technology is based on lasers, which produce highly focused monochromatic beams of light. The disk has an embedded groove that spirals out from the center on which are impressed a sequence of pits and peaks illuminated by the laser beam. Each pit or peak represents a bit of information that is detected by the reflection of the beam. Typical storage capacity for a

CD is 650 MB. DVDs were originally designed for storing video information with multichannel sound and were adopted by the computer industry as well. A typical DVD storage capacity is 4.7 GB.

Example 1.3   You have 20 GB of information on your hard disk that you want to transfer to a set of CDs. How many CDs are required?

The exact number of bytes on the hard disk is $20 \times 10{,}737{,}412{,}824$, and on each CD it is $650 \times 1{,}048{,}576$. However, if you are content with approximate values, you can estimate 20×10^9 bytes for the hard disk and 650×10^6 bytes for each CD. The number of CDs required is $(20 \times 10^9)/(650 \times 10^6) = 31$ CDs.   ∎

A *USB flash drive*, also known as a thumb drive, is really not a disk drive at all. It is a solid state device with no moving parts that is designed to mimic the behavior of a hard drive. The acronym USB stands for Universal Serial Bus, which defines the connection protocol between many hard drives and computer systems. When you plug a thumb drive into a computer, the thumb drive appears to the computer as if it were a hard drive. Because there are no moving parts in a thumb drive, they are more rugged than hard drives. Also unlike hard drives, they are removeable. Storage capacities are up to about 16 GB.

The *mouse* is a popular hand-held input device. Inside an optical mouse is a small light-emitting diode that shines a beam of light down onto the surface of the desk or mouse pad. The light reflects back onto a sensor that samples the light 1,500 times per second. A digital signal processor inside the mouse acts like a tiny computer programmed for only one task: to detect patterns in the images of the desk or mouse pad and determine how far they have moved since the previous sample. The processor inside the mouse computes the direction and velocity of the mouse from the patterns and sends the data to the personal computer, which in turn draws the cursor image on the screen.

The *bar code reader* is another efficient input device. Perhaps the most common bar code is the Universal Product Code (UPC) on grocery store items (Figure 1.13). Each digit in the UPC symbol has seven vertical data elements. Each data element can be light or dark. Photocells inside the bar code reader detect the light and dark regions and convert them to bits. Light elements are read as zeros, and dark elements as ones. Figure 1.14 shows the correspondence between light and dark regions and bits for two digits from the right half of the UPC symbol in Figure 1.13.

Figure 1.15 shows the UPC correspondence between decimal and binary values. The code is different for the characters on the left half and those on the right half. A dark bar is composed of from one to four adjacent dark regions. Each decimal digit has two dark bars and two light spaces. The characters on the left half begin with a light space and end with a dark bar, and the characters on the right half begin with a dark bar and end with a light space. Each left character has an odd number of ones, and each right character has an even number of ones.

Checkout clerks at the supermarket work at the highest level of abstraction. They do not need to know the details of the UPC symbol. They only know that if they try to input the UPC symbol and they do not hear the confirmation beep, an input error has

USB flash drive

Figure 1.13

The UPC symbol from a package of cereal. The left five digits identify the manufacturer. The right five digits identify the product. The Quaker company code is 30000, and the 100% Natural Cereal code is 06700.

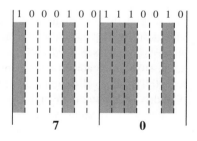

Figure 1.14

Part of the UPC symbol from the Quaker cereal box. Visually, groups of adjacent dark regions look like thick bars.

occurred and they must rescan the bar code. Programmers at a lower level, however, must know the details of the code. Their programs, for example, must check the number of ones, or dark elements, in each left character. If a left character has an even number of ones, the program must not issue the confirmation beep.

Decimal value	Left chars.	Right chars.
0	0001101	1110010
1	0011001	1100110
2	0010011	1101100
3	0111101	1000010
4	0100011	1011100
5	0110001	1001110
6	0101111	1010000
7	0111011	1000100
8	0110111	1001000
9	0001011	1110100

Figure **1.15**

Bit patterns for the decimal digits in the UPC symbol.

Output Devices

Output devices transmit information from the memory of the computer to the outside world. Figure 1.16 shows the path that the data takes from main memory to an output device. On output, data flows on the same bus used by the input devices. Output devices include

- Disk drives
- USB flash drives
- Screens
- Printers

Notice that disk and USB flash drives can serve as both input and output devices. When disks are used for input, the process is called *reading*. When they are used for output, the process is called *writing*.

The *screen* is a visual display similar to the picture screen of a television set. It can be either a cathode ray tube (CRT) or a flat panel. A monitor is packaged separately from the keyboard and the CPU. A *terminal* is a monitor together with a keyboard. It is not a self-contained, general-purpose personal computer, although it may resemble one. Terminals communicate with workstations and mainframes and are useless without them. Personal computers, on the other hand, are self-contained and can process information without being connected to larger machines. Personal computers can also behave like terminals and communicate with other machines. In the early days of computing, a standard terminal screen held 24 lines of text with a maximum of 80 characters in a line. Since the advent of graphical user interfaces, screen size is no longer specified as a fixed number of lines of text, because windows and dialog boxes can be of various sizes. However, the terminal emulator programs on personal computers sometimes conform to the old standard of 24 lines and 80 characters in the window that represents the terminal.

Individual characters on a screen are actually composed of a rectangular grid of dots. Each dot is called a *pixel*, which stands for picture element. In a black-and-white screen, a pixel can be either bright or dark. The pattern of bright pixels in the rectangular grid forms an image of the character. Figure 1.17 shows a grid of pixels with five columns and seven rows that forms an image of the character 'B.' Higher-quality screens have more pixels in the rectangular grid to form a smoother image of the character. See how much clearer the image of the 'B' is in the field of 9×13 pixels.

Printers range widely in performance and cost. Ink jet printers operate on the same basis as the pixels in a screen. As the print head moves across the paper, small jets of ink are sprayed onto the paper at just the right moment to form the desired image. A computer program controls the timing of the release of the ink. As with

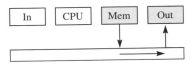

Figure **1.16**

The data path for output. Information flows from main memory on the bus to the output device.

Printers

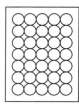

(a) A 5 ×7 pixel grid.

(b) An image of a 'B' in a 5 × 7 pixel grid.

(c) An image of a 'B' in a 9 × 13 pixel grid.

Figure **1.17**

Picture elements (pixels) on a rectangular grid. The pixels in (b) have the same diameter as the ones in (c).

the screen, the greater the number of dots for an individual character, the higher the quality of the print. Many printers have several modes of operation, ranging from lower quality but faster to higher quality but slower.

The page printer is a high-quality output device. Most page printers use a laser beam to form the image on the page. Page printers also use pixels for their imaging systems, but the pixels are spaced closely enough to be unnoticeable. A typical desktop laser printer has 600 or 1,200 pixels per inch. A 600 pixel-per-inch printer has 600 × 600 or 360,000 pixels per square inch. Commercial typesetting machines have 2,400 pixels per inch or more.

Main Memory

Main memory stores both the data being processed and the programs processing the data. As with disk, the capacity of main memory is measured in bytes. Small personal computers usually have about 1 GB of main memory; larger ones can have up to about 8 GB. Workstations usually have more than 8 GB, and mainframes have hundreds of GB of main memory.

An important characteristic of main memory is that it is volatile. That is, if the power source to the computer is discontinued, whether intentionally or unintentionally, the information in main memory is lost. That is not true with disks. You can unplug a USB flash drive from a computer, turn off the machine, come back the next day, and the information will still be on your flash drive.

Another important characteristic of main memory is its access method, which is random. In fact, the electronic components that make up main memory are often referred to as RAM (for *random access memory*) circuits. Unlike a hard drive, if you have just fetched some information from one end of main memory, you can immediately get information from the other end at random without passing over the information in-between.

Central Processing Unit

The *central processing unit* (CPU) contains the circuitry to control all the other parts of the computer. It has its own small set of memory, called *registers*. The

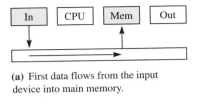

(a) First data flows from the input device into main memory.

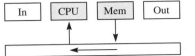

(b) Next the CPU brings the data into its registers for processing.

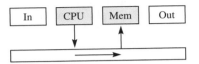

(c) Then the CPU sends the processed data back to memory.

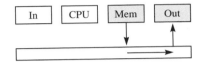

(d) Finally the results go to the output device.

Figure **1.18**

The data flow for a complete job. Steps (b) and (c) usually repeat many times.

CPU also has a set of instructions permanently wired into its circuitry. The instructions do such things as fetch information from memory into a register, add, subtract, compare, and store information from a register back into memory, and so on. What is not permanent is the order in which these instructions are executed. The order is determined by a program written in machine language at Level 3.

A single machine instruction is fast by human standards. CPU speeds are commonly measured in GHz, which stands for gigahertz. A hertz is one instruction per second. So, a GHz is a billion instructions per second.

Example 1.4   Suppose a CPU is rated at 2.5 GHz. What is the average length of time needed to execute one instruction?

2.5 GHz is 2.5×10^9 instructions per second. That is $1/2.5 \times 10^9 = 0.4 \times 10^{-9}$ or 400 picoseconds per instruction.   ∎

To process data stored in main memory, the CPU must first bring it into its local registers. Then the CPU can process the data in the registers and send the results back to main memory. Eventually, to be useful to the user, the data must be sent to an output device. Figure 1.18 shows the data flow for a complete job.

1.3   Software

An *algorithm* is a set of instructions that, when carried out in the proper sequence, solves a problem in a finite amount of time. Algorithms do not require computers.

Figure 1.19 is an algorithm in English that solves the problem of making six servings of stirred custard.

Ingredients

    3 slightly beaten eggs

    $\frac{1}{4}$ cup sugar

    2 cups milk, scalded

    $\frac{1}{2}$ teaspoon vanilla

Algorithm

    Combine eggs, sugar, and $\frac{1}{4}$ teaspoon salt.

    Slowly stir in slightly cooled milk.

    Cook in double boiler over hot, not boiling, water, stirring constantly.

    As soon as custard coats metal spoon, remove from heat.

    Cool at once—place pan in cold water and stir a minute or two.

    Add vanilla.

    Chill.

Figure 1.19

An algorithm for making stirred custard. (**Source:** Adapted from *Better Homes and Gardens New Cook Book*. Copyright Meredith Corporation, 1981. All rights reserved.)

This recipe illustrates two important properties of algorithms—the finite number of instructions and execution in a finite amount of time. The algorithm has seven instructions—combine, stir, cook, remove, cool, add, and chill. Seven is a finite number. An algorithm cannot have an infinite number of instructions.

Even though the number of instructions in the custard algorithm is finite, there is a potential problem with its execution. The recipe instructs us to cook until the custard coats the metal spoon. What if it never coats the spoon? Then, if we strictly followed the instructions, we would be cooking forever! A valid algorithm must never execute endlessly. It must provide a solution in a finite amount of time. Assuming that the custard will always coat the spoon, this recipe is indeed an algorithm.

The finite requirement for an algorithm

A *program* is an algorithm written for execution on a computer. Programs cannot be written in English. They must be written in a language for one of the seven levels of a computer system.

Definition of a program

General-purpose computers can solve many different kinds of problems, from computing the company payroll to correcting a spelling mistake in a memorandum. The hardware gets its versatility from its ability to be programmed to do the different jobs. Programs that control the computer are called *software*.

Software

Software is classified into two broad groups:

- Systems software
- Applications software

Systems software makes the computer accessible to the applications designers. *Applications software*, in turn, makes the computer system accessible to the end user at Level App7. Generally speaking, a systems software engineer designs programs at Level HOL6 and below. These programs take care of the many details of the computer system with which the applications programmer does not want to bother.

Systems software versus applications software

Operating Systems

The most important software for a computer is the operating system. The *operating system* is the systems program that makes the hardware usable. Every general-purpose computer system includes both hardware and an operating system.

To study this text effectively you must have access to a computer with an operating system. Some common commercial operating systems are Microsoft Windows, Mac OS X, UNIX, and Linux. Unfortunately, each operating system has unique commands. This book cannot explain how to use all of the different operating systems. You must learn the specifics of your operating system from your instructor or from another source.

An operating system has three general functions:

- File management
- Memory management
- Processor management

Functions of an operating system

Of these three functions, file management is the most visible to the user. The first thing a new computer user must learn is how to manipulate the files of information on the operating system.

Files in an operating system are analogous to files in an office. They contain information to be retrieved and processed on request. In an office, the filing cabinet stores files. In an operating system, peripheral memory devices store files. Although tapes and disks can store files, the following discussion concentrates on disks.

Files in the operating system

In an office, an individual file is in a file folder. The office worker names each file and places the name on the tab of the folder. The name indicates the contents of the folder and makes it easy to pick out an individual file from the cabinet. In an operating system, every file also has a name. The name serves the same purpose as the name on a folder—to make it easy to pick out an individual file from a disk.

When a computer user creates a file, the operating system requests a name for the file. Depending on the system, there are usually some restrictions on the length of the name and the allowable characters in the name. Sometimes the system will automatically attach a prefix or a suffix to the name. Other files are created by the system and automatically named by it.

Files can contain three types of information:

- Documents
- Programs
- Data

Three types of information contained in files

Documents may be company memoranda, letters, reports, and the like. Files also store programs to be executed by the computer. To be executed, first they must be loaded from disk into main memory. Input data for an executing program can come from a file, and output data can also be sent to a file.

The files are physically scattered over the surface of the disk. To keep track of all these files of information, the operating system maintains a directory of them. The directory is a list of all the files on the disk. Each entry in the directory has the file's name, its size, its physical location on the disk, and any other information the operating system needs to manage the files. The directory itself is also stored on the disk.

The operating system provides the user with a way to manipulate the files on the disk. Some typical operating system commands include

- List the names of the files from the directory.
- Delete a file from the disk.
- Change the name of a file.
- Print the contents of a file.
- Execute an applications program.

Some typical operating system commands

These are the commands you need to learn for your operating system in order to work the problems in this book.

Your operating system is a program written for your computer by a team of systems programmers. When you issue the command to delete a file from the disk, a systems program executes that command. You, the user, are using a program that someone else, the systems programmer, wrote.

Software Analysis and Design

Software, whether systems or applications, has much in common with literature. Human authors write both. Other people read both, although computers can also read and execute programs. Both novelists and programmers are creative in that the solutions they propose are not unique. When a novelist has something to communicate, there is always more than one way to express it. The difference between a good novel and a bad one lies not only in the idea communicated, but also in the

(a) Analysis—The input and processing are given. The output is to be determined.

(b) Design—The input and desired output are given. The processing is to be determined.

Figure **1.20**
The difference between analysis and design.

way the idea is expressed. Likewise, when a programmer has a problem to solve, there is always more than one way to program the solution. The difference between a good program and a bad one lies not only in the correctness of the solution to the problem, but also in other characteristics of the program, such as clarity, execution speed, and memory requirement.

As a student of literature, you participate in two distinct activities—reading and writing. Reading is analysis; you read what someone else has written and analyze its contents. Writing is design or synthesis; you have an idea to express, and your problem is to communicate that idea effectively. Most people find writing much more difficult than reading, because it requires more creativity. That is why there are more readers in the general population than authors.

Similarly, as a student of software you will analyze and design programs. Remember that the three activities of a program are input, processing, and output. In analysis, you are given the input and the processing instructions. Your problem is to determine the output. In design, you are given the input and the desired output. Your problem is to write the processing instructions, that is, to design the software. Figure 1.20 shows the difference between analysis and design.

As in reading and writing English literature, designing good software is much more difficult than analyzing it. A familiar complaint of computer science students is "I understand the concepts, but I can't write the programs." This is a natural complaint because it reflects the difficulty of synthesis as opposed to analysis. Our ultimate goal is for you to be able to design software as well as analyze it. The following chapters will give you specific software design techniques.

Analysis versus design

But first you should become familiar with these general problem-solving guidelines, which also apply to software design:

General problem-solving guidelines

- Understand the problem.
- Outline a solution.
- Solve each part of your outlined problem.
- Test your solution by hand.
- Test your solution on the computer.

When faced with a software design problem, test your understanding of the problem by writing down some sample input and the corresponding output. You cannot solve a problem by computer if you do not know how to solve it by hand. To outline a solution, you must break down the problem into several subproblems. Because the subproblems are smaller than the original problem, they are easier to solve. If you have doubts about the correctness of your program, you should test it by hand before entering it on the computer. You can test it with the sample input you wrote in the first step.

Many students find these steps unnecessary for the small programs found in an introductory textbook. If the problem is easy for you, it is all right not to organize your thoughts on paper this way before programming your solution to the problem. In that case, you are mentally following these steps anyway. On the other hand, you may eventually encounter a large design problem for which these problem-solving steps will be indispensable.

1.4   Database Systems

Database systems are one of the most common applications at Level App7. A *database* is a collection of files that contain interrelated information, and a *database system* (also called a database management system, or DBMS) is a program that lets the user add, delete, and modify records in the database. A database system also permits queries of the database. A *query* is a request for information, usually from different parts of the database.

An example of a database is the information a furniture manufacturer maintains about his inventory, parts suppliers, and shipments. A query might be a request for a report showing the number of each part in storage that is required to manufacture a particular sofa. To produce the report, the database system combines the information from different parts of the database, in this case from an inventory file and from a required-materials file for the sofa.

Database systems come in three main varieties: hierarchical systems, network systems, and relational systems. Of these three types of database systems, the hierarchical is the fastest but the most restrictive for the user. This system is appropriate if you can naturally organize the information in the database into the same structure as a hierarchy chart. The network system is more flexible than the hierarchical system but more difficult for a user than the relational database system. *Three types of database systems*

The relational system is the most popular of the three. It is the most flexible and easiest to use at Level App7. But in computer science, nothing is free. This high flexibility comes at the cost of low speed compared to the other database systems. This section describes the basic idea behind a relational DBMS.

Relations

Relational database systems store information in files that appear to have a table structure. Each table has a fixed number of columns and a variable number of rows. Figure 1.21 is an example of the information in a relational database. Each table has a name. The table named Sor contains information about the members of a sorority, and the one named Frat contains information about the members of a fraternity. The user at Level App7 fixed the number of vertical columns in each table before *Relational database systems*

Edgar Codd

Edgar Codd was born in Portland Bill, Dorset, England in 1923, the youngest of seven children. He majored in mathematics and chemistry at Oxford University, and was a pilot with the Royal Air Force during World War II. He moved to New York in 1948, where he went to work for IBM. Angered by Senator Joseph McCarthy's attacks on supposed Communist sympathizers, he then moved to Ottawa where he lived during the early 1950s.

Codd eventually received his doctorate in computer science at the University of Michigan at Ann Arbor and then moved to San Jose, California, to work at IBM's research laboratory. In 1970 he wrote a landmark paper titled "A Relational Model of Data for Large Shared Data Banks." At the time of its publication, the user interface for database systems was at a low level of abstraction. To perform a query, a user had to use a complicated query language that depended on the details of how the data was stored on the disk. Codd's relational database language placed the user at a higher level of abstraction, hiding the details that users of the old language needed to know to make a query. Codd was the co-inventor along with Don Chamberlin and Ray Boyce of Structured Query Language (SQL), which has become the industry-

standard language for querying relational databases.

Unfortunately for Codd, IBM was not as quick to see the commercial possibilities of his work as were their competitors. It remained for Larry Ellison to use Codd's research as the basis for a start-up company that has since become Oracle. In 1973, IBM began work on the System R project to test Codd's relational ideas. Finally, in 1978, a full eight years after the publication of Codd's paper, IBM began to build a commercial relational database product.

Edgar Codd is widely recognized as the inventor of the relational database. In 1981, he received the A. M. Turing Award for his fundamental and continuing contributions to the theory and practice of database management systems. Codd died in 2003 at the age of 79 at his home in Williams Island, Florida.

entering the information in the body of the tables. The number of horizontal rows is variable so that individuals can be added to or deleted from the tables.

In relational database terminology, a table is called a *relation*. A column is an *attribute*, and a row is a *tuple* (rhymes with couple). In Figure 1.21, Sor and Frat are relations, (Nancy, Jr, Math, NY) is a 4-tuple of Sor because it has four elements, and F.Major is an attribute of Frat. The *domain* of an attribute is the set of all possible values of the attribute. The domain of S.Major and F.Major is the set {Hist, Math, CompSci, PolySci, English}.

Relations, attributes, tuples, and domains

Queries

Examples of queries from this database are requests for Ron's home state and for the names of all the sophomores in the sorority. Another query is a request for a list of those sorority and fraternity members who have the same major, and what that common major is.

Sor

S.Name	S.Class	S.Major	S.State
Beth	Soph	Hist	TX
Nancy	Jr	Math	NY
Robin	Sr	Hist	CA
Allison	Soph	Math	AZ
Lulwa	Sr	CompSci	CA

Frat

F.Name	F.Major	F.State
Emile	PolySci	CA
Sam	CompSci	WA
Ron	Math	OR
Mehdi	Math	CA
David	English	AZ
Jeff	Hist	TX
Craig	English	CA
Gary	CompSci	CA

Figure **1.21**

An example of a relational database. This database contains two relations—Sor and Frat.

In this small example, you can manually search through the database to determine the result of each of these queries. Ron's home state is OR, and Beth and Allison are the sophomores in the sorority. The third query is a little more difficult to tabulate. Beth and Jeff are both history majors. Nancy and Ron are both math majors, as are Nancy and Mehdi. Robin and Jeff are both history majors, and so on.

It is interesting that the result of each of these queries can be written in table form (Figure 1.22). The result of the first query is a table with one column and one row, while the result of the second is a table with one column and two rows. The

Result1

F.State
OR

Result2

S.Name
Beth
Allison

Result3

S.Name	F.Name	Major
Beth	Jeff	Hist
Nancy	Ron	Math
Nancy	Mehdi	Math
Robin	Jeff	Hist
Allison	Ron	Math
Allison	Mehdi	Math
Lulwa	Sam	CompSci
Lulwa	Gary	CompSci

Figure **1.22**

The result of three queries from the database of Figure 1.21. Each result is a relation.

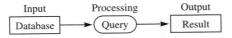

Figure **1.23**

The relationship between the database, a query, and the result.

result of the third is a table with three columns and eight rows. So the result of a query of a relational database, which is a collection of relations, is itself a relation!

The fact that the result of a query is itself a relation is a powerful idea in relational database systems. The user at Level App7 views the database as a collection of relations. Her query is a request for another relation that the system derives from the existing relations in the database.

Remember that each level has a language. The language of a Level App7 relational DBMS is a set of commands that combines or modifies existing relations and produces new relations. The user at Level App7 issues the commands to produce the desired result. Figure 1.23 shows the relationship between the database, a query, and the result. The database is the input. The query is a set of commands in the Level App7 language. As it does in every level in the computer system, the relationship takes this form: input, processing, output.

This chapter cannot describe every language of every relational database system on the market. Instead, it describes a simplified language typical of such systems. Most relational DBMS languages have many powerful commands. But three commands are fundamental—`select`, `project`, and `join`.

The `select` and `project` statements are similar because they both operate on a single relation to produce a modified relation. The `select` statement takes a set of rows from a given table that satisfies the condition specified in the statement. The `project` statement takes a set of columns from a given table according to the attributes specified in the statement. Figure 1.24 illustrates the effect of the statements

```
select Frat where F.Major = English giving Temp1
```

and

```
project Sor over S.Name giving Temp2
```

The `project` statement can specify more than one column, in which case the attributes are enclosed in parentheses and separated by commas. For example,

```
project Sor over (S.Class, S.State) giving Temp3
```

selects two attributes from the `Sor` relation.

Note in Figure 1.24(c) that the pair (Sr, CA) is common from both 4-tuples (Robin, Sr, Hist, CA) and (Lulwa, Sr, CompSci, CA) in relation `Sor` (Figure 1.21). But the pair is not repeated in relation `Temp3`. A basic property of relations is that no row in any table may be duplicated. The `project` operator checks for duplicated rows and does not permit them. Mathematically, a relation is a set of tuples, and elements of a set cannot be duplicated.

Query as a relation result

Temp1

F.Name	F.Major	F.State
David	English	AZ
Craig	English	CA

(a) `select Frat where F.Major = English giving Temp1`

Temp2

S.Name
Beth
Nancy
Robin
Allison
Lulwa

(b) `project Sor over S.Name giving Temp2`

Temp3

S.Class	S.State
Soph	TX
Jr	NY
Sr	CA
Soph	AZ

(c) `project Sor over (S.Class, S.State) giving Temp3`

Figure **1.24**

The `select` and `project` operators.

join differs from select and project because its input is two tables, not one. A column from the first table and a column from the second table are specified as the join column. The join column from each table must have a common domain. The result of a join of two tables is one wide table whose columns are duplicates of the original columns, except that the join column appears only once. The rows of the resulting table are copies of those rows of the two original tables that have equal elements in the join column.

For example, in Figure 1.21 the columns S.Major and F.Major have a common domain. The statement

```
join Sor and Frat over Major giving Temp4
```

specifies that Major is the join column and that the relations Sor and Frat are to be joined over it. Figure 1.25 shows that the only rows included in the join of the two tables are the ones with equal majors. The 4-tuple (Robin, Sr, Hist, CA) from Sor and the 3-tuple (Jeff, Hist, TX) from Frat are joined in Temp4 because their majors, Hist, are equal.

Structure of the Language

The statements in this Level App7 language have the following form:

select *relation* where *condition* giving *relation*
project *relation* over *attributes* giving *relation*
join *relation* and *relation* over *attribute* giving *relation*

The reserved words of the language are

select	project
join	and
where	over
giving	

Reserved words

Temp4

S.Name	S.Class	S.State	Major	F.Name	F.State
Beth	Soph	TX	Hist	Jeff	TX
Nancy	Jr	NY	Math	Ron	OR
Nancy	Jr	NY	Math	Mehdi	CA
Robin	Sr	CA	Hist	Jeff	TX
Allison	Soph	AZ	Math	Ron	OR
Allison	Soph	AZ	Math	Mehdi	CA
Lulwa	Sr	CA	CompSci	Sam	WA
Lulwa	Sr	CA	CompSci	Gary	CA

Figure **1.25**

The join operator. The relation is from the statement
join Sor and Frat over Major giving Temp4

Each reserved word has a special meaning in the language, as the previous examples demonstrate. Words to identify objects in the language, such as `Sor` and `Temp2` to identify relations and `F.State` to identify an attribute, are not reserved. They are created arbitrarily by the user at Level App7 and are called *identifiers*. The existence of reserved words and user-defined identifiers is common in languages at all the levels of a typical computer system.

Do you see how to use the `select`, `project`, and `join` statements to generate the results of the query in Figure 1.22? The statements for the first query, which asks for Ron's home state, are

```
select Frat where F.Name = Ron giving Temp5
project Temp5 over F.State giving Result1
```

The statements for the second query, which asks for the names of all the sophomores in the sorority, are

```
select Sor where S.Class = Soph giving Temp6
project Temp6 over S.Name giving Result2
```

The statements for the third query, which asks for a list of those sorority and fraternity members who have the same major and what that common major is, are

```
join Sor and Frat over Major giving Temp4
project Temp4 over (S.Name, F.Name, Major) giving  Result3
```

SUMMARY

The fundamental question of computer science is: What can be automated? Computers automate the processing of information. The theme of this book is levels of abstraction in computer systems. Abstraction includes suppression of detail to show the essence of the matter, an outline structure, division of responsibility through a chain of command, and subdivision of a system into smaller systems. The seven levels of abstraction in a typical computer system are

Level 7 (App7):	Application
Level 6 (HOL6):	High-order language
Level 5 (Asmb5):	Assembly
Level 4 (OS4):	Operating system
Level 3 (ISA3):	Instruction set architecture
Level 2 (Mc2):	Microcode
Level 1 (LG1):	Logic gate

Each level has its own language, which serves to hide the details of the lower levels.

A computer system consists of hardware and software. Four components of hardware are input devices, the central processing unit, main memory, and output devices. Programs that control the computer are called software.

An algorithm is a set of instructions that, when carried out in the proper sequence, solves a problem in a finite amount of time. A program is an algorithm written for execution on a computer. A program inputs information, processes it, and outputs the results.

Database systems are one of the most common applications at Level App7. Relational database systems store information in files that appear to have a table structure; this table is called a relation. The result of a query in a relational database system is itself a relation. The three fundamental operations in a relational database system are `select`, `project`, and `join`. A query is a combination of these three operations.

EXERCISES

At the end of each chapter in this book is a set of exercises and problems. Work the exercises on paper by hand. Answers to the starred exercises are in the back of the book. (For some multipart exercises, answers are supplied only for selected parts.) The problems are programs to be entered into the computer. This chapter contains only exercises.

Section 1.1

1. **(a)** Draw a hierarchy diagram that corresponds to the United States Constitution. **(b)** Based on Figure 1.5, draw a nesting diagram that corresponds to the organization of the hypothetical publishing company.

2. Genghis Khan organized his men into groups of 10 soldiers under a "leader of 10." Ten "leaders of 10" were under a "leader of 100." Ten "leaders of 100" were under a "leader of 1,000." *__(a)__ If Khan had an army of 10,000 soldiers at the lowest level, how many men in total were under him in his organization? **(b)** If Khan had an army of 5,763 soldiers at the lowest level, how many men in total were under him in his organization? Assume that the groups of 10 should contain 10 if possible, but that one group at each level may need to contain fewer.

3. In the Bible, Exodus Chapter 18 describes how Moses was overwhelmed as the single judge of Israel because of the large number of trivial cases that were brought before him. His father-in-law, Jethro, recommended a hierarchical system of appellate courts where the lowest-level judge had responsibility for 10 citizens. Five judges of 10 sent the difficult cases that they could not resolve to a judge of 50 citizens. Two judges of 50 were under a judge of 100, and 10 judges of 100 were under a judge of 1,000. The judges of 1,000 citizens reported to Moses, who had to decide only the most difficult cases. *__(a)__ If the population were exactly 2,000 citizens (excluding judges), draw the three top levels of the hierarchy diagram. **(b)** In part (a), what would be the total population, including Moses, all the judges, and citizens? **(c)** If the population were exactly 10,000 citizens (excluding judges), what would be the total population, including Moses, all the judges, and citizens?

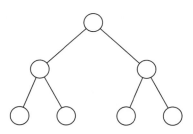

Figure **1.26**

Exercise 4: The full binary tree with three levels.

4. A full binary tree is a tree whose leaves are all at the same level, and every node that is not a leaf has exactly two nodes under it. Figure 1.26 is a full binary tree with three levels. *__(a)__ Draw the full binary tree with four levels. *__(b)__ How many nodes total are in a full binary tree with five levels? **(c)** with six levels? **(d)** with *n* levels in general?

Section 1.2

*5. A typist is entering text on a keyboard at the rate of 40 words per minute. If each word is 5 characters long on average, how many bits per second are being sent to main memory? A space is also a character. Assume that each word is followed by one space on average.

6. A typist is entering text on a keyboard at the rate of 30 words per minute. If each word is 6 characters long on average, how many bits per second are being sent to main memory? A space is also a character. Assume that each word is followed by one space on average.

7. You have a digital music collection of 2,300 songs with an average of 4.6 MB storage required for each song. **(a)** How many 650 MB CDs will it take for you to burn your entire collection? **(b)** If you could burn it to 4.7 GB DVDs, how many DVDs would it take?

8. You have a digital photo collection with photos that require an average of 75 KB of storage each. **(a)** How many photos can you fit on a 650 MB CD? **(b)** How many photos can you fit on a 4.7 GB DVD?

*9. A screen has an 8 × 10 rectangular grid of pixels for each character. It can display 24 rows by 80 columns of characters. **(a)** How many pixels in total are on the screen? **(b)** If each pixel is stored as one bit, how many KB does it take to store the screen?

10. A screen has a 5 × 7 rectangular grid of pixels for each character. It can display 24 rows of 80 columns of characters. **(a)** How many pixels are on the screen? **(b)** If each pixel is stored as one bit, how many KB does it take to store a screen image?

11. A desktop laser printer has a 300-pixel-per-inch resolution. If each pixel is stored in one bit of memory, how many bytes of memory are required to store the complete image of one $8\frac{1}{2}$ –by–11-inch page of paper?

12. A medium-sized book contains about 1 million characters. *(a)** How many hours would it take to print it on a letter-quality printer at 15 characters per second? **(b)** Assuming an average of 55 characters per line, how many hours would it take on a 600-line-per-minute line printer?

13. What two decimal digits does the UPC symbol in Figure 1.27 represent?

Section 1.3

14. Answer the following questions about file names for your operating system. **(a)** Is there a limit to the number of characters in a file name? If so, what is the limit? **(b)** Are certain characters not allowed or, if allowed, problematic? **(c)** Does your operating system distinguish between uppercase and lowercase characters in a file name?

15. Determine how to perform each of the following procedures with your operating system. **(a)** Sign onto the system if it is a mainframe or minicomputer, or start up the system if it is a personal computer. **(b)** List the names of the files from the directory. **(c)** Delete a file from the disk. **(d)** Change the name of a file. **(e)** Duplicate a file. **(f)** Print the contents of a file.

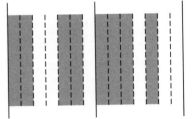

Figure **1.27**

Exercise 13: The digits are characters on the right half of the UPC symbol.

Section 1.4

*16.   Write the relations Temp5 and Temp6 from the discussion in Section 1.4 of the chapter.

17.   Write the statements for the following queries of the database in Figure 1.21. *(a) Find Beth's home state. (b) List the fraternity members who are English majors. (c) List the sorority and fraternity members who have the same home state and indicate what that home state is.

18.   (a) Write the statements to produce Result2 in Figure 1.22, but with the project command before the select. (b) Write the statements to produce Result3 in Figure 1.22, but with join as the last statement.

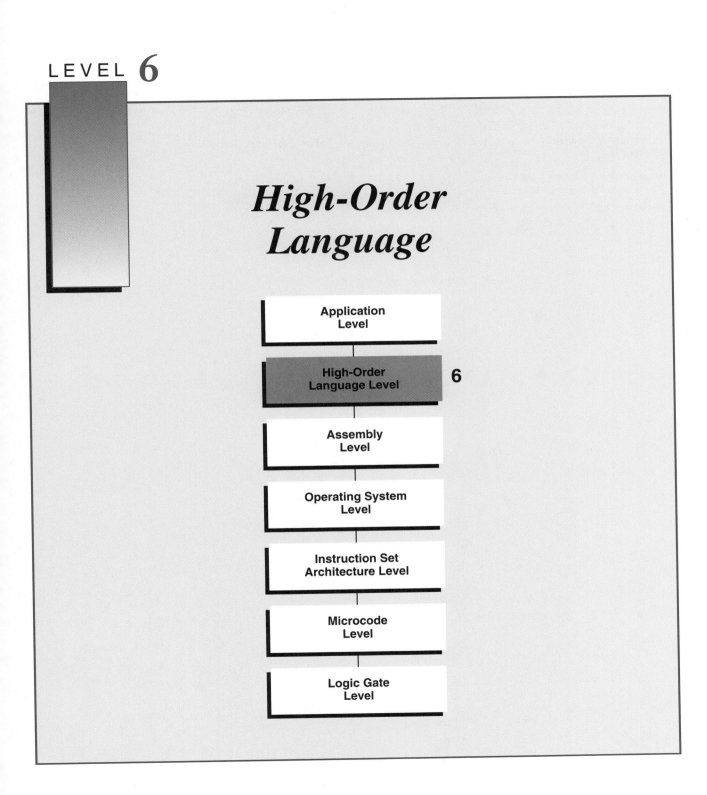

LEVEL **6**

High-Order Language

Application Level

High-Order Language Level   6

Assembly Level

Operating System Level

Instruction Set Architecture Level

Microcode Level

Logic Gate Level

2

C++

A program inputs information, processes it, and outputs the results. This chapter shows how a C++ program inputs, processes, and outputs values. It reviews programming at Level HOL6 and assumes that you have experience writing programs in some high-order language—not necessarily C++—such as C, Java, or Ada. Because this book presents concepts that are common to all those languages, you should be able to follow the discussion despite any differences in the language with which you are familiar.

2.1 Variables

A computer can directly execute statements in machine language only at Level ISA3, the instruction set architecture level. So a Level HOL6 statement must first be translated to Level ISA3 before executing. Figure 2.1 shows the function of a compiler, which performs the translation from a Level HOL6 language to the Level ISA3 language. The figure shows translation to Level 3. Some compilers translate from Level 6 to Level 5, which then requires another translation from Level 5 to Level 3.

The C++ Compiler

To execute the programs in this book you need access to a C++ compiler. Running a program is a three-step process:

- Write the program in C++ using a text editor. This version is called the source program.
- Invoke the compiler to translate, or compile, the source program from C++ to machine language. The machine language version is called the object program.
- Execute the object program.

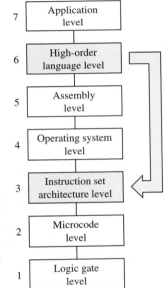

Figure **2.1**

The function of a compiler, which translates a program in a Level 6 language to an equivalent program in a language at a lower level.

Some systems allow you to specify the last two of these steps with a single command, usually called the "run" command. Whether or not you specify the compilation and execution separately, some translation is required before a Level HOL6 program can be executed.

When you write the source program, it will be saved in a file on disk just as any other text document would be. The compiler will produce another file, called a code file, for the object program. Depending on your compiler, the object program may or may not be visible on your file directory after the compilation.

If you want to execute a program that was previously compiled, you do not need to translate it again. You can simply execute the object program directly. If you ever delete the object program from your disk, you can always get it back from the source program by compiling again. But the translation can only go from a high level to a low level. If you delete the source program, you cannot recover it from the object program.

Your C++ compiler is software, not hardware. It is a program that is stored in a file on your disk. Like all programs, the compiler has input, does processing, and produces output. Figure 2.2 shows that the input to the compiler is the source program and the output is the object program.

Figure **2.2**

The compiler as a program.

Machine Independence

Level ISA3 languages are machine dependent. If you write a program in a Level ISA3 language for execution on a Brand X computer, it cannot run on a Brand Y computer. An important property of the languages at Level HOL6 is their machine independence. If you write a program in a Level HOL6 language for execution on a Brand X computer, it will run with only slight modification on a Brand Y computer.

Figure 2.3 shows how C++ achieves its machine independence. Suppose you write an applications program in C++ to do some statistical analysis. You want to sell it to people who own Brand X computers and to others who own Brand Y. The statistics program can be executed only if it is in machine language. Because machine language is machine dependent, you will need two machine-language versions, one for Brand X and one for Brand Y. Because C++ is a common high-order language, you will probably have access to a C++ compiler for the Brand X machine and a C++ compiler for the Brand Y machine. If so, you can simply invoke the Brand X C++ compiler on one machine to produce the Brand X machine language version, and invoke the Brand Y C++ compiler on the other machine for the Brand Y version. You need to write only one C++ program.

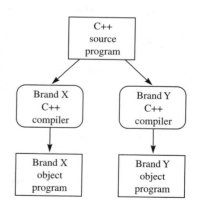

Figure **2.3**

The machine independence of a Level HOL6 language.

The C++ Memory Model

The C++ programming language has three different kinds of variables—global variables, local variables, and dynamically allocated variables. The value of a variable is stored in the main memory of a computer, but the way in which it is stored depends on the kind of variable. There are three special sections of memory corresponding to the three kinds of variables:

- Global variables are stored at a fixed location in memory.
- Local variables are stored on the run-time stack.
- Dynamically allocated variables are stored on the heap.

Global variables are declared outside of any function and remain in place throughout the execution of the entire program. Local variables are declared within a function. They come into existence when the function is called and cease to exist when the function terminates. Dynamically allocated variables come into existence with the execution of the new operator and cease to exist with the execution of the delete operator.

A stack is a container of values that stores values with the push operation and retrieves them with the pop operation. The policy for storage and retrieval is last in, first out. That is, when you pop a value from a stack, the value you get is the last one that was pushed. For this reason, a stack is sometimes called a LIFO list, where LIFO is an acronym for "last in, first out". *The push and pop operations*

Every C++ statement that executes is part of a function. A C++ function has a return type, a name, and a list of parameters. A program consists of a special function whose name is main. A program executes by executing the statements in the main function. It is possible for a main statement to call another function. When a function executes, allocation on the run-time stack takes place in the following order:

- Push storage for the returned value. *Function call*
- Push the parameters.
- Push the return address.
- Push storage for the local variables.

Then, when the function terminates, deallocation from the run-time stake takes place in the opposite order:

- Deallocate the local variables. *Function return*
- Pop the return address and use it to determine the next instruction to execute.
- Deallocate the parameters.
- Pop the returned value and use it as specified in the calling statement.

These actions occur whether the function is the main function or is a function called by a statement in another function.

The programs in this chapter illustrate the memory model of the C++ programming language. Later chapters show the object code for the same programs after the compiler translates them to level Asmb5.

Global Variables and Assignment Statements

Every C++ variable has three attributes:

- Name
- Type
- Value

The three attributes of a C++ variable

A variable's name is an identifier determined arbitrarily by the programmer. A variable's type specifies the kind of values it can have. Figure 2.4 shows a program that declares two global variables, inputs values for them, operates on the values, and outputs the result. This is a nonsense program whose sole purpose is to illustrate some features of the C++ language.

```
// Stan Warford
// A nonsense program to illustrate global variables.

#include <iostream>
using namespace std;

char ch;
int j;

int main () {
   cin >> ch >> j;
   j += 5;
   ch++;
   cout << ch << endl << j << endl;
   return 0;
}
```

Input

M 419

Output

N
424

Figure **2.4**

The assignment statement with global variables at levels HOL6 and Asmb5.

The first two lines in Figure 2.4 are comments, which are ignored by the compiler. Comments in a C++ source program begin with two slash characters // and continue until the end of the line. The next line in the program is

```
#include <iostream>
```

which is a compiler directive to make a library of functions available to the program. In this case, the library file iostream contains the input function >> and the output function << used later in the program. This directive, or one similar to it, is necessary for all programs that use >> and <<. The statement

```
using namespace std;
```

is necessary to use the identifiers cin and cout, which are defined in the namespace std. Without the using statement, cin and cout would have to be fully qualified. For example, the first line in main() would have to be written

```
std::cin >> ch >> j;
```

The next two lines in the program

```
char ch;
int j;
```

declare two global variables. The name of the first variable is ch. Its type is character, as specified by the word char, which precedes its name. As with most variables, its value cannot be determined from the listing. Instead, it gets its value from an input statement. The name of the second variable is j with type integer, as specified by int. Every C++ program has a main function, which contains the executable statements of the program. In Figure 2.4, because the variables are declared outside the main program, they are global variables.

Global variables are declared outside of main().

The next line in the program

```
int main () {
```

declares the main program to be a function that returns an integer. The C++ compiler must generate code that executes on a particular operating system. It is up to the operating system to interpret the value returned. The standard convention is that a returned value of 0 indicates that no errors occurred during the program's execution. If an execution error does occur, the program is interrupted and returns some nonzero value without reaching the last executable statement of main(). What happens in such a case depends on the particular operating system and the nature of the error. All the C++ programs in this book use the common convention of returning 0 as the last executable statement in the main function.

The returned value for main().

The first executable statement in Figure 2.4 is

```
cin >> ch >> j;
```

This statement uses the input operator >> in conjunction with cin, which denotes the standard input device. The standard input device can be either the keyboard or a disk file. In a UNIX environment, the default input device is the keyboard. You can redirect the input to come from a disk file when you execute the program. This input statement gives the first value in the input stream to `ch` and the second value to `j`.

The second executable statement is

```
j += 5;
```

The assignment operator in C++ is =, which is pronounced "gets." The above statement is equivalent to the assignment statement

```
j = j + 5;
```

which is pronounced "j gets j plus five."

Unlike some programming languages, C++ treats characters as if they were integers. You can perform arithmetic on them. The next executable statement

```
ch++;
```

adds 1 to `ch` with the increment operator. It is identical to the assignment statement

```
ch = ch + 1;
```

The C++ programming language is an extension of the C language (which was itself a successor of the B language). The language designers used a little play on words with this increment operator when they decided on the name for C++.

The next executable statement is

```
cout << ch << endl << j << endl;
```

This statement uses the output operator `<<` in conjunction with `cout`, which denotes the standard output device. The standard output device can be either the screen or a disk file. In a UNIX environment, the default output device is the screen. You can redirect the input to go to a disk file when you execute the program. `endl` stands for "end line." This output statement sends the value of variable `ch` to the output device, moves the cursor to the start of the next line, sends the value of variable `j` to the output device, and then moves the cursor to the start of the next line.

Figure 2.5 shows the memory model for the program of Figure 2.4 just before the program terminates. Storage for the global variables `ch` and `j` is allocated at a fixed location in memory as Figure 2.5(a) shows.

(a) Fixed location.

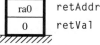

(b) Run-time stack.

Figure **2.5**

The memory model for the program of Figure 2.4.

Remember that when a function is called, four items are allocated on the run-time stack: returned value, parameters, return address, and local variables. Because the main function in this program has no parameters and no local variables, the only items allocated on the stack are storage for the returned value, labeled `retVal`, and the return address, labeled `retAddr`, in Figure 2.5(b). The figure shows the value for the return address as ra0, which is the address of the instruction in the operating system that will execute when the program terminates. The details of the operating system at level OS4 are hidden from us at level HOL6.

Local Variables

Global variables are allocated at a fixed position in main memory. Local variables, however, are allocated on the run-time stack. In a C++ program, local variables are declared within the main program. The program in Figure 2.6 declares a constant and three local variables that represent two scores on exams for a course, and the total score computed as their average plus a bonus.

Local variables are declared within `main()`.

```
#include <iostream>
using namespace std;

int main () {
   const int bonus = 5;
   int exam1;
   int exam2;
   int score;
   cin >> exam1 >> exam2;
   score = (exam1 + exam2) / 2 + bonus;
   cout << "score = " << score << endl;
   return 0;
}
```

Input

68 84

Output

score = 81

Figure **2.6**

A C++ program that processes three local integer values.

Before the first variable is the constant `bonus`. A constant is like a variable in that it has a name, a type, and a value. Unlike a variable, however, the value of a constant cannot change. The value of this constant is 5, as specified by the initialization operator `=`.

The first executable statement in Figure 2.6 is

```
cin >> exam1 >> exam2;
```

which gives the first value in the input stream to `exam1` and the second value to `exam2`. The second executable statement is

```
score = (exam1 + exam2) / 2 + bonus;
```

which adds the values in `exam1` and `exam2`, divides the sum by 2 to get their average, adds the bonus to the average, and then assigns the value to the variable `score`. Because `exam1`, `exam2`, and 2 are all integers, the division operator / represents integer division. If either `exam1` or `exam2` is declared to be a floating point value, or if the divisor is written as `2.0` instead of 2, then the division operator represents floating point division. Integer division truncates the remainder, whereas floating point division maintains the fractional part.

Integer versus floating-point division

Example 2.1   If the input of the program in Figure 2.6 is

```
68 85
```

then the output is still

```
score = 81
```

The sum of the exams is 153. If you divide 153 by 2.0 you get the floating point value 76.5. But if you divide 153 by 2 the / operator represents integer division and the fractional part is truncated, in other words chopped off, yielding 76.   ∎

Example 2.2   If you declare `score` to have a double-precision, floating-point type as follows

```
double score;
```

and if you force the division to be floating point by changing 2 to `2.0` as follows

```
score = (exam1 + exam2) / 2.0 + bonus;
```

then the output is

```
score = 81.5
```

when the input is 68 and 85.   ∎

Floating point division of two numbers produces only one value, the quotient. However, integer division produces two values—the quotient and the remainder—both of which are integers. You can compute the remainder of an integer division with the C++ modulus operator %. Figure 2.7 shows some examples of integer division and the modulus operation.

Expression	Value	Expression	Value
15 / 3	5	15 % 3	0
14 / 3	4	14 % 3	2
13 / 3	4	13 % 3	1
12 / 3	4	12 % 3	0
11 / 3	3	11 % 3	2

Figure **2.7**

Some examples of integer division and the modulus operation.

Figure 2.8 shows the memory model for the local variables in the program of Figure 2.6. The computer allocates storage for all local variables on the run-time stack. When `main()` executes, storage for the returned value, the return address, and local variables `exam1`, `exam2`, and `score` are pushed onto the stack. Because `bonus` is not a variable, it is not pushed onto the stack.

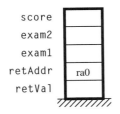

(a) Before the input statement executes.

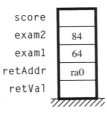

(b) After the input statement executes.

Figure **2.8**

The memory model for the local variables in the program of Figure 2.6.

2.2   Flow of Control

A program operates by executing its statements sequentially, that is, one statement after the other. You can alter the sequence by changing the flow of control in two ways: selection and repetition. C++ has the `if` and `switch` statements for selec-tion, and the `while`, `do`, and `for` statements for repetition. Each of these statements per-forms a test to possibly alter the sequential flow of control. The most common tests use one of the six relational operators shown in Figure 2.9.

Operator	Meaning
==	Equal to
<	Less than
<=	Less than or equal to
>	Greater than
>=	Greater than or equal to
!=	Not equal to

Figure **2.9**

The relational operators.

The If/Else Statement

Figure 2.10 shows a simple use of the C++ `if` statement to perform a test with the greater-than-or-equal-to relational operator `>=`. The program inputs a value for the integer variable `num` and compares it with the constant integer `limit`. If the value of `num` is greater than or equal to the value of `limit`, which is 100, the word high is output. Otherwise, the word `low` is output. It is legal to write an `if` statement without an `else` part.

Figure **2.10**

The C++ `if` statement.

```
#include <iostream>
using namespace std;

int main () {
   const int limit = 100;
   int num;
   cin >> num;
   if (num >= limit) {
      cout << "high";
   }
   else {
      cout << "low";
   }
   return 0;
}
```

Input

75

Output

low

You can combine several relational tests with the boolean operators shown in Figure 2.11. The double ampersand (`&&`) is the symbol for the AND operation, the double vertical bar (`||`) is for the OR operation, and the exclamation point (`!`) is for the NOT operation.

Example 2.3   If `age`, `income`, and `tax` are integer variables, the `if` statement

```
if ((age < 21) && (income <= 4000)) {
   tax = 0;
}
```

Meaning	Symbol
AND	&&
OR	||
NOT	!

Figure **2.11**

The boolean operators.

sets the value of `tax` to 0 if `age` is less than 21 and `income` is less than $4,000. ∎

The `if` statement in Figure 2.10 has a single statement in each alternative. If you want more than one statement to execute in an alternative, you must enclose the statements in braces {}. Otherwise the braces are optional.

Example 2.4   The `if` statement in Figure 2.10 can be written

```
if (num >= limit)
   cout << "high";
```

```
else
    cout << "low";
```

without the braces around the output statements.   ∎

The Switch Statement

The program in Figure 2.12 uses the C++ switch statement to play a little guessing game with the user. It asks the user to pick a number. Then, depending on the number input, it outputs an appropriate message.

You can achieve the same effect yielded by the switch statement using the if statement. However, the equivalent if statement is not quite as efficient as switch.

Example 2.5   The switch statement in Figure 2.12 can be written using the logically equivalent nested if statement:

```
if (guess == 0) {
    cout << "Not close";
}
else if (guess == 1) {
    cout << "Close";
}
```

```
#include <iostream>
using namespace std;

int main () {
    int guess;
    cout << "Pick a number 0..3: ";
    cin >> guess;
    switch (guess) {
        case 0: cout << "Not close"; break;
        case 1: cout << "Close"; break;
        case 2: cout << "Right on"; break;
        case 3: cout << "Too high";
    }
    cout << endl;
    return 0;
}
```

Interactive Input/Output

```
Pick a number 0..3: 1
Close
```

Figure **2.12**

The C++ switch statement.

```
else if (guess == 2) {
   cout << "Right on";
}
else if (guess == 3) {
   cout << "Too high";
}
```

However, this code is not as efficient as the switch. With this code, if the user guesses 3, all four tests will execute. With the switch statement, if the user guesses 3, the program jumps immediately to the "Too high" statement without having to compare guess with 0, 1, and 2.   ∎

The While Loop

The program in Figure 2.13 is a nonsense program whose sole purpose is to illustrate the C++ while loop. It takes as input a sequence of characters that are terminated with the asterisk *. It outputs all the characters up to but not including the asterisk. An experienced C++ programmer would not use this technique. Figure 2.13 and all the programs in this chapter are presented so that they can be analyzed at a lower level of abstraction in later chapters.

```
#include <iostream>
using namespace std;

char letter;

int main () {
   cin >> letter;
   while (letter != '*') {
      cout << letter;
      cin >> letter;
   }
   return 0;
}
```

Input

```
happy*
```

Output

```
happy
```

Figure **2.13**

The C++ while loop.

The program inputs the value of the first character into global variable `letter` before entering the loop. The statement

```
while (letter != '*')
```

compares the value of `letter` with the asterisk character. If they are not equal, the body of the loop executes, which outputs the character and inputs the next one. Flow of control then returns to the test at the top of the loop.

This program would produce identical output if `letter` were local instead of global. Whether to declare a variable as local instead of global is a software design issue. The rule of thumb is to always declare variables to be local unless there is a good reason to do otherwise. Local variables enhance the modularity of software systems and make long programs easier to read and debug. The global variables in Figures 2.4 and 2.13 do not represent good software design. They are presented because they illustrate the C++ memory model. Later chapters show how a C++ compiler would translate the programs presented in this chapter.

The Do Loop

The program in Figure 2.14 illustrates the `do` statement. It is unusual because it has no input. The program produces the same output each time it executes. This is another nonsense program whose purpose is to illustrate flow of control.

```cpp
#include <iostream>
using namespace std;

int cop;
int driver;

int main () {
   cop = 0;
   driver = 40;
   do {
      cop += 25;
      driver += 20;
   }
   while (cop < driver);
   cout << cop;
   return 0;
}
```

Output

```
200
```

Figure **2.14**

The C++ do loop.

A police officer is initially at a position of 0 units when he begins to pursue a driver who is initially at a position of 40 units. Each execution of the loop represents one time interval, during which the officer travels 25 units and the driver 20. The statement

```
cop += 25;
```

is C++ shorthand for

```
cop = cop + 25;
```

Unlike in the loop in Figure 2.13, the do statement has its test at the bottom of the loop. Consequently, the body of the loop is guaranteed to execute at least one time. When the statement

```
while (cop < driver);
```

executes, it compares the value of cop with the value of driver. If cop is less than driver, flow of control transfers to do, and the body of the loop repeats.

Arrays and the For Loop

The program in Figure 2.15 illustrates the for loop and the array. It allocates a local array of four integers, inputs values into the array, and then outputs the values in reverse order.

```
#include <iostream>
using namespace std;

int main () {
   int vector[4];
   int j;
   for (j = 0; j < 4; j++) {
      cin >> vector[j];
   }
   for (j = 3; j >= 0; j--) {
      cout << j << ' ' << vector[j] << endl;
   }
   return 0;
}
```

Figure **2.15**

The C++ for loop with an array.

Input

2 26 -3 9

Output

Figure **2.15**

(Continued)

```
3 9
2 -3
1 26
0 2
```

The statement

```
int vector[4];
```

declares variable `vector` to be an array of four integers. In C++, all arrays have their first index at 0. Hence, this declaration allocates storage for array elements

```
vector[0] vector[1] vector[2] vector[3]
```

The number in the declaration that specifies how many elements will be allocated is always one more than the index of the last element. In this program, 4, which is the number of elements, is one more than 3, which is the index of the last element.

Every `for` statement has a pair of parentheses whose interior is divided into three compartments, each compartment separated from its neighbor by a semicolon. The first compartment initializes, the second compartment tests, and the third compartment increments. In this program, the `for` statement

```
for (j = 0; j < 4; j++)
```

has `j = 0` for the initialization, `j < 4` for the test, and `j++` for the increment.

When the program enters the loop, `j` is set to 0. Because the test is at the top of the loop, the value of `j` is compared to 4. Because `j` is less than 4, the body of the loop

```
cin >> vector[j];
```

executes. The first integer value from the input stream is read into `v[0]`. Control returns to the `for` statement, which increments `j` because of the expression `j++` in the third compartment. The value of `j` is then compared to 4, and the process repeats.

The values are printed in reverse order by the second loop because of the decrement expression

```
j--
```

which is C++ shorthand for

```
j = j - 1
```

2.3   Functions

In C++, there are two kinds of functions: those that return void and those that return some other type. Function `main()` returns an integer, not void. The operating system uses the integer to determine if the program terminated normally. Functions that return void perform their processing without returning a value at all. One common use of void functions is to input or output a collection of values.

Void Functions and Call-By-Value Parameters

The program in Figure 2.16 uses a void function to print a bar chart of data values. The program reads the first value into the integer variable `numPts`. The global variable `j` controls the `for` loop in the main program, which executes `numPts` times. Each time the loop executes, it calls the void function `printBar`. Figure 2.17 shows a trace of the beginning of execution of the program in Figure 2.16.

```
#include <iostream>
using namespace std;

int numPts;
int value;
int j;

void printBar (int n) {
   int k;
   for (k = 1; k <= n; k++) {
      cout << '*';
   }
   cout << endl;
}

int main () {
   cin >> numPts;
   for (j = 1; j <= numPts; j++) {
      cin >> value;
      printBar (value);
   }  // ra1
   return 0;
}
```

Input

12   3 13 17 34 27 23 25 29 16 10 0 2

Figure 2.16

A program that prints a bar chart. The void function prints a single bar.

Output

Figure **2.16**

(Continued)

```
***
*************
******************
**********************************
****************************
***********************
************************
******************************
****************
**********


**
```

Allocation takes place on the run-time stack in the following order when you call a void function:

- Push the actual parameters.

- Push the return address.

- Push storage for the local variables.

The allocation process for a void function

Figure 2.17(e) is the start of the allocation process for Figure 2.16. The program pushes the value of `value` for the formal parameter `n`. It pushes the return address in Figure 2.17(f). In Figure 2.17(g), it pushes storage for the local variable, `k`. After the allocation process, the last local variable in the listing, `k`, is on top of the stack.

The collection of all the items pushed onto the run-time stack is called a stack frame or activation record. In the program of Figure 2.16, the stack frame for the void function consists of three items—`n`, the return address, and `k`. The return address indicated by ra1 in the figure is the address of the end of the for statement of the main program. The stack frame for the `main` function consists of two items—the returned value and the return address.

After the procedure prints a single bar, control returns to the main program. The items on the run-time stack are deallocated in reverse order compared to their allocation. The process is:

- Deallocate storage for the local variables.

- Pop the return address.

- Deallocate the actual parameters.

The deallocation process for a void function

The program uses the return address to know which statement to execute next in the main program after executing the last statement in the void function. That statement is denoted ra1 in the listing of the main program. It is the statement after the procedure call.

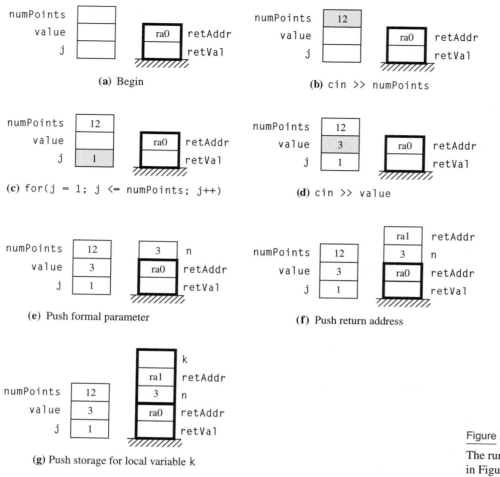

Figure **2.17**

The run-time stack for the program in Figure 2.16.

Functions

The program in Figure 2.18 uses a function to compute the value of the factorial of an integer. It prompts the user for a small integer and passes that integer as a parameter to function fact.

```
#include <iostream>
using namespace std;

int num;
```

Figure **2.18**

A program to compute the factorial of an integer with a function.

```
int fact (int n) {
   int f, j;
   f = 1;
   for (j = 1; j <= n; j++) {
      f *= j;
   }
   return f;
}


int main () {
   cout << "Enter a small integer: ";
   cin >> num;
   cout << "Its factorial is: " << fact (num) << endl; // ra1
   return 0;
}
```

Figure 2.18

(Continued)

Interactive Input/Output

```
Enter a small integer: 3
Its factorial is: 6
```

Figure 2.19 shows the allocation process for the function in Figure 2.18, which returns the factorial of the actual parameter. Figure 2.19(c) shows storage for the returned value pushed first. Figure 2.19(d) shows the value of num, 3, pushed for the formal parameter n. The return address is pushed in Figure 2.19(e). Storage for local variables f and j are pushed in Figure 2.19(f) and (g).

The stack frame for this function has five items. The return address indicated by ra1 in the figure represents the address of the cout statement in the main program. Control returns from the function to the calling statement. This is in contrast to a void function, in which control returns to the statement *following* the calling statement.

Call-By-Reference Parameters

The procedures and functions in the previous programs all pass their parameters by value. In call by value, the formal parameter gets the value of the actual parameter. If the called procedure changes the value of its formal parameter, the corresponding actual parameter in the calling program does not change. Any changes made by the called procedure are made to the value on the run-time stack. When the stack frame is deallocated, any changed values are deallocated with it.

Call by value

If the intent of the procedure is to change the value of the actual parameter in the calling program, then call by reference is used instead of call by value. In call by reference, the formal parameter gets a reference to the actual parameter. If the called procedure changes the value of its formal parameter, the corresponding actual parameter in the calling program changes. To specify that a parameter is

Call by reference

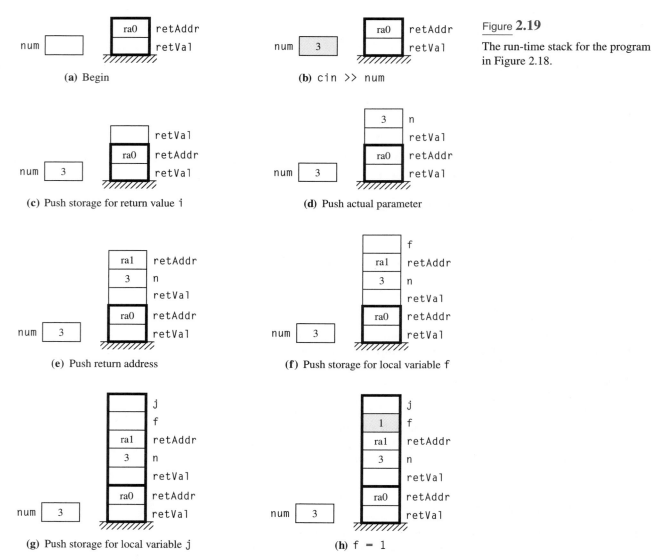

(a) Begin

(b) `cin >> num`

(c) Push storage for return value i

(d) Push actual parameter

(e) Push return address

(f) Push storage for local variable f

(g) Push storage for local variable j

(h) f = 1

Figure **2.19**

The run-time stack for the program in Figure 2.18.

called by reference, you place the ampersand symbol & after the type in the parameter list. If the ampersand is not present, the compiler assumes the parameter is called by value (with one important exception described later).

The program in Figure 2.20 uses call by reference to change the values of the actual parameters. It prompts the user for two integer values and puts them in order. It has one void function, order, that calls another void function, swap. Figure 2.21 shows the allocation and deallocation sequence for the entire program.

```
#include <iostream>
using namespace std;

int a, b;

void swap (int& r, int& s) {
    int temp;
    temp = r;
    r = s;
    s = temp;
}

void order (int& x, int& y) {
    if (x > y) {
        swap (x, y);
    }  // ra2
}

int main () {
    cout << "Enter an integer: ";
    cin >> a;
    cout << "Enter an integer: ";
    cin >> b;
    order (a, b);
    cout << "Ordered they are: " << a << ", " << b << endl; // ra1
    return 0;
}
```

Figure 2.20

A program to put two values in order. The void functions pass parameters by reference.

Interactive Input/Output

```
Enter an integer: 6
Enter an integer: 2
Ordered they are: 2, 6
```

The stack frame for order in Figure 2.21(c) has three items. The formal parameters, x and y, are called by reference. The arrow pointing from x on the run-time stack to a in the main program indicates that x refers to a. Similarly, the arrow from y to b indicates that y refers to b. The return address indicated by ra1 is the address of the cout statement that follows the call to order in the main program.

The stack frame for swap in Figure 2.21(d) has four items. r refers to x, which refers to a. Therefore, r refers to a. The arrow pointing from r on the run-time stack points to a, as does the arrow from x. Similarly, the arrow from s points to b, as does the arrow from y. The return address indicated by ra2 is the address after

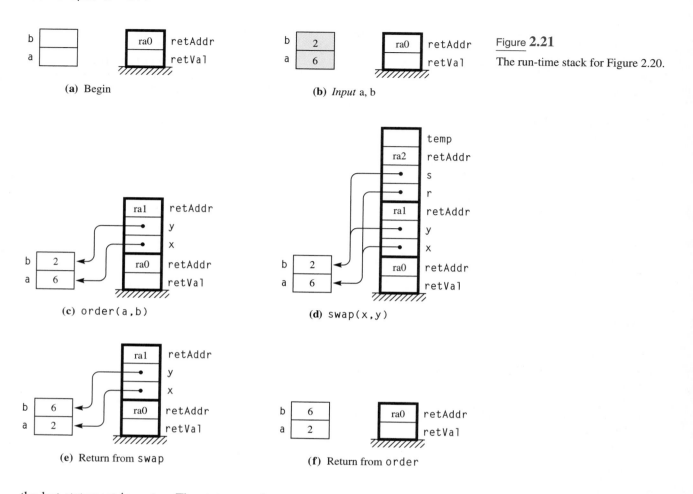

Figure 2.21
The run-time stack for Figure 2.20.

(a) Begin

(b) *Input* a, b

(c) order(a,b)

(d) swap(x,y)

(e) Return from swap

(f) Return from order

the last statement in order. The statements in swap exchange the values of r and s. Because r refers to a and s refers to b, they exchange the values of a and b in the main program.

When a void function terminates and it is time to deallocate its stack frame, the return address in the frame tells the computer which instruction to execute next. Figure 2.21(e) shows the return from void function swap, deallocating its stack frame. The return address in the stack frame for swap tells the computer to execute the statement labeled ra2 in order after deallocation. Although the listing shows no statement at ra2 in Figure 2.20, there is an implied return statement at the end of the void function that is invisible at Level HOL6.

In Figure 2.21(f), the stack frame for order is deallocated. The return address in the stack frame for order tells the computer to execute the cout statement in the main program after deallocation.

Because a stack is a LIFO structure, the last stack frame pushed onto the run-time stack will be the first one popped off at the completion of a function. The return address will, therefore, return control to the most recent calling function. This LIFO property of the run-time stack will be basic to your understanding of recursion in Section 2.4.

You may have noticed that `main()` is always a function that returns an integer and that all the programs thus far have returned 0 to the operating system. Furthermore, all the main program functions thus far have no parameters. Although it is common for a main program to have parameters, none of the programs in this book do. To keep the figures simple, from now on they will omit the `retVal` and `retAddr` for the main program. A real C++ compiler must account for both of them.

A simplification for `main()` *in this book.*

2.4 Recursion

Did you ever look up the definition of some unknown word in the dictionary, only to discover that the dictionary defined it in terms of another unknown word? Then, when you looked up the second word, did you discover that it was defined in terms of the first word? That is an example of circular or indirect recursion. The problem with the dictionary is that you did not know the meaning of the first word to begin with. Had the second word been defined in terms of a third word that you knew, you would have been satisfied.

In mathematics, a *recursive definition* of a function is a definition that uses the function itself. For example, suppose a function, $f(n)$, is defined as follows:

Recursive definitions in mathematics

$$f(n) = nf(n - 1)$$

You want to use this definition to determine $f(4)$, so you substitute 4 for n in the definition:

$$f(4) = 4f(3)$$

But now you do not know what $f(3)$ is. So you substitute 3 for n in the definition and get

$$f(3) = 3f(2)$$

Substituting this into the formula for $f(4)$ gives

$$f(4) = 4(3)f(2)$$

But now you do not know what $f(2)$ is. The definition tells you it is 2 times $f(1)$. So the formula for $f(4)$ becomes

$$f(4) = 4(3)(2)f(1)$$

You can see the problem with this definition. With nothing to stop the process, you will continue to compute $f(4)$ endlessly.

$$f(4) = 4(3)(2)(1)(0)(-1)(-2)(-3) \ldots$$

It is as if the dictionary gave you an endless string of definitions, each based on another unknown word. To be complete, the definition must specify the value of $f(n)$ for a specific value of n. Then the preceding process will terminate, and you can compute $f(n)$ for any n.

Here is a complete recursive definition of $f(n)$:

$f(n) = nf(n - 1)$ for $n > 1$
$f(1) = 1$

This definition says you can stop the previous process at $f(1)$. So $f(4)$ is

$$\begin{aligned} f(4) &= 4f(3) \\ &= 4(3)f(2) \\ &= 4(3)(2)f(1) \\ &= 4(3)(2)(1) \\ &= 24 \end{aligned}$$

You should recognize this definition as the factorial function.

A Factorial Function

A *recursive function* in C++ is a function that calls itself. There is no special recursion statement with a new syntax to learn. The method of storage allocation on the run-time stack is the same as with nonrecursive functions. The only difference is that a recursive function contains a statement that calls itself.   *Recursive functions in C++*

The function in Figure 2.22 computes the factorial of a number recursively. It is a direct application of the recursive definition of $f(n)$, which was just shown.

Figure 2.23 is a trace that shows the run-time stack with the simplification of not showing the stack frame of the main program. The first function call is from the main program. Figure 2.23(c) shows the stack frame for the first call. The return address is ra1, which represents the address of the cout call in the main program.

Figure **2.22**

A program to compute the factorial recursively.

```
#include <iostream>
using namespace std;

int num;

int fact (int n) {
   if (n <= 1) {
      return 1;
   }
   else {
      return n * fact(n - 1); // ra2
   }
}

int main () {
   cout << "Enter a small integer: ";
   cin >> num;
   cout << "Its factorial is: " << fact (num) << endl; // ra1
   return 0;
}
```

Interactive Input/Output

```
Enter a small integer: 4
Its factorial is: 24
```

The first statement in the function tests n for 1. Because the value of n is 4, the else part executes. But the statement in the else part

```
return n * fact (n - 1) // ra2
```

contains a call to function fact on the right side of the return statement.

This is a recursive call because it is a call to the function within the function itself. The same sequence of events happens as with any function call. A new stack frame is allocated, as Figure 2.23(d) shows. The return address in the second stack frame is the address of the calling statement in the function, represented by ra2.

The actual parameter is n - 1, whose value is 3 because the value of n in Figure 2.23(c) is 4. The formal parameter, n, is called by value. Therefore, the value of 3 is given to the formal parameter n in the top frame of Figure 2.23(d).

Figure 2.23(d) shows a curious situation that is typical of recursive calls. The program listing of Figure 2.22 shows only one declaration of n in the formal parameter list of fact. But Figure 2.23(d) shows two instances of n. The old instance of n

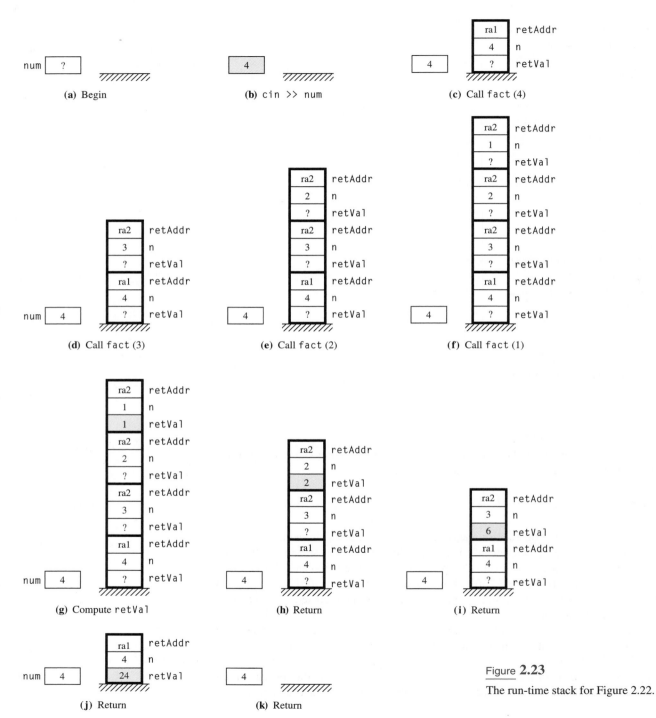

(a) Begin

(b) cin >> num

(c) Call fact (4)

(d) Call fact (3)

(e) Call fact (2)

(f) Call fact (1)

(g) Compute retVal

(h) Return

(i) Return

(j) Return

(k) Return

Figure **2.23**

The run-time stack for Figure 2.22.

has the value 4 from the main program. But the new instance of `n` has the value 3 from the recursive call.

Multiple instances of local variables and parameters

The computer suspends the old execution of the function and begins a new execution of the same function from its beginning. The first statement in the function tests `n` for 1. But which `n`? Figure 2.23(d) shows two `n`s on the run-time stack. The rule is that any reference to a local variable or formal parameter is to the one on the top stack frame. Because the value of `n` is 3, the `else` part executes.

But now the function makes another recursive call. It allocates a third stack frame, as Figure 2.23(e) shows, and then a fourth, as Figure 2.23(f) shows. Each time, the newly allocated formal parameter gets a value one less than the old value of `n` because the function call is

```
fact(n - 1)
```

Finally, in Figure 2.23(g), `n` has the value 1. The function gives 1 to the cell on the stack labeled `retVal`. It skips the `else` part and terminates. That triggers a return to the calling statement.

The same events transpire with a recursive return as with a nonrecursive return. `retVal` contains the returned value, and the return address tells which statement to execute next. In Figure 2.22(g), `retVal` is 1 and the return address is the calling statement in the function. The top frame is deallocated, and the calling statement

```
return n * fact(n - 1) // ra2
```

completes its execution. It multiplies its value of `n`, which is 2, by the value returned, which is 1, and assigns the result to `retVal`. So, `retVal` gets 2, as Figure 2.23(h) shows.

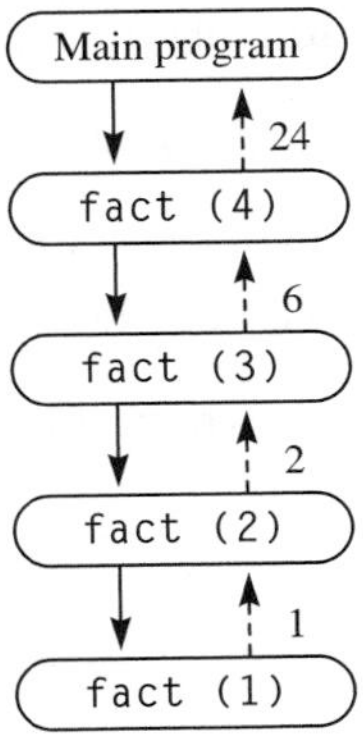

Figure **2.24**

The calling sequence for Figure 2.22. The solid arrows represent function calls. The dotted arrows represent returns. The value returned is next to each return arrow.

A similar sequence of events occurs on each return. Figures 2.23(i) and (j) show that the value returned from the second call is 6 and from the first call is 24. Figure 2.24 shows the calling sequence for Figure 2.22. The main program calls `fact`. Then `fact` calls itself three times. In this example, `fact` is called a total of four times.

You see that the program computes the factorial of 4 the same way you would compute *f*(4) from its recursive definition. You start by computing *f*(4) as 4 times *f*(3). Then you must suspend your computation of *f*(4) to compute *f*(3). After you get your result for *f*(3), you can multiply it by 4 to get *f*(4).

Similarly, the program must suspend its execution of the function to call the same function again. The run-time stack keeps track of the current values of the variables so they can be used when that instance of the function resumes.

Thinking Recursively

The microscopic and macroscopic viewpoints of recursion

You can take two different viewpoints when dealing with recursion: microscopic and macroscopic. Figure 2.23 illustrates the microscopic viewpoint and shows precisely what happens inside the computer during execution. It is the viewpoint that considers the details of the run-time stack during a trace of the program. The macroscopic viewpoint does not consider the individual trees. It considers the forest as a whole.

You need to know the microscopic viewpoint to understand how C++ implements recursion. The details of the run-time stack will be necessary when you study how recursion is implemented at Level Asmb5. But to write a recursive function, you should think macroscopically, not microscopically.

The most difficult aspect of writing a recursive function is the assumption that you can call the procedure that you are in the process of writing. To make that assumption, you must think macroscopically and forget about the run-time stack.

Proof by mathematical induction can help you think macroscopically. The two key elements of proof by induction are

- Establish the basis.

- Given the formula for n, prove it for $n + 1$.

Similarly, the two key elements of designing a recursive function are

The relation between proof by mathematical induction and recursion

- Compute the function for the basis.

- Assuming the function for $n - 1$, write it for n.

Imagine you are writing function `fact`. You get to this point:

```
int fact (int n) {
   if (n <= 1) {
      return 1;
   }
   else {
```

and wonder how to continue. You have computed the function for the basis, n = 1. But now you must assume that you can call function `fact`, even though you have not finished writing `fact`. You must assume that `fact(n - 1)` will return the correct value for the factorial.

Here is where you must think macroscopically. If you start wondering how `fact(n - 1)` will return the correct value, and if visions of stack frames begin dancing in your head, you are not thinking correctly. In proof by induction, you must assume the formula for n. Similarly, in writing `fact`, you must assume that you can call `fact(n - 1)` with no questions asked.

The importance of thinking macroscopically when you design a recursive function

Recursive programs are based on a divide and conquer strategy, which is appropriate when you can solve a large problem in terms of a smaller one. Each recursive call makes the problem smaller and smaller, until the program reaches the smallest problem of all, the basis, which is simple to solve.

The divide and conquer strategy

Recursive Addition

Here is another example of a recursive problem. Suppose `list` is an array of integers. You want to find the sum of all integers in the list recursively.

The first step is to formulate the solution of the large problem in terms of a smaller problem. If you knew how to find the sum of the integers between `list[0]` and `list[n - 1]`, you could simply add it to `list[n]`. You would then have the sum of all the integers.

The next step is to design a function with the appropriate parameters. The function will compute the sum of `n` integers by calling itself to compute the sum of `n - 1` integers. So the parameter list must have a parameter that tells how many integers in the array to add. That should lead you to the following function head:

```
int sum (int a[], int n) {
// Returns the sum of the elements of a between a[0] and a[n].
```

How do you establish the basis? That is simple. If `n` is 0, the function should add the sum of the elements between `a[0]` and `a[0]`. The sum of one element is just `a[0]`.

Now you can write

```
if (n == 0) {
    return a[0];
}
else {
```

Now think macroscopically. You can assume that `sum(a, n - 1)` will return the sum of the integers between `a[0]` and `a[n - 1]`. Have faith. All you need to do is add that sum to `a[n]`. Figure 2.25 shows the function in a finished program.

Even though you write the function without considering the microscopic view, you can still trace the run-time stack. Figure 2.26 shows the stack frames for the first two calls to `sum`. The stack frame consists of the value returned, the parameters `a` and `n`, and the return address. Because there are no local variables, no storage for them is allocated on the run-time stack.

In C++, arrays are always called by reference. Hence, variable `a` in procedure `sum` refers to `list` in the main program. The arrows in Figure 2.26(b) and (c) that point from the cells labeled `a` in the stack frame to the cell labeled `list` indicate the reference of `a` to `list`.

Arrays always called by reference

A Binomial Coefficient Function

The next example of a recursive function has a more complex calling sequence. It is a function to compute the coefficient in the expansion of a binomial expression.

Consider the following expansions:

$$(x + y)^1 = x + y$$
$$(x + y)^2 = x^2 + 2xy + y^2$$

```cpp
#include <iostream>
using namespace std;

int list[4];

int sum (int a[], int n) {
// Returns the sum of the elements of a between a[0] and a[n].
   if (n == 0) {
      return a[0];
   }
   else {
      return a[n] + sum(a, n - 1); // ra2
   }
}

int main () {
   cout << "Enter four integers: ";
   cin >> list[0] >> list[1] >> list[2] >> list[3];
   cout << "Their sum is: " << sum(list, 3) << endl; // ra1
   return 0;
}
```

Interactive Input/Output

```
Enter four integers: 3 2 6 4
Their sum is: 15
```

Figure **2.25**

A recursive function that returns the sum of the first n numbers in an array.

Figure **2.26**

The run-time stack for the program in Figure 2.25.

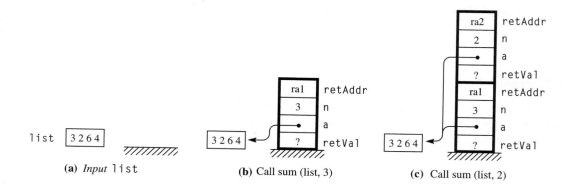

(a) *Input* list　　(b) Call sum (list, 3)　　(c) Call sum (list, 2)

$(x + y)^3 = x^3 + 3x^2y + 3xy^2 + y^3$

$(x + y)^4 = x^4 + 4x^3y + 6x^2y^2 + 4xy^3 + y^4$

The coefficients of the terms are called *binomial coefficients*. If you write the coefficients without the terms, they form a triangle of values called *Pascal's triangle*. Figure 2.27 is Pascal's triangle for the coefficients up to the seventh power.

You can see from Figure 2.27 that each coefficient is the sum of the coefficient immediately above and the coefficient above and to the left. For example, the binomial coefficient in row 5, column 2, which is 10, equals 4 plus 6. Six is above 10, and 4 is above and to the left.

Mathematically, the binomial coefficient $b(n, k)$ for power n and term k is

$$b(n, k) = b(n - 1, k) + b(n - 1, k - 1) \quad \text{for} \quad 0 \le k \le n.$$

That is a recursive definition because it defines the function $b(n, k)$ in terms of itself. You can also see that if k equals 0, or if n equals k, the value of the binomial coefficient is 1. Mathematically,

$b(n, 0) = 1$

$b(k, k) = 1$

which is the basis for the recursive function.

Figure 2.28 computes the value of a binomial coefficient recursively. It is based directly on the recursive definition of $b(n, k)$. Figure 2.29 shows a trace of the run-time stack. Figure 2.29(b), (c), and (d) show the allocation of the first three stack frames. They represent calls to `binCoeff(3, 1)`, `binCoeff(2, 1)`, and `binCoeff(1, 1)`. The first stack frame has the return address of the calling program in the main program. The next two stack frames have the return address of the `y1` assignment statement. `ra2` represents that statement.

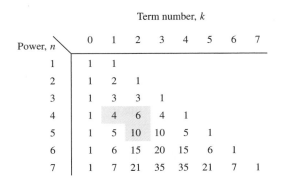

Term number, k

Power, n	0	1	2	3	4	5	6	7
1	1	1						
2	1	2	1					
3	1	3	3	1				
4	1	4	6	4	1			
5	1	5	10	10	5	1		
6	1	6	15	20	15	6	1	
7	1	7	21	35	35	21	7	1

Figure **2.27**

Pascal's triangle of binomial coefficients.

```cpp
#include <iostream>
using namespace std;

int binCoeff (int n, int k) {
   int y1, y2;
   if ((k == 0) || (n == k)) {
      return 1;
   }
   else {
      y1 = binCoeff (n - 1, k); // ra2
      y2 = binCoeff (n - 1, k - 1); // ra3
      return y1 + y2;
   }
}

int main () {
   cout << "binCoeff (3, 1) = " << binCoeff (3, 1); // ra1
   cout << endl;
   return 0;
}
```

Output

```
binCoeff(3, 1) = 3
```

Figure **2.28**

A recursive computation of the binomial coefficient.

Figure 2.29(e) shows the return from `binCoeff(1, 1)`. `y1` gets the value 1 returned by the function. Then the `y2` assignment statement calls the function `binCoeff(1, 0)`. Figure 2.29(f) shows the run-time stack during execution of `bin-Coeff(1, 0)`. Each stack frame has a different return address.

The calling sequence for this program is different from those of the previous recursive programs. The other programs keep allocating stack frames until the run-time stack reaches its maximum height. Then they keep deallocating stack frames until the run-time stack is empty. This program allocates stack frames until the run-time stack reaches its maximum height. It does not deallocate stack frames until the run-time stack is empty, however. From Figure 2.29(d) to (e) it deallocates, but from 2.29(e) to (f) it allocates. From 2.29(f) to (g) to (h) it deallocates, but from 2.29(h) to (i) it allocates. Why? Because this function has two recursive calls instead of one. If the basis step is true, the function makes no recursive call. But if the basis step is false, the function makes two recursive calls, one for `y1` and one for `y2`. Figure 2.30 shows the calling sequence for the program. Notice that it is in the shape of a tree. Each node of the tree represents a function call. Except for the main

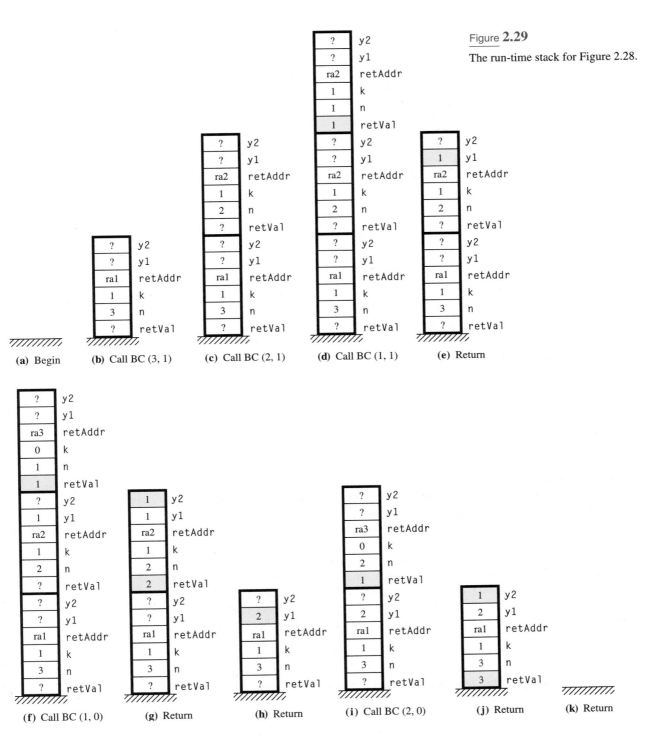

Figure **2.29**

The run-time stack for Figure 2.28.

(a) Begin (b) Call BC (3, 1) (c) Call BC (2, 1) (d) Call BC (1, 1) (e) Return

(f) Call BC (1, 0) (g) Return (h) Return (i) Call BC (2, 0) (j) Return (k) Return

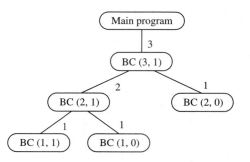

Figure **2.30**

The call tree for the program in Figure 2.28.

program, a node has either two children or no children, corresponding to two recursive calls or no recursive calls.

Referring to Figure 2.30, the sequence of calls and returns is

Main program
    Call BC(3, 1)
        Call BC(2, 1)
            Call BC(1, 1)
        Return to BC(2, 1)
            Call BC(1, 0)
        Return to BC(2, 1)
    Return to BC(3, 1)
        Call BC(2, 0)
    Return to BC(3, 1)
Return to main program

The sequence of calls and returns for the program in Figure 2.28

You can visualize the order of execution on the call tree by imagining that the tree is a coastline in an ocean. A boat starts from the left side of the main program and sails along the coast, always keeping the shore to its left. The boat visits the nodes in the same order from which they are called and returned. Figure 2.31 shows the visitation path.

When analyzing a recursive program from a microscopic point of view, it is easier to construct the call tree before you construct the trace of the run-time stack. Once you have the tree, it is easy to see the behavior of the run-time stack. Every time the boat visits a lower node in the tree, the program allocates one stack frame. Every time the boat visits a higher node in the tree, the program deallocates one stack frame.

You can determine the maximum height of the run-time stack from the call tree. Just keep track of the net number of stack frames allocated when you get to the lowest node of the call tree. That will correspond to the maximum height of the run-time stack.

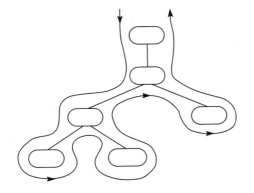

Figure **2.31**

The order of execution of the program in Figure 2.28.

Drawing the call tree in the order of execution is not the easiest way. The previous execution sequence started

Main program
    Call BC(3, 1)
        Call BC(2, 1)
            Call BC(1, 1)

You should not draw the call tree in that order. It is easier to start with

Main program
    Call BC(3, 1)

    Return to BC(3, 1)

    Return to BC(3, 1)
Return to main program

recognizing from the program listing that BC(3, 1) will call itself twice, BC(2, 1) once, and BC(2, 0) once. Then you can go back to BC(2, 1) and determine its children. In other words, determine all the children of a node before analyzing the deeper calls from any one of the children.

This is a "breadth first" construction of the tree as opposed to the "depth first" construction, which follows the execution sequence. The problem with the depth-first construction arises when you return up several levels in a complicated call tree to some higher node. You might forget the state of execution the node is in and not be able to determine its next child node. If you determine all the children of a node at once, you no longer need to remember the state of execution of the node.

Constructing the call tree breadth first

Reversing the Elements of an Array

Figure 2.32 has a recursive procedure instead of a function. It reverses the elements in an array of characters.

```
#include <iostream>
using namespace std;

char word[32] = "Backward";

void reverse (char str[], int j, int k) {
   char temp;
   if (j < k) {
      temp = str[j];
      str[j] = str[k];
      str[k] = temp;
      reverse(str, j + 1, k - 1);
   } // ra2
}

int main () {
   reverse (word, 0, 7);
   cout << word << endl; // ra1
   return 0;
}
```

Output

```
drawkcaB
```

Figure 2.32

A recursive procedure to reverse the elements of an array.

The procedure reverses the characters in the array str between str[j] and str[k]. The main program wants to reverse the characters between 'B' and 'd.' So it calls reverse with 0 for j and 7 for k.

The procedure solves this problem by breaking it down into a smaller problem. Because 0 is less than 7, the procedure knows the characters between 0 and 7 need to be reversed. So it switches str[0] with str[7] and calls itself recursively to switch all the characters between str[1] and str[6]. If j is ever greater than or equal to k, no switching is necessary and the procedure does nothing. Figure 2.33 shows the beginning of a trace of the run-time stack.

Towers of Hanoi

The Towers of Hanoi puzzle is a classic computer science problem that is conveniently solved by the recursive technique. The puzzle consists of three pegs and a set of disks with different diameters. The pegs are numbered 1, 2, and 3. Each disk

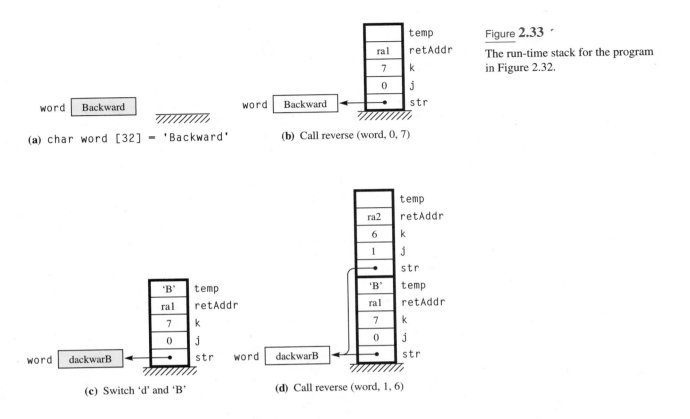

word
Backward
(a) char word [32] = 'Backward'
temp
ra1
retAddr
7
k
0
j
word
Backward
str
(b) Call reverse (word, 0, 7)
'B'
temp
ra1
retAddr
7
k
0
j
word
dackwarB
str
(c) Switch 'd' and 'B'
temp
ra2
retAddr
6
k
1
j
str
'B'
temp
ra1
retAddr
7
k
0
j
word
dackwarB
str
(d) Call reverse (word, 1, 6)

Figure **2.33**

The run-time stack for the program in Figure 2.32.

has a hole at its center so that it can fit onto one of the pegs. The initial configuration of the puzzle consists of all the disks on one peg in a way that no disk rests directly on another disk with a smaller diameter. Figure 2.34 is the initial configuration for four disks.

1
2
3

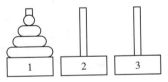

Figure **2.34**

The Towers of Hanoi puzzle.

The problem is to move all the disks from the starting peg to another peg under the following conditions:

- You may move only one disk at a time. It must be the top disk from one peg, which is moved to the top of another peg.
- You may not place one disk on another disk having a smaller diameter.

The procedure for solving this problem has three parameters, `n`, `j`, and `k`, where

- `n` is the number of disks to move
- `j` is the starting peg
- `k` is the goal peg

Bjarne Stroustrup

Bjarne Stroustrup was born in Aarhus, Denmark, in 1950. Although not from an academic family, he worked his way to a master's degree in mathematics from Aarhus University and later to a PhD in computer science from Cambridge University.

Stroustrup did not grow up with computers. The first one he saw was at his university's math department. It filled an entire room, and he learned how to program it with a language called Algol 60. For his PhD work, he wrote a distributed systems simulator in a programming language called Simula67. He financed much of his formal education by writing small commercial programs that other people would rely on for their livelihoods. He credits this experience with helping him to understand the real-world importance of programming.

After completing his studies at Cambridge in 1979, Stroustrup moved with his family to New Jersey, where he worked as a research scientist for AT&T Bell Labs at Murray Hill. The C language and the UNIX operating system were gaining in popularity at the Labs, where they were both developed.

Stroustrup was not satisfied with the programming languages at the time, so he invented a new one called C with Classes by adding object-oriented programming features, such as those found in Simula67, to the C language. Eventually, he evolved the language into C++, and he is now known primarily as its inventor. Stroustrup decided early on that he wanted his language to support real users. He knew that his language would be widely used if

people did not have to learn a completely new language, so he made C++ with few exceptions compatible with C. That is, most programs written in C could be translated by a C++ compiler (although not vice versa, obviously). This goal placed constraints on the language design but was instrumental in its adoption. Stroustrup has stated, "Had C not been there to be compatible with, I would have chosen some other language to be compatible with. I was—and am—convinced that my time would not have been well spent inventing yet another way of writing a loop." In practice, the language is extremely successful in the market. It is used to write such applications as Microsoft Word, Adobe Photoshop, and Google's search engine.

Stroustrup was elected to the National Academy of Engineering, is an AT&T Bell Laboratories Fellow, and received the ACM Grace Murray Hopper award. At the time of this writing, he holds the College of Engineering Chair in Computer Science at Texas A&M University.

"I have always wished that my computer would be as easy to use as my telephone. My wish has come true. I no longer know how to use my telephone."

—*Bjarne Stroustrup*

j and k are integers that identify the pegs. Given the values of j and k, you can calculate the intermediate peg, which is the one that is neither the starting peg nor the goal peg, as 6 - j - k. For example, if the starting peg is 1 and the goal peg is 3, then the intermediate peg is 6 − 1 − 3 = 2.

To move the n disks from peg j to peg k, first check whether n = 1. If it does, then simply move the one disk from peg j to peg k. But if it does not, then decompose the problem into several smaller parts:

- Move n - 1 disks from peg j to the intermediate peg.
- Move one disk from peg j to peg k.
- Move n - 1 disks from the intermediate peg to peg k.

Figure **2.35**

The solution for moving four disks from peg 1 to peg 3, assuming that you can move three disks from one peg to any other peg.

Figure 2.35 shows this decomposition for the problem of moving four disks from peg 1 to peg 3.

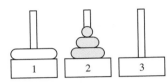 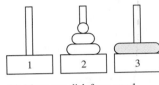 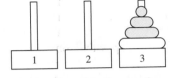

(a) Move three disks from peg 1 to peg 2.

(b) Move one disk from peg 1 to peg 3.

(c) Move three disks from peg 2 to peg 3.

This procedure guarantees that a disk will not be placed on another disk with a smaller diameter, assuming that the original n disks are stacked correctly. Suppose, for example, that four disks are to be moved from peg 1 to peg 3, as in Figure 2.35. The procedure says that you should move the top three disks from peg 1 to peg 2, move the bottom disk from peg 1 to peg 3, and then move the three disks from peg 2 to peg 3.

In moving the top three disks from peg 1 to peg 2, you will leave the bottom disk on peg 1. Remember that it is the disk with the largest diameter, so any disk you place on it in the process of moving the other disks will be smaller. In order to move the bottom disk from peg 1 to peg 3, peg 3 must be empty. You will not place the bottom disk on a smaller disk in this step either. When you move the three disks from peg 2 to peg 3, you will place them on the largest disk, now on the bottom of peg 3. So the three disks will be placed on peg 3 correctly.

The procedure is recursive. In the first step, you must move three disks from peg 1 to peg 2. To do that, move two disks from peg 1 to peg 3, then one disk from peg 1 to peg 2, then two disks from peg 3 to peg 2. Figure 2.36 shows this sequence. Using the previous reasoning, these steps will be carried out correctly. In the process of moving two disks from peg 1 to peg 3, you may place any of these two disks on the bottom two disks of peg 1 without fear of breaking the rules.

Figure **2.36**

The solution for moving three disks from peg 1 to peg 2, assuming that you can move two disks from one peg to any other peg.

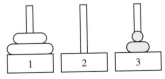 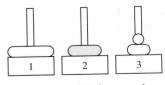 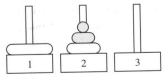

(a) Move two disks from peg 1 to peg 3.

(b) Move one disk from peg 1 to peg 2.

(c) Move two disks from peg 3 to peg 2.

Eventually you will reduce the problem to the basis step where you need to move only one disk. But the solution with one disk is easy. Programming the solution to the Towers of Hanoi puzzle is a problem at the end of the chapter.

Mutual Recursion

Some problems are best solved by procedures that do not call themselves directly but that are recursive nonetheless. Suppose a main program calls procedure a, and procedure a contains a call to procedure b. If procedure b contains a call to procedure a, then a and b are mutually recursive. Even though procedure a does not call itself directly, it does call itself indirectly through procedure b.

There is nothing different about the implementation of mutual recursion compared to plain recursion. Stack frames are allocated on the run-time stack the same way, with parameters allocated first, followed by the return address, followed by local variables.

There is one slight problem in specifying mutually recursive procedures in a C++ program, however. It arises from the fact that procedures must be declared before they are used. If procedure a calls procedure b, the declaration of procedure b must appear before the declaration of procedure a in the listing. But if procedure b calls procedure a, the declaration of procedure a must appear before the declaration of procedure b in the listing. The problem is that if each calls the other, each must appear before the other in the listing, an obvious impossibility.

For this situation, C++ provides the *function prototype*, which allows the programmer to write the first procedure heading without the body. In a function prototype, you include the complete formal parameter list, but in place of the body, you put ;. After the function prototype comes the declaration of the second procedure, followed by the body of the first procedure.

The function prototype

Example 2.6   Here is an outline of the structure of the mutually recursive procedures a and b as just discussed:

Constants, types, variables of main program

```
void a (SomeType x);

void b (SomeOtherType y) {

    Body for b
}

void a (SomeType x) {

    Body for a
}
```

```
int main() {
    Executable statements of main program
}
```

If b has a call to a, the compiler will be able to verify that the number and types of the actual parameters match the formal parameters of a scanned earlier in the function prototype. If a has a call to b, the call will be in the body of a. The compiler will have scanned the declaration of b because it occurs before the block of a. ∎

Although mutual recursion is not as common as recursion, some compilers are based on a technique called *recursive descent*, which uses mutual recursion heavily. You can get an idea of why this is so by considering the structure of C++ statements. It is possible to nest an if inside a while, which is nested in turn inside another if. A compiler that uses recursive descent has a procedure to translate if statements and another procedure to translate while statements. When the procedure that is translating the outer if statement encounters the while statement, it calls the procedure that translates while statements. But when that procedure encounters the nested if statement, it calls the statement that translates if statements; hence the mutual recursion.

Mutual recursion in a recursive descent compiler

The Cost of Recursion

The selection of examples in this section was based on only one criterion: the ability of the example to illustrate recursion. You can see that recursive solutions require much storage for the run-time stack. It also takes time to allocate and deallocate the stack frames. Recursive solutions are expensive in both space and time.

If you can solve a problem easily without recursion, the nonrecursive solution will usually be better than the recursive solution. Figure 2.18, the nonrecursive function to calculate the factorial, is certainly better than the recursive factorial function of Figure 2.22. Both Figure 2.25, to find the sum of the numbers in an array, and Figure 2.32 can easily be programmed nonrecursively with a loop.

The binomial coefficient $b(n, k)$ has a nonrecursive definition that is based on factorials:

$$b(n,k) = \frac{n!}{k!(n-k)!}$$

If you compute the factorials nonrecursively, a program based on this definition may be more efficient than the corresponding recursive program. Here the choice is a little less clear because the nonrecursive solution requires multiplication and division, but the recursive solution requires only addition.

Some problems are recursive by nature and can be solved only nonrecursively with great difficulty. The problem of solving the Towers of Hanoi puzzle is recursive by nature. You can try to solve it without recursion to see how difficult it would be. Quick sort, one of the best-known sorting algorithms, falls in this category also. It is much more difficult to program quick sort nonrecursively than recursively.

2.5   Dynamic Memory Allocation

In C++, values are stored in three distinct areas of main memory:

- Fixed locations in memory for global variables
- The run-time stack for local variables
- The heap for dynamically allocated variables

The C++ memory model

You do not control allocation and deallocation from the heap during procedure calls and returns. Instead, you allocate from the heap with the help of pointer variables. Allocation on the heap, which is not triggered automatically on the run-time stack by procedure calls, is known as dynamic memory allocation.

Pointers

When you declare a global or local variable, you specify its type. For example, you can specify the type to be an integer, or a character, or an array. Similarly, when you declare a pointer, you must declare that it points to some type. The pointer itself can be global or local. The value to which it points, however, resides in the heap and is neither global nor local.

C++ provides two operators to control dynamic memory allocation:

- `new`, to allocate from the heap
- `delete`, to deallocate from the heap

Two operators that control dynamic memory allocation

Although memory deallocation with the `delete` operator is important, this book does not describe how it operates. The programs that use pointers in this book are bad examples of software design because of this omission. The intent of the programs is to show the relationship between levels HOL6 and Asmb5, as will become evident in Chapter 6, which describes the translation of the programs.

The `new` operator expects a type on its right-hand side. It does two things when it executes:

Omitting `delete` is a simplification.

- It allocates a memory cell from the heap large enough to hold a value of the type that is on its right-hand side.

- It returns a pointer to the newly allocated storage.

Two assignments are possible with pointers. You can assign a value to a pointer, or you can assign a value to the cell to which the pointer points. The first assignment is called a pointer assignment, which behaves according to the following rule:

- If p and q are pointers, the assignment p = q makes p point to the same cell to which q points.

Figure 2.37 is a nonsense program that illustrates the actions of the new operator and the pointer assignment rule. It uses global pointers, but the output would be the same if the pointers were local. If they were local, they would be allocated on the run-time stack instead of being at a fixed location in memory.

```
#include <iostream>
using namespace std;

int *a, *b, *c;

int main () {
    a = new int;
    *a = 5;
    b = new int;
    *b = 3;
    c = a;
    a = b;
    *a = 2 + *c;
    cout << "*a = " << *a << endl;
    cout << "*b = " << *b << endl;
    cout << "*c = " << *c << endl;
    return 0;
}
```

Output

```
*a = 7
*b = 7
*c = 5
```

Figure 2.37

A C++ nonsense program that illustrates the pointer type.

In the declaration of the global pointers

```
int *a, *b, *c;
```

the asterisk before the variable name indicates that the variable, instead of being an integer, is a pointer to an integer. Figure 2.38(a) shows the pictorial representation of a pointer value to be a small black dot.

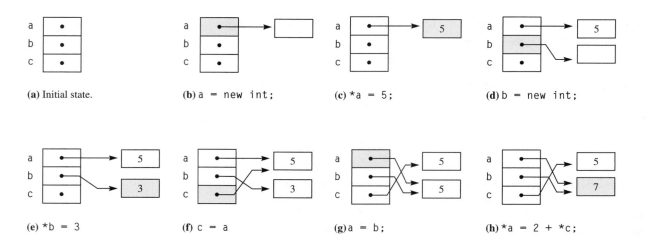

(a) Initial state.   **(b)** a = new int;   **(c)** *a = 5;   **(d)** b = new int;

(e) *b = 3   **(f)** c = a   **(g)** a = b;   **(h)** *a = 2 + *c;

Figure 2.38(b) illustrates the action of the new operator. It allocates a cell from the heap large enough to store an integer value and it returns a pointer to the value. The assignment makes a point to the newly allocated cell. Figure 2.38(c) shows how to access the cell to which a pointer points. Because a is a pointer, *a is the cell to which a points. Figure 2.38(f) illustrates the pointer assignment rule. The assignment c = a makes c point to the same cell to which a points. Similarly, the assignment a = b makes a point to the same cell to which b points. In Figure 2.38(h), the assignment is not to pointer a, but to the cell to which a points.

Figure **2.38**

A trace of the program in Figure 2.37.

Structures

Structures are the key to data abstraction in C++. They let the programmer consolidate variables with primitive types into a single abstract data type. Both arrays and structures are groups of values. However, all cells of an array must have the same type. Each cell is accessed by the numeric integer value of the index. With a structure, the cells can have different types. C++ provides the struct construct to group the values. The C++ programmer gives each cell, called a field, a field name.

Figure 2.39 shows a program that declares a struct named person that has four fields named first, last, age, and gender. The program declares a global variable named bill that has type person. Fields first, last, and gender have type char, and field age has type int.

To access the field of a structure, you place a period between the name of the variable and the name of the field you want to access. For example, the test of the if statement

```
if (bill.gender == 'm')
```

accesses the field named gender in the variable named bill.

Figure **2.39**

The C++ structure.

```
#include <iostream>
using namespace std;

struct person {
   char first;
   char last;
   int age;
   char gender;
};
person bill;

int main () {
   cin >> bill.first >> bill.last >> bill.age >> bill.gender;
   cout << "Initials: " << bill.first << bill.last << endl;
   cout << "Age: " << bill.age << endl;
   cout << "Gender: ";
   if (bill.gender == 'm') {
      cout << "male\n";
   }
   else {
      cout << "female\n";
   }
   return 0;
}
```

Input

```
bj 32 m
```

Output

```
Initials: bj
Age: 32
Gender: male
```

Linked Data Structures

Programmers frequently combine pointers and structures to implement linked data structures. The struct is usually called a node, a pointer points to a node, and the node has a field that is a pointer. The pointer field of the node serves as a link to another node in the data structure. Figure 2.40 is a program that implements a linked list data structure. The first loop inputs a sequence of integers terminated by the sentinel value -9999, placing the first value in the input stream at the end of the linked list. The second loop outputs each element of the linked list. Figure 2.41 is a trace of the first few statement executions of the program in Figure 2.40.

Figure **2.40**

A C++ program to input and output
a linked list.

```cpp
#include <iostream>
using namespace std;

struct node {
   int data;
   node* next;
};

int main () {
   node *first, *p;
   int value;
   first = 0;
   cin >> value;
   while (value != -9999) {
      p = first;
      first = new node;
      first->data = value;
      first->next = p;
      cin >> value;
   }
   for (p = first; p != 0; p = p->next) {
      cout << p->data << ' ';
   }
   return 0;
```

Input

10 20 30 40 -9999

Output

40 30 20 10

The value 0 for a pointer is a special value that is guaranteed to point to no cell
at all. It is commonly used in C++ programs as a sentinel value of linked structures.
The statement

0 is a special pointer value.

```cpp
first = 0;
```

assigns this special value to local pointer first. Figure 2.41(b) shows the value pic-
torially as a dashed triangle.

You use an asterisk to access the cell to which a pointer points, and a period to
access the field of a structure. If a pointer points to a struct, you access a field of
the struct using both the asterisk and the period.

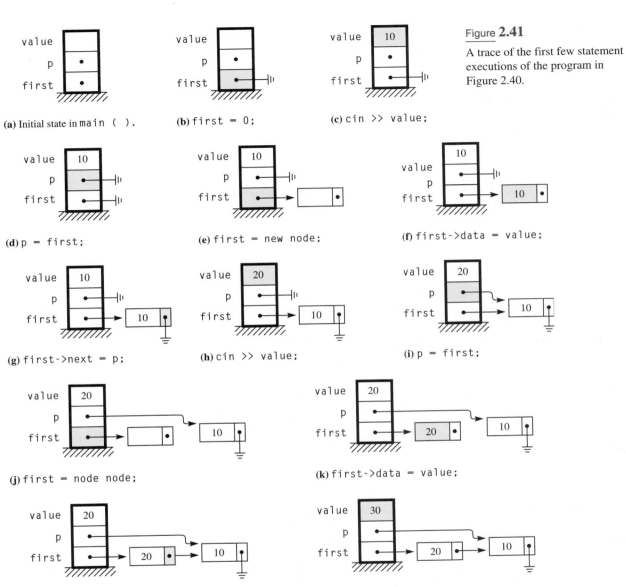

Figure 2.41

A trace of the first few statement executions of the program in Figure 2.40.

(a) Initial state in `main ( )`.

(b) `first = 0;`

(c) `cin >> value;`

(d) `p = first;`

(e) `first = new node;`

(f) `first->data = value;`

(g) `first->next = p;`

(h) `cin >> value;`

(i) `p = first;`

(j) `first = node node;`

(k) `first->data = value;`

(l) `first->next = p;`

(m) `cin >> value;`

Example 2.7   The following statement assigns the value of variable `value` to the data field of the structure to which it points.

```
(*first).data = value;
```

■

Because this combination of asterisk and period is so common, C++ provides the arrow operator `->` formed by a hyphen followed immediately by a greater-than symbol. The statement in Example 2.7 can be written using this abbreviation as

The `->` operator

```
first->data = value;
```

which Figure 2.41(f) and (k) shows. The program uses the same abbreviation to access the `next` field, which Figure 2.41(g) and (l) shows.

SUMMARY

In C++, values are stored in three distinct areas of main memory: fixed locations in memory for global variables, the run-time stack for local variables, and the heap. The two ways in which flow of control can be altered from the normal sequential flow are selection and repetition. The C++ `if` and `switch` statements implement selection, and the `while`, `do`, and `for` statements implement repetition. All five statements use the relational operators to test the truth of a condition.

The LIFO nature of the run-time stack is required to implement function and procedure calls. The allocation process for a function is the following: Push storage for the returned value, push the actual parameters, push the return address, and push storage for the local variables. The allocation process for a procedure is identical except that storage for the returned value is not pushed. The stack frame consists of all the items pushed onto the run-time stack in one function or procedure call.

A recursive procedure is one that calls itself. To avoid calling itself endlessly, a recursive procedure must have an `if` statement that serves as an escape hatch to stop the recursive calls. Two different viewpoints in thinking about recursion are the microscopic and the macroscopic viewpoints. The microscopic viewpoint considers the details of the run-time stack during execution. The macroscopic viewpoint is based on a higher level of abstraction and is related to proof by mathematical induction. The microscopic viewpoint is useful for analysis; the macroscopic viewpoint is useful for design.

Allocation on the heap with the `new` operator is known as dynamic memory allocation. The `new` operator allocates a memory cell from the heap and returns a pointer to the newly allocated cell. A structure is a collection of values that need not all be the same type. Each value is stored in a field, and each field has a name. Linked data structures consist of nodes, which are structures that have pointers to other nodes. The node for a linked list has a field for a value and a field usually named next that points to the next node in the list.

EXERCISES

Section 2.4

1. The function sum in Figure 2.25 is called for the first time by the main program. From the second time on it is called by itself. *(a) How many times is it called altogether? (b) Draw a picture of the main program variables and the run-time stack just after the function is called for the third time. You should have three stack frames. (c) Draw a picture of the main program variables and the run-time stack just before the return from the call of part (b). You should have three stack frames, but with different contents from part (b).

2. Draw the call tree, as in Figure 2.30, for the function binCoeff of Figure 2.28 for the following call statements from the main program:

   *(a) binCoeff (4, 1)   (b) binCoeff (5, 1)
   (c) binCoeff (3, 2)   (d) binCoeff (4, 4)
   (e) binCoeff (4, 2)

   How many times is the function called? What is the maximum number of stack frames on the run-time stack during the execution? In what order does the program make the calls and returns?

3. For Exercise 2, draw the run-time stack as in Figure 2.29 just before the return from the following function calls:

   *(a) binCoeff (2, 1)   (b) binCoeff (3, 1)
   (c) binCoeff (1, 0)   (d) binCoeff (4, 4)
   (e) binCoeff (2, 1)

   In part (e), binCoeff (2, 1) is called twice. Draw the run-time stack just before the return from the second call of the function.

4. Draw the call tree, as in Figure 2.30, for the program in Figure 2.32 to reverse the letters of an array of characters. How many times is function reverse called? What is the maximum number of stack frames allocated on the run-time stack? Draw the run-time stack just after the third call to function reverse.

5. The Fibonacci sequence is

   0 1 1 2 3 5 8 13 21 ...

   Each Fibonacci number is the sum of the preceding two Fibonacci numbers. The sequence starts with the first two Fibonacci numbers, and is defined recursively as

   $fib (0) = 0$
   $fib (1) = 1$
   $fib (n) = fib (n - 1) + fib (n - 2)$ for $n > 1$

   Draw the call tree for the following Fibonacci numbers:

   (a) *fib* (3)   (b) *fib* (4)   (c) *fib* (5)

   For each of these calls, how many times is *fib* called? What is the maximum number of stack frames allocated on the run-time stack?

6. For your solution to the Towers of Hanoi in Problem 2.15, draw the call tree for the four-disk problem. How many times is your procedure called? What is the maximum number of stack frames on the run-time stack?

7. The mystery numbers are defined recursively as

   $myst\ (0) = 2$
   $myst\ (1) = 1$
   $myst\ (n) = 2 \times myst\ (n-1) + myst\ (n-2)$ for $n > 1$

   (a) Draw the calling sequence for *myst* (4). (b) What is the value of *myst* (4)?

8. Examine the C++ program that follows. (a) Draw the run-time stack just after the procedure is called for the last time. (b) What is the output of the program?

```cpp
#include <iostream>
using namespace std;

void what (char word [], int j) {
   if (j > 1) {
      word [j] = word [3 - j];
      what (word, j - 1);
   }  // ra2
}

int main () {
   char str [5] = "abcd";
   what (str, 3);
   cout << str << endl;
   // ra1
   return 0;
}
```

PROBLEMS

Section 2.1

9. Write a C++ program that inputs two integers and outputs their quotient and remainder.

Sample Input

13   4

Sample Output

```
13/4 has value 3
13%4 has value 1
```

Section 2.2

10. Write a C++ program that inputs an integer and outputs whether the integer is even.

Sample Input
<hr>

```
15
```

Sample Output
<hr>

```
15 is not even.
```

11. Write a C++ program that inputs two integers and outputs the sum of the integers between them.

Sample Input
<hr>

```
9   12
```

Sample Output
<hr>

```
The sum of the numbers between 9 and 12 inclusive is 42.
```

Section 2.3

12. Write a C++ function

```
int rectArea (int len, int wid)
```

that returns the area of a rectangle with length `len` and width `wid`. Test it with a main program that inputs the length and width of a rectangle and outputs its area. Output the value in the main program, not in the function.

Sample Input
<hr>

```
6   10
```

Sample Output
<hr>

```
The area of a 6 by 10 rectangle is 60.
```

13. Write a C++ function

```
void rect (int& ar, int& per, int len, int wid)
```

that computes the area `ar` and perimeter `per` of a rectangle with length `len` and width `wid`. Test it with a main program that inputs the length and width of a rectangle and outputs its area and perimeter. Output the value in the main program, not in the procedure.

Sample Input
<hr>

```
6   10
```

Sample Output
<hr>

```
Length: 6
Width: 10
Area: 60
Perimeter: 32
```

Section 2.4

14. Write a C++ program that asks the user to input a small integer. Then use a recursive function that returns the value of that Fibonacci number as defined in Exercise 5. Do not use a loop. Output the value in the main program, not in the function.

Sample Input/Output

```
Which Fibonacci number? 8
The number is 21
```

15. Write a C++ program that prints the solution to the Towers of Hanoi puzzle. It should ask the user to input the number of disks in the puzzle, the peg on which all the disks are placed initially, and the peg on which the disks are to be moved.

Sample Input/Output

```
How many disks do you want to move? 3
From which peg? 3
To which peg? 2

Move a disk from peg 3 to peg 2.
Move a disk from peg 3 to peg 1.
Move a disk from peg 2 to peg 1.
Move a disk from peg 3 to peg 2.
Move a disk from peg 1 to peg 3.
Move a disk from peg 1 to peg 2.
Move a disk from peg 3 to peg 2.
```

16. Write a recursive void function called rotateLeft that rotates the first n integers in an array to the left. To rotate n items left, rotate the first $n - 1$ items left recursively, and then exchange the last two items. For example, to rotate the five items

50   60   70   80   90

to the left, recursively rotate the first four items to the left:

60   70   80   50   90

and then exchange the last two items:

60   70   80   90   50

Test it with a main program that takes as input an integer count followed by the values to rotate. Output the original values and the rotated values. Do not use a loop in rotateLeft. Output the value in the main program, not in the procedure.

Sample Input

5   50 60 70 80 90

Sample Output

```
Original list: 50  60  70  80  90
Rotated list: 60  70  80  90  50
```

17. Write a function

```
int maximum (int list[], int n)
```

that recursively finds the largest integer between `list[0]` and `list[n]`. Assume at least one element is in the list. Test it with a main program that takes as input an integer count followed by the values. Output the original values followed by the maximum. Do not use a loop in maximum. Output the value in the main program, not in the function.

Sample Input

```
5   50 30 90 20 80
```

Sample Output

```
Original list: 50   30   90   20   80
Largest value: 90
```

Section 2.5

18. The program in Figure 2.40 creates a linked list whose elements are in reverse order compared to their input order. Modify the first loop of the program to create the list in the same order as the input order. Do not modify the second loop.

Sample Input

```
10 20 30 40 -9999
```

Sample Output

```
10 20 30 40
```

19. Declare the following node for a binary search tree.

```
struct node {
    node* leftCh;
    int data;
    node* rightCh;
};
```

where `leftCh` is a pointer to the left subtree and `rightCh` is a pointer to the right subtree. Write a C++ program that inputs a sequence of integers with -9999 as a sentinel and inserts them into a binary search tree. Output them in ascending order with a recursive procedure that makes an inorder traversal of the search tree.

Sample Input

```
40 90 50 10 80 30 70 60 20 -9999
```

Sample Output

```
10 20 30 40 50 60 70 80 90
```

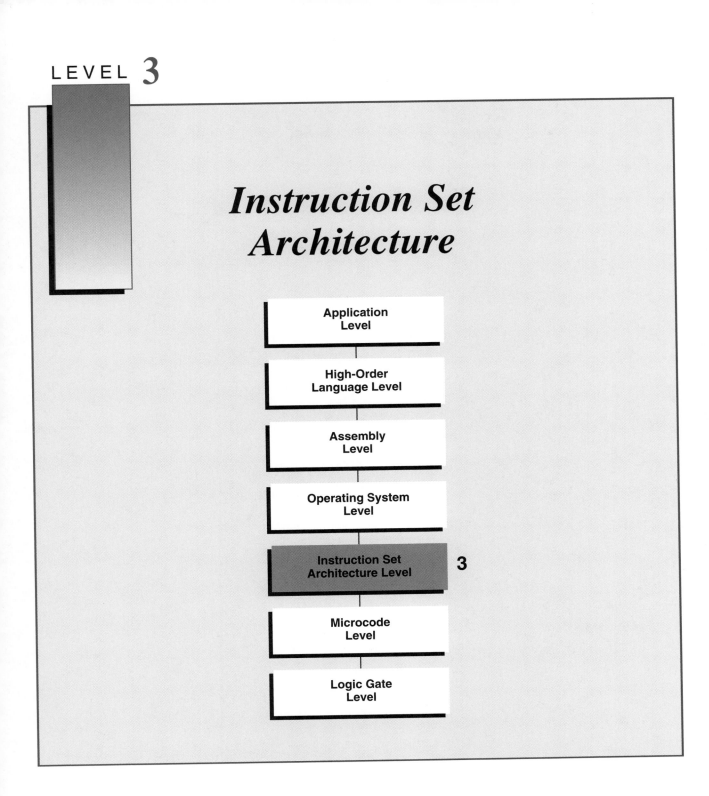

LEVEL 3

Instruction Set Architecture

Application Level

High-Order Language Level

Assembly Level

Operating System Level

Instruction Set Architecture Level — 3

Microcode Level

Logic Gate Level

Chapter

3

Information Representation

One of the most significant inventions of mankind is the printed word. The words on this page represent information stored on paper, which is conveyed to you as you read. Like the printed page, computers have memories for storing information. The central processing unit (CPU) has the ability to retrieve information from its memory much as you take information from words on a page.

Some computer terminology is based on this analogy. The CPU *reads* information from memory and *writes* information into memory. The information itself is divided into *words*. In some computer systems large sets of words, usually anywhere from a few hundred to a few thousand, are grouped into *pages*.

Reading and writing, words and pages

In C++, at Level HOL6, information takes the form of values that you store in a variable in main memory or in a file on disk. This chapter shows how the computer stores that information at Level ISA3. Information representation at the machine level differs significantly from that at the high-order languages level. At Level ISA3, information representation is less human-oriented. Later chapters discuss information representation at the intermediate levels, Levels Asmb5 and OS4, and show how they relate to Levels HOL6 and ISA3.

Information representation at Level ISA3

3.1   Unsigned Binary Representation

Early computers were electromechanical. That is, all their calculations were performed with moving switches called *relays*. The Mark I computer, built in 1944 by Howard H. Aiken of Harvard University, was such a machine. Aiken had procured financial backing for his project from Thomas J. Watson, president of International Business Machines (IBM). The relays in the Mark I computer could compute much faster than the mechanical gears that were used in adding machines at that time.

The Mark I computer

Even before the completion of Mark I, John V. Atanasoff, working at Iowa State University, had finished the construction of an electronic computer to solve systems of linear equations. In 1941 John W. Mauchly visited Atanasoff's laboratory and in 1946, in collaboration with J. Presper Eckert at the University of Pennsylvania, built the famous Electronic Numerical Integrator and Calculator (ENIAC). ENIAC's 19,000 vacuum tubes could perform 5,000 additions per second compared to 10 additions per second with the relays of the Mark I. Like the ENIAC, present-day computers are electronic, although their calculations are performed with integrated circuits (ICs) instead of with vacuum tubes. Each IC contains thousands of transistors similar to the transistors in radios.

The ENIAC computer

Binary Storage

Electronic computer memories cannot store numbers and letters directly. They can only store electrical signals. When the CPU reads information from memory, it is detecting a signal whose voltage is about equal to that produced by two flashlight batteries.

Computer memories are designed with a most remarkable property. Each storage location contains either a high-voltage signal or a low-voltage signal—never anything in between. The storage location is like being pregnant. Either you are or you are not. There is no halfway.

The word *digital* means that the signal stored in memory can have only a fixed number of values. *Binary* means that only two values are possible. Practically all computers on the market today are binary. Hence, each storage location contains either a high voltage or a low voltage. The state of each location is also described as being either on or off, or, alternatively, as containing either a 1 or a 0.

Each individual storage unit is called a *binary digit* or *bit*. A bit can be only 1 or 0, never anything else, such as 2, 3, A, or Z. This is a fundamental concept. Every piece of information stored in the memory of a computer, whether it is the amount you owe on your credit card or your street address, is stored in binary as 1's and 0's.

In practice, the bits in a computer memory are grouped together into *cells*. A seven-bit computer, for example, would store its information in groups of seven bits, as Figure 3.1 shows. You can think of a cell as a group of boxes, each box containing a 1 or a 0, and nothing else. The first two lines in Figure 3.1(c) are impossible because the values in some boxes differ from 0 or 1. The last is impossible because each box must contain a value. A bit of storage cannot contain nothing.

Different computers have different numbers of bits in each cell, although most computers these days have eight bits per cell. This chapter shows examples with several different cell sizes to illustrate the general principle.

Information such as numbers and letters must be represented in binary form to be stored in memory. The representation scheme used to store information is called

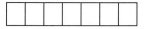

(a) A seven-bit cell.

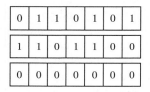

(b) Some possible values in a seven-bit cell.

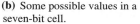

(c) Some impossible values in a seven-bit cell.

Figure **3.1**

A seven-bit memory cell in main memory.

a *code*. This section examines a code for storing unsigned integers. The remainder of this chapter describes codes for storing other kinds of data. The next chapter examines codes for storing program commands in memory.

▌ Integers

Numbers must be represented in binary form to be stored in a computer's memory. The particular code depends on whether the number has a fractional part or is an integer. If the number is an integer, the code depends on whether it is always positive or whether it can be negative as well.

The *unsigned binary* representation is for integers that are always positive. *Unsigned binary* Before learning the binary system we will review our own base 10 (*decimal*, or *dec* for short) system, and then work our way down to the binary system.

Our decimal system was probably invented because we have 10 fingers with which we count and add. A book of arithmetic using this elegant system was written in India in the eighth century A.D. It was translated into Arabic and was eventually carried by merchants to Europe, where it was translated from Arabic into Latin. The numbers came to be known as Arabic numerals because at the time it was thought that they originated in Arabia. But Hindu-Arabic numerals would be a more appropriate name because they actually originated in India.

Counting with Arabic numerals in base 10 looks like this (reading down, of course):

0	7	14	21	28	35
1	8	15	22	29	36
2	9	16	23	30	37
3	10	17	24	31	38
4	11	18	25	32	.
5	12	19	26	33	.
6	13	20	27	34	.

Counting in decimal

Starting from 0, the Indians simply invented a symbol for the next number 1, then 2, and so on until they got to the symbol 9. At that point they looked at their hands and thought of a fantastic idea. On their last finger they did not invent a new symbol. Instead they used the first two symbols, 1 and 0, together to represent the next number, 10.

You know the rest of the story. When they got to 19 they saw that the 9 was as high as they could go with the symbols they had invented. So they dropped it down to 0 and increased the 1 to 2, creating 20. They did the same for 29 to 30 and, eventually, 99 to 100. On and on it went.

What if we only had 8 fingers instead of 10? What would have happened? At 7, the next number would be on our last finger, and we would not need to invent a new symbol. The next number would be represented as 10. Counting in base eight (*octal*, or *oct* for short) looks like this:

Counting in octal

0	7	16	25	34	43
1	10	17	26	35	44
2	11	20	27	36	45
3	12	21	30	37	46
4	13	22	31	40	.
5	14	23	32	41	.
6	15	24	33	42	.

The next number after 77 is 100 in octal.

Comparing the decimal and octal schemes, notice that 5 (oct) is the same number as 5 (dec), but that 21 (oct) is not the same number as 21 (dec). Instead, 21 (oct) is the same number as 17 (dec). Numbers have a tendency to look larger than they actually are when written in octal.

But what if we only had 3 fingers instead of 10 or 8? The pattern is the same. Counting in base 3 looks like this:

Counting in base 3

0	21	112	210	1001	1022
1	22	120	211	1002	1100
2	100	121	212	1010	1101
10	101	122	220	1011	1102
11	102	200	221	1012	.
12	110	201	222	1020	.
20	111	202	1000	1021	.

Finally, we have arrived at unsigned binary representation. Computers have only two fingers. Counting in base 2 (*binary*, or *bin* for short) follows the exact same method as counting in octal and base 3:

Counting in binary

0	111	1110	10101	11100	100011
1	1000	1111	10110	11101	100100
10	1001	10000	10111	11110	100101
11	1010	10001	11000	11111	100110
100	1011	10010	11001	100000	.
101	1100	10011	11010	100001	.
110	1101	10100	11011	100010	.

Binary numbers look a lot larger than they actually are. The number 10110 (bin) is only 22 (dec).

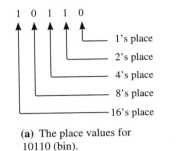

Figure **3.2**

Converting from binary to decimal.

(a) The place values for 10110 (bin).

(b) Converting 10110 (bin) to decimal.

Base Conversions

Given a number written in binary, there are several ways to determine its decimal equivalent. One way is to simply count up to the number in binary and in decimal. That method works well for small numbers. Another method is to add up the place values of each 1 bit in the binary number.

Example 3.1   Figure 3.2(a) shows the place values for 10110 (bin). Starting with the 1's place on the right (called the least significant bit), each place has a value twice as great as the previous place value. Figure 3.2(b) shows the addition that produces the 22 (dec) value.   ∎

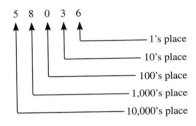

Figure **3.3**

The place values for 58,036 (dec).

Example 3.2   The unsigned binary number system is analogous to our familiar decimal system. Figure 3.3 shows the place values for 58,036 (dec). The figure 58,036 represents six 1's, three 10's, no 100's, eight 1,000's, and five 10,000's. Starting with the 1's place from the right, each place value is 10 times greater than the previous place value. In binary, each place value is 2 times greater than the previous place value.   ∎

The value of an unsigned number can be conveniently represented as a polynomial in the base of the number system. (The base is also called the *radix* of the number system.) Figure 3.4 shows the polynomial representation of 10110 (bin) and 58,036 (dec). The value of the least significant place is always the base to the zeroth power, which is always 1. The next significant place is the base to the first power, which is the value of the base itself. You can see from the structure of the polynomial that the value of each place is the base times the value of the previous place.

$$1 \cdot 2^4 + 0 \cdot 2^3 + 1 \cdot 2^2 + 1 \cdot 2^1 + 0 \cdot 2^0$$

(a) The binary number 10110.

$$5 \cdot 10^4 + 8 \cdot 10^3 + 0 \cdot 10^2 + 3 \cdot 10^1 + 6 \cdot 10^0$$

(b) The decimal number 58,036.

Figure **3.4**

The polynomial representation of unsigned numbers.

In binary, the only place with an odd value is the 1's place. All the other places (2's, 4's, 8's, and so on) are even. If there is a 0 in the 1's place, the value of the binary number will come from adding several even numbers, and it therefore will be even. On the other hand, if there is a 1 in the 1's place of a binary number, its value will come from adding one to several even numbers, and it will be odd. As in the decimal system, you can tell whether a binary number is even or odd simply by inspecting the digit in the 1's place.

Determining the binary equivalent of a number written in decimal is a bit tricky. One method is to successively divide the original number by two, keeping track of the remainders, which will form the binary number when listed in reverse order from which they were obtained.

Example 3.3   Figure 3.5 converts 22 (dec) to binary. The number 22 divided by 2 is 11 with a remainder of 0, which is written in the right column. Then, 11 divided by 2 is 5, with a remainder of 1. Continuing until the number gets down to 0 produces a column of remainders, which, when read from the bottom up, form the binary number 10110. ∎

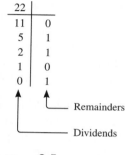

Figure **3.5**

Converting from decimal to binary.

Notice that the least significant bit is the remainder when you divide the original value by 2. This fact is consistent with the observation that you can determine whether a binary number is even or odd by inspecting only the least significant bit. If the original value is even, the division will produce a remainder of 0, which will be the least significant bit. Conversely, if the original value is odd, the least significant bit will be 1.

Range for Unsigned Integers

All these counting schemes based on Arabic numerals let you represent arbitrarily large numbers. A real computer, however, has a finite number of bits in each cell. Figure 3.6 shows how a seven-bit cell would store the number 22 (dec). Notice the two leading 0's, which do not affect the value of the number, but which are necessary for specifying the contents of the memory location. In dealing with a seven-bit computer, you should write the number without showing the boxes as

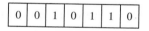

Figure **3.6**

The number 22 (dec) in a seven-bit cell.

    001 0110

The two leading 0's are still necessary. This book displays bit strings with a space (for legibility) between each group of four bits starting from the right.

The range of unsigned values depends on the number of bits in a cell. A sequence of all 0's represents the smallest unsigned value, and a sequence of all 1's represents the largest.

Example 3.4   The smallest unsigned integer a seven-bit cell can store is

    000 0000 (bin)

and the largest is

111 1111 (bin)

The smallest is 0 (dec) and the largest is 127 (dec). A seven-bit cell cannot store an unsigned integer greater than 127. ∎

Unsigned Addition

Addition with unsigned binary numbers works like addition with unsigned decimal numbers. But it is easier because you only need to learn the addition rules for 2 bits instead of 10 digits. The rules for adding bits are

$0 + 0 = 0$

$0 + 1 = 1$

$1 + 0 = 1$

$1 + 1 = 10$

Binary addition rules

The carry technique that you are familiar with in the decimal system also works in the binary system. If two numbers in a column add to a value greater than 1, you must carry 1 to the next column.

The carry technique in binary

Example 3.5 Suppose you have a six-bit cell. To add the two numbers 01 1010 and 01 0001, simply write one number above the other and start at the least significant column:

```
        01 1010
ADD     01 0001
        10 1011
```

Notice that when you get to the fifth column from the right, 1 + 1 equals 10. You must write down the 0 and carry the 1 to the next column, where 1 + 0 + 0 produces the leftmost 1 in the sum.

To verify that this carry technique works in binary, convert the two numbers and their sum to decimal:

01 1010 (bin) = 26 (dec)

01 0001 (bin) = 17 (dec)

10 1011 (bin) = 43 (dec)

Sure enough, 26 + 17 = 43 in decimal. ∎

Example 3.6   These examples show how the carry can propagate along several consecutive columns:

```
        00 0011              00 1111
ADD     01 0001      ADD     00 1001
        01 0100              01 1000
```

In the second example, when you get to the fourth column from the right, you have a carry from the previous column. Then $1 + 1 + 1$ equals 11. You must write down 1 and carry 1 to the next column.   ∎

The Carry Bit

The range for the six-bit cell of the previous examples is 00 0000 to 11 1111 (bin), or 0 to 63 (dec). It is possible for two numbers to be in range but for their sum to be out of range. In that case the sum is too large to fit into the six bits of the storage cell.

The carry bit in addition

To flag this condition, the CPU contains a special bit called the *carry bit*, denoted by the letter C. When two binary numbers are added, if the sum of the left-most column (called the *most significant bit*) produces a carry, then C is set to 1. Otherwise C is cleared to 0. In other words, C always contains the carry from the leftmost column of the cell. In all the previous examples, the sum was in range. Hence the carry bit was cleared to 0.

Example 3.7   Here are two examples showing the effect on the carry bit:

```
            01 0110                  10 1010
ADD         10 0010      ADD         01 1010
C = 0       11 1000      C = 1       00 0100
```

In the second example, the CPU adds $42 + 26$. The correct result, which is 68, is too large to fit into the six-bit cell. Remember that the range is from 0 to 63. So the lowest order (that is, the rightmost) six bits are stored, giving an incorrect result of 4. The carry bit is also set to 1 to indicate that a carry occurred from the highest-order column.   ∎

The carry bit in subtraction

The computer subtracts two numbers in binary by adding the negative of the second number. For example, to subtract the numbers $42 - 26$, the computer adds $42 + (-26)$. It is impossible to subtract two integers using unsigned binary representation, because there is no way to store a negative number. The next section describes a representation for storing negative numbers. In that representation, the C bit is the carry of the addition of the negation of the second number.

3.2 Two's Complement Binary Representation

The unsigned binary representation works for nonnegative integers only. If a computer is to process negative integers, it must use a different representation.

Suppose you have a six-bit cell and you want to store the number −5 (dec). Because 5 (dec) is 101 (bin), you might try the pattern shown in Figure 3.7. But this is impossible because all bits, including the first, must be 0 or 1. Remember that computers are binary. The above storage value would require each box to be capable of storing a 0, or a 1, or a dash. Such a computer would have to be ternary instead of binary.

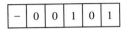

Figure **3.7**

An attempt to store a negative number in binary.

The solution to this problem is to reserve the first box in the cell to indicate the sign. Thus, the six-bit cell will have two parts—a one-bit sign and a five-bit magnitude, as Figure 3.8 shows. Because the sign bit must be 0 or 1, one possibility is to let a 0 sign bit indicate a positive number and a 1 sign bit indicate a negative number. Then +5 could be represented as

00 0101

and −5 could be represented as

10 0101

In this code the magnitudes for +5 and −5 would be identical. Only the sign bits would differ.

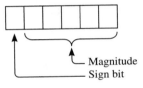

Magnitude
Sign bit

Figure **3.8**

The structure of a signed integer.

Few computers use the previous code, however. The problem is that if you add +5 and −5 in decimal, you get 0, but if you add 00 0101 and 10 0101 in binary (sign bits and all), you get

```
          00 0101
ADD       10 0101
C = 0    10 1010
```

which is definitely not 0. It would be much more convenient if the hardware of the CPU could add the numbers for +5 and −5, complete with sign bits using the ordinary rules for unsigned binary addition, and get 0.

A convenient property of negative numbers

The *two's complement* binary representation has that property. The positive numbers have a 0 sign bit and a magnitude as in the unsigned binary representation. For example, the number +5 (dec) is still represented as 00 0101.

But the representation of −5 (dec) is not 10 0101. Instead it is 11 1011 because adding +5 and −5 gives

```
          00 0101
ADD       11 1011
C = 1    00 0000
```

Note that the six-bit sum is all 0's, as advertised.

Under the rules of binary addition for a six-bit cell, the number 11 1011 is called the *additive inverse* of 00 0101. The operation of finding the additive inverse is referred to as *negation*, abbreviated NEG. To negate a number is also called *taking its two's complement.*

The NEG operation

All we need now is the rule for taking the two's complement of a number. A simple rule is based on the *ones' complement*, which is simply the binary sequence with all the 1's changed to 0's and all the 0's changed to 1's. The ones' complement is also called the NOT operation.

The NOT operation.

Example 3.8   The ones' complement of 00 0101 is

   NOT 00 0101 = 11 1010

assuming a six-bit cell.   ∎

A clue to finding the rule for two's complement is to note the effect of adding a number to its ones' complement. Because 1 plus 0 is 1, and 0 plus 1 is 1, any number, when added to its ones' complement, will produce a sequence of all 1's. But then, adding a single 1 to a number of all 1's produces a number of all 0's.

Example 3.9   Adding 00 0101 to its ones' complement produces

```
            00 0101
ADD      11 1010
C = 0    11 1111
```

which is all 1's. Adding 1 to this produces

```
            11 1111
ADD      00 0001
C = 1    00 0000
```

which is all 0's.   ∎

In other words, adding a number to its ones' complement plus 1 gives all 0's. So the two's complement of a binary number must be found by adding 1 to its ones' complement.

Example 3.10   To find the two's complement of 00 0101, add 1 to its ones' complement.

```
NOT    00 0101 = 11 1010

            11 1010
ADD      00 0001
            11 1011
```

The two's complement of 00 0101 is therefore 11 1011. That is,

NEG 00 0101 = 11 1011

Recall that 11 1011 is indeed the negative of 00 0101 because they add to 0 as shown. ∎

The general rule for negating a number regardless of how many bits the number contains is

- The two's complement of a number is 1 plus its ones' complement.

The two's complement rule

Or, in terms of the NEG and NOT operations,

- NEG x = 1 + NOT x

In our familiar decimal system, if you take the negative of a value that is already negative, you get a positive value. Algebraically,

$$-(-x) = x$$

where x is some positive value. If the rule for taking the two's complement is to be useful, the two's complement of a negative value should be the corresponding positive value.

Example 3.11 What happens if you take the two's complement of -5 (dec)?

NOT   11 1011 = 00 0100

$$
\begin{array}{r}
00\ 0100 \\
\text{ADD} \quad 00\ 0001 \\
\hline
00\ 0101
\end{array}
$$

Voilà! You get +5 (dec) back again, as you would expect. ∎

Two's Complement Range

Suppose you have a four-bit cell to store integers in two's complement representation. What is the range of integers for this cell?

The positive integer with the greatest magnitude is 0111 (bin), which is +7 (dec). It cannot be 1111 as in unsigned binary because the first bit is reserved for the sign and must be 0. In unsigned binary, you can store numbers as high as +15 (dec) with four bits. All four bits are used for the magnitude. In two's complement representation, you can only store numbers as high as +7 (dec), because only three bits are reserved for the magnitude.

What is the negative number with the greatest magnitude? The answer to this question might not be obvious. Figure 3.9 shows the result of taking the two's complement of each positive number up to +7. What pattern do you see in the figure?

Notice that the two's complement operation automatically produces a 1 in the sign bit of the negative numbers, as it should. Even numbers still end in 0, and odd numbers end in 1.

Also, −5 is obtained from −6 by adding 1 to −6 in binary, as you would expect. Similarly, −6 is obtained from −7 by adding 1 to −7 in binary. We can squeeze one more negative integer out of our four bits by including −8. When you add 1 to −8 in binary, you get −7. The number −8 should therefore be represented as 1000. Figure 3.10 shows the complete table for signed integers assuming a four-bit memory cell.

The number −8 (dec) has a peculiar property not shared by any of the other negative integers. If you take the two's complement of −7 you get +7, as follows:

NOT   1001 = 0110

```
       0110
ADD    0001
       0111
```

But if you take the two's complement of −8, you get −8 back again:

NOT   1000 = 0111

```
       0111
ADD    0001
       1000
```

This property exists because there is no way to represent +8 with only four bits.

We have determined the range of numbers for a four-bit cell with two's complement binary representation. It is

1000 to 0111

as written in binary, or

−8 to +7

as written in decimal.

Decimal	Binary
−7	1001
−6	1010
−5	1011
−4	1100
−3	1101
−2	1110
−1	1111

Figure **3.9**

The result of taking the two's complement in a four-bit computer.

Decimal	Binary
−8	1000
−7	1001
−6	1010
−5	1011
−4	1100
−3	1101
−2	1110
−1	1111
0	0000
1	0001
2	0010
3	0011
4	0100
5	0101
6	0110
7	0111

Figure **3.10**

The signed integers for a four-bit cell.

The same patterns hold regardless of how many bits are contained in the cell. The largest positive integer is a single 0 followed by all 1's. The negative integer with the largest magnitude is a single 1 followed by all 0's. Its magnitude is 1 greater than the magnitude of the largest positive integer. The number -1 (dec) is represented as all 1's.

Example 3.12   The range for six-bit two's complement representation is

10 0000 to 01 1111

as written in binary, or

-32 to 31

as written in decimal. Unlike all the other negative integers, the two's complement of 10 0000 is itself, 10 0000. Also notice that -1 (dec) = 11 1111 (bin).   ∎

Base Conversions

To convert a negative number from decimal to binary is a two-step process. First, convert its magnitude from decimal to binary as in unsigned binary representation. Then negate it by taking the two's complement.

Converting from decimal to binary

Example 3.13   For -7 (dec) in a 10-bit cell

$+7$ (dec) = 00 0000 0111 (bin)

NOT   00 0000 0111 = 11 1111 1000

$$\begin{array}{r} 11\ 1111\ 1000 \\ \text{ADD}\quad \underline{00\ 0000\ 0001} \\ 11\ 1111\ 1001 \end{array}$$

So -7 (dec) is 11 1111 1001 (bin).   ∎

To convert a number from binary to decimal in a computer that uses two's complement representation, always check the sign bit first. If it is 0, the number is positive and you may convert as in unsigned representation. If it is 1, the number is negative and you can choose one of two methods. One method is to make the number positive by negating it. Then convert to decimal as in unsigned representation.

Converting from binary to decimal

Example 3.14   Say you have a 10-bit cell that contains 11 1101 1010. What decimal number does it represent? The sign bit is 1, so the number is negative. First negate the number:

NOT   11 1101 1010 = 00 0010 0101

$$
\begin{array}{r}
00\ 0010\ 0101 \\
\text{ADD}\quad 00\ 0000\ 0001 \\
\hline
00\ 0010\ 0110
\end{array}
$$

00 0010 0110 (bin) = 32 + 4 + 2 = 38 (dec)

So the original binary number must have been the negative of 38. That is,

11 1101 1010 (bin) = −38 (dec)   ∎

The other method is to convert directly without taking the two's complement. Simply add 1 to the sum of the place values of the 0's in the original binary number. This method works because the first step in taking the two's complement of a positive integer is to invert the bits. Those bits that were 1's, and thus contributed to the magnitude of the positive integer, become 0's. The 0's, not the 1's, of a negative integer contribute to its magnitude.

Example 3.15   Figure 3.11 shows the place values of the 0's in 11 1101 1010 (bin). Adding 1 to their sum gives

11 1101 1010 (bin) = −(1 + 32 + 4 + 1) = −38 (dec)

which is the same result as with the previous method.   ∎

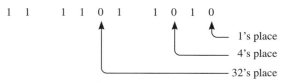

Figure **3.11**

The place values of the 0's in 11 1101 1010 (bin).

The Number Line

Another way of viewing binary representation is with the number line. Figure 3.12 shows the number line for a three-bit cell with unsigned binary representation. Eight numbers are represented.

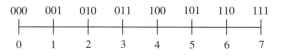

Figure **3.12**

The number line for a three-bit unsigned system.

You add by moving to the right on the number line. For example, to add 4 and 3, start with 4 and move three positions to the right to get 7. If you try to add 6 and 3 on the number line, you will fall off the right end. If you do it in binary, you will get an incorrect result because the answer is out of range:

```
          110
ADD       011
C = 1     001
```

The two's complement number line comes from the unsigned number line by breaking it between 3 and 4 and shifting the right part to the left side. Figure 3.13 shows that the binary number 111 is now adjacent to 000, and what used to be +7 (dec) is now −1 (dec).

Addition is still performed by moving to the right on the number line, even if you pass through 0. To add −2 and 3, start with −2 and move three positions to the right to get 1. If you do it in binary, the answer is in range and correct:

```
          110
ADD       011
C = 1     001
```

These bits are identical to those for 6 + 3 in unsigned binary. Notice that the carry bit is 1, even though the answer is in range. With two's complement representation, the carry bit no longer indicates whether the result of the addition is in range.

Sometimes you can avoid the binary representation altogether by considering the shifted number line entirely in decimal. Figure 3.14 shows the two's complement number line with the binary number replaced by its unsigned decimal equivalent.

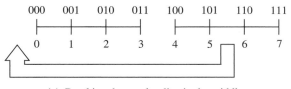

(a) Breaking the number line in the middle.

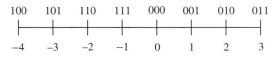

(b) Shifting the right part to the left side.

Figure **3.13**

The number line for a three-bit two's complement system.

Figure **3.14**

The two's complement number line
with unsigned decimals.

In this example, there are three bits in each memory location. Thus, there are 2^3, or 8, possible numbers.

Now the unsigned and signed numbers are the same from 0 up to 3. Furthermore, you can get the signed negative numbers from the unsigned numbers by subtracting 8:

$$7 - 8 = -1$$
$$6 - 8 = -2$$
$$5 - 8 = -3$$
$$4 - 8 = -4$$

Example 3.16   Suppose you have an eight-bit cell. There are 2^8, or 256, possible integer values. The nonnegative numbers go from 0 to 127. Assuming two's complement binary representation, what do you get if you add 97 and 45? In unsigned binary the sum is

$$97 + 45 = 142 \text{ (dec, unsigned)}$$

But in two's complement binary the sum is

$$142 - 256 = -114 \text{ (dec, signed)}$$

Notice that we get this result by avoiding the binary representation altogether. To verify the result, first convert 97 and 45 to binary and add:

97 (dec) = 0110 0001 (bin)
45 (dec) = 0010 1101 (bin)

```
          0110 0001
ADD       0010 1101
C = 0     1000 1110
```

This is a negative number because of the 1 in the sign bit. And now, to determine its magnitude

NEG 1000 1110 = 0111 0010 (bin)

= 114 (dec)

This produces the expected result.   ∎

The Overflow Bit

An important characteristic of binary storage at Level ISA3 is the absence of a type associated with a value. In the previous example, the sum 1000 1110, when interpreted as an unsigned number, is 142 (dec), but when interpreted in two's complement representation is −114 (dec). Although the value of the bit pattern depends on its type, whether unsigned or two's complement, the hardware makes no distinction between the two types. It only stores the bit pattern.

When the CPU adds the contents of two memory cells, it uses the rules for binary addition on the bit sequences, regardless of their types. In unsigned binary, if the sum is out of range, the hardware simply stores the (incorrect) result, sets the C bit accordingly, and goes on. It is up to the software to examine the C bit after the addition to see if a carry out occurred from the most significant column and to take appropriate action if necessary.

The C bit detects overflow for unsigned integers.

We noted above that in two's complement binary representation, the carry bit no longer indicates whether a sum is in range or out of range. An *overflow condition* occurs when the result of an operation is out of range. To flag this condition for signed numbers, the CPU contains another special bit called the *overflow bit* denoted by the letter V. When the CPU adds two binary integers, if their sum is out of range when interpreted in the two's complement representation, then V is set to 1. Otherwise V is cleared to 0.

The V bit detects overflow for signed integers.

The CPU performs the same addition operation regardless of the interpretation of the bit pattern. As with the C bit, the CPU does not stop if a two's complement overflow occurs. It sets the V bit and continues with its next task. It is up to the software to examine the V bit after the addition.

Example 3.17   Here are some examples with a six-bit cell showing the effects on the carry bit and on the overflow bit:

Adding two		00 0011			01 0110
positives:	ADD	01 0101		ADD	00 1100
	V = 0	01 1000		V = 1	10 0010
	C = 0			C = 0	

Adding a positive		00 0101			00 1000
and a negative:	ADD	11 0111		ADD	11 1010
	V = 0	11 1100		V = 0	00 0010
	C = 0			C = 1	

Adding two		11 1010			10 0110
negatives:	ADD	11 0111		ADD	10 0010
	V = 0	11 0001		V = 1	00 1000
	C = 1			C = 1	

Notice that all combinations of values are possible for V and C.   ∎

How can you tell if an overflow condition will occur? One way would be to convert the two numbers to decimal, add them, and see if their sum is outside the range as written in decimal. If so, an overflow has occurred.

The hardware detects an overflow by comparing the carry into the sign bit with the C bit. If they are different, an overflow has occurred, and V gets 1. If they are the same, V gets 0.

Instead of comparing the carry into the sign bit with C, you can tell directly by inspecting the signs of the numbers and the sum. If you add two positive numbers and get a negative sum or if you add two negative numbers and get a positive sum, then an overflow occurred. It is not possible to get an overflow by adding a positive number and a negative number.

The Negative and Zero Bits

In addition to the C bit, which detects an overflow condition for unsigned integers, and the V bit, which detects an overflow condition for signed integers, the CPU maintains two other bits that the software can test after it performs an operation. They are the N bit, for detecting a negative result, and the Z bit, for detecting a zero result. In summary, the function of these four status bits is

- N = 1 if the result is negative.
  N = 0 otherwise.

- Z = 1 if the result is all zeros.
  Z = 0 otherwise.

- V = 1 if a signed integer overflow occurred.
  V = 0 otherwise.

- C = 1 if an unsigned integer overflow occurred.
  C = 0 otherwise.

The N bit is easy for the hardware to determine as it is simply a copy of the sign bit. It takes a little more work for the hardware to determine the Z bit, because it must determine if every bit of the result is zero. Chapter 10 shows how the hardware computes the status bits from the result.

Example 3.18   Here are three examples of addition that show the effect of all four status bits on the result.

```
        01  0110              00  1000              00  1101
ADD     00  1100        ADD   11  1010        ADD   11  0011
N = 1   10  0010        N = 0 00  0010        N = 0 00  0000
Z = 0                   Z = 0                 Z = 1
V = 1                   V = 0                 V = 0
C = 0                   C = 1                 C = 1        ■
```

3.3   Operations in Binary

Because all information in a computer is stored in binary form, the CPU processes it with binary operations. The previous sections presented the binary operations NOT, ADD, and NEG. NOT is a logical operator; ADD and NEG are arithmetic operators. This section describes some other logical and arithmetic operators that are available in the CPU of the computer.

Logical Operators

You are familiar with the logical operations AND and OR. Another logical operator is the exclusive or, denoted XOR. The exclusive or of logical values p and q is true if p is true, or if q is true, but not both. That is, p must be true exclusive of q, or q must be true exclusive of p.

One interesting property of binary digits is that you can interpret them as logical quantities. At Level ISA3, a 1 bit can represent true, and a 0 bit can represent false. Figure 3.15 shows the truth tables for the AND, OR, and XOR operators at Level ISA3.

At Level HOL6, AND and OR operate on boolean expressions whose values are either true or false. They are used in `if` statements and loops to test conditions that control the execution of statements. An example of the AND operator is the C++ phrase

```
if ((ch >= 'a') && (ch <= 'z'))
```

Figure 3.16 shows the truth tables for AND, OR, and XOR at Level HOL6. They are identical to Figure 3.15 with 1 at Level ISA3 corresponding to true at Level HOL6, and 0 at Level ISA3 corresponding to false at Level HOL6.

Logical operations are easier to perform than addition because no carries are involved. The operation is applied bitwise to the corresponding bits in the sequence. Neither the carry bit nor the overflow bit is affected by logical operations.

Figure **3.15**

The truth tables for the AND, OR, and XOR operators at Level ISA3.

p	q	p AND q
0	0	0
0	1	0
1	0	0
1	1	1

(a)

p	q	p OR q
0	0	0
0	1	1
1	0	1
1	1	1

(b)

p	q	p XOR q
0	0	0
0	1	1
1	0	1
1	1	0

(c)

p	*q*	*p* AND *q*
true	true	true
true	false	false
false	true	false
false	false	false

(a)

p	*q*	*p* OR *q*
true	true	true
true	false	true
false	true	true
false	false	false

(b)

p	*q*	*p* XOR *q*
true	true	false
true	false	true
false	true	true
false	false	false

(c)

Figure **3.16**

The truth tables for the AND, OR, and XOR operators at Level HOL6.

Example 3.19   Some examples for a six-bit cell are

```
        01 1010              01 1010              01 1010
AND     01 0001       OR     01 0001       XOR    01 0001
N = 0   01 0000       N = 0  01 1011       N = 0  00 1011
Z = 0                 Z = 0                Z = 0
```

Note that when you take the AND of 1 and 1, the result is 1 with no carry.   ■

Each of the operations AND, OR, and XOR combines two groups of bits to produce its result. But NEG operates on only a single group of bits. It is, therefore, called a *unary operation*.

Register Transfer Language

The purpose of Register Transfer Language (RTL) is to specify precisely the effect of a hardware operation. The RTL symbols might be familiar to you from your study of logic. Figure 3.17 shows the symbols.

The AND and OR operations are known as conjunction and disjunction in logic. The NOT operator is negation. The implies operator can be translated into English as "if/then." The transfer operator is the hardware equivalent of the assignment operator = in C++. The memory cell on the left of the operator gets the quantity on the right of the operator. The bit index operator treats the memory cell as an array of bits starting with an index of 0 for the leftmost bit, the same way C++ indexes an array of elements. The braces enclose an informal English description when a more formal specification would not be helpful.

There are two separators. The sequential separator (semicolon) separates two actions that occur one after the other. The concurrent separator (comma) separates two actions that occur simultaneously.

Operation	RTL Symbol
AND	$\wedge$
OR	$\vee$
XOR	$\oplus$
NOT	$\neg$
Implies	$\Rightarrow$
Transfer	$\leftarrow$
Bit index	$\langle\,\rangle$
Informal description	$\{\ \}$
Sequential separator	;
Concurrent separator	,

Figure **3.17**

The Register Transfer Language operations and their symbols.

Example 3.20 In the third computation of Example 3.19, suppose the first six-bit cell is denoted a, the second six-bit cell is denoted b, and the result is denoted c. An RTL specification of the exclusive OR operation is

$$c \leftarrow a \oplus b \,; \mathrm{N} \leftarrow c < 0 \,, \mathrm{Z} \leftarrow c = 0$$

First, c gets the exclusive OR of a and b. After that action, two things happen simultaneously—N gets a boolean value and Z gets a boolean value. The boolean expression $c < 0$ is 1 when c is less than zero and 0 when it is not. ∎

Arithmetic Operators

Two other unary operations are ASL, which stands for *arithmetic shift left*, and ASR, which stands for *arithmetic shift right*. As the name ASL implies, each bit in the cell shifts one place to the left. The bit that was on the leftmost end shifts into the carry bit. The rightmost bit gets 0. Figure 3.18 shows the action of the ASL operation for a six-bit cell.

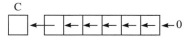

Figure **3.18**

The action of the ASL operation for a six-bit cell.

Example 3.21 Three examples of the arithmetic shift left operation are

$$\text{ASL } 11\ 1100 = 11\ 1000, \quad \text{N} = 1, \text{Z} = 0, \text{V} = 0, \text{C} = 1$$
$$\text{ASL } 00\ 0011 = 00\ 0110, \quad \text{N} = 0, \text{Z} = 0, \text{V} = 0, \text{C} = 0$$
$$\text{ASL } 01\ 0110 = 10\ 1100, \quad \text{N} = 1, \text{Z} = 0, \text{V} = 1, \text{C} = 0$$

∎

The operation is called an arithmetic shift because of the effect it has when the bits represent an integer. Assuming unsigned binary representation, the three integers in the previous example before the shift are

60 3 22   (dec, unsigned)

After the shift they are

56 6 44   (dec, unsigned)

The effect of ASL is to double the number. ASL could not double the 60 because 120 is out of range for a six-bit unsigned integer. If the carry bit is 1 after the shift, an overflow has occurred when you interpret the binary sequence as an unsigned integer.

ASL doubles the number.

In the decimal system, a left shift produces the same effect, but the integer is multiplied by 10 instead of by 2. For example, a decimal ASL applied to 356 would give 3560, which is 10 times the original value.

What if you interpret the numbers in two's complement representation? Then the three integers before the shift are

−4 3 22   (dec, signed)

After the shift they are

−8 6 −20 (dec, signed)

Again, the effect of the ASL is to double the number, even if it is negative. This time ASL could not double the 22 because 44 is out of range when you assume two's complement representation. This overflow condition causes the V bit to be set to 1. The situation is similar to the ADD operation, where the C bit detects overflow of unsigned values, but the V bit is necessary to detect overflow of signed values.

The RTL specification for an arithmetic shift left on a six-bit cell r is

$$C \leftarrow r\langle 0 \rangle \, , \; r\langle 0..4 \rangle \leftarrow r\langle 1..5 \rangle \, , \; r\langle 5 \rangle \leftarrow 0;$$
$$N \leftarrow r < 0 \, , \; Z \leftarrow r = 0 \, , \; V \leftarrow \{overflow\}$$

Simultaneously, C gets the leftmost bit of r, the leftmost five bits of r get the values of the bits immediately to their right, and the last bit on the right gets 0. After the values are shifted, the N, Z, and V status bits are set according to the new values in r. It is important to distinguish between the semicolon, which separates two events, each of which has three parts, and the comma, which separates simultaneous events within the parts. The braces indicate less formally that the V bit is set according to whether the result overflowed when you interpret the value as a signed integer.

In the ASR operation, each bit in the group shifts one place to the right. The least significant bit shifts into the carry bit, and the most significant bit remains unchanged. Figure 3.19 shows the action of the ASR operation for a six-bit cell. The ASR operation does not affect the V bit.

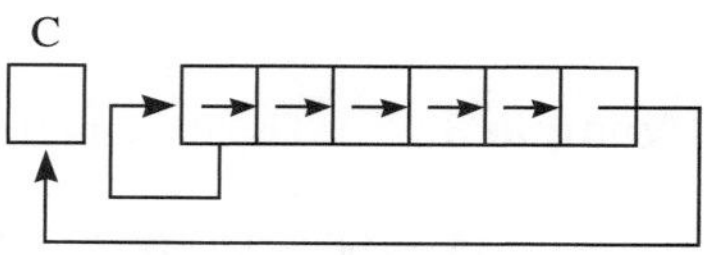

Figure **3.19**

The action of the ASR operation for a six-bit cell.

Example 3.22 Four examples of the arithmetic shift right operation are

$$\text{ASR } 01\ 0100 = 00\ 1010, \quad N = 0, Z = 0, C = 0$$
$$\text{ASR } 01\ 0111 = 00\ 1011, \quad N = 0, Z = 0, C = 1$$
$$\text{ASR } 11\ 0010 = 11\ 1001, \quad N = 1, Z = 0, C = 0$$
$$\text{ASR } 11\ 0101 = 11\ 1010, \quad N = 1, Z = 0, C = 1 \qquad \blacksquare$$

The ASR operation is designed specifically for the two's complement representation. Because the sign bit does not change, negative numbers remain negative and positive numbers remain positive.

Shifting to the left multiplies an integer by 2, whereas shifting to the right divides it by 2. Before the shift, the four integers in the previous example are

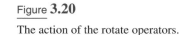

ASR halves the number.

$$20 \quad 23 \quad -14 \quad -11 \quad \text{(dec, signed)}$$

After the shift they are

$$10 \quad 11 \quad -7 \quad -6 \quad \text{(dec, signed)}$$

The even integers can be divided by 2 exactly, so there is no question about the effect of ASR on them. When odd integers are divided by 2, the result is always rounded down. For example, $23 \div 2 = 11.5$, and 11.5 rounded down is 11. Similarly, $-11 \div 2 = -5.5$, and -5.5 rounded down is -6. Note that -6 is less than -5.5 because it lies to the left of -5.5 on the number line.

Rotate Operators

In contrast to the arithmetic operators, the rotate operators do not interpret a binary sequence as an integer. Consequently, the rotate operations do not affect the N, Z, or V bits, but only the C bit. There are two rotate operators—rotate left, denoted ROL, and rotate right, denoted ROR. Figure 3.20 shows the actions of the rotate operators for a six-bit cell. Rotate left is similar to arithmetic shift left, except that the C bit is rotated into the rightmost bit of the cell instead of 0 shifting into the rightmost bit. Rotate right does the same thing but in the opposite direction.

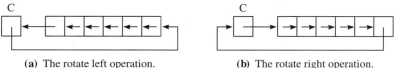

(a) The rotate left operation.   (b) The rotate right operation.

Figure 3.20

The action of the rotate operators.

The RTL specification for a rotate left on a six-bit cell is

$$C \leftarrow r\langle 0 \rangle, r\langle 0..4 \rangle \leftarrow r\langle 1..5 \rangle, r\langle 5 \rangle \leftarrow c$$

Example 3.23   Four examples of the rotate operation are

C = 1, ROL 01 1101 = 11 1011, C = 0
C = 0, ROL 01 1101 = 11 1010, C = 0
C = 1, ROR 01 1101 = 10 1110, C = 1
C = 0, ROR 01 1101 = 00 1110, C = 1

where the value of C before the rotate is on the left and the value of C after the rotate is on the right.   ∎

3.4   Hesadecimal and Character Representations

The binary representations in the previous sections are integer representations. This section deals with yet another number base, which will be used with the computer introduced in the next chapter. It also shows how that computer stores alphabetic information.

Hexadecimal

Suppose humans had 16 fingers instead of 10. What would have happened when Arabic numerals were invented? Remember the pattern. With 10 fingers, you start from 0 and keep inventing new symbols—1, 2, and so on until you get to your penultimate finger, 9. Then on your last finger you combine 1 and 0 to represent the next number, 10.

With 16 fingers, when you get to 9 you still have plenty of fingers left. You must go on inventing new symbols. These extra symbols are usually represented by the letters at the beginning of the English alphabet. So counting in base 16 (*hexadecimal*, or *hex* for short) looks like this:

0	7	E	15	1C	23
1	8	F	16	1D	24
2	9	10	17	1E	25
3	A	11	18	1F	26
4	B	12	19	20	.
5	C	13	1A	21	.
6	D	14	1B	22	.

Counting in hexadecimal

When the hexadecimal number contains many digits, counting can be a bit tricky. Consider counting the next five numbers in hexadecimal, starting with 8BE7, C9D, or 9FFE:

8BE7	C9D	9FFE
8BE8	C9E	9FFF
8BE9	C9F	A000
8BEA	CA0	A001
8BEB	CA1	A002
8BEC	CA2	A003

When written in octal, numbers have a tendency to look larger than they actually are. In hexadecimal, the effect is the opposite. Numbers have a tendency to look smaller than they actually are. Comparing the list of hexadecimal numbers with the list of decimal numbers shows that 18 (hex) is 24 (dec).

Base Conversions

In hexadecimal, each place value is 16 times greater than the previous place value. To convert from hexadecimal to decimal, simply multiply the place value by its digit and add.

Example 3.24   Figure 3.21 shows how to convert 8BE7 from hexadecimal to decimal. The decimal value of B is 11, and the decimal value of E is 14.   ∎

The procedure for converting from decimal to hexadecimal is analogous to the procedure for converting from decimal to binary. Instead of successively dividing the number by 2, you divide it by 16 and keep track of the remainders, which are the hexadecimal digits of the converted number.

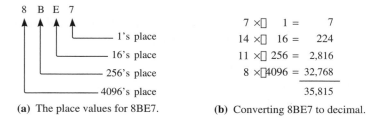

(a) The place values for 8BE7.   (b) Converting 8BE7 to decimal.

Figure **3.21**

Converting from hexadecimal to decimal.

For numbers up to 255 (dec) or FF (hex), converting either way is easily done with the table in Figure 3.22. The body of the table contains decimal numbers. The left column and top row contain hexadecimal digits.

	0	**1**	**2**	**3**	**4**	**5**	**6**	**7**	**8**	**9**	**A**	**B**	**C**	**D**	**E**	**F**
0_	0	1	2	3	4	5	6	7	8	9	10	11	12	13	14	15
1_	16	17	18	19	20	21	22	23	24	25	26	27	28	29	30	31
2_	32	33	34	35	36	37	38	39	40	41	42	43	44	45	46	47
3_	48	49	50	51	52	53	54	55	56	57	58	59	60	61	62	63
4_	64	65	66	67	68	69	70	71	72	73	74	75	76	77	78	79
5_	80	81	82	83	84	85	86	87	88	89	90	91	92	93	94	95
6_	96	97	98	99	100	101	102	103	104	105	106	107	108	109	110	111
7_	112	113	114	115	116	117	118	119	120	121	122	123	124	125	126	127
8_	128	129	130	131	132	133	134	135	136	137	138	139	140	141	142	143
9_	144	145	146	147	148	149	150	151	152	153	154	155	156	157	158	159
A_	160	161	162	163	164	165	166	167	168	169	170	171	172	173	174	175
B_	176	177	178	179	180	181	182	183	184	185	186	187	188	189	190	191
C_	192	193	194	195	196	197	198	199	200	201	202	203	204	205	206	207
D_	208	209	210	211	212	213	214	215	216	217	218	219	220	221	222	223
E_	224	225	226	227	228	229	230	231	232	233	234	235	236	237	238	239
F_	240	241	242	243	244	245	246	247	248	249	250	251	252	253	254	255

Example 3.25   To convert 9C (hex) to decimal, look up row 9 and column C to find 156 (dec). To convert 125 (dec), look it up in the body of the table and read off 7D (hex) from the left column and top row.   ∎

Figure **3.22**

The hexadecimal conversion chart.

If computers store information in binary format, why learn the hexadecimal system? The answer lies in the special relationship between hexadecimal and binary, as Figure 3.23 shows. There are 16 possible combinations of four bits, and there are exactly 16 hexadecimal digits. Each hexadecimal digit, therefore, represents four bits.

Bit patterns are often written in hexadecimal notation to save space on the printed page. A computer manual for a 16-bit machine might state that a memory location contains 01D3. That is shorter than saying it contains 0000 0001 1101 0011.

Hexadecimal as a shorthand for binary

To convert from unsigned binary to hexadecimal, partition the bits into groups of four starting from the rightmost end, and use the hexadecimal from Figure 3.23 for each group. To convert from hexadecimal to unsigned binary, simply reverse the procedure.

Example 3.26   To write the 10-bit unsigned binary number 10 1001 1100 in hexadecimal, start with the rightmost four bits, 1100:

10 1001 1100 (bin) = 29C (hex)

Because 10 bits cannot be partitioned into groups of four exactly, you must assume two additional leading 0's when looking up the leftmost digit in Figure 3.23. The leftmost hexadecimal digit comes from

10 (bin) = 0010 (bin) = 2 (hex)

in this example. ∎

Example 3.27 For a 14-bit cell,

0D60 (hex) = 00 1101 0110 0000 (bin)

Note that the last hexadecimal 0 represents four binary 0's, but the first hexadecimal 0 represents only two binary 0's. ∎

To convert from decimal to unsigned binary, you may prefer to use the hexadecimal table as an intermediate step. You can avoid any computation by looking up the hexadecimal value in Figure 3.22, and then converting each digit to binary according to Figure 3.23.

Example 3.28 For a six-bit cell,

29 (dec) = 1D (hex) = 01 1101 (bin)

where each step in the conversion is a simple table lookup. ∎

In machine language program listings or program traces, numbers are rarely written in hexadecimal notation with negative signs. Instead, the sign bit is implicit in the bit pattern represented by the hexadecimal digits. You must remember that hexadecimal is only a convenient shorthand for a binary sequence. The hardware stores only binary values.

Example 3.29 If a 12-bit memory location contains F7A (hex), then the number in decimal is found by considering the following bit pattern:

F7A (hex) = 1111 0111 1010 (bin)

The sign bit is 1, so the number is negative. Converting to decimal gives

F7A (hex) = −134 (dec)

Notice that the hexadecimal number is not written with a negative sign, even though it may be interpreted as a negative number. ∎

Hexadecimal	Binary
0	0000
1	0001
2	0010
3	0011
4	0100
5	0101
6	0110
7	0111
8	1000
9	1001
A	1010
B	1011
C	1100
D	1101
E	1110
F	1111

Figure **3.23**

The relationship between hexadecimal and binary.

Characters

Because computer memories are binary, alphabetic characters must be coded to be stored in memory. A widespread binary code for alphabetic characters is the

American Standard Code for Information Interchange, also known as ASCII (pronounced *askey*).

ASCII contains all the uppercase and lowercase English letters, the 10 numeric
digits, and special characters such as punctuation signs. Some of its symbols are
nonprintable and are used mainly to transmit information between computers or to
control peripheral devices.

ASCII is a seven-bit code. Since there are $2^7 = 128$ possible combinations of
seven bits, there are 128 ASCII characters. Figure 3.24 shows all these characters.
The first column of the table shows the nonprintable characters, whose meanings
are listed at the bottom. The rest of the table lists the printable characters.

Example 3.30   The sequence 000 0111, which stands for *bell*, causes a terminal
to beep. Another example is the set of commands necessary for a paper printer to
begin printing at the start of a new line. The computer sends a carriage return character (CR, which is 000 1101) followed by a line feed character (LF, which is
000 1010). CR makes the "print carriage," or cursor, return to the left side of the
page, and LF advances the paper by one line.   ■

Example 3.31   The name

Tom

would be stored in ASCII as

101 0100
110 1111
110 1101

If that sequence of bits were sent to an output terminal, the word "Tom" would be
displayed.   ■

Example 3.32   The street address

52 Elm

would be stored in ASCII as

011 0101
011 0010
010 0000
100 0101
110 1100
110 1101

The blank space between 2 and E is a separate ASCII character.   ■

Char	Bin	Hex	Char	Bin	Hex	Char	Bin	Hex	Char	Bin	Hex
NUL	000 0000	00	SP	010 0000	20	@	100 0000	40	`	110 0000	60
SOH	000 0001	01	!	010 0001	21	A	100 0001	41	a	110 0001	61
STX	000 0010	02	"	010 0010	22	B	100 0010	42	b	110 0010	62
ETX	000 0011	03	#	010 0011	23	C	100 0011	43	c	110 0011	63
EOT	000 0100	04	$	010 0100	24	D	100 0100	44	d	110 0100	64
ENQ	000 0101	05	%	010 0101	25	E	100 0101	45	e	110 0101	65
ACK	000 0110	06	&	010 0110	26	F	100 0110	46	f	110 0110	66
BEL	000 0111	07	'	010 0111	27	G	100 0111	47	g	110 0111	67
BS	000 1000	08	(	010 1000	28	H	100 1000	48	h	110 1000	68
HT	000 1001	09	)	010 1001	29	I	100 1001	49	i	110 1001	69
LF	000 1010	0A	*	010 1010	2A	J	100 1010	4A	j	110 1010	6A
VT	000 1011	0B	+	010 1011	2B	K	100 1011	4B	k	110 1011	6B
FF	000 1100	0C	,	010 1100	2C	L	100 1100	4C	l	110 1100	6C
CR	000 1101	0D	-	010 1101	2D	M	100 1101	4D	m	110 1101	6D
SO	000 1110	0E	.	010 1110	2E	N	100 1110	4E	n	110 1110	6E
SI	000 1111	0F	/	010 1111	2F	O	100 1111	4F	o	110 1111	6F
DLE	001 0000	10	0	011 0000	30	P	101 0000	50	p	111 0000	70
DC1	001 0001	11	1	011 0001	31	Q	101 0001	51	q	111 0001	71
DC2	001 0010	12	2	011 0010	32	R	101 0010	52	r	111 0010	72
DC3	001 0011	13	3	011 0011	33	S	101 0011	53	s	111 0011	73
DC4	001 0100	14	4	011 0100	34	T	101 0100	54	t	111 0100	74
NAK	001 0101	15	5	011 0101	35	U	101 0101	55	u	111 0101	75
SYN	001 0110	16	6	011 0110	36	V	101 0110	56	v	111 0110	76
ETB	001 0111	17	7	011 0111	37	W	101 0111	57	w	111 0111	77
CAN	001 1000	18	8	011 1000	38	X	101 1000	58	x	111 1000	78
EM	001 1001	19	9	011 1001	39	Y	101 1001	59	y	111 1001	79
SUB	001 1010	1A	:	011 1010	3A	Z	101 1010	5A	z	111 1010	7A
ESC	001 1011	1B	;	011 1011	3B	[	101 1011	5B	{	111 1011	7B
FS	001 1100	1C	<	011 1100	3C	\	101 1100	5C	|	111 1100	7C
GS	001 1101	1D	=	011 1101	3D	]	101 1101	5D	}	111 1101	7D
RS	001 1110	1E	>	011 1110	3E	^	101 1110	5E	~	111 1110	7E
US	001 1111	1F	?	011 1111	3F	_	101 1111	5F	DEL	111 1111	7F

Abbreviations for Control Characters

NUL null, or all zeros
SOH start of heading
STX start of text
ETX end of text

EOT end of transmission
ENQ enquiry
ACK acknowledge
BEL bell

BS backspace
HT horizontal tabulation
LF line feed
VT vertical tabulation

FF form feed
CR carriage return
SO shift out
SI shift in

DLE data link escape
DC1 device control 1
DC2 device control 2
DC3 device control 3

DC4 device control 4
NAK negative acknowledge
SYN synchronous idle
ETB end of transmission block

CAN cancel
EM end of medium
SUB substitute
ESC escape

FS file separator
GS group separator
RS record separator
US unit separator

SP space
DEL delete

Figure **3.24**

The American Standard Code for Information Interchange (ASCII).

Although ASCII is widespread, it is by no means the only code possible for representing string characters. It is limited because the seven-bit code has no provision for accent marks common in languages other than English. Because of this limitation, there is an extension that uses the eighth bit to provide many of the accented characters that are not in the seven-bit code.

But even this extension is not sufficient to handle non-Latin characters. Because of the importance of global information exchange, a standard called Unicode was developed. The goal of Unicode is to encode the alphabets of all the languages in the world, and eventually even ancient languages no longer spoken. The Unicode character set uses 32 bits, or four bytes. Because most applications would not use most of these characters, the Unicode standard specifies a technique for using less than four bytes. A subset of common Unicode characters is contained in the Basic Multilingual Plane, with each character occupying just two bytes. This is still twice the storage necessary to store the one-byte extended ASCII code. However, the Basic Multilingual Plane contains practically all the world's written languages including Arabic, Armenian, Chinese, Cyrillic, Greek, Hebrew, Japanese, Korean, Syriac, many African languages, and even Canadian Aboriginal Syllabics and Braille patterns.

Unicode

3.5 Floating Point Representation

The numeric representations described in previous sections of this chapter are for integer values. C++ has three numeric types that have fractional parts:

- float   single-precision floating point
- double   double-precision floating point
- long double   extended-precision floating point

Values of these types cannot be stored at Level ISA3 with two's complement binary representation because provisions must be made for locating the decimal point within the number. Floating point values are stored using a binary version of scientific notation.

Binary Fractions

Binary fractions have a binary point, which is the base-two version of the base-ten decimal point.

Example 3.33   Figure 3.25(a) shows the place values for 101.011 (bin). The bits to the left of the binary point have the same place values as the corresponding bits in unsigned binary representation as in Figure 3.2, page 93. Starting with the 1/2's place to the right of the binary point, each place has a value one half as great as the

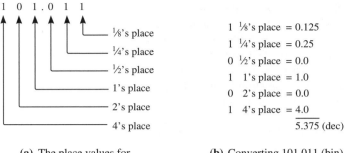

(a) The place values for 101.011 (bin).

(b) Converting 101.011 (bin) to decimal.

Figure **3.25**

Converting from binary to decimal.

previous place value. Figure 3.25(b) shows the addition that produces the 5.375 (dec) value.   ∎

Figure 3.26 shows the polynomial representation of numbers with fractional parts. The value of the bit to the left of the radix point is always the base to the zeroth power, which is always 1. The next significant place to the left is the base to the first power, which is the value of the base itself. The value of the bit to the right of the radix point is the base to the power -1. The next significant place to the right is the base to the power -2. The value of each place to the right is 1/base times the value of the place on its left.

$$1 \times 2^2 + 0 \times 2^1 + 1 \times 2^0 + 0 \times 2^{-1} + 1 \times 2^{-2} + 1 \times 2^{-3}$$

(a) The binary number 101.011.

$$5 \times 10^2 + 0 \times 10^1 + 6 \times 10^0 + 7 \times 10^{-1} + 2 \times 10^{-2} + 1 \times 10^{-3}$$

(b) The decimal number 506.721.

Figure **3.26**

The polynomial representation of floating point numbers.

To determine the decimal value of a binary fraction requires two steps. First, convert the bits to the left of the binary point using the technique of Example 3.3, page 94, for converting unsigned binary values. Then, use the algorithm of successive doubling to convert the bits to the right of the binary point.

Example 3.34   Figure 3.27 shows the conversion of 6.5859375 (dec) to binary. The conversion of the whole part gives 101 (bin) to the left of the binary point. To convert the fractional part, write the digits to the right of the decimal point in the heading of the right column of the table. Double the fractional part, writing the digit to the left of the decimal point in the column on the left and the fractional part in the column on the right. The next time you double, do not include the whole number part. For example, the value 0.34375 comes from doubling .171875, not from doubling 1.171875. The digits on the left from top to bottom are the bits of the binary fractional part from left to right. So, 6.5859375 (dec) = 110.1001011 (bin).   ∎

6.5859375

6 (dec) = 110 (bin)

(a) Convert the whole part.

	.5859375
1	.171875
0	.34375
0	.6875
1	.375
0	.75
1	.5
1	.0

(b) Convert the fractional part.

Figure **3.27**

Converting from decimal to binary.

The algorithm for converting the fractional part from decimal to binary is the mirror image of the algorithm for converting the whole part from decimal to binary. Figure 3.5 shows that to convert the whole part you use the algorithm of successive division by two. The bits you generate are the remainders of the division, and you generate them from right to left starting at the binary point. To convert the fractional part you use the algorithm of successive multiplication by two. The bits you generate are the whole part of the multiplication, and you generate them from left to right starting at the binary point.

A number that can be represented with a finite number of digits in decimal may require an endless representation in binary.

Example 3.35   Figure 3.28 shows the conversion of 0.2 (dec) to binary. The first doubling produces 0.4. A few more doublings produce 0.4 again. It is clear that the process will never terminate and that 0.2 (dec) = 0.001100110011... (bin) with the bit pattern 011 endlessly repeating.   ■

	.2
0	.4
0	.8
1	.6
1	.2
0	.4
0	.8
1	.6
⋮	⋮

Because all computer cells can store only a finite number of bits, the value 0.2 (dec) cannot be stored exactly, but must be approximated. You should realize that if you add 0.2 + 0.2 in a Level HOL6 language like C++ you will probably not get 0.4 exactly because of the roundoff error inherent in the binary representation of the values. For that reason, good numeric software rarely tests two floating point numbers for strict equality. Instead, the software maintains a small but nonzero tolerance that represents how close two floating point values must be to be considered equal. If the tolerance is, say 0.0001, then the numbers 1.38264 and 1.38267 would be considered equal because their difference, which is 0.00003, is less than the tolerance.

Figure **3.28**

A decimal value with an unending binary representation.

Excess Representations

Floating point numbers are represented with a binary version of the scientific notation common with decimal numbers. A nonzero number is normalized if it is written in scientific notation with the first nonzero digit immediately to the left of the radix point. The number zero cannot be normalized because it does not have a first nonzero digit.

Example 3.36   The decimal number -328.4 is written in normalized form in scientific notation as -3.284×10^2. The effect of the exponent 2 as the power of 10 is to shift the decimal point two places to the right. Similarly, the binary number -10101.101 is written in normalized form in scientific notation as -1.0101101×2^4. The effect of the exponent 4 as the power of 2 is to shift the binary point four places to the right.   ■

Example 3.37   The binary number 0.00101101 is written in normalized form in scientific notation as 1.01101×2^{-3}. The effect of the exponent -3 as the power of 2 is to shift the binary point three places to the left.   ■

In general, a floating point number can be positive or negative, and its exponent can be a positive or negative integer. Figure 3.29 shows a cell in memory that stores a floating point value. The cell is divided into three fields. The first field stores one bit for the sign of the number. The second field stores the bits representing the exponent of the normalized binary number. The third field, called the significand, stores bits that represent the magnitude of the value.

Any signed representation for integers could be used to store the exponent. You might think that two's complement binary representation would be used, because that is the representation that most computers use to store signed integers. However, two's complement is not used. Instead, a biased representation is used for a reason that will be explained shortly.

An example of a biased representation for a five-bit cell is excess 15. The range of numbers for the cell is −15 to 16 as written in decimal and 00000 to 11111 as written in binary. To convert from decimal to excess 15, you add 15 to the decimal value and then convert to binary as you would an unsigned number. To convert from excess 15 to decimal, you write the decimal value as if it were an unsigned number and subtract 15 from it. In excess 15, the first bit denotes whether a value is positive or negative. But unlike two's complement representation, 1 signifies a positive value, and 0 signifies a negative value.

Example 3.38   To convert 5 from decimal to excess 15, add 5 + 15 = 20. Then convert 20 to binary as if it were unsigned, 20 (dec) = 10100 (excess 15). The first bit is 1, indicating a positive value.   ∎

Example 3.39   To convert 00011 from excess 15 to decimal, convert 00011 as an unsigned value, 00011 (bin) = 3 (dec). Then subtract decimal values 3 − 15 = −12. So, 00011 (excess 15) = −12 (dec).   ∎

Figure 3.30 shows the bit patterns for a three-bit cell that stores integers with excess 3 representation compared to two's complement representation. Each representation stores eight values. The excess 3 representation has a range of −3 to 4 (dec), while the two's complement representation has a range of −4 to 3 (dec).

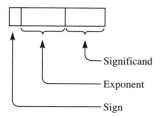

Figure **3.29**

Storage for a floating point value.

Decimal	Excess 3	Two's Complement
−4		100
−3	000	101
−2	001	110
−1	010	111
0	011	000
1	100	001
2	101	010
3	110	011
4	111	

Figure **3.30**

The signed integers for a three-bit cell.

The Hidden Bit

Suppose you store floating point numbers in normalized form with the first nonzero digit immediately to the left of the binary point. Then you do not need to explicitly store the binary point, because it is always at the same location. Assuming the sign field in Figure 3.29 contains 1 for negative values and 0 for positive values, the exponent field is three bits, and the significand is four bits, you could store a number with four significant bits. To store a decimal value, first convert it to binary, write it in normalized scientific notation, store the exponent in excess 3 representation, and store the most significant bits of the magnitude in the significand.

Example 3.40   To store 0.34, convert to binary as 0.34 (dec) = 0.010101110.... The sequence of bits for the value is endless, so you can only store the most significant bits. In normalized scientific notation, the value is $1.0101110...\times 2^{-2}$. The exponent of -2 written in excess 3 representation from Figure 3.30 is 001. The first four significant bits are 1010, with the implied decimal point after the first bit. The number is positive, so the sign bit is 0. The bit pattern for the stored value is 0 001 1010.

To see how close the approximation is, convert the stored value back to decimal. The stored value is 1.010×2^{-2} (bin) = 0.3125, which differs from the original decimal value by 0.0275. ∎

It is unfortunate that you cannot store more significant bits in the significand. Of course, three bits for the exponent and four bits for the significand are tiny compared to floating point formats in real machines. The example is small to keep the illustrations simple. However, even in a real machine with much larger fields for the significand, the approximations are better but still unavoidable because the memory cell is finite.

You can take advantage of the fact that there will always be a 1 to the left of the binary point when the number is normalized. Because the 1 will always be there you can simply not store it, which gives you room in the significand for an extra bit of accuracy. The bit that is assumed to be to the left of the binary point but that is not stored explicitly is called the *hidden bit*.

Example 3.41   Using a representation that assumes a hidden bit in the significand, the value 0.34 (dec) is stored as 0 001 0101. The first four bits to the right of the binary point are 0101. The 1 bit to the left of the binary point is assumed. To see the improvement in accuracy, the stored value is now 1.0101×2^{-2} (bin) = 0.328125, which differs from the original decimal value by 0.011875. The difference without the hidden bit is 0.0275, so using the hidden bit improves the approximation. ∎

Of course, the hidden bit is assumed, not ignored. When you write a decimal floating point value in a program, the compiler generates code to convert the value to binary. It discards the assumed hidden bit and stores as many bits to the right of the binary point as it can. If the program multiplies two floating point stored values, the computer extracts the bits from the significands and inserts the assumed hidden bit before performing the multiply operation. Then, the product is stored after removing the hidden bit from the result of the operation.

Special Values

Some real values require special treatment. The most obvious is zero, which cannot *Zero* be normalized because there is no 1 bit in its binary representation. You must set aside a special bit pattern for zero. Standard practice is to put all 0's in the exponent field and all 0's in the significand as well. What do you put for the sign? Most common is to have two representations for zero, one positive and one negative. For a three-bit exponent and four-bit significand, the bit patterns are

1 000 0000 (bin) = −0.0 (dec)

0 000 0000 (bin) = +0.0 (dec)

This solution for storing zero has ramifications for some other bit patterns, however. If the bit pattern for +0.0 were not special, then 0 000 0000 would be interpreted with the hidden bit as 1.0000×2^{-3} (bin) = 0.125, the smallest positive value that could be stored had the value not been reserved for zero. If this pattern is reserved for zero, then the smallest positive value that can be stored is 0 000 0001 = 1.0001×2^{-3} (bin) = 0.1328125, which is slightly larger. The negative number with the smallest possible magnitude would be identical but with a 1 in the sign bit. The numbers with the smallest nonzero magnitudes would be

1 000 0001 (bin) = −0.1328125 (dec)

0 000 0001 (bin) = +0.1328125 (dec)

The largest positive number that can be stored is the bit pattern with the largest exponent and the largest significand. The negative number with the largest magnitude would have an identical bit pattern, but with a one in the sign bit. The bit patterns for the largest magnitudes and their decimal values would be

1 111 1111 (bin) =−31.0 (dec)

0 111 1111 (bin) =+31.0 (dec)

Figure 3.31 shows the number line for the representation where zero is the only special value. As with integer representations, there is a limit to how large a value you can store. If you try to multiply 9.5 times 12.0, both of which are in range, the true value is 114.0, which is in the positive overflow region.

Unlike integer values, however, the real number line has an underflow region. If you try to multiply 0.125 times 0.125, which are both in range, the true value is 0.015625, which is in the positive underflow region. The smallest positive value that can be stored is 0.132815.

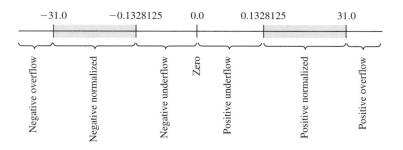

Figure **3.31**

The real number line with zero as the only special value.

Numeric calculations with approximate floating point values need to have results that are consistent with what would be expected when calculations are done with exact precision. For example, suppose you multiply 9.5 and 12.0. What should be stored for the result? Suppose you store the largest possible value, 31.0 as an approximation. Suppose further that this is an intermediate value in a longer computation. If you later need to compute half of the result, you will get 15.5, which is far from what the correct value would have been.

The same problem occurs in the underflow region. If you store 0.0 as an approximation of 0.015625, and you later want to multiply the value by 12.0, you will get 0.0. You risk being misled by what appears to be a reasonable value.

The problems encountered with overflow and underflow are alleviated somewhat by introducing more special values for the bit patterns. As is the case with zero, you must use some bit patterns that would otherwise be used to represent values on the number line. In addition to zero, three special values are common:

- Infinity

- Not a Number

- Denormalized numbers

Infinity is used for values that are in the overflow regions. If the result of an operation overflows, the bit pattern for infinity is stored. If further operations are done on this bit pattern, the result is what you would expect for an infinite value. For example, $3/\infty = 0$, $5 + \infty = \infty$, and the square root of infinity is infinity. You can produce infinity by dividing by 0. For example $3/0 = \infty$, and $-4/0 = -\infty$. If you ever do a computation with real numbers and get infinity, you know that an overflow occurred somewhere in your intermediate results. *Infinity*

A bit pattern for a value that is not a number is called a NaN (rhymes with plan). NaNs are used to indicate floating point operations that are illegal. For example, taking the square root of a negative number produces NaN, and so does dividing 0/0. Any floating point operation with at least one NaN operand produces NaN. For example, $7 + \text{NaN} = \text{NaN}$, and $7/\text{NaN} = \text{NaN}$. *Not a number*

Both infinity and NaN use the largest possible value of the exponent for their bit patterns. That is, the exponent field is all 1's. The significand is all 0's for infinity and can be any nonzero pattern for NaN. Reserving these bit patterns for infinity and NaN has the effect of reducing the range of values that can be stored. For a three-bit exponent and four-bit significand, the bit patterns for the largest magnitudes and their decimal values are

1 111 0000 (bin) = $-\infty$

1 110 1111 (bin) = -15.5 (dec)

0 110 1111 (bin) = $+15.5$ (dec)

0 111 0000 (bin) = $+\infty$

There is no infinitesimal value for the underflow region in Figure 3.31 that corresponds to the infinite value in the overflow region. However, denormalized numbers are special values that have a desirable behavior called gradual underflow. With gradual underflow, the gap between the smallest positive value and zero is reduced considerably. The idea is to take the nonzero values that would be stored with an exponent field of all 0's and distribute them evenly in the underflow gap.

Denormalized numbers

Because the exponent field of all 0's is reserved for denormalized numbers, the smallest positive normalized number becomes 0 001 0000 = 1.000×2^{-2} (bin) = 0.25 (dec). It might appear that we have made matters worse because the smallest positive normalized number with 000 in the exponent field is 0.1328125. But, the denormalized values are spread throughout the gap in such a way as to actually reduce it.

When the exponent field is all 0's and the significand contains at least one 1, special rules apply to the representation. Assuming a three-bit exponent and a four-bit significand,

- The hidden bit to the left of the binary point is assumed to be 0 instead of 1.

- The exponent is assumed to be stored in excess 2 instead of excess 3.

Example 3.42 For a representation with a three-bit exponent and four-bit significand, what decimal value is represented by 0 000 0110? Because the exponent is all 0's and the significand contains at least one 1, the number is denormalized. Its exponent is 000 (excess 2) = 0 − 2 = −2, its hidden bit is 0, so its binary scientific notation is 0.0110×2^{-2}. The exponent is in excess 2 instead of excess 3 because this is the special case of a denormalized number. Converting to decimal yields 0.09375. ∎

To see how much better the underflow gap is, compute the values having the smallest possible magnitudes, which are denormalized.

$$1\ 000\ 0001 \text{ (bin)} = -0.015625 \text{ (dec)}$$
$$1\ 000\ 0000 \text{ (bin)} = -0.0$$
$$0\ 000\ 0000 \text{ (bin)} = +0.0$$
$$0\ 000\ 0001 \text{ (bin)} = +0.015625 \text{ (dec)}$$

Without denormalized numbers, the smallest positive number is 0.1328125, so the gap has been reduced considerably.

Figure 3.32 shows some of the key values for a three-bit operand and a four-bit significand using all the special values. The values are listed in numeric order from smallest to largest. The figure shows why an excess representation is common for floating point exponents. Consider all the positive numbers from +0.0 to +∞ ignoring

	Binary	Scientific notation	Decimal
Not a Number	1 111 nonzero		
Negative infinity	1 111 0000		$-\infty$
Negative normalized	1 110 1111	-1.1111×2^3	-15.5
	1 110 1110	-1.1110×2^3	-15.0
	...	...	...
	1 011 0001	-1.0001×2^0	-1.0625
	1 011 0000	-1.0000×2^0	-1.0
	1 010 1111	-1.1111×2^{-1}	-0.96875
	...	...	...
	1 001 0001	-1.0001×2^{-2}	-0.265625
	1 001 0000	-1.0000×2^{-2}	-0.25
Negative denormalized	1 000 1111	-0.1111×2^{-2}	-0.234375
	1 000 1110	-0.1110×2^{-2}	-0.21875
	...	...	...
	1 000 0010	-0.0010×2^{-2}	-0.03125
	1 000 0001	-0.0001×2^{-2}	-0.015625
Negative zero	1 000 0000		-0.0
Positive zero	0 000 0000		$+0.0$
Positive denormalized	0 000 0001	0.0001×2^{-2}	0.015625
	0 000 0010	0.0010×2^{-2}	0.03125
	...	...	...
	0 000 1110	0.1110×2^{-2}	0.21875
	0 000 1111	0.1111×2^{-2}	0.234375
Positive normalized	0 001 0000	1.0000×2^{-2}	0.25
	0 001 0001	1.0001×2^{-2}	0.265625
	...	...	...
	0 010 1111	1.1111×2^{-1}	0.96875
	0 011 0000	1.0000×2^0	1.0
	0 011 0001	1.0001×2^0	1.0625
	...	...	...
	0 110 1110	1.1110×2^3	15.0
	0 110 1111	1.1111×2^3	15.5
Positive infinity	0 111 0000		$+\infty$
Not a Number	0 111 nonzero		

Figure **3.32**

Floating point values for a three-bit operand and four-bit significand.

the sign bit. You can see that if you treat the rightmost seven bits to be a simple unsigned integer, the successive values increase by one all the way from 000 0000 for 0 (dec) to 111 0000 for ∞. To do a comparison of two positive floating point values, say in a C++ statement like

```
if (x < y)
```

the computer does not need to extract the exponent field or insert the hidden bit. It can simply compare the rightmost seven bits as if they represented an integer to determine which floating point value has the larger magnitude. The circuitry for integer operations is considerably faster than that for floating point operations, so using an excess representation for the exponent really improves performance.

The same pattern occurs for the negative numbers. The rightmost seven bits can be treated like an unsigned integer to compare magnitudes of the negative quantities. Floating point quantities would not have this property if the exponents were stored using two's complement representation.

If the value of x has been computed as −0.0 and y as +0.0 then the programmer should expect the expression (x < y) to be false. With real numbers there is no distinction between positive and negative zero. Computers must be programmed to return false in this special case, even though the bit patterns indicate that x is negative and y is positive.

The IEEE 754 Floating Point Standard

The Institute of Electrical and Electronic Engineers, Inc. (IEEE) is a professional society supported by its members that provides services in various engineering fields, one of which is computer engineering. The society has various groups that propose standards for the industry. Before the IEEE proposed its standard for floating point numbers, every computer manufacturer designed its own representation for floating point values, and they all differed from each other. In the early days before networks became prevalent and little data was shared between computers, this arrangement was tolerated.

Even without the widespread sharing of data, however, the lack of a standard hindered research and development in numerical computations. It was possible for two identical programs to run on two separate machines with the same input and produce different results because of the different approximations of the representations.

The IEEE set up a committee to propose a floating point standard, which it did in 1985. There are two standards: number 854, which is more applicable to handheld calculators than to other computing devices, and number 754, which was widely adopted for computers. Virtually every computer manufacturer now

William V. Kahan

William Kahan was born in 1933 in Canada. He attended the University of Toronto, where he earned his PhD in mathematics in 1958.

In 1976, Intel had plans to build a floating point coprocessor for one of its lines of microprocessors. John Palmer was in charge of the project and persuaded Intel that it needed an arithmetic standard so that different chips made by the company would produce identical output from identical floating point input. Ten years earlier at Stanford University, Palmer had heard Kahan analyze the representations of floating point values of some popular computers of that day. He hired Kahan as a consultant to establish the details of the representation.

Soon thereafter, the IEEE established a committee to develop an industry-wide floating point standard. Kahan was on the committee and his work at Intel became the basis of the IEEE 754 standard, although it was controversial at the beginning. At the time, the Digital Equipment Corporation (DEC) used a well-respected representation on its VAX line of computers. Kahan had even suggested that Intel copy it when he was first contacted by Palmer. But the VAX representation did not have denormalized numbers with gradual underflow. That feature became a big issue in the deliberations of the committee because it was thought that any implementation of this representation would execute too slowly. The battle over gradual underflow raged on for years, with DEC claiming that computations with the feature would never outperform the VAX. Finally, George Taylor, a graduate student of Dave Patterson at UC Berkeley, built a working prototype circuit board with Kahan's floating point specifications. They found they could plug it into a VAX without slowing the machine down.

This chapter omits many details of IEEE 754, including specifications for guard digits, exceptions, and flags. Kahan has dedicated himself to "making the world safe for numerical computations." Practically all hardware conforms to the standard, but some software systems do not make proper use of the exceptions and flags. When that happens, Kahan is quick to publicize the shortcoming. Sun Microsystems, which promotes its Java language with the slogan "Write Once—Run Anywhere," has been taken to task by Kahan in his paper entitled "How Java's Floating-Point Hurts Everyone Everywhere." When a recent version of the Matlab software was released with less conformance to IEEE 754 than earlier versions, Kahan's paper was entitled "Matlab's Loss Is Nobody's Gain."

In 1989, William Kahan received the A. M. Turing Award for his fundamental contributions to numerical analysis. At the time of this writing he is a Professor of Mathematics and of Electrical Engineering and Computer Science at the University of California, Berkeley.

provides floating point numbers for their computers that conform to the IEEE 754 standard.

The floating point representation described earlier in this section is identical to the IEEE 754 standard except for the number of bits in the exponent field and in the significand. Figure 3.33 shows the two formats for the standard. The single precision format has an eight-bit cell for the exponent using excess 127 representation

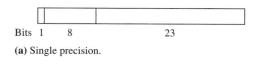

Bits 1   8   23

(a) Single precision.

Bits 1   11   52

(b) Double precision.

Figure **3.33**

The IEEE 754 floating point standard.

(except for denormalized numbers, which use excess 126) and 23 bits for the significand. The double precision format has an 11-bit cell for the exponent using excess 1023 representation (except for denormalized numbers, which use excess 1022) and a 52-bit cell for the significand.

The single precision format has the following bit values. Positive infinity is

0 1111 1111 000 0000 0000 0000 0000 0000

The hexadecimal abbreviation for the full 32-bit pattern arranges the bits into groups of four as

0111 1111 1000 0000 0000 0000 0000 0000

which is written 7F80 0000 (hex). The largest positive value is

0 1111 1110 111 1111 1111 1111 1111 1111

which works out to approximately 2^{128} or 10^{38}. Its hexadecimal representation is 7F7F FFFF (hex). The smallest positive normalized number is

0 0000 0001 000 0000 0000 0000 0000 0000

with a hexadecimal representation of 0080 0000 (hex). The smallest positive denormalized number is

0 0000 0000 000 0000 0000 0000 0000 0001

with a hexadecimal representation of 0000 0001 (hex), which works out to approximately 10^{-45}.

Example 3.43 What is the hexadecimal representation of -47.25 in single precision floating point? The integer 47 (dec) = 101111 (bin), and the fraction 0.25 (dec) = 0.01 (bin). So, 47.25 (dec) = 101111.01 = 1.0111101×2^5. The number is negative, so the first bit is 1. The exponent 5 is converted to excess 127 by adding

5 + 127 = 132 (dec) = 1000 0100 (excess 127). The significand stores the bits to the right of the binary point, 0111101. So, the bit pattern is

1 1000 0100 011 1101 0000 0000 0000 0000

which is C23D 0000 (hex).   ∎

Example 3.44   What is the number, as written in binary scientific notation, whose hexadecimal representation is 3CC8 0000? The bit pattern is

0 0111 1001 100 1000 0000 0000 0000 0000

The sign bit is zero, so the number is positive. The exponent is 0111 1001 (excess 127) = 121 (unsigned) = 121 − 127 = −6 (dec). From the significand, the bits to the right of the binary point are 1001. The hidden bit is 1, so the number is 1.1001 $\times 2^{-6}$.   ∎

Example 3.45   What is the number, as written in binary scientific notation, whose hexadecimal representation is 0050 0000? The bit pattern is

0 0000 0000 101 0000 0000 0000 0000 0000

The sign bit is 0, so the number is positive. The exponent field is all 0's, so the number is denormalized. The exponent is 0000 0000 (excess 126) = 0 (unsigned) = 0 − 126 = −126 (dec). The hidden bit is 0 instead of 1, so the number is 0.101 $\times 2^{-126}$.   ∎

3.6   Representations Across Levels

C++ is a Level HOL6 language. When programmers declare variables in C++, they must specify the type of values that the variables can have. At Level ISA3, the values are binary.

Suppose you declare

```
int i, j;
char ch1, ch2;
```

in a C++ program and run it on a seven-bit computer. At Level ISA3, values of type int are stored in two's complement binary representation. If the values of i and j are 8 and −2, respectively, and the program contains the expression

```
i + j
```

then the expression is evaluated at Level ISA3 as

$$
\begin{array}{ll}
& 000\ 1000 \\
\underline{\text{ADD}} & \underline{111\ 1110} \\
\text{N} = 0 & 000\ 0110 \\
\text{Z} = 0 & \\
\text{V} = 0 & \\
\text{C} = 1 &
\end{array}
$$

At Level ISA3, values of type `char` are stored in ASCII or some other character code. If `ch1` has the value − and `ch2` has the value 2, then at Level ISA3 these values are stored as

010 1101   011 0010

This bit pattern is certainly different from the integer value for j, which is 111 1110.

In C++, at Level HOL6, each character has a position on the number line with an ordinal value. At Level ISA3, the machine level, the ordinal value is simply the binary value of the character code interpreted as an unsigned integer. Because different computers may choose to use different binary character codes, the ordinal values of their characters may differ.

Example 3.46   From the ASCII table, D is represented as 100 0100. Furthermore, 100 0100 (bin) = 68 (dec). On a computer that uses the ASCII code, the ordinal value of D will therefore be 68.   ∎

Example 3.47   To ring the bell on your output device, you can execute the C++ statements

```
int j = 7;
char ch = j;
cout << ch;
```

which makes the bell ring.   ∎

At Level HOL6, a typical statement in a high-order language is

```
cout << "Tom";
```

where the string constant Tom is sent to the output device. This statement is not so simple at Level ISA3. In machine language you cannot "write Tom." Instead you must send the sequence of bits

101 0100

110 1111

110 1101

to the output device.

Why must we deal with bits instead of the English letters and decimal digits that we are accustomed to? Because computers are electronic. The cheapest, most reliable way to manufacture the electronic parts that make up a computer is to make them binary. So we are stuck with binary machines for processing our information. The problem at Level ISA3 is that the information we want to process is in the form of decimal numbers and English letters, whereas the machine language to represent it is in the form of 1's and 0's. Hence the need for codes, such as two's complement binary representation and ASCII.

The reason for binary

This mismatch between the form of the information to be processed and the language to represent it is not unique to Level ISA3. It is the major area of concern at all the higher levels as well.

A basic problem at all levels

The situation can be illustrated for Level HOL6 by the traveling-salesman problem. A salesman is responsible for accounts in 8 different cities, which he visits by commercial airline. The cities are connected by 14 airline routes. The data to be processed is in the form of a map supplied by the airline showing the routes of all the flights connecting the cities in the salesman's territory. The map, Figure 3.34, also shows the cost of the flights along each route.

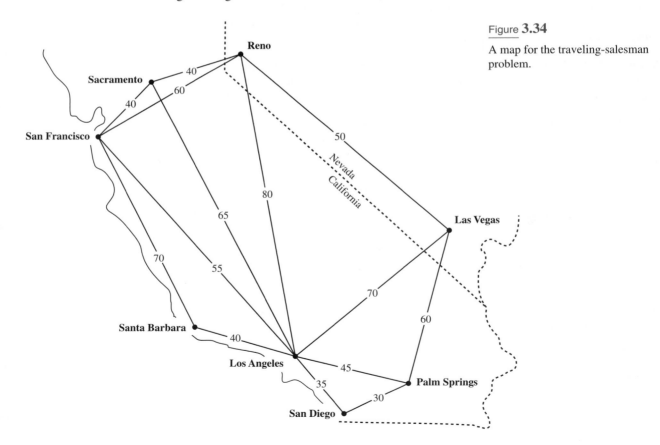

Figure **3.34**

A map for the traveling-salesman problem.

The salesman must start from Los Angeles, visit every city in his territory, and then return to Los Angeles. Naturally, he wants to plan his trip to minimize the total cost.

Determining the optimum itinerary sounds like a perfect job for a computer. The salesman gives the map to a programmer who knows how to speak in some Level HOL6 language such as C++.

But now the programmer faces this fundamental problem of computer science. There is a mismatch between the data, which is in the form of a map, and the Level HOL6 language. C++ does not understand maps. It only understands things such as real numbers, integers, and arrays.

The programmer must decide how to represent the data in a form that C++ can process. For example, she might represent the map as a two-dimensional array of real numbers, as shown in Figure 3.35. In this scheme, the integers in the top row and left column represent the cities in the salesman's territory. Each real number represents the cost in dollars to travel from the city indicated by the row index to the city indicated by the column index. If the name of the two-dimensional array is `cost`, then

```
cost[0][5] = 65
```

represents the fact that to fly from city 0 (Los Angeles) to city 5 (Sacramento) costs $65. The fact that

```
cost[1][7] = 1e30
```

	0	1	2	3	4	5	6	7
0	1e30	35	45	40	55	65	80	70
1	35	1e30	30	1e30	1e30	1e30	1e30	1e30
2	45	30	1e30	1e30	1e30	1e30	1e30	60
3	40	1e30	1e30	1e30	70	1e30	1e30	1e30
4	55	1e30	1e30	70	1e30	40	60	1e30
5	65	1e30	1e30	1e30	40	1e30	40	1e30
6	80	1e30	1e30	1e30	60	40	1e30	50
7	70	1e30	60	1e30	1e30	1e30	50	1e30

Figure **3.35**

One array representation of the airline map of Figure 3.34.

City Numbers

0 Los Angeles
1 San Diego
2 Palm Springs
3 Santa Barbara
4 San Francisco
5 Sacramento
6 Reno
7 Las Vegas

indicates that there is no airline route between city 1 (San Diego) and city 7 (Las Vegas).

After the original data is transformed into a representation that C++ can handle, the Level HOL6 programmer can proceed with her algorithm design and eventually solve the problem. But the first step is to represent the data in a form that the language can deal with.

At Level ISA3 the problem is how to represent numbers and letters with machine language bits. At Level HOL6 the problem is how to represent a map of cities, routes, and airline costs with C++ integers, real numbers, and arrays. At both levels it is the fundamental data representation problem.

Alternative Representations

One challenging aspect of the representation problem is that usually there are several different ways to represent the data. The particular representation selected depends on how the data is to be processed.

An example at Level ISA3 is an alternative representation for positive integers. Although this chapter presents the unsigned binary representation for positive numeric values, it is not the only possibility. Positive integers can also be stored in *binary coded decimal* (BCD) representation.

Binary coded decimal (BCD)

In BCD, each decimal digit requires exactly four bits. The decimal number 142 would be stored in binary as

0001 0100 0010

Because there are only 10 decimal digits, a group of 4 BCD bits is only allowed to be 0000, 0001, 0010, 0011, 0100, 0101, 0110, 0111, 1000, or 1001. The bit patterns 1010 through 1111 are unused.

Unsigned binary is usually chosen when the data is subjected more to arithmetic operations within the computer than to I/O operations. BCD is frequently chosen when the data is financial in nature and is subjected to many I/O operations. BCD is easier to convert to decimal for printed reports. The circuitry for BCD arithmetic operations is usually slower than the circuitry for unsigned binary arithmetic operations, however.

The same kind of option is available in the traveling-salesman problem. For example, airlines do not offer a flight between all possible pairs of cities, especially small ones. To get from Palm Springs to Reno, you must first fly from Palm Springs to Los Angeles and then from Los Angeles to Reno. In Figure 3.35, cost has 64 elements even though there are only 14 routes. Most of the elements are 1e30, and of the 28 that are not 1e30, only 14 are really necessary.

For example, the two entries

```
cost[0][5] = 65
cost[5][0] = 65
```

represent the fact that there is a single route between Los Angeles and Sacramento. Assuming that the air fares are equal in both directions, only one entry is really necessary. The other is redundant.

The programmer may therefore opt to represent the map as in Figure 3.36. In a Level HOL6 language, the list of routes can be implemented as an array, `route`, of records with three fields—`from`, `to`, and `cost`. Then

```
route[4].from = 0
route[4].to = 5
route[4].cost = 65
```

represents the fact that to fly between Los Angeles and Sacramento costs $65.

With this representation of the map, no storage is wasted on nonexistent routes. If there is no air route from city 9 to city 11, it is simply not stored in the list.

Having an alternate representation of the map at Level HOL6 is just like having an alternate representation of unsigned integers at Level ISA3. At any level, you may have several methods to represent the data, any one of which can produce correct results.

It is often difficult to determine which representation is best. Indeed, it is often difficult even to define what "best" means. If your computer has a great deal of memory, the best representation for you might be one that is a bit wasteful of storage, since you have plenty to spare. If memory is scarce, on the other hand, the best representation for you might take less storage, even though the algorithm to process the data in that representation is slow. This space/time tradeoff applies at all levels of abstraction in a computer system. As with any creative endeavor, the choice is not always clear-cut.

What is best?

Models

A model is a simplified representation of some physical system. Workers in every scientific discipline, including computer science, construct models and investigate their properties. Consider some models of the solar system that astronomers have constructed and investigated.

Aristotle, who lived in Greece about 350 B.C., proposed a model in which the earth was at the center of the universe. Surrounding the earth were 55 celestial spheres. The sun, moon, planets, and stars were each carried around the heavens on one of these spheres.

How well did this model match reality? It was successful in explaining the appearance of the sky, which looks like the top half of a sphere. It was also successful in explaining the approximate motion of the planets. Aristotle's model was accepted as accurate for hundreds of years.

Then in 1543 the Polish astronomer Copernicus published *De Revolutionibus*. In it he modeled the solar system with the sun at the center. The planets revolved

Route number	From	To	Cost
0	0	1	35
1	0	2	45
2	0	3	40
3	0	4	55
4	0	5	65
5	0	6	80
6	0	7	70
7	1	2	30
8	2	7	60
9	3	4	70
10	4	5	40
11	4	6	60
12	5	6	40
13	6	7	50

Figure **3.36**

Another representation of the airline map of Figure 3.34.

around the sun in circles. This model was a better approximation to the physical system than the earth-centered model.

In the latter part of the sixteenth century the Danish astronomer Tycho Brahe made a series of precise astronomical observations that showed a discrepancy in Copernicus's model. Then in 1609 Johannes Kepler proposed a model in which the earth and all the planets revolved around the sun not in circles, but in flattened circles called ellipses. This model was successful in explaining in detail the intricate motion of the planets as observed by Tycho Brahe.

Each of these models is a simplified representation of the solar system. None of the models is a completely accurate description of the real physical world. We know now, in light of Einstein's theories of relativity, that even Kepler's model is an approximation. No model is perfect. Every model is an approximation to the real world.

When information is represented in a computer's memory, that representation is only a model as well. Just as each model of the solar system describes some aspects of the underlying real system more accurately than other aspects, so does a representation scheme describe some property of the information more accurately than other properties.

Models as approximations of reality

For example, one property of positive integers is that there is an infinite number of them. No matter how large an integer you write down, someone else can always write down a larger integer. The unsigned binary representation in a computer does not describe that property very accurately. There is a limit to the size of the integer when stored in memory.

You may be aware that

$$\sqrt{2} = 1.4142136 \ldots$$

The digits go on forever, never repeating. The representation scheme for storing real numbers is a model that only approximates numbers such as the square root of 2. It cannot represent the square root of 2 exactly.

Solving a problem at any level involves constructing an imperfect model and investigating its properties. The traveling-salesman problem at Level HOL6 is to determine the itinerary that minimizes his cost. His expenses are modeled by the airline map. The model does not include the fact that some hotels in some cities may charge a different rate on weekends than on weekdays. Taking a more realistic model of expenses may change the optimum itinerary.

The previous examples illustrate that any time a computer solves a problem, approximations are always involved because of limitations in the models. These approximations can arise from limitations in the representation scheme, such as the limited precision of real numbers in trying to store the square root of 2, or from simplifications of the problem, such as failing to take into account different hotel rates.

Two sources of approximations in computer-based models

All sorts of physical systems are commonly modeled with computers—inventories, national economies, accounting systems, and biological population systems, to name a few. In computer science, it is often the computer itself that is modeled.

Modeling the computer itself

The only physically real part of the computer is at Level LG1. Ultimately, a computer is just a complicated, organized mass of circuits and electrical signals. At Level ISA3 the high signals are modeled as 1's and the low signals as 0's. The programmer at Level ISA3 does not need to know anything about electrical circuits and signals to work with his model. Remember that at Level ISA3 the 1's and 0's represent the word Tom as

101 0100

110 1111

110 1101

The programmer at Level HOL6 does not need to know anything about bits to work with his model. In fact, programming the computer at any level requires only a knowledge of the model of the computer at that level.

A programmer at Level HOL6 can model the computer as a C++ machine. This model accepts C++ programs and uses them to process data. When the programmer instructs the machine to

```
cout << "Tom";
```

he need not be concerned with how the computer is modeled as a binary machine at Level ISA3. Similarly, when a programmer at Level ISA3 writes a sequence of bits, he need not be concerned with how the computer is modeled as a combination of circuits at Level LG1.

This modeling of computer systems at successively higher levels is an idea that is not unique to computer science. Consider a large corporation with six divisions throughout the country. The president's model of the corporation is six divisions, with a vice president of each division reporting to him. He views the overall performance of the company in terms of the performance of each of the divisions. When he tells the vice president of the Widget Division to increase earnings, he does not need to be concerned with the vice president's model of the Widget Division.

And when the vice president goes to each department manager within the Widget Division with an order, she does not need to be concerned with the department manager's model of his department. To have the president himself deal with the organization at the department level would be just about impossible. There are simply too many details at the department level of the entire corporation for one person to manage.

The computer user at Level App7 is like the president. He gives an instruction such as "compute the grade point average of all the sophomores" to a program originally written by a programmer at Level HOL6. He need not be concerned with the Level HOL6 model to issue the instruction. Eventually this command at Level App7 is transformed through successively lower levels to Level LG1. The end result is that the user at Level App7 can control the mass of electrical circuitry and signals with a very simplified model of the computer.

SUMMARY

A binary quantity is restricted to one of two values. At the machine level, computers store information in binary. A bit is a binary digit whose value can be either 0 or 1. Nonnegative integers use unsigned binary representation. The rightmost bit is in the 1's place, the next bit to the left is in the 2's place, the next bit to the left is in the 4's place, and so on with each place value double the preceding place value. Signed integers use two's complement binary representation in which the first bit is the sign bit and the remaining bits determine the magnitude. For positive numbers, the two's complement representation is identical to the unsigned representation. For negative numbers, however, the two's complement of a number is obtained by taking 1 plus the ones' complement of the corresponding positive number.

Every binary integer, signed or unsigned, has a range that is determined by the number of bits in the memory cell. The smaller the number of bits in the cell, the more limited the range. The carry bit, C, is used to flag an out-of-range condition for an unsigned integer, and the overflow bit, V, is used to flag an out-of-range condition for an integer in two's complement representation. Operations on binary integers include ADD, AND, OR, and NOT. ASL, which stands for arithmetic shift left, multiplies a binary value by 2, and ASR, which stands for arithmetic shift right, divides a binary value by 2.

The hexadecimal number system, which is a base 16 system, provides a compact notation for expressing bit patterns. The 16 hexadecimal digits are 0, 1, 2, 3, 4, 5, 6, 7, 8, 9, A, B, C, D, E, and F. One hexadecimal digit represents four bits. The American Standard Code for Information Interchange, abbreviated ASCII, is a common code for storing characters. It is a seven-bit code with 128 characters, including the uppercase and lowercase letters of the English alphabet, the decimal digits, punctuation marks, and nonprintable control characters.

A floating point number is stored in a cell with three fields—a one-bit sign field, a field for the exponent, and a field for the significand. Except for special values, numbers are stored in binary scientific notation with a hidden bit to the left of the binary point that is assumed to be 1. The exponent is stored in an excess representation. Four special values are zero, infinity, NaN, and denormalized numbers. The IEEE 754 standard defines the number of bits in the exponent and significand fields to be 8 and 23 for single precision, and 11 and 52 for double precision.

A basic problem at all levels of abstraction is the mismatch between the form of the information to be processed and the language to represent it. A program in machine language processes bits. A program in a high-order language processes items such as arrays and records. Regardless of the level in which the program is written, the information must be cast into a format that the language can recognize. Matching the information to the language is a basic problem at all levels of abstraction and is a source of approximation in the modeling process of problem solving.

EXERCISES

Section 3.1

*1. Count the next 10 numbers (a) in octal starting from 267, (b) in base 3 starting from 2102, (c) in binary starting from 10101, and (d) in base 5 starting from 2433.

2. Count the next 10 numbers (a) in octal starting from 466, (b) in base 3 starting from 1201, (c) in binary starting from 11011, and (d) in base 5 starting from 3434.

*3. Convert the following numbers from binary to decimal, assuming unsigned binary representation:

(a) 10010 (b) 110 (c) 1011
(d) 1000 (e) 11111 (f) 1010101

4. Convert the following numbers from binary to decimal, assuming unsigned binary representation:

(a) 10110 (b) 10 (c) 10101
(d) 10000 (e) 1111 (f) 11110000

*5. Convert the following numbers from decimal to binary, assuming unsigned binary representation:

(a) 25 (b) 16 (c) 1 (d) 14 (e) 5 (f) 41

6. Convert the following numbers from decimal to binary, assuming unsigned binary representation:

(a) 12 (b) 35 (c) 3 (d) 0 (e) 27 (f) 16

7. With unsigned binary representation, what is the range of numbers as written in binary and in decimal for the following cells?

*(a) a two-bit cell *(b) a three-bit cell (c) a four-bit cell
(d) a five-bit cell (e) an n-bit cell in general

*8. Perform the following additions on unsigned integers, assuming a seven-bit cell. Show the effect on the carry bit:

(a)
```
        010 1011
ADD     100 1001
C =
```

(b)
```
        101 1001
ADD     011 0111
C =
```

(c)
```
        111 1111
ADD     111 1111
C =
```

(d)
```
        111 1111
ADD     000 0001
C =
```

9. Perform the following additions on unsigned integers, assuming a nine-bit cell. Show the effect on the carry bit:

(a)   0 0100 1011   (b)   1 0001 1101
    ADD   0 1101 0001   ADD   0 1110 1000
    C =   C =

(c)   1 1111 1111   (d)   1 1111 1111
    ADD   0 0000 0001   ADD   1 1111 1111
    C =   C =

10. Suppose you have a 12-bit cell. Find a binary number such that when you add it to 0110 0101 0111, the sum is all 0's. That is, find the missing number in the following operation:

                0110   0101   0111
    ADD   ????   ????   ????
                0000   0000   0000

The number you find might set the carry bit to 1. Without reading Section 3.2, can you determine the rule for finding the missing number from any number in general? Hint: A simple rule involves the NOT operation.

11. Section 3.1 states that you can tell whether a binary number is even or odd only by inspecting the digit in the 1's place. Is that always possible for an arbitrary base? Explain.

12. Converting between octal and decimal is analogous to the technique of converting between binary and decimal. *(a) Write the polynomial representation of the octal number 70146 as in Figure 3.4. (b) Use the technique of Figure 3.5 to convert 7291 (dec) to octal.

13. Fractional numbers in binary are analogous to fractional numbers in decimal. Instead of a decimal point, however, a binary fraction contains a binary point. *(a) Write the polynomial representation of the decimal number 29.458 as in Figure 3.4. (b) Write the polynomial representation of the binary number 1011.100101 as in Figure 3.4. (c) What is the decimal value of the binary number in (b)?

14. Why do programmers at Level ISA3 confuse Halloween and Christmas? Hint: What does 31 (oct) equal?

Section 3.2

*15. Convert the following numbers from decimal to binary, assuming seven-bit two's complement binary representation:

(a) 49   (b) −27   (c) 0
(d) −64   (e) −1   (f) −2
(g) What is the range for this computer as written in binary and in decimal?

16. Convert the following numbers from decimal to binary, assuming nine-bit two's complement binary representation:

    (a) 51   **(b)** −29   **(c)** −2
    (d) 0   **(e)** −256   **(f)** −1
    (g) What is the range for this cell as written in binary and in decimal?

*17. Convert the following numbers from binary to decimal, assuming seven-bit two's complement binary representation:

    (a) 001 1101   **(b)** 101 0101   **(c)** 111 1100
    (d) 000 0001   **(e)** 100 0000   **(f)** 100 0001

18. Convert the following numbers from binary to decimal, assuming nine-bit two's complement binary representation:

    (a) 0 0001 1010   **(b)** 1 0110 1010   **(c)** 1 1111 1100
    (d) 0 0000 0001   **(e)** 1 0000 0000   **(f)** 1 0000 0001

*19. Perform the following additions, assuming seven-bit two's complement binary representation. Show the effect on the status bits:

    (a)   010 1011   **(b)**   111 1001
         ADD   000 1110   ADD   000 1101
         N =   N =
         Z =   Z =
         V =   V =
         C =   C =

    (c)   100 0110   **(d)**   110 0001
         ADD   101 0101   ADD   111 0101
         N =   N =
         Z =   Z =
         V =   V =
         C =   C =

    (e)   000 1101   **(f)**   100 1001
         ADD   011 0100   ADD   010 1011
         N =   N =
         Z =   Z =
         V =   V =
         C =   C =

20. Perform the following additions, assuming nine-bit two's complement binary representation. Show the effect on the status bits:

    (a)   0 1010 1100   **(b)**   1 1110 0101
         ADD   0 0011 1010   ADD   0 0011 0101
         N =   N =
         Z =   Z =
         V =   V =
         C =   C =

(c)   1 0001 1011   **(d)**   1 1000 0101
    ADD   1 0101 0100   ADD   1 1101 0110
    N =   N =
    Z =   Z =
    V =   V =
    C =   C =

(e)   0 0011 0100   **(f)**   1 0010 0111
    ADD   0 1101 0010   ADD   0 1010 0111
    N =   N =
    Z =   Z =
    V =   V =
    C =   C =

21. With two's complement binary representation, what is the range of numbers as written in binary and in decimal notation for the following cells?

*(a) a two-bit cell   *(b) a three-bit cell   (c) a four-bit cell
(d) a five-bit cell   (e) an *n*-bit cell in general

Section 3.3

*22. Perform the following logical operations, assuming a seven-bit cell:

(a)   010 1100   **(b)**   000 1111
    AND   110 1010   AND   101 0101
    N =   N =
    Z =   Z =

(c)   010 1100   **(d)**   000 1111
    OR   110 1010   OR   101 0101
    N =   N =
    Z =   Z =

(e)   010 1100   **(f)**   000 1111
    XOR   110 1010   XOR   101 0101
    N =   N =
    Z =   Z =

(g) NEG   010 1100   **(h)** NOT   110 1010

23. Perform the following logical operations, assuming a nine-bit cell:

(a)   0 1001 0011   **(b)**   0 0000 1111
    AND   1 0111 0101   AND   1 0111 0101
    N =   N =
    Z =   Z =

(c)   0 1001 0011   **(d)**   0 0000 1111
    OR   1 0111 0101   OR   1 0111 0101
    N =   N =
    Z =   Z =

(e)   0 1001 0011   **(f)**   0 0000 1111

    XOR   1 0111 0101   XOR   1 0111 0101

    N =   N =

    Z =   Z =

(g) NEG   1 1001 0011   **(h)** NOT   1 0111 0101

*24. Assuming seven-bit two's complement representation, convert each of the following decimal numbers to binary, show the effect of the ASL operation on it, and then convert the result back to decimal. Repeat with the ASR operation:

    (a) 24   **(b)** 37   **(c)** −26

    (d) 1   **(e)** 0   **(f)** −1

25. Assuming nine-bit two's complement representation, convert each of the following decimal numbers to binary, show the effect of the ASL operation on it, and then convert the result back to decimal. Repeat with the ASR operation:

    (a) 94   **(b)** 135   **(c)** −62

    (d) 1   **(e)** 0   **(f)** −1

26. **(a)** Write the RTL specification for an arithmetic shift right on a six-bit cell. **(b)** Write the RTL specification for an arithmetic shift left on a 16-bit cell.

* 27. Assuming a seven-bit cell, show the effect of the rotate operation on each of the following values with the given initial value of C:

    (a) C = 1, ROL 010 1101   **(b)** C = 0, ROL 010 1101

    (c) C = 1, ROR 010 1101   **(d)** C = 0, ROR 010 1101

28. Assuming a nine-bit cell, show the effect of the rotate operation on each of the following values with the given initial value of C:

    (a) C = 1, ROL 0 0110 1101   **(b)** C = 0, ROL 0 0110 1101

    (c) C = 1, ROR 0 0110 1101   **(d)** C = 0, ROR 0 0110 1101

29. **(a)** Write the RTL specification for a rotate right on a six-bit cell. **(b)** Write the RTL specification for a rotate left on a 16-bit cell.

Section 3.4

30. Count the next five numbers in hexadecimal, starting with the following:

    *(a) 3AB7   **(b)** 6FD   **(c)** B9E

31. Convert the following numbers from hexadecimal to decimal:

    *(a) 2D5E   **(b)** 2F   **(c)** 7

32. This chapter mentions the method of converting from decimal to hexadecimal but gives no examples. Use the method to convert the following decimal numbers to hexadecimal:

    *(a) 26,831   **(b)** 4,096   **(c)** 9

33. The technique for converting from decimal to any base will work, with some modification, for bases other than binary. **(a)** Explain the method to convert from decimal to octal. **(b)** Explain the method to convert from decimal to base *n* in general.

*34. Assuming seven-bit two's complement binary representation, convert the following numbers from hexadecimal to decimal. Remember to check the sign bit:

　　(a) 5D　　**(b)** 2F　　**(c)** 40

35. Assuming nine-bit two's complement binary representation, convert the following numbers from hexadecimal to decimal. Remember to check the sign bit:

　　(a) 1B4　　**(b)** 0F5　　**(c)** 100

*36. Assuming seven-bit two's complement binary representation, write the bit patterns for the following decimal numbers in hexadecimal:

　　(a) −27　　**(b)** 63　　**(c)** −1

37. Assuming nine-bit two's complement binary representation, write the bit patterns for the following decimal numbers in hexadecimal:

　　(a) −73　　**(b)** −1　　**(c)** 94

*38. Decode the following secret ASCII message (reading across):

100 1000	110 0001	111 0110	110 0101
010 0000	110 0001	010 0000	110 1110
110 1001	110 0011	110 0101	010 0000
110 0100	110 0001	111 1001	010 0001

39. Decode the following secret ASCII message (reading across):

100 1101	110 0101	110 0101	111 0100
010 0000	110 0001	111 0100	010 0000
110 1101	110 1001	110 0100	110 1110
110 1001	110 0111	110 1000	111 0100
010 1110			

*40. How is the following string of 9 characters stored in ASCII?

　　Pay $0.92

41. How is the following string of 13 characters stored in ASCII?

　　(321)497-0015

42. You are the chief communications officer for the Lower Slobovian army at war with the Upper Slobovians. Your spies will infiltrate the enemy's command headquarters in an attempt to gain the "upper" hand. You know the Uppers are planning a major assault, and you also know the following: (1) It will be at either sunrise or sunset. (2) It will come by land, air, or sea. (3) It will occur on March 28, 29, 30, or 31, or on April 1. Your spies must communicate with you in binary. Devise a suitable binary code for transmitting the information. Try to use the fewest number of bits possible.

43. Octal numbers are sometimes used instead of hexadecimal numbers to represent bit sequences.

    *(a) How many bits does one octal number represent?

    How would you represent the decimal number -13 in octal with the following cells?

    (b) a 15-bit cell   (c) a 16-bit cell   (d) an 8-bit cell

Section 3.5

*44. Convert the following numbers from binary to decimal:

    (a) 110.101001   (b) 0.000011   (c) 1.0

45. Convert the following numbers from binary to decimal:

    (a) 101.101001   (b) 0.000101   (c) 1.0

*46. Convert the following numbers from decimal to binary:

    (a) 13.15625   (b) 0.0390625   (c) 0.6

47. Convert the following numbers from decimal to binary:

    (a) 12.28125   (b) 0.0234375   (c) 0.7

48. Construct a table similar to Figure 3.30 that compares all the values with a four-bit cell for excess 7 and two's complement representation.

49. (a) With excess 7 representation, what is the range of numbers as written in binary and in decimal for a 4-bit cell? (b) With excess 15 representation, what is the range of numbers as written in binary and in decimal for a 5-bit cell? (c) With excess $2^{n-1} - 1$ representation, what is the range of numbers as written in binary and in decimal for an n-bit cell in general?

50. Assuming a three-bit exponent field and a four-bit significand, write the bit pattern for the following decimal values:

    *(a) -12.5 (b) 13.0   (c) 0.43   (d) 0.1015625

51. Assuming a three-bit exponent field and a four-bit significand, what decimal values are represented by the following bit patterns?

    *(a) 0 010 1101   (b) 1 101 0110   (c) 1 111 1001
    (d) 0 001 0011   (e) 1 000 0100   (f) 0 111 0000

52. For IEEE 754 single precision floating point, write the hexadecimal representation for the following decimal values:

    *(a) 27.1015625   (b) -1.0 (c) -0.0
    (d) 0.5   (e) 0.6   (f) 256.015625

53. For IEEE 754 single precision floating point, what is the number, as written in binary scientific notation, whose hexadecimal representation is the following?

   *(a) 4280 0000   (b) B350 0000   (c) 0061 0000
   (d) FF80 0000   (e) 7FE4 0000   (f) 8000 0000

54. For IEEE 754 single precision floating point, write the hexadecimal representation for

   (a) positive zero
   (b) the smallest positive denormalized number
   (c) the largest positive denormalized number
   (d) the smallest positive normalized number
   (e) 1.0
   (f) the largest positive normalized number
   (g) positive infinity

55. For IEEE 754 double precision floating point, write the hexadecimal representation for

   (a) positive zero
   (b) the smallest positive denormalized number
   (c) the largest positive denormalized number
   (d) the smallest positive normalized number
   (e) 1.0
   (f) the largest positive normalized number
   (g) positive infinity

PROBLEMS

Section 3.1

56. Write a program in C++ that takes as input a four-digit octal number and prints the next 10 octal numbers. Define an octal number as

```
int octNum[4];
```

Use `octNum[0]` to store the most significant (i.e., leftmost) octal digit, and `octNum[3]` the least significant octal digit. Test your program with interactive input.

57. Write a program in C++ that takes as input an eight-bit binary number and prints the next 10 binary numbers. Define a binary number as:

```
int binNum[8];
```

Use `binNum[0]` to store the most significant (i.e., leftmost) bit, and `binNum[7]` the least significant bit. Ask the user to input the first binary number with each bit separated by at least one space.

58. Write a function in C++ to convert an eight-bit unsigned binary number to a positive decimal integer. Use the definition of a binary number as given in Problem 57. Test your function with interactive input.

59. Write a void function in C++ to convert a positive decimal integer to an eight-bit unsigned binary number. Use the definition of a binary number as given in Problem 57. Test your void function with interactive input.

60. Defining a binary number as in Problem 57, write the void function

```
void BinaryAdd (int* sum, int& cBit,
                const int* bin1, const int* bin2)
```

to compute `sum` as the sum of the two binary numbers, `bin1` and `bin2`. `cBit` should be the value of the carry bit after the addition. Test your void function with interactive input.

Section 3.2

61. Write a function in C++ to convert an eight-bit two's complement binary number to a decimal integer. Use the definition of a binary number as given in Problem 57. Test your function with interactive input.

62. Write a void function in C++ to convert a decimal integer to an eight-bit two's complement binary number. Use the definition of a binary number as given in Problem 57. Test your void function with interactive input.

Section 3.3

63. Defining a binary number as in Problem 57, write the void function

```
void BinaryAnd (int* bAnd,
                const int* bin1, const int* bin2)
```

to compute `bAnd` as the AND of the two binary numbers `bin1` and `bin2`. Test your void function with interactive input.

64. Write the void function for Problem 63, using the OR operation.

65. Defining a binary number as in Problem 57, write the function

```
void ShiftLeft (int* binNum, int& cBit)
```

to perform an arithmetic shift left on `binNum`. `cBit` should be the value of the carry bit after the shift. Test your function with interactive input.

66. Write the function for Problem 65, using the arithmetic shift right operation.

Section 3.4

67. Write a program in C++ that takes as input a four-digit hexadecimal number and prints the next 10 hexadecimal numbers. Define a hexadecimal number as

```
int hexNum[4]
```

Use the uppercase letters of the alphabet for the hexadecimal I/O. For example, 3C6 F should be valid input.

68. Write a function in C++ to convert a four-digit hexadecimal number to a positive decimal integer. Use the definition of a hexadecimal number as given in Problem 67. Test your function with interactive input. Use the uppercase letters of the alphabet for the hexadecimal input.

69. Write a void function in C++ to convert a positive decimal integer to a four-digit hexadecimal number. Use the definition of a hexadecimal number as given in Problem 67. Test your void function with interactive input. Use the uppercase letters of the alphabet for the hexadecimal output.

70. Write a function in C++ to convert a four-digit hexadecimal number to a possibly negative decimal integer. Use the definition of a hexadecimal number as given in Problem 67. Assume that the hexadecimal value represents the bits of a 16-bit cell with two's complement representation. Test your function with interactive input. Use the uppercase letters of the alphabet for the hexadecimal input.

71. Write a void function in C++ to convert a possibly negative decimal integer to a four-digit hexadecimal number. Use the definition of a hexadecimal number as given in Problem 67. Assume that the hexadecimal value represents the bits of a 16-bit cell with two's complement representation. Test your void function with interactive input. Use the uppercase letters of the alphabet for the hexadecimal output.

72. Write a function in C++ to convert a positive number in an arbitrary base to decimal. For four-digit base 6 numbers, for example, declare

```
const int base = 6;
const int numDigits = 4;
int number[numDigits];
```

Test your function with interactive input. Read the number to be converted into an array of characters. Use the uppercase letters of the alphabet for input if required by the value of base. Write a void function to convert it to the proper value of type array of int before converting it to decimal.

You must be able to modify your program for operation with a different base by changing only the constant base. You must be able to modify the program for a different number of digits by changing only the constant numDigits.

73. Write a void function in C++ to convert a positive decimal integer to a number in an arbitrary base. Declare number as in Problem 72. Test your procedure with interactive input. Use the uppercase letters of the alphabet for output if required by the value of base.

You must be able to modify your program for operation with a different base by changing only the constant base. You must be able to modify the program for a different number of digits by changing only the constant numDigits.

Chapter

4 *Computer Architecture*

An architect takes components such as walls, doors, and ceilings and arranges them together to form a building. Similarly, the computer architect takes components such as input devices, memories, and CPU registers and arranges them together to form a computer.

Buildings come in all shapes and sizes, and so do computers. This fact raises a problem. If we select one computer to study out of the dozens of popular models that are available, then our knowledge will be somewhat obsolete when that model is inevitably discontinued by its manufacturer. Also, this book would be less valuable to people who use the computers we chose not to study.

But there is another possibility. In the same way that a book on architecture could examine a hypothetical building, this book can explore a virtual computer that contains important features similar to those found on all real computers. This approach has its advantages and disadvantages.

A virtual computer

One advantage is that the virtual computer can be designed to illustrate only the fundamental concepts that apply to most computer systems. We can then concentrate on the important points and not have to deal with the individual quirks that are present on all real machines. Concentrating on the fundamentals is also a hedge against obsolete knowledge. The fundamentals will continue to apply even as individual computers come and go in the marketplace.

Advantages and disadvantages of a virtual computer

The primary disadvantage of studying a virtual computer is that some of its details will be irrelevant to those who need to work with a specific real machine at the assembly language level or at the instruction set architecture level. If you understand the fundamental concepts, however, then you will easily be able to learn the details of any specific machine.

There is no 100% satisfactory solution to this dilemma. We have chosen the virtual computer approach mainly for its advantages in illustrating fundamental concepts. Our hypothetical machine is called the Pep/8 computer.

The Pep/8 computer

4.1   Hardware

The Pep/8 hardware consists of four major components at the instruction set architecture level (level ISA3):

- The central processing unit (CPU)
- The main memory
- The input device
- The output device

The block diagram of Figure 4.1 shows each of these components as a rectangular block. The bus is a group of wires that connects the four major components. It carries the data signals and control signals sent between the blocks.

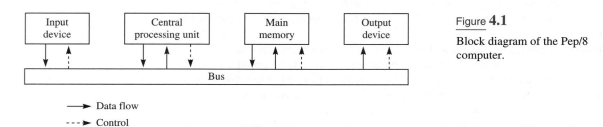

Figure **4.1**

Block diagram of the Pep/8 computer.

Central Processing Unit (CPU)

The CPU contains six specialized memory locations called registers. As shown in Figure 4.2, they are

- The 4-bit status register (NZVC)
- The 16-bit accumulator (A)
- The 16-bit index register (X)
- The 16-bit program counter (PC)
- The 16-bit stack pointer (SP)
- The 24-bit instruction register (IR)

The N, Z, V, and C bits in the status register are the negative, zero, overflow, and carry bits, as discussed in Sections 3.1 and 3.2. The accumulator is the register that contains the result of an operation. The next three registers—X, PC, and SP—help the CPU access information in main memory. The index register is for accessing elements of an array. The program counter is for accessing instructions. The stack pointer is for accessing elements on the run-time stack. The instruction register holds an instruction after it has been accessed from memory.

Central processing unit (CPU)

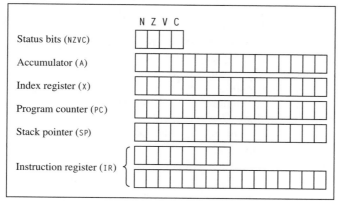

Figure **4.2**

The central processing unit of the Pep/8 computer.

In addition to these six registers, the CPU contains all the electronics (not shown in Figure 4.2) to execute the Pep/8 instructions.

Main Memory

Figure 4.3 shows the main memory of the Pep/8 computer. It contains 65,536 eight-bit storage locations. A group of eight bits is called a byte (pronounced bite). Each byte has an address similar to the number address on a mailbox. In decimal form the addresses range from 0 to 65,535, in hexadecimal from 0000 to FFFF. Main memory is sometimes called core memory.

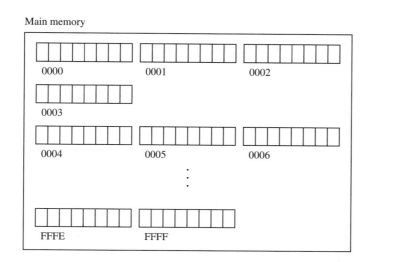

Figure **4.3**

The main memory of the Pep/8 computer.

Figure 4.3 shows the first three bytes of main memory on the first line, the next byte on the second line, the next three bytes on the next line, and, finally, the last two bytes on the last line. Whether you should visualize a line of memory as containing one, two, or three bytes depends on the context of the problem. Sometimes it is more convenient to visualize one byte on a line, sometimes two or three. Of course, in the physical computer a byte is a sequence of eight signals stored in an electrical circuit. The bytes would not be physically lined up as shown in the figure.

Frequently it is convenient to draw main memory as in Figure 4.4, with the addresses along the left side of the block. Even though the lines have equal widths visually in the block, a single line may represent one or several bytes. The address on the side of the block is the address of the left-most byte in the line.

You can tell how many bytes the line contains by the sequence of addresses. In Figure 4.4, the first line must have three bytes because the address of the second line is 0003. The second line must have one byte because the address of the third line is 0004, which is one more than 0003. Similarly, the third and fourth lines each have three bytes, the fifth has one, and the sixth has two. From the figure, it is impossible to tell how many bytes the seventh line has. The first three lines of Figure 4.4 correspond to the first seven bytes in Figure 4.3.

Regardless of the way the bytes of main memory are laid out on paper, the bytes with small addresses are referred to as the "top" of memory, and those with large addresses are referred to as the "bottom."

Most computer manufacturers specify a word to be a certain number of bytes. In the Pep/8 computer a word is two adjacent bytes. A word, therefore, contains 16 bits. Most of the registers in the Pep/8 CPU are word registers. In main memory, the address of a word is the address of the first byte of the word. For example, Figure 4.5(a) shows two adjacent bytes at addresses 000B and 000C. The address of the 16-bit word is 000B.

It is important to distinguish between the content of a memory location and its address. Memory addresses in the Pep/8 computer are 16 bits long. Hence, the memory address of the word in Figure 4.5(a) could be written in binary as 0000 0000 0000 1011. The content of the word at this address, however, is 0000 0010 1101 0001. Do not confuse the content of the word with its address. They are different.

To save space on the page, the content of a byte or word is usually written in hexadecimal. Figure 4.5(b) shows the content in hexadecimal of the same word at address 000B. In a machine-language listing, the address of the first byte of a group is printed, followed by the content in hexadecimal, as in Figure 4.5(c). In this format, it is especially easy to confuse the address of a byte with its content.

In the example in Figure 4.5, you can interpret the content of the memory location several ways. If you consider the bit sequence 0000 0010 1101 0001 as an integer in two's complement representation, then the first bit is the sign bit, and the binary sequence represents decimal 721. If you consider the right-most seven bits as an ASCII character, then the binary sequence represents the character Q. The main

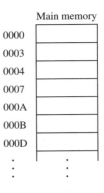

Figure 4.4

Another style for depicting main memory.

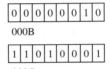

(a) The content in binary.

(b) The content in hexadecimal.

000B   02D1

(c) The content in a machine language listing.

Figure 4.5

The distinction between the content of a memory location and its address.

memory cannot determine which way the byte will be interpreted. It simply remembers the binary sequence 0000 0010 1101 0001.

Input Device

You may be wondering where this Pep/8 hardware is located and whether you will ever be able to get your hands on it. The answer is, the hardware does not exist! At least it does not exist as a physical machine. Instead, it exists as a set of programs that you can execute on your computer system. The programs simulate the behavior of the Pep/8 machine described in these chapters.

The Pep/8 system simulates two input devices—a text file and the keyboard. You cannot specify both in a single Pep/8 program. Before executing a program, you must specify whether you want the input to come from a file or the keyboard. If you are using one of the simulators with a graphical user interface, the input will come from the focus window instead of a file.

Output Device

The Pep/8 system also simulates two output devices—a text file and the screen. As with input, you cannot specify both in one program. If you specify a text file as output, the system will ask you for the name you want to give the file that the program will create. If you are using one of the simulators with a graphical user interface, the output will go to a new window, which you can then save to a new file.

Data and Control

The solid lines connecting the blocks of Figure 4.1 are data flow lines. Data can flow from the input device on the bus to main memory. It can also flow from main memory on the bus to the CPU. It cannot flow directly from the input device to the CPU.

Similarly, data cannot flow directly from the CPU to the output device. If you want to transfer data from the CPU to the output device, you must send it to main memory first. It can then go from main memory to the output device.

The dashed lines are control lines. Control signals all originate from the CPU, which means that the CPU controls all the other parts of the computer. For example, to make data flow from the memory to the output device along the solid data flow lines, the CPU must transmit a send signal along the dashed control line to the memory, and a receive signal along the dashed control line to the output device. The important point is that the processor really is central. It controls all the other parts of the computer.

Instruction Format

Each computer has its own set of instructions wired into its CPU. The instruction set varies from manufacturer to manufacturer. It often varies among computers made by the same company, although many manufacturers produce a family of models, each of which contains the same instruction set as the other models in that family.

The Pep/8 computer has 39 instructions in its instruction set shown in Figure 4.6. Each instruction consists of either a single byte called the *instruction specifier,* or the instruction specifier followed immediately by a word called the *operand specifier.* Instructions that do not have an operand specifier are called unary instructions. Figure 4.7 shows the structure of nonunary and unary instructions.

The instruction specifier and operand specifier

The eight-bit instruction specifier can have several parts. The first part is called the operation code, often referred to as the *opcode.* The opcode may consist of as many as eight bits and as few as four. For example, Figure 4.6 shows the instruction to move the stack pointer to the accumulator as having an eight-bit opcode of 0000 0010. The character input instruction, however, has the five-bit opcode 0100 1. Instructions with fewer than eight bits in the opcode subdivide their instruction specifier into several fields depending on the instruction. Figure 4.6 indicates these fields by the letters a, r, and n. Each one of these letters can be either zero or 1.

The opcode

Example 4.1   Figure 4.6 shows that the "branch if equal to" instruction has an instruction specifier of 0000 101a. Because the letter a can be zero or one, there are really two versions of the instruction—0000 1010 and 0000 1011. Similarly, there are eight versions of the decimal output trap instruction. Its instruction specifier is 0011 1aaa where aaa can be any combination from 000 to 111.   ∎

Figure 4.8 summarizes the meaning of the possible fields in the instruction specifier for the letters a and r. The meaning of the letters nn in the unary trap instruction and nnn in the return from call instruction are described in a later chapter.

Generally, the letter a stands for addressing mode, and the letter r stands for register. When r is 0, the instruction operates on the accumulator. When r is 1, the instruction operates on the index register. Pep/8 executes each nonunary instruction in one of eight addressing modes—immediate, direct, indirect, stack-relative, stack-relative deferred, indexed, stack-indexed, or stack-indexed deferred. Later chapters describe the meaning of the addressing modes. For now, it is only important that you know how to use the tables of Figures 4.7 and 4.8 to determine which register and addressing mode a given instruction uses.

Example 4.2   Determine the opcode, register, and addressing mode of the 1100 1011 instruction. Starting from the left, determine with the help of Figure 4.6 that the opcode is 1100. The next bit after the opcode is the r bit, which is 1, indicating the index register. The three bits after the r bit are the aaa bits, which are 011, indicating stack-relative addressing. Therefore, the instruction loads a value from memory into the index register using stack-relative addressing.   ∎

Instruction Specifier	Instruction
0000 0000	Stop execution
0000 0001	Return from trap
0000 0010	Move stack pointer (SP) to accumulator (A)
0000 0011	Move NZVC flags to accumulator (A)
0000 010a	Branch unconditional
0000 011a	Branch if less than or equal to
0000 100a	Branch if less than
0000 101a	Branch if equal to
0000 110a	Branch if not equal to
0000 111a	Branch if greater than or equal to
0001 000a	Branch if greater than
0001 001a	Branch if V
0001 010a	Branch if C
0001 011a	Call subroutine
0001 100r	Bitwise invert register r
0001 101r	Negate register r
0001 110r	Arithmetic shift left register r
0001 111r	Arithmetic shift right register r
0010 000r	Rotate left register r
0010 001r	Rotate right register r
0010 01nn	Unimplemented opcode, unary trap
0010 1aaa	Unimplemented opcode, nonunary trap
0011 0aaa	Unimplemented opcode, nonunary trap
0011 1aaa	Unimplemented opcode, nonunary trap
0100 0aaa	Unimplemented opcode, nonunary trap
0100 1aaa	Character input
0101 0aaa	Character output
0101 1nnn	Return from call with n local bytes
0110 0aaa	Add to stack pointer (SP)
0110 1aaa	Subtract from stack pointer (SP)
0111 raaa	Add to register r
1000 raaa	Subtract from register r
1001 raaa	Bitwise AND to register r
1010 raaa	Bitwise OR to register r
1011 raaa	Compare register r
1100 raaa	Load register r from memory
1101 raaa	Load byte register r from memory
1110 raaa	Store register r to memory
1111 raaa	Store byte register r to memory

Figure **4.6**

The Pep/8 instruction set at Level ISA3.

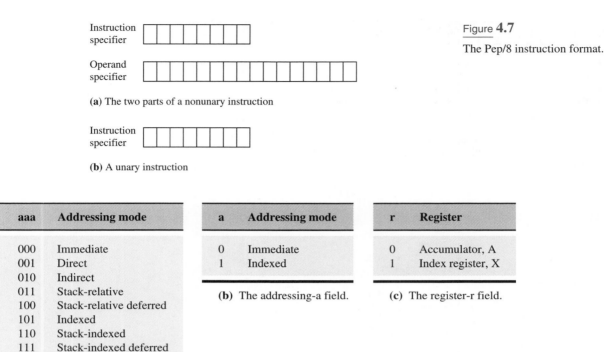

Figure **4.7**

The Pep/8 instruction format.

(a) The two parts of a nonunary instruction

(b) A unary instruction

aaa	Addressing mode
000	Immediate
001	Direct
010	Indirect
011	Stack-relative
100	Stack-relative deferred
101	Indexed
110	Stack-indexed
111	Stack-indexed deferred

(a) The addressing-aaa field.

a	Addressing mode
0	Immediate
1	Indexed

(b) The addressing-a field.

r	Register
0	Accumulator, A
1	Index register, X

(c) The register-r field.

Figure **4.8**

The Pep/8 instruction specifier fields.

The operand specifier, for those instructions that are not unary, indicates the operand to be processed by the instruction. The CPU can interpret the operand specifier several different ways, depending on the bits in the instruction specifier. For example, it may interpret the operand specifier as an ASCII character, as an integer in two's complement representation, or as an address in main memory where the operand is stored.

Instructions are stored in main memory. The address of an instruction in main memory is the address of the first byte of the instruction.

Example 4.3   Figure 4.9 shows two adjacent instructions stored in main memory at locations 01A3 and 01A6. The instruction at 01A6 is unary; the instruction at 01A3 is not.

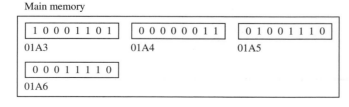

Figure **4.9**

Two instructions in main memory.

In this example, the instruction at 01A3 has

Opcode: 1000

Register-r field: 1

Addressing-aaa field: 101

Operand specifier: 0000 0011 0100 1110

where all the quantities are written in binary. According to the opcode chart of Figure 4.6, this is a subtract instruction. The register-r field indicates that the index register, as opposed to the accumulator, is affected. So this instruction subtracts the operand from the index register. The addressing-aaa field indicates indexed addressing, so the operand specifier is interpreted accordingly. In this chapter, we confine our study to the direct addressing mode. The other modes are taken up in later chapters.

The unary instruction at 01A6 has

Opcode: 0001 111

Register-r field: 0

The opcode indicates that the instruction will do an arithmetic shift right. The register-r field indicates that the accumulator is the register in which the shift will take place. Because this is a unary instruction, there is no operand specifier. ∎

In Example 4.3, the following form of the instructions is called machine language:

1000 1101 0000 0011 0100 1110

0001 1110

Machine language is a binary sequence—that is, a sequence of ones and zeros—that the CPU interprets according to the opcodes of its instruction set. A machine language listing would show these two instructions in hexadecimal, preceded by their memory addresses, as follows:

Machine language

01A3   8D034E

01A6   1E

If you have only the hexadecimal listing of an instruction, you must convert it to binary and examine the fields in the instruction specifier to determine what the instruction will do.

4.2 Direct Addressing

This section describes the operation of some of the Pep/8 instructions at Level ISA3. It describes how they operate in conjunction with the direct addressing mode. Later chapters describe the other addressing modes.

The addressing field determines how the CPU interprets the operand specifier. An addressing-aaa field of 001 indicates direct addressing. With direct addressing, the CPU interprets the operand specifier as the address in main memory of the cell that contains the operand. In mathematical notation

Oprnd = Mem[OprndSpec]   *Direct addressing*

where Oprnd stands for operand, OprndSpec stands for operand specifier, and Mem stands for main memory.

The bracket notation indicates that you can think of main memory as an array and the operand specifier as the index of the array. In C++, if v is an array and i is an integer, v[i] is the "cell" in the array that is determined by the value of the integer i. Similarly, the operand specifier in the instruction identifies the cell in main memory that contains the operand.

What follows is a description of some instructions from the Pep/8 instruction set. Each description lists the opcode and gives an example of the operation of the instruction when used with the direct addressing mode. Values of N, Z, V, and C are always given in binary. Values of other registers and of memory cells are given in hexadecimal. At the machine level, all values are ultimately binary. After describing the individual instructions, this chapter concludes by showing how you can put them together to construct a machine language program.

The Stop Instruction

The stop instruction has instruction specifier 0000 0000. When this instruction is executed, it simply makes the computer stop. Because Pep/8 is a simulated computer, you execute it by running the Pep/8 simulator on your computer. The simulator has a menu of command options for you to choose from. One of those options is to execute your Pep/8 program. When your Pep/8 program is executing, if it encounters this instruction it will stop and return the simulator to the menu of command options. The stop execution instruction is unary. It has no operand specifier.

The Load Instruction

The load instruction has instruction specifier 1100 raaa. This instruction loads one word (two bytes) from a memory location into either the accumulator or the index register depending on the value of r. It affects the N and Z bits. If the operand is negative, it sets the N bit to 1; otherwise it clears the N bit to 0. If the operand consists of 16 0's, it sets the Z bit to 1; otherwise it clears the Z bit to 0. The register transfer language (RTL) specification of the load instruction is

$r \leftarrow$ Oprnd; $N \leftarrow r < 0$, $Z \leftarrow r = 0$

Example 4.4 Suppose the instruction to be executed is C1004A in hexadecimal, which Figure 4.10 shows in binary. The register-r field in this example is 0, which indicates a load to the accumulator instead of the index register. The addressing-aaa field is 001, which indicates direct addressing.

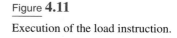

Instruction specifier

| Opcode | r | aaa |

| 1 1 0 0 | 0 | 0 0 1 |
| C | | 1 |

Operand specifier

| 0 0 0 0 0 0 0 0 | 0 1 0 0 1 0 1 0 |
| 0 | 0 | 4 | A |

Figure **4.10**

The load instruction.

Figure 4.11 shows the effect of executing the load instruction assuming Mem[004A] has an initial content of 92EF. The load instruction does not change the content of the memory location. It sends a copy of the two memory cells (at addresses 004A and 004B) to the register. Whatever was in the register before the instruction was executed, in this case 036D, is destroyed. The N bit is set to 1 because the bit pattern loaded has 1 in the sign bit. The Z bit is set to 0 because the bit pattern is not all 0's. The V and C bits are unaffected by the load instruction.

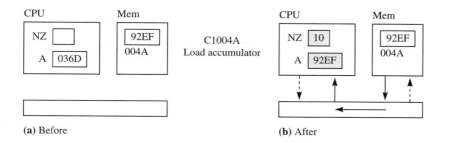

(a) Before   **(b)** After

Figure **4.11**

Execution of the load instruction.

Figure 4.11 shows the data flow lines and control lines that the load instruction activates. As indicated by the solid lines, data flows from the main memory on the bus to the CPU, and then into the register. For this data transfer to take place, the CPU must send a control signal, as indicated by the dashed lines, to main memory telling it to put the data on the bus. The CPU also tells main memory the address from which to fetch the data. ∎

The Store Instruction

The store instruction has instruction specifier 1110 raaa. This instruction stores one word (two bytes) from either the accumulator or the index register to a memory location. With direct addressing, the operand specifies the memory location in which the information is stored. The RTL specification for the store instruction is

Oprnd ← r

Example 4.5   Suppose the instruction to be executed is E9004A in hexadecimal, which Figure 4.12 shows in binary. This time, the register-r field indicates that the instruction will affect the index register. The addressing-aaa field, 001, indicates direct addressing.

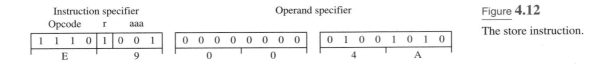

Instruction specifier	Operand specifier

Figure **4.12**

The store instruction.

Figure 4.13 shows the effect of executing the store instruction, assuming the index register has an initial content of 16BC. The store instruction does not change the content of the register. It sends a copy of the register to two memory cells (at addresses 004A and 004B). Whatever was in the memory cells before the instruction was executed, in this case F082, is destroyed. The store instruction affects none of the status bits.   ∎

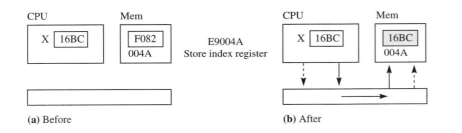

(a) Before   (b) After

Figure **4.13**

Execution of the store instruction.

The Add Instruction

The add instruction has instruction specifier 0111 raaa. It is similar to the load instruction in that data is transferred from main memory to register r in the CPU. But with the add instruction, the original content of the register is not just written over by the content of the word from main memory. Instead, the content of the word from main memory is added to the content of the register. The sum is placed in the register, and all four status bits are set accordingly. As with the load instruction, a copy of the memory word is sent to the CPU. The original content of the memory word is unchanged. The RTL specification of the add instruction is

$$r \leftarrow r + Oprnd; \ N \leftarrow r < 0, \ Z \leftarrow r = 0, \ V \leftarrow \{overflow\}, \ C \leftarrow \{carry\}$$

Example 4.6   Suppose the instruction to be executed is 79004A in hexadecimal, which Figure 4.14 shows in binary. The register-r field indicates that the instruction

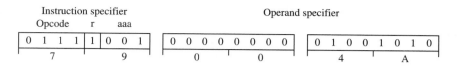

Figure **4.14**

The add instruction.

will affect the index register. The addressing-aaa field, 001, indicates direct addressing.

Figure 4.15 shows the effect of executing the add instruction, assuming the index register has an initial content of 0005 and Mem[004A] has −7 (dec) = FFF9 (hex). In decimal, the sum 5 + (−7) is −2, which is shown as FFFE (hex) in Figure 4.15(b). The figure shows the NZVC bits in binary. The N bit is 1 because the sum is negative. The Z bit is 0 because the sum is not all 0's. The V bit is 0 because an overflow did not occur, and the C bit is 0 because a carry did not occur out of the most significant bit. ∎

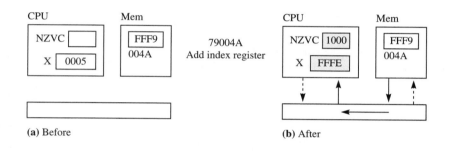

(a) Before   **(b)** After

Figure **4.15**

Execution of the add instruction.

The Subtract Instruction

The subtract instruction has instruction specifier 1000 raaa. It is similar to the add instruction, except that the operand is subtracted from the register. The result is placed in the register, and the operand is unchanged. With subtraction, the C bit represents a carry from adding the negation of the operand. The RTL specification of the subtract instruction is

$$r \leftarrow r - \text{Oprnd}; \ N \leftarrow r < 0, \ Z \leftarrow r = 0, \ V \leftarrow \{overflow\}, \ C \leftarrow \{carry\}$$

Example 4.7 Suppose the instruction to be executed is 81004A in hexadecimal, which Figure 4.16 shows in binary. The register-r field indicates that the instruction will affect the accumulator.

Figure 4.17 shows the effect of executing the subtract instruction, assuming the accumulator has an initial content of 0003 and Mem[004A] has 0009. In decimal, the difference 3 − 9 is −6, which is shown as FFFA (hex) in Figure 4.17(b). The figure shows the NZVC bits in binary. The N bit is 1 because the sum is negative. The Z bit

Instruction specifier
Opcode   r   aaa

1	0	0	0	0	0	0	1

8   1

Operand specifier

0	0	0	0	0	0	0	0

0   0

0	1	0	0	1	0	1	0

4   A

Figure **4.16**

The subtract instruction.

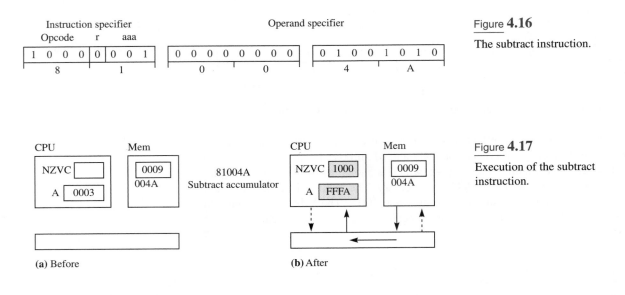

(a) Before   **(b)** After

Figure **4.17**

Execution of the subtract instruction.

is 0 because the sum is not all 0's. The V bit is 0 because an overflow did not occur, and the C bit is 0 because a carry did not occur when –9 was added to 3.   ∎

The And and Or Instructions

The and instruction has instruction specifier 1001 raaa, and the or instruction has instruction specifier 1010 raaa. Both instructions are similar to the add instruction. Rather than add the operand to the register, each instruction performs a logical operation on the register. The AND operation is useful for masking out undesired 1 bits from a bit pattern. The OR operation is useful for inserting 1 bits into a bit pattern. Both instructions affect the N and Z bits and leave the V and C bits unchanged. The RTL specifications for the and and or instructions are

$r \leftarrow r \wedge Oprnd; N \leftarrow r < 0, Z \leftarrow r = 0$
$r \leftarrow r \vee Oprnd; N \leftarrow r < 0, Z \leftarrow r = 0$

Example 4.8   Suppose the instruction to be executed is 99004A in hexadecimal, which Figure 4.18 shows in binary. The opcode indicates that the and instruction

Instruction specifier
Opcode   r   aaa

1	0	0	1	1	0	0	1

9   9

Operand specifier

0	0	0	0	0	0	0	0

0   0

0	1	0	0	1	0	1	0

4   A

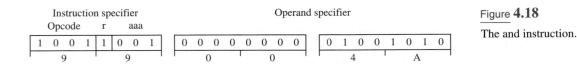

Figure **4.18**

The and instruction.

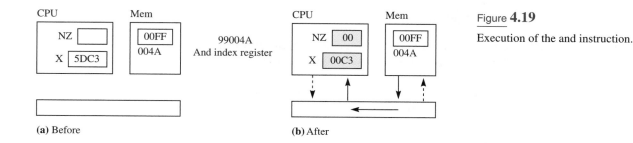

Figure **4.19**

Execution of the and instruction.

will execute and the register-r field indicates that the instruction will affect the index register.

Figure 4.19 shows the effect of executing the and instruction assuming the index register has an initial content of 5DC3 and Mem[004A] has 00FF. In binary, 00FF is 0000 0000 1111 1111. At every position where there is a 1 in Mem[004A], the corresponding bit in the index register is unchanged. At every position where there is a 0, the corresponding bit is cleared to 0. The figure shows the NZ bits in binary. The N bit is 0 because the quantity in the index register is not negative when interpreted as a signed integer. The Z bit is 0 because the index register is not all 0's. ∎

Example 4.9 Figure 4.20 shows the operation of the or instruction. The initial state is identical to that of Example 4.8 except that the opcode of the instruction specifier A9 is 1010, which indicates the or instruction. This time, at every position where there is a 0 in Mem[004A], the corresponding bit in the index register is unchanged. At every position where there is a 1, the corresponding bit is set to 1. The N bit is 0 because the index register would not be negative if it were interpreted as a signed integer. ∎

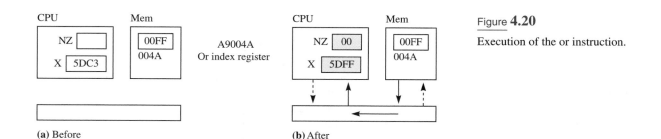

Figure **4.20**

Execution of the or instruction.

The Invert and Negate Instructions

The invert instruction has instruction specifier 0001 100r, and the negate instruction has instruction specifier 0001 101r. Both instructions are unary. They have no operand specifier. The invert instruction performs the NOT operation on the register. That is, each 1 is changed to 0, and each 0 is changed to 1. It affects the N and Z bits. The RTL specification of the invert instruction is

$$r \leftarrow \neg r; \; N \leftarrow r < 0, \; Z \leftarrow r = 0$$

The negate instruction interprets the register as a signed integer and negates it. The 16-bit register stores signed integers in the range −32768 to 32767. The negate instruction affects the N, Z, and V bits. The V bit is set only if the original value in the register is −32768, because there is no corresponding positive value of 32768. The RTL specification of the negate instruction is

$$r \leftarrow -r; \; N \leftarrow r < 0, \; Z \leftarrow r = 0, \; V \leftarrow \{overflow\}$$

Example 4.10   Suppose the instruction to be executed is 18 in hexadecimal, which Figure 4.21 shows in binary. The opcode indicates that the invert instruction will execute, and the register-r field indicates that the instruction will affect the accumulator.

Figure 4.22 shows the effect of executing the not instruction, assuming the accumulator has an initial content of 0003 (hex), which is 0000 0000 0000 0011 (bin). The not instruction changes the bit pattern to 1111 1111 1111 1100. The N bit is 1 because the quantity in the accumulator is negative when interpreted as a signed integer. The Z bit is 0 because the accumulator is not all 0's. ∎

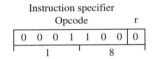

Instruction specifier

Opcode   r

Figure 4.21

The invert instruction.

(a) Before   (b) After

18
Invert accumulator

Figure 4.22

Execution of the invert instruction.

Example 4.11   Figure 4.23 shows the operation of the negate instruction. The initial state is identical to that of Example 4.10 except that the opcode of the instruction specifier 1A is 0001 101, which indicates the negate instruction. The negation of 3 is −3, which is 1111 1111 1111 1101 (bin) = FFFD (hex). ∎

Figure **4.23**

Execution of the negate instruction.

CPU

NZ [ ]

A [0003]

1A
Negate accumulator

CPU

NZ [10]

A [FFFD]

(a) Before

(b) After

▆ The Load Byte and Store Byte Instructions

These instructions, along with the two that follow, are byte instructions. Byte instructions operate on a single byte of information instead of a word. The load byte instruction has instruction specifier 1101 raaa, and the store byte instruction has instruction specifier 1111 raaa. The load byte instruction loads the operand into the right half of either the accumulator or the index register, and affects the N and Z bits. It leaves the left half of the register unchanged. The store byte instruction stores the right half of either the accumulator or the index register into a one-byte memory location and does not affect any status bits. The RTL specification of the load byte instruction is

$$r\langle 8..15\rangle \leftarrow \text{byte Oprnd}; \ N \leftarrow r < 0, \ Z \leftarrow r = 0$$

and the RTL specification of the store byte instruction is

$$\text{byte Operand} \leftarrow r\langle 8..15\rangle$$

Example 4.12   Suppose the instruction to be executed is D1004A in hexadecimal, which Figure 4.24 shows in binary. The register-r field in this example is 0, which indicates a load to the accumulator instead of the index register. The addressing-aaa field is 001, which indicates direct addressing.

Figure 4.25 shows the effect of executing the load byte instruction, assuming Mem[004A] has an initial content of 92. The N bit is set to 0 because the final bit pattern in the accumulator has 0 in the sign bit. The Z bit is set to 0 because the bit pattern is not all 0's. ∎

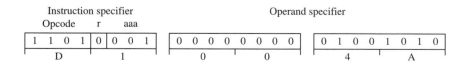

Instruction specifier			Operand specifier		
Opcode	r	aaa			
1 1 0 1	0	0 0 1	0 0 0 0 0 0 0 0	0 1 0 0 1 0 1 0	
D		1	0	0	4 A

Figure **4.24**

The load byte instruction.

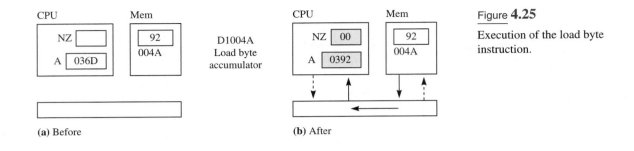

Figure **4.25**

Execution of the load byte instruction.

Example 4.13   Figure 4.26 shows the effect of executing the store byte instruction. The initial state is the same as in Example 4.12 except that the instruction is store byte instead of load byte. The right half of the accumulator is 6D, which is sent to the memory cell at address 004A.   ■

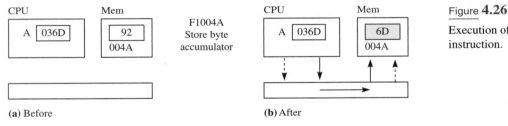

Figure **4.26**

Execution of the store byte instruction.

The Character Input and Output Instructions

The character input instruction has instruction specifier 0100 1aaa, and the character output instruction has instruction specifier 0101 0aaa. Both are byte instructions. The character input instruction takes the next ASCII character from the input device and stores the corresponding binary code for that character in a byte in main memory. The character output instruction sends the content of a byte in memory to the output device, which prints the corresponding ASCII character. Neither instruction has any effect on any register in the CPU. The RTL specification of the character input instruction is

byte Oprnd ← {*character input*}

and the RTL specification of the character output instruction is

{*character output*} ← byte Oprnd

Example 4.14   Suppose the instruction to be executed is 49004A in hexadecimal, which Figure 4.27 shows in binary. There is no register-r field. The addressing-aaa field is 001, which indicates direct addressing.

Instruction specifier | | Operand specifier

Opcode   aaa

| 0 1 0 0 1 | 0 0 1 | 0 0 0 0 0 0 0 0 | 0 1 0 0 1 0 1 0 |
| 4 | 9 | 0   0 | 4   A |

Figure **4.27**

The character input instruction.

Figure 4.28 shows the effect of executing the character input instruction, assuming that the next character in the input stream is W. The character from the input stream can come from the keyboard or from a file. The ASCII value of the letter W is 57 (hex), which is sent to the memory cell at address 004A.

The figure shows no registers in the CPU being affected by the instruction. However, the CPU is the part of the computer system that controls the other parts via the control signals it sends over the bus. The dashed lines from the CPU to the input device represent control signals that instruct the input device to put the next character from the input stream onto the bus. The control signals from the CPU to the memory system instruct the memory subsystem to take the data from the bus and store it into the memory cell. The control signal includes the address of where the memory system is to store the data. ∎

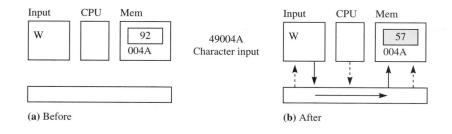

(a) Before   **(b)** After

Figure **4.28**

Execution of the character input instruction.

Example 4.15   Figure 4.29 shows the effect of executing the character output instruction assuming that the content of the memory cell at address 004A is 48

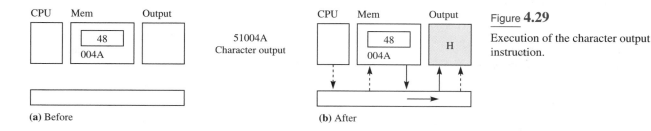

(a) Before   **(b)** After

Figure **4.29**

Execution of the character output instruction.

(hex). The CPU sends a control signal to the memory system telling it to put the data from memory location 004A onto the bus. It sends a control signal to the output device to take the data from the bus, interpret it as an ASCII character, and output it on the device. The ASCII character corresponding to the value 48 (hex) is the letter H.   ∎

4.3   von Neumann Machines

In the earliest electronic computers, each program was hand-wired. To change the program, the wires had to be manually reconnected, a tedious and time-consuming process. The ENIAC computer described in Section 3.1 was an example of this kind of machine. Its memory was used only to store data.

In 1945, John von Neumann had proposed in a report from the University of Pennsylvania that the United States Ordnance Department build a computer that would store in main memory not only the data, but the program as well. The stored-program concept was a radical idea at the time. Maurice V. Wilkes built the Electronic Delay Storage Automatic Calculator (EDSAC) at Cambridge University in England in 1949. It was the first computer to be built that used von Neumann's stored-program idea. Practically all commercial computers today are based on the stored-program concept, with programs and data sharing the same main memory. Such computers are called von Neumann machines, although some believe that J. Presper Eckert, Jr. originated the idea several years before von Neumann's paper.

The von Neumann Execution Cycle

The Pep/8 computer is a classical von Neumann machine. Figure 4.30 is a pseudocode description of the steps required to execute a program:

Load the machine language program
Initialize PC *and* SP
do {
  Fetch the next instruction
  Decode the instruction specifier
  Increment PC
  Execute the instruction fetched
}
while (*the stop instruction does not execute*)

Figure **4.30**

A pseudocode description of the steps necessary to execute a program on the Pep/8 computer.

The do loop is called the von Neumann execution cycle. The cycle consists of five operations

- Fetch
- Decode
- Increment
- Execute
- Repeat

The von Neumann cycle is wired into the central processing unit. The following is a more detailed description of the steps in the execution process.

To load the machine language program into main memory, the first instruction is placed at address 0000 (hex). The second instruction is placed adjacent to the first. If the first instruction is unary, then the address of the second instruction is 0001. Otherwise the operand specifier of the first instruction will be contained in the bytes at 0001 and 0002. The address of the second instruction would then be at 0003. The third instruction is placed adjacent to the second similarly, and so on for the entire machine language program.

To initialize the program counter and stack pointer, PC is set to 0000 (hex), and SP is set to Mem[FFF8]. The purpose of the program counter is to hold the address of the next instruction to be executed. Because the first instruction was loaded into main memory at address 0000, the PC must be set initially to 0000. The purpose of the stack pointer is to hold the address of the top of the run-time stack. A later section explains why SP is set to Mem[FFF8].

The first operation in the von Neumann execution cycle is fetch. To fetch an instruction, the CPU examines the 16 bits in the PC and interprets them as an address. It then goes to that address in main memory to fetch the instruction specifier (one byte) of the next instruction. It brings the eight bits of the instruction specifier into the CPU and holds them in the first byte of the instruction register (IR).

The second operation in the von Neumann cycle is decode. The CPU extracts the opcode from the instruction specifier to determine which instruction to execute. Depending on the opcode, the CPU extracts the register specifier if there is one and the addressing field if there is one. Now the CPU knows from the opcode whether the instruction is unary. If it is not unary, the CPU fetches the operand specifier (one word) from memory and stores it in the last two bytes of the IR.

The third operation in the von Neumann execution cycle is increment. The CPU adds 0001 to the PC if the instruction was unary. Otherwise it adds 0003. Regardless of which number is added to the PC, its value after the addition will be the address of the following instruction because the instructions are loaded adjacent to one another in main memory.

The fourth operation in the von Neumann execution cycle is execute. The CPU executes the instruction that is stored in the IR. The opcode tells the CPU which of the 39 instructions to execute.

The fifth operation in the von Neumann execution cycle is repeat. The CPU returns to the fetch operation unless the instruction just executed was the stop instruction. Pep/8 will also terminate at this point if the instruction attempts an illegal operation. Some instructions are not allowed to use certain addressing modes. The most common illegal operation that makes Pep/8 terminate is attempting execution of an instruction with a forbidden addressing mode.

Repeat the cycle

Figure 4.31 is a more detailed pseudocode description of the steps to execute a program on the Pep/8 computer.

Load the machine language program into memory starting at address 0000.
PC ← 0000
SP ← Mem [FFF8]
do {
    Fetch the instruction specifier at address in PC
    PC ← PC + 1
    Decode the instruction specifier
    if (*the instruction is not unary*) {
        Fetch the operand specifier at address in PC
        PC ← PC + 2
    }
    Execute the instruction fetched
}
while ((*the stop instruction does not execute*) && (*the instruction is legal*))

Figure **4.31**

A more detailed pseudocode description of the steps necessary to execute a program on the Pep/8 computer.

A Character Output Program

The Pep/8 system can take its input from the keyboard and send its output to the screen. These I/O devices are based on the ASCII character set. When you press a key, a byte of information representing a single ASCII character goes from the keyboard along the bus to main memory. When the CPU sends a byte to the screen along the bus, the screen interprets the byte as an ASCII character, which it displays.

At Level ISA3, the machine level, computers usually have no input or output instructions for any type of data except bytes. The interpretation of the byte occurs in the input or output device, not in main memory. Pep/8's only input instruction transfers a byte from the input device to main memory, and its only output instruction transfers a byte from main memory to the output device. Because these bytes are usually interpreted as ASCII characters, the I/O at Level ISA3 of the Pep/8 system is called character I/O.

Figure 4.32 shows a simple machine-language program that outputs the characters Hi on the output device. It uses two instructions: 0101 0, which is the character output instruction, and 0000 0000, which is the stop instruction. The first listing shows the machine language program in binary. Main memory stores this sequence of ones and zeros. The first column gives the address in hex of the first byte of the bit pattern on each line.

Address	Machine Language (bin)
0000	0101 0001 0000 0000 0000 0111
0003	0101 0001 0000 0000 0000 1000
0006	0000 0000
0007	0100 1000
0008	0110 1001

Address	Machine Language (hex)	
0000	510007	;Character output
0003	510008	;Character output
0006	00	;Stop
0007	48	;ASCII H character
0008	69	;ASCII i character

Output

Hi

Figure **4.32**

A machine language program to output the characters Hi.

The second listing shows the same program abbreviated to hexadecimal. Even though this format is slightly easier to read, remember that memory stores bits, not literal hexadecimal characters as in this listing. Each line in the second listing has a comment that begins with a semicolon to separate it from the machine language. The comments are not loaded into memory with the program.

Figure 4.33 (pp. 172–173) shows each step the computer takes to execute the program. Figure 4.33(a) is the initial state of the Pep/8 computer. The input device is not shown. Several of the CPU registers not used by this program are also omitted. Each question mark indicates four bits. Initially, the contents of the main memory cells and the CPU registers are unknown.

Figure 4.33(b) shows the first step of the process. The program is loaded into main memory, starting at address 0000. The details of where the program comes from and what puts it into memory are described in later chapters.

Figure 4.33(c) shows the second step of the process. The program counter is cleared to 0000 (hex). The figure does not show the initialization of SP because this program does not use the stack pointer.

Figure 4.33(d) shows the fetch part of the execution cycle. The CPU examines the bits in the PC and finds 0000 (hex). It signals the main memory to send the byte at that address to the CPU. When the CPU gets the byte, it stuffs it into

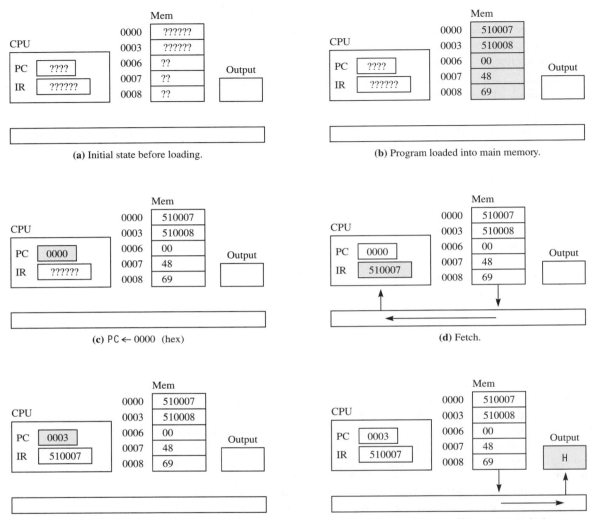

(a) Initial state before loading.

(b) Program loaded into main memory.

(c) PC ← 0000 (hex)

(d) Fetch.

(e) Increment PC.

(f) Execute. Character H sent to output device.

Figure **4.33**

The von Neumann execution cycle for the program of Figure 4.32.

the first part of the instruction register. Then it decodes the instruction specifier, determines from the opcode that the instruction is not unary, and brings the operand specifier into IR as well. The original bits at addresses 0000, 0001, and 0002 are not changed by the fetch. Main memory has sent a copy of the 24 bits to the CPU.

Figure 4.33(e) shows the increment part of the execution cycle. The CPU adds 0003 to the PC.

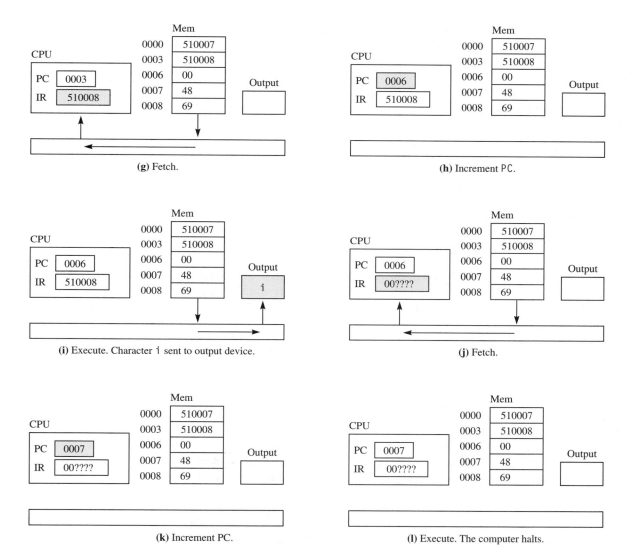

(g) Fetch.

(h) Increment PC.

(i) Execute. Character i sent to output device.

(j) Fetch.

(k) Increment PC.

(l) Execute. The computer halts.

Figure **4.33**

(Continued)

Figure 4.33(f) shows the execute part of the execution cycle. The CPU examines the first five bits of IR and finds 0101 0. This opcode signals the circuitry to execute the character output instruction.

Consequently, the CPU examines the addressing mode bits and finds 001, which indicates direct addressing. It then examines the operand specifier and finds 0007 (hex). It sends a control signal back to main memory to go directly to address 0007 and put the byte at that address on the bus. Simultaneously, it sends a control signal to the output device to get the byte from the bus. The output device interprets the byte as an ASCII character and displays it. If the addressing mode had not been direct, the CPU would not have signaled main memory to go directly to address 0007 for the byte.

Figure 4.33(g) shows the fetch part of the execution cycle. This time the CPU finds 0003 (hex) in the PC. It fetches a copy of the byte at address 0003, determines that the instruction is not unary, and then fetches the word at 0004. As a result, the original content of IR is destroyed.

Figure 4.33(h) shows the increment part of the execution cycle. The CPU adds 0003 to PC, making it 0006 (hex).

Figure 4.33(i) shows the execute part of the execution cycle. As in part (f), the CPU finds the opcode for the character output instruction and the addressing mode bits for direct addressing. But this time the operand specifier is 0008 (hex). The byte at address 0008 is 69 (hex), which is 0110 1001 (bin). Because the right-most seven bits are 110 1001, the output device displays the ASCII character i.

Figure 4.33(j) shows the fetch part of the execute cycle. Because PC contains 0006 (hex), the byte at that address comes to the CPU. This time when the CPU examines the opcode, it discovers that the instruction is unary. So the CPU does not fetch the word at address 0007.

Figure 4.33(k) shows the increment part of the execution cycle. The CPU adds 0001 to PC, making it 0007 (hex).

Figure 4.33(l) shows the execute part of the execution cycle. This time the CPU finds the opcode for the stop instruction in IR. Therefore, it ignores the addressing mode bits and simply stops the execution cycle.

Just outputting a couple characters may seem a rather involved process, but it all happens rather quickly in human terms. The fetch part of the execution cycle takes less than about one nanosecond on many computers. Because the execution part of the execution cycle depends on the particular instruction, a complex instruction may take many nanoseconds to execute, whereas a simple instruction may take a few nanoseconds.

The computer does not attach any meaning to the electrical signals in its circuitry. Specifically, main memory does not know whether the bits at a particular address represent data or an instruction. It remembers only individual 1's and 0's.

von Neumann Bugs

In the program of Figure 4.32, the bits at addresses 0000 to 0006 are used by the CPU as instructions, and the bits at 0007 and 0008 are used as data. The programmer placed the instruction bits at the beginning because she knew the PC would be initially cleared to 0000 and would be incremented by 0001 or 0003 on each iteration of the execution cycle. If the stop instruction (opcode 0000 0000) were omitted

Executing data as instructions

by mistake, the execution cycle would continue to fetch the next byte and interpret it as the instruction specifier of the next instruction, even though the programmer intended to have it interpreted as data.

Because programs and data share the same memory, programmers at the machine level must be careful in allocating memory for each of them. Otherwise two types of problems can arise. The CPU may interpret a sequence of bits as an instruction when the programmer intended them to be data. Or the CPU may interpret a sequence of bits to be data when the programmer intended them to be an instruction. Both types of bugs occur at the machine level.

Although the sharing of memory by both data and instructions can produce bugs if the programmer is not careful, it also presents an exciting possibility. A program is simply a set of instructions that is stored in memory. The programmer, therefore, can view the program as data for yet another program. It becomes possible to write programs that process other programs. Compilers, assemblers, and loaders are programs that adopt this viewpoint of treating other programs as data.

Interpreting instructions as data

A Character Input Program

The program of Figure 4.34 inputs two characters from the input device and outputs them in reverse order on the output device. It uses the character input instruction with direct addressing to get the characters from the input device.

Address	Machine Language (bin)
0000	0100 1001 0000 0000 0000 1101
0003	0100 1001 0000 0000 0000 1110
0006	0101 0001 0000 0000 0000 1110
0009	0101 0001 0000 0000 0000 1101
000C	0000 0000

Address	Machine Language (hex)	
0000	49000D	;Character input
0003	49000E	;Character input
0006	51000E	;Character output
0009	51000D	;Character output
000C	00	;Stop

Input

up

Output

pu

Figure **4.34**

A machine language program to input two characters and output them in reverse order.

The first instruction, 49000D, has an opcode that specifies the character input instruction and addressing mode bits that specify direct addressing. It puts the first character from the input device into the byte at Mem[000D]. Although this byte is not shown on the listing, it is surely available because memory goes all the way up to address FFFF. The second instruction, 49000E, also specifies character input, but to Mem[000E].

The third instruction, 51000E, has an opcode that specifies the character output instruction. It outputs the byte that was previously stored at Mem[000E]. The fourth instruction, 51000D, outputs the byte that was previously stored at Mem[000D].

Converting Decimal to ASCII

Figure 4.35 shows a program that adds two single-digit numbers and outputs their single-digit sum. It illustrates the inconvenience of dealing with output at the machine level.

Address	Machine Language (bin)
0000	1100 0001 0000 0000 0001 0001
0003	0111 0001 0000 0000 0001 0011
0006	1010 0001 0000 0000 0001 0101
0009	1111 0001 0000 0000 0001 0000
000C	0101 0001 0000 0000 0001 0000
000F	0000 0000
0010	0000 0000
0011	0000 0000 0000 0101
0013	0000 0000 0000 0011
0015	0000 0000 0011 0000

Address	Machine Language (hex)	
0000	C10011	;A := first number
0003	710013	;Add the two numbers
0006	A10015	;Convert sum to character
0009	F10010	;Store the character
000C	510010	;Output the character
000F	00	;Stop
0010	00	;Character to output
0011	0005	;Decimal 5
0013	0003	;Decimal 3
0015	0030	;Mask for ASCII char

Figure **4.35**

A machine language program to add 5 and 3 and output the single-character result.

Output

8

Figure **4.35**

(Continued)

The two numbers to be added are 5 and 3. The program stores them at Mem[0011] and Mem[0013]. The first instruction loads the 5 into the accumulator, and then the second instruction adds the 3. At this point the sum is in the accumulator.

Now a problem arises. We want to output this result, but the only output instruction for this Level ISA3 machine is the character output instruction. The problem is that our result is 0000 1000 (bin). If the character output instruction tries to output that, it will be interpreted as the backspace character, BS, as shown on the ASCII chart of Figure 3.24.

So, the program must convert the decimal number 8, 0000 1000 (bin), to the ASCII character 8, 0011 1000 (bin). The ASCII bits differ from the unsigned binary bits by the two extra 1's in the third and fourth bits. To do the conversion, the program inserts those two extra 1's into the result by ORing the accumulator, with the mask 0000 0000 0011 0000 using the OR register instruction:

$$
\begin{array}{ll}
 & 0000\ 0000\ 0000\ 1000 \\
\text{OR} & \underline{0000\ 0000\ 0011\ 0000} \\
 & 0000\ 0000\ 0011\ 1000
\end{array}
$$

The accumulator now contains the correct sum in ASCII form. The store byte instruction stores the character in Mem[0010], and the character output instruction outputs it.

If you replace the word at Mem[0013] with 0009, what does this program output? Unfortunately, it does not output 14, even though the sum in the accumulator is

14 (dec) = 0000 0000 0000 1110 (bin)

after the add accumulator instruction executes. The OR instruction changes this bit pattern to 0000 0000 0011 1110 (bin), producing an output of >. Because the only output instruction at Level ISA3 is one that outputs a single byte, the program cannot output a result that should contain more than one character. We will see in Chapter 5 how to remedy this shortcoming.

A Self-Modifying Program

Figure 4.36 illustrates a curious possibility based on the von Neumann design principle. Notice that the program from 0006 to 001B is identical to Figure 4.35 from 0000 to 0015. This program has two instructions at the beginning that are not in

Figure 4.35, however. Because the instructions are shifted down six bytes, their operand specifiers are all greater by six than the operand specifiers of the previous program. Other than the adjustment by six bytes, however, the instructions beginning at 0006 would appear to duplicate the processing of Figure 4.35.

Address	Machine Language (bin)
0000	1101 0001 0000 0000 0001 1101
0003	1111 0001 0000 0000 0000 1001
0006	1100 0001 0000 0000 0001 0111
0009	0111 0001 0000 0000 0001 1001
000C	1010 0001 0000 0000 0001 1011
000F	1111 0001 0000 0000 0001 0110
0012	0101 0001 0000 0000 0001 0110
0015	0000 0000
0016	0000 0000
0017	0000 0000 0000 0101
0019	0000 0000 0000 0011
001B	0000 0000 0011 0000
001D	1000 0001

Address	Machine Language (hex)	
0000	D1001D	;Load byte accumulator
0003	F10009	;Store byte accumulator
0006	C10017	;A := first number
0009	710019	;Add the two numbers
000C	A1001B	;Convert sum to character
000F	F10016	;Store the character
0012	510016	;Output the character
0015	00	;Stop
0016	00	;Character to output
0017	0005	;Decimal 5
0019	0003	;Decimal 3
001B	0030	;Mask for ASCII char
001D	81	;Byte to modify instruction

Output

2

Figure 4.36

A machine language program that modifies itself. The add accumulator instruction changes to a subtract instruction.

In particular, it appears that the load accumulator instruction would load the 5 into the accumulator, the add instruction would add the 3, the OR instruction would change the 8 (dec) to ASCII 8, the store byte accumulator instruction would put the 8 in Mem[0016], and the character output instruction would print the 8. Instead, the output is 2.

Because program and data share the same memory in a von Neumann machine, it is possible for a program to treat itself as data and modify itself. The first instruction loads the byte 81 (hex) into the right half of the accumulator, and the second instruction puts it in Mem[0009]. What was at Mem[0009] before this change? The instruction specifier of the add accumulator instruction. Now the bits at Mem[0009] are 1000 0001. When the computer gets these bits in the fetch part of the von Neumann execution cycle, the CPU detects the opcode as 1000, the opcode for the subtract register instruction. The register specifier indicates the accumulator, and the addressing mode bits indicate direct addressing. The instruction subtracts 3 from 5 instead of adding it.

Of course, this is not a very practical program. If you wanted to subtract the two numbers, you would simply write the program of Figure 4.35 with the subtract instruction in place of the add instruction. But it does show that in a von Neumann machine, main memory places no significance on the bits it is storing. It simply remembers 1's and 0's and has no idea which are program bits, which are data bits, which are ASCII characters, and so on. Furthermore, the CPU cranks out the von Neumann execution cycle and interprets the bits accordingly, with no idea of their history. When it fetches the bits at Mem[0009], it does not know, or care, how they got there in the first place. It simply repeats the fetch, decode, increment, execute cycle over and over.

4.4 Programming at Level ISA3

To program at Level ISA3 is to write a set of instructions in binary. To execute the binary sequence, first you must load it into main memory. The operating system is responsible for loading the binary sequence into main memory.

An operating system is a program. Like any other program, a software engineer must design, write, test, and debug it. Most operating systems are so large and complex that teams of engineers must write them. The primary function of an operating system is to control the execution of application programs on the computer. Because the operating system is itself a program, it must reside in main memory in order to be executed. So main memory must store not only the application programs, but also the operating system.

In the Pep/8 computer, the bottom part of main memory is reserved for the operating system. The top part is reserved for the application program. Figure 4.37 shows the place of the operating system in main memory. It starts at memory location FBCF and occupies the rest of main memory. That leaves memory locations 0000 to FBCE for the application program.

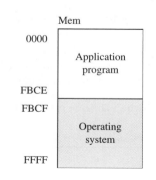

Figure **4.37**

The location of the Pep/8 operating system in main memory.

John von Neumann

John von Neumann was a brilliant mathematician, physicist, logician, and computer scientist. Legends have been passed down about the phenomenal speed at which von Neumann solved problems and of his astonishing memory. He used his talents not only for furthering his mathematical theories, but also for memorizing entire books and reciting them years after he had read them. But ask a highway patrolman about von Neumann's driving ability, and he would be liable to throw up his hands in despair; behind the wheel, the mathematical genius was as reckless as a rebel teenager.

John von Neumann was born in Hungary in 1903, the oldest son of a wealthy Jewish banker. He entered high school by the time he was 11, and it wasn't long before his math teachers recommended he be tutored by university professors. At only 19, with the publication of his first paper, he was recognized as a brilliant mathematician.

von Neumann left Nazi Germany for the United States before the outbreak of World War II. During the war, von Neumann was hired as a consultant for the U.S. armed forces and related civilian agencies because of his knowledge of hydrodynamics. He was also called upon to participate in the construction of the atomic bomb in 1943. It was not surprising that, following this work, President Eisenhower appointed him to the Atomic Energy Commission in 1955.

A fortuitous meeting in 1944 with Herbert Goldstine, a pioneer of one of the first operational electronic digital computers, introduced

the scientist to computers. von Neumann's chance conversation in a train station with Goldstine sparked the beginning of a new fascination for him. He started working on the stored program concept and concluded that by internally storing a program, the hours of tedious labor required to reprogram computers in those days could be eliminated. He also developed a new computer architecture to perform this storage task based on the now-famous von Neumann cycle. Changes in computers since the beginning have been primarily in terms of the speed and composition of the fundamental circuits, but the basic architecture designed by von Neumann has persisted.

During his lifetime, von Neumann taught at many respected institutions, including Berlin, Hamburg, and Princeton Universities. While at Princeton, he worked with the talented and as-yet-unknown British student Alan Turing. He received many awards, including honorary PhDs from Princeton, Harvard, and Istanbul Universities. In 1957 von Neumann died of bone cancer in Washington, D.C., at the age of 54.

"There's no sense in being precise when you don't even know what you're talking about."

—John von Neumann

The loader is that part of the operating system that loads the application program into main memory so it can be executed. What loads the loader? The Pep/8 loader, along with many other parts of the operating system, is permanently stored in main memory.

Read-Only Memory

There are two types of electronic-circuit elements from which memory devices are manufactured—read/write circuit elements and read-only circuit elements.

In the program of Figure 4.36, when the store byte instruction, F10016, executed, the CPU transferred the content of the right half of the accumulator to Mem[0016]. The original content of Mem[0016] was destroyed, and the memory location then contained 0011 0010 (bin). When the character output instruction was executed next, the bits at location 0016 were sent to the output device.

The circuit element at memory location 0016 is a read/write circuit. The store instruction did a write operation on it, which changed its content. The character output instruction did a read operation on it, which sent a copy of its content to the output device. If the circuit element at location 0016 were a read-only circuit, the store instruction would not have changed its content.

Both types of main-memory circuit elements—read/write and read-only—are random-access devices, as opposed to serial devices. When the character output instruction does a read from memory location 0016, it does not need to start at location 0000 and sequentially go through 0001, 0002, 0003, and so on until it gets to 0016. Instead, it can go directly to location 0016. Because it can go to a random location in memory directly, the circuit element is called a random-access device.

RAM should be called RWM

Read-only memory devices are known as ROM. Read/write memory devices should be known as RWM. Unfortunately, they are known as RAM, which stands for random-access memory. That name is unfortunate because both read-only and read/write devices are random-access devices. The characteristic that distinguishes a read-only memory device from a read/write memory device is that the content of a read-only device cannot be changed by a store instruction. Because use of the term RAM is so pervasive in the computer industry, we also will use it to refer to read/write devices. But in our hearts we will know that ROMs are random also.

Main memory usually contains some ROM devices. Those parts of main memory that are ROM contain permanent binary sequences, which the store instruction cannot alter. Furthermore, when power to the computer is switched off at the end of the day and then switched on at the beginning of the next day, the ROM will retain those binary sequences in its circuitry. RAM will not retain its memory if the power is switched off. It is therefore called volatile.

There are two ways a computer manufacturer can buy ROM for a memory system. She can specify to the circuit manufacturer the bit sequences desired in the memory devices. The circuit manufacturer can then manufacture the devices accordingly. Or the manufacturer can order a programmable read-only memory

(PROM), which is a ROM with all zeros. The computer manufacturer can then permanently change any desired location to a one, in such a way that the device will contain the proper bit sequence. This process is called "burning in" the bit pattern.

The Pep/8 Operating System

Most of the Pep/8 operating system has been burned into ROM. Figure 4.38 shows the ROM part of the operating system. It begins at location FC57 and continues down to FFFF. That part of main memory is permanent. A store instruction cannot change it. If the power is ever turned off, when it is turned on again, that part of the operating system will still be there. The region from FBCF to FC56 is the RAM part of the operating system for our computer.

The RAM part of the operating system is for storing the system variables. Their values will change while the operating system program is executing. The ROM part of the operating system contains the loader, which is a permanent fixture. Its job is to load the application program into RAM, starting at address 0000. On the Pep/8 machine, you invoke the loader by choosing the loader option from the menu of the simulator program.

Figure 4.39 is a more detailed memory map of the Pep/8 system. As in Figure 4.38, the shaded area represents the operating system region, and the clear area represents the application region.

The run-time stack for the application program, called the user stack, begins at memory location FBCF, just above the operating system. The stack pointer register in the CPU contains the address of the top of the stack. When procedures are called, storage for the parameters, the return address, and the local variables are allocated on the stack at successively lower addresses. Hence the stack "grows upward" in memory.

The run-time stack for the operating system begins at memory location FC4F, which is 128 bytes below the start of the user stack. When the operating system executes, the stack pointer in the CPU contains the address of the top of the system stack. Like the user stack, the system stack grows upward in memory. The operating system never needs more than 128 bytes on its stack, so there is no possibility that the system stack will try to store its data in the user stack region.

The Pep/8 operating system consists of two programs—the loader, which begins at address FC57, and the trap handler, which begins at address FC9B. You will recall from Figure 4.6 that the instructions with opcodes 0010 01 through 0100 0 are unimplemented at Level ISA3. The trap handler implements these three instructions for the assembly language programmer. Chapter 5 describes the instructions at Level Asmb5, the assembly level, and Chapter 8 shows how they are implemented at Level OS4, the operating system level.

Associated with these two parts of the operating system are four words at the very bottom of ROM that are reserved for special use by the operating system. They are called machine vectors and are at addresses FFF8, FFFA, FFFC, and FFFE, as shown in Figure 4.39.

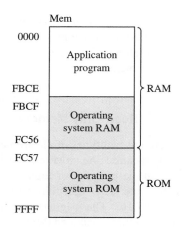

Figure **4.38**

The read-only memory in the Pep/8 system.

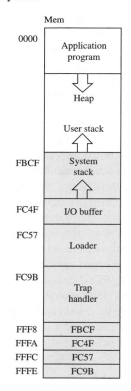

Figure **4.39**

A memory map of the Pep/8 system.

When you choose the load option from the Pep/8 simulator menu, the following two events occur:

SP ← Mem[FFFA]
PC ← Mem[FFFC]

In other words, the content of memory location FFFA is copied into the stack pointer, and the content of memory location FFFC is copied into the program counter. After these events occur, the execution cycle begins. Figure 4.40 illustrates these two events.

Selecting the load option in effect initializes the stack pointer and program counter to the predetermined values stored at FFFA and FFFC. It just so happens that the value at address FFFA is FC4F, the bottom of the system stack. FC4F is the value the stack pointer should have when the system stack is empty. It also happens that the value at address FFFC is FC57. In fact, FC57 is the address of the first instruction to be executed in the loader.

The system programmer who wrote the operating system decided where the system stack and the loader should be located. Realizing that the Pep/8 computer would fetch the vectors from locations FFFA and FFFC when the load option is selected, she placed the appropriate values in those locations. Because the first step in the execution cycle is fetch, the first instruction to be executed after selecting the load option is the first instruction of the loader program.

If you wish to revise the operating system, your loader might not begin at FC57. Suppose it begins at 7BD6 instead. When the user selects the load option, the computer will still go to location FFFC to fetch the vector. So you would need to place 7BD6 in the word at address FFFC.

This scheme of storing addresses at special reserved memory locations is flexible. It allows the system programmer to place the loader anywhere in memory that is convenient. A more direct but less flexible scheme would be to design the computer to execute the following operations when the user selects the load option:

SP ← FC4F
PC ← FC57

If selecting the load option produced these two events, the loader of the current operating system would still function correctly. However, it would be difficult to modify the operating system. The loader would always have to start at FC57, and the system stack would always have to start at FC4F. The system programmer would have no choice in the placement of the various parts of the system.

(a) Initial state.

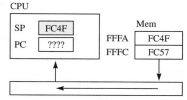

(b) SP ← Mem[FFFA]

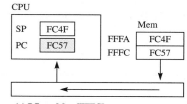

(c) PC ← Mem[FFFC]

Figure **4.40**

The Pep/8 load option.

Using the Pep/8 System

To load a machine language program on the Pep/8 computer, fortunately you do not need to write it in binary. You may write it with ASCII hexadecimal characters in a text file. The loader will convert from ASCII to binary for you when it loads the program.

The listing in Figure 4.41 shows how to prepare a machine language program for loading. It is the program of Figure 4.32, which outputs `Hi`. You simply write in a text file the binary sequence in hexadecimal without any addresses or comments. Terminate the list of bytes with lowercase zz, which the loader detects as a sentinel. The loader will put the bytes in memory one after the other, starting at address 0000 (hex).

Address	Machine Language (hex)	
0000	510007	;Character output
0003	510008	;Character output
0006	00	;Stop
0007	48	;ASCII H character
0008	69	;ASCII i character

Hex Version for the Loader

51 00 07 51 00 08 00 48 69 zz

Output

Hi

Figure **4.41**

Preparing a program for the loader.

The Pep/8 loader is extremely particular about the format of your machine-language program. To work correctly, the very first character in your text file must be a hexadecimal character. No leading blank lines or spaces are allowed. There must be exactly one space between bytes. If you wish to continue your byte stream on another line, you must not leave trailing spaces on the preceding line.

After you write your machine-language program and load it with the loader option, you must select the execute option to run it. The following two events occur when you select the execute option:

SP ← Mem[FFF8]
PC ← 0000

Then the von Neumann execution cycle begins. Because PC has the value 0000, the CPU will fetch the first instruction from Mem[0000]. Fortunately, that is where the loader put the first instruction of the application program.

Figure 4.39 shows that Mem[FFF8] contains FBCF, the address of the bottom of the user stack. The application program in this example does not use the run-time stack. If it did, the application program could access the stack correctly because SP would be initialized to the address of the bottom of the user stack.

Enjoy!

SUMMARY

Virtually all commercial computers are based on the von Neumann design principle, in which main memory stores both data and instructions. The four components of a von Neumann machine are input devices, the central processing unit (CPU), main memory, and output devices. The CPU contains a set of registers, one of which is the program counter (PC), which stores the address of the instruction to be executed next.

The CPU has an instruction set wired into it. An instruction consists of an instruction specifier and an operand specifier. The instruction specifier, in turn, consists of an opcode and possibly a register field and an addressing mode field. The opcode determines which instruction in the instruction set is to be executed. The register field determines which register participates in the operation. The addressing mode field determines which addressing mode is used for the source or destination of the data.

Each addressing mode corresponds to a relationship between the operand specifier (OprndSpec) and the operand (Oprnd). In the direct addressing mode, the operand specifier is the address in main memory of the operand. In mathematical notation, Oprnd = Mem[OprndSpec].

To execute a program, a group of instructions and data are loaded into main memory and then the von Neumann execution cycle begins. The von Neumann execution cycle consists of the following steps: (1) fetch the instruction specified by PC, (2) decode the instruction specifier, (3) increment PC, (4) execute the instruction fetched, and (5) repeat by going to Step 1.

Because main memory stores instructions as well as data, two types of errors at the machine level are possible. You may interpret data bits as instructions, or you may interpret instruction bits as data. Another possibility that is a direct result of storing instructions in main memory is that a program may be processed as if it were data. Loaders and compilers are important programs that take the viewpoint of treating instruction bits as data.

The operating system is a program that controls the execution of applications programs. It must reside in main memory along with the applications programs and data. On some computers, a portion of the operating system is burned into read-only memory (ROM). One characteristic of ROM is that a store instruction cannot change the content of a memory cell. The run-time stack for the operating system is located in random-access memory (RAM). A machine vector is an address of an operating system component, such as a stack or a program, used to access that component. Two important functions of an operating system are the loader and the trap handler.

EXERCISES

Section 4.1

*1. (a) How many bytes are in the main memory of the Pep/8 computer? (b) How many words are in it? (c) How many bits are in it? (d) How many total bits are in the Pep/8 CPU? (e) How many times bigger in terms of bits is the main memory than the CPU?

2. (a) Suppose the main memory of the Pep/8 were completely filled with unary instructions. How many instructions would it contain? (b) What is the maximum number of instructions that would fit in the main memory if none of the instructions is unary? (c) Suppose the main memory is completely filled with an equal number of unary and nonunary instructions. How many total instructions would it contain?

*3. Answer the following questions for the machine language instructions 7AF82C and D623D0. **(a)** What is the opcode in binary? **(b)** What does the instruction do? **(c)** What is the register-r field in binary? **(d)** Which register does it specify? **(e)** What is the addressing-aaa field in binary? **(f)** Which addressing mode does it specify? **(g)** What is the operand specifier in hexadecimal?

4. Answer the questions in Exercise 3 for the machine language instructions 8B00AC and F70BD3.

Section 4.2

*5. Suppose Pep/8 contains the following four hexadecimal values:

A: 19AC
X: FE20
Mem[0A3F]: FF00
Mem[0A41]: 103D

If it has these values before each of the following statements executes, what are the four hexadecimal values after each statement executes?

(a) C10A3F	**(b)** D10A3F	**(c)** D90A41
(d) F10A41	**(e)** E90A3F	**(f)** 890A41
(g) 810A3F	**(h)** A10A3F	**(i)** 19

6. Repeat Exercise 5 for the following statements:

(a) C90A3F	**(b)** D90A3F	**(c)** F10A41
(d) E10A41	**(e)** 790A3F	**(f)** 810A41
(g) 990A3F	**(h)** A90A3F	**(i)** 18

Section 4.3

*7. Determine the output of the following Pep/8 machine-language program. The left column is the memory address of the first byte on the line:

```
0000   51000A
0003   51000B
0006   51000C
0009   00
000A   4A6F
000C   79
```

8. Determine the output of the following Pep/8 machine-language program if the input is tab. The left column is the memory address of the first byte on the line:

```
0000   490010
0003   490011
0006   490012
0009   510011
000C   510010
000F   00
```

9. Determine the output of the following Pep/8 machine-language program. The left column in each part is the memory address of the first byte on the line:

*(a)

```
0000   C1000E
0003   910010
0006   F1000D
0009   51000D
000C   00
000D   00
000E   A94F
0010   FFFD
```

(b)

```
0000   C1000C
0003   18
0004   F1000B
0007   51000B
000A   00
000B   00
000C   F0D4
```

Section 4.4

10. Suppose you need to process a list of 31,000 integers contained in Pep/8 memory at one integer per word. You estimate that 20% of the instructions in a typical program are unary instructions. What is the maximum number of instructions you can expect to be able to use in the program that processes the data? Keep in mind that your applications program must share memory with the operating system and with your data.

11. **(a)** What company manufactured the computer you are using? **(b)** How many bytes are in its main memory? **(c)** How many registers are in its CPU? How many bits are in each register? **(d)** How many bits are contained in a single instruction? **(e)** How many bits of the instruction are reserved for the opcode?

PROBLEMS

Section 4.4

12. Write a machine-language program to output your first name on the output device. Write it in a format suitable for the loader and execute it on the Pep/8 simulator.

13. Write a machine-language program to output the four characters Frog on the output device. Write it in a format suitable for the loader and execute it on the Pep/8 simulator.

14. Write a machine-language program to output the three characters Cat on the output device. Write it in a format suitable for the loader and execute it on the Pep/8 simulator.

15. Write a machine-language program to add the three numbers 2, –3, and 6 and output the sum on the output device. Write it in a format suitable for the loader and execute it on the Pep/8 simulator.

16. Write a machine-language program to input two one-digit numbers, add them, and output the one-digit sum. Write it in a format suitable for the loader and execute it on the Pep/8 simulator.

17. Write the program in Figure 4.35 in hexadecimal format for input to the loader. Verify that it works correctly by running it on the Pep/8 simulator. Then modify the store byte instruction and the character output instruction so that the result is stored at Mem[FCF5] and the character output is also from Mem[FCF5]. What is the output? Explain.

LEVEL 5

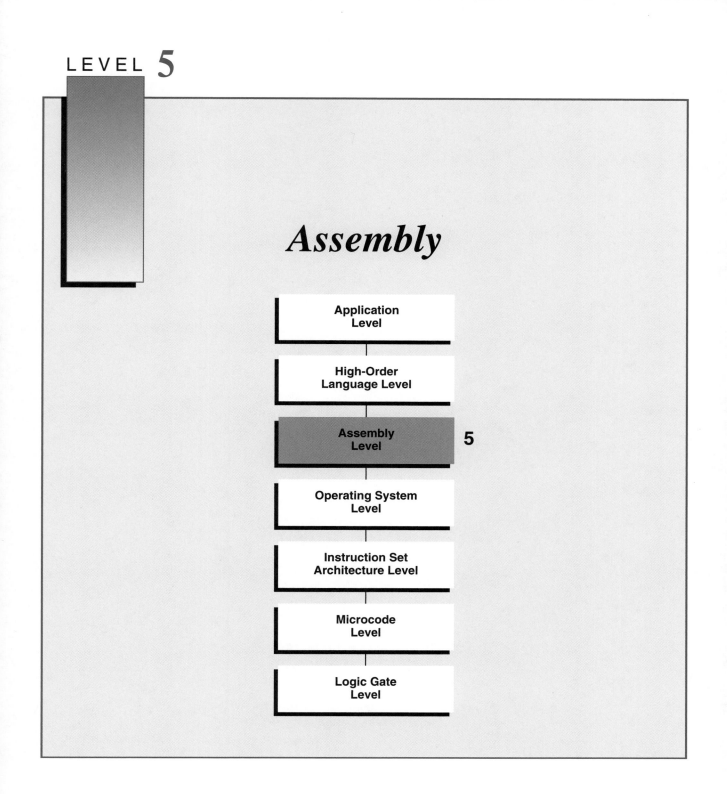

Assembly

Application
Level

High-Order
Language Level

Assembly
Level   5

Operating System
Level

Instruction Set
Architecture Level

Microcode
Level

Logic Gate
Level

Chapter

5

Assembly Language

The level-ISA3 language is machine language, sequences of 1's and 0's sometimes abbreviated to hexadecimal. Computer pioneers had to program in machine language, but they soon revolted against such an indignity. Memorizing the opcodes of the machine and having to continually refer to ASCII charts and hexadecimal tables to get their programs into binary was no fun. The assembly level was invented to relieve programmers of the tedium of programming in binary.

Chapter 4 describes the Pep/8 computer at level ISA3, the machine level. This chapter describes level Asmb5, the assembly level. Between these two levels lies the operating system. Remember that the purpose of levels of abstraction is to hide the details of the system at the lower levels. This chapter illustrates that principle of information hiding. You will use the trap handler of the operating system without knowing the details of its operation. That is, you will learn what the trap handler does without learning how the handler does it. Chapter 8 reveals the inner workings of the trap handler.

The assembly level uses the operating system below it.

5.1 Assemblers

The language at level Asmb5 is called assembly language. It provides a more convenient way of writing machine language programs than binary does. The program of Figure 4.32, which outputs Hi, contains two types of bit patterns, one for instructions and one for data. These two types are a direct consequence of the von Neumann design, where program and data share the same memory with a binary representation for each.

Assembly language contains two types of statements that correspond to these two types of bit patterns. Mnemonic statements correspond to the instruction bit patterns, and pseudo-operations correspond to the data bit patterns.

The two types of bit patterns at level ISA3

The two types of statements at level Asmb5

191

Instruction Mnemonics

Suppose the machine language instruction

```
C0009A
```

is stored at some memory location. This is the load register r instruction. The register-r bit is 0, which indicates the accumulator and not the index register. The addressing-aaa field is 000, which specifies immediate addressing.

This instruction is written in the Pep/8 assembly language as

```
LDA 0x009A,i
```

The mnemonic LDA, which stands for load accumulator, is written in place of the opcode, 1100, and the register-r field, 0. A mnemonic is a memory aid. It is easier to remember that LDA stands for the load accumulator instruction than to remember that opcode 1100 and register-r 0 stand for the load accumulator instruction. The operand specifier is written in hexadecimal, 009A, preceded by 0x, which stands for hexadecimal constant. In Pep/8 assembly language, you specify the addressing mode by placing one or more letters after the operand specifier with a comma between them. Figure 5.1 shows the letters that go with each of the eight addressing modes.

A mnemonic for the opcode

Letters for the addressing mode

aaa	Addressing Mode	Letters
000	Immediate	i
001	Direct	d
010	Indirect	n
011	Stack-relative	s
100	Stack-relative deferred	sf
101	Indexed	x
110	Stack-indexed	sx
111	Stack-indexed deferred	sxf

Figure **5.1**

The letters that specify the addressing mode in Pep/8 assembly language.

Example 5.1   Here are some examples of the load register r instruction written in binary machine language and in assembly language. LDX corresponds to the same machine language statement as LDA, except that the register-r bit for LDX is 1 instead of 0.

```
1100 0011 0000 0000 1001 1010        LDA 0x009A,s
1100 0110 0000 0000 1001 1010        LDA 0x009A,sx
1100 1011 0000 0000 1001 1010        LDX 0x009A,s
1100 1110 0000 0000 1001 1010        LDX 0x009A,sx
```
∎

Figure 5.2 summarizes the 39 instructions of the Pep/8 instruction set at level Asmb5. It shows the mnemonic that goes with each opcode and the meaning of

Instruction Specifier	Mnemonic	Instruction	Addressing Modes	Status Bits
0000 0000	STOP	Stop execution	U	
0000 0001	RETTR	Return from trap	U	
0000 0010	MOVSPA	Move SP to A	U	
0000 0011	MOVFLGA	Move NZVC flags to A	U	
0000 010a	BR	Branch unconditional	i, x	
0000 011a	BRLE	Branch if less than or equal to	i, x	
0000 100a	BRLT	Branch if less than	i, x	
0000 101a	BREQ	Branch if equal to	i, x	
0000 110a	BRNE	Branch if not equal to	i, x	
0000 111a	BRGE	Branch if greater than or equal to	i, x	
0001 000a	BRGT	Branch if greater than	i, x	
0001 001a	BRV	Branch if V	i, x	
0001 010a	BRC	Branch if C	i, x	
0001 011a	CALL	Call subroutine	i, x	
0001 100r	NOTr	Bitwise invert r	U	NZ
0001 101r	NEGr	Negate r	U	NZV
0001 110r	ASLr	Arithmetic shift left r	U	NZVC
0001 111r	ASRr	Arithmetic shift right r	U	NZC
0010 000r	ROLr	Rotate left r	U	C
0010 001r	RORr	Rotate right r	U	C
0010 01nn	NOPn	Unary no operation trap	U	
0010 1aaa	NOP	Nonunary no operation trap	i	
0011 0aaa	DECI	Decimal input trap	d, n, s, sf, x, sx, sxf	NZV
0011 1aaa	DECO	Decimal output trap	i, d, n, s, sf, x, sx, sxf	
0100 0aaa	STRO	String output trap	d, n, sf	
0100 1aaa	CHARI	Character input	d, n, s, sf, x, sx, sxf	
0101 0aaa	CHARO	Character output	i, d, n, s, sf, x, sx, sxf	
0101 1nnn	RETn	Return from call with n local bytes	U	
0110 0aaa	ADDSP	Add to stack pointer (SP)	i, d, n, s, sf, x, sx, sxf	NZVC
0110 1aaa	SUBSP	Subtract from stack pointer (SP)	i, d, n, s, sf, x, sx, sxf	NZVC
0111 raaa	ADDr	Add to r	i, d, n, s, sf, x, sx, sxf	NZVC
1000 raaa	SUBr	Subtract from r	i, d, n, s, sf, x, sx, sxf	NZVC
1001 raaa	ANDr	Bitwise AND to r	i, d, n, s, sf, x, sx, sxf	NZ
1010 raaa	ORr	Bitwise OR to r	i, d, n, s, sf, x, sx, sxf	NZ
1011 raaa	CPr	Compare r	i, d, n, s, sf, x, sx, sxf	NZVC
1100 raaa	LDr	Load r from memory	i, d, n, s, sf, x, sx, sxf	NZ
1101 raaa	LDBYTEr	Load byte from memory	i, d, n, s, sf, x, sx, sxf	NZ
1110 raaa	STr	Store r to memory	d, n, s, sf, x, sx, sxf	
1111 raaa	STBYTEr	Store byte r to memory	d, n, s, sf, x, sx, sxf	

Figure **5.2**

The Pep/8 instruction set at level Asmb5.

each instruction. The addressing modes column tells what addressing modes are allowed or whether the instruction is unary (U). The status bits column lists the status bits the instruction affects when it executes.

Figure 5.2 shows the unimplemented opcode instructions replaced by five new instructions:

NOPn	Unary no operation trap
NOP	Nonunary no operation trap
DECI	Decimal input trap
DECO	Decimal output trap
STRO	String output trap

The unimplemented opcode instructions at level Asmb5

These new instructions are available to the assembly language programmer at level Asmb5, but they are not part of the instruction set at level ISA3. The operating system at level OS4 provides them with its trap handler. At the assembly level, you may simply program with them as if they were part of the level-ISA3 instruction set, even though they are not. Chapter 8 shows in detail how the operating system provides these instructions. You do not need to know the details of how they are implemented to program with them.

Pseudo-Operations

Pseudo-operations (pseudo-ops) are assembly language statements. Pseudo-ops do not have opcodes and do not correspond to any of the 39 instructions in the Pep/8 instruction set. Pep/8 assembly language has eight pseudo-ops:

.ADDRSS	The address of a symbol
.ASCII	A string of ASCII bytes
.BLOCK	A block of bytes
.BURN	Initiate ROM burn
.BYTE	A byte value
.END	The sentinel for the assembler
.EQUATE	Equate a symbol to a constant value
.WORD	A word value

The eight pseudo-ops of Pep/8 assembly language

All the pseudo-ops except .BURN, .END, and .EQUATE insert data bits into the machine-language program. Pseudo means false. Pseudo-ops are so called because the bits that they generate do not correspond to opcodes, as do the bits generated by the 39 instruction mnemonics. They are not true instruction operations. Pseudo-ops are also called *assembler directives* or *dot commands* because each must be preceded by a . in assembly language.

The next three programs show how to use the .ASCII, .BLOCK, .BYTE, .END, and .WORD pseudo-ops. The other pseudo-ops are described later.

The .ASCII and .END Pseudo-ops

Figure 5.3 is Figure 4.32 written in assembly language instead of machine language. Pep/8 assembly language, unlike C++, is line oriented. That is, each assembly language statement must be contained on only one line. You cannot continue a statement onto another line, nor can you place two statements on the same line.

The line-oriented nature of assembly language

Assembler Input

```
;Stan Warford
;January 13, 2009
;A program to output "Hi"
;
CHARO     0x0007,d    ;Output 'H'
CHARO     0x0008,d    ;Output 'i'
STOP
.ASCII    "Hi"
.END
```

Assembler Output

```
51 00 07 51 00 08 00 48 69 zz
```

Program Output

```
Hi
```

Figure **5.3**

An assembly-language program to output Hi. It is the assembly-language version of Figure 4.32.

Comments begin with a semicolon ; and continue until the end of the line. It is permissible to have a line with only a comment on it, but it must begin with a semicolon. The first four lines of this program are comment lines. The CHARO instructions also contain comments, but only after the assembly language statements. As in C++, your assembly language programs should contain, at a minimum, your name, the date, and a description of the program. To conserve space in this book, however, the rest of the programs do not contain such a heading.

Assembly language comments

CHARO is the mnemonic for the character output instruction. The statement

```
CHARO   0x0007,d   ;Output 'H'
```

means "Output one character from Mem [0007] using the direct addressing mode."

The .ASCII pseudo-op generates contiguous bytes of ASCII characters. In assembly language, you simply write .ASCII followed by a string of ASCII characters enclosed by double quotes. If you want to include a double quote in your string, you must prefix it with a backslash \. To include a backslash, prefix it with a backslash. You can put a newline character in your string by prefixing the letter n with a backslash and a tab character by prefixing the letter t with a backslash.

The .ASCII *pseudo-op*

The backslash prefix

Example 5.2   Here is a string that includes two double quotes:

```
"She said, \"Hello\"."
```

Here is one that includes a backslash character:

```
"My bash is \\."
```

And here is one with the newline character:

```
"\nThis sentence will output on a new line."
```
∎

Any arbitrary byte can be included in a string constant using the \x feature. When you include \x in a string constant, the assembler expects the next two characters to be hexadecimal digits, which specify the byte to be included in the string.

Example 5.3   The dot commands

```
.ASCII "Hello\nworld."
```

and

```
.ASCII "Hello\x0Aworld\x2E"
```

both generate the same sequence of bytes, namely

```
48 65 6C 6C 6F 0A 77 6F 72 6C 64 2E
```
∎

You must end your assembly language program with the .END command. It does not insert data bits into the program the way the .ASCII command does. It simply indicates the end of the assembly language program. The assembler uses .END as a sentinel to know when to stop translating.

The .END *pseudo-op*

Assemblers

Compare this program written in assembly language with the same program written in machine language. Assembly language is much easier to understand because of the mnemonics used in place of the opcodes. Also, the characters H and i written directly as ASCII characters are easier to read.

Unfortunately, you cannot simply write a program in assembly language and expect the computer to understand it. The computer can only execute programs by performing its von Neumann execution cycle (fetch, decode, increment, execute, repeat), which is wired into the CPU. As shown in Chapter 4, the program must be stored in binary in main memory starting at address 0000 for the execution cycle to process it correctly. The assembly language statements must somehow be translated into machine language before they are loaded and executed.

In the early days, programmers wrote in assembly language and then translated each statement into machine language by hand. The translation part was straightforward. It only involved looking up the binary opcodes for the instructions and the binary codes for the ASCII characters in the ASCII table. The hexadecimal operands could similarly be converted to binary with hexadecimal conversion tables. Only after the program was translated could it be loaded and executed.

The translation of a long program was a routine and tedious job. Soon programmers realized that a computer program could be written to do the translation. Such a program is called an assembler, and Figure 5.4 illustrates how it functions.

An assembler is a program whose input is an assembly-language program and whose output is that same program translated into machine language in a format suitable for a loader. Input to the assembler is called the source program. Output from the assembler is called the object program. Figure 5.5 shows the effect of the Pep/8 assembler on the assembly language of Figure 5.3.

It is important to realize that an assembler merely translates a program into a format suitable for a loader. It does not execute the program. Translation and execution are separate processes, and translation always occurs first.

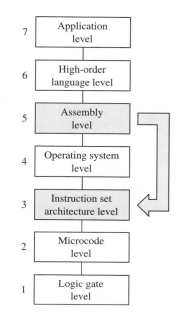

Figure **5.4**

The function of an assembler.

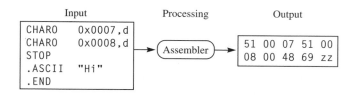

Figure **5.5**

The action of the Pep/8 assembler on the program of Figure 5.3.

Because the assembler is itself a program, it must be written in some programming language. The computer pioneers who wrote the first assemblers had to write them in machine language. Or, if they wrote them in assembly language, they had to translate them into machine language by hand because no assemblers were available at the time. The point is that a machine can only execute programs that are written in machine language.

The .BLOCK Pseudo-op

Figure 5.6 is the assembly language version of Figure 4.34. It inputs two characters and outputs them in reverse order.

Figure **5.6**

An assembly language program to input two characters and output them in reverse order. It is the assembly language version of Figure 4.34.

Assembler Input

```
CHARI    0x000D,d    ;Input first character
CHARI    0x000E,d    ;Input second character
CHARO    0x000E,d    ;Output second character
CHARO    0x000D,d    ;Output first character
STOP
.BLOCK   1           ;Storage for first char
.BLOCK   1           ;Storage for second char
.END
```

Assembler Output

```
49 00 0D 49 00 0E 51 00 0E 51 00 0D 00 00 00 zz
```

Program Input

```
up
```

Program Output

```
pu
```

You can see from the assembler output that the first input statement, CHARI 0x000D,d, translates to 49000D, and the last output statement, CHARO 0x000D,d, translates to 51000D. After that, the STOP statement translates to 00.

The .BLOCK pseudo-ops generate the next two bytes of 0's. The dot command

```
.BLOCK   1
```

means "Generate a block of one byte of storage." The assembler interprets any number not prefixed with 0x as a decimal integer. The digit 1 is therefore interpreted as a decimal integer. The assembler expects a constant after the .BLOCK and will generate that number of bytes of storage, setting them to 0's. In the program, you could replace both .BLOCK commands by a single

```
.BLOCK   2
```

which means "Generate a block of two bytes of storage." Although the assembler output would be the same, you could not write the two separate comments on the .BLOCK lines in the assembly-language program.

The .WORD and .BYTE Pseudo-ops

Figure 5.7 is the same as Figure 4.35, computing 5 plus 3. It illustrates the .WORD pseudo-op.

Assembler Input

```
LDA      0x0011,d   ;A <- first number
ADDA     0x0013,d   ;Add the two numbers
ORA      0x0015,d   ;Convert sum to character
STBYTEA  0x0010,d   ;Store the character
CHARO    0x0010,d   ;Output the character
STOP
.BLOCK   1          ;Character to output
.WORD    5          ;Decimal 5
.WORD    3          ;Decimal 3
.WORD    0x0030     ;Mask for ASCII char
.END
```

Assembler Output

```
C1 00 11 71 00 13 A1 00 15 F1 00 10 51 00 10 00
00 00 05 00 03 00 30 zz
```

Program Output

```
8
```

Figure **5.7**

An assembly language program to add 3 and 5 and output the single-character result. It is the assembly language version of Figure 4.35.

Like the .BLOCK command, the .WORD command generates code for the loader, but with two differences. First, it always generates one word (two bytes) of code, not an arbitrary number of bytes. Second, the programmer can specify the content of the word. The dot command

.WORD 5

means "Generate one word with a value of 5 (dec)." The dot command

.WORD 0x0030

means "Generate one word with a value of 0030 (hex)."

The .BYTE command works like the .WORD command, except that it generates a byte value instead of a word value. In this program, you could replace

.WORD 0x0030

with

.BYTE 0x00
.BYTE 0x30

and generate the same machine language.

You can compare the assembler output of this assembly language program with the hexadecimal machine language of Figure 4.35 to see that they are identical. The assembler was designed to generate output that carefully follows the format expected by the loader. There are no leading blank lines or spaces. There is exactly one space between bytes, with no trailing spaces on a line. The byte sequence terminates with zz.

Using the Pep/8 Assembler

Execution of the program in Figure 5.6, the application program that outputs the two input characters in reverse order, requires the computer runs shown in Figure 5.8.

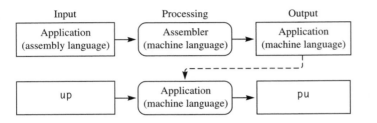

Figure 5.8

Two computer runs necessary for execution of the program in Figure 5.6.

First the assembler is loaded into main memory and the application program is taken as the input file. The output from this run is the machine language version of the application program. It is then loaded into main memory for the second run. All the programs in the center boxes must be in machine language.

The Pep/8 system comes with an assembler as well as the simulator. When you execute the assembler, you must provide it with your assembly language program, previously created with a text editor. If you have made no errors in your program, the assembler will generate the object code in a format suitable for the loader. Otherwise it will protest with one or more error messages and state that no code was generated. After you generate code from an error-free program, you can use it with the simulator as described in Chapter 4.

When writing an assembly language program, you must place at least one space after the mnemonic or dot command. Other than that, there are no restrictions on spacing. Your source program may be in any combination of uppercase or lowercase letters. For example, you could write your source of Figure 5.6 as in Figure 5.9, and the assembler would accept it as valid and generate the correct code.

In addition to generating object code for the loader, the assembler gives you the option of requesting a program listing. The assembler listing converts the source program to a consistent format of uppercase and lowercase letters and spacing. The figure shows the assembler listing from the unformatted source program.

The listing also shows the hexadecimal object code that each line generates and the address of the first byte where it will be loaded by the loader. Note that the .END command did not generate any object code.

Assembler Input

```
chari 0x000D,d    ;Input first character
CHARI    0x000E,d   ;Input second character
charo 0x000E,        d   ;Output second character
CHarO    0x000D,D   ;Output first character
      stop
.bloCK  1 ;Storage for first char
.BLOCK  1            ;Storage for second char
            .END
```

Assembler Listing

```
Addr   Code    Mnemon   Operand    Comment
0000   49000D  CHARI    0x000D,d   ;Input first character
0003   49000E  CHARI    0x000E,d   ;Input second character
0006   51000E  CHARO    0x000E,d   ;Output second character
0009   51000D  CHARO    0x000D,d   ;Output first character
000C   00      STOP
000D   00      .BLOCK   1          ;Storage for first char
000E   00      .BLOCK   1          ;Storage for second char
000F           .END
```

Figure **5.9**

A valid source program and the resulting assembler listing.

This book presents the remaining assembly language programs as assembler listings, but without the column headings produced by the assembler, which are shown in the figure. The second column is the machine language object code, and the first column is the address where the loader will place it in main memory. This layout is typical of most assemblers. It is a vivid presentation of the correspondence between machine language at level ISA3 and assembly language at level Asmb5.

Cross Assemblers

Machines built by one manufacturer generally have different instruction sets from those in machines built by another manufacturer. Hence, a program in machine language for one brand of computer will not run on another machine.

If you write an application in assembly language for a personal computer, you will probably assemble it on the same computer. An assembler written in the same language as the language to which it translates is called a resident assembler. The assembler resides on the same machine as the application program. The two runs of Figure 5.8 are on the same machine.

Resident assemblers

However, it is possible for the assembler to be written in Brand X machine language, but to translate the application program into Brand Y machine language for a different machine. Then the application program cannot be executed on the same machine on which it was translated. It must first be moved from Brand X machine to Brand Y machine.

Cross assemblers

A cross assembler is an assembler that produces an object program for a different machine from the one that runs the assembler. Moving the machine language version of the application program from the output file of Brand X to the main memory of Brand Y is called downloading. Brand X is called the host machine, and Brand Y is called the target machine. In Figure 5.8, the first run would be on the host, and the second run would be on the target.

This situation often occurs when the target machine is a small special-purpose computer, such as the computer that controls the cooking cycles in a microwave oven. Assemblers are large programs that require significant main memory, as well as input and output peripheral devices. The processor that controls a microwave oven has a very small main memory. Its input is simply the buttons on the control panel and perhaps the input signal from the temperature probe. Its output includes the digital display and the signals to control the cooking element. Because it has no input/output files, it cannot be used to run an assembler for itself. Its program must be downloaded from a larger host machine that has previously assembled the program into the target language.

5.2 Immediate Addressing and the Trap Instructions

With direct addressing, the operand specifier is the address in main memory of the operand. Mathematically,

Oprnd = Mem [OprndSpec]

Direct addressing

But with immediate addressing, the operand specifier *is* the operand:

Oprnd = OprndSpec

Immediate addressing

An instruction that uses direct addressing contains the address of the operand. But an instruction that uses immediate addressing contains the operand itself.

Immediate Addressing

Figure 5.10 shows how to write the program in Figure 5.3 with immediate addressing. It outputs the message `Hi`.

```
0000    500048  CHARO   'H',i       ;Output 'H'
0003    500069  CHARO   'i',i       ;Output 'i'
0006    00      STOP
0007            .END
```

Output

```
Hi
```

Figure **5.10**

A program to output `Hi` using immediate addressing.

The assembler translates the character output instruction

```
CHARO 'H',i
```

into object code 500048 (hex), which is

```
0101 0000 0000 0000 0100 1000
```

in binary. A check of Figure 5.2 verifies that 0101 0 is the correct opcode for the CHARO instruction. Also, the addressing-aaa field is 000 (bin), which indicates immediate addressing. As Figure 5.1 shows, the ,i specifies immediate addressing.

Character constants are enclosed in single quotes and always generate one byte of code. In the program of Figure 5.10, the character constant is placed in the operand specifier, which occupies two bytes. In this case, the character constant is positioned in the rightmost byte of the two-byte word.

Character constants

That is how the assembler translates the statement to binary. But what happens when the loader loads the program and the first instruction executes? If the addressing mode were direct, the CPU would interpret 0048 as an address, and it would instruct main memory to put Mem [0048] on the bus for the output device. Because the addressing mode is immediate, the CPU interprets 0048 as the operand itself (not the address of the operand) and puts 48 on the bus for the output device. The second instruction does likewise with 0069.

Immediate addressing has two advantages over direct addressing. The program is shorter because the ASCII string does not need to be stored separately from the instruction. The program in Figure 5.3 has nine bytes, and this program has seven bytes. The instruction also executes faster because the operand is immediately available to the CPU in the instruction register. With direct addressing, the CPU must make an additional access to main memory to get the operand.

Two advantages of immediate addressing over direct addressing

The DECI, DECO, and BR Instructions

Although the assembly language features we have learned so far are a big improvement over machine language, several irritating aspects remain. They are illustrated in the program of Figure 5.11, which inputs a decimal value, adds 1 to it, and outputs the sum.

The first instruction of Figure 5.7,

```
LDA 0x0011,d ;A <- the number
```

puts the content of Mem [0011] into the accumulator. To write this instruction, the programmer had to know that the first number would be stored at address 0011 (hex) after the instruction part of the program. The problem with placing the data at the end of the program is that you do not know exactly how long the instruction part of the program will be until you have finished it. Therefore, you do not know the address of the data while writing the instructions that require that address.

The problem of address computation.

```
0000    040005  BR      0x0005      ;Branch around data
0003    0000    .BLOCK  2           ;Storage for one integer
                ;
0005    310003  DECI    0x0003,d    ;Get the number
0008    390003  DECO    0x0003,d    ;and output it
000B    500020  CHARO   ' ',i       ;Output " + 1 = "
000E    50002B  CHARO   '+',i
0011    500020  CHARO   ' ',i
0014    500031  CHARO   '1',i
0017    500020  CHARO   ' ',i
001A    50003D  CHARO   '=',i
001D    500020  CHARO   ' ',i
0020    C10003  LDA     0x0003,d    ;A <- the number
0023    700001  ADDA    1,i         ;Add one to it
0026    E10003  STA     0x0003,d    ;Store the sum
0029    390003  DECO    0x0003,d    ;Output the sum
002C    00      STOP
002D            .END
```

Input

-479

Output

-479 + 1 = -478

Figure **5.11**

A program to input a decimal value, add 1 to it, and output the sum.

Another problem is program modification. Suppose you want to insert an extra statement in your program. That one modification will change the addresses of the data, and every instruction that refers to the data will need to be modified to reflect the new addresses. It would be easier to program at level Asmb5 if you could place the data at the top of the program. Then you would know the address of the data when you write a statement that refers to that data.

Another irritating aspect of the program in Figure 5.7 is the restriction to single-character results because of the limitations of CHARO. Because CHARO can only output one byte as a single ASCII character, it is difficult to perform I/O on decimal values that require more than one digit for their ASCII representation.

The problem of restricting numeric operations to a single character

The program in Figure 5.11 alleviates both of these irritations. It is a program to input an integer, add 1 to it, and output the sum. It stores the data at the beginning of the program and permits large decimal values.

When you select the execute option in the Pep/8 simulator, PC gets the value 0000 (hex). The CPU will interpret the bytes at Mem [0000] as the first instruction to execute. To place data at the top of the program, we need an instruction that will cause the CPU to skip the data bytes when it fetches the next instruction. The unconditional branch, BR, is such an instruction. It simply places the operand of the instruction in the PC. In this program,

The unconditional branch, BR

```
BR 0005 ;Branch around data
```

places 0005 in the PC. The RTL specification for the BR instruction is

PC ← Oprnd

During the fetch part of the next execution cycle, the CPU will get the instruction at 0005 instead of 0003, which would have happened if the PC had not been altered.

Because the branch instructions almost always use immediate addressing, the Pep/8 assembler does not require that the addressing mode be specified. If you do not specify the addressing mode for a branch instruction, the assembler will assume immediate addressing and generate 000 for the addressing-aaa field.

BR *defaults to immediate addressing*

The correct operation of the BR instruction depends on the details of the von Neumann execution cycle. For example, you may have wondered why the cycle is fetch, decode, *increment, execute*, repeat instead of fetch, decode, *execute, increment*, repeat. Figure 4.33(f) shows the execution of instruction 510007 to output H while the value of PC is 0003, the address of instruction 510008. If the execute part of the von Neumann execution cycle had been before the increment part, then PC would have had the value 0000 when the instruction at address 0000, which was 510007, executes. It seems to make more sense to have PC correspond to the executing instruction. Why doesn't the von Neumann execution cycle have the execute part before the increment part?

Because then BR would not work properly. In Figure 5.11, PC would get 0000, the CPU would fetch the BR instruction, 040005, and BR would execute, placing 0005 in PC. Then PC would increment to 0008. Instead of branching to 0005, your program would branch to 0008. Because the instruction set contains branching instructions, the increment part of the von Neumann execution cycle must be before the execute part.

The reason increment must come before execute in the von Neumann execution cycle

DECI and DECO are two of the instructions the operating system provides to the assembly level that the Pep/8 hardware does not provide at the machine level. DECI, which stands for decimal input, converts a sequence of ASCII digit characters to a single word that corresponds to the two's complement representation of the value. DECO, decimal output, does the opposite conversion from the two's complement value in a word to a sequence of ASCII characters.

DECI permits any number of leading spaces or line feeds on input. The first printable character must be a decimal digit, a +, or a -. The following characters must be decimal digits. DECI sets Z to 1 if you input 0 and N to 1 if you input a negative value. It sets V to 1 if you enter a value that is out of range. Because a

The DECI *instruction*

word is 16 bits and $2^{16} = 32768$, the range is −32768 to 32767 (dec). DECI does not affect the C bit.

DECO prints a - if the value is negative but does not print + if it is positive. It does not print leading 0's and outputs the minimum number of characters possible to properly represent the value. You cannot specify the field width. DECO does not affect the NZVC bits.

The DECO instruction

In Figure 5.11, the statement

```
DECI 0x0003,d ;Get the number
```

when confronted with input sequence −479, converts it to 1111 1110 0010 0001 (bin) and stores it in Mem [0003]. DECO converts the binary sequence to a string of ASCII characters and outputs them.

The STRO Instruction

You might have noticed the program in Figure 5.11 requires seven CHARO instructions to output the string " + 1 = ", one CHARO instruction for each ASCII character that is output. The program in Figure 5.12 illustrates STRO, which means string output. It is another instruction that triggers a trap at the machine level but is a bona fide instruction at the assembly level. It lets you output the entire string of seven characters with only one instruction.

The STRO instruction

```
0000   04000D BR     0x000D     ;Branch around data
0003   0000   .BLOCK 2          ;Storage for one integer
0005   202B20 .ASCII " + 1 = \x00"
       31203D
       2000
                  ;
000D   310003 DECI   0x0003,d   ;Get the number
0010   390003 DECO   0x0003,d   ;and output it
0013   410005 STRO   0x0005,d   ;Output " + 1 = "
0016   C10003 LDA    0x0003,d   ;A <- the number
0019   700001 ADDA   1,i        ;Add one to it
001C   E10003 STA    0x0003,d   ;Store the sum
001F   390003 DECO   0x0003,d   ;Output the sum
0022   00     STOP
0023          .END
```

Figure 5.12

A program identical to that of Figure 5.11 but with the STRO instruction.

Input

```
-479
```

Output

```
-479 + 1 = -478
```

The operand for STRO is a contiguous sequence of bytes, each one of which is interpreted as an ASCII character. The last byte of the sequence must be a byte of all 0's, which the STRO instruction interprets as the sentinel. The instruction outputs the string of bytes from the beginning up to, but not including, the sentinel. In Figure 5.12, the pseudo-op

```
.ASCII " + 1 = \x00"
```

uses \x00 to generate the sentinel byte. The pseudo-op generates eight bytes including the sentinel, but only seven characters are output by the STRO instruction. All eight bytes must be counted when you calculate the operand for the BR instruction.

The assembler listing only allocates room for three bytes in the object code column. If the string in the .ASCII pseudo-op generates more than three bytes, the assembler listing continues the object code on subsequent lines.

Interpreting Bit Patterns

Chapters 4 and 5 progress from a low level of abstraction (ISA3) to a higher one (Asmb5). Even though assembly language at level Asmb5 hides the machine language details, those details are there nonetheless. In particular, the machine is ultimately based on the von Neumann cycle of fetch, decode, increment, execute, repeat. Using pseudo-ops and mnemonics to generate the data bits and instruction bits does not change that property of the machine. When an instruction executes, it executes bits and has no knowledge of how those bits were generated by the assembler. Figure 5.13 shows a nonsense program whose sole purpose is to illustrate this fact. It generates data bits with one kind of pseudo-op that are interpreted by instructions in an unexpected way.

In the program, First is generated as a hexidecimal value with

```
.WORD 0xFFFE ;First
```

but is interpreted as a decimal number with

```
DECO 0x0003,d ;Interpret First as decimal
```

which outputs -2. Of course, if the programmer meant for the bit pattern FFFE to be interpreted as a decimal number, he probably would have written the pseudo-op

```
.WORD -2 ;First
```

This pseudo-op generates the same object code, and the object program would be identical to the original. When DECO executes it does not know how the bits were generated during translation time. It only knows what they are during execution time.

The decimal output instruction

```
DECO 0x0005,d ;Interpret Second and Third as decimal
```

```
0000   040009  BR      0x0009      ;Branch around data
0003   FFFE    .WORD   0xFFFE      ;First
0005   00      .BYTE   0x00        ;Second
0006   55      .BYTE   'U'         ;Third
0007   0470    .WORD   1136        ;Fourth
               ;
0009   390003  DECO    0x0003,d    ;Interpret First as decimal
000C   50000A  CHARO   '\n',i
000F   390005  DECO    0x0005,d    ;Interpret Second and Third as decimal
0012   50000A  CHARO   '\n',i
0015   510006  CHARO   0x0006,d    ;Interpret Third as character
0018   510008  CHARO   0x0008,d    ;Interpret Fourth as character
001B   00      STOP
001C           .END
```

Output

```
-2
85
Up
```

Figure **5.13**

A nonsense program to illustrate the interpretation of bit patterns.

interprets the bits at address 0005 as a decimal number and outputs 85. DECO always outputs the decimal value of two consecutive bytes. In this case, the bytes are 0055 (hex) = 85 (dec). The fact that the two bytes were generated from two different .BYTE dot commands and that one was generated from the hexadecimal constant 0x00 and the other from the character constant 'U' is irrelevant. During execution, the only thing that matters is what the bits are, not where they came from.

The character output instruction

```
CHARO 0x0006,d ;Interpret Third as character
```

interprets the bits at address 0006 as a character. There is no surprise here, because those bits were generated with the .BYTE command using a character constant. As expected, the letter U is output.

The last output instruction

```
CHARO 0x0008,d ;Interpret Fourth as character
```

ouputs the letter p. Why? Because the bits at memory location 0008 are 70 (hex), which are the bits for the ASCII character p. Where did those bits come from? They are the second half of the bits that were generated by

```
.WORD 1136 ;Fourth
```

It just so happens that 1136 (dec) = 0470 (hex) and the second byte of that bit pattern is 70 (hex).

In all these examples, the instruction simply grinds through the von Neumann execution cycle. You must always remember that the translation process is different from the execution process and that translation happens before execution. After translation, when the instructions are executing, the origin of the bits is irrelevant. The only thing that matters is what the bits are, not where they came from during the translation phase.

Disassemblers

An assembler translates each assembly language statement into exactly one machine language statement. Such a transformation is called a *one-to-one mapping*. One assembly language statement maps to one machine language statement. This is in contrast to a compiler, which, as we shall see later, produces a one-to-many mapping.

The one-to-one mapping of an assembler

Given a single assembly language statement, you can always determine the corresponding machine language statement. But can you do the inverse? That is, given a bit sequence in a machine language program, can you determine the original assembly language statement from which the machine language came?

No, you cannot. Even though the transformation is one-to-one, the inverse transformation is not unique. Given the binary machine language sequence

The nonunique nature of the inverse mapping of an assembler

```
0101 0111
```

you cannot tell if the assembly language programmer originally used an ASCII assembler directive for the ASCII character W, or if she wrote the CHARO mnemonic with stack-indexed deferred addressing. The assembler would have produced the exact same sequence of bits, regardless of which of these two assembly language statements was in the original program.

Furthermore, during execution, main memory does not know what the original assembly language statements were. It only remembers the 1's and 0's that the CPU processes via its execution cycle.

Figure 5.14 shows two assembly language programs that produce the same machine language, and so produce identical output. Of course, a serious programmer would not write the second program because it is more difficult to understand than the first program.

Because of pseudo-ops, the inverse assembler mapping is not unique. If there were no pseudo-ops, there would be only one possible way to recover the original assembly language statements from binary object code. Pseudo-ops are for inserting data bits, as opposed to instruction bits, into memory. The fact that data and programs share the same memory is a major cause of the nonunique nature of the inverse assembler mapping.

The cause of the nonunique nature of the inverse mapping

The difficulty of recovering the source program from the object program can be a marketing benefit to the software developer. If you write an application program in assembly language, there are two ways you can sell it. You can sell the

The advantage of object code for software distribution

Assembly Language Program

```
0000  51000A  CHARO   0x000A,d
0003  51000B  CHARO   0x000B,d
0006  51000C  CHARO   0x000C,d
0009  00      STOP
000A  50756E  .ASCII  "Pun"
000D          .END
```

Assembly Language Program

```
0000  51000A  CHARO   0x000A,d
0003  51000B  CHARO   0x000B,d
0006  51000C  CHARO   0x000C,d
0009  00      STOP
000A  50756E  CHARO   0x756E,i
000D          .END
```

Program Output

```
Pun
```

Figure 5.14

Two different source programs that produce the same object program and, therefore, the same output.

source program and let your customer assemble it. Your customer would then have both the source program and the object program. Or you could assemble it yourself and sell only the object program.

In both cases, the customer has the object program necessary for executing the application program. But if he has the source program as well, he can easily modify it to suit his own purposes. He may even enhance it and then try to sell it as an improved version in direct competition with you, with little effort on his part. Modifying a machine language program would be much more difficult. Most commercial software products are sold only in object form to prevent the customer from tampering with the program.

The open-source software movement is a recent development in the computer industry. The idea is that there is a benefit to the customer's having the source program because of support issues. If you own an object program and discover a bug that needs to be fixed or a feature that needs to be added, you must wait for the company who sold you the program to fix the bug or add the feature. But if you own the source, you can modify it yourself to suit your own needs. Some open-source companies actually give away the source code free of charge and derive their income by providing software support for the product. An example of this strategy is the Linux operating system, which is available for free from the Internet. Although such software is free, it requires a higher level of skill to use.

The advantage of source code for software distribution

A *disassembler* is a program that tries to recover the source program from the object program. It can never be 100% successful because of the nonunique nature of the inverse assembler mapping. The programs in this chapter place the data either before or after the instructions. In a large program, sections of data are typically placed throughout the program, making it difficult to distinguish data bits

Disassemblers

from instruction bits in the object code. A disassembler can read each byte and print it out several times—once interpreted as an instruction specifier, once interpreted as an ASCII character, once interpreted as an integer with two's complement binary representation, and so on. A person then can attempt to reconstruct the source program, but the process is tedious.

5.3 Symbols

The previous section introduces `BR` as an instruction to branch around the data at the beginning of the program. Although this technique alleviates the problem of manually determining the address of the data cells, it does not eliminate the problem. You must still determine the addresses by counting in hexadecimal, and if the number of data cells is large, mistakes are likely. Also, if you want to modify the data section, say by removing a `.WORD` command, the addresses of all the data cells following the deletion will change. You must modify any instructions that refer to the modified addresses.

Assembly language symbols eliminate the problem of manually determining addresses. The assembler lets you associate a *symbol*, similar to a C++ identifier, with a *memory address*. Anywhere in the program you need to refer to the address, you can refer to the symbol instead. If you ever modify a program by adding or removing statements, when you reassemble the program the assembler will calculate the new address associated with the symbol. You do not need to rewrite the statements that refer to the changed addresses via the symbols.

The purpose of assembly language symbols

A Program with Symbols

The assembly language of Figure 5.15 produces object code identical to that of Figure 5.12. It uses three symbols, `num`, `msg`, and `main`.

The syntax rules for symbols are similar to the syntax rules for C++ identifiers. The first character must be a letter, and the following characters must be letters or digits. Symbols can be a maximum of only eight characters long. The characters are case sensitive. For example, `Number` would be a different symbol from `number` because of the uppercase `N`.

You can define a symbol on any assembly language line by placing it at the beginning of the line. When you define a symbol, you must terminate it with a colon :. No spaces are allowed between the last character of the symbol and the colon. In this program, the statement

```
num: .BLOCK 2 ;Storage for one integer
```

defines the symbol `num`, in addition to allocating a block of two bytes. Although this line has spaces between the colon and the pseudo-op, the assembler does not require them.

When the assembler detects a symbol definition, it stores the symbol and its value in a symbol table. The value is the address in memory of where the first byte

The value of a symbol is an address.

Assembler Listing

Figure **5.15**

A program that adds 1 to a decimal value. It is identical to Figure 5.12 except that it uses symbols.

```
Addr   Code    Symbol   Mnemon   Operand    Comment
0000   04000D           BR       main       ;Branch around data
0003   0000    num:     .BLOCK   2          ;Storage for one integer
0005   202B20  msg:     .ASCII   " + 1 = \x00"
       31203D
       2000

                  ;
000D   310003  main:    DECI     num,d      ;Get the number
0010   390003           DECO     num,d      ;and output it
0013   410005           STRO     msg,d      ;Output ' + 1 = '
0016   C10003           LDA      num,d      ;A <- the number
0019   700001           ADDA     1,i        ;Add one to it
001C   E10003           STA      num,d      ;Store the sum
001F   390003           DECO     num,d      ;Output the sum
0022   00               STOP
0023                    .END
```

```
Symbol table:
Symbol      Value
main        000D
msg         0005
num         0003
```

Input

```
-479
```

Output

```
-479 + 1 = -478
```

---

of the object code generated from that line will be loaded. If you define any symbols in your program, the assembler listing will include a printout of the symbol table with the values in hexadecimal. Figure 5.15 shows the symbol table printout from the listing of this program. You can see from the table that the value of the symbol num is 0003 (hex).

When you refer to the symbol, you cannot include the colon. The statement

```
LDA num,d ;A <- the number
```

refers to the symbol num. Because num has the value 0003 (hex), this statement generates the same code that

```
LDA 0x0003,d ;A <- the number
```

would generate. Similarly, the statement

```
BR main ;Branch around data
```

generates the same code that

```
BR 0x000D ;Branch around data
```

would generate, because the value of main is 000D (hex).

Note that the value of a symbol is an address, not the content of the cell at that address. When this program executes, Mem [0003] will contain –479 (dec), which it gets from the input device. The value of num will still be 0003 (hex), not –479 (dec), which is different. It might help you to visualize the value of a symbol as coming from the address column on the assembler listing in the line that contains the symbol definition.

Symbols not only relieve you of the burden of calculating addresses manually, they also make your programs easier to read. num is easier on the eyes than 0x0003. Good programmers are careful to select meaningful symbols for their programs to enhance readability.

A von Neumann Illustration

When you program with symbols at level Asmb5, it is easy to lose sight of the von Neumann nature of the computer. The two classic von Neumann bugs—manipulating instructions as if they were data and attempting to execute data as if they were instructions—are still possible.

For example, consider the following assembly language program:

```
this: DECO this,d
      STOP
      .END
```

You might think that the assembler would object to the first statement because it appears to be referring to itself as data in a nonsensical way. But the assembler does not look ahead to the ramifications of execution. Because the syntax is correct, it translates accordingly, as shown in the assembler listing in Figure 5.16.

Assembler Listing

```
0000   390000 this:   DECO    this,d
0003   00             STOP
0004                  .END
```

Output

```
14592
```

Figure **5.16**

A nonsense program that illustrates the underlying von Neumann nature of the machine.

During execution, the CPU interprets 39 as the opcode for the decimal output instruction with direct addressing. It interprets the word at Mem [0000], which is 3900 (hex), as a decimal number and outputs its value, 14592.

It is important to realize that computer hardware has no innate intelligence or reasoning power. The execution cycle and the instruction set are wired into the CPU. As this program illustrates, the CPU has no knowledge of the history of the bits it processes. It has no overall picture. It simply executes the von Neumann cycle over and over again. The same thing is true of main memory, which has no knowledge of the history of the bits it remembers. It simply stores 1's and 0's as commanded by the CPU. Any intelligence or reasoning power must come from software, which is written by humans.

5.4   Translating from Level HOL6

A compiler translates a program in a high-order language (level HOL6) into a lower-level language, so eventually it can be executed by the machine. Some compilers translate directly into machine language (level ISA3), as shown in Figure 5.17(a). Then the program can be loaded into memory and executed. Other compilers translate into assembly language (level Asmb5), as shown in Figure 5.17(b). An assembler then must translate the assembly language program into machine language before it can be loaded and executed.

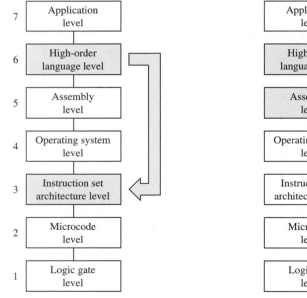

(a) Translation directly to machine language.

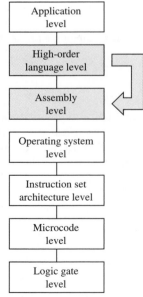

(b) Translation to assembly language.

Figure **5.17**

The function of a compiler.

Like an assembler, a compiler is a program. It must be written and debugged as any other program must be. The input to a compiler is called the source program, and the output from a compiler is called the object program, whether it is machine language or assembly language. This terminology is identical to that for the input and output of an assembler.

Compilers and assemblers are programs.

This section describes the translation process from C++ to Pep/8 assembly language. It shows how a compiler translates cin, cout, and assignment statements, and how it enforces the concept of type at the C++ level. Chapter 6 continues the discussion of the relationship between the high-order languages level (level HOL6) and the assembly level (level Asmb5).

The cout Statement

The program in Figure 5.18 shows how a compiler would translate a simple C++ program with one output statement into assembly language.

High-Order Language

```
#include <iostream>
using namespace std;
int main () {
   cout << "Love" << endl;
   return 0;
}
```

Figure **5.18**

The cout statement at level HOL6 and level Asmb5.

Assembly Language

```
0000   410007           STRO    msg,d
0003   50000A           CHARO   '\n',i
0006   00               STOP
0007   4C6F76 msg:      .ASCII  "Love\x00"
       6500
000C                    .END
```

Output

```
Love
```

The compiler translates the single C++ statement

```
cout << "Love" << endl;
```

into two executable assembly language statements   *Translating* cout

```
STRO msg,d
CHARO '\n',i
```

and one dot command

```
msg: .ASCII "Love\x00"
```

The STRO instruction corresponds to sending "Love" to cout, and the CHARO instruction corresponds to sending endl to cout. This is a one-to-three mapping. In contrast to an assembler, the mapping for a compiler generally is not one-to-one, but one-to-many. This program and all the ones that follow place string constants at the bottom of the program. Data that correspond to variable values are placed at the top of the program to correspond to their placement in the HOL6 program.

The compiler translates the C++ statement

```
return 0;
```
Translating return 0 *in* main()

into the assembly language statement

```
STOP
```

return statements for C++ functions other than main() do not translate to STOP. This tranlation of return for main() is a simplification. A real C++ compiler must generate code that executes on a particular operating system. It is up to the operating system to interpret the value returned. A common convention is that a returned value of 0 indicates that no errors occurred during the program's execution. If an error did occur, the program returns some nonzero value, but what happens in such a case depends on the particular operating system. In the Pep/8 system, returning from main() corresponds to terminating the program. Hence, returning from main() will always translate to STOP. Chapter 6 shows how the compiler translates returns from functions other than main().

Other elements of the C++ program are not even translated directly. For example,

```
#include <iostream>
using namespace std;
```

do not appear in the assembly language program at all. A real compiler would use the include and using statements to make the correct interface to the operating system and its library. The Pep/8 system ignores these kinds of details to keep things simple at the introductory level.

Figure 5.19 shows the input and output of a compiler with this program. Part (a) is a compiler that translates directly into machine language. The object program could be loaded and executed. Part (b) is a compiler that translates to assembly language at level Asmb5. The object program would need to be assembled before it could be loaded and executed.

Input   Processing   Output

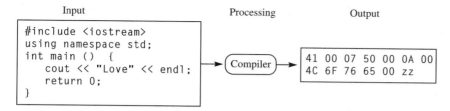

(a) A compiler that translates directly into machine language.

Figure **5.19**

The action of a compiler on the program in Figure 5.18.

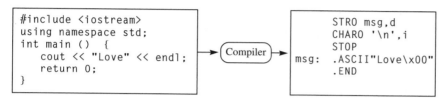

(b) A compiler that translates into assembly language.

Variables and Types

Every C++ variable has three attributes—name, type, and value. For each variable that is declared, the compiler reserves one or more memory cells in the machine language program. A variable in a high-order language is simply a memory location in a low-level language. Level-HOL6 programs refer to variables by names, which are C++ identifiers. Level-ISA3 programs refer to them by addresses. The value of the variable is the value in the memory cell at the address associated with the C++ identifier.

The compiler must remember which address corresponds to which variable name in the level-HOL6 program. It uses a symbol table to make the connection between variable names and addresses.

The symbol table for a compiler is similar to, but inherently more complicated than, the symbol table for an assembler. A variable name in C++ is not limited to eight characters, as is a symbol in Pep/8. In addition, the symbol table for a compiler must store the variable's type as well as its associated address.

The symbol table for a compiler

A compiler that translates directly to machine language does not require a second translation with an assembler. Figure 5.20(a) shows the mapping produced by

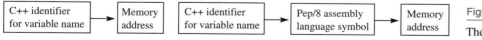

(a) A compiler that translates to machine language.   **(b)** A hypothetical compiler for illustrative purposes.

Figure **5.20**

The mapping a compiler makes between a level-HOL6 variable and a level-ISA3 storage location.

the symbol table for such a compiler. The programs in this book illustrate the translation process for a hypothetical compiler that translates to assembly language, however, because assembly language is easier to read than machine language. Variable names in C++ correspond to symbols in Pep/8 assembly language, as Figure 5.20(b) shows.

The correspondence in Figure 5.20(b) is unrealistic for compilers that translate to assembly language. Consider the problem of a C++ program that has two variables named `discountRate1` and `discountRate2`. Because they are longer than eight characters, the compiler would have a difficult time mapping the identifiers to unique Pep/8 symbols. Our examples will limit the C++ identifiers to, at most, eight characters to make clear the correspondence between C++ and assembly language. Real compilers that translate to assembly language typically do not use assembly language symbols for the variable names.

Global Variables and Assignment Statements

The C++ program in Figure 5.21 is from Figure 2.4 (page 36). It shows assignment statements with global variables at level HOL6 and the corresponding assembly language program, which the compiler produces. The object program contains comments. Real compilers do not generate comments because human programmers usually do not need to read the object program.

Remember that a compiler is a program. It must be written and debugged just like any other program. A compiler to translate C++ programs can be written in any language—even C++! The following program segment illustrates some details of this incestuous state of affairs. It is part of a simplified compiler that translates C++ source programs into assembly language object programs:

```
typedef int HexDigit;
enum KindType {sInt, sBool, sChar, sFloat};
struct SymbolTableEntry {
   char symbol[32];
   HexDigit value[4];
   KindType kind;
};


SymbolTableEntry symbolTable[100];
```

A symbol table definition for a hypothetical compiler

An entry in a symbol table contains three parts—the symbol itself; its value, which is the address in Pep/8 memory where the value of the variable will be stored; and the kind of value that is stored, that is, the variable's type.

Figure 5.22 shows the entries in the symbol table for this program. The first variable has the symbolic name `ch`. The compiler allocates the byte at Mem [0003] by generating the `.BLOCK` command and stores its type as `sChar` in the symbol table, an indication that the variable is a C++ character. The second variable has the sym-

High-Order Language

```
#include <iostream>
using namespace std;

char ch;
int j;

int main () {
   cin >> ch >> j;
   j += 5;
   ch++;
   cout << ch << endl << j << endl;
   return 0;
}
```

Assembly Language

```
0000   040006          BR      main
0003   00      ch:     .BLOCK  1        ;global variable #1c
0004   0000    j:      .BLOCK  2        ;global variable #2d
                       :
0006   490003  main:   CHARI   ch,d     ;cin >> ch
0009   310004          DECI    j,d      ;    >> j
000C   C10004          LDA     j,d      ;j += 5
000F   700005          ADDA    5,i
0012   E10004          STA     j,d
0015   D10003          LDBYTEA ch,d     ;ch++
0018   700001          ADDA    1,i
001B   F10003          STBYTEA ch,d
001E   510003          CHARO   ch,d     ;cout << ch
0021   50000A          CHARO   '\n',i   ;    << endl
0024   390004          DECO    j,d      ;    << j
0027   50000A          CHARO   '\n',i   ;    << endl
002A   00              STOP
002B                   .END
```

Input

M 419

Output

N
424

Figure **5.21**

The assignment statement with global variables at levels HOL6 and Asmb5. The C++ program is from Figure 2.4.

bolic name j. The compiler allocates two bytes at Mem [0004] for its value and stores its type as sInt, indicating a C++ integer. It gets the types from the variable declaration of the C++ program.

During the code generation phase, the compiler translates

```
cin >> ch >> j;
```

into

```
CHARI 0x0003,d
DECI 0x0004,d
```

	symbol	value	kind
[0]	ch	0003	sChar
[1]	j	0004	sInt
[2]	⋮	⋮	⋮

Figure **5.22**

The symbol table for a hypothetical compiler that translates the program in Figure 5.21.

It consults the symbol table, which was filled at an earlier phase of compilation, to determine the addresses for the operands of the CHARI and DECI instructions. As explained previously, our listing shows the generated instructions as

```
CHARI ch,d
DECI j,d
```

for readability.

Note that the value stored in the symbol table is not the value of the variable during execution. It is the memory address of where that value will be stored. If the user enters 419 for j during execution, then the value stored at Mem [0004] will be 01A3 (hex), which is the binary representation of 419 (dec). The symbol table contains 0004, not 01A3, as the value of the symbol j at translation time. Values of C++ variables do not exist at translation time. They exist at execution time.

Assigning a value to a variable at level HOL6 corresponds to storing a value in memory at level Asmb5. The compiler translates the assignment statement

```
j += 5;
```

into

```
LDA j,d
ADDA 5,i
STA j,d
```

An assignment statement at level Asmb5

LDA and ADDA perform the computation on the righthand side of the assignment statement, leaving the result of the computation in the accumulator. STA assigns the result back to j.

This assignment statement illustrates the general rules for accessing global variables:

- The symbol for the variable is the address of the value.
- The value is accessed with direct addressing.

The rules for accessing global variables

In this case, the symbol for the global variable j is the address 0004, and the LDA and STA statements use direct addressing.

Similarly, the compiler translates

```
ch++
```

into

```
LDBYTEA ch,d
ADDA 1,i
STBYTEA ch,d
```

The increment statement at level Asmb5

The same instruction that adds 5 to j, ADDA, performs the increment operation on ch. Again, because ch is a global variable, its value is its address 0003 and the LDBYTEA and STBYTEA instructions use direct addressing.

The compiler translates

```
cout << ch << endl << j << endl;
```

into

```
CHARO ch,d
CHARO '\n',i
DECO j,d
CHARO '\n',i
```

The output operator at level Asmb5

using direct addressing to output the values of the global variables ch and j.

The compiler must search its symbol table to make the connection between a symbol such as ch and its address, 0003. The symbol table is an array. If it is not maintained in alphabetic order by symbolic name, a sequential search would be necessary to locate ch in the table. If the symbolic names are in alphabetic order, a binary search is possible.

Type Compatibility

To see how type compatibility is enforced at level HOL6, suppose you have two variables, integer j and floating-point y, in a C++ program. Also suppose that you have a computer unlike Pep/8 that is able to store and manipulate floating-point values—let's call it Pep/99. Floating-point numbers are not encoded in binary the same way integers are. They are stored in binary scientific notation with separate cells reserved for the exponent part and the magnitude part. The compiler's symbol table for your program might look something like Figure 5.23.

Now consider the operation j % 8 in C++. % is the modulus operator, which is restricted to operate on integer values. In binary, to perform j % 8, you simply set all the bits except the rightmost three bits to 0. For example, if j has the value 61 (dec) = 0011 1101 (bin), then j % 8 has the value 5 (dec) = 0000 0101 (bin), which is 0011 1101 with all bits except the rightmost three set to 0.

	symbol	value	kind
[0]	j	0003	sInt
[1]	y	0005	sFloat
[2]	⋮	⋮	⋮

Figure **5.23**

The symbol table for a Pep/99 compiler.

Suppose the following statement appears in your C++ program:

```
j = j % 8;
```

The compiler would consult the symbol table and determine that `kind` for the variable j is `sInt`. It would also recognize 8 as an integer constant and determine that the % operation is legal. It would then generate the object code

```
LDA j,d
ANDA 0x0007,i
STA j,d
```

Now suppose that the following statement appears in your C++ program:

```
y = y % 8;
```

Illegal at level HOL6

The compiler would consult the symbol table and determine that `kind` for the variable y is `sFloat`. It would determine that the % operation is not legal because it can be applied only to integer types. It would then generate the error message

```
error: float operand for %
```

and would generate no object code. If, however, there were no type checking, the following code would be generated:

```
LOADA y,d
ANDA 0x0007,i
STOREA y,d
```

Legal at level Asmb5

Indeed, there is nothing to prevent an assembly language programmer from writing this code, even though its execution would produce meaningless results.

Having the compiler check for type compatibility is a tremendous help. It keeps you from writing meaningless statements, such as performing a % operation on a float variable. When you program directly in assembly language at level Asmb5, there are no type compatibility checks. All data consists of bits. When bugs occur due to incorrect data movements, they can only be detected at run-time, not at translation time. That is, they are logical errors instead of syntax errors. Logical errors are notoriously more difficult to locate than syntax errors.

Type compatibility enforced by the compiler

Pep/8 Symbol Tracer

Pep/8 has three symbolic trace features corresponding to the three parts of the C++ memory model—the global tracer for global variables, the stack tracer for parameters and local variables, and the heap tracer for dynamically allocated variables. To trace a variable, the programmer embeds trace tags in the comments associated with the variables and single steps through the program. The Pep/8 integrated development environment shows the run-time values of the variables.

There are two kinds of trace tags:

- Format trace tags

Trace tags

- Symbol trace tags

Trace tags are contained in assembly language comments and have no effect on generated object code. Each trace tag begins with the # character and supplies information to the symbol tracer on how to format and label the memory cell in the trace window. Trace tag errors show up as warnings when the code is assembled, allowing program execution without tracing turned on. However, they do prevent tracing until they are corrected.

The global tracer allows the user to specify which global symbol to trace by placing a format trace tag in the comment of the .BLOCK line where the global variable is declared. For example, these two lines from Figure 5.21,

```
ch: .BLOCK  1   ;global variable #1c
j:  .BLOCK  2   ;global variable #2d
```

have format trace tags #1c and #2d. You should read the first format trace tag as "one byte, character." This trace tag tells the symbol tracer to display the content of the one-byte memory cell at the address specified by the value of the symbol, along with the symbol ch itself. Similarly, the second trace tag tells the symbol tracer to display the two-byte cell at the address specified by j as a decimal integer.

The legal format trace tags are:

#1c   One-byte character

The format trace tags

#1d   One-byte decimal

#2d   Two-byte decimal

#1h   One-byte hexadecimal

#2h   Two-byte hexadecimal

Global variables do not require the use of symbol trace tags, because the Pep/8 symbol tracer takes the symbol from the .BLOCK line on which the trace tag is placed. Local variables, however, require symbol trace tags, which are described in Chapter 6.

The Shift and Rotate Instructions

Pep/8 has two arithmetic shift instructions and two rotate instructions. All four are unary with the following instruction specifiers, mnemonics, and status bits that they affect:

0001 110r	ASLr	Arithmetic shift left r	NZVC
0001 111r	ASRr	Arithmetic shift right r	NZC
0010 000r	ROLr	Rotate left r	C
0010 001r	RORr	Rotate right r	C

The shift and rotate instructions

The shift and rotate instructions have no operand specifier. Each one operates on either the accumulator or the index register depending on the value of r. As described in Chapter 3, a shift left multiplies a signed integer by 2, and a shift right divides a signed integer by 2. Rotate left rotates each bit to the left by one bit, sending the most significant bit into C and C into the least significant bit. Rotate right rotates each bit to the right by one bit, sending the least significant bit into C and C into the most significant bit.

The Register Transfer Language (RTL) specification for the ASLr instruction is

$$C \leftarrow r\langle 0 \rangle, \ r\langle 0..14 \rangle \leftarrow r\langle 1..15 \rangle, \ r\langle 15 \rangle \leftarrow 0;$$
$$N \leftarrow r < 0, \ Z \leftarrow r = 0, \ V \leftarrow \{overflow\}$$

The RTL specification for the ASRr instruction is

$$C \leftarrow r\langle 15 \rangle, \ r\langle 1..15 \rangle \leftarrow r\langle 0..14 \rangle; \ N \leftarrow r < 0, \ Z \leftarrow r = 0$$

The RTL specification for the ROLr instruction is

$$C \leftarrow r\langle 0 \rangle, \ r\langle 0..14 \rangle \leftarrow r\langle 1..15 \rangle, \ r\langle 15 \rangle \leftarrow C$$

The RTL specification for the RORr instruction is

$$C \leftarrow r\langle 15 \rangle, \ r\langle 1..15 \rangle \leftarrow r\langle 0..14 \rangle, \ r\langle 0 \rangle \leftarrow C$$

Example 5.4 Suppose the instruction to be executed is 1E in hexadecimal, which Figure 5.24 shows in binary. The opcode indicates that the ASRr instruction will execute, and the register-r field indicates that the instruction will affect the accumulator.

Figure 5.25 shows the effect of executing the ASRA instruction assuming the accumulator has an initial content of 0098 (hex) = 152 (dec). The ASRA instruction changes the bit pattern to 004C (hex) = 76 (dec), which is half of 152. The N bit is 0

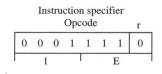

Figure 5.24

The ASRA instruction.

Atanasoff, Mauchly, Eckert

Determining the founder of the modern computer is a complex problem. We must acknowledge contributions such as the ancient Chinese abacus, Charles Babbage's analytical engine of the 1800s, and Lady Lovelace's musings on computation, but the real objects of our search are the immediate inventors of electronic digital computers. Candidates include John Atanasoff, Clifford Berry, John Mauchly, J. Presper Eckert, Konrad Zuse, and John von Neumann; each of these men actively pursued the research and development of electronic computing devices during the late 1930s and early 1940s.

Throughout the 1950s and 1960s, it was generally accepted that Mauchly and Eckert were the fathers of the electronic computer, and that the ENIAC (Electronic Numerical Integrator and Calculator), completed in 1945, was the first electronic computer. Mauchly's and Eckert's successful work on the ENIAC attracted grant money, then spun off into commercial ventures. Their work also became very high profile when the U.S. military decided to use the ENIAC to help compute ballistics tables quickly and accurately.

Sperry Rand bought the patent for the ENIAC and its underlying concepts in 1951. Subsequently, the company required other computer manufacturers to pay royalties to use the important concepts that they owned—in particular, the fundamental architectural structures found in all modern computers, such as circuitry for doing arithmetic via logical switching and memory refresh circuits to prevent the decay of electronically represented information. Honeywell did not want to get into the expensive bind of paying royalties for every computer they would build and sell, so they sent their lawyers to research the history of modern computers.

The lawyers from Honeywell presented evidence that John Atanasoff and Clifford Berry of Iowa State College had beaten Mauchly and Eckert to the punch by several years. ENIAC was not operational

until 1945; however Atanasoff had working prototypes by 1939 and a special-purpose computer by 1942. Atanasoff's machine contained the memory refresh circuitry and electronic adder/subtractor circuits that were used in ENIAC and in almost all other commercially successful machines. Also, the Honeywell lawyers discovered that Mauchly visited Atanasoff for several days during June 1941 and that some of Atanasoff's ideas appeared in Mauchly's project after that time. All this information strongly suggested that Atanasoff's work directly influenced the development of the ENIAC. In the end, the courts invalidated the ENIAC patent in 1973, declaring that Atanasoff's contributions were significant and that Mauchly borrowed on those ideas. Atanasoff could have applied for a patent if he had wanted to protect himself. But Atanasoff and Berry didn't market their research very aggressively, and their project fell into stagnation when they had to serve in World War II.

Konrad Zuse also had a general-purpose computer in mind at about the same time as Atanasoff, Berry, Mauchly, and Eckert did. Unfortunately, Zuse lived and worked in Nazi Germany, so the seeds of his ideas never bore fruit.

"We anticipate a global world market with place for perhaps five computers."

—*Tom Watson*
Chairman, IBM 1949

Figure **5.25**

Execution of the ASRA instruction.

because the quantity in the accumulator is positive. The Z bit is 0 because the accumulator is not all 0's. The C bit is 0 because the least significant bit was 0 before the shift occurred.   ∎

Constants and .EQUATE

.EQUATE is one of the few pseudo-ops to not generate any object code. Furthermore, the normal mechanism of taking the value of a symbol from the address of the object code does not apply. .EQUATE operates as follows:

The operation of .EQUATE

- It must be on a line that defines a symbol.
- It equates the value of the symbol to the value that follows the .EQUATE.
- It does not generate any object code.

The C++ compiler uses the .EQUATE dot command to translate C++ constants.

The C++ program in Figure 5.26 is identical to the one in Figure 2.6 (page 39), except that the variables are global instead of local. It shows how to translate a C++ constant to machine language. It also illustrates the ASRA assembly language statement. The program calculates a value for score as the average of two exam grades plus a five-point bonus.

High-Order Language

```cpp
#include <iostream>
using namespace std;

const int bonus = 5;
int exam1;
int exam2;
int score;

int main () {
   cin >> exam1 >> exam2;
   score = (exam1 + exam2) / 2 + bonus;
   cout << "score = " << score << endl;
   return 0;
}
```

Figure **5.26**

A program for which the compiler translates a C++ constant to machine language.

Assembly Language

Figure **5.26**

(Continued)

```
0000   040009           BR       main
               bonus:   .EQUATE  5         ;constant
0003   0000   exam1:    .BLOCK   2         ;global variable #2d
0005   0000   exam2:    .BLOCK   2         ;global variable #2d
0007   0000   score:    .BLOCK   2         ;global variable #2d
               ;
0009   310003 main:     DECI     exam1,d   ;cin >> exam1
000C   310005           DECI     exam2,d   ;    >> exam2
000F   C10003           LDA      exam1,d   ;score = (exam1
0012   710005           ADDA     exam2,d   ;    + exam2)
0015   1E               ASRA               ;    / 2
0016   700005           ADDA     bonus,i   ;    + bonus
0019   E10007           STA      score,d
001C   410026           STRO     msg,d     ;cout << "score = "
001F   390007           DECO     score,d   ;    << score
0022   50000A           CHARO    '\n',i    ;    << endl
0025   00               STOP
0026   73636F msg:      .ASCII   "score = \x00"
       726520
       3D2000
002F                    .END
```

```
Symbol table:
Symbol     Value      Symbol     Value
bonus      0005       exam1      0003
exam2      0005       score      0007
main       0009       msg        0026
```

Input

68 84

Output

score = 81

The compiler translates

```
const int bonus = 5;
```

as

```
bonus: .EQUATE 5
```

The assembly language listing in Figure 5.26 is notable on two counts. First, the line that contains the .EQUATE has no code in the machine language column. There is not even an address in the address column because there is no code to which the address would apply. This is consistent with the rule that .EQUATE does not generate code. Second, Figure 5.26 includes the symbol table from the assembler listing. You can see from the table that symbol bonus has the value 5. The symbol exam2 also has the value 5 but for a different reason. exam2 has a value of 5 because the code generated for it by the .BLOCK dot command is at address 0005 (hex). But, there is no code for bonus, which has the value 5 because it was set to 5 by the .EQUATE dot command.

The I/O and assignment statements are similar to those in previous programs. cin translates to DECI or CHARI as required, and cout to DECO or CHARO, all with direct addressing for the global variables. In general, assignment statements translate to

- load register,
- evaluate expression if necessary, and
- store register.

Translating assignment statements

To compute the expression

```
(exam1 + exam2) / 2 + bonus
```

the compiler generates code to load the value of exam1 into the accumulator, add the value of exam2 to it, and divide the sum by 2 with the ASRA instruction. The LDA and ADDA instructions use direct addressing because exam1 and exam2 are global variables.

But how does the compiler generate code to add bonus? It cannot use direct addressing, because there is no object code corresponding to bonus, and hence no address. Instead, the statement

```
ADDA bonus,i
```

uses immediate addressing. In this case, the operand specifier is 0005 (hex) = 5 (dec), which is the value to be added. The general rule for translating C++ constants to assembly language is:

- Declare the constant with .EQUATE.
- Access the constant with immediate addressing.

Translating C++ constants

In a more realistic program, score would have type float, and you would compute the average with the real division operator. Pep/8 does not have hardware support for real numbers. Nor does its instruction set contain instructions for multiplying or dividing integers. These operations must be programmed with the shift left and shift right instructions.

Placement of Instructions and Data

The purpose this book is to show the correspondence between the levels of abstraction in a typical computer system. Consequently, the general program structure of an Asmb5 translation corresponds to the structure of the translated HOL6 program. Specifically, global variables appear before the main program in both the Asmb5 program and the HOL6 program. Real compilers do not have that constraint and often alter the placement of programs and data. Figure 5.27 is a different translation of the C++ program in Figure 5.26. One benefit of this translation is the absence of the initial branch to the main program.

```
0000   31001D main:    DECI    exam1,d     ;cin >> exam1
0003   31001F          DECI    exam2,d     ;    >> exam2
0006   C1001D          LDA     exam1,d     ;score = (exam1
0009   71001F          ADDA    exam2,d     ;    + exam2)
000C   1E              ASRA                ;    / 2
000D   700005          ADDA    bonus,i     ;    + bonus
0010   E10021          STA     score,d
0013   410023          STRO    msg,d       ;cout << "score = "
0016   390021          DECO    score,d     ;    << score
0019   50000A          CHARO   '\n',i      ;    << endl
001C   00              STOP
                       ;
               bonus:  .EQUATE 5           ;constant
001D   0000    exam1:  .BLOCK  2           ;global variable #2d
001F   0000    exam2:  .BLOCK  2           ;global variable #2d
0021   0000    score:  .BLOCK  2           ;global variable #2d
0023   73636F  msg:    .ASCII  "score = \x00"
       726520
       3D2000
002C                   .END

Symbol table:
Symbol     Value    Symbol    Value
main       0000     bonus     0005
exam1      001D     exam2     001F
score      0021     msg       0023
```

Figure **5.27**

A translation of the C++ program in Figure 5.26 with a different placement of instructions and data.

SUMMARY

An assembler is a program that translates a program in assembly language into the equivalent program in machine language. The von Neumann design principle calls for instructions as well as data to be stored in main memory. Corresponding to each of these bit sequences are two types of assembly language statements. For program statements, assembly language uses mnemonics in place of opcodes and register-r fields, hexadecimal instead of binary for the operand specifiers, and mnemonic letters for the addressing modes. For data statements, assembly language uses pseudo-ops, also called dot commands.

With direct addressing, the operand specifier is the address in main memory of the operand. But with immediate addressing, the operand specifier is the operand. In mathematical notation, Oprnd = OprndSpec. Immediate addressing is preferable to direct addressing because the operand does not need to be stored separately from the instruction. Such instructions execute faster because the operand is immediately available to the CPU in the instruction register.

Assembly language symbols eliminate the problem of manually determining the addresses of data and instructions in a program. The value of a symbol is an address. When the assembler detects a symbol definition, it stores the symbol and its value in a symbol table. When the symbol is used, the assembler substitutes its value in place of the symbol.

A variable at the high-order languages level (level HOL6) corresponds to a memory location at the assembly level (level Asmb5). An assignment statement at level HOL6 that assigns an expression to a variable translates to a load, followed by an expression evaluation, followed by a store at level Asmb5. Type compatibility at level HOL6 is enforced by the compiler with the help of its symbol table, which is more complex than the symbol table of an assembler. At level Asmb5, the only type is bit, and any operation can be performed on any bit pattern.

EXERCISES

Section 5.1

*1. Convert the following machine language instructions into assembly language, assuming that they were not generated by pseudo-ops:

(a) AAEF2A
(b) 02
(c) D7003D

2. Convert the following machine language instructions into assembly language, assuming that they were not generated by pseudo-ops:

(a) 92B7DE
(b) 03
(c) DF63DF

*3. Convert the following assembly language instructions into hexadecimal machine language:

(a) `ASLA`
(b) `CHARI 0x000F,s`
(c) `BRNE 0x01E6,i`

4. Convert the following assembly language instructions into hexadecimal machine language:

(a) `ADDA 0x01FE,i`
(b) `STRO 0x000D,sf`
(c) `LDX 0x01FF,s`

*5. Convert the following assembly language pseudo-ops into hexadecimal machine language:

   (a) `.ASCII "Bear\x00"`
   (b) `.BYTE 0xF8`
   (c) `.WORD 790`

6. Convert the following assembly language pseudo-ops into hexadecimal machine language:

   (a) `.BYTE 13`
   (b) `.ASCII "Frog\x00"`
   (c) `.WORD -6`

*7. Predict the output of the following assembly language program:

```
CHARO 0x000C,d
CHARO 0x000B,d
CHARO 0x000A,d
STOP
.ASCII "gum"
.END
```

8. Predict the output of the following assembly language program:

```
CHARO 0x0008,d
CHARO 0x0007,d
STOP
.ASCII "is"
.END
```

9. Predict the output of the following assembly language program if the input is g. Predict the output if the input is A. Explain the difference between the two results:

```
CHARI 0x0010,d
LDBYTEA 0x0010,d
ANDA 0x0011,d
STBYTEA 0x0010,d
CHARO 0x0010,d
STOP
.BLOCK 1
.WORD 0x00DF
.END
```

Section 5.2

*10. Predict the output of the program in Figure 5.13 if the dot commands are changed to

```
.WORD 0xFFC7 ;First
.BYTE 0x00 ;Second
.BYTE 'H' ;Third
.WORD 873 ;Fourth
```

11. Predict the output of the program in Figure 5.13 if the dot commands are changed to

```
.WORD 0xFE63 ;First
.BYTE 0x00 ;Second
.BYTE 'b' ;Third
.WORD 1401 ;Fourth
```

12. Determine the object code and predict the output of the following assembly language programs:

*(a)

```
DECO 'm',i
CHARO '\n',i
DECO "mm",i
CHARO '\n',i
CHARO 0x0026,i
STOP
.END
```

(b)

```
DECO 'Q',i
CHARO '\n',i
DECO 0xFFC3,i
CHARO '\n',i
CHARO 0x007D,i
STOP
.END
```

Section 5.3

*13. In the following code, determine the values of the symbols here and there. Write the object code in hexadecimal. (Do not predict the output.)

```
        BR      there
here:   .WORD   9
there:  DECO    here,d
        STOP
        .END
```

14. In the following code, determine the values of the symbols this, that, and theOther. Write the object code in hexadecimal. (Do not predict the output.)

```
         BR      theOther
this:    .WORD   17
that:    .WORD   19
theOther:DECO    this,d
         DECO    that,d
         STOP
         .END
```

*15. In the following code, determine the value of the symbol this. Predict and explain the output of the assembly language program:

```
this:   CHARO   this,d
        STOP
        .END
```

16. In the following code, determine the value of the symbol this. Predict and explain the output of the assembly language program:

```
this:   DECO    this,d
        STOP
        .END
```

Section 5.4

17. How are the symbol table of an assembler and a compiler similar? How do they differ?

*18. How does a C++ compiler enforce type compatibility?

19. Assume that you have a Pep/8-type computer and the following disk files:

■ File A: A Pep/8 assembly language assembler written in machine language

■ File B: A C++-to-assembly-language compiler written in assembly language

■ File C: A C++ program that will read numbers from a data file and print their median

■ File D: A data file for the median program of file C

To compute the median, you must make the four computer runs described schematically in Figure 5.28. Each run involves an input file that will be operated on by a program to produce an output file. The output file produced by one run may be used either as the input file or as the program of a subsequent run. Describe the content of files E, F, G, and H, and label the empty blocks in Figure 5.28 with the appropriate file letter.

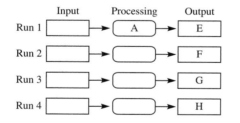

Figure **5.28**

The computer runs for Exercise 19.

PROBLEMS

Section 5.1

20. Write an assembly language program that prints your first name on the screen. Use the .ASCII pseudo-op to store the characters at the bottom of your program. Use the CHARO instruction to output the characters.

Section 5.2

21. Write an assembly language program that prints your first name on the screen. Use immediate addressing with a character constant to designate the operand of CHARO for each letter of your name.

22. Write an assembly language program that prints your first name on the screen. Use immediate addressing with a decimal constant to designate the operand of CHARO for each letter of your name.

23. Write an assembly language program that prints your first name on the screen. Use immediate addressing with a hexadecimal constant to designate the operand of CHARO for each letter of your name.

Section 5.4

24. Write an assembly language program that corresponds to the following C++ program:

```cpp
#include <iostream>
using namespace std;

int num1;
int num2;
main () {
    cin >> num1 >> num2;
    cout << num2 << endl << num1 << endl;
    return 0;
}
```

25. Write an assembly language program that corresponds to the following C++ program:

```cpp
#include <iostream>
using namespace std;

const char chConst = 'a';
char ch1;
char ch2;

int main () {
    cin >> ch1 >> ch2;
    cout << ch1 << chConst << ch2;
    return 0;
}
```

26. Write an assembly language program that corresponds to the following C++ program:

```cpp
#include <iostream>
using namespace std;

const int amount = 20000;
int num;
int sum;

int main () {
    cin >> num;
    sum = num + amount;
    cout << "sum = " << sum << endl;
    return 0;
}
```

Test your program twice. The first time, enter a value for num to make the sum within the allowed range for the Pep/8 computer. The second time, enter a value that is in range but that makes sum outside the range. Note that the out-of-range condition does not cause an error message but just gives an incorrect value. Explain the value.

27. Write an assembly language program that corresponds to the following C++ program:

```
#include <iostream>
using namespace std;

int width;
int length;
int perim;

int main () {
    cin >> width >> length;
    perim = (width + length) * 2;
    cout << "w = " << width << endl;
    cout << "l = " << length << endl;
    cout << endl;
    cout << "p = " << perim << endl;
    return 0;
}
```

28. Write an assembly language program that corresponds to the following C++ program:

```
#include <iostream>
using namespace std;

char ch;

int main () {
    cin >> ch;
    ch--;
    cout << ch << endl;
    return 0;
}
```

29. Write an assembly language program that corresponds to the following C++ program:

```
#include <iostream>
using namespace std;

int num1;
int num2;

int main () {
    cin >> num1;
    num2 = -num1;
    cout << "num1 = " << num1 << endl;
    cout << "num2 = " << num2 << endl;
    return 0;
}
```

30. Write an assembly language program that corresponds to the following C++ program:

```
#include <iostream>
using namespace std;

int num;

int main () {
    cin >> num;
    num = num / 16;
    cout << "num = " << num << endl;
    return 0;
}
```

31. Write an assembly language program that corresponds to the following C++ program:

```
#include <iostream>
using namespace std;

int num;

int main () {
    cin >> num;
    num = num % 16;
    cout << "num = " << num << endl;
    return 0;
}
```

6 *Compiling to the Assembly Level*

The theme of this book is the application of the concept of levels of abstraction to computer science. This chapter continues the theme by showing the relationship between the high-order languages level and the assembly level. It examines features of the C++ language at level HOL6 and shows how a compiler might translate programs that use those features to the equivalent program at level Asmb5.

One major difference between level-HOL6 languages and level-Asmb5 languages is the absence of extensive data types at level Asmb5. In C++, you can define integers, reals, arrays, booleans, and structures in almost any combination. But assembly language has only bits and bytes. If you want to define an array of structures in assembly language, you must partition the bits and bytes accordingly. The compiler does that job automatically when you program at level HOL6.

Another difference between the levels concerns the flow of control. C++ has `if`, `while`, `do`, `for`, `switch`, and function statements to alter the normal sequential flow of control. You will see that assembly language is limited by the basic von Neumann design to more primitive control statements. This chapter shows how the compiler must combine several primitive level-Asmb5 control statements to execute a single, more powerful level-HOL6 control statement.

6.1 Stack Addressing and Local Variables

When a program calls a function, the program allocates storage on the run-time stack for the returned value, the parameters, and the return address. Then the function allocates storage for its local variables. Stack-relative addressing allows the function to access the information that was pushed onto the stack.

You can consider `main()` of a C++ program to be a function that the operating system calls. You might be familiar with the fact that the main program can have parameters named `argc` and `argv` as follows:

```
int main (int argc, char* argv[])
```

With main declared this way, `argc` and `argv` are pushed onto the run-time stack, along with the return address and any local variables.

To keep things simple, this book always declares `main()` without the parameters, and it ignores the fact that storage is allocated for the integer returned value and the return address. Hence, the only storage allocated for `main()` on the run-time stack is for local variables. Figure 2.8 (page 41) shows the memory model with the returned value and the return address on the run-time stack. Figure 2.41 (page 79) shows the memory model with this simplification.

A simplification with `main()`

Stack-Relative Addressing

With stack-relative addressing, the relation between the operand and the operand specifier is

Oprnd = Mem [SP + OprndSpec]

Stack-relative addressing

The stack pointer acts as a memory address to which the operand specifier is added. Figure 4.39 shows that the user stack grows upward in main memory starting at address FBCF. When an item is pushed onto the run-time stack, its address is less than the address of the item that was on the top of the stack.

The stack grows upward in main memory.

You can think of the operand specifier as the offset from the top of the stack. If the operand specifier is 0, the instruction accesses Mem [SP], the value on top of the stack. If the operand specifier is 2, it accesses Mem [SP + 2], the value two bytes below the top of the stack.

The Pep/8 instruction set has two instructions for manipulating the stack pointer directly, `ADDSP` and `SUBSP`. (`CALL`, `RETn`, and `RETTR` manipulate the stack pointer indirectly.) `ADDSP` simply adds a value to the stack pointer, and `SUBSP` subtracts a value. The RTL specification of `ADDSP` is

The `ADDSP` *instruction*

$$\text{SP} \leftarrow \text{SP} + \text{Oprnd}; \text{N} \leftarrow \text{SP} < 0, \text{Z} \leftarrow \text{SP} = 0, \text{V} \leftarrow \{overflow\}, \text{C} \leftarrow \{carry\}$$

and the RTL specification of `SUBSP` is

The `SUBSP` *instruction*

$$\text{SP} \leftarrow \text{SP} - \text{Oprnd}; \text{N} \leftarrow \text{SP} < 0, \text{Z} \leftarrow \text{SP} = 0, \text{V} \leftarrow \{overflow\}, \text{C} \leftarrow \{carry\}$$

Even though you can add to and subtract from the stack pointer, you cannot set the stack pointer with a load instruction. There is no `LDSP` instruction. Then how is the stack pointer ever set? When you select the execute option in the Pep/8 simulator the following two actions occur:

SP ← Mem [FFF8]
PC ← 0000

The first action sets the stack pointer to the content of memory location FFF8. That location is part of the operating system ROM, and it contains the address of the top of the application's run-time stack. Therefore, when you select the execute option, the stack pointer is initialized correctly. The default Pep/8 operating system initializes SP to FBCF. The application never needs to set it to anything else. In general, the application only needs to add to the stack pointer to push items onto the run-time stack, and subtract from the stack pointer to pop items off of the run-time stack.

Accessing the Run-Time Stack

Figure 6.1 shows how to push data onto the stack, access it with stack-relative addressing, and pop it off the stack. The program pushes the string BMW onto the stack followed by the decimal integer 335 followed by the character 'i'. Then it outputs the items and pops them off the stack.

```
0000  C00042  LDA      'B',i      ;push B
0003  F3FFFF  STBYTEA  -1,s
0006  C0004D  LDA      'M',i      ;push M
0009  F3FFFE  STBYTEA  -2,s
000C  C00057  LDA      'W',i      ;push W
000F  F3FFFD  STBYTEA  -3,s
0012  C0014F  LDA      335,i      ;push 335
0015  E3FFFB  STA      -5,s
0018  C00069  LDA      'i',i      ;push i
001B  F3FFFA  STBYTEA  -6,s
001E  680006  SUBSP    6,i        ;6 bytes on the run-time stack
0021  530005  CHARO    5,s        ;output B
0024  530004  CHARO    4,s        ;output M
0027  530003  CHARO    3,s        ;output W
002A  3B0001  DECO     1,s        ;output 335
002D  530000  CHARO    0,s        ;output i
0030  600006  ADDSP    6,i        ;deallocate stack storage
0033  00      STOP
0034          .END
```

Figure **6.1**

Stack-relative addressing.

Output

```
BMW335i
```

Figure 6.2(a) shows the values in the stack pointer (SP) and main memory before the program executes. The machine initializes the stack pointer to FBCF from the vector at Mem [FFF8].

The first two instructions,

```
LDA 'B',i
STBYTEA -1,s
```

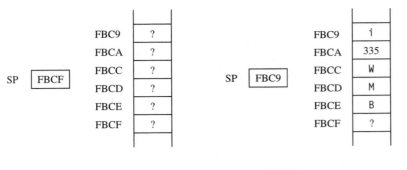

Figure **6.2**

Pushing BMW335i onto the run-time stack in Figure 6.1.

(a) Before the program executes.   **(b)** After SUBSP executes.

put an ASCII 'B' character in the byte just above the top of the stack. LDA puts the 'B' byte in the right half of the accumulator, and STBYTEA puts it above the stack. The store instruction uses stack-relative addressing with an operand specifier of −1 (dec) = FFFF (hex). Because the stack pointer has the value FBCF, the 'B' is stored at Mem [FBCF + FFFF] = Mem [FBCE]. The next two instructions put 'M' and 'W' at Mem [FBCD] and Mem [FBCC], respectively.

The decimal integer 335, however, occupies two bytes. The program must store it at an address that differs from the address of the 'W' by two. That is why the instruction to store the 335 is

```
STA -5,s
```

and not

```
STA -4,s
```

In general, when you push items onto the run-time stack, you must take into account how many bytes each item occupies and set the operand specifier accordingly.

The SUBSP instruction subtracts 6 from the stack pointer, as Figure 6.2(b) shows. That completes the push operation.

Tracing a program that uses stack-relative addressing does not require you to know the absolute value in the stack pointer. The push operation would work the same if the stack pointer were initialized to some other value, say FA18. In that case, 'B', 'M', 'W', 335, and 'i' would be at Mem [FA17], Mem [FA16], Mem [FA15], Mem [FA13], and Mem [FA12], respectively, and the stack pointer would wind up with a value of FA12. The values would be at the same locations relative to the top of the stack, even though they would be at different absolute memory locations.

Figure 6.3 is a more convenient way of tracing the operation and makes use of the fact that the value in the stack pointer is irrelevant. Rather than show the value in the stack pointer, it shows an arrow pointing to the memory cell whose address is contained in the stack pointer. Rather than show the address of the cells in memory, it shows their offsets from the stack pointer. Figures depicting the state of the run-time stack will use this drawing convention from now on.

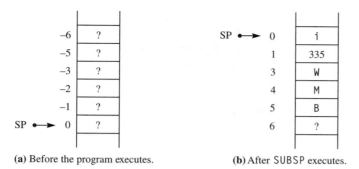

Figure **6.3**

The stack of Figure 6.2 with relative addresses.

(a) Before the program executes.   **(b)** After SUBSP executes.

The instruction

```
CHARO 5,s
```

outputs the ASCII 'B' character from the stack. Note that the stack-relative address of the 'B' before SUBSP executes is –1, but its address after SUBSP executes is 5. Its stack-relative address is different because the stack pointer has changed. Both

```
STBYTEA -1,s
```

and

```
CHARO 5,s
```

access the same memory cell. The other items are output similarly using their stack offsets shown in Figure 6.3(b).

The instruction

```
ADDSP 6,i
```

deallocates six bytes of storage from the run-time stack by adding 6 to SP. Because the stack grows upward toward smaller addresses, you allocate storage by subtracting from the stack pointer, and you deallocate storage by adding to the stack pointer.

Local Variables

The previous chapter shows how the compiler translates programs with global variables. It allocates storage for a global variable with a .BLOCK dot command and it accesses it with direct addressing. Local variables, however, are allocated on the run-time stack. To translate a program with local variables, the compiler

- allocates local variables with SUBSP,
- accesses local variables with stack-relative addressing, and
- deallocates storage with ADDSP.

The rules for accessing local variables

An important difference between global and local variables is the time at which the allocation takes place. The .BLOCK dot command is not an executable statement. Storage for global variables is reserved at a fixed location before the program executes. In contrast, the SUBSP statement is executable. Storage for local variables is created on the run-time stack during program execution.

The C++ program in Figure 6.4 is from Figure 2.6 (page 39). It is identical to the program of Figure 5.26 except that the variables are declared local to main().

The memory model for global versus local variables

Figure **6.4**

A program with local variables. The C++ program is from Figure 2.6.

High-Order Language

```
#include <iostream>
using namespace std;

int main () {
   const int bonus = 5;
   int exam1;
   int exam2;
   int score;
   cin >> exam1 >> exam2;
   score = (exam1 + exam2) / 2 + bonus;
   cout << "score = " << score << endl;
   return 0;
}
```

Assembly Language

```
0000   040003          BR      main
               bonus:  .EQUATE 5               ;constant
               exam1:  .EQUATE 4               ;local variable #2d
               exam2:  .EQUATE 2               ;local variable #2d
               score:  .EQUATE 0               ;local variable #2d
                       ;
0003   680006 main:    SUBSP   6,i             ;allocate #exam1 #exam2 #score
0006   330004          DECI    exam1,s         ;cin >> exam1
0009   330002          DECI    exam2,s         ;    >> exam2
000C   C30004          LDA     exam1,s         ;score = (exam1
000F   730002          ADDA    exam2,s         ;    + exam2)
0012   1E              ASRA                    ;    / 2
0013   700005          ADDA    bonus,i         ;    + bonus
0016   E30000          STA     score,s
0019   410026          STRO    msg,d           ;cout << "score = "
001C   3B0000          DECO    score,s         ;    << score
001F   50000A          CHARO   '\n',i          ;    << endl
0022   600006          ADDSP   6,i             ;deallocate #score #exam2 #exam1
0025   00              STOP
0026   73636F msg:     .ASCII  "score = \x00"
       726520
       3D2000
002F                   .END
```

Figure **6.5**

The run-time stack for the program of Figure 6.4.

(a) Before SUBSP executes.   **(b)** After SUBSP executes.

Although this difference is not perceptible to the user of the program, the translation performed by the compiler is significantly different. Figure 6.5 shows the run-time stack for the program. As in Figure 5.26, bonus is a constant and is defined with the .EQUATE command. However, local variables are also defined with .EQUATE. With a constant, .EQUATE specifies the value of the constant, but with a local variable, .EQUATE specifies the stack offset on the run-time stack. For example, Figure 6.5 shows that the stack offset for local variable exam1 is 6. Therefore, the assembly language program equates the symbol exam1 to 6. Note from the assembly language listing that .EQUATE does not generate any code for the local variables.

.EQUATE specifies the stack offset for a local variable.

Translation of the executable statements in main() differs in two respects from the version with global variables. First, SUBSP and ADDSP allocate and deallocate storage on the run-time stack for the locals. Second, all accesses to the variables use stack-relative addressing instead of direct addressing. Other than these differences, the translation of the assignment and output statements is the same.

Figure 6.4 shows how to write trace tags for debugging with local variables. The assembly language program uses the format trace tag #2d with the .EQUATE pseudo-op to tell the debugger that the values of exam1, exam2, and score should be displayed as two-byte decimal values.

Format trace tags

These local variables are allocated on the run-time stack with the SUBSP instruction. Consequently, to debug your program you specify the three symbol trace tags #exam1, #exam2, and #score in the comment for SUBSP. When you single-step through the program, the Pep/8 system displays a figure on the screen like that of Figure 6.5(b) with the symbolic labels of the cells on the right of the run-time stack. For the debugger to function accurately, you must list the symbol trace tags in the comment field in the exact order they are pushed onto the run-time stack. In this program, exam1 is pushed first followed by exam2 and then score. Furthermore, this order must be consistent with the offset values in the .EQUATE pseudo-op.

Symbol trace tags

The variables are deallocated with the ADDSP instruction. So, you must list the variables that are popped off the run-time stack in the proper order. Because the variables are popped off in the opposite order they are pushed on, you list them in the opposite order from the order in the SUBSP instruction. In this program, score is popped off, followed by exam2 and then exam1.

Although trace tags are not necessary for the program to execute, they serve to document the program. The information provided by the symbol trace tags is valuable for the reader of the program, because it describes the purpose of the SUBSP and ADDSP instructions. The assembly language programs in this chapter all include trace tags for documentation purposes, and your programs should as well.

6.2   Branching Instructions and Flow of Control

The Pep/8 instruction set has eight conditional branches:

BRLE	Branch on less than or equal to
BRLT	Branch on less than
BREQ	Branch on equal to
BRNE	Branch on not equal to
BRGE	Branch on greater than or equal to
BRGT	Branch on greater than
BRV	Branch on V
BRC	Branch on C

Each of these conditional branches tests one or two of the four status bits, N, Z, V, and C. If the condition is true, the operand is placed in PC, causing the branch. If the condition is not true, the operand is not placed in PC, and the instruction following the conditional branch executes normally. You can think of them as comparing a 16-bit result to 0000 (hex). For example, BRLT checks whether a result is less than zero, which happens if N is 1. BRLE checks whether a result is less than or equal to zero, which happens if N is 1 or Z is 1. Here is the Register Transfer Language (RTL) specification of each conditional branch instruction.

BRLE	$N = 1 \lor Z = 1 \Rightarrow PC \leftarrow Oprnd$
BRLT	$N = 1 \Rightarrow PC \leftarrow Oprnd$
BREQ	$Z = 1 \Rightarrow PC \leftarrow Oprnd$
BRNE	$Z = 0 \Rightarrow PC \leftarrow Oprnd$
BRGE	$N = 0 \Rightarrow PC \leftarrow Oprnd$
BRGT	$N = 0 \land Z = 0 \Rightarrow PC \leftarrow Oprnd$
BRV	$V = 1 \Rightarrow PC \leftarrow Oprnd$
BRC	$C = 1 \Rightarrow PC \leftarrow Oprnd$

The conditional branch instructions

Whether a branch occurs depends on the value of the status bits. The status bits are in turn affected by the execution of other instructions. For example,

```
LDA num,s
BRLT place
```

causes the content of num to be loaded into the accumulator. If the word represents a negative number, that is, if its sign bit is 1, then the N bit is set to 1. BRLT tests the N bit and causes a branch to the instruction at place. On the other hand, if the word loaded into the accumulator is not negative, then the N bit is cleared to 0. When BRLT tests the N bit, the branch does not occur and the instruction after BRLT executes next.

▌ Translating the If Statement

Figure 6.6 shows how a compiler would translate an `if` statement from C++ to assembly language. The program computes the absolute value of an integer.

The assembly language comments show the statements that correspond to the high-level program. The `cin` statement translates to `DECI` and the `cout` statement translates to `DECO`. The assignment statement translates to the sequence `LDA`, `NEGA`, `STA`.

The compiler translates the `if` statement into the sequence `LDA`, `BRGE`. When `LDA` executes, if the value loaded into the accumulator is positive or zero, the N bit is cleared to 0. That condition calls for skipping the body of the `if` statement. Figure 6.7(a) shows the structure of the `if` statement at level HOL6. S1 represents the statement `cin >> number`, C1 represents the condition `number < 0`, S2

High-Order Language

```
#include <iostream>
using namespace std;

int main () {
   int number;
   cin >> number;
   if (number < 0) {
      number = -number;
   }
   cout << number;
   return 0;
}
```

Assembly Language

```
0000  040003          BR      main
              number: .EQUATE 0              ;local variable #2d
              ;
0003  680002 main:    SUBSP   2,i            ;allocate #number
0006  330000          DECI    number,s       ;cin >> number
0009  C30000 if:      LDA     number,s       ;if (number < 0)
000C  0E0016          BRGE    endIf
000F  C30000          LDA     number,s       ;    number = -number
0012  1A              NEGA
0013  E30000          STA     number,s
0016  3B0000 endIf:   DECO    number,s       ;cout << number
0019  600002          ADDSP   2,i            ;deallocate #number
001C  00              STOP
001D                  .END
```

Figure **6.6**

The `if` statement at level HOL6 and level Asmb5.

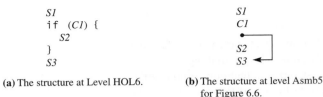

(a) The structure at Level HOL6.   **(b)** The structure at level Asmb5 for Figure 6.6.

Figure **6.7**

The structure of the i f statement at level Asmb5.

represents the statement number = -number, and S3 represents the statement cout <<
number. Figure 6.7(b) shows the structure with the more primitive branching instructions at level Asmb5. The dot following C1 represents the conditional branch, BRGE.

The braces { and } for delimiting a compound statement have no counterpart in
assembly language. The sequence

```
Statement 1
if (number >= 0) {
    Statement 2
    Statement 3
}
Statement 4
```

translates to

```
        Statement 1
if:     LDA number,d
        BRLT endIf
        Statement 2
        Statement 3
endIf:  Statement 4
```

Optimizing Compilers

You may have noticed an extra load statement that was not strictly required in Figure 6.6. You can eliminate the LDA at 000F because the value of number will still
be in the accumulator from the previous load at 0009.

The question is, what would a compiler do? The answer depends on the compiler.
A compiler is a program that must be written and debugged. Imagine that you must
design a compiler to translate from C++ to assembly language. When the compiler
detects an assignment statement, you program it to generate the following sequence:
(a) load accumulator, (b) evaluate expression if necessary, (c) store result to variable.
Such a compiler would generate the code of Figure 6.6, with the LDA at 000F.

Imagine how difficult your compiler program would be if you wanted it to eliminate the unnecessary load. When your compiler detected an assignment statement, it
would not always generate the initial load. Instead, it would analyze the previous
instructions generated and remember the content of the accumulator. If it determined
that the value in the accumulator was the same as the value that the initial load put
there, it would not generate the initial load. In Figure 6.6, the compiler would need

to remember that the value of `number` was still in the accumulator from the code generated for the `if` statement.

The purpose of an optimizing compiler

A compiler that expends extra effort to make the object program shorter and faster is called an optimizing compiler. You can imagine how much more difficult an optimizing compiler is to design than a nonoptimizing one. Not only are optimizing compilers more difficult to write, they also take longer to compile because they must analyze the source program in much greater detail.

The advantages and disadvantages of an optimizing compiler

Which is better, an optimizing or a nonoptimizing compiler? That depends on the use to which you put the compiler. If you are developing software, a process that requires many compiles for testing and debugging, then you would want a compiler that translates quickly, that is, a nonoptimizing compiler. If you have a large fixed program that will be executed repeatedly by many users, you would want fast execution of the object program, hence, an optimizing compiler. Frequently, software is developed and debugged with a nonoptimizing compiler and then translated one last time with an optimizing compiler for the users.

Real compilers come in all shades of gray between these two extremes. The examples in this chapter occasionally present object code that is partially optimized. Most assignment statements, such as the one in Figure 6.6, are presented in nonoptimized form.

Translating the If/Else Statement

Figure 6.8 illustrates the translation of the `if/else` statement. The C++ program is identical to the one in Figure 2.10 (page 42). The `if` body requires an extra unconditional branch around the `else` body. If the compiler omitted the `BR` at 0015 and the input were 127, the output would be `highlow`.

Unlike Figure 6.6, the `if` statement in Figure 6.8 does not compare a variable's value with zero. It compares it with another nonzero value using `CPA`, which stands for compare accumulator. `CPA` subtracts the operand from the accumulator and sets the NZVC status bits accordingly. `CPr` is identical to `SUBr` except that `SUBr` stores the result of the subtraction in register r (accumulator or index register), whereas `CPr` ignores the result of the subtraction. The RTL specification of `CPr` is

The `CPr` instruction

$$T \leftarrow r - Oprnd; N \leftarrow T < 0, Z \leftarrow T = 0, V \leftarrow \{overflow\}, C \leftarrow \{carry\}$$

where T represents a temporary value.

This program computes `num - limit` and sets the NZVC bits. `BRLT` tests the N bit, which is set if

`num - limit < 0`

that is, if

`num < limit`

That is the condition under which the `else` part must execute.

High-Order Language

```
#include <iostream>
using namespace std;

int main () {
   const int limit = 100;
   int num;
   cin >> num;
   if (num >= limit) {
      cout << "high";
   }
   else {
      cout << "low";
   }
   return 0;
}
```

Figure 6.8

The if/else statement at level HOL6 and level Asmb5. The C++ program is from Figure 2.10.

Assembly Language

```
0000   040003           BR      main
                 limit:  .EQUATE 100          ;constant
                 num:    .EQUATE 0            ;local variable #2d
                 ;
0003   680002 main:      SUBSP   2,i          ;allocate #num
0006   330000           DECI    num,s        ;cin >> num
0009   C30000 if:        LDA     num,s        ;if (num >= limit)
000C   B00064           CPA     limit,i
000F   080018           BRLT    else
0012   41001F           STRO    msg1,d       ;    cout << "high"
0015   04001B           BR      endIf        ;else
0018   410024 else:      STRO    msg2,d       ;    cout << "low"
001B   600002 endIf:     ADDSP   2,i          ;deallocate #num
001E   00               STOP
001F   686967 msg1:      .ASCII  "high\x00"
       6800
0024   6C6F77 msg2:      .ASCII  "low\x00"
       00
0028                     .END
```

Figure 6.9 shows the structure of the control statements at the two levels. Part (a) shows the level-HOL6 control statement, and part (b) shows the level-Asmb5 translation for this program.

```
S1
if  (C1) {
    S2
}
else
    S3
}
S4
```

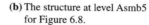

```
S1
C1
S2
S3
S4
```

(a) The structure at Level HOL6.   **(b)** The structure at level Asmb5
                                               for Figure 6.8.

Figure **6.9**

The structure of the if/else statement at level Asmb5.

Translating the While Loop

Translating a loop requires branches to previous instructions. Figure 6.10 shows the translation of a while statement. The C++ program is identical to the one in Figure 2.13. It echoes ASCII input characters to the output, using the sentinel technique with * as the sentinel. If the input is happy*, the output is happy.

The test for a while statement is made with a conditional branch at the top of the loop. This program tests a character value, which is a byte quantity. The load instruction at 0007 clears both bytes in the accumulator, so the most significant byte will be 00 (hex) after the load byte instruction at 000A executes. You must guarantee that the most significant byte is 0 because the compare instruction compares a whole word.

Every while loop ends with an unconditional branch to the test at the top of the loop. The branch at 0019 brings control back to the initial test. Figure 6.11 shows the structure of the while statement at the two levels.

High-Order Language

```
#include <iostream>
using namespace std;

char letter;

int main () {
    cin >> letter;
    while (letter != '*') {
        cout << letter;
        cin >> letter;
    }
    return 0;
}
```

Figure **6.10**

The while statement at level HOL6
and level Asmb5. The C++ program
is from Figure 2.13.

Assembly Language

```
0000  040004           BR      main
0003  00      letter:  .BLOCK  1           ;global variable #1c
                       ;
0004  490003 main:     CHARI   letter,d     ;cin >> letter
0007  C00000           LDA     0x0000,i
000A  D10003 while:    LDBYTEA letter,d     ;while (letter != '*')
000D  B0002A           CPA     '*',i
0010  0A001C           BREQ    endWh
0013  510003           CHARO   letter,d     ;   cout << letter
0016  490003           CHARI   letter,d     ;   cin >> letter
0019  04000A           BR      while
001C  00      endWh:   STOP
001D                   .END
```

Figure **6.10**

(Continued)

S1
while *(C1)* {
    S2
}
S3

(a) The structure at level HOL6.

S1
C1
S2
S3

(b) The structure at level
Asmb5 for Figure 6.10.

Figure **6.11**

The structure of the while
statement at level Asmb5.

Translating the Do Loop

A highway patrol officer parks behind a sign. A driver passes by, traveling
20 meters per second, which is faster than the speed limit. When the driver is
40 meters down the road, the officer gets his car up to 25 meters per second to
pursue the offender. How far from the sign does the officer catch up to the
speeder?

The program in Figure 6.12 solves the problem by simulation. It is identical to
the one in Figure 2.14 (page 45). The values of cop and driver are the positions of
the two motorists, initialized to 0 and 40, respectively. Each execution of the do
loop represents one second of elapsed time, during which the officer travels 25
meters and the driver 20, until the officer catches the driver.

A do statement has its test at the bottom of the loop. In this program, the compiler translates the while test to the sequence LDA, CPA, BRLT. BRLT executes the
branch if N is set to 1. Because CPA computes the difference, cop - driver, N will
be 1 if

cop - driver < 0

High-Order Language

```cpp
#include <iostream>
using namespace std;

int cop;
int driver;

int main () {
   cop = 0;
   driver = 40;
   do {
      cop += 25;
      driver += 20;
   }
   while (cop <=driver);
   cout << cop;
   return 0;
}
```

Assembly Language

```
0000   040007           BR      main
0003   0000    cop:     .BLOCK  2          ;global variable #2d
0005   0000    driver:  .BLOCK  2          ;global variable #2d
                        ;
0007   C00000 main:     LDA     0,i        ;cop = 0
000A   E10003           STA     cop,d
000D   C00028           LDA     40,i       ;driver = 40
0010   E10005           STA     driver,d
0013   C10003 do:       LDA     cop,d      ;    cop += 25
0016   700019           ADDA    25,i
0019   E10003           STA     cop,d
001C   C10005           LDA     driver,d   ;    driver += 20
001F   700014           ADDA    20,i
0022   E10005           STA     driver,d
0025   C10003 while:    LDA     cop,d      ;while (cop < driver)
0028   B10005           CPA     driver,d
002B   080013           BRLT    do
002E   390003           DECO    cop,d      ;cout << cop
0031   00               STOP
0032                    .END
```

Figure **6.12**

The do statement at level HOL6 and level Asmb5. The C++ program is from Figure 2.14.

that is, if

```
cop < driver
```

That is the condition under which the loop should repeat. Figure 6.13 shows the structure of the do statement at levels 6 and 5.

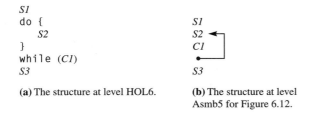

S1
```
do {
    S2
}
while (C1)
```
S3

(a) The structure at level HOL6.

S1
S2
C1
S3

(b) The structure at level Asmb5 for Figure 6.12.

Figure **6.13**

The structure of the do statement at level Asmb5.

Translating the For Loop

for statements are similar to while statements because the test for both is at the top of the loop. The compiler must generate code to initialize and to increment the control variable. The program in Figure 6.14 shows how a compiler would generate code for the for statement. It translates the for statement into the following sequence at level Asmb5:

- Initialize the control variable.
- Test the control variable.
- Execute the loop body.
- Increment the control variable.
- Branch to the test.

High-Order Language

```
#include <iostream>
using namespace std;

int main () {
   int j;
   for (j = 0; j < 3; j++) {
      cout << "j = " << j << endl;
   }
   cout << "j = " << j << endl;
   return 0;
}
```

Figure **6.14**

The for statement at level HOL6 and level Asmb5.

Assembly Language

Figure **6.14**

(Continued)

```
0000   040003           BR      main
               j:       .EQUATE 0               ;local variable #2d
               ;
0003   680002 main:     SUBSP   2,i             ;allocate #j
0006   C00000           LDA     0,i             ;for (j = 0
0009   E30000           STA     j,s
000C   B00003 for:      CPA     3,i             ;    j < 3
000F   0E0027           BRGE    endFor
0012   410034           STRO    msg,d           ;    cout << "j = "
0015   3B0000           DECO    j,s             ;        << j
0018   50000A           CHARO   '\n',i          ;        << endl
001B   C30000           LDA     j,s             ;    j++)
001E   700001           ADDA    1,i
0021   E30000           STA     j,s
0024   04000C           BR      for
0027   410034 endFor:   STRO    msg,d           ;cout << "j = "
002A   3B0000           DECO    j,s             ;    << j
002D   50000A           CHARO   '\n',i          ;    << endl
0030   600002           ADDSP   2,i             ;deallocate #j
0033   00               STOP
0034   6A203D msg:      .ASCII  "j = \x00"
       2000
0039                    .END
```

In this program, CPA computes the difference, j - 3. BRGE branches out of the loop if N is 0—that is, if

j - 3 >= 0

or, equivalently,

j >= 3

The body executes once each for j having the values 0, 1, and 2. The last time through the loop, j increments to 3, which is the value written by the output statement following the loop.

Spaghetti Code

At the assembly level, a programmer can write control structures that do not correspond to the control structures in C++. Figure 6.15 shows one possible flow of control that is not directly possible in many level-HOL6 languages. Condition *C1* is

S1
C1

S2
S3
C2

S4

Figure **6.15**

A flow of control not possible directly in many HOL6 languages.

tested, and if it is true, a branch is taken to the middle of a loop whose test is *C2*. This control flow cannot be written directly in C++.

Assembly language programs generated by a compiler are usually longer than programs written by humans directly in assembly language. Not only that, but they often execute more slowly. If human programmers can write shorter, faster assembly language programs than compilers, why does anyone program in a high-order language? One reason is the ability of the compiler to perform type checking, as mentioned in Chapter 5. Another is the additional burden of responsibility that is placed on the programmer when given the freedom of using primitive branching instructions. If you are not careful when you write programs at level Asmb5, the branching instructions can get out of hand, as the next program shows.

The program in Figure 6.16 is an extreme example of the problem that can occur with unbridled use of primitive branching instructions. It is difficult to understand because of its lack of comments and indentation and its inconsistent branching style. Actually, the program performs a very simple task. Can you discover what it does?

0000	040009		BR	main
0003	0000	n1:	.BLOCK	2
0005	0000	n2:	.BLOCK	2
0007	0000	n3:	.BLOCK	2
		;		
0009	310005	main:	DECI	n2,d
000C	310007		DECI	n3,d
000F	C10005		LDA	n2,d
0012	B10007		CPA	n3,d
0015	08002A		BRLT	L1
0018	310003		DECI	n1,d
001B	C10003		LDA	n1,d
001E	B10007		CPA	n3,d
0021	080074		BRLT	L7
0024	040065		BR	L6
0027	E10007		STA	n3,d
002A	310003	L1:	DECI	n1,d
002D	C10005		LDA	n2,d
0030	B10003		CPA	n1,d
0033	080053		BRLT	L5
0036	390003		DECO	n1,d
0039	390005		DECO	n2,d
003C	390007	L2:	DECO	n3,d
003F	00		STOP	
0040	390005	L3:	DECO	n2,d
0043	390007		DECO	n3,d
0046	040081		BR	L9

Figure **6.16**

A mystery program.

```
0049   390003 L4:      DECO    n1,d
004C   390005          DECO    n2,d
004F   00              STOP
0050   E10003          STA     n1,d
0053   C10007 L5:      LDA     n3,d
0056   B10003          CPA     n1,d
0059   080040          BRLT    L3
005C   390005          DECO    n2,d
005F   390003          DECO    n1,d
0062   04003C          BR      L2
0065   390007 L6:      DECO    n3,d
0068   C10003          LDA     n1,d
006B   B10005          CPA     n2,d
006E   080049          BRLT    L4
0071   04007E          BR      L8
0074   390003 L7:      DECO    n1,d
0077   390007          DECO    n3,d
007A   390005          DECO    n2,d
007D   00              STOP
007E   390005 L8:      DECO    n2,d
0081   390003 L9:      DECO    n1,d
0084   00              STOP
0085                   .END
```

Figure **6.16**

(Continued)

The body of an if statement or a loop in C++ is a block of statements, sometimes contained in a compound statement delimited by braces {}. Additional if statements and loops can be nested entirely within these blocks. Figure 6.17(a) pictures this situation schematically. A flow of control that is limited to nestings of the if/else, switch, while, do, and for statements is called structured flow of control.

Structured flow of control

The branches in the mystery program do not correspond to the structured control constructs of C++. Although the program's logic is correct for performing its intended task, it is difficult to decipher because the branching statements branch all over the place. This kind of program is called spaghetti code. If you draw an arrow from each branch statement to the statement to which it branches, the picture looks rather like a bowl of spaghetti, as shown in Figure 6.17(b).

Spaghetti code

It is often possible to write efficient programs with unstructured branches. Such programs execute faster and require less memory for storage than if they were written in a high-order language with structured flow of control. Some specialized applications require this extra measure of efficiency and are therefore written directly in assembly language.

Balanced against this savings in execution time and memory space is difficulty in comprehension. When programs are hard to understand, they are hard to write, debug, and modify. The problem is economic. Writing, debugging, and modifying

Advantages and disadvantages of programming at level Asmb5

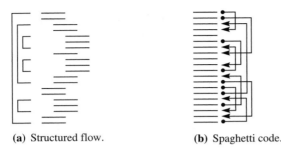

(a) Structured flow.   (b) Spaghetti code.

Figure **6.17**

Two different styles of flow of control.

are all human activities, which are labor intensive and, therefore, expensive. The question you must ask is whether the extra efficiency justifies the additional expense.

Flow of Control in Early Languages

Computers had been around for many years before structured flow of control was discovered. In the early days there were no high-order languages. Everyone programmed in assembly language. Computer memories were expensive, and CPUs were slow by today's standards. Efficiency was all-important. Because a large body of software had not yet been generated, the problem of program maintenance was not appreciated.

The first widespread high-order language was FORTRAN, developed in the 1950s. Because people were used to dealing with branch instructions, they included them in the language. An unconditional branch in FORTRAN is

```
GOTO 260
```

where 260 is the statement number of another statement. It is called a goto statement. A conditional branch is

A goto statement at level HOL6

```
IF (NUMBER .GE. 100) GOTO 500
```

where .GE. means "is greater than or equal to." This statement compares the value of variable NUMBER with 100. If it is greater than or equal to 100, the next statement executed is the one with a statement number of 500. Otherwise the statement after the IF is executed.

FORTRAN's conditional IF is a big improvement over level-Asmb5 branch instructions. It does not require a separate compare instruction to set the status bits. But notice how the flow of control is similar to level-Asmb5 branching: If the test is true, do the GOTO. Otherwise continue to the next statement.

As people developed more software, they noticed that it would be convenient to group statements into blocks for use in if statements and loops. The most notable language to make this advance was ALGOL-60, developed in 1960. It was the first widespread block-structured language, although its popularity was limited mainly to Europe.

The Structured Programming Theorem

The preceding sections show how high-level structured control statements translate into primitive branch statements at a lower level. They also show how you can write branches at the lower level that do not correspond to the structured constructs. That raises an interesting and practical question: Is it possible to write an algorithm with goto statements that will perform some processing that is impossible to perform with structured constructs? That is, if you limit yourself to structured flow of control, are there some problems you will not be able to solve that you could solve if unstructured goto's were allowed?

Corrado Bohm and Giuseppe Jacopini answered this important question in a computer science journal article in 1966.[1] They proved mathematically that any algorithm containing goto's, no matter how complicated or unstructured, can be written with only nested `if` statements and `while` loops. Their result is called the structured programming theorem.

The structured programming theorem

Bohm and Jacopini's paper was highly theoretical. It did not attract much attention at first because programmers generally had no desire to limit the freedom they had with goto statements. Bohm and Jacopini showed what could be done with nested `if` statements and `while` loops, but left unanswered why programmers would want to limit themselves that way.

People experimented with the concept anyway. They would take an algorithm in spaghetti code and try to rewrite it using structured flow of control without goto statements. Usually the new program was much clearer than the original. Occasionally it was even more efficient.

The Goto Controversy

Two years after Bohm and Jacopini's paper appeared, Edsger W. Dijkstra of the Technological University at Eindhoven, the Netherlands, wrote a letter to the editor of the same journal in which he stated his personal observation that good programmers used fewer goto's than poor programmers.[2]

---

1. Corrado Bohm and Giuseppe Jacopini, "Flow-Diagrams, Turing Machines and Languages with Only Two Formation Rules," *Communications of the ACM 9* (May 1966): 366–371.

2. Edsger W. Dijkstra, "Goto Statement Considered Harmful," *Communications of the ACM 11* (March 1968): 147–648. Reprinted by permission.

Edsger Dijkstra

Born to a Dutch chemist in Rotterdam in 1930, Dijkstra grew up with a formalist predilection toward the world. While studying at the University of Leiden in the Netherlands, Dijkstra planned to take up physics as his career. But his father heard about a summer course on computing in Cambridge, England, and Dijkstra jumped aboard the computing bandwagon just as it was gathering speed around 1950.

One of Dijkstra's most famous contributions to programming was his strong advocacy of structured programming principles, as exemplified by his famous letter that disparaged the goto statement. He developed a reputation for speaking his mind, often in inflammatory or dramatic ways that most of us couldn't get away with. For example, Dijkstra once remarked that "the use of COBOL cripples the mind; its teaching should therefore be regarded as a criminal offence." Not one to single out only one lan-

guage for his criticism, he also said that "it is practically impossible to teach good programming to students that have had a prior exposure to BASIC; as potential programmers they are mentally mutilated beyond hope of regeneration."

Besides his work in language design, Dijkstra is also noted for his

work in proofs of program correctness. The field of program correctness is an application of mathematics to computer programming. Researchers are trying to construct a language and proof technique that might be used to certify unconditionally that a program will perform according to its specifications—entirely free of bugs. Needless to say, whether your application is customer billing or flight control systems, this would be an extremely valuable claim to make about a program.

Dijkstra worked in practically every area within computer science. He invented the semaphore, described in Chapter 8 of this book, and invented a famous algorithm to solve the shortest path problem. In 1972 the Association for Computing Machinery acknowledged Dijkstra's rich contributions to the field by awarding him the distinguished Turing Award. Dijkstra died after a long struggle with cancer in 2002 at his home in Nuenen, the Netherlands.

"The question of whether computers can think is like the question of whether submarines can swim."

—*Edsger Dijkstra*

In his opinion, a high density of goto's in a program indicated poor quality. He stated in part:

> For a number of years I have been familiar with the observation that the quality of programmers is a decreasing function of the density of goto statements in the programs they produce. More recently I discovered why the use of the goto state-

An excerpt from Dijkstra's famous letter

ment has such disastrous effects, and I became convinced that the goto statement should be abolished from all "higher level" programming languages (i.e., everything except, perhaps, plain machine code). . . . The goto statement as it stands is just too primitive; it is too much an invitation to make a mess of one's program.

To justify these statements, Dijkstra developed the idea of a set of coordinates that are necessary to describe the progress of the program. When a human tries to understand a program, he must maintain this set of coordinates mentally, perhaps unconsciously. Dijkstra showed that the coordinates to be maintained with structured flow of control were vastly simpler than those with unstructured goto's. Thus he was able to pinpoint the reason that structured flow of control is easier to understand.

Dijkstra acknowledged that the idea of eliminating goto's was not new. He mentioned several people who influenced him on the subject, one of whom was Niklaus Wirth, who had worked on the ALGOL-60 language.

Dijkstra's letter set off a storm of protest, now known as the famous goto controversy. To theoretically be able to program without goto was one thing. But to advocate that goto be abolished from high-order languages such as FORTRAN was altogether something else.

Old ideas die hard. However, the controversy has died down and it is now generally recognized that Dijkstra was, in fact, correct. The reason is cost. When software managers began to apply the structured flow of control discipline, along with other structured design concepts, they found that the resulting software was much less expensive to develop, debug, and maintain. It was usually well worth the additional memory requirements and extra execution time.

FORTRAN 77 is a more recent version of FORTRAN standardized in 1977. The goto controversy influenced its design. It contains a block style IF statement with an ELSE part similar to C++. For example,

```
IF (NUMBER .GE. 100) THEN
    Statement 1
ELSE
    Statement 2
ENDIF
```

You can write the IF statement in FORTRAN 77 without goto.

One point to bear in mind is that the absence of goto's in a program does not guarantee that the program is well structured. It is possible to write a program with three or four nested if statements and while loops when only one or two are necessary. Also, if a language at any level contains only goto statements to alter the flow of control, they can always be used in a structured way to implement if statements and while loops. That is precisely what a C++ compiler does when it translates a program from level HOL6 to level Asmb5.

6.3   Function Calls and Parameters

A C++ function call changes the flow of control to the first executable statement
in the function. At the end of the function, control returns to the statement following the function call. The compiler implements function calls with the CALL
instruction, which has a mechanism for storing the return address on the run-time
stack. It implements the return to the calling statement with RETn, which uses the
saved return address on the run-time stack to determine which instruction to execute next.

Translating a Function Call

Figure 6.18 shows how a compiler translates a function call without parameters.
The program outputs three triangles of asterisks.

   The CALL instruction pushes the content of the program counter onto the run-
time stack and then loads the operand into the program counter. Here is the RTL
specification of the CALL instruction:

The CALL instruction

$$SP \leftarrow SP - 2; \; Mem[SP] \leftarrow PC; \; PC \leftarrow Oprnd$$

In effect, the return address for the procedure call is pushed onto the stack and a
branch to the procedure is executed.

   As with the branch instructions, CALL usually executes in the immediate
addressing mode, in which case the operand is the operand specifier. If you do not
specify the addressing mode, the Pep/8 assembler will assume immediate addressing.

The default addressing mode for
CALL is immediate.

   Figure 5.2 shows that the RETn instruction has a three-bit nnn field. In general,
a procedure can have any number of local variables. There are eight versions of the
RETn instruction, namely RET0, RET1, ..., RET7, where n is the number of bytes occupied by the local variables in the procedure. Procedure printTri in Figure 6.18 has
no local variables. That is why the compiler generated the RET0 instruction at 0015.
Here is the RTL specification of RETn:

The RETn instruction

$$SP \leftarrow SP + n; \; PC \leftarrow Mem[SP]; \; SP \leftarrow SP + 2$$

First, the instruction deallocates storage for the local variables by adding n to the
stack pointer. After the deallocation, the return address should be on top of the run-
time stack. Then, the instruction moves the return address from the top of the stack
into the program counter. Finally, it adds 2 to the stack pointer, which completes
the pop operation. Of course, it is possible for a procedure to have more than seven
bytes of local variables. In that case, the compiler would generate an ADDSP instruction to deallocate the storage for the local variables.

   In Figure 6.18,

```
BR main
```

High-Order Language

```cpp
#include <iostream>
using namespace std;

void printTri () {
   cout << "*" << endl;
   cout << "**" << endl;
   cout << "***" << endl;
}

int main () {
   printTri ();
   printTri ();
   printTri ();
   return 0;
}
```

Figure **6.18**

A procedure call at level HOL6 and level Asmb5.

Assembly Language

```
0000   04001F          BR     main
               ;
               ;******* void printTri ()
0003   410016 printTri:STRO    msg1,d     ;cout << "*"
0006   50000A          CHARO   '\n',i     ;   << endl
0009   410018          STRO    msg2,d     ;cout << "**"
000C   50000A          CHARO   '\n',i     ;   << endl
000F   41001B          STRO    msg3,d     ;cout << "***"
0012   50000A          CHARO   '\n',i     ;   << endl
0015   58              RETO
0016   2A00    msg1:   .ASCII  "*\x00"
0018   2A2A00  msg2:   .ASCII  "**\x00"
001B   2A2A2A  msg3:   .ASCII  "***\x00"
       00
               ;
               ;******* int main ()
001F   160003  main:   CALL    printTri   ;printTri ()
0022   160003          CALL    printTri   ;printTri ()
0025   160003          CALL    printTri   ;printTri ()
0028   00              STOP
0029                   .END
```

puts 001F into the program counter. The next statement to execute is, therefore, the one at 001F, which is the first CALL instruction. The discussion of the program in Figure 6.1 explains how the stack pointer is initialized to FBCF. Figure 6.19 shows the run-time stack before and after execution of the first CALL statement. As usual, the initial value of the stack pointer is FBCF.

Figure **6.19**

Execution of the first CALL instruction in Figure 6.18.

(a) Before execution of the first CALL.　　　　**(b)** After execution of the first CALL.

The operations of CALL and RETn crucially depend on the von Neumann execution cycle: fetch, decode, increment, execute, repeat. In particular, the increment step happens before the execute step. As a consequence, the statement that is executing is not the statement whose address is in the program counter. It is the statement that was fetched before the program counter was incremented and that is now contained in the instruction register. Why is that so important in the execution of CALL and RETn?

Figure 6.19(a) shows the content of the program counter as 0022 before execution of the first CALL instruction. It is not the address of the first CALL instruction, which is 001F. Why not? Because the program counter was incremented to 0022 before execution of the CALL. Therefore, during execution of the first CALL instruction the program counter contains the address of the instruction in main memory located just after the first CALL instruction.

What happens when the first CALL executes? First, SP ← SP – 2 subtracts two from SP, giving it the value FBCD. Then, Mem[SP] ← PC puts the value of the program counter, 0022, into main memory at address FBCD—that is, on top of the run-time stack. Finally, PC ← Oprnd puts 0003 into the program counter, because the operand specifier is 0003 and the addressing mode is immediate. The result is Figure 6.19(b).

The von Neumann cycle continues with the next fetch. But now the program counter contains 0003. So, the next instruction to be fetched is the one at address 0003, which is the first instruction of the printTri procedure. The output instructions of the procedure execute, producing the pattern of a triangle of asterisks.

Eventually the RET0 instruction at 0015 executes. Figure 6.20(a) shows the content of the program counter as 0016 just before execution of RET0. This might seem

Figure **6.20**

The first execution of the RET0 instruction in Figure 6.18.

(a) Before the first execution of RET0.　　　　**(b)** After the first execution of RET0.

strange, because 0016 is not even the address of an instruction. It is the address of the string "*\x00". Why? Because RET0 is a unary instruction and the CPU incremented the program counter by one. The first step in the execution of RET0 is SP ← SP + n, which adds zero to SP because n is zero. Then, PC ← Mem[SP] puts 0022 into the program counter. Finally, SP ← SP + 2 changes the stack pointer back to FBCF.

The von Neumann cycle continues with the next fetch. But now the program counter contains the address of the second CALL instruction. The same sequence of events happens as with the first call, producing another triangle of asterisks in the output stream. The third call does the same thing, after which the STOP instruction executes. Note that the value of the program counter after the STOP instruction executes is 0029 and not 0028, which is the address of the STOP instruction.

Now you should see why increment comes before execute in the von Neumann execution cycle. To store the return address on the run-time stack, the CALL instruction needs to store the address of the instruction following the CALL. It can only do that if the program counter has been incremented before the CALL statement executes.

The reason increment must come before execute in the von Neumann execution cycle

Translating Call-By-Value Parameters with Global Variables

The allocation process when you call a void function in C++ is

- Push the actual parameters.
- Push the return address.
- Push storage for the local variables.

At level HOL6, the instructions that perform these operations on the stack are hidden. The programmer simply writes the function call, and during execution the stack allocation occurs automatically.

At the assembly level, however, the translated program must contain explicit instructions for the allocation. The program in Figure 6.21, which is identical to the program in Figure 2.16 (page 48), is a level-HOL6 program that prints a bar chart, and the program's corresponding level-Asmb5 translation. It shows the level-Asmb5 statements, not explicit at level HOL6, that are required to push the parameters.

High-Order Language

```
#include <iostream>
using namespace std;

int numPts;
int value;
int j;
```

Figure **6.21**

Call-by-value parameters with global variables. The C++ program is from Figure 2.16.

```
void printBar (int n) {
   int k;
   for (k = 1; k <= n; k++) {
      cout << '*';
   }
   cout << endl;
}

int main () {
   cin >> numPts;
   for (j = 1; j <= numPts; j++) {
      cin >> value;
      printBar (value);
   }
   return 0;
}
```

Figure **6.21**

(Continued)

Assembly Language

```
0000   04002B            BR       main
0003   0000    numPts:   .BLOCK   2        ;global variable #2d
0005   0000    value:    .BLOCK   2        ;global variable #2d
0007   0000    j:        .BLOCK   2        ;global variable #2d
                         ;
                         ;******* void printBar (int n)
                         n:       .EQUATE  4        ;formal parameter #2d
                         k:       .EQUATE  0        ;local variable #2d
0009   680002  printBar:SUBSP    2,i      ;allocate #k
000C   C00001            LDA      1,i      ;for (k = 1
000F   E30000            STA      k,s
0012   B30004  for1:     CPA      n,s      ;k <= n
0015   100027            BRGT     endFor1
0018   50002A            CHARO    '*',i    ;   cout << '*'
001B   C30000            LDA      k,s      ;k++)
001E   700001            ADDA     1,i
0021   E30000            STA      k,s
0024   040012            BR       for1
0027   50000A  endFor1:  CHARO    '\n',i   ;cout << endl
002A   5A                RET2              ;deallocate #k, pop retAddr
```

Figure **6.21**

(Continued)

```
          ;
          ;******* main ()
002B  310003 main:    DECI    numPts,d    ;cin >> numPts
002E  C00001          LDA     1,i         ;for (j = 1
0031  E10007          STA     j,d
0034  B10003 for2:    CPA     numPts,d    ;j <= numPts
0037  100058          BRGT    endFor2
003A  310005          DECI    value,d     ;   cin >> value
003D  C10005          LDA     value,d     ;   call by value
0040  E3FFFE          STA     -2,s
0043  680002          SUBSP   2,i         ;   push #n
0046  160009          CALL    printBar    ;   push retAddr
0049  600002          ADDSP   2,i         ;   pop #n
004C  C10007          LDA     j,d         ;j++)
004F  700001          ADDA    1,i
0052  E10007          STA     j,d
0055  040034          BR      for2
0058  00     endFor2: STOP
0059                  .END
```

The calling procedure is responsible for pushing the actual parameters and executing CALL, which pushes the return address onto the stack. The called procedure is responsible for allocating storage on the stack for its local variables. After the called procedure executes, it must deallocate the storage for the local variables, and then pop the return address by executing RETn. Before the calling procedure can continue, it must deallocate the storage for the actual parameters.

In summary, the calling and called procedures do the following:

- Calling pushes actual parameters (executes SUBSP).
- Calling pushes return address (executes CALL).
- Called allocates local variables (executes SUBSP).
- Called executes its body.
- Called deallocates local variables and pops return address (executes RETn).
- Calling pops actual parameters (executes ADDSP).

Note the symmetry of the operations. The last two operations undo the first three operations in reverse order. That order is a consequence of the last-in, first-out property of the stack.

The global variables in the level-HOL6 main program—numPts, value, and j—correspond to the identical level-Asmb5 symbols, whose symbol values are 0003, 0005, and 0007, respectively. These are the addresses of the memory cells that will hold the run-time values of the global variables. Figure 6.22(a) shows the

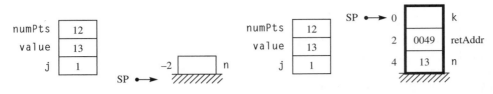

(a) After `cin >> value`.   **(b)** After allocation with `SUBSP` in `printBar`.

Figure **6.22**

Call-by-value parameters with
global variables.

global variables on the left with their symbols in place of their addresses. The values for the global variables are the ones after

```
cin >> value;
```

executes for the first time.

What do the formal parameter, n, and the local variable, k, correspond to at level Asmb5? Not absolute addresses, but stack-relative addresses. Procedure `printBar` defines them with

```
n: .EQUATE 4
k: .EQUATE 0
```

Remember that .EQUATE does not generate object code. The assembler does not reserve storage for them at translation time. Instead, storage for n and k is allocated on the stack at run time. The decimal numbers 4 and 0 are the stack offsets appropriate for n and k during execution of the procedure, as Figure 6.22(b) shows. The procedure refers to them with stack-relative addressing.

The statements that correspond to the procedure call in the calling procedure are

```
LDA    value,d
STA    -2,s
SUBSP 2,i
CALL  printBar
ADDSP 2,i
```

Because the parameter is a global variable that is called by value, LDA uses direct addressing. That puts the run-time value of variable value in the accumulator, which STA then pushes onto the stack. The offset is –2 because value is a two-byte integer quantity, as Figure 6.22(a) shows.

The statements that correspond to the procedure call in the called procedure are

```
SUBSP 2,i
.
.
.
RET2
```

The SUBSP subtracts 2 because the local variable, k, is a two-byte integer quantity. Figure 6.22(a) shows the run-time stack just after the first input of global variable `value` and just before the first procedure call. It corresponds directly to Figure 2.17(d) (page 50). Figure 6.22(b) shows the stack just after the procedure call and corresponds directly to Figure 2.17(g). Note that the return address, which is labeled ra1 in Figure 2.17, is here shown to be 0049, which is the assembly language address of the instruction following the `CALL` instruction.

The stack address of `n` is 4 because both `k` and the return address occupy two bytes on the stack. If there were more local variables, the stack address of `n` would be correspondingly greater. The compiler must compute the stack addresses from the number and size of the quantities on the stack.

In summary, to translate call-by-value parameters with global variables, the compiler generates code as follows:

- To push the actual parameter, it generates a load instruction with direct addressing.

- To access the formal parameter, it generates instructions with stack-relative addressing.

The translation rules for call-by-value parameters with global variables

Translating Call-By-Value Parameters with Local Variables

The program in Figure 6.23 is identical to the one in Figure 6.21 except that the variables in `main()` are local instead of global. Although the program behaves like the one in Figure 6.21, the memory model and the translation to level Asmb5 are different.

High-Order Language

```
#include <iostream>
using namespace std;

void printBar (int n) {
   int k;
   for (k = 1; k <= n; k++) {
      cout << '*';
   }
   cout << endl;
}

int main () {
   int numPts;
   int value;
   int j;
```

Figure **6.23**

Call-by-value parameters with local variables.

```
      cin >> numPts;
      for (j = 1; j <= numPts; j++) {
         cin >> value;
         printBar (value);
      }
      return 0;
}
```

Figure **6.23**

(Continued)

Assembly Language

```
00000   040025              BR       main
                    ;
                    ;******* void printBar (int n)
                    n:        .EQUATE  4          ;formal parameter #2d
                    k:        .EQUATE  0          ;local variable #2d
0003    680002 printBar:SUBSP  2,i               ;allocate #k
0006    C00001              LDA      1,i          ;for (k = 1
0009    E30000              STA      k,s
000C    B30004 for1:       CPA      n,s          ;k <= n
000F    100021              BRGT     endFor1
0012    50002A              CHARO    '*',i        ;   cout << '*'
0015    C30000              LDA      k,s          ;k++)
0018    700001              ADDA     1,i
001B    E30000              STA      k,s
001E    04000C              BR       for1
0021    50000A endFor1:     CHARO    '\n',i       ;cout << endl
0024    5A                  RET2                  ;deallocate #k, pop retAddr
                    ;
                    ;******* main ()
                    numPts:   .EQUATE  4          ;local variable #2d
                    value:    .EQUATE  2          ;local variable #2d
                    j:        .EQUATE  0          ;local variable #2d
0025    680006 main:       SUBSP    6,i          ;allocate #numPts #value #j
0028    330004              DECI     numPts,s     ;cin >> numPts
002B    C00001              LDA      1,i          ;for (j = 1
002E    E30000              STA      j,s
0031    B30004 for2:       CPA      numPts,s     ;j <= numPts
0034    100055              BRGT     endFor2
0037    330002              DECI     value,s      ;   cin >> value
003A    C30002              LDA      value,s      ;   call by value
003D    E3FFFE              STA      -2,s
0040    680002              SUBSP    2,i          ;   push #n
0043    160003              CALL     printBar     ;   push retAddr
0046    600002              ADDSP    2,i          ;   pop #n
0049    C30000              LDA      j,s          ;j++)
004C    700001              ADDA     1,i
```

```
004F   E30000           STA     j,s
0052   040031           BR      for2
0055   600006 endFor2:  ADDSP   6,i        ;deallocate #j #value #numPts
0058   00               STOP
0059                    .END
```

Figure **6.23**

(Continued)

You can see that the versions of void function `printTri` at level HOL6 are identical in Figure 6.21 and Figure 6.23. Hence, it should not be surprising that the compiler generates identical object code for the two versions of `printTri` at level Asmb5. The only difference between the two programs is in the definition of `main()`. Figure 6.24(a) shows the allocation of `numPts`, `value`, and `j` on the run-time stack in the main program. Figure 6.24(b) shows the stack after `printTri` is called for the first time. Because `value` is a local variable, the compiler generates `LDA value,s` with stack-relative addressing to push the actual value of `value` into the stack cell of formal parameter `n`.

In summary, to translate call-by-value parameters with local variables, the compiler generates code as follows:

- To push the actual parameter, it generates a load instruction with stack-relative addressing.

- To access the formal parameter, it generates instructions with stack-relative addressing.

The translation rules for call-by-value parameters with local variables

Translating Non-Void Function Calls

The allocation process when you call a function is

- Push storage for the returned value.
- Push the actual parameters.
- Push the return address.
- Push storage for the local variables.

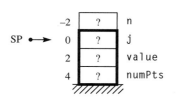

(a) After `cin >> value`.

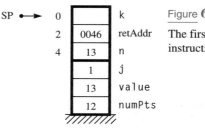

Figure **6.24**

The first execution of the `RET0` instruction in Figure 6.23.

(b) After allocation with `SUBSP` in `printBar`.

Allocation for a non-void function call differs from that for a procedure (void function) call by the extra value that you must allocate for the returned function value.

Figure 6.25 shows a program that computes a binomial coefficient recursively and is identical to the one in Figure 2.28 (page 64). It is based on Pascal's triangle of coefficients, shown in Figure 2.27. The recursive definition of the binomial coefficient is

$$
\begin{cases}
b(n,0) = 1 \\
b(k,k) = 1 \\
b(n,k) = b(n-1,k) + b(n-1,k-1) \quad \text{for } 0 \le k \le n
\end{cases}
$$

The function tests for the base cases with an `if` statement, using the OR boolean operator. If neither base case is satisfied, it calls itself recursively twice—once to compute $b(n-1, k)$ and once to compute $b(n-1, k-1)$. Figure 6.26 shows the run-time stack produced by a call from the main program with actual parameters (3, 1). The function is called twice more with parameters (2, 1) and (1, 1), followed by a return. Then a call with parameters (1, 0) is executed, followed by a second return, and so on. Figure 6.26 shows the run-time stack at the assembly level immediately after the second return. It corresponds directly to the level-HOL6 diagram of Figure 2.29(g) (page 65). The return address labeled ra2 in Figure 2.29(g) is 0031 in Figure 6.29, the address of the instruction after the first CALL in the function. Similarly, the address labeled ra1 in Figure 2.29 is 007A in Figure 6.26.

High-Order Language

```
#include <iostream>
using namespace std;

int binCoeff (int n, int k) {
    int y1, y2;
    if ((k == 0) || (n == k)) {
        return 1;
    }
    else {
        y1 = binCoeff (n - 1, k); // ra2
        y2 = binCoeff (n - 1, k - 1); // ra3
        return y1 + y2;
    }
}

int main () {
    cout << "binCoeff (3, 1) = " << binCoeff (3, 1); // ra1
    cout << endl;
    return 0;
}
```

Figure **6.25**

A recursive nonvoid function at level HOL6 and level Asmb5. The C++ program is from Figure 2.25.

Assembly Language

Figure **6.25**

(Continued)

```
00000   040065              BR      main
                    ;
                    ;******* int binomCoeff (int n, int k)
                    retVal: .EQUATE 10          ;returned value #2d
                    n:      .EQUATE 8           ;formal parameter #2d
                    k:      .EQUATE 6           ;formal parameter #2d
                    y1:     .EQUATE 2           ;local variable #2d
                    y2:     .EQUATE 0           ;local variable #2d
0003    680004 binCoeff:SUBSP 4,i              ;allocate #y1 #y2
0006    C30006 if:     LDA     k,s             ;if ((k == 0)
0009    0A0015          BREQ    then
000C    C30008          LDA     n,s             ;|| (n == k))
000F    B30006          CPA     k,s
0012    0C001C          BRNE    else
0015    C00001 then:    LDA     1,i             ;return 1
0018    E3000A          STA     retVal,s
001B    5C              RET4                    ;deallocate #y2 #y1, pop retAddr
001C    C30008 else:    LDA     n,s             ;push n - 1
001F    800001          SUBA    1,i
0022    E3FFFC          STA     -4,s
0025    C30006          LDA     k,s             ;push k
0028    E3FFFA          STA     -6,s
002B    680006          SUBSP   6,i             ;push #retVal #n #k
002E    160003          CALL    binCoeff        ;binomCoeff (n - 1, k)
0031    600006 ra2:     ADDSP   6,i             ;pop #k #n #retVal
0034    C3FFFE          LDA     -2,s            ;y1 = binomCoeff (n - 1, k)
0037    E30002          STA     y1,s
003A    C30008          LDA     n,s             ;push n - 1
003D    800001          SUBA    1,i
0040    E3FFFC          STA     -4,s
0043    C30006          LDA     k,s             ;push k - 1
0046    800001          SUBA    1,i
0049    E3FFFA          STA     -6,s
004C    680006          SUBSP   6,i             ;push #retVal #n #k
004F    160003          CALL    binCoeff        ;binomCoeff (n - 1, k - 1)
0052    600006 ra3:     ADDSP   6,i             ;pop #k #n #retVal
0055    C3FFFE          LDA     -2,s            ;y2 = binomCoeff (n - 1, k - 1)
0058    E30000          STA     y2,s
005B    C30002          LDA     y1,s            ;return y1 + y2
005E    730000          ADDA    y2,s
0061    E3000A          STA     retVal,s
0064    5C     endIf:   RET4                    ;deallocate #y2 #y1, pop retAddr
                    ;
```

```
                ;******* main ()                                            Figure 6.25
0065   410084 main:   STRO    msg,d    ;cout << "binCoeff (3, 1) = "        (Continued)
0068   C00003         LDA     3,i      ;push 3
006B   E3FFFC         STA     -4,s
006E   C00001         LDA     1,i      ;push 1
0071   E3FFFA         STA     -6,s
0074   680006         SUBSP   6,i      ;push #retVal #n #k
0077   160003         CALL    binCoeff ;binomCoeff (3, 1)
007A   600006 ra1:    ADDSP   6,i      ;pop #k #n #retVal
007D   3BFFFE         DECO    -2,s     ;<< binCoeff (3, 1)
0080   50000A         CHARO   '\n',i   ;cout << endl
0083   00             STOP
0084   62696E msg:    .ASCII  "binCoeff (3, 1) = \x00"
       ...
0097                  .END
```

At the start of the main program when the stack pointer has its initial value, the first actual parameter has a stack offset of −4, and the second has a stack offset of −6. In a procedure call (a void function), these offsets would be −2 and −4, respectively. Their magnitudes are greater by 2 because of the two-byte value returned on the stack by the function. The SUBSP instruction at 0074 allocates six bytes, two each for the actual parameters and two for the returned value.

When the function returns control to ADDSP at 007A, the value it returns will be on the stack below the two actual parameters. ADDSP pops the parameters and returned value by adding 6 to the stack pointer, after which it points to the cell directly below the returned value. So DECO outputs the value with stack-relative addressing and an offset of −2.

The function calls itself by allocating actual parameters according to the standard technique. For the first recursive call, it computes n - 1 and k and pushes those values onto the stack along with storage for the returned value. After the return, the sequence

```
ADDSP 6,i    ;pop #k #n #retVal
LDA   -2,s   ;y1 = binomCoeff (n - 1, k)
STA   y1,s
```

pops the two actual parameters and returned value and assigns the returned value to y1. For the second call, it pushes n − 1 and k − 1 and assigns the returned value to y2 similarly.

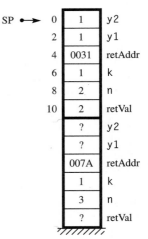

Figure **6.26**

The run-time stack of Figure 6.25 immediately after the second return.

Translating Call-By-Reference Parameters with Global Variables

C++ provides call-by-reference parameters so that the called procedure can change the value of the actual parameter in the calling procedure. Figure 2.20 (page 53) shows a program at level HOL6 that uses call by reference to put two global variables, a and b, in order. Figure 6.27 shows the same program together with the object program that a compiler would produce.

High-Order Language

```
#include <iostream>
using namespace std;

int a, b;

void swap (int& r, int& s) {
   int temp;
   temp = r;
   r = s;
   s = temp;
}
void order (int& x, int& y) {
   if (x > y) {
      swap (x, y);
   }  // ra2
}

int main () {
   cout << "Enter an integer: ";
   cin >> a;
   cout << "Enter an integer: ";
   cin >> b;
   order (a, b);
   cout << "Ordered they are: " << a << ", " << b << endl; // ra1
   return 0;
}
```

Figure **6.27**

Call-by-reference parameters with global variables. The C++ program is from Figure 2.20.

Assembly Language

Figure **6.27**

(Continued)

```
0000   04003C           BR      main
0003   0000    a:       .BLOCK  2              ;global variable #2d
0005   0000    b:       .BLOCK  2              ;global variable #2d
                        ;
                        ;******* void swap (int& r, int& s)
               r:       .EQUATE 6              ;formal parameter #2h
               s:       .EQUATE 4              ;formal parameter #2h
               temp:    .EQUATE 0              ;local variable #2d
0007   680002  swap:    SUBSP   2,i            ;allocate #temp
000A   C40006           LDA     r,sf           ;temp = r
000D   E30000           STA     temp,s
0010   C40004           LDA     s,sf           ;r = s
0013   E40006           STA     r,sf
0016   C30000           LDA     temp,s         ;s = temp
0019   E40004           STA     s,sf
001C   5A               RET2                   ;deallocate #temp, pop retAddr
                        ;
                        ;******* void order (int& x, int& y)
               x:       .EQUATE 4              ;formal parameter #2h
               y:       .EQUATE 2              ;formal parameter #2h
001D   C40004  order:   LDA     x,sf           ;if (x > y)
0020   B40002           CPA     y,sf
0023   06003B           BRLE    endIf
0026   C30004           LDA     x,s            ;    push x
0029   E3FFFE           STA     -2,s
002C   C30002           LDA     y,s            ;    push y
002F   E3FFFC           STA     -4,s
0032   680004           SUBSP   4,i            ;    push #r #s
0035   160007           CALL    swap           ;    swap (x, y)
0038   600004           ADDSP   4,i            ;    pop #s #r
003B   58      endIf:   RET0                   ;pop retAddr


                        ;
                        ;******* main ()
003C   41006D  main:    STRO    msg1,d         ;cout << "Enter an integer: "
003F   310003           DECI    a,d            ;cin >> a
0042   41006D           STRO    msg1,d         ;cout << "Enter an integer: "
0045   310005           DECI    b,d            ;cin >> b
0048   C00003           LDA     a,i            ;push the address of a
004B   E3FFFE           STA     -2,s
004E   C00005           LDA     b,i            ;push the address of b
```

Figure **6.27**

(Continued)

```
0051   E3FFFC         STA      -4,s
0054   680004         SUBSP    4,i        ;push #x #y
0057   16001D         CALL     order      ;order (a, b)
005A   600004  ra1:   ADDSP    4,i        ;pop #y #x
005D   410080         STRO     msg2,d     ;cout << "Ordered they are: "
0060   390003         DECO     a,d        ;    << a
0063   410093         STRO     msg3,d     ;    << ", "
0066   390005         DECO     b,d        ;    << b
0069   50000A         CHARO    '\n',i     ;    << endl
006C   00             STOP
006D   456E74  msg1:  .ASCII   "Enter an integer: \x00"
       ...
0080   4F7264  msg2:  .ASCII   "Ordered they are: \x00"
       ...
0093   2C2000  msg3:  .ASCII   ", \x00"
0096                  .END
```

The main program calls a procedure named order with two formal parameters, x and y, that are called by reference. order in turn calls swap, which makes the actual exchange. swap has call-by-reference parameters r and s. Parameter r refers to s, and s refers to a. The programmer used call by reference so that when procedure swap changes r it really changes a, because r refers to a (via s).

Parameters called by reference differ from parameters called by value in C++ because the actual parameter provides a reference to a variable in the calling routine instead of a value. At the assembly level, the code that pushes the actual parameter onto the stack pushes the address of the actual parameter. When the actual parameter is a global variable, its address is available as the value of its symbol. So, the code to push the address of a global variable is a load instruction with immediate addressing. In Figure 6.27, the code to push the address of a is

```
LDA a,i ;push the address of a
```

The value of the symbol a is 0003, the address of where the value of a is stored. The machine code for this instruction is

```
C00003
```

C0 is the instruction specifier for the load accumulator instruction with addressing-aaa field of 000 to indicate immediate addressing. With immediate addressing, the operand specifier is the operand. Consequently, this instruction loads 0003 into the accumulator. The following instruction pushes it onto the run-time stack.

Similarly, the code to push the address of b is

```
LDA b,i ;push the address of b
```

The machine code for this instruction is

```
C00005
```

where 0005 is the address of b. This instruction loads 0005 into the accumulator with immediate addressing, after which the next instruction puts it on the run-time stack.

In Figure 6.27 at 0026, procedure order calls swap (x, y). It must push x onto the run-time stack. x is called by reference. Consequently, the address of x is on the run-time stack. The corresponding formal parameter r is also called by reference. Consequently, procedure swap expects the address of r to be on the run-time stack. Procedure order simply transfers the address for swap to use. The statement

```
LDA x,s ;push x
```

at 0026 uses stack-relative addressing to put the address in the accumulator. The next instruction puts it on the run-time stack.

In procedure order, however, the compiler must translate

```
temp = r
```

It must load the value of r into the accumulator, and then store it in temp. How does the called procedure access the value of a formal parameter whose address is on the run-time stack? It uses stack-relative deferred addressing.

Remember that the relation between the operand and the operand specifier with stack-relative addressing is

$$Oprnd = Mem [SP + OprndSpec]$$ *Stack-relative addressing*

The operand is on the run-time stack. But with call-by-reference parameters, the address of the operand is on the run-time stack. The relation between the operand and the operand specifier with stack-relative deferred addressing is

$$Oprnd = Mem [Mem [SP + OprndSpec]]$$ *Stack-relative deferred addressing*

In other words, Mem [SP + OprndSpec] is the address of the operand, rather than the operand itself.

At lines 000A and 000D, the compiler generates the following object code to translate the assignment statement:

```
LDA r,sf
STA temp,s
```

The letters sf with the load instruction indicate stack-relative deferred addressing. The object code for the load instruction is

```
C40006
```

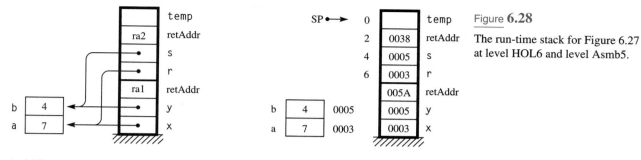

Figure **6.28**

The run-time stack for Figure 6.27 at level HOL6 and level Asmb5.

(a) The run-time stack at level HOL6. **(b)** The run-time stack at level Asmb5.

0006 is the stack relative address of parameter r, as Figure 6.28(b) shows. It contains 0003, the address of a. The load instruction loads 7, which is the value of a, into the accumulator. The store instruction puts it in temp on the stack.

The next assignment statement in procedure swap

```
r = s;
```

has parameters on both sides of the assignment operator. The compiler generates LDA to load the value of s and STA to store the value to r, both with stack-relative addressing.

```
LDA s,sf
STA r,sf
```

In summary, to translate call-by-reference parameters with global variables, the compiler generates code as follows:

- To push the actual parameter, it generates a load instruction with immediate addressing.

- To access the formal parameter, it generates instructions with stack-relative deferred addressing.

The translation rules for call-by-reference parameters with global variables

Translating Call-By-Reference Parameters with Local Variables

Figure 6.29 shows a program that computes the perimeter of a rectangle given its width and height. The main program prompts the user for the width and the height, which it inputs into two local variables named width and height. A third local variable is named perim. The main program calls a procedure (a void function) named rect passing width and height by value and perim by reference. The figure shows the input and output when the user enters 8 for the width and 5 for the height.

High-Order Language

```
#include <iostream>
using namespace std;

void rect (int& p, int w, int h) {
   p = (w + h) * 2;
}


int main () {
   int perim, width, height;
   cout << "Enter width: ";
   cin >> width;
   cout << "Enter height: ";
   cin >> height;
   rect (perim, width, height);
   // ra1
   cout << "perim = " << perim << endl;
   return 0;
}
```

Figure **6.29**

Call-by-reference parameters with local variables.

Assembly Language

```
0000   04000E           BR      main
                ;
                ;******* void rect (int& p, int w, int h)
                p:       .EQUATE 6            ;formal parameter #2h
                w:       .EQUATE 4            ;formal parameter #2d
                h:       .EQUATE 2            ;formal parameter #2d
0003   C30004 rect:     LDA     w,s          ;p = (w + h) * 2
0006   730002           ADDA    h,s
0009   1C               ASLA
000A   E40006           STA     p,sf
000D   58     endIf:    RET0                 ;pop retAddr
                ;
                ;******* main ()
                perim:   .EQUATE 4            ;local variable #2d
                width:   .EQUATE 2            ;local variable #2d
                height:  .EQUATE 0            ;local variable #2d
000E   680006 main:     SUBSP   6,i          ;allocate #perim #width #height
0011   410046           STRO    msg1,d       ;cout << "Enter width: "
0014   330002           DECI    width,s      ;cin >> width
0017   410054           STRO    msg2,d       ;cout << "Enter height: "
```

```
001A   330000    DECI    height,s    ;cin >> height
001D   02        MOVSPA              ;push the address of perim
001E   700004    ADDA    perim,i
0021   E3FFFE    STA     -2,s
0024   C30002    LDA     width,s     ;push the value of width
0027   E3FFFC    STA     -4,s
002A   C30000    LDA     height,s    ;push the value of height
002D   E3FFFA    STA     -6,s
0030   680006    SUBSP   6,i         ;push #p #w #h
0033   160003    CALL    rect        ;rect (perim, width, height)
0036   600006 ra1:  ADDSP 6,i        ;pop #h #w #p
0039   410063    STRO    msg3,d      ;cout << "perim = "
003C   3B0004    DECO    perim,s     ;     << perim
003F   50000A    CHARO   '\n',i      ;     << endl
0042   600006    ADDSP   6,i         ;deallocate #height #width #perim
0045   00        STOP
0046   456E74 msg1:  .ASCII  "Enter width: \x00"
       . . .
0054   456E74 msg2:  .ASCII  "Enter height: \x00"
       . . .
0063   706572 msg3:  .ASCII  "perim = \x00"
       . . .
006C             .END
```

Input/Output

```
Enter width: 8
Enter height: 5
perim = 26
```

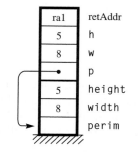

Figure **6.29**

(Continued)

Figure **6.30**

The run-time stack for Figure 6.29 at level HOL6.

Figure 6.30 shows the run-time stack at level HOL6 for the program. Compare it to Figure 6.28(a) for a program with global variables that are called by reference. In that program, formal parameters x, y, r, and s refer to global variables a and b. At level Asmb5, a and b are allocated at translation time with the .EQUATE dot command. Their symbols are their addresses. However, Figure 6.30 shows perim to be allocated on the run-time stack. The statement

```
main: SUBSP 6,i
```

at 000E allocates storage for perim, and its symbol is defined by

```
perim: .EQUATE 4
```

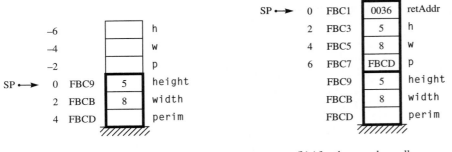

(a) Before the procedure call.

(b) After the procedure call.

Figure **6.31**

The run-time stack for Figure 6.29 at level Asmb5.

Its symbol is not its absolute address. Its symbol is its address relative to the top of the run-time stack, as Figure 6.31(a) shows. Its absolute address is FBCD. Why? Because that is the location of the bottom of the application run-time stack, as the memory map in Figure 4.39 shows.

So, the compiler cannot generate code to push parameter perim with

```
LDA perim,i
STA -2,s
```

as it does for global variables. If it generated those instructions, procedure rect would modify the content of Mem [0004], and 0004 is not where perim is located.

The absolute address of perim is FBCD. Figure 6.31(a) shows that you could calculate it by adding the value of perim, 4, to the value of the stack pointer. Fortunately, there is a unary instruction MOVSPA that moves the content of the stack pointer to the accumulator. The RTL specification of MOVSPA is

$$A \leftarrow SP$$

The MOVSPA *instruction*

To push the address of perim the compiler generates the following instructions at 001D in Figure 6.29:

```
MOVSPA
ADDA    perim,i
STA     -2,s
```

The first instruction moves the content of the stack pointer to the accumulator. The accumulator then contains FBC9. The second instruction adds the value of perim, which is 4, to the accumulator, making it FBCD. The third instruction puts the address of perim in the cell for p, which procedure rect uses to store the perimeter. Figure 6.31(b) shows the result.

Procedure rect uses p as any procedure would use any call-by-reference parameter. Namely, at 000A it stores the value using stack-relative deferred addressing.

```
STA p,sf
```

With stack-relative deferred addressing, the address of the operand is on the stack. The operand is

Oprnd = Mem [Mem [SP + OprndSpec]]

Stack-relative deferred addressing

This instruction adds the stack pointer FBC1 to the operand specifier 6, yielding FBC7. Because Mem [FBC7] is FBCD, it stores the accumulator at Mem [FBCD].

In summary, to translate call-by-reference parameters with local variables, the compiler generates code as follows:

- To push the actual parameter, it generates the unary MOVSPA instruction followed by the ADDA instruction with immediate addressing.

- To access the formal parameter, it generates instructions with stack-relative deferred addressing.

The translation rules for call-by-reference parameters with local variables

Translating Boolean Types

Several schemes exist for storing boolean values at the assembly level. The one most appropriate for C++ is to treat the values true and false as integer constants. The values are

```
const int true = 1;
const int false = 0;
```

Figure 6.32 is a program that declares a boolean function named inRange. The compiler translates the function as if true and false were declared as above.

High-Order Language

```
#include <iostream>
using namespace std;

const int LOWER = 21;
const int UPPER = 65;

bool inRange (int a) {
   if ((LOWER <= a) && (a <= UPPER)) {
      return true;
   }
   else {
      return false;
   }
}
```

Figure **6.32**

Translation of a boolean type.

```
int main () {
   int age;
   cin >> age;
   if (inRange (age)) {
      cout << "Qualified\n";
   }
   else {
      cout << "Unqualified\n";
   }
   return 0;
}
```

Figure **6.32**

(Continued)

Assembly Language

```
0000   040023                  BR       main
               true:   .EQUATE 1
               false:  .EQUATE 0
               ;
               LOWER:  .EQUATE 21            ;const int
               UPPER:  .EQUATE 65            ;const int
               ;
               ;******* bool inRange (int a)
               retVal: .EQUATE 2             ;returned value #2d
               a:      .EQUATE 0             ;formal parameter #2d
0003   C00015 inRange: LDA      LOWER,i     ;if ((LOWER <= a)
0006   B30000 if:      CPA      a,s
0009   10001C          BRGT     else
000C   C30000          LDA      a,s          ;    && (a <= UPPER))
000F   B00041          CPA      UPPER,i
0012   10001C          BRGT     else
0015   C00001 then:    LDA      true,i       ;    return true
0018   E30002          STA      retVal,s
001B   58              RETO
001C   C00000 else:    LDA      false,i      ;    return false
001F   E30002          STA      retVal,s
0022   58              RETO
               ;
               ;******* main ()
               age:    .EQUATE 0             ;local variable #2d
0023   680002 main:    SUBSP    2,i          ;allocate #age
0026   330000          DECI     age,s        ;cin >> age
0029   C30000 if2:     LDA      age,s        ;if (
002C   E3FFFC          STA      -4,s         ;store the value of age
```

```
002F  680004           SUBSP   4,i          ;push #retVal #a
0032  160003           CALL    inRange      ;   (inRange (age))
0035  600004           ADDSP   4,i          ;pop #a #retVal
0038  C3FFFE           LDA     -2,s         ;load retVal
003B  0A0044           BREQ    else2        ;branch if retVal == false (i.e. 0)
003E  41004B then2:    STRO    msg1,d       ;   cout << "Qualified\n"
0041  040047           BR      endif2
0044  410056 else2:    STRO    msg2,d       ;   cout << "Unqualified\n"
0047  600002 endif2:   ADDSP   2,i          ;deallocate #age
004A  00               STOP
004B  517561 msg1:     .ASCII  "Qualified\n\x00"
      ...
0056  556E71 msg2:     .ASCII  "Unqualified\n\x00"
      ...
0063                   .END
```

Figure **6.32**

(Continued)

Representing false and true at the bit level as 0000 and 0001 (hex) has advantages and disadvantages. Consider the logical operations on boolean quantities and the corresponding assembly instructions ANDr, ORr, and NOTr. If p and q are global boolean variables, then

p && q

translates to

```
LDA  p,d
ANDA q,d
```

If you AND 0000 and 0001 with this object code, you get 0000 as desired. The OR operation || also works as desired. The NOT operation is a problem, however, because if you apply NOT to 0000, you get FFFF instead of 0001. Also, applying NOT to 0001 gives FFFE instead of 0000. Consequently, the compiler does not generate the NOT instruction when it translates the C++ assignment statement

p = !q

Instead, it uses the exclusive-or operation XOR, which has the mathematical symbol $\oplus$. It has the useful property that if you take the XOR of any bit value b with 0, you get b. And if you take the XOR of any bit value b with 1, you get the logical negation of b. Mathematically,

$$b \oplus 0 = b$$
$$b \oplus 1 = \neg b$$

Unfortunately, the Pep/8 computer does not have an XORr instruction in its instruction set. If it did have such an instruction, the compiler would generate the following code for the above assignment:

```
LDA  q,d
XORA 0x0001,i
STA  p,d
```

If q is false it has the representation 0000 (hex), and 0000 XOR 0001 equals 0001, as desired. Also, if q is true it has the representation 0001 (hex), and 0001 XOR 0001 equals 0000.

The type bool was not included in the C++ language standard until 1996. Older compilers use the convention that the boolean operators operate on integers. They interpret the integer value 0 as false and any nonzero integer value as true. To preserve backward compatibility, current C++ compilers maintain this convention.

6.4   Indexed Addressing and Arrays

A variable at level HOL6 is a memory cell at level ISA3. A variable at level HOL6 is referred to by its name, at level ISA3 by its address. A variable at level Asmb5 can be referred to by its symbolic name, but the value of that symbol is the address of the cell in memory.

What about an array of values? An array contains many elements, and so consists of many memory cells. The memory cells of the elements are contiguous; that is, they are adjacent to one another. An array at level HOL6 has a name. At level Asmb5, the corresponding symbol is the address of the first cell of the array. This section shows how the compiler translates source programs that allocate and access elements of one-dimensional arrays. It does so with several forms of indexed addressing.

At level Asmb5, the value of the symbol of an array is the address of the first cell of the array.

Figure 6.33 summarizes all the Pep/8 addressing modes. Previous programs illustrate immediate, direct, stack-relative, and stack-relative deferred addressing. Programs with arrays use indexed, stack-indexed, or stack-indexed deferred addressing. The column labeled aaa shows the address-aaa field at level ISA3. The column labeled Letters shows the assembly language designation for the addressing mode at level Asmb5. The column labeled Operand shows how the CPU determines the operand from the operand specifier (OprndSpec).

Addressing Mode	aaa	Letters	Operand
Immediate	000	i	OprndSpec
Direct	001	d	Mem [OprndSpec]
Indirect	010	n	Mem [Mem [OprndSpec]]
Stack-relative	011	s	Mem [SP + OprndSpec]
Stack-relative deferred	100	sf	Mem [Mem [SP + OprndSpec]]
Indexed	101	x	Mem [OprndSpec + X]
Stack-indexed	110	sx	Mem [SP + OprndSpec + X]
Stack-indexed deferred	111	sxf	Mem [Mem [SP + OprndSpec] + X]

Figure **6.33**

The Pep/8 addressing modes.

Translating Global Arrays

The C++ program in Figure 6.34 is the same as the one in Figure 2.15 (page 46), except that the variables are global instead of local. It shows a program at level HOL6 that declares a global array of four integers named vector and a global integer named j. The main program inputs four integers into the array with a for loop and outputs them in reverse order together with their indexes.

High-Order Language

```
#include <iostream>
using namespace std;

int vector[4];
int j;

int main () {
   for (j = 0; j < 4; j++) {
      cin >> vector[j];
   }
   for (j = 3; j >= 0; j--) {
      cout << j  << ' ' << vector[j] << endl;
   }
   return 0;
}
```

Figure **6.34**

A global array.

Assembly Language

Figure **6.34**

(Continued)

```
0000    04000D              BR      main
0003    000000  vector:     .BLOCK  8            ;global variable #2d4a
        000000
        0000
000B    0000    j:          .BLOCK  2            ;global variable #2d
        ;
        ;******* main ()
000D    C80000  main:       LDX     0,i          ;for (j = 0
0010    E9000B              STX     j,d
0013    B80004  for1:       CPX     4,i          ;   j < 4
0016    0E0029              BRGE    endFor1
0019    1D                  ASLX                 ;   an integer is two bytes
001A    350003              DECI    vector,x     ;   cin >> vector[j]
001D    C9000B              LDX     j,d          ;   j++)
0020    780001              ADDX    1,i
0023    E9000B              STX     j,d
0026    040013              BR      for1
0029    C80003  endFor1:    LDX     3,i          ;for (j = 3
002C    E9000B              STX     j,d
002F    B80000  for2:       CPX     0,i          ;   j >= 0
0032    08004E              BRLT    endFor2
0035    39000B              DECO    j,d          ;   cout << j
0038    500020              CHARO   ' ',i        ;       << ' '
003B    1D                  ASLX                 ;   an integer is two bytes
003C    3D0003              DECO    vector,x     ;       << vector[j]
003F    50000A              CHARO   '\n',i       ;       << endl
0042    C9000B              LDX     j,d          ;   j--)
0045    880001              SUBX    1,i
0048    E9000B              STX     j,d
004B    04002F              BR      for2
004E    00      endFor2:    STOP
004F                        .END
```

Input

```
60 70 80 90
```

Output

```
3 90
2 80
1 70
0 60
```

Figure 6.35 shows the memory allocation for integer j and array vector. As with all global integers, the compiler translates

```
int j;
```

at level HOL6 as the following statement at level Asmb5:

```
j: .BLOCK 2
```

The two-byte integer is allocated at address 000B. The compiler translates

```
int vector[4];
```

at level HOL6 as the following statement at level Asmb5:

```
vector: .BLOCK 8
```

It allocates eight bytes because the array contains four integers, each of which is two bytes. The .BLOCK statement is at 0003. Figure 6.35 shows that 0003 is the address of the first element of the array. The second element is at 0005, and each element is at an address two bytes greater than the previous element.

The compiler translates the first for statement

```
for (j = 0; j < 4; j++)
```

as usual. It accesses j with direct addressing because j is a global variable. But how does it access vector[j]? It cannot simply use direct addressing, because the value of symbol vector is the address of the first element of the array. If the value of j is 2, it should access the third element of the array, not the first.

The answer is that it uses indexed addressing. With indexed addressing, the CPU computes the operand as

Oprnd = Mem[OprndSpec + X]

It adds the operand specifier and the index register and uses the sum as the address in main memory from which it fetches the operand.

In Figure 6.34, the compiler translates

```
cin >> vector[j];
```

at level HOL6 as

```
ASLX
DECI vector,x
```

at level Asmb5. This is an optimized translation. The compiler analyzed the previous code generated and determined that the index register already contained the current value of j. A nonoptimizing compiler would generate the following code:

```
LDX    j,d
ASLX
DECI   vector,x
```

Suppose the value of j is 2. LDX puts the value of j in the index register. (Or, an optimizing compiler determines that the current value of j is already in the index

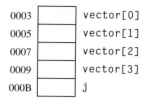

0003		vector[0]
0005		vector[1]
0007		vector[2]
0009		vector[3]
000B		j

Figure 6.35

Memory allocation for the global array of Figure 6.34.

Indexed addressing

register.) `ASLX` multiplies the 2 times 2, leaving 4 in the index register. `DECI` uses indexed addressing. So, the operand is computed as

Mem [OprndSpec + X]
Mem [0003 + 4]
Mem [0007]

which Figure 6.35 shows is `vector[2]`. Had the array been an array of characters, the `ASLX` operation would be unnecessary because each character occupies only one byte. In general, if each cell in the array occupies *n* bytes, the value of `j` is loaded into the index register, multiplied by *n*, and the array element is accessed with indexed addressing.

Similarly, the compiler translates the output of `vector[j]` as

```
ASLX
DECO   vector,x
```

with indexed addressing.

In summary, to translate global arrays, the compiler generates code as follows:

- It allocates storage for the array with `.BLOCK` *tot* where *tot* is the total number of bytes occupied by the array.

- It accesses an element of the array by loading the index into the index register, multiplying it by the number of bytes per cell, and using indexed addressing.

The translation rules for global arrays

Format trace tags for arrays specify how many cells are in the array as well as the number of bytes. In Figure 6.34 at 0003, the declaration for `vector` is

Format trace tags for arrays

```
vector:   .BLOCK 8   ;global variable #2d4a
```

You should read the format trace tag `#2d4a` as "two byte decimal, four cell array." With this specification, the Pep/8 debugger will produce a figure similar to that of Figure 6.35 with each array cell individually labeled.

Translating Local Arrays

Like all local variables, local arrays are allocated on the run-time stack during program execution. The `SUBSP` instruction allocates the array and the `ADDSP` instruction deallocates it. Figure 6.36 is a program identical to the one of Figure 6.34 except that the index `j` and the array `vector` are local to `main()`.

High-Order Language

```
#include <iostream>
using namespace std;

int main () {
    int vector[4];
    int j;
```

Figure **6.36**

A local array. The C++ program is from Figure 2.15.

```
   for (j = 0; j < 4; j++) {
      cin >> vector[j];
   }
   for (j = 3; j >= 0; j--) {
      cout << j  << ' ' << vector[j] << endl;
   }
   return 0;
}
```

Figure **6.36**

(Continued)

Assembly Language

```
0000  040003            BR       main
                  ;
                  ;******* main ()
                  vector:   .EQUATE 2          ;local variable #2d4a
                  j:        .EQUATE 0          ;local variable #2d
0003  68000A main:     SUBSP    10,i        ;allocate #vector #j
0006  C80000            LDX      0,i         ;for (j = 0
0009  EB0000            STX      j,s
000C  B80004 for1:     CPX      4,i         ;   j < 4
000F  0E0022            BRGE     endFor1
0012  1D                ASLX                 ;   an integer is two bytes
0013  360002            DECI     vector,sx   ;   cin >> vector[j]
0016  CB0000            LDX      j,s         ;   j++)
0019  780001            ADDX     1,i
001C  EB0000            STX      j,s
001F  04000C            BR       for1
0022  C80003 endFor1:  LDX      3,i         ;for (j = 3
0025  EB0000            STX      j,s
0028  B80000 for2:     CPX      0,i         ;   j >= 0
002B  080047            BRLT     endFor2
002E  3B0000            DECO     j,s         ;   cout << j
0031  500020            CHARO    ' ',i       ;      << ' '
0034  1D                ASLX                 ;   an integer is two bytes
0035  3E0002            DECO     vector,sx   ;      << vector[j]
0038  50000A            CHARO    '\n',i      ;      << endl
003B  CB0000            LDX      j,s         ;   j--)
003E  880001            SUBX     1,i
0041  EB0000            STX      j,s
0044  040028            BR       for2
0047  60000A endFor2:  ADDSP    10,i        ;deallocate #j #vector
004A  00                STOP
004B                    .END
```

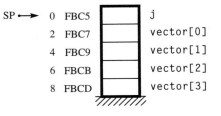

Figure **6.37**

Memory allocation for the local array of Figure 6.36.

Figure 6.37 shows the memory allocation on the run-time stack for the program of Figure 6.36. The compiler translates

```
int vector[4];
int j;
```

at level HOL6 as

```
main: SUBSP 10,i
```

at level Asmb5. It allocates eight bytes for `vector` and two bytes for `j`, for a total of 10 bytes. It sets the values of the symbols with

```
vector: .EQUATE 2
j:      .EQUATE 0
```

where 2 is the stack-relative address of the first cell of `vector` and 0 is the stack-relative address of `j` as Figure 6.37 shows

How does the compiler access `vector[j]`? It cannot use indexed addressing, because the value of symbol `vector` is not the address of the first element of the array. It uses stack-indexed addressing. With stack-indexed addressing, the CPU computes the operand as

Oprnd = Mem[SP + OprndSpec + X]   *Stack-indexed addressing*

It adds the stack pointer plus the operand specifier plus the index register and uses the sum as the address in main memory from which it fetches the operand.

In Figure 6.37, the compiler translates

```
cin >> vector[j];
```

at level HOL6 as

```
ASLX
DECI  vector,sx
```

at level Asmb5. As in the previous program, this is an optimized translation. A nonoptimizing compiler would generate the following code:

```
LDX   j,d
ASLX
DECI  vector,sx
```

Suppose the value of j is 2. LDX puts the value of j in the index register. ASLX multiplies the 2 times 2, leaving 4 in the index register. DECI uses stack-indexed addressing. So, the operand is computed as

Mem [SP + OprndSpec + X]
Mem [FBC5 + 2 + 4]
Mem [FBCB]

which Figure 6.37 shows is vector[2]. You can see how stack-indexed addressing is made for arrays on the run-time stack. SP is the address of the top of the stack. OprndSpec is the stack-relative address of the first cell of the array, so SP + OprndSpec is the absolute address of the first cell of the array. With j in the index register (multiplied by the number of bytes per cell of the array), the sum SP + OprndSpec + X is the address of cell j of the array.

In summary, to translate local arrays, the compiler generates code as follows:

- The array is allocated with SUBSP and deallocated with ADDSP.

- An element of the array is accessed by loading the index into the index register, multiplying it by the number of bytes per cell, and using stack-indexed addressing.

The translation rules for local arrays

Translating Arrays Passed as Parameters

In C++, the name of an array is the address of the first element of the array. When you pass an array, even if you do not use the & designation in the formal parameter list, you are passing the address of the first element of the array. The effect is as if you call the array by reference. The designers of the C language, on which C++ is based, reasoned that programmers almost never want to pass an array by value because such calls are so inefficient. They require large amounts of storage on the run-time stack because the stack must contain the entire array. And they require a large amount of time because the value of every cell must be copied onto the stack. Consequently, the default behavior in C++ is for arrays to be called as if by reference.

Figure 6.38 shows how a compiler translates a program that passes a local array as a parameter. The main program passes an array of integers vector and an integer numItms to procedures getVect and putVect. getVect inputs values into the array and sets numItms to the number of items input. putVect outputs the values of the array.

High-Order Language

```
#include <iostream>
using namespace std;

void getVect (int v[], int& n) {
    int j;
    cin >> n;
```

Figure **6.38**

Passing a local array as a parameter.

```
        for (j = 0; j < n; j++) {
           cin >> v[j];
        }
     }


     void putVect (int v[], int n) {
        int j;
        for (j = 0; j < n; j++) {
           cout << v[j] << ' ';
        }
        cout << endl;
     }


     int main () {
        int vector[8];
        int numItms;
        getVect (vector, numItms);
        putVect (vector, numItms);
        return 0;
     }
```

Figure **6.38**

(Continued)

Assembly Language

```
0000  04004C            BR      main
                ;
                ;******* getVect (int v[], int& n)
                v:      .EQUATE  6          ;formal parameter #2h
                n:      .EQUATE  4          ;formal parameter #2h
                j:      .EQUATE  0          ;local variable #2d
0003  680002 getVect: SUBSP   2,i         ;allocate #j
0006  340004            DECI    n,sf       ;cin >> n
0009  C80000            LDX     0,i        ;for (j = 0
000C  EB0000            STX     j,s
000F  BC0004 for1:      CPX     n,sf       ;   j < n
0012  0E0025            BRGE    endFor1
0015  1D                ASLX               ;   an integer is two bytes
0016  370006            DECI    v,sxf      ;   cin >> v[j]
0019  CB0000            LDX     j,s        ;   j++)
001C  780001            ADDX    1,i
001F  EB0000            STX     j,s
0022  04000F            BR      for1
0025  5A     endFor1:   RET2               ;pop #j and retAddr
                ;
```

```
              ;******* putVect (int v[], int n)
              v2:     .EQUATE 6          ;formal parameter #2h
              n2:     .EQUATE 4          ;formal parameter #2d
              j2:     .EQUATE 0          ;local variable #2d
0026 680002 putVect: SUBSP   2,i        ;allocate #j2
0029 C80000         LDX     0,i        ;for (j = 0
002C EB0000         STX     j2,s
002F BB0004 for2:   CPX     n2,s       ;   j < n
0032 0E0048         BRGE    endFor2
0035 1D             ASLX               ;   an integer is two bytes
0036 3F0006         DECO    v2,sxf     ;   cout << v[j]
0039 500020         CHARO   ' ',i      ;      << ' '
003C CB0000         LDX     j2,s       ;   j++)
003F 780001         ADDX    1,i
0042 EB0000         STX     j2,s
0045 04002F         BR      for2
0048 50000A endFor2: CHARO  '\n',i     ;cout << endl
004B 5A             RET2               ;pop #j2 and retAddr
              ;
              ;******* main ()
              vector:  .EQUATE 2         ;local variable #2d8a
              numItms: .EQUATE 0         ;local variable #2d
004C 680012 main:   SUBSP   18,i       ;allocate #vector #numItms
004F 02             MOVSPA             ;push address of vector
0050 700002         ADDA    vector,i
0053 E3FFFE         STA     -2,s
0056 02             MOVSPA             ;push address of numItms
0057 700000         ADDA    numItms,i
005A E3FFFC         STA     -4,s
005D 680004         SUBSP   4,i        ;push #v #n
0060 160003         CALL    getVect    ;getVect (vector, numItms)
0063 600004         ADDSP   4,i        ;pop #n #v
0066 02             MOVSPA             ;push address of vector
0067 700002         ADDA    vector,i
006A E3FFFE         STA     -2,s
006D C30000         LDA     numItms,s  ;push value of numItms
0070 E3FFFC         STA     -4,s
0073 680004         SUBSP   4,i        ;push #v2 #n2
0076 160026         CALL    putVect    ;putVect (vector, numItms)
0079 600004         ADDSP   4,i        ;pop #n2 #v2
007C 600012         ADDSP   18,i       ;deallocate #numItms #vector
007F 00             STOP
0080                .END
```

Figure **6.38**

(Continued)

Input

Figure **6.38**

(Continued)

5   40 50 60 70 80

Output

40 50 60 70 80

Figure 6.38 shows that the compiler translates the local variables

```
int vector[8];
int numItms;
```

as

```
vector:   .EQUATE 2
numItms: .EQUATE 0
main:     SUBSP 18,i
```

The SUBSP instruction allocates 18 bytes on the run-time stack, 16 bytes for the eight integers of the array, and 2 bytes for the integer. The .EQUATE dot commands set the symbols to their stack offsets, as Figure 6.39(a) shows.

The compiler translates

```
getVect (vector, numItms);
```

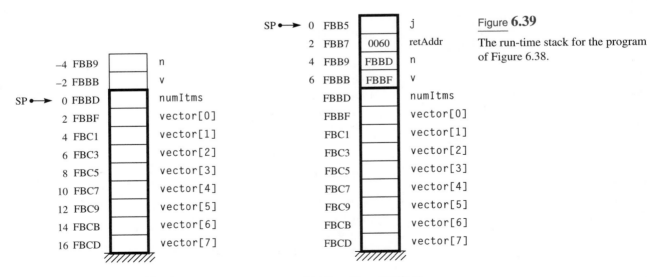

(a) Before calling getVect. (b) After calling getVect.

Figure **6.39**

The run-time stack for the program of Figure 6.38.

by first generating code to push the address of the first cell of `vector`

```
MOVSPA
ADDA    vector,i
STA     -2,s
```

and then by generating code to push the address of `numItms`

```
MOVSPA
ADDA    numItms,i
STA     -4,s
```

Even though the signature of the function

```
void getVect (int v[], int& n)
```

does not have the & with parameter `v[]`, the compiler writes code to push the address of `v` with the `MOVSPA` and `ADDA` instructions. Because the signature does have the & with parameter `n`, the compiler writes code to push the address of `n` in the same way. Figure 6.39(b) shows `v` with FBBF, the address of `vector[0]` and `n` with FBBD, the address of `numItms`.

Figure 6.39(b) also shows the stack offsets for the parameters and local variables in `getVect`. The compiler defines the symbols

```
v:  .EQUATE 6
n:  .EQUATE 4
j:  .EQUATE 0
```

accordingly. It translates the input statement

```
cin >> n;
```

as

```
DECI n,sf
```

where stack-relative deferred addressing is used because `n` is called by reference and the address of `n` is on the stack.

But how does the compiler translate

```
cin >> v[j];
```

It cannot use stack-indexed addressing, because the array of values is not in the stack frame for `getVect`. The value of `v` is 6, which means that the address of the first cell of the array is six bytes below the top of the stack. The array of values is in the stack frame for `main()`. Stack-indexed deferred addressing is designed to access the elements of an array whose address is in the top stack frame but whose actual collection of values is not. With stack-indexed deferred addressing, the CPU computes the operand as

$$\text{Oprnd} = \text{Mem}\,[\text{Mem}\,[\text{SP} + \text{OprndSpec}] + \text{X}]$$

Stack-indexed deferred addressing

It adds the stack pointer plus the operand specifier and uses the sum as the address of the first element of the array, to which it adds the index register. The compiler translates the input statement as

```
ASLX
DECI v,sxf
```

where the letters sxf indicate stack-indexed deferred addressing, and the compiler has determined that the index register will contain the current value of j.

For example, suppose the value of j is 2. The ASLX instruction doubles it to 4. The computation of the operand is

Mem [Mem[SP + OprndSpec] + X]
Mem [Mem[FBB5 + 6] + 4]
Mem [Mem[FBBB] + 4]
Mem [FBBF + 4]
Mem [FBC3]

which is vector[2] as expected from Figure 6.39(b).

The formal parameters in procedures getVect and putVect in Figure 6.39 have the same names. At level HOL6, the scope of the parameter names is confined to the body of the function. The programmer knows that a statement containing n in the body of getVect refers to the n in the parameter list for getVect and not to the n in the parameter list of putVect. The scope of a symbol name at level Asmb5, however, is the entire assembly language program. The compiler cannot use the same symbol for the n in putVect that it uses for the n in getVect, as duplicate symbol definitions would be ambiguous. All compilers must have some mechanism for managing the scope of name declarations in level-HOL6 programs when they transform them to symbols at level Asmb5. The compiler in Figure 6.38 makes the identifiers unambiguous by appending the digit 2 to the symbol name. Hence, the compiler translates variable name n in putVect at level HOL6 to symbol n2 at level Asmb5. It does the same with v and j.

With procedure putVect, the array is passed as a parameter but n is called by value. In preparation for the procedure call, the address of vector is pushed onto the stack as before, but this time the value of numItms is pushed. In procedure putVect, n2 is accessed with stack-relative addressing

```
for2: CPX n2,s
```

because it is called by value. v2 is accessed with stack-indexed deferred addressing

```
ASLX
DECO v2,sxf
```

as it is in getVect.

In Figure 6.38, vector is a local array. If it were a global array, the translations of getVect and putVect would be unchanged. v[j] would be accessed with stack-indexed deferred addressing, which expects the address of the first element of the array to be in the top stack frame. The only difference would be in the code to push the address of the first element of the array in preparation of the call. As in the program of Figure 6.34, the value of the symbol of a global array is the address of the first cell of the array. Consequently, to push the address of the first cell of the array, the compiler would generate a LDA instruction with immediate addressing followed by a STA instruction with stack-relative addressing to do the push.

Passing global arrays as parameters

In summary, to pass an array as a parameter, the compiler generates code as follows:

- The address of the first element of the array is pushed onto the run-time stack, either (a) with MOVSPA followed by ADDA with immediate addressing for a local array, or (b) with LDA with immediate addressing for a global array.

- An element of the array is accessed by loading the index into the index register, multiplying it by the number of bytes per cell, and using stack-indexed deferred addressing.

The translation rules for passing an array as a parameter

Translating the Switch Statement

The program in Figure 6.40, which is also in Figure 2.12 (page 43), shows how a compiler translates the C++ switch statement. It uses an interesting combination of indexed addressing with the unconditional branch, BR. The switch statement is not the same as a nested if statement. If a user enters 2 for guess, the switch statement branches directly to the third alternative without comparing guess to 0 or 1. An array is a random access data structure because the indexing mechanism allows the programmer to access any element at random without traversing all the previous elements. For example, to access the third element of a vector of integers you can write vector[2] directly without having to traverse vector[0] and vector[1] first. Main memory is in effect an array of bytes whose addresses correspond to the indexes of the array. To translate the switch statement, the compiler allocates an array of addresses called a jump table. Each entry in the jump table is the address of the first statement of a section of code that corresponds to one of the cases of the switch statement. With indexed addressing, the program can branch directly to case 2.

High-Order Language

```
#include <iostream>
using namespace std;

int main () {
   int guess;
   cout << "Pick a number 0..3: ";
   cin >> guess;
```

Figure **6.40**

Translation of a switch statement. The C++ program is from Figure 2.12

```
    switch (guess) {
        case 0: cout << "Not close"; break;
        case 1: cout << "Close"; break;
        case 2: cout << "Right on"; break;
        case 3: cout << "Too high";
    }
    cout << endl;
    return 0;
}
```

Figure **6.40**

(Continued)

Assembly Language

```
0000  040003            BR      main
                  ;
                  ;******* main ()
                  guess:   .EQUATE  0          ;local variable #2d
0003  680002 main:     SUBSP   2,i          ;allocate local #guess
0006  410037           STRO    msgIn,d      ;cout << "Pick a number 0..3: "
0009  330000           DECI    guess,s      ;cin >> Guess
000C  CB0000           LDX     guess,s      ;switch (Guess)
000F  1D               ASLX                 ;addresses occupy two bytes
0010  050013           BR      guessJT,x
0013  001B   guessJT: .ADDRSS case0
0015  0021             .ADDRSS case1
0017  0027             .ADDRSS case2
0019  002D             .ADDRSS case3
001B  41004C case0:    STRO    msg0,d       ;cout << "Not close"
001E  040030           BR      endCase      ;break
0021  410056 case1:    STRO    msg1,d       ;cout << "Close"
0024  040030           BR      endCase      ;break
0027  41005C case2:    STRO    msg2,d       ;cout << "Right on"
002A  040030           BR      endCase      ;break
002D  410065 case3:    STRO    msg3,d       ;cout << "Too high"
0030  50000A endCase:  CHARO   '\n',i       ;count << endl
0033  600002           ADDSP   2,i          ;deallocate #guess
0036  00               STOP
0037  506963 msgIn:    .ASCII  "Pick a number 0..3: \x00"
      ...
004C  4E6F74 msg0:     .ASCII  "Not close\x00"
      ...
0056  436C6F msg1:     .ASCII  "Close\x00"
      ...
005C  526967 msg2:     .ASCII  "Right on\x00"
      ...
```

```
0065   546F6F  msg3:    .ASCII   "Too high\x00"
       ...
006E                    .END
```

Figure **6.40**

(Continued)

Figure 6.40 shows the jump table at 0013 in the assembly language program. The code generated at 0013 is 001B, which is the address of the first statement of case 0. The code generated at 0015 is 0021, which is the address of the first statement of case 1, and so on. The compiler generates the jump table with .ADDRSS pseudo-ops. Every .ADDRSS command must be followed by a symbol. The code generated by .ADDRSS is the value of the symbol. For example, case2 is a symbol whose value is 0027, the address of the code to be executed if guess has a value of 2. Therefore, the object code generated by

The .ADDRSS *pseudo-op*

```
.ADDRSS case2
```

at 0017 is 0027.

Suppose the user enters 2 for the value of guess. The statement

```
LDX guess,s
```

puts 2 in the index register. The statement

```
ASLX
```

multiplies the 2, by two leaving 4 in the index register. The statement

```
BR guessJT,x
```

is an unconditional branch with indexed addressing. The value of the operand specifier guessJT is 0013, the address of the first word of the jump table. For indexed addressing, the CPU computes the operand as

Oprnd = Mem[OprndSpec + X]

Indexed addressing

Therefore, the CPU computes

Mem [OprndSpec + X]
Mem [0013 + 4]
Mem [0017]
0027

as the operand. The RTL specification for the BR instruction is

PC ← Oprnd

and so the CPU puts 0027 in the program counter. Because of the von Neumann cycle, the next instruction to be executed is the one at address 0027, which is precisely the first instruction for case 2.

The break statement in C++ is translated as a BR instruction to branch to the end of the switch statement. If you omit the break in your C++ program, the compiler will omit the BR and control will fall through to the next case.

If the user enters a number not in the range 0..3, a run-time error will occur. For example, if the user enters 4 for guess, the ASLX instruction will multiply it by 2, leaving 8 in the index register, and the CPU will compute the operand as

Mem [OprndSpec + X]
Mem [0013 + 8]
Mem [001B]
4100

so the branch will be to memory location 4100 (hex). The problem is that the bits 001B were generated by the assembler for the STRO instruction and were never meant to be interpreted as a branch address. To prevent such indignities from happening to the user, C++ specifies that nothing should happen if the value of guess is not one of the cases. It also provides a default case for the switch statement to handle any case not encountered by the previous cases. The compiler must generate an initial conditional branch on guess to handle the values not covered by the other cases. The problems at the end of the chapter explore this characteristic of the switch statement.

6.5   Dynamic Memory Allocation

The purpose of a compiler is to create a high level of abstraction for the programmer. For example, it lets the programmer think in terms of a single while loop instead of the detailed conditional branches at the assembly level that are necessary to implement the loop on the machine. Hiding the details of a lower level is the essence of abstraction.

Abstraction of control

But abstraction of program control is only one side of the coin. The other side is abstraction of data. At the assembly and machine levels, the only data types are bits and bytes. Previous programs show how the compiler translates character, integer, and array types. Each of these types can be global, allocated with .BLOCK, or local, allocated with SUBSP on the run-time stack. But C++ programs can also contain structures and pointers, the basic building blocks of many data structures. At level HOL6, pointers access structures allocated from the heap with the new operator. This section shows the operation of a simple heap at level Asmb5 and how the compiler translates programs that contain pointers and structures.

Abstraction of data

Translating Global Pointers

Figure 6.41 shows a C++ program with global pointers and its translation to Pep/8 assembly language. The C++ program is identical to the one in Figure 2.37

(page 75). Figure 2.38 (page 76) shows the allocation from the heap as the program executes. The heap is a region of memory different from the stack. The compiler, in cooperation with the operating system under which it runs, must generate code to perform the allocation and deallocation from the heap.

High-Order Language

```
#include <iostream>
using namespace std;

int *a, *b, *c;

int main () {
   a = new int;
   *a = 5;
   b = new int;
   *b = 3;
   c = a;
   a = b;
   *a = 2 + *c;
   cout << "*a = " << *a << endl;
   cout << "*b = " << *b << endl;
   cout << "*c = " << *c << endl;
   return 0;
}
```

Assembly Language

```
0000   040009          BR      main
0003   0000    a:       .BLOCK  2        ;global variable #2d
0005   0000    b:       .BLOCK  2        ;global variable #2d
0007   0000    c:       .BLOCK  2        ;global variable #2d
               ;
               ;******* main ()
0009   C00002 main:     LDA     2,i      ;a = new int
000C   16006A          CALL    new      ;#a
000F   E90003          STX     a,d
0012   C00005          LDA     5,i      ;*a = 5
0015   E20003          STA     a,n
0018   C00002          LDA     2,i      ;b = new int
001B   16006A          CALL    new      ;#b
001E   E90005          STX     b,d
0021   C00003          LDA     3,i      ;*b = 3
0024   E20005          STA     b,n
0027   C10003          LDA     a,d      ;c = a
```

Figure 6.41

Translation of global pointers. The C++ program is from Figure 2.37

Figure **6.41**

(Continued)

```
002A  E10007         STA    c,d
002D  C10005         LDA    b,d        ;a = b
0030  E10003         STA    a,d
0033  C00002         LDA    2,i        ;*a = 2 + *c
0036  720007         ADDA   c,n
0039  E20003         STA    a,n
003C  410058         STRO   msg0,d     ;cout << "*a = "
003F  3A0003         DECO   a,n        ;    << *a
0042  50000A         CHARO  '\n',i     ;    << endl
0045  41005E         STRO   msg1,d     ;cout << "*b = "
0048  3A0005         DECO   b,n        ;    << *b
004B  50000A         CHARO  '\n',i     ;    << endl
004E  410064         STRO   msg2,d     ;cout << "*c = "
0051  3A0007         DECO   c,n        ;    << *c
0054  50000A         CHARO  '\n',i     ;    << endl
0057  00             STOP
0058  2A6120 msg0:   .ASCII "*a = \x00"
      3D2000
005E  2A6220 msg1:   .ASCII "*b = \x00"
      3D2000
0064  2A6320 msg2:   .ASCII "*c = \x00"
      3D2000
             ;
             ;******* operator new
             ;        Precondition: A contains number of bytes
             ;        Postcondition: X contains pointer to bytes
006A  C90074 new:    LDX    hpPtr,d    ;returned pointer
006D  710074         ADDA   hpPtr,d    ;allocate from heap
0070  E10074         STA    hpPtr,d    ;update hpPtr
0073  58             RET0
0074  0076   hpPtr:  .ADDRSS heap      ;address of next free byte
0076  00     heap:   .BLOCK 1          ;first byte in the heap
0077                 .END
```

Output

```
*a = 7
*b = 7
*c = 5
```

When you program with pointers in C++, you allocate storage from the heap with the `new` operator. When your program no longer needs the storage that was allocated, you deallocate it with the `delete` operator. It is possible to allocate several cells of memory from the heap and then deallocate one cell from the middle. The memory management algorithms must be able to handle that scenario. To keep things simple at this introductory level, the programs that illustrate the heap do not show the deallocation process. The heap is located in main memory at the end of the application program. Operator new works by allocating storage from the heap, so that the heap grows downward. Once memory is allocated, it can never be deallocated. This feature of the Pep/8 heap is unrealistic but easier to understand than if it were presented more realistically.

Simplifications in the Pep/8 heap

The assembly language program in Figure 6.41 shows the heap starting at address 0076, which is the value of the symbol heap. The allocation algorithm maintains a global pointer named hpPtr, which stands for heap pointer. The statement

```
hpPtr: .ADDRSS heap
```

at 0074 initializes hpPtr to the address of the first byte in the heap. The application supplies the new operator with the number of bytes needed. The new operator returns the value of hpPtr and then increments it by the number of bytes requested. Hence, the invariant maintained by the new operator is that hpPtr points to the address of the next byte to be allocated from the heap.

The calling protocol for operator new is different from the calling protocol for functions. With functions, information is passed via parameters on the run-time stack. With operator new, the application puts the number of bytes to be allocated in the accumulator and executes the CALL statement to invoke the operator. The operator puts the current value of hpPtr in the index register for the application. So, the precondition for the successful operation of new is that the accumulator contains the number of bytes to be allocated from the heap. The postcondition is that the index register contains the address in the heap of the first byte allocated by new.

The calling protocol for operator new

The calling protocol for operator new is more efficient than the calling protocol for functions. The implementation of new requires only four lines of assembly language code including the RET0 statement. At 006A, the statement

```
new: LDX hpPtr,d
```

puts the current value of the heap pointer in the index register. At 006D, the statement

```
ADDA hpPtr,d
```

adds the number of bytes to be allocated to the heap pointer, and at 0070, the statement

```
STA hpPtr,d
```

updates hpPtr to the address of the first unallocated byte in the heap.

This efficient protocol is possible for two reasons. First, there is no long parameter list as is possible with functions. The application only needs to supply one value to operator new. The calling protocol for functions must be designed to handle arbitrary numbers of parameters. If a parameter list had, say, four parameters, there would not be enough registers in the Pep/8 CPU to hold them all. But the run-time stack can store an arbitrary number of parameters. Second, operator new does not call any other function. Specifically, it makes no recursive calls. The calling protocol for functions must be designed in general to allow for functions to call other functions recursively. The run-time stack is essential for such calls but unnecessary for operator new.

Figure 6.42(a) shows the memory allocation for the C++ program at level HOL6 just before the first cout statement. It corresponds to Figure 2.38(h). Figure 6.42(b) shows the same memory allocation at level Asmb5. Global pointers a, b, and c are stored at 0003, 0005, and 0007. As with all global variables, they are allocated with .BLOCK by the statements

```
a:  .BLOCK  2
b:  .BLOCK  2
c:  .BLOCK  2
```

A pointer at level HOL6 is an address at level Asmb5. Addresses occupy two bytes. Hence, each global pointer is allocated two bytes.   *Pointers are addresses.*

The compiler translates the statement

```
a = new int;
```

as

```
main: LDA  2,i
      CALL new
      STX  a,d
```

The LDA instruction puts 2 in the accumulator. The CALL instruction calls the new operator, which allocates two bytes of storage from the heap and puts the pointer to the allocated storage in the index register. The STX instruction stores the returned pointer in the global variable a. Because a is a global variable, STX uses direct addressing. After this sequence of statements executes, a has the value 0076, and hpPtr has the value 0078 because it has been incremented by two.

How does the compiler translate

```
*a = 5;
```

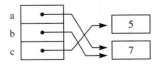

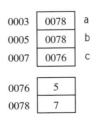

0003 | 0078 | a
0005 | 0078 | b
0007 | 0076 | c

0076 | 5
0078 | 7

Figure **6.42**

Memory allocation for Figure 6.41 just before the first cout statement.

(a) Global pointers at level HOL6.   (b) The global pointers at level Asmb5.

At this point in the execution of the program, the global variable a has the address of where the 5 should be stored. (This point does *not* correspond to Figure 6.42, which is later.) The store instruction cannot use direct addressing, as that would replace the address with 5, which is not the address of the allocated cell in the heap. Pep/8 provides the indirect addressing mode, in which the operand is computed as

Oprnd = Mem[Mem[OprndSpec]]   *Indirect addressing*

With indirect addressing, the operand specifier is the address in memory of the address of the operand. The compiler translates the assignment statement as

```
LDA 5,i
STA a,n
```

where n in the STA instruction indicates indirect addressing. At this point in the program, the operand is computed as

Mem [Mem[OprndSpec]]
Mem [Mem[0003]]
Mem [0076]

which is the first cell in the heap. The store instruction stores 5 in main memory at address 0076.

The compiler translates the assignment of global pointers the same as it would translate the assignment of any other type of global variable. It translates

```
c = a;
```

as

```
LDA a,d
STA c,d
```

using direct addressing. At this point in the program, a contains 0076, the address of the first cell in the heap. The assignment gives c the same value, the address of the first cell in the heap, so that c points to the same cell to which a points.

Contrast the access of a global pointer to the access of the cell to which it points. The compiler translates

```
*a = 2 + *c;
```

as

```
LDA   2,i
ADDA  c,n
STA   a,n
```

where the `add` and `store` instructions use indirect addressing. Whereas access to a global pointer uses direct addressing, access to the cell to which it points uses indirect addressing. You can see that the same principle applies to the translation of the `cout` statement. Because `cout` outputs `*a`, that is, the cell to which `a` points, the `DECO` instruction at 003F uses indirect addressing.

In summary, to access a global pointer, the compiler generates code as follows:

- It allocates storage for the pointer with `.BLOCK 2` because an address occupies two bytes.
- It accesses the pointer with direct addressing.
- It accesses the cell to which the pointer points with indirect addressing.

The translation rules for global pointers

Translating Local Pointers

The program in Figure 6.43 is the same as the program in Figure 6.41 except that the pointers a, b, and c are declared to be local instead of global. There is no difference in the output of the program compared to the program where the pointers are declared to be global. But, the memory model is quite different because the pointers are allocated on the run-time stack.

High-Order Language

```
#include <iostream>
using namespace std;

int main () {
    int *a, *b, *c;
    a = new int;
    *a = 5;
    b = new int;
    *b = 3;
    c = a;
    a = b;
    *a = 2 + *c;
    cout << "*a = " << *a << endl;
    cout << "*b = " << *b << endl;
    cout << "*c = " << *c << endl;
    return 0;
}
```

Figure **6.43**

Translation of local pointers.

Assembly Language

Figure **6.43**

(Continued)

```
0000  040003          BR      main
                  ;
                  ;******* main ()
                  a:      .EQUATE 4           ;local variable #2h
                  b:      .EQUATE 2           ;local variable #2h
                  c:      .EQUATE 0           ;local variable #2h
0003  680006 main:  SUBSP   6,i             ;allocate #a #b #c
0006  C00002        LDA     2,i             ;a = new int
0009  16006A        CALL    new             ;#a
000C  EB0004        STX     a,s
000F  C00005        LDA     5,i             ;*a = 5
0012  E40004        STA     a,sf
0015  C00002        LDA     2,i             ;b = new int
0018  16006A        CALL    new             ;#b
001B  EB0002        STX     b,s
001E  C00003        LDA     3,i             ;*b = 3
0021  E40002        STA     b,sf
0024  C30004        LDA     a,s             ;c = a
0027  E30000        STA     c,s
002A  C30002        LDA     b,s             ;a = b
002D  E30004        STA     a,s
0030  C00002        LDA     2,i             ;*a = 2 + *c
0033  740000        ADDA    c,sf
0036  E40004        STA     a,sf
0039  410058        STRO    msg0,d          ;cout << "*a = "
003C  3C0004        DECO    a,sf            ;   << *a
003F  50000A        CHARO   '\n',i          ;   << endl
0042  41005E        STRO    msg1,d          ;cout << "*b = "
0045  3C0002        DECO    b,sf            ;   << *b
0048  50000A        CHARO   '\n',i          ;   << endl
004B  410064        STRO    msg2,d          ;cout << "*c = "
004E  3C0000        DECO    c,sf            ;   << *c
0051  50000A        CHARO   '\n',i          ;   << endl
0054  600006        ADDSP   6,i             ;deallocate #c #b #a
0057  00            STOP
0058  2A6120 msg0:  .ASCII  "*a = \x00"
      3D2000
005E  2A6220 msg1:  .ASCII  "*b = \x00"
      3D2000
0064  2A6320 msg2:  .ASCII  "*c = \x00"
      3D2000
```

Figure **6.43**

(Continued)

```
            ;
            ;******* operator new
            ;          Precondition: A contains number of bytes
            ;          Postcondition: X contains pointer to bytes
006A C90074 new:    LDX    hpPtr,d      ;returned pointer
006D 710074         ADDA   hpPtr,d      ;allocate from heap
0070 E10074         STA    hpPtr,d      ;update hpPtr
0073 58             RETO
0074 0076   hpPtr:  .ADDRSS heap        ;address of next free byte
0076 00     heap:   .BLOCK  1           ;first byte in the heap
0077                .END
```

Figure 6.44 shows the memory allocation for the program in Figure 6.43 just before execution of the first cout statement. As with all local variables, a, b, and c are allocated on the run-time stack. Figure 6.44(b) shows their offsets from the top of the stack as 4, 2, and 0. Consequently, the compiler translates

```
int *a, *b, *c;
```

as

```
a: .EQUATE 4
b: .EQUATE 2
c: .EQUATE 0
```

Because a, b, and c are local variables, the compiler generates code to allocate storage for them with SUBSP and deallocates storage with ADDSP.

The compiler translates

```
a = new int;
```

as

```
LDA  2,i
CALL new
STX  a,s
```

The LDA instruction puts 2 in the accumulator in preparation for calling the new operator, because an integer occupies two bytes. The CALL instruction invokes the new operator, which allocates the two bytes from the heap and puts their address in the

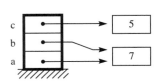

(a) Local pointers at level HOL6.

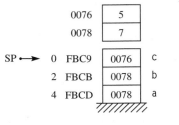

(b) The local pointers at level Asmb5.

Figure **6.44**

Memory allocation for Figure 6.43 just before the cout statement.

index register. In general, assignments to local variables use stack-relative addressing. Therefore, the STX instruction uses stack-relative addressing to assign the address to a.

How does the compiler translate the assignment

```
*a = 5;
```

a is a pointer, and the assignment gives 5 to the cell to which a points. a is also a local variable. This situation is identical to the one where a parameter is called by reference in the programs of Figures 6.27 and 6.29. Namely, the address of the operand is on the run-time stack. The compiler translates the assignment statement as

```
LDA 5,i
STA a,sf
```

where the store instruction uses stack-relative deferred addressing.

The compiler translates the assignment of local pointers the same as it would translate the assignment of any other type of local variable. It translates

```
c = a;
```

as

```
LDA a,s
STA c,s
```

using stack-relative addressing. At this point in the program, a contains 0076, the address of the first cell in the heap. The assignment gives c the same value, the address of the first cell in the heap, so that c points to the same cell to which a points.

The compiler translates

```
*a = 2 + *c;
```

as

```
LDA  2,i
ADDA c,sf
STA  a,sf
```

where the add instruction uses stack-relative deferred addressing to access the cell to which c points and the store instruction uses stack-relative deferred addressing to access the cell to which a points. The same principle applies to the translation of cout statements where the DECO instructions also use stack-relative deferred addressing.

In summary, to access a local pointer, the compiler generates code as follows:

- It allocates storage for the pointer on the run-time stack with SUBSP and deallocates storage with ADDSP.

The translation rules for local pointers

- It accesses the pointer with stack-relative addressing.

- It accesses the cell to which the pointer points with stack-relative deferred addressing.

Translating Structures

Structures are the key to data abstraction at level HOL6, the high-order languages level. They let the programmer consolidate variables with primitive types into a single abstract data type. The compiler provides the struct construct at level HOL6. At level Asmb5, the assembly level, a structure is a contiguous group of bytes, much like the bytes of an array. However, all cells of an array must have the same type and, therefore, the same size. Each cell is accessed by the numeric integer value of the index.

   With a structure, the cells can have different types and, therefore, different sizes. The C++ programmer gives each cell, called a field, a field name. At level Asmb5, the field name corresponds to the offset of the field from the first byte of the structure. The field name of a structure corresponds to the index of an array. It should not be surprising that the fields of a structure are accessed much like the elements of an array. Instead of putting the index of the array in the index register, the compiler generates code to put the field offset from the first byte of the structure in the index register. Apart from this difference, the remaining code for accessing a field of a structure is identical to the code for accessing an element of an array.

   Figure 6.45 shows a program that declares a struct named person that has four fields named first, last, age, and gender. It is identical to the program in Figure 2.39 (page 77). The program declares a global variable name bill that has type person. Figure 6.46 shows the storage allocation for the structure at levels HOL6 and Asmb5. Fields first, last, and gender have type char and occupy one byte each. Field age has type int and occupies two bytes. Figure 6.46(b) shows the address of each field of the structure. To the left of the address is the offset from the first byte of the structure. The offset of a structure is similar to the offset of an element on the stack except that there is no pointer to the top of the structure that corresponds to SP.

High-Order Language

```
#include <iostream>
using namespace std;

struct person {
   char first;
   char last;
   int age;
   char gender;
};
person bill;
```

Figure **6.45**

Translation of a structure. The C++ program is from Figure 2.39.

```
int main () {
   cin >> bill.first >> bill.last >> bill.age >> bill.gender;
   cout << "Initials: " << bill.first << bill.last << endl;
   cout << "Age: " << bill.age << endl;
   cout << "Gender: ";
   if (bill.gender == 'm') {
      cout << "male\n";
   }
   else {
      cout << "female\n";
   }
   return 0;
}
```

Figure **6.45**

(Continued)

Assembly Language

```
0000  040008            BR      main
              first:    .EQUATE 0            ;struct field #1c
              last:     .EQUATE 1            ;struct field #1c
              age:      .EQUATE 2            ;struct field #2d
              gender:   .EQUATE 4            ;struct field #1c
0003  000000 bill:      .BLOCK  5            ;global variable #first #last #age #gender
      0000
                        ;
                        ;******* main ()
0008  C80000 main:      LDX     first,i      ;cin >> bill.first
000B  4D0003            CHARI   bill,x
000E  C80001            LDX     last,i       ;   >>bill.last
0011  4D0003            CHARI   bill,x
0014  C80002            LDX     age,i        ;   >>bill.age
0017  350003            DECI    bill,x
001A  C80004            LDX     gender,i     ;   >>bill.gender
001D  4D0003            CHARI   bill,x
0020  41005A            STRO    msg0,d       ;cout << "Initials: "
0023  C80000            LDX     first,i      ;   << bill.first
0026  550003            CHARO   bill,x
0029  C80001            LDX     last,i       ;   << bill.last
002C  550003            CHARO   bill,x
002F  50000A            CHARO   '\n',i       ;   << endl
0032  410065            STRO    msg1,d       ;cout << "Age: "
0035  C80002            LDX     age,i        ;   << bill.age
0038  3D0003            DECO    bill,x
003B  50000A            CHARO   '\n',i       ;   << endl;
003E  41006B            STRO    msg2,d       ;cout << "Gender: "
0041  C80004            LDX     gender,i     ;if (bill.gender == 'm')
0044  C00000            LDA     0,i
```

```
0047   D50003            LDBYTEA  bill,x                                      Figure 6.45
004A   B0006D            CPA      'm',i                                       (Continued)
004D   0C0056            BRNE     else
0050   410074            STRO     msg3,d       ;    cout << "male\n"
0053   040059            BR       endIf
0056   41007A  else:     STRO     msg4,d       ;    cout << "female\n"
0059   00      endIf:    STOP
005A   496E69  msg0:     .ASCII   "Initials: \x00"
       . . .
0065   416765  msg1:     .ASCII   "Age: \x00"
       . . .
006B   47656E  msg2:     .ASCII   "Gender: \x00"
       . . .
0074   6D616C  msg3:     .ASCII   "male\n\x00"
       . . .
007A   66656D  msg4:     .ASCII   "female\n\x00"
       . . .
0082                     .END
```

Input

```
bj 32 m
```

Output

```
Initials: bj
Age: 32
Gender: male
```

The compiler translates

```
struct person {
   char first;
   char last;
   int age;
   char gender;
};
```

with equate dot commands as

```
first:   .EQUATE 0
last:    .EQUATE 1
age:     .EQUATE 2
gender:  .EQUATE 4
```

The name of a field equates to the offset of that field from the first byte of the structure. `first` equates to 0 because it is the first byte of the structure. `last`

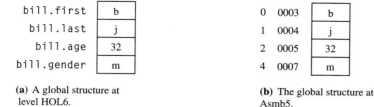

(a) A global structure at level HOL6.

(b) The global structure at Asmb5.

Figure **6.46**

Memory allocation for Figure 6.45 just after the cin statement.

equates to 1 because first occupies one byte. age equates to 2 because first and last occupy a total of two bytes. And gender equates to 4 because first, last, and age occupy a total of four bytes. The compiler translates the global variable

```
person bill;
```

as

```
bill: .BLOCK 5
```

It reserves five bytes because first, last, age, and gender occupy a total of five bytes.

To access a field of a global structure, the compiler generates code to load the index register with the offset of the field from the first byte of the structure. It accesses the field as it would the cell of a global array using indexed addressing. For example, the compiler translates

```
cin >> bill.age
```

as

```
LDX   age,i
DECI  bill,x
```

The load instruction uses immediate addressing to load the offset of field age into the index register. The decimal input instruction uses indexed addressing to access the field.

The compiler translates

```
if (bill.gender == 'm')
```

similarly as

```
LDX      gender,i
LDA      0,i
LDBYTEA  bill,x
CPA      'm',i
```

The first load instruction puts the offset of the gender field into the index register. The second load instruction clears the accumulator to ensure that its left-most byte is all zeros for the comparison. The load byte instruction accesses the field of the

structure with indexed addressing and puts it into the right-most byte of the accumulator. Finally, the compare instruction compares `bill.gender` with the letter m.

In summary, to access a global structure the compiler generates code as follows:

- It equates each field of the structure to its offset from the first byte of the
  structure.

- It allocates storage for the structure with `.BLOCK` *tot* where *tot* is the total
  number of bytes occupied by the structure.

- It accesses a field of the structure by loading the offset of the field into the
  index register with immediate addressing followed by an instruction with
  indexed addressing.

The translation rules for global structures

In the same way that accessing the field of a global structure is similar to
accessing the element of a global array, accessing the field of a local structure is
similar to accessing the element of a local array. Local structures are allocated on
the run-time stack. The name of each field equates to its offset from the first byte of
the structure. The name of the local structure equates to its offset from the top of the
stack. The compiler generates `SUBSP` to allocate storage for the structure and any
other local variables, and `ADDSP` to deallocate storage. It accesses a field of the
structure by loading the offset of the field into the index register with immediate
addressing followed by an instruction with stack-indexed addressing. Translating a
program with a local structure is a problem for the student at the end of this chapter.

The translation rules for local structures

Translating Linked Data Structures

Programmers frequently combine pointers and structures to implement linked data
structures. The `struct` is usually called a node, a pointer points to a node, and the
node has a field that is a pointer. The pointer field of the node serves as a link to
another node in the data structure. Figure 6.47 is a program that implements a
linked list data structure. It is identical to the program in Figure 2.40 (page 78).

High-Order Language

```
#include <iostream>
using namespace std;

struct node {
   int data;
   node* next;
};
```

Figure **6.47**

Translation of a linked list. The C++
program is from Figure 2.40.

```
int main () {
   node *first, *p;
   int value;
   first = 0;
   cin >> value;
   while (value != -9999) {
      p = first;
      first = new node;
      first->data = value;
      first->next = p;
      cin >> value;
   }
   for (p = first; p != 0; p = p->next) {
      cout << p->data << ' ';
   }
   return 0;
}
```

Figure **6.47**

(Continued)

Assembly Language

```
0000   040003          BR      main
               data:   .EQUATE 0               ;struct field #2d
               next:   .EQUATE 2               ;struct field #2h
                       ;
                       ;******* main ()
               first:  .EQUATE 4               ;local variable #2h
               p:      .EQUATE 2               ;local variable #2h
               value:  .EQUATE 0               ;local variable #2d
0003   680006 main:    SUBSP   6,i             ;allocate #first #p #value
0006   C00000          LDA     0,i             ;first = 0
0009   E30004          STA     first,s
000C   330000          DECI    value,s         ;cin >> value
000F   C30000 while:   LDA     value,s         ;while (value != -9999)
0012   B0D8F1          CPA     -9999,i
0015   0A003F          BREQ    endWh
0018   C30004          LDA     first,s         ;   p = first
001B   E30002          STA     p,s
001E   C00004          LDA     4,i             ;   first = new node
0021   160067          CALL    new             ;   allocate #data #next
0024   EB0004          STX     first,s
0027   C30000          LDA     value,s         ;   first->data = value
002A   C80000          LDX     data,i
002D   E70004          STA     first,sxf
0030   C30002          LDA     p,s             ;   first->next = p
0033   C80002          LDX     next,i
```

```
0036   E70004          STA      first,sxf                                    Figure 6.47
0039   330000          DECI     value,s      ;   cin >> value
003C   04000F          BR       while                                        (Continued)
003F   C30004 endWh:   LDA      first,s      ;for (p = first
0042   E30002          STA      p,s
0045   C30002 for:     LDA      p,s          ;   p != 0
0048   B00000          CPA      0,i
004B   0A0063          BREQ     endFor
004E   C80000          LDX      data,i       ;   cout << p->data
0051   3F0002          DECO     p,sxf
0054   500020          CHARO    ' ',i        ;      << ' '
0057   C80002          LDX      next,i       ;   p = p->next)
005A   C70002          LDA      p,sxf
005D   E30002          STA      p,s
0060   040045          BR       for
0063   600006 endFor:  ADDSP    6,i          ;deallocate #value #p #first
0066   00              STOP
                ;
                ;******* operator new
                ;       Precondition: A contains number of bytes
                ;       Postcondition: X contains pointer to bytes
0067   C90071 new:     LDX      hpPtr,d      ;returned pointer
006A   710071          ADDA     hpPtr,d      ;allocate from heap
006D   E10071          STA      hpPtr,d      ;update hpPtr
0070   58              RET0
0071   0073   hpPtr:   .ADDRSS  heap         ;address of next free byte
0073   00     heap:    .BLOCK   1            ;first byte in the heap
0074                   .END
```

Input
___

10 20 30 40 -9999

Output
___

40 30 20 10

The compiler equates the fields of the struct

```
struct node {
   int data;
   node* next;
};
```

to their offsets from the first byte of the struct. data is the first field, with an off-set of 0. next is the second field, with an offset of 2 because data occupies two bytes. The translation is

```
data: .EQUATE 0
next: .EQUATE 2
```

The compiler translates the local variables

```
node *first, *p;
int value;
```

as it does all local variables. It equates the variable names with their offsets from the top of the run-time stack. The translation is

```
first: .EQUATE 4
p:     .EQUATE 2
value: .EQUATE 0
```

Figure 6.48(b) shows the offsets for the local variables. The compiler generates SUBSP at 0003 to allocate storage for the locals and ADDSP at 0063 to deallocate storage.

When you use the new operator in C++, the computer must allocate enough memory from the heap to store the item to which the pointer points. In this program, a node occupies four bytes. Therefore, the compiler translates

```
first = new node;
```

by allocating four bytes in the code it generates to call the new operator. The transla-tion is

```
LDA  4,i
CALL new
STX  first,s
```

Figure **6.48**

Memory allocation for Figure 6.47 just after the third execution of the while loop.

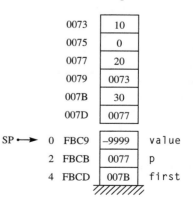

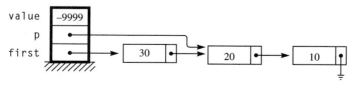

(a) The linked list at level HOL6.

(b) The linked list at level Asmb5.

The load instruction puts 4 in the accumulator in preparation for the call to new. The call instruction calls the new operator, which puts the address of the first byte of the allocated node in the index register. The store index instruction completes the assignment to local variable first using stack-relative addressing.

How does the compiler generate code to access the field of a node to which a local pointer points? Remember that a pointer is an address. A local pointer implies that the address of the node is on the run-time stack. Furthermore, the field of a struct corresponds to the index of an array. If the address of the first cell of an array is on the run-time stack, you access an element of the array with stack-indexed deferred addressing. That is precisely how you access the field of a node. Instead of putting the value of the index in the index register, you put the offset of the field in the index register. The compiler translates

```
first->data = value;
```

as

```
LDA value,s
LDX data,i
STA first,sxf
```

Similarly, it translates

```
first->next = p;
```

as

```
LDA p,s
LDX next,i
STA first,sxf
```

To see how stack-indexed deferred addressing works for a local pointer to a node, remember that the CPU computes the operand as

Oprnd = Mem[Mem[SP + OprndSpec] + X]   *Stack-indexed deferred addressing*

It adds the stack pointer plus the operand specifier and uses the sum as the address of the first field, to which it adds the index register. Suppose that the third node has been allocated as shown in Figure 6.48(b). The call to new has returned the address of the newly allocated node, 007B, and stored it in first. The LDA instruction above has put the value of p, 0077 at this point in the program, in the accumulator. The LDX instruction has put the value of next, offset 2, in the index register. The STA instruction executes with stack-indexed addressing. The operand specifier is 4, the value of first. The computation of the operand is

Mem[Mem[SP + OprndSpec] + X]
Mem[Mem[FBC9 + 4] + 2]
Mem[Mem[FBCD] + 2]
Mem[007B + 2]
Mem[007D]

which is the `next` field of the node to which `first` points.

In summary, to access a field of a node to which a local pointer points, the compiler generates code as follows:

- The field name of the node equates to the offset of the field from the first byte of the node. The offset is loaded into the index register.

- The instruction to access the field of the node uses stack-indexed deferred addressing.

The translation rules for accessing the field of a node to which a local pointer points

You should be able to determine how the compiler translates programs with global pointers to nodes. Formulation of the translation rules is an exercise for the student at the end of this chapter. Translation of a C++ program that has global pointers to nodes is also a problem for the student.

SUMMARY

A compiler uses conditional branch instructions at the machine level to translate `if` statements and loops at the high-order languages level. An `if`/`else` statement requires a conditional branch instruction to test the `if` condition and an unconditional branch instruction to branch around the `else` part. The translation of a `while` or `do` loop requires a branch to a previous instruction. The `for` loop requires, in addition, instructions to initialize and increment the control variable.

The structured programming theorem, proved by Bohm and Jacopini, states that any algorithm containing goto's, no matter how complicated or unstructured, can be written with only nested `if` statements and `while` loops. The goto controversy was sparked by Dijkstra's famous letter, which stated that programs without goto's were not only possible but desirable.

The compiler allocates global variables at a fixed location in main memory. Procedures and functions allocate parameters and local variables on the run-time stack. Values are pushed onto the stack by incrementing the stack pointer (SP) and popped off the stack by decrementing SP. The subroutine call instruction pushes the contents of the program counter (PC), which acts as the return address, onto the stack. The subroutine return instruction pops the return address off the stack into the PC. Instructions access global values with direct addressing and values on the run-time stack with stack-relative addressing. A parameter that is called by reference has its address pushed onto the run-time stack. It is accessed with stack-relative deferred addressing. Boolean variables are stored with a value of 0 for false and a value of 1 for true.

Array values are stored in consecutive main memory cells. You access an element of a global array with indexed addressing, and an element of a local array with stack-indexed addressing. In both cases, the index register contains the index value of the array element. An array passed as a parameter always has the address of the first cell of the array pushed onto the run-time stack. You access an element of the array with stack-indexed deferred addressing. The compiler translates the `switch` statement with an array of addresses, each of which is the address of the first statement of a `case`.

Pointer and `struct` types are common building blocks of data structures. A pointer is an address of a memory location in the heap. The `new` operator allocates memory from the heap. You access a cell to which a global pointer points with indirect addressing. You access a cell to which a local pointer points with stack-relative deferred addressing. A `struct` has several named fields and is stored as a contiguous group of bytes. You access a field of a `global` struct with indexed addressing with the index register containing the offset of the field from the first byte of the `struct`. Linked data structures commonly have a pointer to a `struct` called a node, which in turn contains a pointer to yet another node. If a local pointer points to a node, you access a field of the node with stack-indexed deferred addressing.

EXERCISES

Section 6.1

1. Explain the difference in the memory model between global and local variables. How are each allocated and accessed?

Section 6.2

2. What is an optimizing compiler? When would you want to use one? When would you not want to use one? Explain.

*3. The object code for Figure 6.14 has a `CPA` at 000C to test the value of j. Because the program branches to that instruction from the bottom of the loop, why doesn't the compiler generate a `LDA j,d` at that point before `CPA`?

4. Discover the function of the mystery program of Figure 6.16, and state in one short sentence what it does.

5. Read the papers by Bohm and Jacopini and by Dijkstra that are referred to in this chapter and write a summary of them.

Section 6.3

*6. Draw the values just before and just after the `CALL` at 0022 of Figure 6.18 executes as they are drawn in Figure 6.19.

7. Draw the run-time stack, as in Figure 6.26, that corresponds to the time just before the second return.

Section 6.4

*8. In the Pep/8 program of Figure 6.40, if you enter 4 for `Guess`, what statement executes after the branch at 0010? Why?

9. Section 6.4 does not show how to access an element from a two-dimensional array. Describe how a two-dimensional array might be stored and the assembly language object code that would be necessary to access an element from it.

Section 6.5

10. What are the translation rules for accessing the field of a node to which a global pointer points?

PROBLEMS

Section 6.2

11. Translate the following C++ program to Pep/8 assembly language:

```cpp
#include <iostream>
using namespace std;

int main () {
   int number;
   cin >> number;
   if (number % 2 == 0) {
      cout << "Even\n";
   }
   else {
      cout << "Odd\n";
   }
   return 0;
}
```

12. Translate the following C++ program to Pep/8 assembly language:

```cpp
#include <iostream>
using namespace std;

const int limit = 5;

int main () {
   int number;
   cin >> number;
   while (number < limit) {
      number++;
      cout << number << ' ';
   }
   return 0;
}
```

13. Translate the following C++ program to Pep/8 assembly language:

```cpp
#include <iostream>
using namespace std;

int main () {
   char ch;
   cin >> ch;
   if ((ch >= 'A') && (ch <= 'Z')) {
      cout << 'A';
   }
   else if ((ch >= 'a') && (ch <= 'z')) {
```

```
        cout << 'a';
    }
    else {
        cout << '$';
    }
    cout << endl;
    return 0;
}
```

14. Translate the C++ program in Figure 6.12 to Pep/8 assembly language but with the do loop test changed to

```
while (cop <= driver);
```

15. Translate the following C++ program to Pep/8 assembly language:

```
#include <iostream>
using namespace std;

int main () {
    int numItms, j, data, sum;
    cin >> numItms;
    sum = 0;
    for (j = 1; j <= numItms; j++) {
        cin >> data;
        sum += data;
    }
    cout << "Sum: " << sum << endl;
    return 0;
}
```

Sample Input
---
4   8 -3 7 6

Sample Output

Sum: 18

Section 6.3

16. Translate the following C++ program to Pep/8 assembly language:

```
#include <iostream>
using namespace std;

int myAge;

void putNext (int age) {
    int nextYr;
    nextYr = age + 1;
    cout << "Age: " << age << endl;
    cout << "Age next year: " << nextYr << endl;
}
```

```
int main () {
    cin >> myAge;
    putNext (myAge);
    putNext (64);
    return 0;
}
```

17. Translate the C++ program in Problem 16 to Pep/8 assembly language, but declare myAge to be a local variable in main().

18. Translate the following C++ program to Pep/8 assembly language. It multiplies two integers using a recursive shift-and-add algorithm:

A recursive integer multiplication algorithm

```
#include <iostream>
using namespace std;

int times (int mpr, int mcand) {
    if (mpr == 0) {
        return 0;
    }
    else if (mpr % 2 == 1) {
        return times (mpr / 2, mcand * 2) + mcand;
    }
    else {
        return times (mpr / 2, mcand * 2);
    }
}

int main () {
    int n, m;
    cin >> n >> m;
    cout << "Product: " << times (n, m) << endl;
    return 0;
}
```

16

19. **(a)** Write a C++ program that converts a lowercase character to an uppercase character. Declare

```
char uppercase (char ch);
```

to do the conversion. If the actual parameter is not a lowercase character, the function should return that character value unchanged. Test your function in a main program with interactive I/O. **(b)** Translate your C++ program to Pep/8 assembly language.

20. **(a)** Write a C++ program that defines

```
int minimum (int j1, int j2)
```

which returns the smaller of j1 and j2, and test it with interactive input. **(b)** Translate your C++ program to Pep/8 assembly language.

21. Translate to Pep/8 assembly language your C++ solution from Problem 2.14 that computes a Fibonacci term using a recursive function.

22. Translate to Pep/8 assembly language your C++ solution from Problem 2.15 that outputs the instructions for the Towers of Hanoi puzzle.

23. The recursive binomial coefficient function in Figure 6.25 can be simplified by omitting y1 and y2 as follows:

```
int binCoeff (int n, int k) {
   if ((k == 0) || (n == k)) {
      return 1;
   }
   else {
      return binCoeff (n - 1, k) + binCoeff (n - 1, k - 1);
   }
}
```

Write a Pep/8 assembly language program that calls this function. Keep the value returned from the binCoeff (n - 1, k) call on the stack, and allocate the actual parameters for the binCoeff (n - 1, k - 1) call on top of it. Figure 6.49 shows a trace of the run-time stack where the stack frame contains four words (for retVal, n, k, and retAddr) and the shaded word is the value returned by a function call. The trace is for a call of binCoeff (3,1) from the main program.

24. Translate the following C++ program to Pep/8 assembly language. It multiplies two integers using an iterative shift-and-add algorithm.

An iterative integer multiplication algorithm

```
#include <iostream>
using namespace std;

int product, n, m;

void times (int& prod, int mpr, int mcand) {
   prod = 0;
   while (mpr != 0) {
```

Figure **6.49**

Trace of the run-time stack for Figure 6.25.

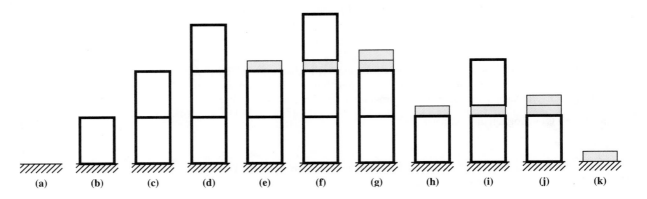

(a)   (b)   (c)   (d)   (e)   (f)   (g)   (h)   (i)   (j)   (k)

```cpp
      if (mpr % 2 == 1) {
         prod = prod + mcand;
      }
      mpr /= 2;
      mcand *= 2;
   }
}

int main () {
   cin >> n >> m;
   times (product, n, m);
   cout << "Product: " << product << endl;
   return 0;
}
```

25. Translate the C++ program in Problem 24 to Pep/8 assembly language, but declare product, n, and m to be local variables in main().

26. **(a)** Rewrite the C++ program of Figure 2.22 to compute the factorial recursively, but use procedure times in Problem 24 to do the multiplication. Use one extra local variable in fact to store the product. **(b)** Translate your C++ program to Pep/8 assembly language.

Section 6.4
27. Translate the following C++ program to Pep/8 assembly language:

```cpp
#include <iostream>
using namespace std;

int list[16];
int j, numItems;
int temp;

int main () {
   cin >> numItems;
   for (j = 0; j < numItems; j++) {
      cin >> list[j];
   }
   temp = list[0];
   for (j = 0; j < numItems - 1; j++) {
      list[j] = list[j + 1];
   }
   list[numItems - 1] = temp;
   for (j = 0; j < numItems; j++) {
      cout << list[j] << ' ';
   }
   cout << endl;
   return 0;
}
```

Sample Input

```
5
11 22 33 44 55
```

Sample Output ,

```
22 33 44 55 11
```

The test in the second `for` loop is awkward to translate because of the arithmetic expression on the right side of the < operator. You can simplify the translation by transforming the test to the following mathematically equivalent test:

```
j + 1 < numItems;
```

28. Translate the C++ program in Problem 27 to Pep/8 assembly language, but declare `list`, `j`, `numItems`, and `temp` to be local variables in `main()`.

29. Translate the following C++ program to Pep/8 assembly language:

```cpp
#include <iostream>
using namespace std;

void getList (int ls[], int& n) {
   int j;
   cin >> n;
   for (j = 0; j < n; j++) {
      cin >> ls[j];
   }
}

void putList (int ls[], int n) {
   int j;
   for (j = 0; j < n; j++) {
       cout << ls[j] << ' ';
   }
   cout << endl;
}

void rotate (int ls[], int n) {
   int j;
   int temp;
   temp = ls[0];
   for (j = 0; j < n - 1; j++) {
      ls[j] = ls[j + 1];
   }
   ls[n - 1] = temp;
}

int main () {
   int list[16];
   int numItems;
```

```
    getList (list, numItems);
    putList (list, numItems);
    rotate (list, numItems);
    putList (list, numItems);
    return 0;
}
```

Sample Input
___

```
5
11 22 33 44 55
```

Sample Output
___

```
11 22 33 44 55
22 33 44 55 11
```

30. Translate the C++ program in Problem 29 to Pep/8 assembly language, but declare list and numItems to be global variables.

31. Translate to Pep/8 assembly language the C++ program from Figure 2.25 that adds four values in an array using a recursive procedure.

32. Translate to Pep/8 assembly language the C++ program from Figure 2.32 that reverses the elements of an array using a recursive procedure.

33. Translate the following C++ program to Pep/8 assembly language:

```
#include <iostream>
using namespace std;

int main () {
    int guess;
    cout << "Pick a number 0..3: ";
    cin >> guess;
    switch (guess) {
        case 0: case 1: cout << "Too low"; break;
        case 2: cout << "Right on"; break;
        case 3: cout << "Too high";
    }
    cout << endl;
    return 0;
}
```

The program is identical to Figure 6.40 except that two of the cases execute the same code. Your jump table must have exactly four entries, but your program must have only three case symbols and three cases.

34. Translate the following C++ program to Pep/8 assembly language:

```
#include <iostream>
using namespace std;

int main () {
```

```
   int guess;
   cout << "Pick a number 0..3: ";
   cin >> guess;
   switch (guess) {
      case 0: cout << "Not close"; break;
      case 1: cout << "Too low"; break;
      case 2: cout << "Right on"; break;
      case 3: cout << "Too high"; break;
      default: cout << "Illegal input";
   }
   cout << endl;
   return 0;
}
```

Section 6.5

35. Translate to Pep/8 assembly language the C++ program from Figure 6.45 that accesses the fields of a structure, but declare `bill` as a local variable in `main()`.

36. Translate to Pep/8 assembly language the C++ program from Figure 6.47 that manipulates a linked list, but declare `first`, `p`, and `value` as global variables.

37. Insert the following C++ code fragment in `main()` of Figure 6.47 just before the `return` statement:

```
sum = 0; p = first;
while (p != 0) {
   sum += p->data;
   p = p->next;
}
cout << "Sum: " << sum << endl;
```

and translate the complete program to Pep/8 assembly language. Declare `sum` to be a local variable along with the other locals as follows:

```
node *first, *p;
int value, sum;
```

38. Insert the following C++ code fragment between the declaration of `node` and `main()` in Figure 6.47:

```
void reverse (node* list) {
   if (list != 0) {
      reverse (list->next);
      cout << list->data << ' ';
   }
}
```

and the following code fragment in `main()` just before the `return` statement:

```
cout << endl;
reverse (first);
```

Translate the complete C++ program to Pep/8 assembly language. The added code outputs the linked list in reverse order.

39. Insert the following C++ code fragment in `main()` of Figure 6.47 just before the `return` statement:

```
first2 = 0; p2 = 0;
for (p = first; p != 0; p = p->next) {
   p2 = first2;
   first2 = new node;
   first2->data = p->data;
   first2->next = p2;
}
for (p2 = first2; p2 != 0; p2 = p2->next) {
   cout << p2->data << ' ';
}
```

Declare `first2` and `p2` to be local variables along with the other locals as follows:

```
node *first, *p, *first2, *p2;
int value;
```

Translate the complete program to Pep/8 assembly language. The added code creates a copy of the first list in reverse order and outputs it.

40. **(a)** Write a C++ program to input an unordered list of integers with –9999 as a sentinel into a binary search tree, then output them with an inorder traversal of the tree.
    (b) Translate your C++ program to Pep/8 assembly language.

41. This problem is a project to write a simulator in C++ for the Pep/8 computer.
    (a) Write a loader that takes a Pep/8 object file in standard format and loads it into the main memory of a simulated Pep/8 computer. Declare main memory as an array of integers as follows:

```
int Mem[65536];   // Pep/8 main memory
```

Take your input as a string of characters from the standard input. Write a memory dump function that outputs the content of main memory as a sequence of decimal integers that represents the program. For example, if the input is

```
51 00 07 51 00 08 00 48 69 zz
```

as in Figure 4.41, then the program should convert the hexadecimal numbers to integers and store them in the first nine cells of `Mem`. The output should be the corresponding integer values as follows:

```
81 0 7 81 0 8 0 72 105
```

(b) Implement instructions `CHARO`, `DECO`, and `STOP` and addressing modes immediate and direct. Implement `DECO` as if it were a native instruction. That is, you should not implement the trap mechanism described in Section 8.2. Use Figure 4.31 as a guide for implementing the von Neumann execution cycle. For example, with the input as in part (a) the output should be `Hi`.

(c) Implement instructions BR, LDr, LDBYTEr, STr, STBYTEr, SUBSP, and ADDSP and addressing mode stack relative. Test your implementation by assembling the program of Figure 6.1 with the Pep/8 assembler then inputting the hexadecimal program into your simulator. The output should be BMW335i.

(d) Implement instructions DECI and STRO as if they were native instructions. Take the input from the standard input of C++. Test your implementation by executing the program of Figure 6.4.

(e) Implement the conditional branch instructions BRLE, BRLT, BREQ, BRNE, BRGE, BRGT, BRV, unary instructions NOTr and NEGr and compare instruction CPr. Test your implementation by executing the programs of Figures 6.6, 6.8, 6.10, 6.12, and 6.14.

(f) Implement instructions CALL and RETn. Test your implementation by executing the programs of Figures 6.18, 6.21, 6.23, and 6.25.

(g) Implement instruction MOVSPA and addressing mode stack relative deferred. Test your implementation by executing the programs of Figures 6.27 and 6.29.

(h) Implement instructions ASLr and ASRr and addressing modes indexed, stack-indexed, and stack-indexed deferred. Test your implementation by executing the programs of Figures 6.34, 6.36, 6.38, 6.40, and 6.47.

(i) Implement the indirect addressing mode. Test your implementation by executing the program of Figure 6.41.

Chapter

7 *Language Translation Principles*

You are now multilingual because you understand at least four languages—English, C++, Pep/8 assembly language, and machine language. The first is a natural language, and the other three are artificial languages.

Keeping that in mind, let's turn to the fundamental question of computer science, which is "What can be automated?" We use computers to automate everything from writing payroll checks to correcting spelling errors in manuscripts. Although computer science has not yet been very successful in automating the translation of natural languages, say from German to English, it has been successful in translating artificial languages. You have already learned how to translate between the three artificial languages of C++, Pep/8 assembly language, and machine language. Compilers and assemblers automate this translation process for artificial languages.

The fundamental question of computer science

Because each level of a computer system has its own artificial language, the automatic translation between these languages is at the very heart of computer science. Computer scientists have developed a rich body of theory about artificial languages and the automation of the translation process. This chapter introduces the theory and shows how it applies to the translation of C++ and Pep/8 assembly language.

Automatic translation

Two attributes of an artificial language are its syntax and semantics. A computer language's *syntax* is the set of rules that a program listing must obey to be declared a valid program of the language. Its *semantics* is the meaning or logic behind the valid program. Operationally, a syntactically correct program will be successfully translated by a translator program. The semantics of the language determine the result produced by the translated program when the object program is executed.

Syntax and semantics

The part of an automatic translator that compares the source program with the language's syntax is called the *parser*. The part that assigns meaning to the source program is called the *code generator*. Most computer science theory applies to the syntactic rather than the semantic part of the translation process.

Three common techniques to describe a language's syntax are   *Techniques to specify syntax*

- Grammars
- Finite state machines
- Regular expressions

This chapter introduces grammars and finite state machines. It shows how to construct a software finite state machine to aid in the parsing process. The last section shows a complete program, including code generation, that automatically translates between two languages. Space limitations preclude a presentation of regular expressions.

7.1   **Languages, Grammars, and Parsing**

Every language has an alphabet. Formally, an *alphabet* is a finite, nonempty set of characters. For example, the C++ alphabet is the nonempty set

```
{ a,  b,  c,  d,  e,  f,  g,  h,  i,  j,  k,  l,  m,  n,
  o,  p,  q,  r,  s,  t,  u,  v,  w,  x,  y,  z,  A,  B,
  C,  D,  E,  F,  G,  H,  I,  J,  K,  L,  M,  N,  O,  P,
  Q,  R,  S,  T,  U,  V,  W,  X,  Y,  Z,  0,  1,  2,  3,
  4,  5,  6,  7,  8,  9,  +,  −,  *,  /,  =,  <,  >,  [,
  ],  (,  ),  {,  },  .,  ,,  :,  ;,  &,  !,  %,  ',  ",
  _,  \,  #,  ?,  ^,  |,  ~}
```

The C++ alphabet

The alphabet for Pep/8 assembly language is similar except for the punctuation characters, as shown in the following set:

```
{ a,  b,  c,  d,  e,  f,  g,  h,  i,  j,  k,  l,  m,  n,
  o,  p,  q,  r,  s,  t,  u,  v,  w,  x,  y,  z,  A,  B,
  C,  D,  E,  F,  G,  H,  I,  J,  K,  L,  M,  N,  O,  P,
  Q,  R,  S,  T,  U,  V,  W,  X,  Y,  Z,  0,  1,  2,  3,
  4,  5,  6,  7,  8,  9,  \,  .,  ,,  :,  ;,  ',  "}
```

The Pep/8 assembly language alphabet

Another example of an alphabet is the alphabet for the language of real numbers, not in scientific notation. It is the set

```
{  0,  1,  2,  3,  4,  5,  6,  7,  8,  9,  +,  −,  .}
```

The alphabet for real numbers

Concatenation

An abstract data type is a set of possible values together with a set of operations on the values. Notice that an alphabet is a set of values. The pertinent operation on this set of values is *concatenation*, which is simply the joining of two or more characters to form a string. An example from the C++ alphabet is the concatenation of ! and = to form the string !=. In the Pep/8 assembly alphabet, you can concatenate d and # to make d#, and in the language of real numbers, you can concatenate −, 2, 3, ., and 7 to make −23.7.

Concatenation applies not only to individual characters in an alphabet to construct a string, but also to strings concatenated to construct bigger strings. From the C++ alphabet, you can concatenate void, printBar, and (int n) to produce the procedure heading

```
void printBar (int n)
```

The length of a string is the number of characters in the string. The string void has a length of four. The string of length zero, called the empty string, is denoted by the Greek letter ϵ to distinguish it from the English characters in an alphabet. Its concatenation properties are *The empty string*

$$\epsilon x = x\epsilon = x$$

where x is a string. The empty string is useful for describing syntax rules.

In mathematics terminology, ϵ is the identity element for the concatenation operation. In general, an *identity element*, i, for an operation is one that does not change a value, x, when x is operated on by i. *Identity elements*

Example 7.1   One is the identity element for multiplication because

$$1 \cdot x = x \cdot 1 = x$$

and true is the identity element for the AND operation because

$$\text{true AND } q = q \text{ AND true} = q$$ ∎

Languages

If T is an alphabet, the closure of T, denoted T^*, is the set of all possible strings formed by concatenating elements from T. T^* is extremely large. For example, if T is the set of characters and punctuation marks of the English alphabet, T^* includes all the sentences in the collected works of Shakespeare, in the English Bible, and in all *The closure of an alphabet*

the English encyclopedias ever published. It includes all strings of those characters ever printed in all the libraries in all the world throughout history, and then some.

Not only does it include all those meaningful strings, it includes meaningless ones as well. Here are some elements of T^* for the English alphabet:

```
To be or not to be, that is the question.
Go fly a kite.
Here over highly toward?
alkeu jfoj ,9nm20mfq23jk l?x!jeo
```

Some elements of T^* where T is the alphabet of the language for real numbers are

```
-2894.01
24
+78.3.80
-234-
6
```

You can easily construct many other elements of T^* with the two alphabets just mentioned. Because strings can be infinitely long, the closure of any alphabet has an infinite number of elements.

What is a language? In the examples of T^* that were just presented, some of the strings are in the language and some are not. In the English example, the first two strings are valid English sentences; that is, they are in the language. The last two strings are not in the language. A *language* is a subset of the closure of its alphabet. Of the infinite number of strings you can construct from concatenating strings of characters from its alphabet, only some will be in the language.

The definition of a language

Example 7.2   Consider the following two elements of T^*, where T is the alphabet for the C++ language:

```
#include <iostream>
int main() {
   cout << "Valid";
   return 0;
}

#include <iostream>
int main(); {
   cout << "Valid";
   return 0;
}
```

The first element of T^* is in the C++ language, but the second is not because it has a syntax error.   ∎

Grammars

To define a language, you need a way to specify which of the many elements of $T*$ are in the language and which are not. A *grammar* is a system that specifies how you can concatenate the characters of alphabet T to form a legal string in a language. Formally, a grammar contains four parts:

The four parts of a grammar

- N, a nonterminal alphabet
- T, a terminal alphabet
- P, a set of rules of production
- S, the start symbol, which is an element of N

An element from the nonterminal alphabet, N, represents a group of characters from the terminal alphabet, T. A nonterminal symbol is frequently enclosed in angle brackets, <>. You see the terminals when you read the language. The rules of production use the nonterminals to describe the structure of the language, which may not be readily apparent when you read the language.

Example 7.3 In the C++ grammar, the nonterminal <compound-statement> might represent the following group of terminals:

```
{
   int i;
   cin >> i;
   i++;
   cout << i;
}
```

The listing of a C++ program always contains terminals, never nonterminals. You would never see a C++ listing such as

```
#include <iostream>
main()
<compound-statement>
```

The nonterminal symbol, <compound-statement>, is useful for describing the structure of a C++ program. ∎

Every grammar has a special nonterminal called the *start symbol*, S. Notice that N is a set, but S is not. S is one of the elements of set N. The start symbol, along with the rules of production, P, enables you to decide whether a string of terminals is a valid sentence in the language. If, starting from S, you can generate the string of terminals using the rules of production, then the string is a valid sentence.

A Grammar for C++ Identifiers

The grammar in Figure 7.1 specifies a C++ identifier. Even though a C++ identifier can use any uppercase or lowercase letter or digit, to keep the example small, this grammar permits only the letters a, b, and c and the digits 1, 2, and 3. You know the rules for constructing an identifier. The first character must be a letter and the remaining characters, if any, can be letters or digits in any combination.

    This grammar has three nonterminals, namely, <identifier>, <letter>, and <digit>. The start symbol is <identifier>, one of the elements from the set of nonterminals.

    The rules of production are of the form

Productions

$$A \rightarrow w$$

where A is a nonterminal and w is a string of terminals and nonterminals. The symbol $\rightarrow$ means "produces." You should read production rule number 3 in Figure 7.1 as, "An identifier produces an identifier followed by a digit."

    The grammar specifies the language by a process called a *derivation*. To derive a valid sentence in the language, you begin with the start symbol and substitute for nonterminals from the rules of production until you get a string of terminals. Here is a derivation of the identifier cab3 from this grammar. The symbol $\Rightarrow$ means "derives in one step":

Derivations

<identifier>	$\Rightarrow$ <identifier> <digit>	Rule 3
	$\Rightarrow$ <identifier> 3	Rule 9
	$\Rightarrow$ <identifier> <letter> 3	Rule 2
	$\Rightarrow$ <identifier> b 3	Rule 5
	$\Rightarrow$ <identifier> <letter> b 3	Rule 2
	$\Rightarrow$ <identifier>a b 3	Rule 4
	$\Rightarrow$ <letter>a b 3	Rule 1
	$\Rightarrow$ c a b 3	Rule 6

$N = \{$<identifier>, <letter>, <digit>$\}$
$T = \{$a, b, c, 1, 2, 3$\}$
$P =$ the productions
    1. <identifier> $\rightarrow$ <letter>
    2. <identifier> $\rightarrow$ <identifier> <letter>
    3. <identifier> $\rightarrow$ <identifier> <digit>
    4. <letter> $\rightarrow$ a
    5. <letter> $\rightarrow$ b
    6. <letter> $\rightarrow$ c
    7. <digit> $\rightarrow$ 1
    8. <digit> $\rightarrow$ 2
    9. <digit> $\rightarrow$ 3
$S =$ <identifier>

Figure **7.1**

A grammar for C++ identifiers.

Next to each derivation step is the production rule on which the substitution is based. For example, Rule 2,

<identifier> → <identifier> <letter>

was used to substitute for <identifier> in the derivation step

<identifier> 3 ⇒ <identifier> <letter> 3

You should read this derivation step as "Identifier followed by 3 derives in one step identifier followed by letter followed by 3."

Analogous to the closure operation on an alphabet is the closure of the derivation operation. The symbol ⇒* means "derives in zero or more steps." You can summarize the previous eight derivation steps as

<identifier> ⇒* c a b 3

This derivation proves that c a b 3 is a valid identifier because it can be derived from the start symbol, <identifier>. A language specified by a grammar consists of all the strings derivable from the start symbol using the rules of production. The grammar provides an operational test for membership in the language. If it is impossible to derive a string, the string is not in the language.

A Grammar for Signed Integers

The grammar in Figure 7.2 defines the language of signed integers, where d represents a decimal digit. The start symbol is I, which stands for integer. F is the first character, which is an optional sign, and M is the magnitude.

Sometimes the rules of production are not numbered and are combined on one line to conserve space on the printed page. You can write the rules of production for this grammar as

I → FM

F → + | − | ε

M → d | dM

where the vertical bar, |, is the alternation operator and is read as "or." Read the last line as "M produces d, or d followed by M."

Here are some derivations of valid signed integers in this grammar:

I ⇒ FM	I ⇒ FM	I ⇒ FM
⇒ FdM	⇒ FdM	⇒ FdM
⇒ FddM	⇒ Fdd	⇒ FddM
⇒ Fddd	⇒ dd	⇒ FdddM
⇒ -ddd		⇒ Fdddd
		⇒ +dddd

$N = \{I, F, M\}$
$T = \{+, -, d\}$
$P =$ the productions
  1. I → FM
  2. F → +
  3. F → -
  4. F → ε
  5. M → dM
  6. M → d
$S = I$

Figure 7.2

A grammar for signed integers.

Note how the last step of the second derivation uses the empty string to derive dd from Fdd. It uses the production F → ε and the fact that εd = d. This production rule with the empty string is a convenient way to express the fact that a positive or negative sign in front of the magnitude is optional.

Some illegal strings from this grammar are ddd+, +-ddd, and ddd+dd. Try to derive these strings from the grammar to convince yourself that they are not in the language. Can you informally prove from the rules of production that each of these strings is not in the language?

The productions in both of the sample grammars have recursive rules in which a nonterminal is defined in terms of itself. Rule 3 of Figure 7.1 defines an <identifier> in terms of an <identifier> as

<identifier> → <identifier> <digit>

Recursive productions

and Rule 5 of Figure 7.2 defines M in terms of M as

M → dM

Recursive rules produce languages with an infinite number of legal sentences. To derive an identifier, you can keep substituting <identifier> <digit> for <identifier> as long as you like to produce an arbitrarily long identifier.

As in all recursive definitions, there must be an escape hatch to provide the basis for the definition. Otherwise, the sequence of substitutions for the nonterminal could never stop. The rule M and d provides the basis for M in Figure 7.2.

A Context-Sensitive Grammar

The production rules for the previous grammars always contain a single nonterminal on the left side. The grammar in Figure 7.3 has some production rules with both a terminal and nonterminal on the left side.

Here is a derivation of a string of terminals with this grammar:

A ⇒ aABC	Rule 1
⇒ aaABCBC	Rule 1
⇒ aaabCBCBC	Rule 2
⇒ aaabBCCBC	Rule 3
⇒ aaabBCBCC	Rule 3
⇒ aaabBBCCC	Rule 3
⇒ aaabbBCCC	Rule 4
⇒ aaabbbCCC	Rule 4
⇒ aaabbbcCC	Rule 5
⇒ aaabbbccC	Rule 6
⇒ aaabbbccc	Rule 6

$N = \{A, B, C\}$
$T = \{a, b, c\}$
$P =$ the productions
    1. A → aABC
    2. A → abC
    3. CB → BC
    4. bB → bb
    5. bC → bc
    6. cC → cc
$S = A$

Figure **7.3**

A context-sensitive grammar.

An example of a substitution in this derivation is using Rule 5 in the step aaabb-bCCC ⇒ aaabbbcCC. Rule 5 says that you can substitute c for C, but only if the C has a b to the left of it.

In the English language, to quote a phrase out of context means to quote it without regard to the other phrases that surround it. Rule 5 is an example of a context-sensitive rule. It does not permit the substitution of C by c unless C is in the proper context, namely, immediately to the right of a b.

Loosely speaking, a *context-sensitive grammar* is one in which the production rules may contain more than just a single nonterminal on the left side. In contrast, grammars that are restricted to a single nonterminal on the left side of every production rule are called *context-free*. (The precise theoretical definitions of context-sensitive and context-free grammars are more restrictive than these definitions. For the sake of simplicity, this chapter uses the previous definitions, although you should be aware that a more rigorous description of the theory would not define them as we have here.)

Context-sensitive grammars

Some other examples of valid strings in the language specified by this grammar are abc, aabbcc, and aaaabbbbcccc. Two examples of invalid strings are aabc and cba. You should derive these valid strings and also try to derive the invalid strings to prove their invalidity to yourself. Some experimentation with the rules should convince you that the language is the set of strings that begins with one or more a's, followed by an equal number of b's, followed by the same number of c's. Mathematically, this language, *L*, can be written

$$L = \{ a^n b^n c^n | \, n > 0 \}$$

which you should read as "The language *L* is the set of strings $a^n b^n c^n$ such that *n* is greater than 0." The notation a^n means the concatenation of *n* a's.

The Parsing Problem

Deriving valid strings from a grammar is fairly straightforward. You can arbitrarily pick some nonterminal on the right side of the current intermediate string and select rules for the substitution repeatedly until you get a string of terminals. Such random derivations can give you many sample strings from the language.

An automatic translator, however, has a more difficult task. You give a translator a string of terminals that is supposed to be a valid sentence in an artificial language. Before the translator can produce the object code, it must determine whether the string of terminals is indeed valid. The only way to determine whether a string is valid is to derive it from the start symbol of the grammar. The translator must attempt such a derivation. If it succeeds, it knows the string is a valid sentence. The problem of determining whether a given string of terminal characters is valid for a specific grammar is called *parsing* and is illustrated schematically in Figure 7.4.

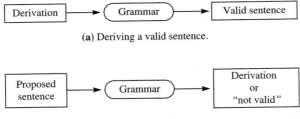

(a) Deriving a valid sentence.

(b) The parsing problem.

Figure **7.4**

The difference between deriving an arbitrary sentence and parsing a proposed sentence.

Parsing a given string is more difficult than deriving an arbitrary valid string. The parsing problem is a form of searching. The parsing algorithm must search for just the right sequence of substitutions to derive the proposed string. Not only must it find the derivation if the proposed string is valid, but it must also admit the possibility that the proposed string may not be valid. If you look for a lost diamond ring in your room and do not find it, that does not mean the ring is not in your room. It may simply mean that you did not look in the right place. Similarly, if you try to find a derivation for a proposed string and do not find it, how do you know that such a derivation does not exist? A translator must be able to prove that no derivation exists if the proposed string is not valid.

A Grammar for Expressions

To see some of the difficulty a parser may encounter, consider Figure 7.5, which shows a grammar that describes an arithmetic infix expression. Suppose you are given the string of terminals

(a * a) + a

and the production rules of this grammar, and are asked to parse the proposed string. The correct parse is

$$
\begin{array}{ll}
E \Rightarrow E + T & \text{Rule 1} \\
\Rightarrow T + T & \text{Rule 2} \\
\Rightarrow F + T & \text{Rule 4} \\
\Rightarrow (E) + T & \text{Rule 5} \\
\Rightarrow (T) + T & \text{Rule 2} \\
\Rightarrow (T * F) + T & \text{Rule 3} \\
\Rightarrow (F * F) + T & \text{Rule 4} \\
\Rightarrow (a * F) + T & \text{Rule 6} \\
\Rightarrow (a * a) + T & \text{Rule 6} \\
\Rightarrow (a * a) + F & \text{Rule 4} \\
\Rightarrow (a * a) + a & \text{Rule 6}
\end{array}
$$

$N = \{E, T, F\}$
$T = \{+, *, (,), a\}$
$P = $ the productions
    1. $E \rightarrow E + T$
    2. $E \rightarrow T$
    3. $T \rightarrow T * F$
    4. $T \rightarrow F$
    5. $F \rightarrow (E)$
    6. $F \rightarrow a$
$S = E$

Figure **7.5**

A grammar for expressions. Nonterminal E represents the expression. T represents a term and F a factor in the expression.

The reason this could be difficult is that you might make a bad decision early in the parse that looks plausible at the time, but that leads to a dead end. For example, you might spot the "(" in the string that you were given and choose Rule 5 immediately. Your attempted parse might be

$E \Rightarrow T$	Rule 2
$\Rightarrow F$	Rule 4
$\Rightarrow (E)$	Rule 5
$\Rightarrow (T)$	Rule 2
$\Rightarrow (T * F)$	Rule 3
$\Rightarrow (F * F)$	Rule 4
$\Rightarrow (a * F)$	Rule 6
$\Rightarrow (a * a)$	Rule 6

Until now, you have seemingly made progress toward your goal of parsing the original expression because the intermediate string looks more like the original string at each successive step of the derivation. Unfortunately, now you are stuck because there is no way to get the + a part of the original string.

After reaching this dead end, you may be tempted to conclude that the proposed string is invalid, but that would be a mistake. Just because you cannot find a derivation does not mean that such a derivation does not exist.

One interesting aspect of a parse is that it can be represented as a tree. The start symbol is the root of the tree. Each interior node of the tree is a nonterminal, and each leaf is a terminal. The children of an interior node are the symbols from the right side of the production rule substituted for the parent node in the derivation. The tree is called a *syntax tree*, for obvious reasons. Figure 7.6 shows the syntax tree for (a * a) + a with the grammar in Figure 7.5, and Figure 7.7 shows it for dd with the grammar in Figure 7.2.

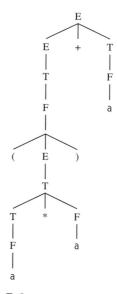

Figure 7.6

The syntax tree for the parse of (a * a) + a in Figure 7.5.

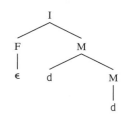

Figure 7.7

The syntax tree for the parse of dd in Figure 7.2.

A C++ Subset Grammar

The rules of production for the grammar in Figure 7.8 (pp. 342–343) specify a small subset of the C++ language. The only primitive types in this language are integer and character. The language has no provision for constant or type declarations and does not permit reference parameters. It also omits switch and for statements. Despite these limitations, it gives an idea of how the syntax for a real language is formally defined.

The nonterminals for this grammar are enclosed in angle brackets, <>. Any symbol not in brackets is in the terminal alphabet and may literally appear in a C++ program listing. The start symbol for this grammar is the nonterminal <translation-unit>.

Figure **7.8**

A grammar for a subset of the C++ language.

```
<translation-unit>  →
    <external-declaration>
    | <translation-unit> <external-declaration>

<external-declaration>  →
    <function-definition>
    | <declaration>

<function-definition>  →
    <type-specifier> <identifier> ( <parameter-list> ) <compound-statement>
    | <identifier> ( <parameter-list> ) <compound-statement>

<declaration> → <type-specifier> <declarator-list>  ;

<type-specifier> → void | char | int

<declarator-list>  →
    <identifier>
    | <declarator-list> , <identifier>

<parameter-list>  →
    ε
    | <parameter-declaration>
    | <parameter-list>  ,  <parameter-declaration>

<parameter-declaration>  →  <type-specifier> <identifier>

<compound-statement>  →  { <declaration-list> <statement-list> }

<declaration-list>  →
    ε
    | <declaration>
    | <declaration-list> <declaration>

<statement-list>  →
    ε
    | <statement>
    | <statement-list> <statement>

<statement>  →
    <compound-statement>
    | <expression-statement>
    | <selection-statement>
    | <iteration-statement>

<expression-statement>  →  <expression>  ;

<selection-statement>  →
    if ( <expression> ) <statement>
    | if ( <expression> ) <statement> else <statement>

<iteration-statement>  →
    while ( <expression> ) <statement>
    | do <statement> while ( <expression> ) ;

<expression>  →
    <relational-expression>
    | <identifier> = <expression>
```

Figure **7.8**

(Continued)

```
<relational-expression> →
    <additive-expression>
    | <relational-expression> < <additive-expression>
    | <relational-expression> > <additive-expression>
    | <relational-expression> <= <additive-expression>
    | <relational-expression> >= <additive-expression>

<additive-expression> →
    <multiplicative-expression>
    | <additive-expression> + <multiplicative-expression>
    | <additive-expression> - <multiplicative-expression>

<multiplicative-expression> →
    <unary-expression>
    | <multiplicative-expression> * <unary-expression>
    | <multiplicative-expression> / <unary-expression>

<unary-expression> →
    <primary-expression>
    | <identifier> ( <argument-expression-list> )

<primary-expression> →
    <identifier>
    | <constant>
    | ( <expression> )

<argument-expression-list> →
    <expression>
    | <argument-expression-list> , <expression>

<constant> →
    <integer-constant>
    | <character-constant>

<integer-constant> →
    <digit>
    | <integer-constant> <digit>

<character-constant> → ' <letter> '

<identifier> →
    <letter>
    | <identifier> <letter>
    | <identifier> <digit>

<letter> →
    a | b | c | d | e | f | g | h | i | j | k | l | m |
    n | o | p | q | r | s | t | u | v | w | x | y | z |
    A | B | C | D | E | F | G | H | I | J | K | L | M |
    N | O | P | Q | R | S | T | U | V | W | X | Y | Z

<digit> →
    0 | 1 | 2 | 3 | 4 | 5 | 6 | 7 | 8 | 9
```

The specification of a programming language by the rules of production of its grammar is called *Backus Naur Form*, abbreviated BNF. In BNF, the production symbol → is sometimes written ::=. The ALGOL–60 language, designed in 1960, popularized BNF.

Backus Naur Form (BNF)

The following example of a parse with this grammar shows that

```
while (a <= 9)
  S1;
```

is a valid <statement>, assuming that *S1* is a valid <expression>. The parse consists of the following derivation:

```
<statement>
  ⇒   <iteration-statement>
  ⇒  while  ( <expression> ) <statement>
  ⇒  while  ( <relational-expression> ) <statement>
  ⇒  while  ( <relational-expression> <= <additive-expression> ) <statement>
  ⇒  while  ( <additive-expression> <= <additive-expression> ) <statement>
  ⇒  while  ( <multiplicative-expression> <= <additive-expression> ) <statement>
  ⇒  while  ( <unary-expression> <= <additive-expression> ) <statement>
  ⇒  while  ( <primary-expression> <= <additive-expression> ) <statement>
  ⇒  while  ( <identifier> <= <additive-expression> ) <statement>
  ⇒  while  ( <letter> <= <additive-expression> ) <statement>
  ⇒  while  ( a <= <additive-expression> ) <statement>
  ⇒  while  ( a <= <multiplicative-expression> ) <statement>
  ⇒  while  ( a <= <unary-expression> ) <statement>
  ⇒  while  ( a <= <primary-expression> ) <statement>
  ⇒  while  ( a <= <constant> ) <statement>
  ⇒  while  ( a <= <integer-constant> ) <statement>
  ⇒  while  ( a <= <digit> ) <statement>
  ⇒  while  ( a <= 9 ) <statement>
  ⇒  while  ( a <= 9 ) <expression-statement>
  ⇒  while  ( a <= 9 ) <expression> ;
  ⇒* while  ( a <= 9 ) S1;
```

Figure 7.9 (p. 345) shows the corresponding syntax tree for this parse. The nonterminal <statement> is the root of the tree because the purpose of the parse is to show that the string is a valid <statement>.

With this example in mind, consider the task of a C++ compiler. The compiler has programmed into it a set of production rules similar to the rules of Figure 7.8. A programmer submits a text file containing the source program, a long string of terminals, to the compiler. First, the compiler must determine whether the string of terminal characters represents a valid C++ translation unit. If the string is a valid <translation-unit>, then the compiler must generate the corresponding object code in a lower-level language. If it is not, the compiler must issue an appropriate syntax error.

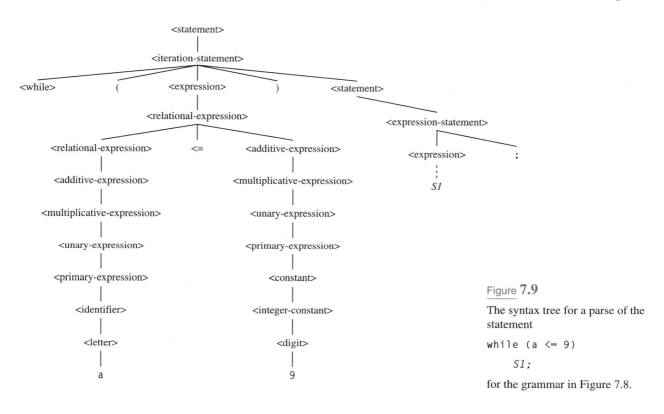

Figure **7.9**

The syntax tree for a parse of the statement

```
while (a <= 9)
    S1;
```

for the grammar in Figure 7.8.

There are literally hundreds of rules of production in the standard C++ grammar. Imagine what a job the C++ compiler has, sorting through those rules every time you submit a program to it! Fortunately, computer science theory has developed to the point where parsing is not difficult for a compiler. When designed using the theory, C++ compilers can parse a program in a way that guarantees they will correctly decide which production to use for the substitution at every step of the derivation. If their parsing algorithm does not find the derivation of <translation-unit> to match the source, they can prove that such a derivation does not exist and that the proposed source program must have a syntax error.

Code generation is more difficult than parsing for compilers. The reason is that the object code must run on a specific machine produced by a specific manufacturer. Because every manufacturer's machine has a different architecture with different instruction sets, code-generation techniques for one machine may not be appropriate for another. A single, standard von Neumann architecture based on theoretical concepts does not exist. Consequently, not as much theory for code generation has been developed to guide compiler designers in their compiler construction efforts.

Context Sensitivity of C++

It appears from Figure 7.8 that the C++ language is context-free. Every production rule has only a single nonterminal on the left side. This is in contrast to a context-sensitive grammar, which can have more than a single nonterminal on the left, as in Figure 7.3. Appearances are deceiving. Even though the grammar for this subset of C++, as well as the full standard C++ language, is context-free, the language itself has some context-sensitive aspects.

Consider the grammar in Figure 7.3. How do its rules of production guarantee that the number of c's at the end of a string must equal the number of a's at the beginning of the string? Rules 1 and 2 guarantee that for each a generated, exactly one C will be generated. Rule 3 lets the C commute to the right of B. Finally, Rule 5 lets you substitute c for C in the context of having a b to the left of C. The language could not be specified by a context-free grammar because it needs Rules 3 and 5 to get the C's to the end of the string.

There are context-sensitive aspects of the C++ language that Figure 7.8 does not specify. For example, the definition of <parameter-list> allows any number of formal parameters, and the definition of <argument-expression-list> allows any number of actual parameters. You could write a C++ program containing a procedure with three formal parameters and a procedure call with two actual parameters that is derivable from <translation-unit> with the grammar in Figure 7.8. If you try to compile the program, however, the compiler will declare a syntax error.

The fact that the number of formal parameters must equal the number of actual parameters in C++ is similar to the fact that the number of a's at the beginning of the string must equal the number of c's at the end of the string in the language defined by the grammar in Figure 7.3. The only way to put that restriction in C++'s grammar would be to include many complicated, context-sensitive rules. It is easier for the compiler to parse the program with a context-free grammar and check for any violations after the parse—usually with the help of its symbol table—that the grammar cannot specify.

7.2 Finite State Machines

Finite state machines are another way to specify the syntax of a sentence in a language. In diagram form, a *finite state machine* is a finite set of states represented by circles called *nodes* and transitions between the states represented by *arcs* between the circles. Each arc begins at one state and ends at another, and contains an arrowhead at the ending state. Each arc is also labeled with a character from the terminal alphabet of the language.

One state of the finite state machine (FSM) is designated as the start state and at least one, possibly more, is designated a final state. On a diagram, the start state has an incoming arrow and a final state is indicated by a double circle.

Mathematically, such a collection of nodes connected by arcs is called a *graph*. When the arcs are directed, as they are in an FSM, the structure is called a *directed graph* or *digraph*.

An FSM to Parse an Identifier

Figure 7.10 shows an FSM that parses an identifier as defined by the grammar in Figure 7.1. The set of states is {A, B, C}. A is the start state, and B is the final state. There is a transition from A to B on a letter, from A to C on a digit, from B to B on a letter or a digit, and from C to C on a letter or a digit.

To use the FSM, imagine that the input string is written on a piece of paper tape. Start in the start state, and scan the characters on the input tape from left to right. Each time you scan the next character on the tape, make a transition to another state of the finite state machine. Use only the transition that is allowed by the arc corresponding to the character you have just scanned. After scanning all the input characters, if you are in a final state, the characters are a valid identifier. Otherwise they are not.

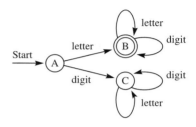

Figure **7.10**

A finite state machine (FSM) to parse an identifier.

Example 7.4   To parse the string `cab3`, you would make the following transitions:

Current state: A	Input: `cab3`	Scan c and go to B.
Current state: B	Input: `ab3`	Scan a and go to B.
Current state: B	Input: `b3`	Scan b and go to B.
Current state: B	Input: `3`	Scan 3 and go to B.
Current state: B	Input:	Check for final state.

Because there is no more input and the last state is B, a final state, `cab3` is a valid identifier. ∎

You can also represent an FSM by its state transition table. Figure 7.11 is the state transition table for the FSM of Figure 7.10. The table lists the next state reached by the transition from a given current state on a given input symbol.

Current State	Next State	
	Letter	Digit
→ A	B	C
Ⓑ	B	B
C	C	C

Figure **7.11**

The state transition table for the FSM of Figure 7.10.

Simplified Finite State Machines

It is often convenient to simplify the diagram for an FSM by eliminating the state whose sole purpose is to provide transitions for illegal input characters. State C in this machine is such a state. If the first character is a digit, the string will not be a valid identifier, regardless of the following characters. State C acts like a failure state. Once you make a transition to C, you can never make a transition to another state, and you know the input string eventually will be declared invalid. Figure 7.12 shows the simplified FSM of Figure 7.10 without the failure state.

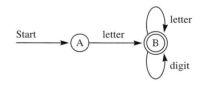

Figure **7.12**

The FSM of Figure 7.10 without the failure state.

When you parse a string with this simplified machine, you will not be able to make a transition when you encounter an illegal character in the input string. There are two ways to detect an illegal sentence in a simplified FSM:

- You may run out of input, and not be in a final state.

- You may be in some state, and the next input character does not correspond to any of the transitions from that state.

Figure 7.13 is the corresponding state transition table for Figure 7.12. The state transition table for a simplified machine has no entry for a missing transition. Note that this table has no entry under the digit column for the current state of A. The remaining machines in this chapter are written in simplified form.

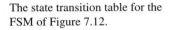

| Current | Next State | |
State	Letter	Digit
→ A	B	
Ⓑ	B	B

Figure **7.13**

The state transition table for the FSM of Figure 7.12.

Nondeterministic Finite State Machines

When you parse a sentence using a grammar, frequently you must choose between several production rules for substitution in a derivation step. Similarly, nondeterministic finite state machines require you to decide between more than one transition when parsing the input string. Figure 7.14 is a nondeterministic FSM to parse a signed integer. It is nondeterministic because there is at least one state that has more than one transition from it on the same character. For example, state A has a transition to both B and C on a digit. There is also some nondeterminism at state B because, given that the next input character is a digit, a transition both to B and to C is possible.

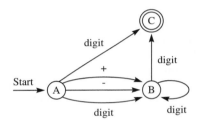

Figure **7.14**

A nondeterministic FSM to parse a signed integer.

Example 7.5   You must make the following decisions to parse +203 with this nondeterministic FSM:

Current state: A	Input: +203	Scan + and go to B.
Current state: B	Input: 203	Scan 2 and go to B.
Current state: B	Input: 03	Scan 0 and go to B.
Current state: B	Input: 3	Scan 3 and go to C.
Current state: C	Input:	Check for final state.

Because there is no more input and you are in the final state C, you have proven that the input string +203 is a valid signed integer.   ∎

When parsing with rules of production, you run the risk of making an incorrect choice early in the parse. You may reach a dead end where no substitution will get your intermediate string of terminals and nonterminals closer to the given string. Just because you reach such a dead end does not necessarily mean that the string is invalid. All invalid strings will produce dead ends in an attempted parse. But even valid strings have the potential for producing dead ends if you make a wrong decision early in the derivation.

The same principle applies with nondeterministic finite state machines. With the machine of Figure 7.14, if you are in the start state, A, and the next input character is 7, you must choose between the transitions to B and to C. Suppose you choose the transition to C and then find that there is another input character to scan. Because there are no transitions from C, you have reached a dead end in your attempted parse. You must conclude, therefore, that either the input string was invalid or it was valid and you made an incorrect choice at an earlier point.

Figure 7.15 is the state transition table for the machine of Figure 7.14. The nondeterminism is evident from the multiple entries (B, C) in the digit column. They represent a choice that must be made when attempting a parse.

Machines with Empty Transitions

In the same way that it is convenient to incorporate the empty string into production rules, it is sometimes convenient to construct finite state machines with transitions on the empty string. Such transitions are called *empty transitions*. Figure 7.17 is an FSM that corresponds closely to the grammar in Figure 7.2 to parse a signed integer, and Figure 7.16 is its state transition table.

In Figure 7.17, F is the state after the first character, and M is the magnitude state analogous to the F and M nonterminals of the grammar. In the same way that a sign can be $+$, $-$, or neither, the transition from I to F can be on $+$, $-$, or ϵ.

Current State	Next State			
	+	−	Digit	ϵ
→I	F	F		F
F			M	
Ⓜ			M	

Example 7.6 To parse 32 requires the following decisions:

Current state: I	Input: 32	Scan ϵ and go to F.
Current state: F	Input: 32	Scan 3 and go to M.
Current state: M	Input: 2	Scan 2 and go to M.
Current state: M	Input:	Check for final state.

The transition from I to F on ϵ does not consume an input character. When you are in state I, you can do one of three things: (a) scan $+$ and go to F, (b) scan $-$ and go to F, or (c) scan nothing (that is, the empty string) and go to F. ∎

Machines with empty transitions are always considered nondeterministic. In Example 7.6, the nondeterminism comes from the decision you must make when you are in state I and the next character is $+$. You must decide whether to go from I to F on $+$ or from I to F on ϵ. These are different transitions because they leave you with different input strings, even though they are transitions to the same state.

Current State	Next State		
	+	−	Digit
→A	B	B	B, C
B			B, C
Ⓒ			

Figure **7.15**

The state transition table for the FSM of Figure 7.14.

Figure **7.16**

The state transition table for the FSM of Figure 7.17.

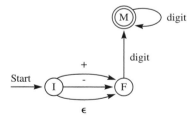

Figure **7.17**

An FSM with an empty transition to parse a signed integer.

Machines with empty transitions are considered nondeterministic.

Given an FSM with empty transitions, it is always possible to transform it to an equivalent machine without the empty transitions. There are two steps in the algorithm to eliminate an empty transition.

- Given a transition from p to q on ∈, for every transition from q to r on a, add a transition from p to r on a.

The algorithm to remove an empty transition

- If q is a final state, make p a final state.

This algorithm follows from the concatenation property of ∈:

∈a = a

Example 7.7   Figure 7.18 shows how to remove an empty transition from the machine in part (a) resulting in the equivalent machine in part (b). Because there is a transition from state X to state Y on ∈, and from state Y to state Z on a, you can eliminate the empty transition if you construct a transition from state X to state Z on a. If you are in X, you might just as well go to Z directly on a. The state and remaining input will be the same as if you went from X to Z via Y on ∈.   ∎

(a) The original FSM.

(b) The equivalent FSM without an empty transition.

Figure **7.18**

Removing an empty transition.

Example 7.8   Figure 7.19 shows this transformation on the FSM of Figure 7.17. The empty transition from I to F is replaced by the transition from I to M on digit, because there is a transition from F to M on digit.   ∎

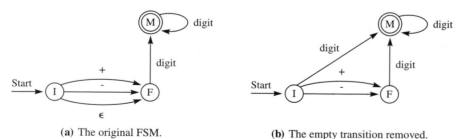

(a) The original FSM.

(b) The empty transition removed.

Figure **7.19**

Removing the empty transition from the FSM of Figure 7.17.

In Example 7.8, there is only one transition from F to M, so the empty transition from I to F is replaced by only one transition from I to M. If an FSM has more than one transition from the destination state of the empty transition, you must add more than one transition when you eliminate the empty transition.

Example 7.9   To eliminate the empty transition from W to X in Figure 7.20(a), you need to replace it with two transitions, one from W to Y on a and one from W to Z on b. In this example, because X is a final state in Figure 7.20(a), W becomes a

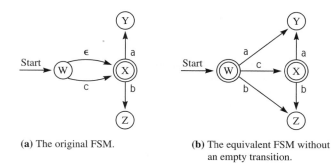

Figure **7.20**

Removing an empty transition.

(a) The original FSM. **(b)** The equivalent FSM without an empty transition.

final state in the equivalent machine of Figure 7.20(b) in accordance with the second step of the algorithm. ∎

Removing the empty transition from Figure 7.17 produced a deterministic machine. In general, however, removing all the empty transitions does not guarantee that the FSM is deterministic. Even though all machines with empty transitions are nondeterministic, an FSM with no empty transitions may still be nondeterministic. Figure 7.14 is such a machine, for example.

Given the choice, you are always better off parsing with a deterministic rather than a nondeterministic FSM. With a deterministic machine, there is no possibility of making a wrong choice with a valid input string and terminating in a dead end. If you ever terminate at a dead end, you can conclude with certainty that the input string is invalid.

The advantage of a deterministic FSM

Computer scientists have been able to prove that for every nondeterministic FSM there is an equivalent deterministic FSM. That is, there is a deterministic machine that recognizes exactly the same language. Unfortunately, the proof of this useful result is beyond the scope of this book. The proof consists of a recipe that tells how to construct an equivalent deterministic machine from the nondeterministic one.

Multiple Token Recognizers

A *token* is a set of terminal characters that has meaning as a group. The characters usually correspond to some nonterminal in a language's grammar. For example, consider the Pep/8 assembly language statement

The definition of a token

```
mask: .WORD 0X00FF
```

The tokens in this statement are `mask:`, `.WORD`, `0X`, and `00FF`. Each is a set of characters from the assembly language alphabet and has meaning as a group. Their individual meanings are a symbol definition, a dot command, a decimal number specification, and a decimal value, respectively.

To a certain extent, the particular grouping of characters that you choose to form one token is arbitrary. For example, you could choose the string of characters `0X00FF` to be a single decimal number token. You would normally choose the characters of a token to be those that make the implementation of the FSM as simple as possible.

A common use of an FSM in a translator is to detect the tokens in the source string. Consider the assembler's job when confronted with this source line. Suppose the assembler has already determined that `mask:` is a symbol definition and `.WORD` is a dot command. It knows that either a decimal or hexadecimal constant can follow the dot command, so it must be programmed to accept either. It needs an FSM that recognizes both.

Figure 7.21(a) shows the two machines for parsing a hexadecimal constant prefix and an unsigned integer. C is the final state in the first machine for 0X, and E is the final state in the second machine for the unsigned integer.

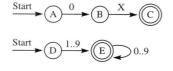

(a) Separate machines for the 0X and unsigned integer tokens.

(b) One nondeterministic FSM that recognizes the 0X or unsigned integer token.

Figure 7.21

Combining two machines to construct one FSM that recognizes both tokens.

To construct an FSM that will recognize both 0X and the unsigned integer, draw a new start state for the combined machine, in this example state F. Then draw empty transitions from the new start state to the start state of each individual machine, in this example from F to A and F to D. The result is one nondeterministic FSM that will recognize either token. The final state on termination tells you what token you have recognized. After the parse, if you terminate in state C you have detected 0X and if you terminate in state E you have detected the unsigned integer.

To get the machine into a more useful form, you should eliminate the empty transitions. Figure 7.22(a) shows removal of the empty transitions for the FSM of Figure 7.21(b). After their removal, states A and D are inaccessible; that is, you can never reach them starting from the start state, regardless of the input string. Consequently, they can never affect the parse and can be eliminated from the machine, as shown in Figure 7.22(b).

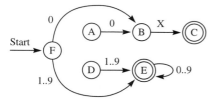

(a) Removing the empty transitions.

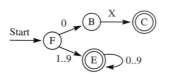

(b) Removing the inaccessible states.

Figure 7.22

Transforming the FSM of Figure 7.21(b).

As another example of when the translator needs to recognize multiple tokens, consider the assembler's job when confronted with the following two source lines:

```
NOTE:   LDA this,d ;comment 1
        NOTA       ;comment 2
```

Michael O. Rabin, Dana S. Scott

Michael O. Rabin and Dana S. Scott received their PhD degrees from Princeton in 1956 and 1958, respectively. They studied under Alonzo Church (1903–1995). Church was an influential professor of mathematics at Princeton. He studied the foundations of mathematical logic long before computers were invented, but his work had a lasting influence on the discipline. He was also the graduate advisor of many students who distinguished themselves in computer science. Alan Turing himself was a student of Church, receiving his PhD under him in 1938. Others included John Kemeny, the co-inventor of the BASIC programming language, and Stephen Kleene, who discovered Kleene's theorem, a statement about the equivalence of finite state machines and regular sets.

Rabin was born in 1931 in what was then Breslau, Germany, but is now a city in Poland. Although Rabin's father was a rabbi, Rabin wanted to attend a school that was well-known for science instead of a religious high school. He persuaded his father to let him study science and eventually entered Hebrew University in the early 1950s. It was there that Rabin read a book by Kleene entitled *Introduction to Metamathematics*. The book had a chapter on computability and the Turing machine and helped influence Rabin to work on the foundations of computer science.

Scott was born in 1932 in Berkeley, California. He was fascinated with mathematics as a youngster and entered UC Berkeley determined to be a mathematics major. He earned his BA there before entering Princeton to work on his PhD, also in mathematics. Scott met Rabin at Princeton and remembers him as always very lively and full of ideas. Although Rabin graduated a few years before Scott, the two of them collaborated after their Princeton years.

Dana Scott and Michael Rabin were both associated with the IBM Research Center in the summer of 1957. Because the classic Turing machine is assumed to have infinite memory, and all real machines have finite memory, the Turing machine is not as accurate a model of real machines as a model with finite memory. Scott and Rabin developed the concept of the nondeterministic finite state machine and investigated its properties. Because the number of states in such a machine is finite, so is its memory. They proved the result stated in this chapter that for every nondeterministic FSM there exists an equivalent deterministic FSM. Dana Scott and Michael Rabin won the A.M. Turing Award in 1976 for their joint 1959 paper "Finite Automata and Their Decision Problem," based on their work together at IBM.

Dana Scott is currently Hillman University Professor of Computer Science, Philosophy, and Mathematical Logic (Emeritus) at Carnegie Mellon University. Rabin is the distinguished Thomas J. Watson, Sr. Professor of Computer Science at Harvard University and is affiliated with Hebrew University in Jerusalem. One of his accomplishments was to devise an algorithm for rapidly finding extremely large prime numbers but with a tiny possibility of error, which is the basis of this quote:

"We should give up the attempt to derive results and answers with complete certainty."

—*Michael O. Rabin*

The first token on the first line is a symbol definition. The first token on the second line is a mnemonic for a unary instruction. At the beginning of each line, the translator needs an FSM to recognize a symbol definition (which is in the form of an identifier followed immediately by a colon) or a mnemonic (which is in the form of an identifier). Figure 7.23 shows the appropriate multiple token FSM.

In the first line, this machine makes the following transitions:

A to B on N

B to B on O

B to B on T

B to B on E

B to C on :

after which the translator knows it has detected a symbol definition. In the second line, it makes the transitions

A to B on N

B to B on O

B to B on T

B to B on A

Because the next input character is not a colon, the FSM does not make the transition to state C. The translator knows it has detected an identifier because the terminal state is B.

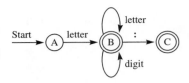

Figure 7.23

An FSM to parse a Pep/8 assembly language identifier or symbol definition.

7.3 Implementing Finite State Machines

The syntax of a programming language is usually specified by a formal grammar, which forms the basis of the parsing algorithm for the translator. Rather than specifying all the syntax, as the grammar in Figure 7.8 does, the formal grammar frequently specifies an upper level of abstraction and leaves the lower level to be specified by regular expressions or finite state machines.

Figure 7.24 shows the steps in a typical compilation process. The low-level syntax analysis is called *lexical analysis*, and the high-level syntax analysis is called *parsing*. (This is a more specialized meaning of the word *parse*. It is sometimes used in a more general sense to include all syntax analysis.) In most translators for artificial languages, the lexical analyzer is based on a deterministic FSM whose

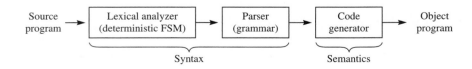

Figure 7.24

Steps in the compilation process.

input is a string of characters. The parser is usually based on a grammar whose input is the sequence of tokens taken from the lexical analyzer.

A nonterminal symbol for the lexical analyzer becomes a terminal symbol for the parser. A common example of such a symbol is an identifier. The FSM has individual letters and digits as its terminal alphabet, and inputs a string of them as it makes its state transitions. If the string `abc3` is input, the FSM declares that an identifier has been detected and passes that information on to the parser. The parser uses <identifier> as a terminal symbol in its parse of the sentence from the language.

When you design software that requires a parse of the input, the specification is sometimes not given in the form of an FSM and a grammar. If the structure of the input is not too complex, however, you may be able to combine the lexical analysis and parsing, and draw an FSM directly from the specification of the problem in order to analyze the syntax. If the FSM is nondeterministic, you would need to convert it to an equivalent deterministic FSM. After you draw a deterministic FSM, you can implement it with a program.

More complex structures, such as those encountered by compilers that translate high-order languages, are usually specified with a formal grammar. Typically, you cannot analyze the syntax for such a language with just one FSM. Instead, you must use both stages for the syntax analysis, as shown in Figure 7.24, and employ more advanced techniques that are beyond the scope of this book.

An algorithm that implements an FSM has an enumerated variable called the *state variable* whose possible values correspond to the possible states of the FSM. The algorithm initializes the state variable to the start state of the machine and gets the string of terminal characters one at a time in a loop. Each character causes a change of state. There are two common implementation techniques:

The state variable

- Table-lookup
- Direct-code

The two FSM implementation techniques

They differ in the way that the state variable gets its next value. The table-lookup technique stores the state transition table and looks up the next state based on the current state and input character. The direct-code technique tests the current state and input character in the code itself and assigns the next state to the state variable directly.

A Table-Lookup Parser

The program in Figure 7.25 implements the FSM of Figure 7.10 with the table-lookup technique. Variable FSM is the state transition table shown in Figure 7.11. The program classifies each input character as a letter or digit. Because B is the final state, it declares that the input string is a valid identifier if the state on termination of the loop is B.

The program assumes that the user will enter only letters and digits. If the user enters some other character, it will detect the character as a digit. For example, if the user enters cab#, the program will detect it as a valid identifier even though it is not. A problem for the student provided at the end of this chapter suggests an improved FSM and corresponding implementation.

```
#include <iostream>
#include <cctype> // isalpha
#include <string> // string
using namespace std;

enum State {eA, eB, eC};
enum Alphabet {eLETTER, eDIGIT};
State FSM[eC + 1][eDIGIT + 1] = {  // Three rows, two columns
   eB, eC,  // The state transition table of Figure 7.11
   eB, eB,
   eC, eC
};

int main () {
   char ch;
   string line;
   Alphabet FSMChar;
   State state = eA;
   cout << "Enter a string of letters and digits: ";
   cin >> line;
   for (int i = 0; i < line.size (); i++) {
      ch = line[i];
      if (isalpha (ch)) {
         FSMChar = eLETTER;
      }
      else {
         FSMChar = eDIGIT;
      }
      state = FSM[state][FSMChar];
   }
   if (state == eB) {
      cout << line << " is a valid identifier." << endl;
   }
   else {
      cout << line << " is not a valid identifier." << endl;
   }
   return 0;
}
```

Figure 7.25

Implementation of the FSM of Figure 7.10 with the table-lookup technique.

Input/Output

```
Enter a string of letters and digits: cab3
cab3 is a valid identifier.
```

Input/Output

```
Enter a string of letters and digits: 3cab
3cab is not a valid identifier.
```

Figure **7.25**

(Continued)

A Direct-Code Parser

The program in Figure 7.26 uses the direct-code technique to parse an integer. Function parseNum allows the user to enter any string of characters. If the string is not a valid integer, parseNum will return false for valid and the program will issue an error message. Otherwise, valid will be true and num will be the correct integer value entered.

```cpp
#include <iostream>
#include <cctype> // isdigit
#include <string> // string, getline
using namespace std;

// Global buffer
string line;
int lineIndex;

void getLine () {
    // Get a line of characters.
    // Install a newline character as sentinel.
    getline (cin, line);
    line.push_back ('\n');
    lineIndex = 0;
}

enum State {eI, eF, eM, eSTOP};

void parseNum (bool& v, int& n) {
    int sign;
    State state;
    char nextChar;
    v = true;
    state = eI;
```

Figure **7.26**

A programmer-designed parse of an integer string.

```
do {
   nextChar = line[lineIndex++];
   switch (state) {
      case eI:
         if (nextChar == '+') {
            sign = +1;
            state = eF;
         }
         else if (nextChar == '-') {
            sign = -1;
            state = eF;
         }
         else if (isdigit (nextChar)) {
            sign = +1;
            n = nextChar - '0';
            state = eM;
         }
         else {
            v = false;
         }
         break;
      case eF:
         if (isdigit (nextChar)) {
            n = nextChar - '0';
            state = eM;
         }
         else {
            v = false;
         }
         break;
      case eM:
         if (isdigit (nextChar)) {
            n = 10 * n + nextChar - '0';
         }
         else if (nextChar == '\n') {
            n = sign * n;
            state = eSTOP;
         }
         else {
            v = false;
         }
         break;
   }
}
while ((state != eSTOP) && v);
}
```

Figure **7.26**

(Continued)

```
int main () {
   bool valid;
   int num;
   cout << "Enter number: ";
   getLine ();
   parseNum (valid, num);
   if (valid) {
      cout << "Number = " << num << endl;
   }
   else {
      cout << "Invalid entry." << endl;
   }
   return 0;
}
```

Figure **7.26**

(Continued)

Input/Output

```
Enter a number: q
Invalid entry.
```

Input/Output

```
Enter a number: -58
Number = -58
```

The input function, getLine, reads the characters from the keyboard into a string of characters. It always installs a newline character as a sentinel, regardless of how many or few characters the user enters. If the user enters no characters and simply presses the Return key, getLine will install the newline character at line[0].

Function parseNum corresponds to the FSM of Figure 7.19(b). The procedure has a local enumerated variable called state, whose possible values are eI, eF, or eM, corresponding to the states I, F, and M of the FSM. An additional state called eSTOP is for terminating the loop. The formal parameter, v, corresponds to the actual parameter, valid, in the main program. The function initializes v to true and state to the start state, eI.

A do loop simulates the transitions in the finite state machine, which is the direct code technique. A single switch statement determines the current state, and a single nested if statement within each case determines the next character. Assignment statements in the code change the state variable directly.

In a simplified FSM, there are two ways to stop—either you run out of input or you reach a state with no transitions from it on the next character, in which case the string is not valid. Corresponding to these termination conditions, there are two ways to quit the do loop—when the input sentinel is reached in a final state or when the string is discovered to be invalid.

The body of a do loop always executes at least once. Nevertheless, the code executes correctly even if the Return key is the first that is pressed. getLine installs the newline character in line[0]. ParseNum initializes state to I, enters the do loop, and immediately sets nextChar to the newline character. Then v gets false, and the loop terminates correctly.

In addition to determining whether the string is valid, parseNum converts the string of characters to the proper integer value. If the first character is + or a digit, it sets sign to +1. If the first character is -, it sets sign to −1. The first digit detected sets n to its proper value in state I or F. Its value is maintained correctly in state M each time a succeeding digit is detected. The magnitude is multiplied by the sign when the loop terminates with a valid number.

The computation of the correct integer value is a semantic action, and the state assignment is a syntax action. It is easy with the direct code technique to integrate the semantic processing with the syntactic processing because there is a distinct place in the syntax code to include the required semantic processing. For example, you know in state I if the character is - that sign must be set to −1. It is easy to determine where to include that assignment in the syntax code.

Integrating semantic actions with syntactic actions

If the user enters leading spaces before a legal string of digits, the FSM will declare the string invalid. The next program shows how to correct this deficiency.

An Input Buffer Class

The following two programs use the same technique to get characters from the input stream. Instead of duplicating the code for the input processing in each program, this section shows an implementation of an input buffer class that both programs use. It is stored in a separate file named inBuffer.hpp and is included with the #include directive in each program. Figure 7.27 shows the .hpp file, which is known as a header file.

As shown in the following two programs, the FSM function sometimes detects a character from the input stream that terminates the current token, yet will be required from the input stream in a subsequent call to the function. Conceptually, the function must push the character back into the input stream so it will be retrieved on the subsequent call. backUpInput provides that operation on the buffer class. Although the FSM function needs to access characters from the input buffer, it does not access the buffer directly. Only procedures getLine, advanceInput, and backUpInput access the global buffer. The reason for this design is to provide the FSM function with a more convenient abstract structure of the input stream.

```
// File: inBuffer.hpp

#include <string> // string, getline

class InBuffer {
private:
   string line;
   int lineIndex;

public:
   void getLine () {
      getline (cin, line);
      line.push_back ('\n');
      lineIndex = 0;
   }

   void advanceInput (char& ch) {
      ch = line[lineIndex++];
   }

   void backUpInput () {
      lineIndex--;
   }
};
```

Figure **7.27**

The input buffer class included in the programs of Figures 7.29 and 7.32.

A Multiple-Token Parser

If the parser of a C++ compiler is analyzing the string

```
total =
```

it knows that the next nonterminal could be an identifier such as amount, or an integer such as 100. Because it does not know which token to expect, it calls a finite state machine that can recognize either, as in Figure 7.28.

The state labeled Ident is a final state for detecting the identifier token. Int is the final state for detecting an integer. The transition from Start to Start is on the space character. It allows for leading spaces before either token. If the only characters left to scan are trailing spaces at the end of a line, the FSM procedure will return the empty token. That is why the start state is also a final state.

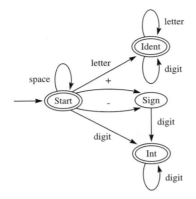

Figure **7.28**

The FSM of a program that
recognizes identifiers and integers.

Figure 7.29 shows two input/output runs from a program that implements the
multiple-token recognizer of Figure 7.28. The first run has an input of two lines, the
first line with five nonempty tokens and the second line with six nonempty tokens.
Here is an explanation of the first run of Figure 7.29.

The machine starts in the start state and scans the first terminal, H. That takes it
to the Ident state. The following terminals, e, r, and e, make transitions to the same
state. The next terminal is a space. There is no transition from state Ident on the terminal space. Because the machine is in the final state for identifiers, it concludes

Figure **7.29**

The input/output of a program that
recognizes identifiers and integers.

Input	Input
`Here     is A47 48B`	`Here     is A47+ 48B`
`   C-49 ALongIdentifier +50 D16-51`	`   C+49`
	`ALongIdentifier`

Output	Output
`Identifier = Here`	`Identifier = Here`
`Identifier = is`	`Identifier = is`
`Identifier = A47`	`Identifier = A47`
`Integer   = 48`	`Syntax error`
`Identifier = B`	`Identifier = C`
`Empty token`	`Integer   = 49`
`Identifier = C`	`Empty token`
`Integer   = -49`	`Empty token`
`Identifier = ALongIdentifier`	`Identifier = ALongIdentifier`
`Integer   = 50`	`Empty token`
`Identifier = D16`	
`Integer   = -51`	
`Empty token`	

(**a**) First run.   (**b**) Second run.

that an identifier has been scanned. It puts the space terminal, which it could not use in this state, back into the input for use as the first terminal for the next token. It then declares that an identifier has been scanned.

The machine starts over in the start state. It uses the leftover space to make a transition to Start. A few more spaces produce a few more transitions to Start, after which the i and s characters produce the recognition of a second identifier, as shown in the sample output. Similarly, A47 is recognized as an identifier.

For the next token, the initial 4 sends the machine into the Integer state. The 8 makes the transition to the same state. Now the machine inputs the B. There is no transition from state Integer on the terminal B. Because the machine is in the final state for integers, it concludes that an integer has been scanned. It puts the B terminal, which it could not use in this state, back into the input for use as the first terminal for the next token. It then declares that an integer has been scanned. Notice that B is detected as an identifier the next time around.

The machine continues recognizing tokens until it gets to the end of the line, at which point it recognizes the empty token. It will recognize the empty token whether or not there are trailing spaces in the input.

The second sample input shows how the machine handles a string of characters that contains a syntax error. After recognizing Here, is, and A47, on the next call, the FSM gets the + and goes to state Sign. Because the next character is space, and there is no transition from Sign on space, the FSM returns the invalid token.

Like all multiple-token recognizers, this machine operates on the following design principle:

> You can never fail once you reach a final state. Instead, if the final state does *A design principle for multiple-*
> not have a transition from it on the terminal just input, you have recognized a *token recognizers*
> token and should back up the input. The character will then be available as the
> first terminal for the next token.

The machine handles an empty line (or a line with only spaces) correctly, returning the empty token on the first call.

Figure 7.30 is a Unified Modeling Language (UML) diagram of the class structure of a token. AToken is an abstract token with no attributes and two public abstract operations, tokenType and printToken. The plus sign in front of the operations is the UML notation for public access. The open triangle is the UML symbol for inheritance; Figure 7.30 shows that the concrete classes TEmpty, TInvalid, TInteger, and TIdentifier inherit from AToken. The UML convention is to show abstract class names and methods in a slanted font.

Each of the concrete classes must implement the abstract methods they inherit from their superclass. Method printToken prints the output shown in Figure 7.29. Method tokenType returns an enumerated value that indicates the type of token detected. In addition to the inherited methods, class TInteger has a private attribute intValue, which stores the integer value detected by the parser, and a public constructor. The minus sign in front of the attribute is the UML symbol

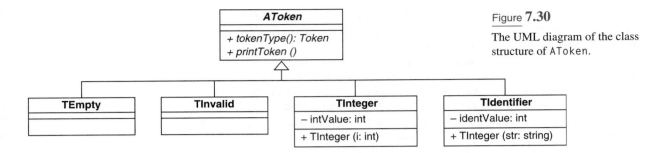

Figure 7.30

The UML diagram of the class
structure of AToken.

for private access. Class TInteger has a similar attribute of type string and its
own constructor.

Figure 7.31 shows the corresponding C++ implementation of the token class
structure of Figure 7.30. It is the first part of a complete listing of the program that
continues in Figures 7.32 and 7.33. Token is a C++ enum type with values that correspond to the four concrete classes.

Figure 7.32 is the direct-code implementation of the FSM of Figure 7.28.
Method getToken takes as input a pointer pAT called by reference. The mnemonic
pAT stands for "pointer to an abstract token." A precondition for getToken is that
pAT is already set to an allocated token whose initial value is irrelevant. Whenever
the method needs to change pAT, it deletes the old value and allocates a new value
with the new operator. This programming style of always matching each new with a
delete helps to prevent memory leaks.

```
#include <iostream>
#include <cctype> // isalpha, isdigit
#include <string> // string, getline
using namespace std;

#include "inBuffer.hpp" // InBuffer
InBuffer inBuffer;

enum Token {eT_IDENTIFIER, eT_INTEGER, eT_EMPTY, eT_INVALID};

class AToken {
public:
   virtual Token tokenType () = 0;
   virtual void printToken () = 0;
};
```

Figure 7.31

The C++ implementation of class
AToken in Figure 7.30.

Figure **7.31**

(Continued)

```
class TEmpty : public AToken {
public:
   Token tokenType () { return eT_EMPTY; }
   void printToken () { cout << "Empty token" << endl; }
};

class TInvalid : public AToken {
public:
   Token tokenType () { return eT_INVALID; }
   void printToken () { cout << "Syntax error" << endl; }
};

class TInteger : public AToken {
private:
   int intValue;
public:
   TInteger (int i) { intValue = i; }
   Token tokenType () { return eT_INTEGER; }
   void printToken () { cout << "Integer   = " << intValue << endl; }
};

class TIdentifier : public AToken {
private:
   string identValue;
public:
   TIdentifier (string str) { identValue = str; }
   Token tokenType () { return eT_IDENTIFIER; }
   void printToken () { cout << "Identifier = " << identValue << endl;
};
```

Figure 7.33 shows the main program. It has a single abstract token pAToken, which it initializes on the first line. The corresponding delete operation executes just before the program terminates, maintaining the programming style of matching each new with a delete. The outer while loop executes once for each line of input and the inner do loop executes once for each token in the line. The output relies on polymorphic dispatch to display the tokens that are detected. That is, the main program does not explicitly test the dynamic type of the token to choose how to output its value. It simply uses its abstract token to invoke the printToken method.

```
enum State {eS_START, eS_IDENT, eS_SIGN, eS_INTEGER, eS_STOP};

void getToken (AToken*& pAT) {
   // Pre: pAT is set to a token object.
   // Post: pAT is set to a token object that corresponds to
   // the next token in the input buffer.
   State state;
   char nextChar;
   int sign;
   int localIntValue;
   string localIdentValue;
   delete pAT;
   pAT = new TEmpty;
   state = eS_START;
   do {
      inBuffer.advanceInput (nextChar);
      switch (state) {
      case eS_START:
         if (isalpha(nextChar)) {
            localIdentValue = nextChar;
            state = eS_IDENT;
         }
         else if (nextChar == '-') {
            sign = -1;
            state = eS_SIGN;
         }
         else if (nextChar == '+') {
            sign = +1;
            state = eS_SIGN;
         }
         else if (isdigit(nextChar)) {
            localIntValue = nextChar - '0';
            sign = +1;
            state = eS_INTEGER;
         }
         else if (nextChar == '\n') {
            state = eS_STOP;
         }
         else if (nextChar != ' ') {
            delete pAT;
            pAT = new TInvalid;
         }
         break;
```

Figure **7.32**

A C++ implementation of the FSM of Figure 7.28.

```
    case eS_IDENT:
        if (isalpha (nextChar) || isdigit (nextChar)) {
            localIdentValue.push_back (nextChar);
        }
        else {
            inBuffer.backUpInput ();
            delete pAT;
            pAT = new TIdentifier (localIdentValue);
            state = eS_STOP;
        }
        break;
    case eS_SIGN:
        if (isdigit (nextChar)) {
            localIntValue = nextChar - '0';
            state = eS_INTEGER;
        }
        else {
            delete pAT;
            pAT = new TInvalid;
        }
        break;
    case eS_INTEGER:
        if (isdigit (nextChar)) {
            localIntValue = 10 * localIntValue + nextChar - '0';
        }
        else {
            inBuffer.backUpInput ();
            delete pAT;
            pAT = new TInteger (sign * localIntValue);
            state = eS_STOP;
        }
        break;
    }
}
while ((state != eS_STOP) && (pAT->tokenType () != eT_INVALID));
}
```

Figure **7.32**

(Continued)

```
int main () {
   AToken* pAToken = new TEmpty;
   inBuffer.getLine ();
   while (!cin.eof ()) {
      do {
         getToken (pAToken);
         pAToken->printToken ();
      }
      while ((pAToken->tokenType () != eT_EMPTY)
         && (pAToken->tokenType () != eT_INVALID));
      inBuffer.getLine ();
   }
   delete pAToken;
   return 0;
}
```

Figure 7.33

The main program for the tokenizer of Figure 7.32.

 7.4   Code Generation

To *translate* is to transform a string of characters from some input alphabet to another string of characters from some output alphabet. The typical phases in such a translation are lexical analysis, parsing, and code generation. This section consists of a program that translates from one language to another. It illustrates all three phases of a simple automatic translator.

A Language Translator

Figure 7.34 shows the input/output of the translator. The input is the source and the output is the object. The source and object languages are line oriented, as are assembly languages. The source language has the syntax of C++ function calls, and the object language has the syntax of assignment statements with the assignment operator :=. A sample statement from the input language is

```
set (Time, 15)
```

The corresponding object statement is

```
Time := 15
```

The word `set` is reserved in the source language. The other reserved words are `add`, `sub`, `mul`, `div`, `neg`, and `end`.

Input	Input	Figure **7.34**
``` set (Time, 15) set (Accel, 3) set (TSquared, Time) MUL (TSquared, Time) set (Position, TSquared) mul (Position, Accel) div (Position, 2) end ```	``` set (Alpha,, 123) set (Alpha) sit (Alpha, 123) set, (Alpha) mul (Alpha, Beta set (123, Alpha) neg (Alpha, Beta) set (Alpha, 123) x ```	The input/output of a program that translates from one language to another.

Output	Output
``` Time := 15 Accel := 3 TSquared := Time TSquared := TSquared * Time Position := TSquared Position := Position * Accel Position := Position / 2 ```	``` Error: Second argument not an identifier or integer. Error: Comma expected after first argument. Error: Line must begin with function identifier. Error: Left parenthesis expected after function. Error: Right parenthesis expected after argument. Error: First argument not an identifier. Error: The argument of "neg" is malformed. Error: Illegal trailing character. Error: Missing "end" sentinel. ```

(a) First run.   **(b)** Second run.

Time is a user-defined identifier. Identifiers follow the same rules as in the C++ language. Integers, such as 15 in the previous example, also follow the C++ syntax.

The set procedure takes two arguments, separated by a comma and surrounded by parentheses. The first argument must be an identifier, but the second can be an identifier or an integer constant.

Another example of a translation is

```
mul (TSquared, Time)
```

which is written in the object language as

```
TSquared := TSquared * Time
```

As with the set procedure, the first argument of a mul procedure call must be an identifier. To translate the mul statement, the translator must duplicate its first argument, which appears on both sides of the assignment operator.

The other procedure calls are similar except for `neg`, which takes a single argument and translates it, prefixed with a dash character on the right side of the assignment operator. For example, the source statement

```
neg (Alpha)
```

is translated to

```
Alpha := -Alpha
```

Reserved word `end` is the sentinel for the translator. It generates no code and corresponds to `.END` of Pep/8 assembly language. Any number of spaces can occur anywhere in a source line, except within an identifier or integer.

The translator must not crash if syntax errors occur in the input stream. In Figure 7.34, there is also a run that shows a source file full of errors. The program generates appropriate error messages to help the user find the bugs in the source program.

This program is based on a two-stage analysis of the syntax, as shown in Figure 7.24. Instead of using a grammar to specify the parsing problem as indicated in the figure, however, the structure of this source language is simple enough for the parser to be based on an FSM.

Figure 7.35 is the start of a partial listing of the program that produces the output of Figure 7.34. The program listing continues in Figures 7.37, 7.39, 7.41, 7.42, 7.44, and 7.45. Figure 7.35 does not show the `#include` statements at the beginning of the program. The operator table and mnemonic table use the `map` data structure from the C++ Standard Template Library (STL). To use the map data structure, you must include the `<map>` library. The operator table uses enumerated mnemonic values as the key to look up the string symbol to place in the generated code. The mnemonic table uses the lowercase string representation of the source code reserved word to look up the corresponding mnemonic.

The function `lookUpMnemon` takes the string `id` as an input parameter and checks to see if it is in the mnemonic table. If it is, it sets parameter `mn` to the corresponding enumerated mnemonic type and sets `fnd` to true. Otherwise, it sets `fnd` to false. The program allows the source code to be case insensitive.

Figure 7.36 is the UML diagram of an abstract argument, and Figure 7.37 is its C++ implementation. Because an argument in the source code can be either an identifier or an integer, the program stores a general argument as an `AArg`, which at runtime is either an `IdentArg` or an `IntArg`. Class `AArg` defines the abstract method `putArg`, which contributes to code generation when the value of an argument must be output.

Figure 7.38 is the UML diagram of an abstract token, and Figure 7.39 is a partial listing of its C++ implementation. This structure of a token is similar to the one in Figure 7.30 of the previous section. Method `tokenType` serves the same purpose as before. Method `getArg` returns a pointer to an abstract argument. It is only

```
// ======== Global tables
enum Mnemon {
   eM_ADD, eM_SUB, eM_MUL, eM_DIV,
   eM_NEG, eM_SET, eM_END, eM_EMPTY
};

map <Mnemon, string> operatorTable;
map <string, Mnemon> mnemonTable;

void initGlobalTables () {
   operatorTable [eM_ADD] = "+";
   operatorTable [eM_SUB] = "-";
   operatorTable [eM_MUL] = "*";
   operatorTable [eM_DIV] = "/";
   mnemonTable ["add"] = eM_ADD;
   mnemonTable ["sub"] = eM_SUB;
   mnemonTable ["mul"] = eM_MUL;
   mnemonTable ["div"] = eM_DIV;
   mnemonTable ["neg"] = eM_NEG;
   mnemonTable ["set"] = eM_SET;
   mnemonTable ["end"] = eM_END;
}

void lookUpMnemon (string id, Mnemon& mn, bool& fnd) {
   string lowerId = "";
   for (int i = 0; i < id.size (); i++) {
      lowerId.push_back (tolower (id[i]));
   }
   if (mnemonTable.count (lowerId) == 1) {
      mn = mnemonTable[lowerId];
      fnd = true;
   }
   else {
      fnd = false;
   }
}
```

Figure **7.35**

The global tables and lookup function for the translator program.

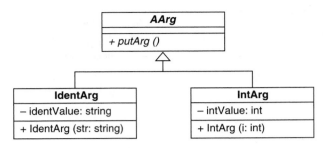

Figure **7.36**

The UML diagram of the class structure of AArg.

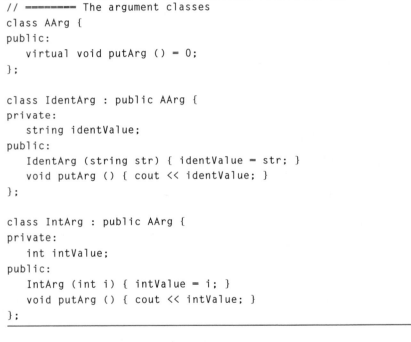

```
// ======== The argument classes
class AArg {
public:
   virtual void putArg () = 0;
};

class IdentArg : public AArg {
private:
   string identValue;
public:
   IdentArg (string str) { identValue = str; }
   void putArg () { cout << identValue; }
};

class IntArg : public AArg {
private:
   int intValue;
public:
   IntArg (int i) { intValue = i; }
   void putArg () { cout << intValue; }
};
```

Figure **7.37**

The C++ implementation of class AArg in Figure 7.36.

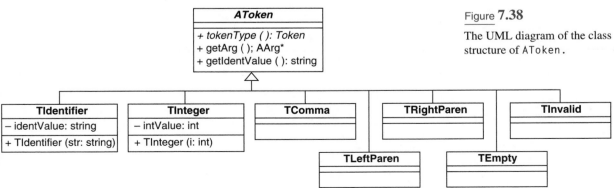

Figure **7.38**

The UML diagram of the class structure of AToken.

```
// ======== The token classes
enum Token {
   eT_IDENTIFIER, eT_INTEGER, eT_COMMA, eT_LEFT_PAREN,
   eT_RIGHT_PAREN, eT_EMPTY, eT_INVALID
};

class AToken {
public:
   virtual Token tokenType () = 0;
   virtual AArg* getArg () { return 0; }
   virtual string getIdentValue () { return ""; }
};

class TIdentifier : public AToken {
private:
   string identValue;
public:
   TIdentifier (string str) { identValue = str; }
   AArg* getArg () {
     AArg* pArg = new IdentArg (identValue);
     return pArg;
   }
   Token tokenType () { return eT_IDENTIFIER; }
   string getIdentValue () { return identValue; }
};

class TInteger : public AToken {
private:
   int intValue;
public:
   TInteger (int i) { intValue = i; }
   AArg* getArg () {
     IntArg* pArg = new IntArg (intValue);
     return pArg;
   }
   Token tokenType () { return eT_INTEGER; }
};

class TComma : public AToken {
public:
   Token tokenType () { return eT_COMMA; }
};

...
```

Figure **7.39**

The C++ implementation of class
AToken in Figure 7.38.

applicable to TIdentifier and TInteger, because these subclasses of AToken are the only ones that contain attributes from which the code generator generates the object code. For TIdentifer, getArg returns a newly allocated IdentArg based on its identValue. For TInteger, getArg returns a newly allocated IntArg based on its intValue.

Method getIdentValue is only applicable to TIdentifer. The lexical analyzer returns an identifier when it encounters a reserved word and when it encounters an argument. When it encounters a reserved word, the parser needs to look up the word in the mnemonic table. It uses getIdentValue to get the identifier value from the token.

Figure 7.40 is the UML diagram of the abstract code class ACode, and Figure 7.41 is a partial listing of its C++ implementation. An object of class ACode represents one line of object code. Execution of method generateCode outputs that line of code to cout. Consequently, a code object must contain all the data it needs to output the code on that line. For example, Figure 7.40 shows that an object of class TwoArgs has two attributes itself, pFirstArg, which is a pointer to an abstract argument, and pSecondArg, also a pointer to an abstract argument. In addition, it has mnemonic, which it inherits from its superclass Valid. Consider the last line of input from Figure 7.34(a)

```
div (Position, 2)
```

The code object would have eM_DIV for mnemonic, pFirstArg would point to an IdentArg with an identValue of "Position" and pSecondArg would point to an IntArg with an intValue of 2. The OneArg class is for the neg statement, which has only one argument.

The UML symbol for protected access is #, as in the attribute for the Valid class in Figure 7.40. The UML symbol for class composition is the solid diamond touching the OneArg class box and the TwoArgs class box. The meaning of class composition is "has a" as opposed to the meaning of inheritance, which is "is a." A OneArg object "is a" Valid object, and a OneArg object "has a" AArg object.

Figure 7.42 is a partial listing of the lexical analyzer. Function getToken works like the getToken function in Figure 7.32 except that it detects one of the seven tokens in Figure 7.38. As before, formal parameter pAT is a pointer to an abstract token called by reference.

Figure 7.43 shows a deterministic FSM that describes the source language, and Figure 7.44 is a partial listing of its implementation. The transitions of the machine are on the tokens from the lexical analyzer, indicated in the figure by the words that begin with eT as in Figure 7.39. The final state ePS_FINISH can only be reached by input of token eT_EMPTY. The transition from ePS_START to ePS_FINISH will occur if there is a blank line or if there is a line that contains only spaces. The terminal string end is the only identifier that makes the transition from ePS_START to ePS_END. The identifiers that correspond to the other reserved words—set, add, sub, mul, div, and neg—make the transition from

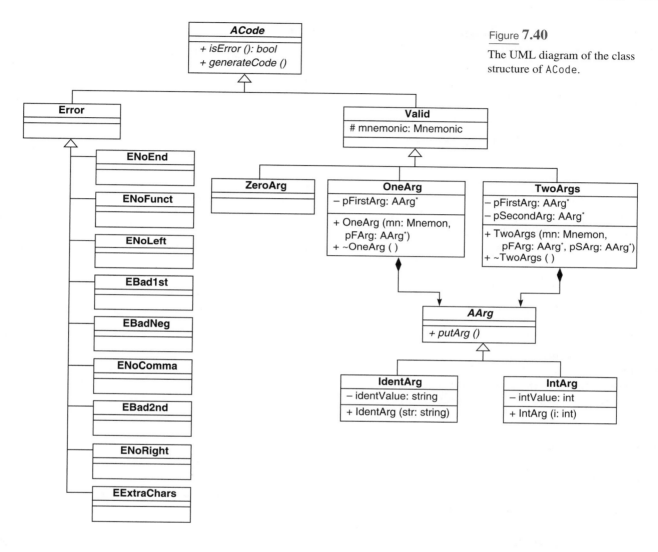

Figure **7.40**

The UML diagram of the class
structure of ACode.

```
// ======== The code classes
class ACode {
public:
   virtual bool isError () = 0;
   virtual void generateCode () = 0;
};

// ======== The error code classes
class Error : public ACode {
```

Figure **7.41**

The C++ implementation of class
ACode in Figure 7.40.

Figure **7.41**

(Continued)

```cpp
public:
   bool isError () { return true; }
};

class ENoEnd : public Error {
public:
   void generateCode () {
      cout << "Error: Missing \"end\" sentinel.";
   }
};


...


// ======== The valid code classes
class Valid : public ACode {
protected:
   Mnemon mnemonic;
public:
   bool isError () { return false; }
};

class ZeroArg : public Valid {
public:
   ZeroArg (Mnemon mn) { mnemonic = mn; }
   void generateCode () { } // cout nothing
};

class OneArg : public Valid {
private:
   AArg *pFirstArg;
public:
   OneArg (Mnemon mn, AArg* pFArg) {
      mnemonic = mn;
      pFirstArg = pFArg;
   }
   ~OneArg () { delete pFirstArg; }
   void generateCode () {
      pFirstArg->putArg ();
      cout << " := -";
      pFirstArg->putArg ();
   }
};


...
```

```
// ========= The lexical analyzer
enum LexState {
   eLS_START, eLS_IDENT, eLS_SIGN, eLS_INTEGER, eLS_STOP
};

void getToken (AToken*& pAT) {
   // Pre: pAT is allocated to an irrelevant value.
   char nextChar;
   string localIdentValue;
   int localIntValue;
   int sign;
   delete pAT;
   pAT = new TEmpty;
   LexState state = eLS_START;
   do {
      inBuffer.advanceInput (nextChar);
      switch (state) {
      case eLS_START:
         if (isalpha (nextChar)) {
            localIdentValue = nextChar;
            state = eLS_IDENT;
         }

...

      case eLS_INTEGER:
         if (isdigit (nextChar)) {
            localIntValue = 10 * localIntValue + nextChar - '0';
         }
         else {
            inBuffer.backUpInput();
            delete pAT;
            pAT = new TInteger (sign * localIntValue);
            state = eLS_STOP;
         }
         break;
      }
   }
   while ((state != eLS_STOP) && (pAT->tokenType () != eT_INVALID));
}
```

Figure **7.42**

The lexical analyzer.

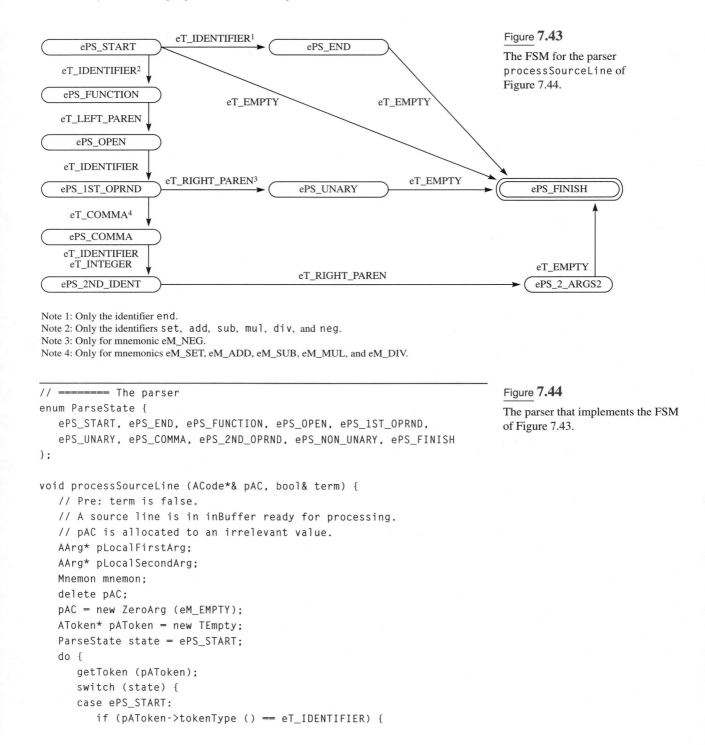

Figure **7.43**

The FSM for the parser
`processSourceLine` of
Figure 7.44.

Note 1: Only the identifier `end`.
Note 2: Only the identifiers `set`, `add`, `sub`, `div`, and `neg`.
Note 3: Only for mnemonic eM_NEG.
Note 4: Only for mnemonics eM_SET, eM_ADD, eM_SUB, eM_MUL, and eM_DIV.

```
// ========= The parser
enum ParseState {
   ePS_START, ePS_END, ePS_FUNCTION, ePS_OPEN, ePS_1ST_OPRND,
   ePS_UNARY, ePS_COMMA, ePS_2ND_OPRND, ePS_NON_UNARY, ePS_FINISH
};

void processSourceLine (ACode*& pAC, bool& term) {
   // Pre: term is false.
   // A source line is in inBuffer ready for processing.
   // pAC is allocated to an irrelevant value.
   AArg* pLocalFirstArg;
   AArg* pLocalSecondArg;
   Mnemon mnemon;
   delete pAC;
   pAC = new ZeroArg (eM_EMPTY);
   AToken* pAToken = new TEmpty;
   ParseState state = ePS_START;
   do {
      getToken (pAToken);
      switch (state) {
      case ePS_START:
         if (pAToken->tokenType () == eT_IDENTIFIER) {
```

Figure **7.44**

The parser that implements the FSM
of Figure 7.43.

```
         string tempStr = pAToken->getIdentValue ();
         bool found;
         lookUpMnemon (tempStr, mnemon, found);
         if (found) {
            if (mnemon == eM_END) {
               delete pAC;
               pAC = new ZeroArg (eM_END);
               term = true;
               state = ePS_END;
            }
            else {
               state = ePS_FUNCTION;
            }
         }
         else {
            delete pAC;
            pAC = new ENoFunct;
         }
      }
      else if (pAToken->tokenType () == eT_EMPTY) {
         // pAC initialized to ZeroArg (eM_EMPTY)
         state = ePS_FINISH;
      }
      else {
         delete pAC;
         pAC = new ENoFunct;
      }
      break;

...

   case ePS_COMMA:
      if ((pAToken->tokenType () == eT_IDENTIFIER)
      || (pAToken->tokenType () == eT_INTEGER)) {
         pLocalSecondArg = pAToken->getArg ();
         delete pAC;
         pAC = new TwoArgs (mnemon, pLocalFirstArg, pLocalSecondArg);
         state = ePS_2ND_OPRND;
      }
      else {
         delete pAC;
         pAC = new EBad2nd;
      }
      break;
```

Figure **7.44**

(Continued)

```
      case ePS_2ND_OPRND:
         if (pAToken->tokenType () == eT_RIGHT_PAREN) {
            state = ePS_NON_UNARY;
         }
         else {
            delete pAC;
            pAC = new ENoRight;
         }
         break;
      case ePS_NON_UNARY:
         if (pAToken->tokenType () == eT_EMPTY) {
            state = ePS_FINISH;
         }
         else {
            delete pAC;
            pAC = new EExtraChars;
         }
         break;
      }
   }
   while ((state != ePS_FINISH) && (!pAC->isError ()));
   delete pAToken;
}
```

Figure **7.44**

(Continued)

ePS_START to ePS_FUNCTION. All other identifiers are invalid when detected in the ePS_START state.

Figure 7.45 is a complete listing of the main program that produces the output of Figure 7.34. The boolean variable `terminateWithEnd`, initialized to false and passed by reference to `processSourceLine`, controls termination of the loop. Only the end statement sets `terminateWithEnd` to true, because end is the sentinel for the translator. If the user omits the end statement, the main program detects that the end of file was reached without it, and issues the appropriate error.

The functions that perform the three phases of the automatic translation are as follows:

- Lexical analyzer: `getToken`
- Parser: `processSourceLine`
- Code generator: `generateCode`

The three translation phases of the program

The parser calls the lexical analyzer, and the main program calls the parser for each line of source code. The main program calls the code generator, whose code generated methods are distributed among separate objects.

```
// ======== The main program
int main () {
    bool terminateWithEnd = false;
    ACode* pACode = new ZeroArg (eM_EMPTY);
    initGlobalTables ();
    inBuffer.getLine ();
    while (! (cin.eof() || terminateWithEnd)) {
        processSourceLine (pACode, terminateWithEnd);
        pACode->generateCode ();
        cout << endl;
        inBuffer.getLine ();
    }
    if (!terminateWithEnd) {
        delete pACode;
        pACode = new ENoEnd;
        pACode->generateCode ();
        cout << endl;
    }
    delete pACode;
    return 0;
}
```

Figure **7.45**

The main program for the translator that produces the output of Figure 7.34.

Parser Characteristics

Rather than define the syntax of the source language with the FSM of Figure 7.43, you could define it with a grammar. A formal grammar for the source language would have a simple structure. For example, a production rule for a set statement might be

<set-statement> → set (<identifier> , <argument>)

where <argument> would be defined in another production rule as <identifier> or <integer>. Unlike in C++, this grammar would contain no recursive definitions.

The simple nature of the source syntax allows the parsing of this language to be based on a deterministic FSM. Parsers for most programming languages cannot be this simple. Although it is common for lexical analyzers to be based on finite state machines, it is rare that a parser can also be based on an FSM. In practice, most languages are too complex for such a technique to be possible.

Parsers are usually not based on an FSM.

Because the production rules of a real grammar invariably contain many recursive definitions, the parsing algorithm itself may contain recursive procedures that reflect the recursion of the grammar. Such an algorithm is called a *recursive descent parser.*

Regardless of the complexity of the source language or the parsing technique of the translator, the relationship of the parser to the lexical analyzer in a translation program is always the same. The parser is at a higher level of abstraction than the lexical analyzer. The lexical analyzer scans the characters and recognizes tokens, which it passes to the parser. The parser scans the tokens and recognizes a program in the source language.

SUMMARY

The fundamental question of computer science is "What can be automated?" The automatic translation of artificial languages is at the heart of computer science. Each artificial language has an alphabet. The closure of a set, T^*, is the set of all possible strings formed by concatenating elements from T. A language is a subset of the closure of its alphabet. A grammar describes the syntax of a language and has four parts: a nonterminal alphabet, a terminal alphabet, a set of rules of production, and a start symbol. Derivation is the process by which a grammar specifies a language. To derive a sentence in the language, you begin with the start symbol and substitute production rules until you get a string of terminals. The parsing problem is to determine the substitution sequence to match a given string of terminals. There are hundreds of rules of production in the standard C++ grammar. A context-free grammar is one that restricts the left side of all the production rules to contain a single nonterminal. Although the C++ grammar is context-free, certain aspects of the language are context-sensitive.

A finite state machine (FSM) also describes the syntax of a language. It consists of a set of states and transitions between the states. Each transition is marked with an input terminal symbol. One state is the start state, and at least one, possibly more, is the final state. A nondeterministic FSM may have more than one transition from a given state on one input terminal symbol. A sentence is valid if, starting at the start state, you can make a sequence of transitions dictated by the symbols in the sentence and end in a final state.

Two software implementation techniques of FSMs are the table lookup technique and the direct code technique. Both techniques contain loops that are controlled by a state variable, which is initialized to the start state. Each execution of the loop corresponds to a transition in the FSM. In the table-lookup technique, the transitions are assigned from a two-dimensional transition table. In the direct-code technique, the transitions are assigned with selection statements in the body of the loop.

The three translation phases of an automatic translator are the lexical analyzer, the parser, and the code generator. For most high-level languages, the lexical analyzer is based on an FSM and the parser is based on a context-free grammar. The code generator is highly dependent on the nature of the object language.

EXERCISES

Section 7.1
*1. What is the fundamental question of computer science?

2. What is the identity element for the addition operation on integers? What is the identity element for the OR operation on booleans?

3. Derive the following strings with the grammar of Figure 7.1 and draw the corresponding syntax tree:

   *(a) `abc123`   **(b)** `a1b2c3`   **(c)** `a321bc`

4. Derive the following strings with the grammar of Figure 7.2 and draw the corresponding syntax tree:

   *(a) `-d`   **(b)** `+ddd`   **(c)** `d`

5. Derive the following strings with the grammar of Figure 7.3:

   *(a) `abc`   **(b)** `aabbcc`

6. For each of the following strings, state whether it can be derived from the rules of the grammar of Figure 7.5. If it can, draw the corresponding syntax tree:

   *(a) `a + ( a )`   **(b)** `a * ( + a )`   **(c)** `a * ( a + a )`
   (d) `a * ( a + a ) * a`   **(e)** `a + ( - a )`   **(f)** `( ( ( a ) ) )`

7. For the grammar of Figure 7.8, draw the syntax tree for <statement> from the following strings, assuming that S1, S2, S3, S4, C1, and C2 are valid <expression>s:

   *(a)
   ```
   {  if ( C1 )
         S1 ;
       S2 ;
   }
   ```

   (b)
   ```
   {  if ( C1 )
           if ( C2 )
             S1 ;
           else
             S2 ;
        S3 ;
   }
   ```

   (c)
   ```
   {  if ( C1 )
          if ( C2 )
             S1 ;
          else
             S2 ;
        else
           S3 ;
      S4 ;
   }
   ```

   (d)
   ```
   {  S1 ;
       while ( C1 )
       {  if ( C2 )
             S2 ;
           S3 ;
       }
   }
   ```

8. For the grammar of Figure 7.8, draw the syntax tree for <statement> from the following strings, assuming that `alpha`, `beta`, and `gamma` are valid <identifier>s and 1 and 24 are valid <constant>s:

   *(a) `alpha = 1 ;`
   (b) `alpha = alpha + 1 ;`
   (c) `alpha = (beta * 1) ;`
   (d) `alpha = ((beta + 1) * (gamma + 24)) ;`
   (e) `alpha (beta) ;`
   (f) `alpha (beta, 24) ;`

9. For the grammar of Figure 7.8, draw the syntax tree for <translation-unit> from the following string, assuming that `alpha`, `beta`, `gamma`, and `main` are valid <identifier>s and `C1`, `S1`, and `S2` are <expression>s:

```
int main()
{  int gamma;
   alpha (gamma);
   if (C1)
      S1;
   else
      S2;
}
```

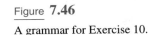

$N = \{A, B\}$
$T = \{0,1\}$
P = the productions
    1. A → 0 B
    2. B → 1 0 B
    3. B → ε
$S = A$

Figure **7.46**

A grammar for Exercise 10.

10. The question this exercise poses is "Can two different grammars produce the same language?" The grammars in Figures 7.46 and 7.47 are not the same because they have different nonterminal sets and different production rules. Experiment with these two grammars by deriving some terminal strings. From your experiments, describe the languages produced by these grammars. Is it possible to derive a valid string of terminals with the grammar in Figure 7.46 that is not in 7.47 or vice versa? Prove your conjecture.

$N = \{C\}$
$T = \{0, 1\}$
P = the productions
    1. C → C 1 0
    2. C → 0
$S = C$

Figure **7.47**

Another grammar for Exercise 10.

Section 7.2
11. For each of the machines shown in Figure 7.48, **(a)** state whether the FSM is deterministic or nondeterministic and **(b)** identify any states that are inaccessible.

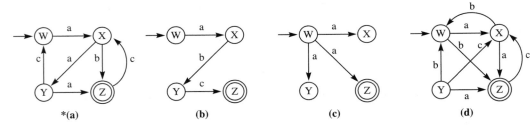

*(a)   **(b)**   **(c)**   **(d)**

12. Remove the empty transitions to produce the equivalent machine for each of the finite state machines in Figure 7.49.

Figure **7.48**

The FSMs for Exercise 11.

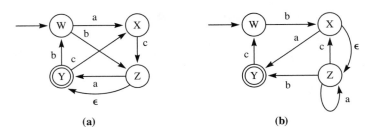

(a)   **(b)**

Figure **7.49**

The FSMs for Exercise 12

13. Draw a deterministic FSM that recognizes strings of 1's and 0's specified by each of the following criteria. Each FSM should reject any characters that are not 0 or 1. *(a) The string of three characters, 101. (b) All strings of arbitrary length that end in 101. For example, the FSM should accept 1101 but reject 1011. (c) All strings of arbitrary length that begin with 101. For example, the FSM should accept 1010 but reject 0101. (d) All strings of arbitrary length that contain a 101 at least once anywhere. For example, the FSM should accept all the strings mentioned in parts (a), (b), and (c) as well as strings such as 11100001011111100111.

Section 7.4

14. Design a grammar that describes the source language of the translator in Figure 7.44.

15. Draw a state transition diagram for the FSM in procedure getToken in Figure 7.32.

PROBLEMS

Section 7.3

16. Improve the program in Figure 7.25 as suggested in the text by defining a third enumeration in Alphabet called other, which represents a symbol that is neither a letter nor a digit.

17. Implement each FSM in Exercise 13 using the table-lookup technique of the program in Figure 7.25. Classify a character as eONE, eZERO, or eOTHER in the transition table. Take the input from the keyboard.

18. Implement each FSM in Exercise 13 using the direct-code technique of the program in Figure 7.26. Take the input from the keyboard. Write a procedure called parsePat for parse pattern that corresponds to parseNum. Do not include formal parameter n in the procedure.

19. A hexadecimal digit is '0'..'9', or 'a'..'f', or 'A'..'F'. A hexadecimal constant consists of one to four hexadecimal digits. Examples are 3, a, 0d, FF4e. Use the direct-code technique for implementing a finite state machine as in the program of Figure 7.26 to parse a hexadecimal constant and convert it to a nonnegative integer. The input/output should be similar to that in the figure, with invalid input producing an error message and a valid hexadecimal input string producing the nonnegative integer value. You might find the following functions in <cctype> helpful. ch has type char.

isxdigit(ch), returns true if ch is a hexadecimal digit
isdigit(ch), returns true if ch is a decimal digit
isupper(ch), returns true if ch is an upper-case letter
islower(ch), returns true if ch is a lower-case letter
toupper(ch), returns uppercase of ch if ch is a lowercase letter, otherwise, returns ch
tolower(ch), returns lowercase of ch if ch is an uppercase letter, otherwise, returns ch

Section 7.4

20. Write a limited assembler for Pep/8 assembly language. The source program contains an assembly language program without symbols with mnemonics; `BR`, `DECI`, `LDA`, `ADDA`, `STA`, `DECO`, and `STOP`; dot commands `.BLOCK` and `.END`; and hexadecimal and decimal constants. For example, if the source contains

```
BR    0x0007,  i
.BLOCK 4
deci    0x2  ,d
LDA     +2,d
AdDa -5,  i
STA     0x0004,d
    DECO    0x04,d
STOP
.END
```

then your assembler should output the object program

```
04 00 07 00 00 00 00 31 00 02 C1 00 02 70 FF FB
E1 00 04 39 00 04 00 zz
```

The loader will not accept trailing spaces at the end of an object program line.

Assume that the source lines contain no comments. All addressing modes are explicit, even with the `BR` instruction. Verify that an instruction has a valid addressing mode, and issue an error if it does not. Mnemonics and dot commands can have any mixture of uppercase or lowercase characters. Zero or more spaces can occur anywhere between tokens, except that there must be at least one space immediately after a mnemonic or dot command. If the source file contains one or more errors, print appropriate messages and suppress the output to the object file. Complete the following milestones in the order they are listed.

(a) Write procedure `getToken`, which should implement the FSM of Figure 7.50. Declare the following enumerated type:

```
enum Token {
    eT_IDENTIFIER, eT_DOT_COMMAND, eT_DEC_CONST,
    eT_HEX_CONST, eT_ADDR_MODE, eT_EMPTY, eT_INVALID
};
```

Design an abstract token like that in Figure 7.31, and draw its UML diagram like that in Figure 7.30.

Test your program thoroughly with a `main()` similar to that in Figure 7.33 that prints a list of tokens and their values. The attribute of a dot command and an addressing mode should be a string. The attribute of a decimal constant and a hexidecimal constant should be an integer. Include in your tests strings of characters that produce syntax errors as well as strings that contain sequences of valid tokens. Use `inBuffer.hpp` in Figure 7.27 for input.

(b) Draw the state transition diagram for the FSM of the parser that corresponds to Figure 7.43. Assume that each transition is on one of the tokens listed in part (a).

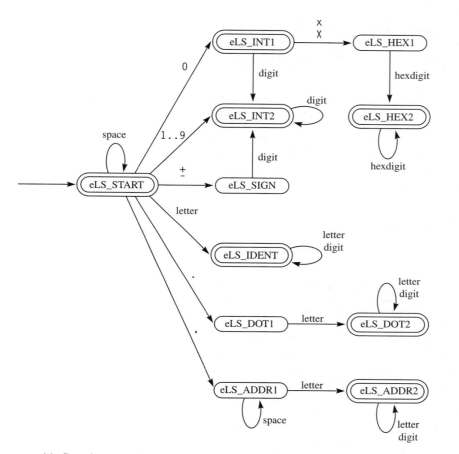

Figure **7.50**

The FSM for getToken in Problem 20(a).

(c) Complete procedure processSourceLine based on your state transition diagram of part (b). Declare the following enumerated types:

```
enum Mnemon {
    eM_BR, eM_DECI, eM_LDA, eM_ADDA,
    eM_STA, eM_DECO, eM_STOP
}
enum AddrMode {
    eA_IMMED, eA_DIRECT, eA_INDIRECT, eA_STACK_REL
    eA_STACK_REL_DEF, eA_INDEXED, eA_STACK_INDEXED,
    eA_STACK_INDEXED_DEF
};
```

Design an abstract argument AArg with two subclasses for a hexadecimal constant and a decimal constant, each with an integer attribute. Add method getArg to your token class. Design your abstract code class ACode as in Figure 7.40. Your Valid class should not have a mnemonic attribute. It should have five subclasses: Empty for the empty line; Unary for the unary STOP instruction; NonUnary for the BR, DECI, LDA, ADDA, STA, and DECO instructions; DotBlock for the .BLOCK pseudo-op; and DotEnd for the .END pseudo-op. The Unary and NonUnary classes should have an enumerated mnemonic. The NonUnary and DotBlock classes should have one abstract argument. The NonUnary class should have an enumerated AddrMode attribute. Use an addressing mode table with a C++ map to convert the string representation of the addressing mode from the token to the enumerated value.

Test your program with a main program similar to that in Figure 7.45. For now, your generateCode methods can simply output descriptions of each instruction and dot command parsed with any argument and addressing mode. Include in your tests strings of characters that produce errors as well as strings that contain sequences of valid instructions.

(d) Add hexadecimal code generation to your assembler. In addition to the single variable pACode, declare an array of code structures as follows:

```
ACode* codeTable[256];
int codeIndex;
```

Initialize codeIndex to 0 at the beginning of your main program. Each time you parse a source line, store the information from the line in a CodeTable[codeIndex] and increment codeIndex. After all the lines have been parsed and if there were no errors, loop through the code array to generate the object code.

(e) Extend the assembler by including all 39 instructions in the Pep/8 instruction set.

(f) Extend the assembler by permitting the branch instructions to not specify an addressing mode, in which case use immediate addressing as the default mode.

(g) Extend the assembler by producing a listing that shows the object code next to the source line that produced it. Print the source line with the standard spacing conventions and uppercase and lowercase conventions of the Pep/8 assembler.

(h) Extend the assembler by permitting character constants enclosed in single quotes.

(i) Extend the assembler by permitting the dot commands .WORD and .BYTE.

(j) Extend the assembler by permitting the .ASCII dot command with strings enclosed in double quotes.

(k) Extend the assembler by permitting a source line to contain a comment prefixed by a semicolon. A line may contain only a comment, or a valid instruction followed by a comment.

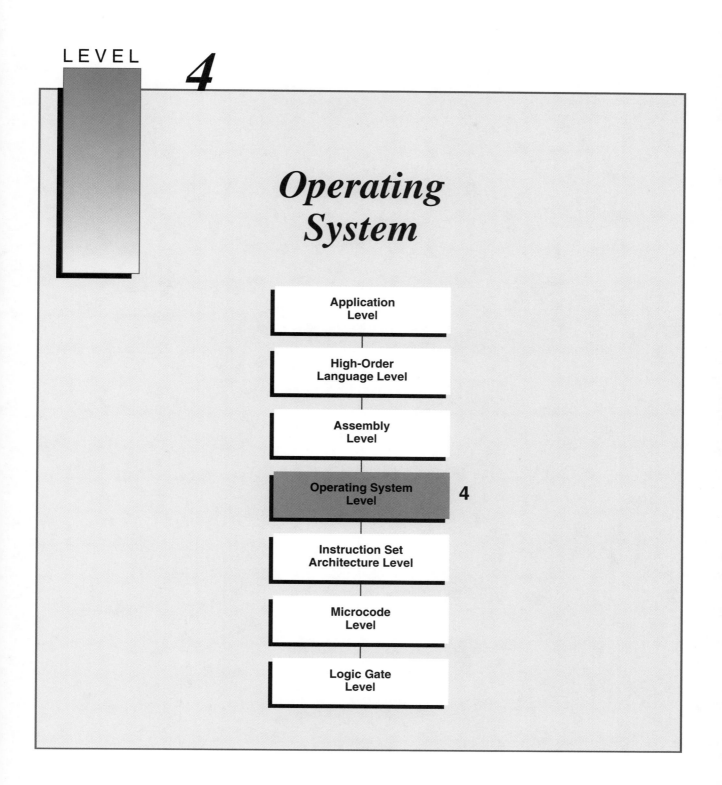

LEVEL 4

Operating System

- Application Level
- High-Order Language Level
- Assembly Level
- Operating System Level — 4
- Instruction Set Architecture Level
- Microcode Level
- Logic Gate Level

Chapter

8

Process Management

An operating system defines a more abstract machine that is easier to program than the machine at Level ISA3. Its purpose is to provide a convenient environment for higher-level programming and to allocate the resources of the system efficiently. The operating system level is between the assembly and machine levels. As is the case with abstraction in general, the operating system hides the details of the Level ISA3 machine from users at higher levels.

The purposes of an operating system

The resources of a typical computer system include CPU time, main memory, and disk memory. This chapter describes how an operating system allocates CPU time. Chapter 9 shows how it allocates main memory and disk memory.

There are three general categories of operating systems:

- Single-user
- Multi-user
- Real-time

Three types of operating systems

Many personal computers have single-user operating systems. These computers are inexpensive enough for an individual to purchase and to use without sharing it with anyone else. Larger computers, which are almost always owned by an organization rather than an individual, have multi-user operating systems. Such computers usually have only one CPU, but it is sufficiently fast to be able to execute many users' jobs simultaneously. Real-time systems are used in computers that are dedicated to controlling equipment. Their inputs are from sensors and their outputs are the control signals for the equipment. A real-time system is in the computer that controls an automobile engine, for example.

The Pep/8 operating system is a single-user system. It illustrates some of the techniques used to allocate CPU time. However, it does not illustrate the management of main memory or disk memory. The first two sections of this chapter include a complete listing of the Pep/8 operating system.

8.1   Loaders

An important function of an operating system is to manage the jobs that users submit to be executed. In a multi-user system, several users continually submit jobs. The operating system must decide which job to run from a list of pending jobs. After it decides which job to execute next, it must load the appropriate program into main memory and turn control of the CPU over to that program for execution.

The Pep/8 Operating System

Figure 8.1 shows the location of the Pep/8 operating system in main memory. It consists of the system stack and I/O buffer in RAM, the loader at address FC57, the interrupt service routine at FC9B, and the four machine vectors at FFF8 through FFFE. Although the Pep/8 operating system illustrates the operation of a loader, it does not illustrate the process by which the operating system must decide which job to run from a list of pending jobs.

This chapter describes the operating system, which is about 475 lines of assembly language code, including documentation comments. Common practice is to write operating systems in a mixture of a high-order language and the assembly language for the particular computer controlled by the operating system. Typically, 90% of the system is in the high-order language and 10% is in the assembly language. The assembly language portion is reserved for those parts of the operating system that cannot be programmed with the features available in the high-order language, or that require an extra measure of efficiency that even an optimizing compiler cannot achieve.

Figure 8.2 shows the global constants and variables of the Pep/8 operating system. Symbols TRUE and FALSE are declared with the .EQUATE command, and thus generate no object code. They are used throughout the rest of the program.

Symbols osRAM, wordBuff, byteBuff, wordTemp, byteTemp, addrMask, and opAddr are all defined with the .BLOCK command. Normally, .BLOCK generates code, and any code generated starts at address 0000 (hex). The listing shows these .BLOCK commands generating no code and osRAM starting at FBCF instead of at 0000.

The reason for this peculiar assembler behavior is the .BURN command at FC57. When you include .BURN in a program, the assembler assumes that the program will be burned into ROM. It generates code for those instructions that follow the burn directive, but not for those that precede it. The assembler also assumes that the ROM will be installed at the bottom of memory, leaving the top of memory for the application programs. It therefore calculates the addresses for the symbol table, such that the last byte generated will have the address specified by the burn directive. In this listing, the burn directive indicates that the last byte should be at

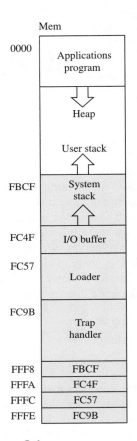

Figure **8.1**

A memory map of the Pep/8 system.

```
            ;****** Pep/8 Operating System
            ;
            TRUE:     .EQUATE 1
            FALSE:    .EQUATE 0
            ;
            ;****** Operating system RAM
FBCF        osRAM:    .BLOCK  128         ;System stack area
FC4F        wordBuff:.BLOCK  1           ;Input/output buffer
FC50        byteBuff:.BLOCK  1           ;Least significant byte of wordBuff
FC51        wordTemp:.BLOCK  1           ;Temporary word storage
FC52        byteTemp:.BLOCK  1           ;Least significant byte of wordTemp
FC53        addrMask:.BLOCK  2           ;Addressing mode mask
FC55        opAddr:   .BLOCK  2           ;Trap instruction operand address
            ;
            ;****** Operating system ROM
FC57                  .BURN   0xFFFF
```

Figure **8.2**

The global constants and variables of the Pep/8 operating system.

address FFFF. Figure 8.16 (p. 418), at the end of the operating system, shows that the last byte, 9B (hex), is indeed at address FFFF. Because FFFF (hex) is 65,536 (dec), the Pep/8 computer is configured with a total of 64 KB of main memory.

The Pep/8 Loader

Figure 8.3 shows the Pep/8 loader. To invoke the loader, you select the load option from the simulator. This triggers the following two events:

$$SP \leftarrow Mem[FFFA]$$
$$PC \leftarrow Mem[FFFC]$$

Invoking the Pep/8 loader

Because Mem[FFFA] contains FC4F, as shown in both Figure 8.1 and Figure 8.16, the stack pointer is initialized to FC4F. Similarly, the program counter is initialized to FC57, the address of the first instruction of the loader.

The loader begins by clearing the index register to zero. It also clears word-Buff to zero. Figure 8.2 shows wordBuff declared as a single byte. Because byteBuff is declared as a single byte immediately after wordBuff, the program considers wordBuff a two-byte buffer with byteBuff its right-most byte. The CHARI instructions all input to byteBuff, but they are followed by a LDA from wordBuff.

```
                 ;******* System Loader
                 ;Data must be in the following format:
                 ;Each hex number representing a byte must contain
                 ;exactly two characters. Each character must be
                 ;in 0..9, A..F, or a..f and must be followed by exactly
                 ;one space. There must be no leading spaces at the beginning
                 ;of a line and no trailing spaces at the end of a line. The last two
                 ;characters in the file must be lowercase zz, which is used as the
                 ;terminating sentinel by the loader.
                 ;
FC57  C80000 loader:  LDX      0,i           ;X := 0
FC5A  E9FC4F          STX      wordBuff,d    ;Clear input buffer word
                 ;
FC5D  49FC50 getChar: CHARI    byteBuff,d    ;Get first hex character
FC60  C1FC4F          LDA      wordBuff,d    ;Put ASCII into low byte of A
FC63  B0007A          CPA      'z',i         ;If end of file sentinel 'z'
FC66  0AFC9A          BREQ     stopLoad      ;then exit loader routine
FC69  B00039          CPA      '9',i         ;If characer <= '9', assume decimal
FC6C  06FC72          BRLE     shift         ;and right nybble is correct digit
FC6F  700009          ADDA     9,i           ;else convert nybble to correct digit
FC72  1C       shift:  ASLA                  ;Shift left by four bits to send
FC73  1C              ASLA                   ;the digit to the most significant
FC74  1C              ASLA                   ;position in the byte
FC75  1C              ASLA
FC76  F1FC52          STBYTEA  byteTemp,d    ;Save the most significant nybble
FC79  49FC50          CHARI    byteBuff,d    ;Get second hex character
FC7C  C1FC4F          LDA      wordBuff,d    ;Put ASCII into low byte of A
FC7F  B00039          CPA      '9',i         ;If characer <= '9', assume decimal
FC82  06FC88          BRLE     combine       ;and right nybble is correct digit
FC85  700009          ADDA     9,i           ;else convert nybble to correct digit
FC88  90000F combine: ANDA     0x000F,i      ;Mask out the left nybble
FC8B  A1FC51          ORA      wordTemp,d    ;Combine both hex digits in binary
FC8E  F50000          STBYTEA  0,x           ;Store in Mem[X]
FC91  780001          ADDX     1,i           ;X := X + 1
FC94  49FC50          CHARI    byteBuff,d    ;Skip blank or <LF>
FC97  04FC5D          BR       getChar       ;
                 ;
FC9A  00       stopLoad:STOP                 ;
```

Figure 8.3

The loader of the Pep/8 operating system.

The LDA moves the character just input to the accumulator and guarantees that the left-most byte of the accumulator is zero.

The loader is in the form of a single loop that inputs a character and compares it with sentinel z. If the character is not the sentinel, the program checks whether it is in '0'..'9'. If it is not in that range, the right-most four bits, called a nybble

The definition of a nybble

because it is half a byte, is converted to the proper value by adding 9 to it. Note that ASCII A is 0100 0001 (bin), so that when 9 is added to it the sum is 0100 1010. The right-most nybble is the correct bit pattern for hexadecimal digit A. It will similarly be correct for hexadecimal digits B through F. If the character is in '0'..'9', the right-most nybble is already correct.

The loader shifts the nybble four bits to the left and stores it temporarily in byteTemp. It inputs the second character of the pair, adjusts the nybble similarly, and combines both nybbles into a single byte with the ANDA at FC88. The instruction that places the program byte in memory is STBYTEA at FC8E. It uses indexed addressing, with the index register incremented by 1 each time through the loop. The loader terminates with the STOP instruction, which returns control to the simulator options.

Programs to be loaded typically are not in the format of hexadecimal ASCII characters. They are already in binary, ready to be loaded. Pep/8 uses ASCII characters for the object file, so you can program directly in machine language and view the object file with a text editor.

Load modules are typically not in ASCII

Program Termination

The application programs presented thus far have all terminated with the STOP instruction. The STOP instruction in a real computer is rarely executed. Rather than generate a STOP instruction at the end of a program, a C++ compiler generates an instruction that returns control to the operating system. If your program ran on a personal computer, the operating system would set up the screen to wait for you to request another service. If your program ran on a timesharing system, the operating system would continue to process other users' jobs. In no case would the computer itself simply stop.

Because there is only one CPU, it alternates between executing operating system jobs and application jobs. Figure 8.4 shows a time line of CPU usage when the operating system loads and executes a sequence of jobs. The shaded parts represent that part of the time spent executing the operating system.

Loader   Job 1   Loader   Job 2   Loader

Figure **8.4**

A time line of CPU usage when the operating system loads and executes a sequence of jobs.

The operating system represents the overhead necessary for doing business. When you shop at a mall, the price you pay for a widget does not reflect just the cost of production and transportation of the widget to the store. It also reflects the salesperson's salary, the electricity for the store lighting, the fringe benefits for the store manager, and so on. Similarly, 100% of a computer's resources does not go toward executing user programs. A certain fraction of the resources, in this case CPU time, must be reserved for the operating system.

8.2   Traps

When programming in assembly language at Level Asmb5, you may use instructions DECI, DECO, and STRO. Figure 4.6 shows no such instructions in the Level ISA3 machine. Instead, when the computer fetches the instructions with these opcodes (00110 through 01000), the hardware executes a trap. A trap is similar to a subroutine jump, but more elaborate. The code that executes is called a trap routine or trap handler instead of a subroutine. The operating system returns control to the application program by executing a return from trap instruction, RETTR, instead of a return from subroutine instruction, RETn.

The trap handler implements the three instructions as if they were part of the Level ISA3 machine. Remember that one purpose of an operating system is to provide a convenient environment for higher-level programming. The abstract machine provided by the Pep/8 operating system is a more convenient machine because it contains these three additional instructions not present at Level ISA3. In addition to DECI, DECO, and STRO, the operating system provides one nonunary and four unary trap instructions called no-operations with mnemonics NOP, NOP0, NOP1, NOP2, and NOP3. These instructions do nothing when they execute, and are provided so you can reprogram them to implement new instructions of your own choosing.

The NOP *trap instructions*

The Trap Mechanism

Here is the Register Transfer Language (RTL) specification for a trap instruction:

A Pep/8 trap

Temp	$\leftarrow$ Mem[7FFA];
Mem[Temp − 1]	$\leftarrow$ IR$\langle 0..7 \rangle$;
Mem[Temp − 3]	$\leftarrow$ SP;
Mem[Temp − 5]	$\leftarrow$ PC;
Mem[Temp − 7]	$\leftarrow$ X;
Mem[Temp − 9]	$\leftarrow$ A;
Mem[Temp − 10]$\langle 4..7 \rangle$	$\leftarrow$ NZVC;
SP	$\leftarrow$ Temp − 10;
PC	$\leftarrow$ Mem[FFFE]

Temp represents a temporary value for notational convenience. Mem[FFFA] contains FC4F, the address of the system stack. In the first event, Temp gets FC4F. The next six events show the CPU pushing the content of all the registers onto the system stack, starting with the instruction specifier of the IR and ending with the NZVC flags. The stack pointer is then modified to point to the new top of the system stack, and the program counter gets the content of Mem[FFFE].

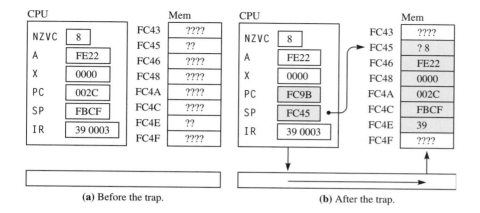

(a) Before the trap. **(b)** After the trap.

Figure **8.5**

A trap triggered by the execution of the DECO trap instruction 390003.

Figure 8.5 shows an example of such a trap from Figure 5.11. The program in Figure 5.11 contains the following decimal output trap

```
0029   390003 DECO 0x0003,d ;Output the sum
```

where 0029 is the address of the instruction and 390003 is the object code that triggered the trap during execution.

Figure 8.5(a) shows the state of the CPU before the trap executes, and Figure 8.5(b) shows the state after the trap executes. Only the instruction specifier part of the IR is pushed onto the stack. Also note that the four NZVC bits are right justified in the byte at Mem[FC45]. The left-most nybble of the byte is undefined. SP contains FC45, the new top of the system stack, and PC contains Mem[FFFE], which is FC9B, the address of the first instruction of the trap handler. Figure 8.16 shows how the operating system sets up the machine vectors at FFFA and FFFE with the .ADDRSS commands.

The RETTR Instruction

A program during execution is called a process. The trap mechanism temporarily suspends the process so the operating system can perform a service. The block of information in main memory that contains a copy of the trapped process's registers is called a process control block (PCB). The PCB for this example is stored in Mem[FC45] to Mem[FC4F], as shown in Figure 8.5(b).

The definition of a process

The process control block (PCB)

After the operating system performs its service, it must eventually return control of the CPU to the suspended process so the process can complete its execution. In this example, the service performed by the Pep/8 operating system is execution of the DECO instruction. It returns control back to the process by executing the return from trap instruction, RETTR.

Here is the RTL specification for the RETTR instruction: *The* RETTR *instruction*

NZVC $\leftarrow$ Mem[SP]$\langle 4..7 \rangle$;
A $\leftarrow$ Mem[SP + 1];
X $\leftarrow$ Mem[SP + 3];
PC $\leftarrow$ Mem[SP + 5];
SP $\leftarrow$ Mem[SP + 7]

RETTR pops the top nine bytes off the stack into the NZVC, A, X, PC, and SP registers. This reverses the events of the trap, except that IR is not popped. The next instruction to execute will be the one specified by the new value of PC. The last register to change is SP.

   If the trap handler does not modify any of the values in the PCB, RETTR will restore the original values in the CPU registers when the process resumes. In particular, the SP will again point to the top of the application stack, as it did at the time of the trap. On the other hand, any changes that the trap handler makes to the values in the PCB will be reflected in the CPU registers when the process resumes.

The Trap Handlers

Figure 8.6 shows the entry and exit points of the trap handlers. oldIR is the stack address of the copy of the IR register stored on the system stack from the trap mechanism. Figure 8.7(a) shows the stack addresses of all the registers.

   When a trap instruction executes, the next instruction to execute is the one at FC9B, the first instruction in Figure 8.6. The trap could have been triggered by any of the following instructions:

   0010 01nn, NOPn, Unary no-operation trap

   0010 1aaa, NOP,   Nonunary no-operation trap

   0011 0aaa, DECI, Nonunary decimal-input trap

   0011 1aaa, DECO, Nonunary decimal-output trap

   0100 0aaa, STRO, Nonunary string-output trap

The code in Figure 8.6 determines which instruction triggered the trap and calls the specific handler that implements that instruction. There are eight trap handlers, four for the unary NOPn instructions and four for the nonunary instructions. Remember that the fetch part of the von Neumann cycle puts the instruction specifier in the instruction register (IR). After the trap occurs, the instruction specifier of the instruction that caused the trap is available on the system stack, because it was pushed there by the trap mechanism. The code in Figure 8.6 accesses the saved instruction specifier to determine which instruction triggered the trap.

```
                ;******* Trap handler
                oldIR:    .EQUATE  9                 ;Stack address of IR on trap
                ;
FC9B  C80000  trap:     LDX      0,i               ;Clear X for a byte compare
FC9E  DB0009            LDBYTEX  oldIR,s           ;X := trapped IR
FCA1  B80028            CPX      0x0028,i          ;If X >= first nonunary trap opcode
FCA4  0EFCB7            BRGE     nonUnary          ;trap opcode is nonunary
                ;
FCA7  980003  unary:    ANDX     0x0003,i          ;Mask out all but rightmost two bits
FCAA  1D                ASLX                        ;An address is two bytes
FCAB  17FCAF            CALL     unaryJT,x         ;Call unary trap routine
FCAE  01                RETTR                       ;Return from trap
                ;
FCAF  FDB6    unaryJT:  .ADDRSS  opcode24          ;Address of NOP0 subroutine
FCB1  FDB7              .ADDRSS  opcode25          ;Address of NOP1 subroutine
FCB3  FDB8              .ADDRSS  opcode26          ;Address of NOP2 subroutine
FCB5  FDB9              .ADDRSS  opcode27          ;Address of NOP3 subroutine
                ;
FCB7  1F      nonUnary: ASRX                        ;Trap opcode is nonunary
FCB8  1F                ASRX                        ;Discard addressing mode bits
FCB9  1F                ASRX
FCBA  880005            SUBX     5,i               ;Adjust so that NOP opcode = 0
FCBD  1D                ASLX                        ;An address is two bytes
FCBE  17FCC2            CALL     nonUnJT,x         ;Call nonunary trap routine
FCC1  01      return:   RETTR                       ;Return from trap
                ;
FCC2  FDBA    nonUnJT:  .ADDRSS  opcode28          ;Address of NOP subroutine
FCC4  FDC4              .ADDRSS  opcode30          ;Address of DECI subroutine
FCC6  FF3B              .ADDRSS  opcode38          ;Address of DECO subroutine
FCC8  FFC6              .ADDRSS  opcode40          ;Address of STRO subroutine
```

Figure 8.6

The entry and exit points of the trap handlers in the Pep/8 operating system.

The first instruction in Figure 8.6 gets the opcode from the copy of IR that was pushed onto the system stack. The NOP instruction has the first nonunary opcode, 0010 1aaa. Furthermore, 0010 1000 (bin) is 28 (hex). The CPX instruction at FCA1 compares the trap opcode with 28 (hex). If the trap opcode is less than this value, the trap instruction is unary; otherwise, it is nonunary.

If the trap instruction is unary, it must be one of the following four instructions:

The test for the NOPn instructions

0010 0100, NOP0, right-most two bits are 00

0010 0101, NOP1, right-most two bits are 01

0010 0110, NOP2, right-most two bits are 10

0010 0111, NOP3, right-most two bits are 11

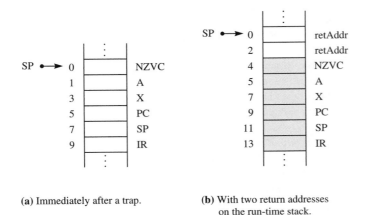

Figure **8.7**

The stack addresses of the copies of
the CPU registers.

(a) Immediately after a trap.

(b) With two return addresses
on the run-time stack.
The shaded region is the PCB.

The ANDX instruction at FCA7 masks out all but the right-most two bits, which are
sufficient to determine which of the four instructions caused the trap. The CALL
instruction at FCAB uses the jump table technique with indexed addressing as
described in the program of Figure 6.40. That figure shows how the compiler translates a C++ switch statement using an array of addresses with the unconditional
branch instruction BR. The code in Figure 8.6 differs slightly from that in Figure 6.40
because it uses CALL instead of BR, but the principle is the same. The jump
table at FCAF is an array of addresses, each element of which is the address of the
first statement to execute in the trap handler for the specific instruction that triggered
the trap. Because a CALL executes, it pushes a return address onto the stack. The last
instruction to execute in a specific trap handler is RETO, which returns control back
to FCAE. The instruction at FCAE is RETTR, which restores the registers in the CPU
from the PCB and returns control to the instruction following the trap instruction.

The instructions at FCB7 through FCC8 do the same thing for the group of
nonunary instructions. The three ASRX instructions discard the addressing mode bits,
and the SUBX instruction makes an adjustment so that the content of the index register will be

The test for the nonunary trap
instructions

   0 if the trap IR contains 0010 1aaa, NOP

   1 if the trap IR contains 0011 0aaa, DECI

   2 if the trap IR contains 0011 1aaa, DECO

   3 if the trap IR contains 0100 0aaa, STRO

As with the unary instructions, the CALL at FCBE branches to the trap handler for
the specific instruction. After the trap handler implements the instruction, it returns
control to the RETTR instruction at FCC1, which in turn returns control to the statement after the one that caused the trap.

Trap Addressing Mode Assertion

Different instructions have different allowed addressing modes. For example, Figure 5.2 shows that the CHARI instruction is not allowed to have immediate addressing, while the STRO instruction is only allowed to have direct, indirect, and stack-relative deferred addressing. Because the CHARI instruction is hard-wired into the CPU, the hardware detects whether an addressing error has occurred. But the trap instructions, such as STRO, are not native to the CPU. The trap handler implements them in software. The question then arises, how does a trap handler detect whether a trap instruction is attempting to use an illegal addressing mode? It does so with the addressing mode assert routine of Figure 8.8.

```
          ;******* Assert valid trap addressing mode
          oldIR4:  .EQUATE 13          ;oldIR + 4 with two return addresses
FCCA C00001 assertAd:LDA    1,i        ;A := 1
FCCD DB000D          LDBYTEX oldIR4,s   ;X := OldIR
FCD0 980007          ANDX    0x0007,i   ;Keep only the addressing mode bits
FCD3 0AFCDD          BREQ    testAd     ;000 = immediate addressing
FCD6 1C      loop:   ASLA               ;Shift the 1 bit left
FCD7 880001          SUBX    1,i        ;Subtract from addressing mode count
FCDA 0CFCD6          BRNE    loop       ;Try next addressing mode
FCDD 91FC53 testAd:  ANDA    addrMask,d ;AND the 1 bit with legal modes
FCE0 0AFCE4          BREQ    addrErr
FCE3 58              RETO               ;Legal addressing mode, return
FCE4 50000A addrErr: CHARO   '\n',i
FCE7 C0FCF4          LDA     trapMsg,i  ;Push address of error message
FCEA E3FFFE          STA     -2,s
FCED 680002          SUBSP   2,i        ;Call print subroutine
FCF0 16FFE2          CALL    prntMsg
FCF3 00              STOP               ;Halt: Fatal runtime error
FCF4 455252 trapMsg: .ASCII  "ERROR: Invalid trap addressing mode.\x00"
     ...
```

Figure 8.8

The trap addressing mode assertion in the Pep/8 operating system

The addressing mode assert routine must access the trap IR, which is saved on the system stack. Immediately after the trap, the IR has a stack address of 9, as Figure 8.7(a) shows. However, by the time the trap addressing mode is called, two additional return addresses are on top of the system stack. One comes from a CALL instruction in the trap handler code of Figure 8.6, and one comes from the CALL in the specific trap handler. Figure 8.7(b) shows the PCB on the system stack after the addressing-mode assert routine is called and the two return addresses are on the stack. The stack address of the trap IR is now 13 instead of 9 because of the four bytes occupied by the two return addresses.

The routine in Figure 8.8 has the following pre- and postconditions:

- Precondition: `addrMask` is a bit mask representation of the set of allowable addressing modes, and the PCB of the stack instruction is on the system stack.

  Pre- and postconditions for the addressing mode assert routine

- Postcondition: If the addressing mode of the trap instruction is in the set of allowable addressing modes, control is returned to the trap handler. Otherwise, an invalid addressing mode message is output and the program halts with a fatal run-time error.

The addressing mode assert routine is the Asmb5 version of the `assert` statement found in some HOL6 languages. In C++, the assert facility is in the `<assert>` library that you can include in your programs with the `#include` compiler directive.

A trap handler uses the assert routine by first setting the value in global variable `addrMask` shown at FC53 in Figure 8.2 to indicate the allowable addressing modes for that particular instruction. Then it calls `assertAd` at FCCA in Figure 8.8. The routine assumes a common representation of a set known as the bit-mapped representation. In machine language, each bit can have a value of either 0 or 1. The bit-mapped representation of the set of allowable addressing modes associates each addressing mode with one bit in `addrMask`. If the bit has the value 0, the associated addressing mode is not in the set. If the bit has the value 1, the addressing mode is in the set.

The bit-mapped representation of a set

Figure 8.9 shows the right-most byte in `addrMask` with the precondition set by the trap handler for the `STRO` instruction, which can use direct, indirect, or stack-relative deferred addressing. The bits associated with those addressing modes have a value of 1, and the others have a value of 0. Mathematically, the mask represents the set {Direct, Indirect, Stack-relative deferred}.

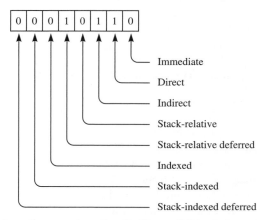

Figure **8.9**

The bits in `addressMask` associated with the allowable addressing modes of the `STRO` trap instruction.

To illustrate how the assert routine in Figure 8.8 tests for set membership, suppose the `STRO` instruction executes with stack-relative deferred addressing, so that its addressing-aaa field is 100. This is an allowable addressing mode. First, the `LDA` statement at FCCA sets the right-most byte of the accumulator to 0000 0001. The next two statements set the index register to 4 (dec) based on the addressing-aaa field of the trap instruction. A loop then counts down to zero starting from this value, shifting the 1 bit in the accumulator left each time through the loop. The accumulator ends up with 0001 0000, so that the 1 bit is at the bit position associated with stack-relative deferred addressing. The ANDA statement at FCCD takes the AND of the accumulator with the address mask in Figure 8.9. Because the 1's line up at the fifth bit from the right, the result is not zero, and control returns to the trap handler. If stack-relative deferred addressing were not allowed, the address mask would have a 0 at the fifth bit from the right, the result of the AND operation would be zero, and the assertion would fail.

Trap Operand Address Computation

The trap operand address computation is another routine called by the nonunary trap handlers. The addressing modes for the native instructions are hard-wired into the CPU. But the trap instructions are implemented in software instead of hardware. So, the eight addressing modes must be simulated in software. Figure 8.10 shows the routine that performs the computation.

```
                ;******* Set address of trap operand
                oldX4:   .EQUATE 7            ;oldX + 4 with two return addresses
                oldPC4:  .EQUATE 9            ;oldPC + 4 with two return addresses
                oldSP4:  .EQUATE 11           ;oldSP + 4 with two return addresses
FD19  DB000D    setAddr: LDBYTEX oldIR4,s     ;X := old instruction register
FD1C  980007             ANDX    0x0007,i     ;Keep only the addressing mode bits
FD1F  1D                 ASLX                 ;An address is two bytes
FD20  05FD23             BR      addrJT,x
FD23  FD33     addrJT:   .ADDRSS addrI        ;Immediate addressing
FD25  FD3D               .ADDRSS addrD        ;Direct addressing
FD27  FD4A               .ADDRSS addrN        ;Indirect addressing
FD29  FD5A               .ADDRSS addrS        ;Stack-relative addressing
FD2B  FD6A               .ADDRSS addrSF       ;Stack-relative deferred addressing
FD2D  FD7D               .ADDRSS addrX        ;Indexed addressing
FD2F  FD8D               .ADDRSS addrSX       ;Stack-indexed addressing
FD31  FDA0               .ADDRSS addrSXF      ;Stack-indexed deferred addressing
                ;
FD33  CB0009   addrI:    LDX     oldPC4,s     ;Immediate addressing
FD36  880002             SUBX    2,i          ;Oprnd = OprndsSpec
FD39  E9FC55             STX     opAddr,d
FD3C  58                 RETO
                ;
```

Figure 8.10

The trap operand address computation in the Pep/8 operating system.

```
FD3D  CB0009 addrD:   LDX   oldPC4,s   ;Direct addressing
FD40  880002          SUBX  2,i        ;Oprnd = Mem[OprndSpec]
FD43  CD0000          LDX   0,x
FD46  E9FC55          STX   opAddr,d
FD49  58              RETO
                 ;
FD4A  CB0009 addrN:   LDX   oldPC4,s   ;Indirect addressing
FD4D  880002          SUBX  2,i        ;Oprnd = Mem[Mem[OprndSpec]]
FD50  CD0000          LDX   0,x
FD53  CD0000          LDX   0,x
FD56  E9FC55          STX   opAddr,d
FD59  58              RETO
                 ;
FD5A  CB0009 addrS:   LDX   oldPC4,s   ;Stack-relative addressing
FD5D  880002          SUBX  2,i        ;Oprnd = Mem[SP + OprndSpec]
FD60  CD0000          LDX   0,x
FD63  7B000B          ADDX  oldSP4,s
FD66  E9FC55          STX   opAddr,d
FD69  58              RETO
                 ;
FD6A  CB0009 addrSF:  LDX   oldPC4,s   ;Stack-relative deferred addressing
FD6D  880002          SUBX  2,i        ;Oprnd = Mem[Mem[SP + OprndSpec]]
FD70  CD0000          LDX   0,x
FD73  7B000B          ADDX  oldSP4,s
FD76  CD0000          LDX   0,x
FD79  E9FC55          STX   opAddr,d
FD7C  58              RETO
                 ;
FD7D  CB0009 addrX:   LDX   oldPC4,s   ;Indexed addressing
FD80  880002          SUBX  2,i        ;Oprnd = Mem[OprndSpec + X]
FD83  CD0000          LDX   0,x
FD86  7B0007          ADDX  oldX4,s
FD89  E9FC55          STX   opAddr,d
FD8C  58              RETO
                 ;
FD8D  CB0009 addrSX:  LDX   oldPC4,s   ;Stack-indexed addressing
FD90  880002          SUBX  2,i        ;Oprnd = Mem[SP + OprndSpec + X]
FD93  CD0000          LDX   0,x
FD96  7B0007          ADDX  oldX4,s
FD99  7B000B          ADDX  oldSP4,s
FD9C  E9FC55          STX   opAddr,d
FD9F  58              RETO
```

Figure **8.10**

(Continued)

```
FDA0   CB0009  addrSXF:  LDX    oldPC4,s    ;Stack-indexed deferred addressing
FDA3   880002            SUBX   2,i         ;Oprnd = Mem[Mem[SP + OprndSpec] + X]
FDA6   CD0000            LDX    0,x
FDA9   7B000B            ADDX   oldSP4,s
FDAC   CD0000            LDX    0,x
FDAF   7B0007            ADDX   oldX4,s
FDB2   E9FC55            STX    opAddr,d
FDB5   58                RET0
```

Figure **8.10**

(Continued)

The routine in Figure 8.10 has the following pre- and postconditions:

- Precondition: The PCB of the stack instruction is on the system stack.
- Postcondition: opAddr contains the address of the operand according to the addressing mode of the trap instruction.

Pre- and postconditions for the addressing mode computation routine

As with the addressing-mode assert routine in Figure 8.8, the register copies on the PCB have a stack offset four bytes greater than when the trap occurs, as Figure 8.7(b) shows. The routine uses oldIR4 defined in the addressing-mode assert routine, as well as the similarly defined oldX4, oldPC4, and oldSP4 to access the copies of the saved index register, program counter, and stack pointer.

The first four statements beginning at FD19 determine the addressing mode of the trap instruction and branch to the computation for that addressing mode. It uses the jump-table technique to switch between one of eight alternatives. The code for each of the eight alternatives computes the address of the operand by inspecting the state of the CPU at the time of the trap.

The first two instructions of each computation are

```
LDX oldPC4,s
SUBX 2,i
```

The first two instructions of each computation

Because the trap instruction is nonunary, the program counter at the time of the trap points to the byte after the two-byte operand specifier. The first instruction loads the saved program counter into the index register, and the second instruction subtracts two from it. After these two instructions execute, the index register contains the address of the operand specifier in the instruction that caused the trap.

For immediate addressing, the operand specifier is the operand. Consequently, the statements at FD39

```
STX opAddr,d
RET0
```

The computation for immediate addressing

simply store the address of the operand specifier in opAddr as required.

For direct addressing, the operand specifier is the address of the operand. The first of the statements at FD43

```
LDX  0,x
STX  opAddr,d
RETO
```

The computation for direct addressing

replaces the index register with the content in memory whose address is in the index register. Before the instruction executes, the index register contains the address of the operand specifier. After the instruction executes, the index register contains the operand specifier itself. Because the operand specifier is the address of the operand, that is what gets stored in opAddr.

For indirect addressing, the operand specifier is the address of the address of the operand. As with direct addressing, the first of the statements at FD50

```
LDX  0,x
LDX  0,x
STX  opAddr,d
RETO
```

The computation for indirect addressing

replaces the index register with the operand specifier itself, which is the address of the address of the operand. The second instruction fetches the address of the operand, which gets stored in opAddr.

For stack-relative addressing, the stack pointer plus the operand specifier is the address of the operand. The first of the statements at FD60

```
LDX  0,x
ADDX oldSP4,s
STX  opAddr,d
RETO
```

The computation for stack-relative addressing

puts the operand specifier in the index register. The second instruction adds the copy of the stack pointer to it. The result is the address of the operand, which gets stored in opAddr.

The remaining four addressing modes use similar techniques to compute the address of the operand. Stack-relative deferred addressing is one extra level of indirection compared with stack-relative addressing, requiring one additional execution of LDX 0,x. Indexed addressing is like stack-relative addressing, except the operand specifier is added to the index register instead of the stack pointer. Stack-indexed and stack-indexed deferred are variations on the same theme.

The No-Operation Trap Handlers

Figure 8.11 shows the code for implementation of the no-operation trap handlers. Because the NOP instructions do not do anything, the trap handlers do no processing other than to execute RETO, returning control to the exit points in Figure 8.6, and eventually to the statement following the trap.

Figure **8.11**

The NOP trap handlers.

```
             ;******* Opcode 0x24
             ;The NOP0 instruction.
FDB6  58     opcode24:RETO
             ;
             ;******* Opcode 0x25
             ;The NOP1 instruction.
FDB7  58     opcode25:RETO
             ;
             ;******* Opcode 0x26
             ;The NOP2 instruction.
FDB8  58     opcode26:RETO
             ;
             ;******* Opcode 0x27
             ;The NOP3 instruction.
FDB9  58     opcode27:RETO
             ;
             ;******* Opcode 0x28
             ;The NOP instruction.
FDBA  C00001 opcode28:LDA    0x0001,i    ;Assert i
FDBD  E1FC53          STA    addrMask,d
FDC0  16FCCA          CALL   assertAd
FDC3  58              RETO
```

The NOP instructions are provided for you to write your own trap handlers. Some problems at the end of the chapter ask you to implement instructions that are not in the Pep/8 instruction set. The Pep/8 assembler lets you redefine the mnemonics for the trap instructions. To write a trap handler, you change the mnemonic of one of the NOP instructions in Figure 8.11 to the mnemonic of your new instruction. Then, you edit the trap handler in the operating system by inserting your code at its entry point. For example, to redefine NOP0 you insert the code for your handler at FDB6. The last executable statement in your handler should be RETO.

Figure 8.11 shows the implementation of nonunary NOP at FDBA. Figure 5.2 specifies that its only allowable addressing mode is immediate addressing. Therefore, the value in addrMask is set to 0000 0001, where the last 1 is at the bit position for immediate addressing, as Figure 8.9 shows.

The DECI Trap Handler

Figure 8.14 is the trap handler for the DECI instruction. DECI must parse the input, converting the string of ASCII characters to the proper bits in two's complement representation. It uses the finite state machine (FSM) of Figure 8.12. An outline of the logic of the FSM in the DECI trap handler appears in Figure 8.13. state has enumerated type with possible values init, sign, or digit.

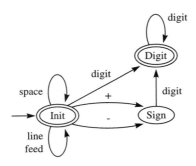

Figure **8.12**

The finite state machine in the DECI interrupt handler.

The first four statements at FDC4 in Figure 8.14 call the addressing-mode assert routine and the routine to compute the trap operand address. At FDD0, the handler allocates six local variables on the stack—total, valAscii, isOvfl, isNeg, state, and temp. Each variable occupies two bytes, so SUBSP subtracts 12 from the stack pointer for the allocation. With application programs, SUBSP is the first executable statement in procedures with local variables. Here, SUBSP must execute after the first two routine calls, because those calls access quantities from the PCB. They assume only two return addresses on the stack, as Figure 8.7(b) shows.

The DECI trap handler must access the NZVC bits from the PCB. The handler is called by the CALL instruction at FCBE, which pushed a two-byte return address on the stack. When the handler accesses the value of NZVC stored on the stack at the trap, its stack address will be 14 greater than it is immediately after the trap because of the local variables and the return address. That is why old NZVC equates to 14 instead of 0.

Beginning with the LDA statement at FDD3, the processing in the DECI interrupt handler follows the logic in Figure 8.13. The routine tests the input string for a value that is out of range. If so, it sets the V bit stored in the PCB during the trap. When RETTR returns control to the application, the programmer at Level Asmb5 will be able to test for overflow after executing DECI. isOvfl is a boolean flag that indicates the overflow condition.

FDE5 is the start of the FSM loop, identified by the do symbol. ANDA at FDEB masks out all but the right-most four bits of the input character, which leaves the binary value that corresponds to the decimal ASCII digit. For example, ASCII 5 is

```
isOvfl := false
state := init
do
    CHARI asciiCh
    switch state
    case init:
        if (asciiCh == '+') {
            isNeg := false
            state := sign
        }
        else if (asciiCh == '-') {
            isNeg := true
            state := sign
        }
        else if (asciiCh is a digit) {
            isNeg := false
            total := Value (asciiCh)
            state := digit
        }
        else if (asciiCh is not <SPACE> or <LF>) {
            Exit with DECI error
        }
    case sign:
        if (asciiCh is a digit) {
            total := Value (asciiCh)
            state := digit
        }
        else {
            Exit with DECI error
        }
    case digit:
        if (asciiCh is a digit) {
            total := 10 * total + Value (asciiCh)
            if (overflow) {
                isOvfl := true
            }
        }
        else {
            Exit normally
        }
    end switch
while (not exit)
```

Figure **8.13**

The program logic of the DECI trap handler.

```
              ;******* Opcode 0x30
              ;The DECI instruction.
              ;Input format: Any number of leading spaces or line feeds are
              ;allowed, followed by '+', '-', or a digit as the first character,
              ;after which digits are input until the first nondigit is
              ;encountered. The status flags N, Z, and V are set appropriately
              ;by this DECI routine. The C status flag is not affected.
              ;
              oldNZVC: .EQUATE 14        ;Stack address of NZVC on interrupt
              ;
              total:   .EQUATE 10        ;Cumulative total of DECI number
              valAscii:.EQUATE 8         ;Value(asciiCH)
              isOvfl:  .EQUATE 6         ;Overflow boolean
              isNeg:   .EQUATE 4         ;Negative boolean
              state:   .EQUATE 2         ;State variable
              temp:    .EQUATE 0
              ;
              init:    .EQUATE 0         ;Enumerated values for state
              sign:    .EQUATE 1
              digit:   .EQUATE 2
              ;
FDC4 C000FE opcode30:LDA     0x00FE,i   ;Assert d, n, s, sf, x, sx, sxf
FDC7 E1FC53          STA     addrMask,d
FDCA 16FCCA          CALL    assertAd
FDCD 16FD19          CALL    setAddr    ;Set address of trap operand
FDD0 68000C          SUBSP   12,i       ;Allocate storage for locals
FDD3 C00000          LDA     FALSE,i    ;isOvfl := FALSE
FDD6 E30006          STA     isOvfl,s
FDD9 C00000          LDA     init,i     ;state := init
FDDC E30002          STA     state,s
FDDF C00000          LDA     0,i        ;wordBuff := 0 for input
FDE2 E1FC4F          STA     wordBuff,d
              ;
FDE5 49FC50 do:      CHARI   byteBuff,d ;Get asciiCh
FDE8 C1FC4F          LDA     wordBuff,d ;Set value(asciiCH)
FDEB 90000F          ANDA    0x000F,i
FDEE E30008          STA     valAscii,s
FDF1 C1FC4F          LDA     wordBuff,d ;A = asciiCh throughout the loop
FDF4 CB0002          LDX     state,s    ;switch (state)
FDF7 1D              ASLX               ;An address is two bytes
FDF8 05FDFB          BR      stateJT,x
              ;
FDFB FE01   stateJT: .ADDRSS sInit
FDFD FE5B            .ADDRSS sSign
FDFF FE76            .ADDRSS sDigit
              ;
```

Figure **8.14**

The DECI trap handler.

```
FE01  B0002B  sInit:   CPA    '+',i        ;if (asciiCh == '+')
FE04  0CFE16           BRNE   ifMinus
FE07  C80000           LDX    FALSE,i       ;isNeg := FALSE
FE0A  EB0004           STX    isNeg,s
FE0D  C80001           LDX    sign,i        ;state := sign
FE10  EB0002           STX    state,s
FE13  04FDE5           BR     do
              ;
FE16  B0002D  ifMinus: CPA    '-',i        ;else if (asciiCh == '-')
FE19  0CFE2B           BRNE   ifDigit
FE1C  C80001           LDX    TRUE,i        ;isNeg := TRUE
FE1F  EB0004           STX    isNeg,s
FE22  C80001           LDX    sign,i        ;state := sign
FE25  EB0002           STX    state,s
FE28  04FDE5           BR     do
              ;
FE2B  B00030  ifDigit: CPA    '0',i        ;else if (asciiCh is a digit)
FE2E  08FE4C           BRLT   ifWhite
FE31  B00039           CPA    '9',i
FE34  10FE4C           BRGT   ifWhite
FE37  C80000           LDX    FALSE,i       ;isNeg := FALSE
FE3A  EB0004           STX    isNeg,s
FE3D  CB0008           LDX    valAscii,s   ;total := Value(asciiCh)
FE40  EB000A           STX    total,s
FE43  C80002           LDX    digit,i       ;state := digit
FE46  EB0002           STX    state,s
FE49  04FDE5           BR     do
              ;
FE4C  B00020  ifWhite: CPA    ' ',i        ;else if (asciiCh is not a space
FE4F  0AFDE5           BREQ   do
FE52  B0000A           CPA    '\n',i       ;or line feed)
FE55  0CFF11           BRNE   deciErr      ;exit with DECI error
FE58  04FDE5           BR     do
              ;
FE5B  B00030  sSign:   CPA    '0',i        ;if asciiCh (is not a digit)
FE5E  08FF11           BRLT   deciErr
FE61  B00039           CPA    '9',i
FE64  10FF11           BRGT   deciErr      ;exit with DECI error
FE67  CB0008           LDX    valAscii,s   ;else total := Value(asciiCh)
FE6A  EB000A           STX    total,s
FE6D  C80002           LDX    digit,i       ;state := digit
FE70  EB0002           STX    state,s
FE73  04FDE5           BR     do
              ;
```

Figure 8.14

(Continued)

```
FE76  B00030 sDigit:  CPA    '0',i        ;if (asciiCh is not a digit)
FE79  08FEC7          BRLT   deciNorm
FE7C  B00039          CPA    '9',i
FE7F  10FEC7          BRGT   deciNorm     ;exit normally
FE82  C80001          LDX    TRUE,i       ;else X := TRUE for later assignments
FE85  C3000A          LDA    total,s      ;Multiply total by 10 as follows:
FE88  1C              ASLA                ;First, times 2
FE89  12FE8F          BRV    ovfl1        ;If overflow then
FE8C  04FE92          BR     L1
FE8F  EB0006 ovfl1:   STX    isOvfl,s     ;isOvfl := TRUE
FE92  E30000 L1:      STA    temp,s       ;Save 2 * total in temp
FE95  1C              ASLA                ;Now, 4 * total
FE96  12FE9C          BRV    ovfl2        ;If overflow then
FE99  04FE9F          BR     L2
FE9C  EB0006 ovfl2:   STX    isOvfl,s     ;isOvfl := TRUE
FE9F  1C     L2:      ASLA                ;Now, 8 * total
FEA0  12FEA6          BRV    ovfl3        ;If overflow then
FEA3  04FEA9          BR     L3
FEA6  EB0006 ovfl3:   STX    isOvfl,s     ;isOvfl := TRUE
FEA9  730000 L3:      ADDA   temp,s       ;Finally, 8 * total + 2 * total
FEAC  12FEB2          BRV    ovfl4        ;If overflow then
FEAF  04FEB5          BR     L4
FEB2  EB0006 ovfl4:   STX    isOvfl,s     ;isOvfl := TRUE
FEB5  730008 L4:      ADDA   valAscii,s   ;A := 10 * total + valAscii
FEB8  12FEBE          BRV    ovfl5        ;If overflow then
FEBB  04FEC1          BR     L5
FEBE  EB0006 ovfl5:   STX    isOvfl,s     ;isOvfl := TRUE
FEC1  E3000A L5:      STA    total,s      ;Update total
FEC4  04FDE5          BR     do
               ;
FEC7  C30004 deciNorm:LDA    isNeg,s      ;If isNeg then
FECA  0AFEE3          BREQ   setNZ
FECD  C3000A          LDA    total,s      ;If total != 0x8000 then
FED0  B08000          CPA    0x8000,i
FED3  0AFEDD          BREQ   L6
FED6  1A              NEGA                ;Negate total
FED7  E3000A          STA    total,s
FEDA  04FEE3          BR     setNZ
FEDD  C00000 L6:      LDA    FALSE,i      ;else -32768 is a special case
FEE0  E30006          STA    isOvfl,s     ;isOvfl := FALSE
               ;
```

Figure **8.14**

(Continued)

```
FEE3  DB000E  setNZ:    LDBYTEX  oldNZVC,s   ;Set NZ according to total result:
FEE6  980001            ANDX     0x0001,i    ;First initialize NZV to 000
FEE9  C3000A            LDA      total,s     ;If total is negative then
FEEC  0EFEF2            BRGE     checkZ
FEEF  A80008            ORX      0x0008,i    ;set N to 1
FEF2  B00000  checkZ:   CPA      0,i         ;If total is not zero then
FEF5  0CFEFB            BRNE     setV
FEF8  A80004            ORX      0x0004,i    ;set Z to 1
FEFB  C30006  setV:     LDA      isOvfl,s    ;If not isOvfl then
FEFE  0AFF04            BREQ     storeFl
FF01  A80002            ORX      0x0002,i    ;set V to 1
FF04  FB000E  storeFl:  STBYTEX  oldNZVC,s   ;Store the NZVC flags
         ;
FF07  C3000A  exitDeci: LDA      total,s     ;Put total in memory
FF0A  E2FC55            STA      opAddr,n
FF0D  60000C            ADDSP    12,i        ;Deallocate locals
FF10  58                RETO                 ;Return to trap handler
         ;
FF11  50000A  deciErr:  CHARO    '\n',i
FF14  C0FF21            LDA      deciMsg,i   ;Push address of message onto stack
FF17  E3FFFE            STA      -2,s
FF1A  680002            SUBSP    2,i
FF1D  16FFE2            CALL     prntMsg     ;and print
FF20  00                STOP                 ;Fatal error: program terminates
         ;
FF21  455252  deciMsg:  .ASCII   "ERROR: Invalid DECI input\x00"
      ...
```

Figure **8.14**

(Continued)

represented in binary as 0011 0101. The right-most four bits are 0101, the corresponding binary value of the decimal digit. The accumulator gets the ASCII character at FDF1 and keeps it throughout the loop. stateJT at FDFB is a jump table for the switch statement in the FSM.

The code from FE01 to FE58 is the case for state having the value sInit, the start state of the FSM. The assignments are all made via the index register instead of the accumulator, because the accumulator maintains the ASCII character for comparison throughout the loop. For example, the assignment of isNeg to FALSE at FE07 is implemented by LDX followed by STX, instead of LDA followed by STA.

The code from FE5B to FE73 is the case for state having the value sSign, and from FE76 to FEC4 is the case for state having the value sDigit. Pep/8 has no instruction to multiply a value by 10 (dec). This section of code performs the multiply with several left-shift operations. Each ASLA multiplies the value by 2. Three ASLA operations multiply the value by 8, which can be added to the value multiplied by 2 to get the value multiplied by 10. After each ASLA operation and the addition, the routine checks for overflow and sets isOvfl accordingly.

The code from FEC7 to FF20 is outside the loop. The algorithm exits the loop under two conditions: normally, or when it has detected an input error. If it exits normally, it checks the isNeg flag to see if the string of digits was preceded by a negative sign. If it was, the instruction at FED6 negates the number by taking the two's complement.

The number 232768 (dec), which is 8000 (hex), must be treated as a special case. If the input is −32768, the FSM will set isOvfl to true when it adds 32760 to 8 at FEB5. The problem is that 32768 is out of range, even though −32768 is in range. The routine adjusts isOvfl for this special case at FEE0.

The code from FEE3 to FF04 adjusts the copies of the N, Z, and V flags that were stored at the trap. ANDX at FEE6 sets NZV to 000. Note that the mask is 01 (hex), which is 0000 0001 (bin). Because C is the right-most bit, it remains unchanged by the AND operation. LDA at FEE9 puts the parsed value into the accumulator, setting the current N, Z, and V bits in the CPU accordingly. The code sets the copies of N and Z in the PCB equal to the current values of N and Z in the CPU. It sets the copy of V in the PCB according to the value of isOvfl computed earlier in the parse.

Now that the decimal value has been input and parsed, the trap handler must store it in memory at the location specified by the operand of the DECI that caused the trap. The instructions

```
LDA total,s
STA opAddr,n
```

at FF07 perform the store. LDA loads the computed value into the accumulator. STA stores it to opAddr with indirect addressing, for which the operand specifier is the address of the address of the operand. Recall that the address of the operand is computed earlier at FDCD and stored in opAddr. opAddr is itself, therefore, the address of the address of the operand, as required.

The code from FF11 to FF20 executes when the input string cannot be parsed legally. It prints an error message by calling prntMsg, a procedure shown in Figure 8.16 to output a null-terminated string, and terminates the application program immediately.

The DECO Trap Handler

Figure 8.15 is the trap handler for the DECO instruction. This routine outputs the operand of DECO in a format that is equivalent to a C++ cout << operation on an integer

```
              ;****** Opcode 0x38
              ;The DECO instruction.
              ;Output format: If the operand is negative, the algorithm prints
              ;a single '-' followed by the magnitude. Otherwise it prints the
              ;magnitude without a leading '+'. It suppresses leading zeros.
              ;
              remain:   .EQUATE 0         ;Remainder of value to output
              chOut:    .EQUATE 2         ;Has a character been output yet?
              place:    .EQUATE 4         ;Place value for division
              ;
FF3B C000FF  opcode38:LDA    0x00FF,i    ;Assert i, d, n, s, sf, x, sx, sxf
FF3E E1FC53          STA     addrMask,d
FF41 16FCCA          CALL    assertAd
FF44 16FD19          CALL    setAddr      ;Set address of trap operand
FF47 680006          SUBSP   6,i          ;Allocate storage for locals
FF4A C2FC55          LDA     opAddr,n     ;A := oprnd
FF4D B00000          CPA     0,i          ;If oprnd is negative then
FF50 0EFF57          BRGE    printMag
FF53 50002D          CHARO   '-',i        ;Print leading '-' and
FF56 1A              NEGA                 ;make magnitude positive
FF57 E30000 printMag:STA     remain,s     ;remain := abs(oprnd)
FF5A C00000          LDA     FALSE,i      ;Initialize chOut := FALSE
FF5D E30002          STA     chOut,s
FF60 C02710          LDA     10000,i      ;place := 10,000
FF63 E30004          STA     place,s
FF66 16FF91          CALL    divide       ;Write 10,000's place
FF69 C003E8          LDA     1000,i       ;place := 1,000
FF6C E30004          STA     place,s
FF6F 16FF91          CALL    divide       ;Write 1000's place
FF72 C00064          LDA     100,i        ;place := 100
FF75 E30004          STA     place,s
FF78 16FF91          CALL    divide       ;Write 100's place
FF7B C0000A          LDA     10,i         ;place := 10
FF7E E30004          STA     place,s
FF81 16FF91          CALL    divide       ;Write 10's place
FF84 C30000          LDA     remain,s     ;Always write 1's place
FF87 A00030          ORA     0x0030,i     ;Convert decimal to ASCII
FF8A F1FC50          STBYTEA byteBuff,d
FF8D 51FC50          CHARO   byteBuff,d
FF90 5E              RET6
              ;
```

Figure **8.15**

The DECO trap handler.

```
                ;Subroutine to print the most significant decimal digit of the
                ;remainder. It assumes that place (place2 here) contains the
                ;decimal place value. It updates the remainder.
                ;
                remain2: .EQUATE 2          ;Stack addresses while executing a
                chOut2:  .EQUATE 4          ;subroutine are greater by two because
                place2:  .EQUATE 6          ;the retAddr is on the stack
                ;
FF91  C30002 divide:  LDA    remain2,s  ;A := remainder
FF94  C80000          LDX    0,i        ;X := 0
FF97  830006 divLoop: SUBA   place2,s   ;Division by repeated subtraction
FF9A  08FFA6          BRLT   writeNum   ;If remainder is negative then done
FF9D  780001          ADDX   1,i        ;X := X + 1
FFA0  E30002          STA    remain2,s  ;Store the new remainder
FFA3  04FF97          BR     divLoop
                ;
FFA6  B80000 writeNum:CPX    0,i        ;If X != 0 then
FFA9  0AFFB5          BREQ   checkOut
FFAC  C00001          LDA    TRUE,i     ;chOut := TRUE
FFAF  E30004          STA    chOut2,s
FFB2  04FFBC          BR     printDgt   ;and branch to print this digit
FFB5  C30004 checkOut:LDA    chOut2,s   ;else if a previous char was output
FFB8  0CFFBC          BRNE   printDgt   ;then branch to print this zero
FFBB  58              RETO              ;else return to calling routine
                ;
FFBC  A80030 printDgt:ORX    0x0030,i   ;Convert decimal to ASCII
FFBF  E9FC4F          STX    wordBuff,d ;for output
FFC2  51FC50          CHARO  byteBuff,d
FFC5  58              RETO              ;return to calling routine
```

Figure **8.3**
(Continued)

value. Because the largest value that can be stored is 32767, the routine will output, at most, five digit characters. It precedes the value by a negative sign if necessary.

As usual, the statements at the beginning of the trap handler at FF3B assert the legal addressing modes, call the routine to compute the address of the operand, and allocate storage for the local variables. In contrast to the DECI trap handler, the statement at FF4A

```
LDA opAddr,n
```

accesses the operand with a load instead of a store because DECO is an output statement instead of an input statement. As with the DECI handler, the operand is accessed through opAddr with indirect addressing.

The code from FF4D to FF56 tests for a negative value. If the operand is negative, the CHARO at FF53 outputs the negative sign, and the following code negates the operand. At FF57 the accumulator contains the magnitude of the operand, which is stored in remain, which stands for remainder.

The code from FF5A to FF81 writes the 10,000's, 1000's, 100's, and 10's place of the magnitude of the operand. To suppress any leading zeros, it initializes chOut to false, which indicates that no digit characters have yet been output.

Subroutine divide outputs the digit character for the place value in place and decreases remain for the next call. For example, if remain is 24873 before the call to divide at FF66, then divide will output 2 and leave 4873 in remain. It will also set chOut to true.

Before outputting character 0, divide tests chOut to check whether any digit characters have been output yet. If chOut is false, the character is a leading zero and is not output. Otherwise it is an embedded zero and is output. For example, if remain is 761 before the call at FF6F, divide prints nothing and leaves 761 in remain and false in chOut. The code beginning at FF84 writes the 1's place regardless of the value of chOut. Thus, a value of zero for the original operand gets output as 0.

The code from FF91 to FFC5 is the subroutine to print the most significant digit of remain. It determines the value to output by repeatedly subtracting place from remain, counting the number of subtractions until remain is less than zero. The effect is to compute the value to output as remain / place.

The STRO Trap Handler and OS Vectors

Figure 8.16 is the trap handler for the STRO instruction. It is similar in function to the DECO trap handler. Because it is an output instruction, the address of the operand is first fetched with

```
LDA opAddr,d
```

at FFD2. Then it calls the prntMsg subroutine at FFE2, pushing the address of the string to print on the run-time stack. In effect, a string is an array of characters, so the processing is similar to the translations of a C++ program where an array is passed as a parameter. The print subroutine, therefore, uses stack-indexed deferred addressing in the statements

```
LDBYTEA msgAddr,sxf
```

```
              ;******* Opcode 0x40
              ;The STRO instruction.
              ;Outputs a null-terminated string from memory.
              ;
FFC6  C00016  opcode40:LDA    0x0016,i   ;Assert d, n, sf
FFC9  E1FC53          STA     addrMask,d
FFCC  16FCCA          CALL    assertAd
FFCF  16FD19          CALL    setAddr    ;Set address of trap operand
FFD2  C1FC55          LDA     opAddr,d   ;Push address of string to print
FFD5  E3FFFE          STA     -2,s
FFD8  680002          SUBSP   2,i
FFDB  16FFE2          CALL    prntMsg    ;and print
FFDE  600002          ADDSP   2,i
FFE1  58              RETO
              ;
              ;******* Print subroutine
              ;Prints a string of ASCII bytes until it encounters a null
              ;byte (eight zero bits). Assumes one parameter, which
              ;contains the address of the message.
              ;
              msgAddr: .EQUATE 2         ;Address of message to print
              ;
FFE2  C80000  prntMsg: LDX    0,i        ;X := 0
FFE5  C00000           LDA    0,i        ;A := 0
FFE8  D70002  prntMore:LDBYTEA msgAddr,sxf;Test next char
FFEB  0AFFF7           BREQ   exitPrnt   ;If null then exit
FFEE  570002           CHARO  msgAddr,sxf;else print
FFF1  780001           ADDX   1,i        ;X := X + 1 for next character
FFF4  04FFE8           BR     prntMore
              ;
FFF7  58      exitPrnt:RETO
              ;
              ;******* Vectors for System Memory Format
FFF8  FBCF             .ADDRSS osRAM     ;User stack pointer
FFFA  FC4F             .ADDRSS wordBuff  ;System stack pointer
FFFC  FC57             .ADDRSS loader    ;Loader program counter
FFFE  FC9B             .ADDRSS trap      ;Trap program counter
```

Figure **8.16**

The trap handler for the STRO instruction.

and

```
CHARO msgAddr,sxf
```

to access an element of the character array.

The machine vectors are established with the .ADDRSS assembler directive. Compare this code with Figure 8.1 and Figure 8.2. The vector at FFF8 is the address of osRAM, which is the top byte of operating system RAM. The hardware initializes SP to this value when the user selects the execute option from the simulator. It is the byte at the bottom of the user stack.

The vector at FFFA is the address of wordBuff. Figure 8.2 shows wordBuff as the next byte below the 128-byte block of storage reserved for the system stack. The hardware initializes SP to this value when the user selects the load option from the simulator. It also pushes the PCB onto the stack starting from this point when a trap instruction executes.

The vector at FFFC is the address of the loader, as Figure 8.3 shows. The hardware initializes PC to this value when the user selects the load option. The vector at FFFE is the address of the interrupt handler entry point, as Figure 8.6 shows. The hardware initializes PC to this value when a trap instruction executes.

8.3 Concurrent Processes

Remember that a process is a program during execution. Section 8.2 shows how the operating system can suspend a process during its execution to provide a service. A time line of CPU activity for a process that uses DECI and DECO would look like Figure 8.17. The shaded regions represent those times that the CPU executes the trap service routine. The time line is similar in form to Figure 8.4 except that this figure shows the operating system suspending a process before it terminates, and then restarting it when the service is complete.

Application   DECI   Application   DECO   Application
           trap   trap

Figure **8.17**

A time line of CPU usage when the operating system executes a single program containing DECI and DECO instructions.

The traps described in Section 8.2 are called *software interrupts* because the executing process initiates them by the unimplemented opcodes in its listing. They are also called *synchronous interrupts,* because each time the process executes, the interrupts occur at the same time. The interrupts are synchronized with the code and are predictable.

Another way to initiate a synchronous interrupt is to execute an operating system call. A common assembly-level mnemonic for an operating system call is SVC, which stands for *supervisor call*. The operand specifier normally acts as a parameter for the system call and tells the system which service the program wants to request. For example, if you want to flush the contents of a buffered stream with the equivalent of cout.flush() in C++ and the code for flush() is 27, you might execute

Supervisor calls

```
SVC 27, i
```

Asynchronous Interrupts

Another type of interrupt is the *asynchronous interrupt*, which does not occur at a predictable time during execution. Two common sources of asynchronous interrupts are

- Time outs

- I/O completions

Two common asynchronous interrupts

To see how asynchronous interrupts can occur from time outs, consider a multiuser system, which allows several users to access the computer simultaneously. Because most computers have only one CPU, the operating system must allocate the CPU to each user's job in turn with a technique known as *time sharing*. The operating system allocates a quantum of time called a *time slice*, typically about 100 ms (one tenth of a second), to a job. If the job is not completed within that time (a condition known as *time out*), the operating system suspends the job temporarily and allocates another quantum of CPU time to the next job.

Time outs

To implement time sharing, the hardware must provide an alarm clock that the operating system can set to produce an interrupt after an interval of time.

The reason such an interrupt is unpredictable is that it depends on how busy the system is servicing the requests of its users. If no other job is waiting for the CPU, the system may let your job run longer than the standard time slice. Then if another user suddenly requests a service, the operating system may suspend your process immediately and allocate the CPU to the requesting job. Your process would not be interrupted at the same point as if it timed out after one time slice.

The second common source of asynchronous interrupts is I/O completions. A basic property of I/O devices is their slow speed compared to the processing speed of

I/O completions

the CPU. If a running process requests some input from a keyboard, in the fraction of a second that it takes the user to respond, the CPU can execute hundreds of thousands of instructions for another process. Even if the process requests input from a disk file, which is much faster than keyboard input, the CPU could still execute thousands of instructions while waiting for the information to come from the disk.

To keep from wasting CPU time, the operating system can suspend the process that makes an I/O request if it appears that the process will need to wait for the I/O to complete. It can temporarily assign the CPU to a second process with the understanding that when the I/O does complete, the first process may immediately get the CPU back. Because the second process cannot predict when the I/O device will complete the I/O operation for the first process, it cannot know when the operating system might interrupt it to give the CPU back to the first process.

An operating system that can switch back and forth between processes to keep the CPU busy is called a *multiprogramming system*. To implement multiprogramming, the hardware must provide connections for the I/O devices to send interrupt signals to the CPU when the devices complete their I/O operations.

Multiprogramming

Processes in the Operating System

One purpose of an operating system is to allocate the resources of the system efficiently. A multiprogramming time-sharing system allocates CPU time among the jobs in the system. The objective is to keep the CPU as busy as possible executing user jobs instead of being idle waiting for I/O. The operating system tries to be fair in scheduling CPU time so that all the jobs will be completed in a reasonable time.

At any given time, the operating system must maintain many suspended processes that are waiting their turn for CPU time. It maintains all these processes by allocating a separate PCB for each one, similar to the PCB the interrupt handler maintains in the Pep/8 system. A common practice is to link the PCBs together with pointers in a linked list called a *queue*. Figure 8.18 shows a queue of PCBs.

Each PCB includes copies of all the CPU register values at the time of the process's most recent interrupt. The register set must include a copy of the program counter so the process can continue executing from where it was when the interrupt occurred.

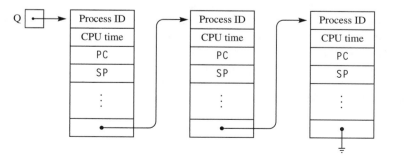

Figure **8.18**

A queue of process control blocks.

The PCB contains additional information to help the operating system schedule the CPU. An example is a unique process identification number assigned by the system, labeled Process ID in Figure 8.18, that serves to reference the process. Suppose a user wants to terminate a process before it completes execution normally, and he knows the ID number is 782. He could issue a KILL(782) command that would cause the operating system to search through the queue of PCBs, find the PCB with ID 782, remove it from the queue, and deallocate it.

Another example of information stored in the PCB is a record of the total amount of CPU time used so far by the suspended process. If the CPU becomes available and the operating system must decide which of several suspended processes gets the CPU, it can use the recorded time to make a fair decision.

As a job progresses through the system toward completion, it passes through several states, as Figure 8.19 shows. The figure is in the form of a state transition diagram and is another example of a finite state machine. Each transition is labeled with the event that causes the change of state.

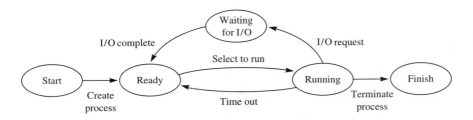

Figure 8.19

The state transition diagram for a job in an operating system.

When a user submits a job for processing, the operating system creates a process for it by allocating a new PCB and attaching it to a queue of processes that are waiting for CPU time. It loads the program into main memory and sets the copy of PC in the PCB to the address of the first instruction of the process. That puts the job in the ready state.

Eventually, the operating system should select the job to receive some processing time. It sets the alarm clock to generate an interrupt after a quantum of time and puts the copies of the registers from the PCB into the CPU. That puts the job in the running state.

Transitions from the running state

While in the running state, three things can happen: (1) The running process may time out if it is still executing when the alarm clock interrupts. If so, the operating system attaches the process's PCB to the ready queue, which puts it back in the ready state. (2) The process may complete its execution normally, in which case the last instruction it executes is an SVC to request that the operating system terminate it. (3) The process may need some input, in which case it executes an SVC for the request. The operating system would transfer the request to the appropriate I/O device and put the PCB in another queue of processes that are waiting for their I/O operations to complete. That puts the process in the waiting-for-I/O state.

While the process is in the waiting-for-I/O state, the I/O device should eventually interrupt the system with the requested input. When that happens, the system puts the input in a buffer in main memory, removes the process's PCB from the waiting-for-I/O queue, and puts it in the ready queue. That puts the process in the ready state, from which it will eventually receive more CPU time. Then it can access the input from the buffer.

Transition from the waiting-for-I/O state

Multiprocessing

As far as the user is concerned, a job simply executes from start to finish. The interruptions are invisible the same way that the DECI interrupt is invisible to the assembly language programmer at Level Asmb5. The details at the operating system level are invisible to the users at a higher level of abstraction.

The only perceptible difference to the user is that it will take longer for the program to execute if many jobs are in the system. One way to speed the progress is to attach more than one CPU to the system. Such a configuration is called a *multiprocessing system*. Figure 8.20 shows a multiprocessing system with two processors.

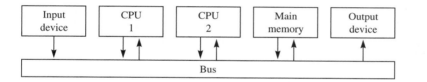

Figure **8.20**

Block diagram of a multiprocessing system.

In multiprogramming, the processes appear to be executing concurrently because the CPU switches between them so rapidly. In multiprocessing, the operating system can schedule more than one process to execute concurrently because there is more than one processor.

It would be nice if increasing the number of processors in the system increased the performance proportionally. Unfortunately, that is not usually the case. When you add more processors to the system, you place a greater demand on the communication links of the system. For example, if you attach the processors to a common bus, as in Figure 8.20, the bus may limit the performance of the system. If both CPUs request a read from the input device at the same time, one CPU will have to wait. The more processors you add, the more frequently those conflicts occur.

The communication overhead inherent in a multiprocessor system typically yields a performance curve as in Figure 8.21. The dashed line shows the theoretical maximum benefit of adding processors. On the dashed line, for example, if you double the number of processors, you double the performance. In practice, the performance does not increase that much.

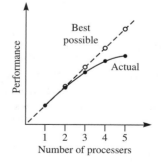

Figure **8.21**

The increase in performance by adding processors in a multiprocessing system.

A Concurrent Processing Program

The processes considered thus far have all been independent of each other. Each process belongs to a different user, and there is no interaction between the processes. Under those circumstances, the result of a computation does not depend on when an interrupt occurs. The only effect the interrupt has is to increase the amount of time it takes to execute the process.

In practice, processes managed by an operating system frequently need to cooperate with one another to perform their tasks. The program in Figure 8.22 describes a situation in which two processes must cooperate to avoid producing incorrect results.

Cooperating processes

C++ Level

Process P1   Process P2

```
...                           ...
numRes++                      numRes++
...                           ...
```

Assembly Level

Process P1   Process P2

```
...                           ...
LDA   numRes,d                LDA   numRes,d
ADDA  1,i                     ADDA  1,i
STA   numRes,d                STA   numRes,d
...                           ...
```

Figure **8.22**

Concurrent processes at two levels of abstraction.

Suppose the operating system must manage an airline's database, with records accessed concurrently by several users. Each flight has a record in the database that contains, among other things, the number of reservations that have been made for that flight. Travel agencies from throughout the city access the system on behalf of prospective passengers. Requests for information from the database are somewhat random because it is impossible to predict when a given agent will need to access the system.

One day, two different agents have customers who want to make reservations at exactly the same time for the same future flight. The operating system creates a process for each job called P1 and P2. Figure 8.22 shows a code fragment from each process. numRes stands for number of reservations. It is an integer variable whose value is in main memory while P1 and P2 progress through the system.

Suppose numRes has the value 47 before either agent makes a reservation for her customer. After both transactions, numRes should have the value 49. At the C++ level, each process wants to increment numRes by 1 with the assignment statement numRes++. If assignment statements are *atomic*, that is, indivisible, then the code fragment at the C++ level will produce correct results regardless of which process executes its assignment statement first. If P1 executes first, it will make numRes 48, and P2 will make numRes 49. If P2 executes first, it will make numRes 48, and P1 will make numRes 49. In either case, numRes gets the correct value of 49.

The problem is that assignment statements at the C++ level are not atomic. They are compiled to LDA, ADDA, and STA, and are executed in a system in which an interrupt may occur between any assembly language statements. Figure 8.23 is a trace of an execution sequence that shows what can go wrong. A(P1) is the content of P1's accumulator, either in the CPU when P1 is running or in the PCB when P1 is suspended. A(P2) is P2's accumulator.

Nonatomic statements

In this sequence, P1 executes LDA, which puts 47 in its accumulator, then ADDA, which increments the accumulator to 48. Then the operating system interrupts P1 and gives P2 some processor time. P2 executes all three of its statements, changing numRes in memory to 48. When P1 eventually resumes, it gives 48 to numRes as well. The net result is that numRes has the value 48 instead of 49, even though each process executed all its statements.

Statement Executed		A (P1)	A (P2)	numRes
		?	?	47
(P1) LDA	numRes,d	47	?	47
(P1) ADDA	1,i	48	?	47
(P2) LDA	numRes,d	48	47	47
(P2) ADDA	1,i	48	48	47
(P2) STA	numRes,d	48	48	48
(P1) STA	numRes,d	48	48	48

Figure **8.23**

A trace of one possible execution sequence of Figure 8.22.

This problem can occur whether the processes execute in a multiprocessing system with true concurrency or in a multiprogramming system where the concurrency is only apparent. In a multiprocessing system it would be possible for P1 and P2 to execute their ADDA instructions at exactly the same time. But if they tried to execute their STA instructions at exactly the same time, the hardware would force one process to wait while the other wrote the value to memory. From a logical point of view, the problems that can occur are the same whether the concurrency is real or not.

The logical equivalence of multi-programming and multiprocessing

Critical Sections

The basic problem arises because P1 and P2 share the part of main memory that contains the value of `numRes`. Whenever concurrent processes share a variable, there is always the possibility that the results depend on the timing of the interrupts. To solve the problem, we need a way to ensure that when one process accesses the shared variable, the other process is prevented from accessing it until the first process has completed its access.

Sections of code in two processes that are mutually exclusive are called *critical sections*. For concurrent programs to execute correctly, the software must guarantee that if one process is executing a statement in a critical section, the other process cannot be executing a statement in its critical section. To solve the problem of Figure 8.22, we need a way of putting the assignment statements in critical sections so that the interleaved execution will not occur at the assembly level.

A critical section requires two additional pieces of code called the *entry section* and the *exit section*. The entry section for P1 is written just before its critical section. Its function is to test whether P2 is executing in its critical section and, if so, to delay somehow the execution of P1's critical section until P2 is finished with its critical section. The exit section for P1 is written just after its critical section. Its function is to alert P2 that P1 is no longer in a critical section so P2 may enter its critical section.

Entry and exit sections

The code fragment at the C++ level for each process of Figure 8.22 must be modified as follows:

```
remainder section
entry section
numRes++ //the critical section
exit section
remainder section
```

The remainder sections are all those parts of the code that can execute concurrently with the other process with no ill effects. The critical sections are those parts of the code that must be mutually exclusive.

The following programs show attempts to implement the entry and exit sections that guard the process's access to its critical section. Each program assumes that P1 and P2 have the general form of Figure 8.24.

Process P1	Process P2
do	do
entry section	*entry section*
critical section	*critical section*
exit section	*exit section*
remainder section	*remainder section*
while (! done1);	while (! done2);

Figure **8.24**

The general form of critical section programs.

done1 and done2 are local boolean variables (not shared) that are modified somewhere in the remainder sections.

A First Attempt at Mutual Exclusion

The program in Figure 8.25, our first attempt at designing the entry and exit sections, uses turn, a shared integer variable. The entry section consists of a do loop that tests turn, and the exit section consists of an assignment statement that modifies turn. Although the listing does not show it, assume that turn is initialized either to 1 or 2 before the processes enter the do loops.

Process P1	Process P2
do	do
while (turn != 1)	while (turn != 2)
; //nothing	; //nothing
critical section	*critical section*
turn = 2;	turn = 1;
remainder section	*remainder section*
while (! done1);	while (! done2);

Figure **8.25**

An attempt at programming mutual exclusion.

The body of the do loop in the entry section is an empty C++ statement that generates no code at the assembly level. The code for the entry section of P1 translates to

```
Loop: LDA    turn,d
      COMPA  1,i
      BRNE   Loop
```

The nonatomic nature of the do *statement*

Suppose turn is initialized to 1 and both processes try to enter their critical sections at the same time. No matter how you interleave the executions of the assembly statements in the entry section, P2 will continually loop until P1 enters its critical section. When P1 finishes its critical section, its exit section will set `turn` to 2, after which P2 will be able to enter its critical section.

This algorithm guarantees that the critical sections are mutually exclusive. P2 can be in its critical section only if `turn` is 2, during which time P1 cannot be in its critical section, and vice versa. When P2 leaves its critical section, it sets `turn` to 1, which acts as a signal to P1 that it may enter its critical section.

Although the algorithm guarantees mutual exclusion, it has the undesirable property of requiring the processes to strictly alternate their do loops. The processes communicate through the shared variable `turn`, which keeps track of whose turn it is to execute a critical section. The user may want P1 to execute its do loop several times without P2 executing its loop at all. That could never happen with these entry and exit sections.

A Second Attempt at Mutual Exclusions

To allow a process to execute its do loops unrestrained by the execution of the other process (except for the mutual exclusion requirement), the program in Figure 8.26 uses two shared boolean variables, `enter1` and `enter2`. Assume that `enter1` and `enter2` are both initialized to false.

Process P1	Process P2
```do```	```do```
``` enter1 = TRUE;```	``` enter2 = TRUE;```
``` while (enter2)```	``` while (enter1)```
``` ; //nothing```	``` ; //nothing```
critical section	*critical section*
``` enter1 = FALSE;```	``` enter2 = FALSE;```
remainder section	*remainder section*
```while (! done1);```	```while (! done2);```

Figure **8.26**

Another attempt at programming mutual exclusion.

If P2 is in its remainder section, `enter2` must be false. Then P1 can execute its do loop as often as it likes. It simply sets `enter1` to true, tests `enter2` once in the `while` loop, executes its critical section, sets `enter1` to false, and executes its remainder section. It can repeat the sequence as long as it likes. Similarly, P2 can loop repeatedly if P1 is in its remainder section.

This implementation guarantees mutual exclusion. When P1 sets `enter1` to true, it is signaling P2 that it is trying to enter a critical section. If P2 has just a little earlier fetched `enter1` with

```
LDA enter1,d
```

in its `while` test, P2 will not immediately know of P1's intentions. P2 may be executing its critical section already. However, if P2 is in its critical section, `enter2` must be true, and P1's `while` loop will keep it from entering its critical section at the same time. When P2 finally exits, it sets `enter2` to false, which allows P1 into its critical section.

The problems that confront the designer of cooperating processes can be quite subtle and unexpected. This algorithm is a case in point. Although it guarantees mutual exclusion and does not constrain the `do` loop execution as in the previous program, it nevertheless has a serious bug.

Figure 8.27 shows a trace where P1 sets `enter1` to true and then experiences an interrupt. P2 sets `enter2` to true and then begins executing its `while` loop. The `while` loop will continue executing until P2 times out and P1 resumes, because `enter1` is true. But P1 will also loop indefinitely because `enter2` is true.

Statement Executed	enter1	enter2
	false	false
(P1) `enter1 = TRUE;`	true	false
(P2) `enter2 = TRUE;`	true	true
(P2) `while (enter1);`	true	true
(P1) `while (enter2);`	true	true

Figure **8.27**

A trace of the program in Figure 8.26 that produces deadlock.

P1 and P2 are in a state in which each one wants to enter a critical section. P1 cannot enter until P2 enters, executes its critical section, and sets `enter2` to false. But P2 cannot enter until P1 enters, executes its critical section, and sets `enter1` to false. Each process is waiting for an event that will never occur, a condition called *deadlock*. Deadlocks, like endless loops, are conditions to avoid.

Definition of deadlock

Peterson's Algorithm for Mutual Exclusion

We need a solution that guarantees mutual exclusion, allows the outer `do` loops of each process to execute without restraint, and avoids deadlock. Figure 8.28, an implementation of Peterson's algorithm, combines features from Figures 8.25 and 8.26 to achieve all these objectives. The basic idea is that `enter1` and `enter2` provide the mutual exclusion as in Figure 8.26, and `turn` allows one of the processes to enter its critical section even if both processes try to enter at the same time. `enter1` and `enter2` initially are false, and `turn` initially can be 1 or 2.

To see that mutual exclusion is guaranteed, consider the situation if P1 and P2 were both executing their critical sections simultaneously. `enter1` and `enter2`

Proof that Peterson's algorithm guarantees mutual exclusion

Process P1	Process P2
`do`	`do`
`    enter1 = TRUE;`	`    enter2 = TRUE;`
`    turn = 2;`	`    turn = 1;`
`    while (enter2 && (turn == 2))`	`    while (enter1 && (turn == 1))`
`        ; //nothing`	`        ; //nothing`
`    `*critical section*	`    `*critical section*
`    enter1 = FALSE;`	`    enter2 = FALSE;`
`    `*remainder section*	`    `*remainder section*
`while (! done1);`	`while (! done2);`

Figure **8.28**

Peterson's algorithm for mutual exclusion.

would both be true. In P1, the `while` test would imply that `turn` has the value 1 because `enter2` is true. But in P2, the `while` test would imply that `turn` has the value 2 because `enter1` is true. This contradiction implies that P1 and P2 cannot execute their critical sections simultaneously.

But what if P1 and P2 try to enter their critical sections at about the same time? Is there some interleaving of the executions in the entry section that will permit them to both execute their critical sections simultaneously? No there is not, even though the `while` test with the AND operation is not atomic at the assembly level. There are two ways that P1 can get past the `while` test into its critical section: if `enter2` is false, or if `turn` is 1. If either of these conditions holds, P1 can enter regardless of the other condition.

Suppose that P1 gets past the `while` test because when it gets the value of `enter2` with

```
LDA enter2,d
```

`enter2` has the value false. That can only happen when P2 is in its remainder section. Even if P1 is interrupted after it loads the value of `enter2`, and P2 then sets `enter2` to true and `turn` to 1, P2 will not be able to enter its critical section because P1 has set `enter1` to true and `turn` is now 1.

Suppose that P1 gets past the `while` test because when it gets the value of `turn` with

```
LDA turn,d
```

`turn` has the value 1. Because the previous instruction in P1 set `turn` to 2, that can only happen if P1 was interrupted between its previous instruction and the `while` test, and P2 set `turn` to 1. But then, P2 again will be prevented from getting past its `while` loop into its critical section, because P1 has set `enter1` to true and `turn` now has the value 1.

To see that deadlock cannot occur, assume that both processes are deadlocked, both executing their `while` loops concurrently (in a multiprocessing system) or during alternate time slices (in a multiprogramming system). The `while` test in P1 implies that `turn` must have the value 2, but the test in P2 implies that `turn` must have the value 1. This contradiction shows that both processes cannot be looping together.

Proof that Peterson's algorithm avoids deadlock

Suppose both processes try to set `turn` at the same time with

```
STA turn,d
```

In a multiprogramming system, P1's assignment to `turn` will occur either before or after P2's assignment because they must execute in different time slices. In a multiprocessing system, if both processes try to store a value to `turn` in main memory at exactly the same time, the hardware will force one of the processes to wait while the other executes its `STA`. In either system, the process that stores to `turn` first will enter its critical section and deadlock will not occur.

Semaphores

Although the program in Figure 8.28 solves the critical section problem while avoiding deadlock, it does have an undesirable inefficiency. The mechanism that prevents a process from entering its critical section is a `while` loop. The loop's only purpose is to stall the process until it is interrupted, allowing time for the other process to finish executing its critical section. Such a loop is called a *spin lock* because the process is locked out of its critical section by spinning around the loop.

Spin locks

Spin locks are a waste of CPU time, especially if the process is executing in a multiprogramming system and has just been allocated a new time slice. It would be more efficient if the CPU were allocated to another process that could use the time to perform useful work. *Semaphores* are shared variables that most operating systems provide for concurrent programming. They enable the programmer to implement critical sections without spin locks.

A semaphore is an integer variable whose value can only be modified by an operating system call. The three operations on semaphore s are

- `init(s)`
- `wait(s)`
- `signal(s)`

The three operations on a semaphore

where `init`, `wait`, and `signal` are procedures provided by the operating system. At the assembly level, the procedures would be invoked by an `SVC` with the appropriate operand specifier. A semaphore is another example of an abstract data type

(ADT) with operations whose meanings are known to the programmer but whose implementations are hidden at a lower level of abstraction. (wait(s) and signal(s) are frequently written p(s) and v(s), respectively.)

Each semaphore, s, has associated with it a queue of process control blocks, called sQueue, that represents suspended processes. The meanings of the operations are

init(s)
_____
s = 1;
sQueue = *an empty list of process control blocks*

wait(s)
_____
s--
if (s < 0)
    Suspend this process by adding it to sQueue

signal(s)
_____
s++
if (s <= 0)
    Transfer a process from sQueue *to the ready queue*

An important characteristic of each operation is that the operating system guarantees them to be atomic. For example, it is impossible for two processes to execute signal(s) simultaneously with s incremented only by 1 as numRes is in Figure 8.22. The assembly-level statements for the assignments will never be interleaved.

Figure 8.29 is the state transition diagram for a job in an operating system that provides semaphores. A process in the waiting-for-s state is suspended, its PCB in sQueue, in the same way that a process in the ready state is suspended, its PCB in the ready queue. Such a process is blocked from running, because it must make a transition to the ready state before it can run.

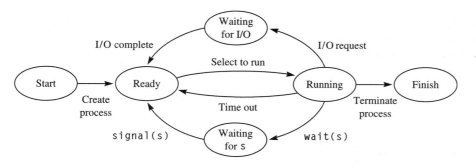

Figure **8.29**

The state transition diagram for a job in an operating system that provides a semaphore.

If a running process executes `wait(s)` when s is greater than 0, then `wait(s)` simply decrements s by 1 and the process continues executing. A running process makes a transition to the waiting-for-s state by executing `wait(s)` when s is less than or equal to 0. If a running process executes `signal(s)` when s is greater than or equal to 0, it simply increments s by 1 and continues executing. A running process that executes `signal(s)` when s is less than 0 causes some other process that is waiting for s to be selected by the operating system and placed in the ready state. The process that executed `signal(s)` continues to run.

From the definitions of `wait` and `signal`, it follows that a negative value of s means that one or more processes are blocked in `sQueue`. Furthermore, the magnitude of s is the number of processes blocked. For example, if the value of s is −3, then three processes are blocked in `sQueue`.

The meaning of a negative semaphore value

If more than one process is blocked when `signal(s)` executes, the operating system tries to be fair in selecting the process to transfer to the ready state. A common strategy is to use *first in, first out* (FIFO) scheduling so the process that was blocked for the longest period of time gets sent to the ready state. FIFO is the characteristic that distinguishes a queue from a stack, which is a *last in, first out* (LIFO) list.

Figure 8.29 shows only one semaphore wait state. In a system that provides semaphores, the programmer can declare as many different semaphores as she likes. The operating system will maintain a queue of blocked processes for each one.

Critical Sections with Semaphores

Critical sections are trivial to program if the operating system provides semaphores. The program in Figure 8.30 assumes that `mutEx` is a semaphore initialized to 1 with `init(mutEx)`.

The first process to execute `wait(mutEx)` will change `mutEx` from 1 to 0 and enter its critical section. If the other process executes `wait(mutEx)` in the meantime, it will change `mutEx` from 0 to −1, and the operating system will immediately block it. When the first process eventually leaves its critical section, it will execute `signal(mutEx)`, which will put the other process in the ready state.

Process P1	Process P2

```
do                          do
   wait(mutEx);                wait(mutEx);
   critical section           critical section
   signal(mutEx);             signal(mutEx);
   remainder section          remainder section
while (! done1);            while (! done2);
```

Figure **8.30**

Critical sections with semaphore.

Fernando J. Corbató

Fernando J. Corbató was born July 1, 1926 in Oakland, California. He received his BS degree from Cal Tech in 1950 and his PhD in Physics from MIT in 1956. He is renowned for his work on two pioneering operating systems—the Compatible Time-Sharing System (CTSS) and the Multiplexed Information and Computing Service (Multics).

Before the advent of operating systems, the user of a computer at an organization would sign up for a particular time of day to physically operate the computer, during which time no other user could have access to it. The first rudimentary operating systems used batch processing, in which one person ran the computer for the various users by accepting their jobs in the format of stacks of punched cards. Debugging was time-consuming, because a programmer had to wait sometimes for hours between each compile run just to get the syntax errors out of the program.

In the late 1950s various computer scientists, including John McCarthy at MIT and Christopher Strachey at Oxford, began proposing the concept of time-sharing where several users could simultaneously log in to the computer remotely with dialup modems and typewriter consoles. It would appear that each user had complete access to the machine and the resulting online debugging would drastically reduce the software development time.

Corbató led the team at MIT that produced CTSS, one of the first time-sharing systems. It was designed for the IBM 709 and 7090 machines and could support four users simultaneously—three with typewriter consoles and one passive user. There were 32K 36-bit words of memory with the user job in the upper 27K and the time-sharing supervisor in the lower 5K. The team had to modify the hardware to provide memory protection between user jobs.

The Multics system was a far more ambitious project based on the

lessons learned from the CTSS project. Two prominent characteristics were the use of PL/I as the implementation language and the ring scheme of memory protection. Before Multics, most operating systems were written in assembly language. When the Multics project began IBM had just introduced the specifications of Programming Language One (PL/I). Corbató's team had to develop their own compiler for it, as IBM had yet to deliver a commercial compiler.

It is ironic that many current personal computer operating systems are vulnerable to viruses to which Multics was completely immune. By far the most common virus mechanism is the buffer overflow, which happens when a program attempts to access an array outside its boundaries. Most operating systems today are implemented in C, which allows such accesses. But PL/I does not, which contributed to the security of Multics.

Fernando Corbató won the Turing Award in 1990 for his pioneering leadership of the CTSS and Multics projects. He is currently Professor Emeritus in the Department of Electrical Engineering and Computer Science at the Massachusetts Institute of Technology.

Because the operating system guarantees that `wait` and `signal` are atomic, the programmer need not worry about interleaving within the entry and exit sections. Also, time is not wasted on spin locks because the system immediately puts the second process on the wait queue for `mutEx`. Of course, hiding the details does not eliminate them. The operating system designer must use the features of the hardware, along with algorithmic reasoning such as that employed in the previous programs, to provide the semaphores. Semaphores satisfy both goals of the operating system—to provide a convenient environment for higher-level programming and to allocate the resources of the system efficiently.

8.4 Deadlocks

The program in Figure 8.26 shows how concurrent processing can produce a deadlock between two processes that share a variable in main memory. The deadlock phenomenon can occur when processes share other resources as well. Resources that an operating system must manage include printers, compact disc (CD) drives, and disk files. Sharing any of these resources among concurrent processes can lead to deadlock.

As an example of a deadlock with these resources, suppose process P1 requests the computer's single CD drive for data input. The operating system allocates the CD drive to P1, which holds it until it does not need the drive any longer. P2 may then request input from a disk file, which the operating system opens and allocates to that process.

Now suppose P1 needs to read from the same disk file P2 is accessing. It requests access, but the operating system cannot grant the request because the file is already open for P2. The operating system blocks P1 until the file becomes available. If P2 requests the CD drive, the operating system will block it as well until P1 releases the drive.

In this case, the processes are in a state of deadlock. P1 cannot proceed until P2 relinquishes the disk file, and P2 cannot proceed until P1 relinquishes the CD drive. Both are waiting for an event that will never happen, suspended by the operating system.

Resource Allocation Graphs

To manage its resources effectively, the operating system needs a way to detect possible deadlocks. It does so with a structure called a *resource allocation graph*. A resource allocation graph is a visual depiction of the processes and resources in the system that shows which resources are allocated to which processes and which processes are blocked by a request on which resources.

Figure 8.31 shows the resource allocation graph for the state in which P1 and P2 are deadlocked over the CD drive and disk file. Processes and resources are nodes in the graph, with processes in circles and resources as solid dots inside boxes. There are two types of edges, allocation edges and request edges.

An *allocation edge* (al) from a resource to a process means the resource is allocated to the process. In the figure, the edge labeled al from the CD drive to P1 means the operating system has allocated the CD drive to process P1. A *request edge* (req) from a process to a resource means the process is blocked, waiting for the resource. The edge labeled req from P2 to the CD drive means P2 is blocked waiting for the CD drive.

The deadlock is evident from the fact that the edges describe a closed path from P1 to R2 to P2 to R1 and back to P1. Such a closed path in a graph is called a

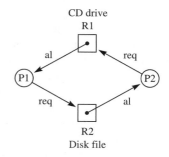

Figure 8.31

A resource allocation graph with a deadlock cycle.

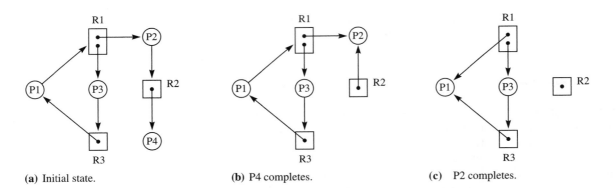

(a) Initial state.　　　　　　**(b)** P4 completes.　　　　　　**(c)**　P2 completes.

cycle. A cycle in a resource allocation graph means that a process is blocked on a resource because it is allocated to another process that is blocked on another resource, and so on, with the last resource allocated to the first process. If the cycle cannot be broken, there is a deadlock.

Sometimes the resources in a class are indistinguishable from each other. A process may request one resource from the class and not be concerned with which particular resource it gets because they are all equivalent. An example is a group of identical CD drives or identical laser printers. If a process needs a laser printer and it does not care which one, the operating system can allocate any printer that is free.

A resource allocation graph represents a class of n identical resources with n solid dots inside the rectangular box. When the operating system allocates a resource from the class, the allocation edge starts from one of the dots that represents the individual resource. A request edge, however, points to the box because the requesting process does not care which resource within the class it gets.

Figure 8.32(a) shows a situation in which both resources in class R1 are allocated. P1 has a request outstanding for one of those resources and does not care which resource it gets.

Even though this graph has cycle (P1, R1, P3, R3, P1), it does not represent a deadlock because the cycle can be broken. Any process in a resource allocation graph that has no request edge from it is not blocked. P4 is not blocked in this figure, and you can assume that it will eventually complete, releasing R2. The operating system will grant P2's request for R2 changing the request edge from P2 to R2, to an allocate edge from R2 to P2, as Figure 8.32(b) shows.

Now P2 can use R2 and R1 and run to completion, eventually releasing those resources. When P2 releases an R1 resource, the operating system can allocate the resource to P1, yielding Figure 8.32(c). P1 can run to completion because it has all the resources it needs, after which P3 can complete also. All the processes can complete, so there is no deadlock.

You must consider the direction of the edges when looking for a cycle. You may be tempted to consider (R1, P1, R2, P2, R1) a cycle in Figure 8.33, but it is not. There is no edge from R2 to P2, or from P2 to R1. A cycle is a necessary but not sufficient condition for a deadlock. In this figure, there is no cycle and, therefore, no deadlock.

Figure **8.32**

A resource allocation graph with a cycle but with no deadlock.

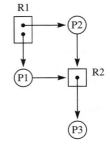

Figure **8.33**

A resource allocation graph with no cycle and, therefore, no deadlock.

Deadlock Policy

An operating system may employ one of three general policies for dealing with deadlock:

- Prevent
- Detect and recover
- Ignore

Three deadlock policies

Several different policies may be found in a given operating system. The system may use one policy for one set of resources and another policy for another set.

The prevention policy employs techniques to ensure that deadlock will not occur. One technique is to require that a job request and be granted once, at the beginning of execution, all the resources it will need to run to completion. The deadlock of Figure 8.31 could not have occurred if P1 had been granted R1 and R2 simultaneously. A deadlock cycle can only be set up if a process is granted a resource and later requests another resource to complete the cycle.

The prevention policy

The detect and recover policy allows deadlocks to occur. With it, the operating system periodically executes a program to detect a deadlock cycle in the system. If the operating system discovers a deadlock, it takes away one of the resources held by a process in the cycle. Because the process has partially executed, the operating system usually must terminate the process, unless the state of the resource can be reconstructed later when it is granted to the process.

The detect and recover policy

All these policies have a cost. The prevention policy puts a constraint on the user, particularly if the resources required depend on the input and cannot be known in advance. The detect and recover policy requires CPU time for the detection and recovery algorithms—time that could be spent on user jobs.

The third policy is to ignore deadlocks. This policy is effective if the costs of the other policies are considered too great, the probability of deadlock is small, or the occurrence of deadlock is inconsequential. For example, a time-shared system may be shut down periodically for routine maintenance, at which time all jobs, including any that are deadlocked, will be removed.

The ignore policy

SUMMARY

The goals of an operating system are to provide a convenient environment for higher-level programming and to allocate the resources of the system efficiently. One important function of an operating system is to manage the jobs that users submit to be executed. A loader is the part of the operating system that places a job into main memory for execution. After the job finishes executing, it turns control of the CPU back to the operating system, which can then load another application program.

A trap handler performs processing for a job, hiding the lower-level details from the programmer. When a trap occurs, the running job's process control block (PCB) is stored while the operating system services the interrupt. The PCB consists of the state of the process: copies of the program counter, the status bits, and the contents of all the CPU registers. To resume the job, the operating system places the PCB back into the CPU. An asynchronous interrupt functions in the same fashion as a procedure call, except that an interrupt is initiated by the operating system, not by the application programmer's code.

A process is a program during execution. In a multiprogramming system, one CPU switches between several processes. In a multiprocessing system, there is more than one CPU. Both multiprogramming and multiprocessing systems maintain concurrently executing processes. To execute cooperating processes concurrently, the operating system must be able to guarantee mutual exclusion of critical sections and avoid deadlock. Peterson's algorithm fills both these requirements. A semaphore is an integer variable provided by the operating system. Its operations include wait and signal, each of which is atomic, or indivisible. Semaphores can also be used to satisfy the mutual exclusion and deadlock requirements.

The deadlock phenomenon can also occur when processes share resources managed by the operating system. A resource allocation graph consists of nodes representing resources and processes, and edges between the nodes representing resource allocations and requests. If the resource allocation graph contains a cycle that cannot be broken, a deadlock has occurred.

EXERCISES

Section 8.1

1. What are the two purposes of an operating system?

2. The loader in Figure 8.3 executes with the following input:

```
04 00 05 00 00 31 00 03 39 00 03 50 00 0A 41 00
12 00 54 68 61 74 27 73 20 61 6C 6C 2E 0A 00 zz
```

Assume that the loop from FC5D to FC97 is executing for the 27th time. State the values in the following registers as four hexadecimal digits:

*(a) A after LDA at F6C0   *(b) A before ASLA at FC72
*(c) A after ASLA at FC75   (d) A after LDA at FC7C
(e) A after ANDA at FC88   (f) A after ORA at FC8B
(g) X after ADDX at FC91

3. Do Exercise 2 for the 29th execution of the loop.

Section 8.2

4. The following program executes, generating an interrupt for DECI:

```
0000   040005            BR      main        ;Branch around data
0003   0000     num:     .BLOCK  2           ;Global variable
                  ;
0005   310003 main:     DECI    num,d       ;Input decimal value
0008   390003            DECO    num,d       ;Output decimal value
000B   50000A            CHARO   '\n',i
000E   410012            STRO    msg,d       ;Output message
0011   00                STOP
```

```
0012   546861 msg:      .ASCII  "That's all.\n\x00"
       742773
       20616C
       6C2E0A
       00
001F                    .END
```

For Figure 8.6, the entry to and exit from the trap handler, state the values in the following registers as four hexadecimal digits:

*(a) X after LDBYTEX at FC9E   *(b) X after ASRX at FCB9
(c) X after SUBX at FCBA   (d) PC after CALL at FCBE
(e) PC after RETTR at FCC1

*5. Do Exercise 4 for the DECO instruction.

*6. Do Exercise 4 for the STRO instruction.

7. The program in Exercise 4 runs with an input of 37. For Figure 8.14, the DECI trap handler, state the values in registers a–h as four hexadecimal digits and answer the question in (i):

*(a) A after ANDA at FDEB the first time it executes
*(b) A after ANDA at FDEB the second time it executes
*(c) X after LDX at FDF4 the first time it executes
(d) X after LDX at FDF4 the second time it executes
(e) PC after BR at FDF8 the first time it executes
(f) PC after BR at FDF8 the second time it executes
(g) A after LDA at FEE9
(h) X before STBYTEX at FF04, assuming that the carry bit is zero before the trap
(i) What statement executes just before LDA at FEC7?

*8. Do Exercise 7 with an input of −295.

9. The program in Exercise 4 runs with an input of 37. For Figure 8.15, the DECO trap handler, state the values in the following registers as four hexadecimal digits:

*(a) A after LDA at FF4A   *(b) A before STA at FF57

In the following parts, assume that subroutine divide is called from CALL at FF78:

*(c) A after LDA at FF91   (d) X before CPX at FFA6
(e) A after LDA at FFBC

In the following parts, assume that subroutine divide is called from CALL at FF81:

(f) A after LDA at FF91   (g) X before CPX at FFA6
(h) X after ORX at FFBC

10. Do Exercise 9 with an input of −2068.

11. The program in Exercise 4 runs and executes the STRO instruction. For Figure 8.16, the STRO trap handler, state the values in the registers as four hexadecimal digits:

(a) A after LDA at FFD2
(b) A after LDBYTEA at FFE8 the first time it executes

   (c) X after ADDX at FFF1 the first time it executes
   (d) A after LDBYTEA at FFE8 the fifth time it executes
   (e) X after ADDX at FFF1 the fifth time it executes

12. The DECI instruction with direct addressing at 0005 in Figure 5.11 executes generating a trap. The trap handler calls the setAddr routine in Figure 8.10. State the values in the index register as four hexadecimal digits:

   (a) after LDX at FD3D   **(b)** after SUBX at FD40
   (c) after LDX at FD43

13. The DECO instruction with indirect addressing at 0048 in Figure 6.41 executes generating a trap. The trap handler calls the setAddr routine in Figure 8.10. State the values in the index register as four hexadecimal digits:

   (a) after LDX at FD4A   **(b)** after SUBX at FD4D
   (c) after LDX at FD50   **(d)** after LDX at FD53

14. The DECI instruction with stack-relative addressing at 0009 in Figure 6.4 executes generating a trap. The trap handler calls the setAddr routine in Figure 8.10. State the values in the index register as four hexadecimal digits:

   (a) after LDX at FD5A   **(b)** after SUBX at FD5D
   (c) after LDX at FD60   **(d)** after ADDX at FD63

15. The DECI instruction with stack-indexed addressing at 0013 in Figure 6.36 executes for the second time, generating a trap. The trap handler calls the setAddr routine in Figure 8.10. State the values in the index register as four hexadecimal digits:

   (a) after LDX at FD8D   **(b)** after SUBX at FD90
   (c) after LDX at FD93   **(d)** after ADDX at FD96
   (e) after ADDX at FD99

16. The DECI instruction with stack-indexed deferred addressing at 0016 in Figure 6.38 executes for the second time, generating a trap. The trap handler calls the setAddr routine in Figure 8.10. State the values in the index register as four hexadecimal digits:

   (a) after LDX at FDA0   **(b)** after SUBX at FDA3
   (c) after LDX at FDA6   **(d)** after ADDX at FDA9
   (e) after LDX at FDAC   **(f)** after ADDX at FDAF

Section 8.3

17. A short notation for the interleaved execution sequence in Figure 8.23 is 112221, which represents statements executed by P1, P1, P2, P2, P2, P1 in Figure 8.22. **(a)** How many different execution sequences are possible? List each possible sequence in the short notation. For each sequence, state whether numRes has the correct value. **(b)** What percentage of the total number of possible sequences produces an incorrect value? **(c)** Would you expect that percentage to be approximately the probability of an incorrect value when the program runs? Explain.

18. The following attempt to implement critical sections is similar to the program in Figure 8.26 except for the order of the statements in the entry section:

```
Process P1                    Process P2
do                            do
    while (enter2)                while (enter1)
        ; //nothing                  ; //nothing
    enter1 = TRUE                 enter2 = TRUE
    critical section             critical section
    enter1 = FALSE;              enter2 = FALSE;
    remainder section            remainder section
while (! done1);              while (! done2);
```

*(a) Does the algorithm guarantee mutual exclusion? If not, show an execution sequence that lets both processes in their critical sections simultaneously. (b) Does the algorithm prevent deadlock? If not, show an execution sequence that deadlocks P1 and P2.

19. Show from the definitions of `wait` and `signal` that the magnitude of s is the number of processes blocked.

20. Let I represent an execution of `init(s)`, W of `wait(s)`, and S of `signal(s)`. Then, for example, IWWS represents the sequence of calls `init(s)`, `wait(s)`, `wait(s)`, and `signal(s)` by some processes in an operating system. For each of the following sequences of calls, state the value of s and the number of processes blocked after the last call in the sequence:

*(a) IW   (b) IS   (c) ISSSW

(d) IWWWS   (e) ISWWWW

21. Suppose three concurrent processes execute the following code:

```
Process P1                Process P2                Process P3
do                        do                        do
    wait(mutEx);              wait(mutEx);              wait(mutEx);
    critical section         critical section         critical section
    signal(mutEx);           signal(mutEx);           signal(mutEx);
    remainder section        remainder section        remainder section
while (! done1);          while (! done2);          while (! done3);
```

Explain how the code guarantees mutual exclusion of all three critical sections.

22. Suppose s and t are two semaphores initialized with `init(s)` and `init(t)`. Consider the following code fragment of two concurrent processes:

```
Process P1                Process P2
wait(s);                  wait(t);
wait(t);                  wait(s);
critical section          critical section
signal(s);                signal(t);
signal(t);                signal(s);
remainder section         remainder section
```

*(a) Does the algorithm guarantee mutual exclusion? If not, show an execution sequence that lets both processes in their critical sections simultaneously. **(b)** Does the algorithm prevent deadlock? If not, show an execution sequence that deadlocks P1 and P2.

23. Consider the code fragment of two concurrent processes:

Process P1	Process P2
Statement 1	*Statement 4*
Statement 2	*Statement 5*
Statement 3	*Statement 6*

Modify the code fragment to guarantee that Statement 5 occurs before Statement 2. Use a semaphore.

24. Each of the following code fragments contains a bug in the entry or exit section. For each fragment, state whether mutual exclusion still holds. If not, show an execution sequence that violates it. State whether deadlock can occur. If so, show an execution sequence that produces it.

*(a)

Process P1	Process P2
do	do
wait(mutEx);	signal(mutEx);
critical section	*critical section*
signal(mutEx);	wait(mutEx);
remainder section	*remainder section*
while (! done1);	while (! done2);

(b)

Process P1	Process P2
do	do
signal(mutEx);	signal(mutEx);
critical section	*critical section*
wait(mutEx);	wait(mutEx);
remainder section	*remainder section*
while (! done1);	while (! done2);

(c)

Process P1	Process P2
do	do
wait(mutEx);	wait(mutEx);
critical section	*critical section*
signal(mutEx);	wait(mutEx);
remainder section	*remainder section*
while (! done1);	while (! done2);

(d)

Process P1
```
do
    wait(mutEx);
    critical section
    signal(mutEx);
    remainder section
while (! done1);
```

Process P2
```
do
    wait(mutEx);
    critical section
    remainder section
while (! done2);
```

(e)

Process P1
```
do
    wait(mutEx);
    critical section
    signal(mutEx);
    remainder section
while (! done1);
```

Process P2
```
do
    critical section
    signal(mutEx);
    remainder section
while (! done2);
```

Section 8.4

25. An operating system has processes P1, P2, P3, and P4 and resources R1 (one resource), R2 (one resource), R3 (two resources), and R4 (three resources). The notation (1, 1), (2, 2), (1, 2) means that P1 requests R1, then P2 requests R2, then P1 requests R2. Note that the first two requests produce allocation edges on the resource allocation graph, but the third request produces a request edge on the graph because R2 is already allocated to P2.

    Draw the resource allocation graph after each sequence of requests. State whether the graph contains a cycle. If it does, state whether it is a deadlock cycle.

    *(a) (1, 1), (2, 2), (1, 2), (2, 1)
    *(b) (1, 4), (2, 4), (3, 4), (4, 4)
    (c) (1, 1), (2, 1), (3, 1), (4, 1)
    (d) (3, 3), (4, 3), (2, 2), (3, 2), (2, 3)
    (e) (1, 2), (1, 3), (1, 4), (2, 2), (2, 3), (2, 4)
    (f) (2, 1), (1, 2), (2, 3), (3, 3), (2, 2), (1, 3)
    (g) (2, 1), (1, 2), (2, 3), (3, 3), (2, 2), (1, 3), (3, 1)
    (h) (1, 4), (2, 3), (3, 3), (2, 1), (3, 4), (1, 3), (4, 4), (3, 1), (2, 4)
    (i) (1, 4), (2, 3), (3, 3), (2, 1), (3, 4), (1, 3), (4, 4), (3, 1), (2, 4), (4, 3)

PROBLEMS

Section 8.2

26. Implement a new unary instruction in place of NOP0 called ASL2 that does two left shifts on the accumulator. V should remain unchanged, but N and Z should correlate with the new value in the accumulator, and C should be the carry from the second shift. Write a program that tests all the features of the new instruction.

27. Implement a new nonunary instruction in place of NOP called ASLMANY whose operand is the number of times the accumulator is shifted left. Allow immediate, direct, and

stack-relative addressing. V should remain unchanged, but N and Z should correlate with the value in the accumulator, and C should be the carry from the last shift. Write a program that tests all the features of the new instruction.

28. Implement a new nonunary instruction in place of NOP called MULA that multiplies the operand by the accumulator and puts the result in the accumulator. Allow immediate, direct, and stack-relative addressing. V and C should remain unchanged, but N and Z should correlate with the value in the accumulator. Write a program that tests all the features of the new instruction.

29. Direct addressing is immediate addressing deferred. Indirect addressing is direct addressing deferred. You can carry this concept one level further with double indirect addressing, which is indirect addressing deferred. Implement a new instruction in place of NOP0 with mnemonic STADI, which stands for Store Accumulator Double Indirect. It should store the accumulator using double indirect addressing. Execute it with the following program as a test.

```
0000  04000F         BR     main
0003  0000   num1:   .BLOCK 2         ;num1
0005  0003   num1ad: .ADDRSS num1     ;Address of num1
0007  0005   num1adad:.ADDRSS num1ad  ;Address of address of num1
0009  0000   num2:   .BLOCK 2         ;num2
000B  0009   num2ad: .ADDRSS num2     ;Address of num2
000D  000B   num2adad:.ADDRSS num2ad  ;Address of address of num2
000F  C0001B main:   LDA    27,i      ;Load accumulator
0012  24             STADI            ;Store num1 double indirect
0013  0007           .ADDRSS num1adad
0015  C00022         LDA    34,i      ;Load accumulator
0018  24             STADI            ;Store num2 double indirect
0019  000D           .ADDRSS num2adad
001B  390003         DECO   num1,d    ;Output num1
001E  500020         CHARO  ' ',i
0021  390009         DECO   num2,d    ;Output num2
0024  50000A         CHARO  '\n',i
0027  00             STOP
0028                 .END
```

NOP0 is a unary instruction as far as the assembler and CPU are concerned, but your program must implement it as a nonunary instruction. You will need to increment the saved PC to skip over the operand specifier.

30. Implement a new unary instruction in place of NOP called HEXO that outputs the content of the operand in hexadecimal. Allow immediate, direct, and stack-relative addressing. Write a program that tests all the features of the new instruction.

31. Implement a new nonunary instruction in place of NOP called BOOLO, which means boolean output. It should output false if the operand is zero and true otherwise. Allow immediate, direct, and stack-relative addressing. Write a program that tests all the features of the new instruction.

32. Implement a new unary instruction in place of NOPO called STACKADD. It should replace the two topmost items on the stack with their sum. For example, the code fragment

```
LDA        5,i        ;Push 5
STA        -2,s
LDA        9,i        ;Push 9
STA        -4,s
SUBSP      4,i
STACKADD              ;Add 5 + 9
DECO       0,s        ;Output top of stack
ADDSP      2,i        ;Pop the sum
```

should output the sum of 5 and 9.

33. This problem is to implement new nonunary instructions to process floating point numbers. Assume floating point numbers are stored with all the special values of IEEE 754 but with a two-byte cell having one sign bit, six exponent bits, nine significand bits, and a hidden bit. The exponent uses excess 31 notation except for denormalized numbers, which use excess 30.

   (a) Implement a new unary instruction in place of DECO called BINFO, which stands for binary floating point output. Permit the same addressing modes as with DECO. The value 3540 (hex), which represents the normalized number 1.101×2^{-5}, should be output as 1.101000000b011010, where the letter b stands for two raised to a power and the bit sequence following the b is the excess 30 representation of -5. The value 0050 (hex), which represents the denormalized number 0.00101×2^{-30}, should be output as 0.001010000b-30, where the power will always be -30 for denormalized numbers. Output a NaN value as NaN, positive infinity as inf, and negative infinity as -inf.

   (b) Implement a new unary instruction in place of DECI called BINFI, which stands for binary floating point input. Permit the same addressing modes as with DECI. Assume that the input will be a normalized binary number. The input 1.101000000b011010, which represents the normalized number 1.101×2^{-5}, should be stored as 3540 (hex).

   (c) Implement a new unary instruction in place of NOP called ADDFA, which stands for add floating point accumulator. Permit the same addressing modes as with ADDA. For normalized and denormalized numbers you may assume that the exponent fields of the two numbers to add are identical, but the exponent field of the sum may not be the same as the initial exponent fields. Your implementation will need to insert the hidden bit before performing the addition and remove it when storing the result. Take into account the possibility that one or both of the operands may be a NaN or infinity.

   (d) Work Part (c) assuming the exponent fields of the normalized or denormalized numbers may not be identical.

Chapter

9

Storage Management

The purpose of an operating system is to provide a convenient environment for higher-level programming and to allocate the resources of the system efficiently. Chapter 8 shows how the operating system allocates CPU time to the processes in the system. This chapter shows how it allocates space. The two primary classes of storage space are main memory and peripheral memory. Disk memory is the most common peripheral storage and is the type described here.

Two primary classes of storage space

9.1 Memory Allocation

Normally, programs that are not executing reside in a disk file. To execute, a program needs main memory space and CPU time. The operating system allocates space by loading the program from disk into main memory. It allocates time by setting the program counter to the address of the first instruction loaded into main memory.

The first two sections of this chapter describe five techniques for allocating main memory space:

- Uniprogramming
- Fixed-partition multiprogramming
- Variable-partition multiprogramming
- Paging
- Virtual memory

Main memory allocation techniques

The techniques are listed in order of increasing complexity. Each improves on the previous technique by solving a performance problem. A sixth technique, segmentation, is beyond the scope of this book.

Uniprogramming

The simplest memory allocation technique is *uniprogramming*, exemplified by the Pep/8 operating system. The operating system resides at one end of memory, and the application resides at the other end. The system executes only one job at a time.

Because every job will be loaded at the same place, the translators can generate object code accordingly. For example, the Pep/8 assembler computes the symbols for the symbol table assuming that the first byte will be loaded at address 0000 (hex). Or, if the program contains a burn directive, it assumes that the last byte will be loaded at the address at the bottom of memory.

Uniprogramming has advantages and disadvantages. Its main advantage comes from its size. The system can be small, simple to design, and therefore, relatively bug-free. It also executes with little overhead. Once an application is loaded, that application is guaranteed 100% of the processor's time, since no other process will interrupt it. Uniprocessing systems are appropriate for embedded systems.

Advantages of uniprogramming

The primary disadvantages are the inefficient use of CPU time and the inflexibility of job scheduling. Compared to main memory, disk memory has long access time. If the application executes a read from disk, the CPU will remain idle while waiting for the disk to deliver the input. The time could better be used executing another user's job. You can tolerate some waste of CPU time in a microcomputer, but in a computer that costs an organization hundreds of thousands of dollars you cannot, especially in a multiuser system in which other processes are executing concurrently.

Disadvantages of uniprogramming

Even in a single-user system, the inflexibility of job scheduling can be a nuisance. The user may want to start up two programs and switch back and forth between them without quitting either one. For example, you may want to run a word processor for a while, switch to a drawing program to create an illustration for your document, and then switch back to the word processor where you left off to continue the text.

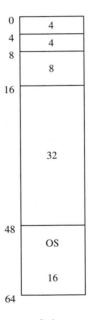

Fixed-Partition Multiprogramming

Multiprogramming solves the problem of inefficient CPU usage by allowing more than one application to run concurrently. To switch between two processes, the operating system loads both applications into main memory. When the running process is suspended, the operating system stores its process control block and gives the CPU to the other process.

To implement multiprogramming, the operating system needs to partition main memory into different regions for storing the different processes while they execute. In a fixed-partition scheme, it subdivides memory into several regions whose sizes and locations do not change with time. Figure 9.1 shows one possible subdivision in a fixed-partition multiprogramming system with 64 KB of main memory. The operating system occupies 16 KB at the bottom of memory. It assumes that the jobs will not all be the same size, so it partitions the remaining 48 KB into two 4-KB regions, one 8-KB region, and one 32-KB region.

Figure **9.1**

Fixed partitions in a 64-KB main memory. Partition sizes and addresses are in kilobytes. The operating system occupies the bottom 16 KB.

A problem with providing different regions of memory for different processes is that the memory references in the object code must be adjusted accordingly. Suppose an assembly language programmer writes an application that is 20 KB long, and the operating system loads it into the 32-KB partition. If the assembler assumes that the object code will be loaded starting at address zero, all the memory references will be wrong.

The address problem

For example, suppose the first few lines of code are

```
0000 040005          BR      AbsVal
0003 0000    number:  .BLOCK  2
0005 310003 AbsVal:   DECI    number,d
```

The assembler has computed the value of symbol AbsVal to be 0005 because BR is a three-byte instruction and number occupies two bytes. The problem is that BR branches to 0005, the address of the code for the process in the first partition. Not only would this process work incorrectly, but it also may destroy some data in the other process. The operating system needs to protect processes from unauthorized tampering by other concurrent processes.

A loader that has the capability of loading a program anywhere in memory is called a relocatable loader. The Pep/8 loader described in Section 8.1 is not a relocatable loader because it loads every program into memory at the same location, namely 0000 (hex).

Relocatable loaders

There are several approaches to this problem. The operating system could require the assembly language programmer to decide where in memory to load the application. The assembler would need a directive that allows the programmer to specify the address of the first byte of object code. A common designation for such a directive is .ORG, which means origin. In this example, the starting address of the 32-KB partition is 16K or 8000 (hex). The first few lines of the listing would be modified as follows:

```
            .ORG    0x8000
8000 048005          BR      AbsVal
8003 0000    number:  .BLOCK  2
8005 318003 AbsVal:   DECI    number,d
```

The net effect is to add 8000 to all the memory references in the application code.

If a compiler generates the object code for an application, the programmer has no concept of memory addresses. The translator would need to cooperate with the operating system to generate the correct memory references in the object code.

Logical Addresses

Requiring the programmer or the compiler to specify in advance where the object code will be loaded has several drawbacks. An applications programmer should not have to worry about partition sizes and locations. That information is not relevant to the programmer. The scheme defeats the purpose of the operating system to provide a convenient environment for higher-level programming.

It also defeats the purpose of allocating the resources of the system efficiently. Suppose the programmer specifies a 3-KB program to be loaded in the second 4-KB partition at address 4K and sets the .ORG directive accordingly. During the course of events, the job may be waiting to be loaded while another job occupies that partition, even though the first 4-KB partition is free. The unused memory represents an inefficient allocation of a resource.

To alleviate these problems, the operating system can let the programmer or compiler generate the object code as if it will be loaded at address zero. An address generated under this assumption is called a *logical address*. If the program is loaded into a partition whose address is not zero, the operating system must translate logical addresses to *physical addresses*.

The following equation depicts the relationship between the physical address, logical address, and address of the first byte of the partition in which the program is loaded:

Physical address = logical address + partition address

Logical address versus physical address

An example is the previous code fragment, in which the logical address of number is 0003 and the physical address is 8003.

Two address-translation techniques are possible. The operating system could provide a software utility that adds the partition address to all the memory references in the object code. The translator would need to specify those parts of the object code that need to be adjusted, because the utility cannot tell by inspection of the raw object code which parts are memory references.

Another technique depends on the availability of specialized hardware called base and bound registers. The *base register* solves the address-translation problem. The *bound register* solves the protection problem. Figure 9.2 shows how base and bound registers work with the previous example.

Operation of base and bound registers

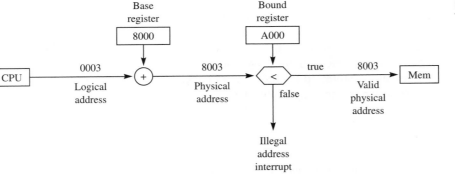

Figure **9.2**

Transformation of a logical address to a physical address with base and bound registers.

The operating system loads the object program with unmodified logical addresses into the partition at 8000. It loads the base register with a value of 8000 and the bound register with a value of A000 (hex) = 48K, the address of the upper bound of the partition in which the program is loaded. It turns the CPU over to the process by setting the program counter to 0000, the logical address of the first instruction.

Whenever the CPU issues a memory read request, the hardware adds the content of the base register to the address supplied by the CPU to form the physical address. It compares the physical address to the content of the bound register. If the physical address is less than the bound register, the hardware completes the memory access. Otherwise, it generates an illegal-address interrupt that the operating system must service. The bound register prevents a process from invading another process's memory partition.

The first memory read request in this example will be from the fetch part of the von Neumann execution cycle. The CPU will request a fetch of the instruction from 0000, which the hardware will translate to a fetch from 8000. Figure 9.2 shows the translation of logical address 0003 from the DECI operand specifier. (Actually, at a lower level of abstraction, it is the operand of the STA instruction at FF0A in the DECI trap handler.)

To switch to another process, the operating system sets the base register to the address of the partition where the process has been loaded and the bound register to the address of the next-higher partition. When it restores the CPU registers (including the program counter) from the PCB, the process will continue executing from where it was suspended.

Consider some of the problems that confront the operating system when it must schedule jobs to occupy the fixed partitions. Assume that all the partitions in Figure 9.1 are occupied except the 32-KB partition. If a 4-KB job requests execution, should the system put it in the 32-KB partition or should it wait until a smaller partition becomes available? Suppose it starts the job in the 32-KB partition, and then a 4-KB process terminates. If a 32-KB job now enters the system, it cannot be loaded. In retrospect, it would have been better to not schedule the small job in the large partition. Then the large job could use the large partition as soon as it requested execution, and the small job could be loaded soon anyway. Because the operating system cannot predict when a process will terminate or when a job will request execution, it cannot achieve the optimum schedule.

Scheduling problems with fixed partitions

Another problem is how the operating system should set up the partitions in the first place. In Figure 9.1, if a 16-KB job and a 32-KB job request execution at the same time, only one can be loaded, even though a total of 48 KB is available in user memory. On the other hand, if the operating system sets up user memory in two large partitions, and six or eight 4-KB jobs request execution, all but two will be delayed. Again, the optimum partition cannot be established because the operating system cannot predict the future.

Variable-Partition Multiprogramming

To alleviate the inefficiencies inherent in fixed-partition scheduling, the operating system can maintain partitions with variable boundaries. The idea is to establish a partition only when a job is loaded into memory. The size of the partition can exactly match the size of the job so more memory will be available to jobs as they enter the system.

When a job stops execution, the region of memory that it occupied becomes available for other jobs. A region of memory that is available for use by incoming jobs is called a *hole*. Holes are filled when the operating system allocates them to subsequent jobs. As in the fixed-partition scheme, the operating system attempts to schedule the jobs to maintain the largest number of processes in memory at any given point in time.

Figure 9.3 shows an example of a 48-KB region of available memory before any jobs are scheduled. Figure 9.4 is a hypothetical sequence of job requests for the user memory in Figure 9.3. The table also indicates when a job stops executing, thereby releasing its memory for another job to use.

Figure 9.5 illustrates the scheduling process. The question that must be resolved is the selection criterion for determining which hole to fill when a new job requests some memory. Figure 9.5 uses what is called the *best-fit algorithm*. Of all the holes that are larger than the memory required for the job, the operating system selects the smallest. That is, the system selects the hole that the job fits the best.

When J1 requests 12 KB, there is only one hole from which to allocate memory, the initial hole in Figure 9.3. The system gives the first 12 KB to J1, leaving a 36-KB hole. When J2 requests 8 KB, the system gives the first part of the smaller hole to it, and similarly for J3, J4, and J5. The result is the memory allocation in Figure 9.5(a).

Figure 9.5(b) shows the allocation when J1 stops executing, relinquishing its 12 KB and creating a second hole at the top of main memory. When J6 requests a 4-KB region, the operating system has the option of allocating memory for it from either hole. According to the best-fit algorithm, the system selects the 8-KB hole rather than the 12-KB hole, because the smaller hole is a better fit. Figure 9.5(c) shows the result.

Figure 9.5(d) shows the allocation after J5 stops, and (e) shows it after the system allocates memory from the top hole to J7. There are now three small holes scattered throughout memory. This phenomenon is called *fragmentation*. Even though J8 wants 8 KB and available memory totals 12 KB, J8 cannot run because the memory is not contiguous.

When confronted with a request that cannot be satisfied because of fragmented memory, the operating system could simply wait for enough processes to complete until a large enough hole becomes available. In this example, the request is so small that any job that completes will free enough memory for J8 to be loaded.

In a crowded system running many small jobs with a large request outstanding, the request may be pending for a long time before allocation. In such a case, the

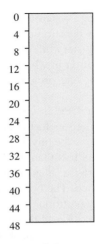

Figure **9.3**

The initial available user memory. Addresses are in kilobytes.

Job	Size	Action
J1	12	Start
J2	8	Start
J3	12	Start
J4	4	Start
J5	4	Start
J1	12	Stop
J6	4	Start
J5	4	Stop
J7	8	Start
J8	8	Start

Figure **9.4**

A job execution sequence for a variable-partition multiprogramming system. Job size is in kilobytes.

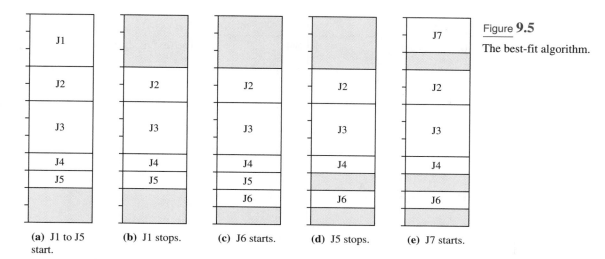

Figure **9.5**

The best-fit algorithm.

(a) J1 to J5 start. **(b)** J1 stops. **(c)** J6 starts. **(d)** J5 stops. **(e)** J7 starts.

operating system may take time to move some processes to make a large enough hole to satisfy the request. This operation is called *compaction*.

Figure 9.6(a) shows the most straightforward compaction technique. The operating system shifts the processes up in memory, eliminating all the holes between them. Another possible compaction scheme is to move only enough processes to create a hole big enough to satisfy the request. In Figure 9.6(b), the system shifts only J6, leaving a large enough hole to load J8.

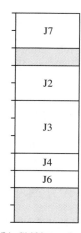

Figure **9.6**

Compacting main memory.

(a) Shifting all jobs to the top.   **(b)** Shifting only J6.

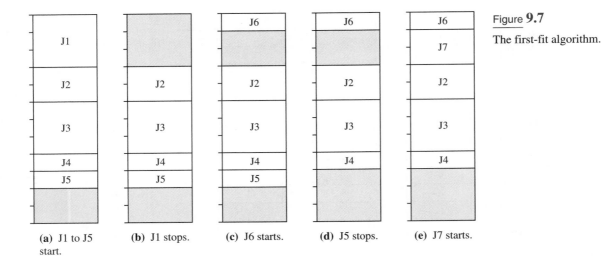

Figure **9.7**

The first-fit algorithm.

(a) J1 to J5 start.   (b) J1 stops.   (c) J6 starts.   (d) J5 stops.   (e) J7 starts.

The idea behind the best-fit algorithm is to minimize fragmentation by using the smallest hole possible, leaving the larger holes available for future scheduling. Another scheduling technique that may not appear as reasonable is the *first-fit algorithm*. Rather than search for the smallest possible hole, this algorithm begins its search from the top of main memory, allocating memory from the first hole that can accommodate the request. Figure 9.7 is a trace of the first-fit algorithm for the request sequence of Figure 9.4.

Figure 9.7(a) and (b) are identical to the best-fit algorithm of Figure 9.5. In Figure 9.7(c), J6 requests a 4-KB partition. Rather than allocate from the smaller hole at the bottom of memory, the first-fit algorithm finds the hole at the top of memory first, from which it allocates storage for J6.

Figure 9.7(d) shows J5 terminating. In (e), the 8-KB request from J7 is filled by the first available hole, which is between J6 and J2. When J8 requests 8 KB, a hole is available, and the system does not need to compact memory.

One example does not prove that first fit is better than best fit. In fact, you can devise a sequence of requests and releases that will require compaction under the first-fit algorithm before best fit. The question is "What happens on the average?" It turns out that in practice, neither algorithm is substantially superior to the other in terms of memory utilization.

First fit versus best fit

The reason first fit works so well is that storage tends to be allocated from the top of main memory. Therefore, large holes tend to form at the bottom of main memory. That is what happens in Figure 9.7.

Regardless of the allocation strategy, fragmentation is unavoidable in a variable-partition system. Noncontiguous holes represent an inefficient allocation of a resource. Even though unusable memory regions can be reclaimed with compaction, that is a time-consuming procedure.

Paging

Paging is an ingenious idea to alleviate the fragmentation problem. Rather than coalesce several small holes to form one big hole for the program, paging fragments the program to fit the holes. Programs are no longer contiguous, but broken up and scattered throughout main memory.

The idea behind paging

Figure 9.8 shows three jobs executing in a paged system. Each job is subdivided into pages, and main memory is subdivided into frames that are the same size as the pages. The figure shows the first 12 KB of a 64-KB memory with 1-KB frames. The page size is always a power of 2, in practice usually 512, 1024, or 2048 bytes.

The code for job J3 is distributed to four noncontiguous frames in main memory. J3, P0 in the frame at 1800 represents page 0 of job J3. The second page is at 2C00, and the third and fourth pages are at 0800 and 2000, respectively. Jobs J1 and J2 are similarly scattered throughout memory. If job J4 comes along and needs 3 KB of memory, the operating system can distribute its pages to 0400, 1000, and 1400. The system does not need to compact memory to allocate it to the incoming job.

As with the previous multiprogramming memory management techniques, the application programs in paging assume logical addresses. The operating system must convert logical addresses to physical addresses during execution.

Figure 9.9 shows the relationship between a logical address and a physical address in the paged system of Figure 9.8. Because a page contains 1 KB, which

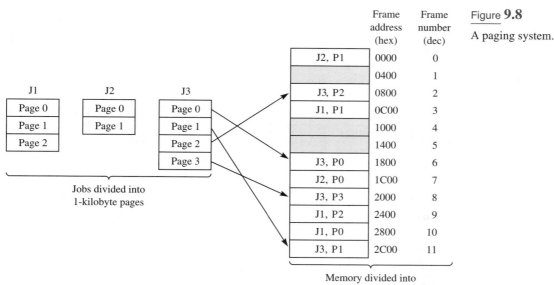

Figure 9.8

A paging system.

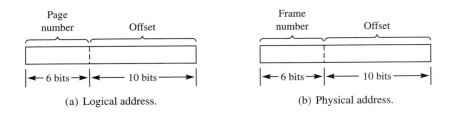

|← 6 bits →|← 10 bits →| |← 6 bits →|← 10 bits →|

(a) Logical address.   (b) Physical address.

Figure **9.9**

The logical and physical addresses
in a paging system.

is 2^{10}, the rightmost 10 bits of a logical address are the offset from the top of the page. The leftmost 6 bits are the page number.

For example, consider the address 058F, which is 0000 0101 1000 1111 in binary. The leftmost 6 bits are 0000 01, which means that the address corresponds to a memory location in page number 1. Because 01 1000 1111 is 399 (dec), the logical address represents the 399th byte from the first byte in page number 1.

Referring to Figure 9.8, the physical address of this byte is the 399th byte from the first byte in the frame at address 2C00. To translate the logical address to the physical address, the operating system must replace the 6-bit page number, 0000 01, with the 6-bit frame number, 0010 11, leaving the offset unchanged.

One base register was enough to transform a logical address to a physical address in the previous memory management schemes. Paging requires a set of frame numbers, however—one for each page of the job. Such a set is called a *page table*. Figure 9.10 shows the page table associated with job J3 of Figure 9.8. Each entry in the page table is the frame number that must replace the page number in the logical address.

Figure **9.10**

Transformation of a logical address to a physical address with a page table.

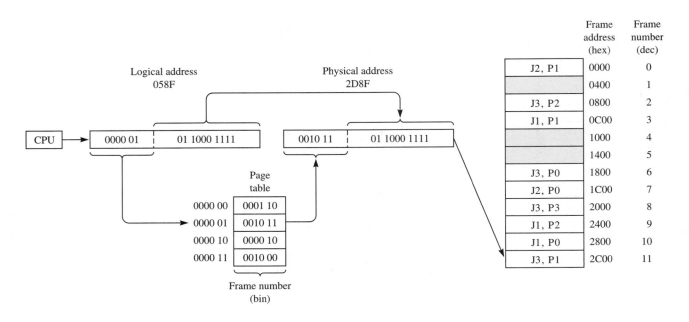

Suppose job J3 executes the statement

```
LDBYTEA 0x058F,d
```

which causes the CPU to request a memory read from logical address 058F. The operating system extracts the first 6 bits, 0000 01, and uses them as an address in the page table, a special-purpose hardware memory that stores the frame numbers for the job. The frame number from the page table replaces the page number in the logical address to produce the physical address.

The byte is read from physical location 2D8F, even though the CPU issued a request for a read from location 058F. The program executes under the illusion that it has been loaded into a contiguous memory region starting at address 0000. The operating system perpetrates the illusion by maintaining a page table for each process loaded into memory. It is the ultimate scam. A process is continually interrupted in time and scattered through space without being aware of either indignity.

It is important to note that paging does not eliminate fragmentation altogether. It is rare that a job's size will be an exact multiple of the page size for the system. In that case, the last page will contain some unused memory, as Figure 9.11 shows for job J3. The unused memory at the end of the last page in a job is called *internal fragmentation* in contrast to the external fragmentation that is visible to the operating system in the variable-partition scheme.

The smaller the page size, the less the internal fragmentation, on the average. Unfortunately, there is a tradeoff. The smaller the page size, the greater the number of frames for a given main memory size and, therefore, the longer the page table. Because every reference to memory includes an access from a page table, the page tables usually are designed with the fastest possible circuitry. Such circuitry is expensive, so the page tables must be small to minimize the cost.

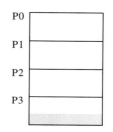

P0

P1

P2

P3

Figure **9.11**

Internal fragmentation.

9.2 Virtual Memory

It may seem unlikely that you could improve on the memory utilization of a paged system, but the paging concept can be carried one step further. Consider the structure of a large program, say one that would fill 50 pages. To execute the program, is it really necessary for all 50 pages to be loaded into main memory at the same time?

Large Program Behavior

Most large programs consist of dozens of procedures, some of which may never execute. For example, procedures that are responsible for processing some input error condition will not execute if the input has no errors. Other procedures, such as those that initialize data, may execute only once and never be needed during the remainder of the execution.

A common control structure in any large program is the loop. As the body of a loop executes repeatedly, only that code in the loop need reside in main memory.

Any code that is far from the loop (from an execution point of view) does not need to be in memory.

A program may also contain large regions of data that are never accessed. For example, if you declare an array of structures in C++ without knowing how many structures will be encountered when the program runs, you allocate more than you would reasonably expect to have. Pages that consist of unaccessed structures never need to be loaded.

These considerations of the typical large program show that it may be feasible to have only the active pages of the program loaded in memory. The active pages are those that contain code that is repeatedly executing and data that is repeatedly being accessed.

The set of active pages is called the *working set*. As the program progresses, new pages enter the working set and old ones leave. For example, at the beginning of execution the pages that contain initialization procedures will be in the working set. Later, the working set will include the pages that contain the processing procedures and not the initialization procedures.

The working set

Virtual Memory

Remember that the programmer at a higher level of abstraction is under the illusion that the program executes in contiguous memory with logical addresses beginning at zero. Suppose the system can be designed to load only a few pages at a time from the executing job while still maintaining the illusion. It then becomes possible for the programmer to write a program that is too large to fit in main memory, but that will execute nonetheless. The user sees not the limited physically installed memory, but a virtual memory that is limited only by the virtual addresses.

For example, in the older Pep/7 computer, an address contains 16 bits. It is, therefore, theoretically possible to access 2^{16} bytes (64 KB) of memory. However, only 32 KB of memory are installed. The application program starts at 0000 and cannot contain more than about 31,000 (dec) bytes without running into the operating system. It is common for a system to contain less memory than that permitted by the number of address bits. That situation allows the owner to upgrade the system at a later date by purchasing additional memory.

Suppose the Pep/7 computer has a virtual memory operating system. The program's physical memory is limited to 3000 bytes, but the programmer still could execute a 64-KB program. The operating system loads the pages from disk into the memory frames as needed to execute the program. When a page needs to be loaded because it contains a statement to execute or some data to access, the operating system removes a page that is no longer active and replaces it with the one that needs to be loaded. The programmer sees the program execute in a 64-KB virtual address space, even though the physical address space is 32 KB.

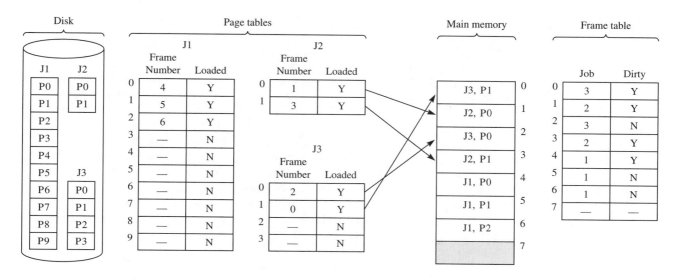

Figure **9.12**

An implementation of virtual memory.

Figure 9.12 shows how paging can be extended to implement a virtual memory system. It shows three jobs in the system, J1 with 10 pages, J2 with 2 pages, and J3 with 4 pages. Notice that physical memory contains only eight frames, but J1 can execute even though it is larger than physical memory. The special hardware required by the operating system includes a page table for each job and one frame table with an entry for each frame. To keep the illustration simple, frame numbers are given in decimal.

The page tables transform logical addresses to physical addresses, as in Figure 9.10. In a virtual memory system, however, some of the pages may not be loaded as the job is running. Each page table contains one extra bit per page that tells the operating system whether the page is loaded. The bit is 1 if the page is loaded and 0 if it is not. Figure 9.12 shows 1 as Y for yes, and 0 as N for no.

The frame table is needed to help the operating system allocate frames from main memory to the various jobs. The first entry is the job allocated to that frame. The second entry is a bit called the *dirty bit*, whose function will be explained shortly.

Demand Paging

Figure 9.12 shows that jobs J1 and J3 do not have all their pages loaded into main memory. Suppose J3 is executing some code in page P1, loaded into frame 0. It will shortly execute a LDA instruction whose operand is in P2. How will the operating system know that J3 is going to need P2 loaded into memory? Because the system cannot predict the future, it cannot know until J3 actually executes the LDA.

Ken Thompson, Dennis M. Ritchie

Ken Thompson was born in 1943 in New Orleans. He earned his master's degree in electrical engineering from The University of California at Berkeley and joined Bell Labs Computing Research in 1966. Dennis Ritchie was born in Bronxville, New York in 1941, and earned his PhD in mathematics from Harvard in 1968. He joined Bell Labs the year after Thompson. At the time, Bell Labs was collaborating with MIT and General Electric on the Multics project headed by Fernando Corbató. Bell Labs pulled out of the project in 1969, however, because it believed that Multics was too ambitious and could not deliver a useable product.

Researchers at Bell Labs did not want to lose the benefits of the Multics time-sharing system and continued to work on developing an operating system that would fill their needs. Their system was named Unix, a pun on the name Multics. So, Unix is not an acronym.

An application prototype for the Bell Labs group was a game Thompson wrote on the Multics system called "Space Travel" that simulated planetary motion in the solar system along with a rocket ship guided by the user. Thompson and Ritchie ported the game to the PDP-7 computer, on which the first Unix file system was implemented.

The earliest versions of Unix were written in assembly language, a tedious process. Thompson and Ritchie did not care for the PL/I language of Multics, as it was too large for the small computers they had at Bell Labs. The BCPL language had been used on the MIT CTSS system but had a few undesirable features. So, Thompson created the B language from it and got it working on the PDP-7.

In 1971, Thompson moved Unix from the PDP-7 to the PDP-11. Porting Unix to a new machine showed the importance of portability considerations in general and the deficiencies of the B language in particular. In 1972, Ritchie created the C language with the express goal of implementing the Unix operating system in an HOL6 language that could be easily ported to different machines. In 1973, Thompson rewrote Unix in Ritchie's C language.

In the mid 1970s, Unix exploded in use at academic research institutions around the world. UC Berkeley created the Berkeley Systems Distribution (BSD) of Unix, which was instrumental in the development of the Internet. In 1987, Andy Tanenbaum wrote an implementation of Unix completely from scratch, called Minix, for use in his operating systems textbook. In 1991, a student in Finland using his book, Linus Torvalds, used the Minix idea to write his own version of Unix known as Linux. Even Apple turned to the BSD version of Unix, on which it based its latest operating system known as OS X.

Ken Thompson and Dennis M. Ritchie won the Turing Award in 1983 for their development of generic operating systems theory and specifically for the implementation of the Unix operating system.

© Alcatel-Lucent. Used with permission.

"Unix is basically a simple operating system, but you have to be a genius to understand the simplicity."

—*Dennis Ritchie*

In the course of translating the logical address to a physical address, the hardware accesses the page table for J3 to determine the frame number of the physical address. Because the loaded bit says N, an interrupt called a *page fault* occurs. The operating system intervenes to service the interrupt.   *Page faults*

When a page fault occurs, the operating system searches the frame table to determine whether there are any empty frames in the system. Figure 9.12 shows that frame 7 is available, so the operating system can load P2 into that frame. It updates the frame table to show that frame 7 contains a page from J3. It updates the page table for J3 to show that P2 is in frame 7, and sets the loaded bit to Y.

When the operating system returns from the interrupt, it sets the program counter to the address of the instruction that caused the page fault. That is, it restarts the instruction. This time, when the hardware accesses the page table for J3, an interrupt will not occur, and the operand of the LDA instruction will be brought into the accumulator.

So when does the operating system load a page into main memory? The answer is, simply, when the program demands it. In the previous example, J3 demanded that P2 be loaded via the page fault interrupt mechanism. The difference between paging and demand paging is that demand paging brings pages into main memory only on demand. If a page is never demanded, it will never be loaded.

Page Replacement

When J3 demanded that P2 be loaded, the operating system had no problem because there was an empty frame in main memory. Suppose, however, that a job demands a page when all the frames are filled. In that case, the operating system must select a page that was previously loaded and replace it, freeing its frame for the demanded page.

The replaced page may subsequently be loaded again, perhaps into a different frame. To ensure that the page is reloaded in the same state that it was in when it was replaced, the operating system may need to save its state by writing the page to disk when the page is replaced. On the other hand, it may not be necessary to write the page to the disk when it is replaced.

Deciding whether the state of the replaced page needs to be updated on disk

In Figure 9.12, J1 has 10 pages stored on disk, 3 of which have been loaded into main memory. When J1 executes instructions such as LDA and ASLA, the effect is to not change the state of a page in main memory. LDA issues a memory read and places the operand in the accumulator. ASLA changes the accumulator, an action that involves neither a memory read nor a memory write. Neither instruction issues a memory write.

But when J1 executes an instruction such as STA, the instruction changes the state of the page in main memory. STA puts the content of the accumulator in the operand, issuing a memory write in the process. If the operand is in P0 in frame 4, P0's state will change in main memory. Page P0 on disk will no longer be an exact copy of the current P0 in main memory. If no store instruction ever executes, the image of the page on disk will be an exact replica of the page in main memory.

When the operating system selects a page for replacement during a page fault, it does not need to write the page back to disk if the disk image is still a replica of the page in memory. To help the operating system decide whether the write is necessary, the hardware contains a special bit, called the dirty bit, in the frame table.

The dirty bit

When a page is first loaded into an empty frame, the operating system sets the dirty bit to 0, indicated by N in Figure 9.12. If a store instruction ever issues a write to memory, the hardware sets the dirty bit for that frame to 1, indicated by Y in the figure. Such a page is said to be dirty because it has been altered from its original clean state. If a page is selected for replacement, the operating system inspects the dirty bit to check whether it must write the page back to disk before overwriting the frame with the new page.

Page-Replacement Algorithms

The operating system has two memory management tasks in a demand paged system. It must allocate frames to jobs, and it must select a page for replacement when a page fault occurs and all the frames are full.

A reasonable allocation strategy for frames is to assume that a large job will need more frames than a small job. The system can allocate frames proportionally. If J1 is twice as big as J2, it gets twice as many frames in which to execute.

Frame allocation strategy

Given that a job has a fixed number of frames in which to execute, how does the operating system decide which page to replace when a page fault occurs and all the job's frames are full? Two possible page-replacement algorithms are *first in, first out* (FIFO) and *least-recently used* (LRU).

Page-replacement strategies

Figure 9.13 shows the behavior of the FIFO page-replacement algorithm in a system that has allocated three frames to a job. As a job executes, the CPU sends a continuous stream of read and write requests to main memory. The first group of bits in each address is the page number, as Figures 9.9 and 9.10 show. The page references are the sequence of page numbers that the executing job generates.

Figure 9.13 shows three empty frames available before the first request. When the job demands P6, a page fault is generated, indicated by F in the figure, and P6 is loaded into a frame.

When the job demands P8, another page fault is generated and P8 is loaded into an empty frame. The boxes do not represent particular page frames. The figure shows P6 shifting to a lower box to accommodate P8. In the computer, P6 does not shift to another frame.

The reference to P3 causes another page fault, but the following reference to P8 does not because P8 is still in the set of loaded pages. Similarly, the reference to P6 does not produce a page fault.

Figure **9.13**

The FIFO page-replacement algorithm with three frames.

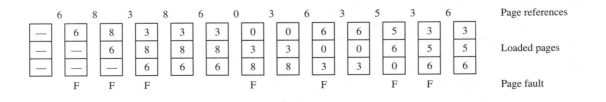

Page references

Loaded pages

Page fault

The reference to P0 triggers a page fault interrupt that must be serviced by selecting a replacement page. The FIFO algorithm replaces the page that was the first to enter the set. Because the figure shifts the pages down to accommodate a new page, the first page in is the one at the bottom, P6. The operating system replaces P6 with P0.

The given sequence of 12 page references produces 7 page faults when the job has three frames. If the job has more frames, the same sequence of page references should generate fewer page faults. Figure 9.14 shows the FIFO algorithm with the same page reference sequence but with four frames. As expected, the sequence generates fewer page faults.

In general, you would expect the number of page faults to decrease with an increase in the number of frames, as Figure 9.15(a) shows, and as the two previous examples illustrate. Early in the development of demand paging systems, however, a curious phenomenon was discovered in which a given page reference sequence with the FIFO page-replacement algorithm actually produced more page faults with a greater number of frames.

A page reference sequence with this property is

0, 1, 2, 3, 0, 1, 4, 0, 1, 2, 3, 4

Figure 9.15(b) is a plot of the number of page faults versus the number of frames for this sequence. It turns out that more page faults are generated with four frames than with three frames. This phenomenon is called *Belady's anomaly* after L.A. Belady, who discovered it.

Belady's anomaly

The FIFO algorithm selects the page that has been in the set of frames the longest. That may appear to be a reasonable criterion. As the job executes it will enter into new regions of code and data, so pages from the old region will no longer be needed. The oldest page is the one replaced.

On further reflection, however, it may be better to consider not how long a page has been in the set of frames, but how long it has been since a page was last referenced. The idea behind LRU is that a page referenced recently in the past is more likely to be referenced in the near future than a page that has not been referenced as recently.

Figure 9.16 illustrates the LRU page-replacement algorithm with the same sequence of page references as in Figure 9.13. The demands for P6, P8, and P3 produce a state identical to that of the FIFO algorithm. The next request for P8 brings

Figure **9.14**

The FIFO page-replacement algorithm with four frames.

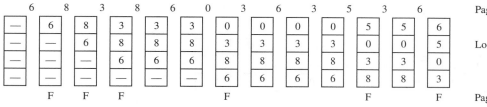

	6	8	3	8	6	0	3	6	3	5	3	6	Page references
—	6	8	3	3	3	0	0	0	0	5	5	6	
—	—	6	8	8	8	3	3	3	3	0	0	5	Loaded pages
—	—	—	6	6	6	8	8	8	8	3	3	0	
—	—	—	—	—	6	6	6	6	6	8	8	3	
	F	F	F			F				F		F	Page fault

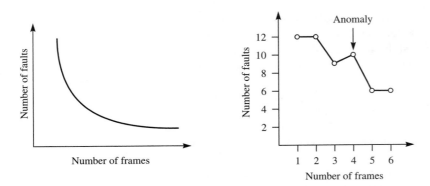

(a) The expected effect of more frames on the number of page faults.

(b) Belady's anomaly with the FIFO replacement algorithm.

Figure **9.15**

The effect of more frames on the number of page faults.

that page to the top box to indicate that P8 is now the most-recently used. The following request for P6 brings it to the top, shifting down P8 and P3. The boxes maintain the pages in order of previous use, with the least-recently used page at the bottom.

For this sequence, the LRU algorithm produced one fewer page fault than the FIFO algorithm did. One example does not prove that LRU is better than FIFO. It is possible to construct a sequence for which FIFO produces fewer faults than LRU.

In practice, operating systems have their own unique page-replacement algorithms that depend on the hardware features available on the particular computer. Most page-replacement algorithms are approximations to LRU, which generally works better than FIFO with the page request sequences from real jobs. An indication that LRU is better from a theoretical point of view is the fact that Belady's anomaly cannot occur with LRU replacement.

The sequences of page references in the previous examples only illustrate the page-replacement algorithms and are not realistic. For a demand paging system to be effective, the page fault rate needs to be kept to less than about one fault per 100,000 memory references.

A properly designed virtual memory system based on demand paging satisfies both goals of an operating system. It offers a convenient environment for higher-level programming because the programmer can develop code without being

Figure **9.16**

The LRU page-replacement algorithm with three frames.

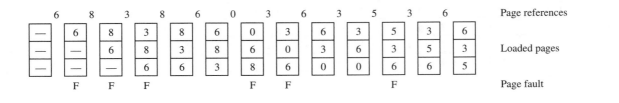

Page references

Loaded pages

Page fault

restricted by the limits of physical memory. It also allocates the memory efficiently because a job's pages are loaded only if needed.

9.3   File Management

The operating system is also responsible for maintaining the collection of files on disk. A file is an abstract data type (ADT). To the user of the system, a file contains a sequence of data and can be manipulated either by a program or by operating system commands. Common operations on files include

- Create a new file.
- Delete a file.
- Rename a file.
- Open a file for reading.
- Read the next data item from the file.

Common operations on files

The operating system makes the connection between the logical organization of the file as seen by a programmer at Level HOL6 or Level Asmb5 and the physical organization on the disk itself.

Disk Drives

Figure 9.17 shows the physical characteristics of a disk drive. Part (a) shows a hard disk drive that consists of several platters coated with magnetic recording material.

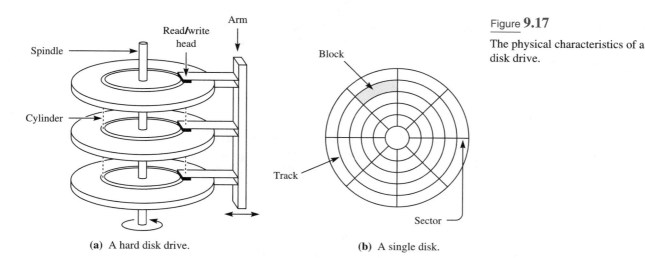

(a) A hard disk drive.   **(b)** A single disk.

Figure **9.17**

The physical characteristics of a disk drive.

They are attached to a central *spindle* that rotates at a typical speed of 5,400 revolutions per minute. Adjacent to each disk surface is a *read/write head* attached to an *arm*. The arm can move the heads in a radial direction across the surface of the platters.

Figure 9.17(b) shows a single disk. With the arm in a fixed position, the area under a read/write head sweeps out a ring as the disk rotates. Each ring is a *track* that stores a sequence of bits. Tracks are divided into pie-shaped *sectors*. A *block* is one sector of one track of one surface. A *cylinder* is the set of tracks on all the surfaces at a fixed arm position. A *block address* consists of three numbers—a cylinder number, a surface number, and a sector number.

Floppy disks are similar to hard disks except that the platter is flexible. In a floppy disk drive, the read/write heads are in physical contact with the surface of the disk. In a hard disk drive, the read/write heads float just above the surface on a small cushion of air. A *head crash* in a hard disk is a mechanical failure in which the head scrapes the surface, damaging the recording material.

Floppy disks

Reading the information from a given block is a four-step process: (1) The arm must move the heads to the designated cylinder. (2) The electronic circuitry must select the read/write head on the designated surface. (3) A period of time must elapse for the designated block to reach the read/write head. (4) The entire block must pass beneath the head to be read. Step 2 is an electronic function, which occurs in negligible time compared to the other three steps.

Reading a block from a disk

Associated with the three mechanical steps are the following times:

- Seek time

- Latency

- Transmission time

Contributions to the disk access time

Seek time is the time it takes the arm to move to the designated cylinder. *Latency* is the time it takes the block to reach the head once the head is in place. *Transmission time* is the time it takes the block to pass beneath the head. The time it takes to access a block is the sum of these three times.

File Abstraction

The user at a high level of abstraction does not want to be bothered with physical tracks and sectors. The operating system hides the details of the physical organization and presents the file with a logical organization to the user as an ADT.

For example, in C++ when you execute the statement

```
someFile >> data1
```

where `someFile` has type `ifstream` from `<fstream>`, you have a logical image of `someFile` as a linear sequence of items with a current position maintained somewhere in the sequence. The >> operation gets the item at the current position and advances the current position to the next item in the sequence.

Physically, the items in the file may be on different tracks and surfaces. Furthermore, there is no physical current position that is maintained by the hardware. The logical behavior of the read statement is due to the operating system software.

Allocation Techniques

The remainder of this section describes three memory-allocation techniques at the physical level—contiguous, linked, and indexed. Each technique requires the operating system to maintain a directory that records the physical location of the files. The directory is itself stored on the disk, along with the files.

If each file were small enough to fit in a single block, the file system would be simple to maintain. The directory would simply contain a list of the files on the disk. Each entry in the directory would have the name of the file and the address of the block in which the file was stored.

If a file is too big to fit in a single block, the operating system must allocate several blocks for it. With *contiguous allocation*, the operating system matches the physical organization of the file to the logical organization by laying out the file sequentially on adjacent blocks of one track.

Contiguous allocation

If the file is too big to fit on a single track, the system continues it on a second track. On a single-sided floppy disk, the second track would be adjacent to the first track on the same surface. On a double-sided floppy or a hard disk, the second track would be on the same cylinder as the first track. If the file is too big to fit on a single cylinder, the file would continue on an adjacent cylinder.

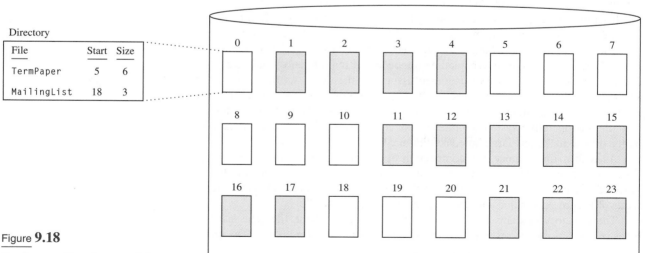

Directory

File	Start	Size
TermPaper	5	6
MailingList	18	3

Figure **9.18**

Contiguous allocation on a disk.

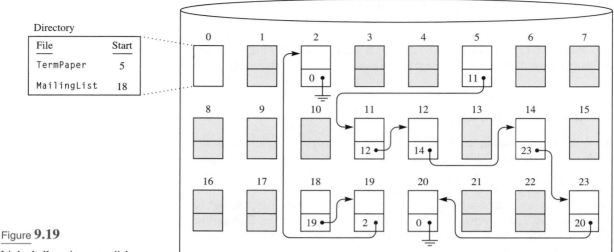

Figure **9.19**

Linked allocation on a disk.

Figure 9.18 is a schematic diagram of contiguous allocation. Each row of eight blocks represents one track divided into eight sectors, as in Figure 9.17(b). The single number above each block is the block address, an abbreviation for the three numbers required to specify the address. Block 0 contains the directory.

The directory lists the name of each file, its starting address, and its size. The file TermPaper starts at block 5 and contains six blocks. Its last three blocks are continued on a second track. Why wouldn't the system allocate blocks 1 through 6 for this file? The configuration in the figure could arise if another file previously occupied blocks 1 through 4, and then was deleted from the disk by the user.

The pattern of occupied and unoccupied disk memory in Figure 9.18 looks suspiciously like the pattern of occupied and unoccupied main memory in Figures 9.5 and 9.7. In fact, the memory management issues are the same. As files are created and deleted, they become fragmented. It may be impossible to create a new file because many small holes are scattered throughout the disk. To make room for the new file, the operating system supplies a disk compaction utility that shifts the files on the disk to make one large hole, as in Figure 9.6.

As with main memory, the compaction operation on disk is time-consuming. To eliminate the need for compaction, the operating system can store the file in blocks that are physically scattered throughout the disk. The linked allocation technique of Figure 9.19 is one way the system can maintain the file.

Linked allocation

The directory contains the address of the first block of the file. The last few bytes of each block are reserved for the address of the following block. The entire

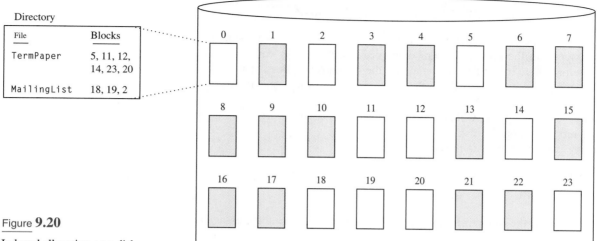

Directory

File	Blocks
TermPaper	5, 11, 12, 14, 23, 20
MailingList	18, 19, 2

Figure **9.20**

Indexed allocation on a disk.

sequence of blocks forms a linked list. The link field in the last block has a nil value that acts like a sentinel.

One disadvantage of the linked technique is its susceptibility to failure. In Figure 9.19, suppose that just one byte in the link field of block 10 is damaged, either by a hardware failure or by a software bug. The operating system can still access the first three blocks of the file, but it will have no way of knowing where the last three blocks are.

The indexed allocation technique in Figure 9.20 collects all the addresses into a single list called an *index* in the directory. Now if a single byte in address 10 in the index is damaged, the operating system will lose track of only one block.

Indexed allocation

Contiguous allocation does have one major advantage over noncontiguous allocation: speed. If a file is contained on one cylinder, you only need to wait for one seek and one latency period to begin the access. You can read the entire file at a speed that is limited only by the transmission time. Even if the file is not all on one cylinder, after you read the first cylinder, you only need to wait for a short seek to an adjacent cylinder.

With the blocks of one file scattered throughout the disk, you must endure a seek time and a latency time to access each block. Even with noncontiguous allocation, it is sometimes worthwhile to periodically reorganize the physical layout of the files to make their blocks contiguous. This operation is called *defragmenting* the disk.

9.4   Error Detecting and Correcting Codes

To be reliable, computer systems must be able to deal with the physical errors that inevitably happen in the real world. For example, if you send an email message over the Internet, there might be some static on the transmission lines that changes one or more of your bits. The result is that the receiver does not get the same bit pattern that you sent. As another example, the system might send some data from main memory to a disk drive, which due to a transient mechanical problem, might store an altered pattern on the disk.

There are two approaches to the error problem.

- Detect the error and retransmit or discard the received message.
- Correct the error.

Both approaches use the same technique of adding redundant bits to the message to detect or correct the error.

Error-Detecting Codes

Suppose you want to send a message about weather conditions. There are four possibilities—sunny, cloudy, raining, or snowing. The sender and receiver agree on the following bit patterns to encode the information:

00, sunny

01, cloudy

10, raining

11, snowing

It is raining, so the sender sends 10. But an error occurs on the transmission line that flips the last 0 to 1. So the receiver gets 11, and concludes erroneously that it is snowing.

A simple way to detect whether an error occurs is to append a redundant bit, called the *parity bit*, to the message using some computation that the sender and receiver agree upon. A common convention is to make the parity bit 0 or 1 in such a way that the total number of 1's is even. With this scheme, the sender and receiver agree on the following bit patterns, where the parity bit is underlined:

00<u>0</u>, sunny

01<u>1</u>, cloudy

10<u>1</u>, raining

11<u>0</u>, snowing

Now the sender would send 101 for the raining message. If an error flips the 0 to 1 so that the receiver gets 111, the receiver can conclude that an error occurred, because 111 is not one of the agreed-upon bit patterns. She can then request a retransmission or discard the received message.

Note that if the error occurs in the parity bit, the received message is just as useless as if it occurs in one of the data bits. For example, if the receiver gets 111 she does not know if the error was in the first bit with 011 sent, the second bit with 101 sent, or the third bit with 110 sent. She only knows that an error occurred.

The scheme would also work if the sender and receiver agreed to use odd parity, where the parity bit is computed to make the total number of 1's odd. The only necessity is for the sender and receiver to agree on the parity computation.

What if two errors occur during transmission, so that not only is the 0 flipped to 1, but the last 1 is flipped to 0? Then the receiver gets 110. But now 110 is one of the agreed-upon patterns and the receiver concludes erroneously that it is snowing.

The set of bit patterns {000, 011, 101, 110} is called a *code*, and an individual pattern from the set, such as 101, is called a *code word*. The above code cannot detect two errors. It is a single-error-detecting code. Error codes operate under the realistic assumption that the probability of error on a single bit is much less than 1.0. Hence, the probability of an error in two bits is much less than the probability of error in one bit. No code can completely eliminate the possibility of an undetectable error with 100% certainty, as it is always possible for multiple errors to occur that would change one code word into another code word. Error codes are still useful because they handle such a large percentage of error events.

Codes and code words

Code Requirements

Suppose you want to be able to detect one or two errors. You will obviously need more parity bits. The questions are "How many parity bits?" and "How do you design the code?" The answers involve the concept of distance. The *Hamming distance* between two code words of the same length is defined as the number of positions in which the bits differ. It is named after Richard Hamming, who developed the theory in 1950 at Bell Labs.

The Hamming distance

Example 9.1 The Hamming distance between the code words for cloudy, 011, and raining, 101, is two, because the code words differ in two positions, namely the first and second positions. ∎

Inspection of the weather code {000, 011, 101, 110} should convince you that the distance between all possible pairs of code words is also two. You can see now that a code to detect a single error cannot have any pair of code words that are separated by a distance of one. Suppose there are two such code words, A and B. Then it would be possible for the sender to send A, have an error in transmission that flipped the single bit where A and B differ, and have the receiver conclude that B was sent. The code would fail to detect the single error.

The *code distance* is the minimum of the Hamming distance between all possible pairs of code words in the code.

The code distance

Example 9.2   The code {00110, 11100, 01010, 11101} has a code distance of one. Although several code words, such as 00110 and 11101, are separated by a Hamming distance as great as four, there exists a pair of words that are separated by a distance of only one, namely 11100 and 11101. If you used this code for sending the weather information, you could not guarantee the detection of all possible single transmission errors. ∎

To design a good code, you must add parity bits in such a way that you make the code distance as large as possible. To detect one error, the code distance must be two. What must the code distance be to detect two errors? The code distance cannot be two, as that would mean that there exists a pair of code words A and B with a Hamming distance of two. The sender could send A, have an error in transmission that flipped both bits where it differs from B, and have the receiver conclude that B was sent.

Figure 9.21 is a schematic representation of this concept. A is the transmitted code word and B is the code word closest to A. The open circles in between represent words not sent but possibly received because of errors in transmission. In Figure 9.21(a), e1 comes from a single error. In Figure 9.21(b), e1 comes from a single error and e2 comes from a double error.

In general, to detect d errors the code distance must satisfy the equation

$$\text{code distance} = d + 1$$

The requirement to detect d errors

For example, to be able to detect three errors, the code distance must be four. The reason is that with a distance of at least $d + 1$ to the closest code word to A, it is impossible to transform A to any other code word by flipping d bits of A.

The concept of distance is also useful with error-correcting codes. Suppose you decide on the following code for the weather messages.

00<u>000</u>, sunny

01<u>101</u>, cloudy

10<u>110</u>, raining

11<u>011</u>, snowing

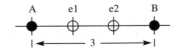

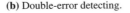

(a) Single-error detecting.   **(b)** Double-error detecting.

Figure **9.21**

Minimum Hamming distances for error-detecting codes.

If you receive 11110, what do you conclude? You could conclude that 000000 was sent for sunny and that four errors occurred. But is that a reasonable conclusion? Not really, because 11110 is closer to 10110, the code word for raining. With that conclusion, you assume that only one error occurred, an event of much higher probability than the event of four errors.

In general, for an error-correction code you add enough parity bits to make the code distance large enough that the receiver can correct the errors. The receiver corrects the errors by computing the Hamming distance between the received word and every code word, and picking the code word that is closest to the received word. "Close" is defined in terms of Hamming distance.

Figure 9.22 is a schematic representation of the error-correction concept. As before, A is the transmitted code word, B is the code word closest to A, and the open circles are words received because of errors in transmission. Figure 9.22(a) shows the situation for a code that is capable of correcting a single error. The code distance is 3, so that even if a single error occurs, the received word e1 will be closer to A than to B, and the receiver can conclude that A was sent. If A is sent and two errors occur, so that e2 is received, then the receiver will erroneously conclude that B was sent.

Figure 9.22(b) shows a code capable of correcting two errors. If A is sent and two errors occur, so that e2 is received, e2 is still closer to A than to B. That can only happen if the distance is 5.

In general, to correct d errors the code distance must satisfy the equation

$$\text{code distance} = 2d + 1$$

The requirement to correct d errors

For example, to be able to correct three errors, the code distance must be 7. The reason is based on the decision process. The receiver concludes that A was sent when it receives words close to A. But it concludes that B was sent when it receives words close to B. The line between A and B must accommodate *both* sets of received words, hence the factor of 2 in the equation. Also the distance must be odd, hence the +1 in the equation. If the distance were even, there would be a received word equidistant between A and B, and the receiver could not conclude which code word had the higher probability of being sent.

A code that can correct single errors can alternatively be used to detect double errors, as both have a code distance of 3. It is simply a question of how the receiver wants to handle the error condition. It can correct the error assuming two errors did

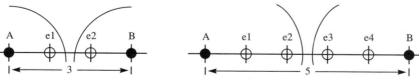

(a) Single-error correcting.   (b) Double-error correcting.

Figure **9.22**

Minimum Hamming distances for error-correcting codes.

not occur, or it can be more conservative, assume that two errors might have occurred, and discard the message or request a retransmission.

Single-Error-Correcting Codes

The previous section describes the requirements on the code distance for error detecting and correcting codes. The question remains of how to pick the code words to achieve the required code distance. Many different schemes have been devised for codes that correct multiple errors. This section investigates the efficiency of single-error-correcting codes and describes one systematic way to construct them.

Figure 9.23(a) shows the structure of a code word. There are m data bits and r parity bits, for a total of $n = m + r$ bits in the code word. Because there are n bits in a code word, there are 2^n possible received patterns. Figure 9.23(b) shows a schematic of how you can group those words that have no errors or one error. The figure shows the pattern for $n = 6$, where e1, e2, e3, e4, e5, and e6 are the six possible received words that could differ from A by one bit. If one of these is received, the receiver concludes that A was sent. Similarly, e7, e8, e9, e10, e11, and e12 are those possible words with a distance of 1 from code word B. There might be other received words that are not included in the grouping, corresponding to the event of more than one error during transmission, but resulting in a received word that is not within a distance of 1 from any code word.

In general there are n words a distance of 1 from A. So, the total number of words, including A, in the first group is $(n + 1)$. Similarly, there are $(n + 1)$ words in the B group, the C group, and so on. There is one group for each code word. So, as there are 2^m code words, there are 2^m groups. The total number of words in Figure

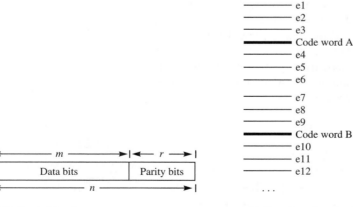

(a) Code word structure.

(b) Grouping of received words with zero or one error.

Figure **9.23**

The single-error-correcting code structure.

9.23(b) is, therefore, $(n + 1)2^m$. There could be other received words not in Figure 9.23(b), but there cannot be more than 2^n words altogether. Therefore,

$$(n + 1)2^m \leq 2^n$$

Substituting $n = m + r$ and dividing both sides by 2^m gives

$$m + r + 1 \leq 2^r$$

which tells how many parity bits r are necessary to correct a single error in a message with m data bits.

A code for which the relationship holds with equality is called a *perfect code*. An example of a perfect code is $m = 4$, $r = 3$. Sending parity bits along with data bits increases the transmission time. For this code, for every four data bits, you must send an additional three parity bits. So, the error correction has added 3/4 = 75% overhead to the transmission time. If you need to send a long stream of bits, you must subdivide the stream into chunks and apply the parity bits to each chunk. The bigger the chunk, the smaller the overhead. With computers, you usually send streams of bytes, so the chunks are usually powers of 2. Figure 9.24 shows the relationship between m and r for a few values of m that are powers of 2.

Perfect codes

Data bits m	Parity Bits r	Percent Overhead
4	3	75
8	4	50
16	5	31
32	6	19
64	7	11
128	8	6

Figure 9.24

The cost of a single-error correcting code.

Hamming devised an ingenious technique for determining the parity bits of a single-error-correcting code. The idea is to not append the parity bits to the end of the code word, but to distribute them throughout the code word. The advantage of this technique is that the receiver can calculate directly which bit is the erroneous one without having to compute the distance between the received word and all the code words. Figure 9.25 shows the positions of the parity bits for the $m = 8$, $r = 4$ case. The bit positions are numbered consecutively from the left, and the parity bits are at locations 1, 2, 4, and 8, all powers of 2. In this example, the data to be transmitted is 1001 1100, but these bits are not stored contiguously in the code word.

The numeric position of each bit can be written as a unique sum of powers of 2 as follows:

Figure 9.25

The position of the four parity bits in a single-error correcting code with eight data bits.

1	2	3	4	5	6	7	8	9	10	11	12
		1		0	0	1		1	1	0	0

$1 = 1$	$5 = 1 + 4$	$9 = 1 + 8$
$2 = 2$	$6 = 2 + 4$	$10 = 2 + 8$
$3 = 1 + 2$	$7 = 1 + 2 + 4$	$11 = 1 + 2 + 8$
$4 = 4$	$8 = 8$	$12 = 4 + 8$

To determine the parity bit at position 1, note that 1 occurs in the sum on the right-hand side for positions 1, 3, 5, 7, 9, and 11. Using even parity, set the parity bit so that the total number of 1's in those positions is even. There are 1's at positions 3, 7, and 9, an odd number of 1's. So, make the parity bit at position 1 a 1. The positions checked by each parity bit are:

Parity bit 1 checks 1, 3, 5, 7, 9, 11

Parity bit 2 checks 2, 3, 6, 7, 10, 11

Parity bit 4 checks 4, 5, 6, 7, 12

Parity bit 8 checks 8, 9, 10, 11, 12

You should verify that a similar computation for the other parity bits results in the code word $\underline{1}$ $\underline{1}$ 1 $\underline{1}$ 0 0 1 $\underline{0}$ 1 1 0 0.

Now, suppose this code word is sent, and during transmission an error occurs at position 10 so that the receiver gets $\underline{1}$ $\underline{1}$ 1 $\underline{1}$ 0 0 1 $\underline{0}$ 1 0 0 0. She calculates the parity bits as $\underline{1}$ $\underline{0}$ 1 $\underline{1}$ 0 0 1 $\underline{1}$ 1 0 0 0, and sees a discrepancy between the received parity and the calculated parity at positions 2 and 8. Because $2 + 8 = 10$, she concludes that the bit at position 10 is in error. So, she flips the bit at position 10 to correct the error. The advantage of this correction technique is that the receiver need not compare the received word with all the code words to determine which code word is closest to it.

9.5   RAID Storage Systems

In the early days of computers, disks were physically large and expensive. As technology advanced they became physically small, their data capacities increased, and they became less expensive. They finally got so cheap that it became advantageous to assemble many individual drives into an array of drives, instead of building one bigger drive when large amounts of data needed to be stored. Such a collection is called a Redundant Array of Inexpensive Disks (RAID) system.

The idea is that an array of disks has more spindles, each with its own set of read/write heads that can operate concurrently compared to the single spindle in one big drive. The concurrency should lead to increased performance. Also, redundancy can provide error correction and detection to increase the reliability of the system. The RAID controller provides a level of abstraction to the operating system, mak-

Advantages of RAID systems

ing the array of disks appear like one big disk to the operating system. Alternatively, the abstraction can be provided in software as part of the operating system.

There are several different ways to organize an array of disks. The industry standard terminology for the most common schemes is:

- RAID Level 0: Nonredundant striped *Common RAID levels*
- RAID Level 1: Mirrored
- RAID Levels 01 and 10: Striped and mirrored
- RAID Level 2: Memory-style ECC
- RAID Level 3: Bit-interleaved parity
- RAID Level 4: Block-interleaved parity
- RAID Level 5: Block-interleaved distributed parity

Each organization has its own set of advantages and disadvantages and is used in different situations. The remainder of this section describes the above RAID levels.

RAID Level 0: Nonredundant Striped

Figure 9.26 shows the organization for RAID Level 0. Data that would be stored in several contiguous blocks is broken up into stripes and distributed over several disks in the array. Figure 9.18 shows blocks 0 through 7 on one track, 8 through 15 on the next track, and so on. A stripe consists of several blocks. For example, if there are two blocks per stripe, then blocks 0 and 1 in Figure 9.18 are stored in stripe 0, blocks 2 and 3 in stripe 1, and so on.

Stripe 0	Stripe 1	Stripe 2	Stripe 3
Stripe 4	Stripe 5	Stripe 6	Stripe 7
Stripe 8	Stripe 9	Stripe 10	Stripe 11
Stripe 12	Stripe 13	Stripe 14	Stripe 15

Figure **9.26**

RAID Level 0: Nonredundant striped.

The operating system sees the logical disk as in Figure 9.18, even though the physical disks are as in Figure 9.26. If the operating system requests a disk read of blocks 0 through 7, the RAID system can read stripes 0 through 3 in parallel, decreasing the access time because of the concurrency. To service a read request of blocks 0 through 10, that is, stripes 0 through 5, the first disk would need to deliver stripes 0 and 4 sequentially, as would the second disk with stripes 1 and 5. This organization requires a minimum of two hard drives.

The advantage of level 0 is increased performance. However, it does not work well in an environment where most read/write requests are for a single block or stripe, as there is no concurrency in that case. Also, there is no redundancy as with the other levels, so reliability is not as high. The probability of a single failure with four disks running is greater than the probability of failure of a single disk running, given that all the disks have equal quality.

RAID Level 1: Mirrored

To mirror a disk is to maintain an exact mirror image of it on a separate drive, as shown in Figure 9.27. There is no striping, just a strict duplication to provide redundancy in case one of the disk drives fails.

Figure **9.27**

RAID Level 1: Mirrored.

A disk write requires a write to each disk, but they can be done in parallel, so the write performance is not much worse than with a single drive. For a disk read, the controller can choose to read from the drive with the shortest seek time and latency. So a disk read is a bit better than with a single drive. If one drive fails, it can be replaced while the other continues to operate. When the replacement drive is installed, it is easily backed up by duplicating the good drive. Mirroring is usually done with only two drives. If four drives are available, it is generally better to take advantage of the increased performance with striping at level 01.

RAID Levels 01 and 10: Striped and Mirrored

There are two ways to combine RAID levels 0 and 1, and hence to obtain the advantages of both. The first is called RAID level 01, or 0+1, or 0/1, or "mirrored stripes" as Figure 9.28(a) shows. With mirrored stripes, you simply mirror the disk organization that you would have with striping at level 0. The second is RAID level 10, or 1+0, or 1/0, or "striped mirrors" as in Figure 9.28(b). Instead of using the redundant disks to duplicate the set of level 0 disks, you mirror pairs of disks, then stripe across the mirrors.

Raid level 10 is more expensive to implement than level 01. With level 01 in Figure 9.28(a), each stripe controller is a system that makes the four striped disks appear as a single disk to the mirror controller. The mirror controller is a system that makes the two mirrored disks appear as a single disk to the computer. With level 10 in Figure 9.28(b), each mirror controller is a system that makes two mirrored disks appear as a single disk to the stripe controller. The stripe controller is a system that makes the four striped disks appear as a single disk to the computer. In this example with eight physical disks, you only need three controllers for level 01 but five controllers for level 10.

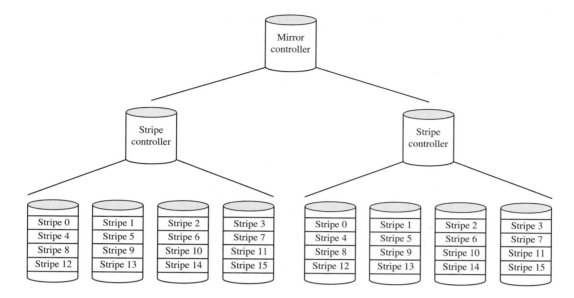

(a) RAID Level 01, mirrored stripes.

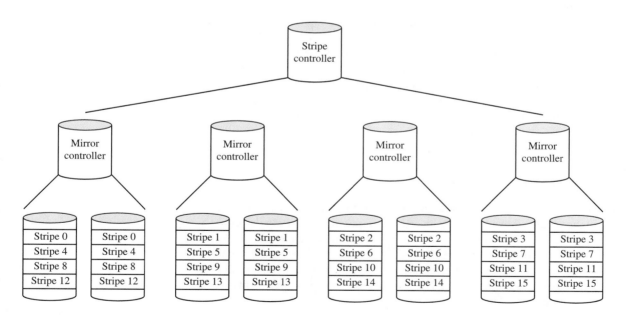

(b) RAID Level 10, striped mirros.

Figure **9.28**

Combining RAID Levels 0 and 1.

The advantage of level 10 over level 01 is reliability. Suppose one physical disk goes bad, say the third one. In Figure 9.28(a), that bad disk will cause the first stripe controller to report an error to the mirror controller, which will then use its rightmost mirrored disk until the faulty drive can be replaced. In effect, during the down time, the four physical disks of the left striped disk are out of commission. In Figure 9.28(b), the bad third disk will cause the second mirror controller to use the fourth disk (its second mirrored disk) until the faulty drive can be replaced. During the down time, only one physical disk is out of commission.

In both cases, the computer sees uninterrupted service from its RAID disk, so it might seem that there is no difference in reliability. However, the problem comes if two disks fail. In Figure 9.28(a), if one of the physical disks fails in the left striped disk and one fails in the right striped disk, the RAID disk fails. If the two disk failures are in the same set of striped disks, the RAID disk does not fail. In Figure 9.28(b), the only way the RAID disk can fail is if both failures are in the same set of paired mirror disks, an event that is less probable than a RAID failure with level 01. See the exercises at the end of this chapter for a quantitative analysis.

Another advantage of level 10 over 01 is the time to do a mirror copy after a failed disk has been replaced. In Figure 9.28(a), the mirror controller sees each striped disk as a single entity, not as four separate disks. Once a repair has been made, the mirror controller has no choice but to copy the entire contents of the good striped disk, that is, four physical disks, to the repaired striped disk. With level 10, all mirrors are with pairs of disks, so only a single disk copy is required to restore a failed disk.

Low-end RAID systems usually support 01 with high-end systems supporting both 01 and 10. You get the performance advantage of striping and the reliability advantage of mirroring. The read performance is even better than level 0 in some cases. Consider the scenario with level 01 of a read request for stripes 0 through 5. Stripes 0 through 3 can be read concurrently on the first set of drives, with stripes 4 and 5 read concurrently on the mirrored set. Both levels 01 and 10 require an even number of hard drives, with a minimum of four.

RAID Level 2: Memory-Style ECC

The storage overhead of mirroring is tremendous, 100% because each drive is duplicated. Figure 9.24 shows that less overhead is possible with single-error-correcting codes (ECC) as commonly used in high-reliability memory systems. Four data bits can be corrected with three parity bits, bringing the overhead down to 75%. With level 2, you stripe at the bit level. Figure 9.29 shows each nybble (half a byte) spread out over the first four drives. The last three drives are the parity bits for the single-error-correcting code.

To maintain performance, the drives must all be rotationally synchronized. To perform a disk write, the disk controller computes the parity bits for each nybble and writes them to the parity drives along with the data. To do a read, the controller computes the parity bits from the data and compares them with the bits from the parity drives, correcting the error on the fly.

Bit 0	Bit 1	Bit 2	Bit 3		P0-3	P0-3	P0-3
Bit 4	Bit 5	Bit 6	Bit 7		P4-7	P4-7	P4-7
Bit 8	Bit 9	Bit 10	Bit 11		P8-11	P8-11	P8-11
Bit 12	Bit 13	Bit 14	Bit 15		P12-15	P12-15	P12-15

Figure **9.29**

RAID Level 2: Memory-style ECC.

This scheme was used on some older supercomputers, usually with 32 data bits and 6 parity bits to get the overhead down. Today, inexpensive drives have their own internal error-correcting capabilities at the bit level, and so level 2 is no longer used commercially.

RAID Level 3: Bit-Interleaved Parity

By far the most common failure in a disk array is the failure of just one of the drives in the array. Furthermore, the disk controller can detect such a failure, so the system knows where the failure is. If you stripe at the bit level, and if you know which bit has failed, then you can correct the error with just one parity bit. For example, suppose you want to store the nybble 1001. With even parity, the parity bit is zero, so you store 1001 0. Figure 9.30 shows 1001 stored at Bit 0, Bit 1, Bit 2, Bit 3, and parity bit 0 stored at P0-3.

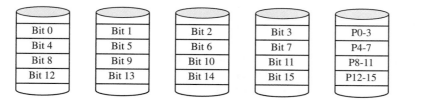

Figure **9.30**

RAID Level 3: Bit-interleaved parity.

Suppose the fourth drive fails, so you know that Bits 3, 7, 11, 15, ... are unavailable. You read your data as $100x\ \underline{0}$ where x is the bit you must correct. Because you are using even parity you know that the number of ones must be even, and hence that x must be 1. Your knowledge of where the error occurred allows you to decrease the overhead for single-error correcting to a single parity bit.

Although the level 3 improves on the efficiency of level 2, it has several disadvantages. Recovering from a failed drive is time consuming. With mirroring, you simply clone the content of the one remaining good drive to the replacement drive. With bit-interleaved parity, the bits on the replacement drive must be computed from the bits on all the other drives, which you must, therefore, access. The rebuild is usually done automatically by the controller.

The parity drive is only used to correct errors when a drive fails and to restore the replacement drive. Consequently, it must be written on every write request to update the parity bit. Because individual disk drives have their own ECC at the bit level, you do not access the parity drive on a read request (unless a drive has failed).

The access time for level 3 is not much worse than it would be for a single drive. But with levels 2 and 3, every read/write request requires you to access every data drive, so you do not get the concurrency that you do with longer stripes.

RAID Level 4: Block-Interleaved Parity

The only difference between level 3 and level 4 is the size of the stripe. In level 3, a stripe is one bit, and in level 4, it can be one or more blocks. In Figure 9.30, P0-3 represents one bit, but in Figure 9.31 P0-3 represents an entire stripe.

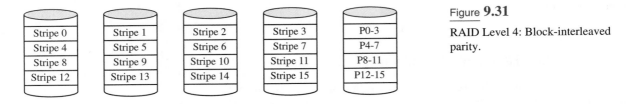

Figure **9.31**

RAID Level 4: Block-interleaved parity.

For example, if each stripe is 1Kbit long, then a file is distributed over the stripes as follows:

Stripe 0: Bits 0 through 1023

Stripe 1: Bits 1024 through 2047

Stripe 2: Bits 2048 through 3071

Stripe 3: Bits 3072 through 4095

The first bit of P0-3 is the parity bit for bits 0, 1024, 2048, and 3072; the second bit of P0-3 is the parity bit for bits 1, 1025, 2049, and 3073; and so on. Because striping is not at the bit level, disks do not need to be rotationally synchronized, as they do with levels 2 and 3.

Level 4 has an advantage over level 3 with small random read requests. If each file is contained on a few stripes on different disks, the seeks, latencies, and transmissions can all happen concurrently. With level 3, to read even one small file requires all the data drives to act in concert; many small files must be read sequentially.

Although overhead with level 4 is much reduced compared to mirrored organizations, its biggest drawback is with write requests. If you are writing a file that spans stripes 0 through 3, you can compute the parity for P0-3 and write it to the parity drive at the same time. But suppose you need to write a file that is wholly contained in stripe 0. Because you are going to alter stripe 0, you also must alter P0-3. But P0-3 is the parity for stripes 1, 2, and 3 as well as 0. It would seem that you have to read stripes 1, 2, and 3 to use with your new stripe 0 to compute the new parity. There is a more efficient way, however. Instead of reading stripes 1, 2, and 3, you can read the old stripe 0 and the old P0-3. For each bit position in the new and old data stripes, if your new bit is different from your old bit, then you will be changing the number of 1's from an even number to an odd number or vice versa, and you must flip that bit in P0-3. If the new and old data bits are the same, you leave the corresponding parity bit unchanged. For four data disks, this technique reduces the number of disk reads from three to two.

Even with this shortcut, every write request requires a write to the parity disk, no matter how small the request. The parity disk becomes the performance bottleneck.

RAID Level 5: Block-Interleaved Distributed Parity

Level 5 alleviates the parity disk bottleneck. Rather than store all the parity on one disk, the parity information is scattered among all the disks, so that no one disk has the responsibility for the parity information of the whole array.

Figure 9.32 shows a common organization, known as left-symmetric parity distribution, for spreading the parity information among all the disks. It has the advantage that if you read a set of stripes sequentially, you access each disk once before accessing any disk twice. In the figure, suppose you access stripes 0, 1, 2, 3, and 4 in that order. You will access the first, second, third, fourth, and fifth disks. If you put stripe 4 where stripe 5 is in the figure and service the same request, you would access the first, second, third, fourth, and first disk; that is, you would access the first disk twice before accessing the fifth disk at all. You can see that the desirable property holds regardless of which stripe you begin with.

Stripe 0	Stripe 1	Stripe 2	Stripe 3	P0-3
Stripe 5	Stripe 6	Stripe 7	P4-7	Stripe 4
Stripe 10	Stripe 11	P8-11	Stripe 8	Stripe 9
Stripe 15	P12-15	Stripe 12	Stripe 13	Stripe 14
P16-19	Stripe 16	Stripe 17	Stripe 18	Stripe 19

Figure 9.32

RAID Level 5: Block-interleaved distributed parity.

RAID level 5 is considered by many to be the ideal combination of good reliability, good performance, high capacity, and low storage overhead. It is one of the most popular high-end RAID systems. The most popular low-end system is probably RAID level 0, which is not really a true RAID because there is no redundancy, and hence no enhanced reliability.

SUMMARY

The operating system allocates time in the form of CPU utilization and space in the form of main memory and disk allocation. Five techniques for allocation of main memory are uniprogramming, fixed-partition multiprogramming, variable-partition multiprogramming, paging, and virtual memory. With uniprogramming, only one job executes at a time from start to finish, and the job has the entire main memory to itself. Fixed-partition multiprogramming allows several jobs to execute concurrently and requires the operating system to determine the partition sizes in memory before executing any jobs. Variable-partition multiprogramming alleviates the inefficiencies inherent in fixed-partition multiprogramming by allowing the partition sizes to vary depending on the job requirements. The best-fit and first-fit algorithms are two different strategies to cope with the fragmentation problem of variable-partition multiprogramming.

Paging alleviates fragmentation by fragmenting the program to fit the memory holes. Programs are no longer contiguous but broken up and scattered throughout main memory. Jobs are divided into equal-sized pages and main memory is divided into frames of the same size. Logical addresses as seen by the programmer are converted to physical addresses with the help of a page table. The page table contains the frame number for each page that is stored in main memory.

Demand paging, also called virtual memory, postpones page loading into memory until the job demands the page. The entire program does not need to reside in main memory to execute. Instead, only its active pages, called the working set, are loaded. A page fault occurs when a page is referenced but has not yet been loaded into memory. First in, first out (FIFO) and least-recently used (LRU) are two algorithms for determining which page to swap out of main memory when a frame is needed for a new page. You would normally expect the number of faults to decrease with increasing number of memory frames. But Belady's anomaly shows that it is possible for an increase in the number of frames to produce an increase in the number of faults with the FIFO replacement algorithm.

Three contributions to disk access time are seek time, which is the time it takes for the arm to move to the designated cylinder; latency, which is the time it takes for the block to rotate to the head once the head is in place; and transmission time, which is the time it takes for the block to pass underneath the head. Three techniques of disk management are contiguous, linked, and indexed. The problem of fragmentation occurs with disk memory, as it does with main memory.

A set of redundant bits can be added to data bits in order to detect or correct errors that may occur during transmission or storage of data. The Hamming distance between two code words is the number of bits that are different. The receiver corrects errors by choosing the code word that is closest to the received word based on the Hamming distance. With a judicious choice of the placement of the redundant bits, you can correct a single error without comparing the received word with all the code words.

A Redundant Array of Inexpensive Disks (RAID) is a grouping of disks that appears to the operating systems as a single large disk. The two benefits of a RAID system are performance, based on the concurrent access of the data with multiple spindles in the system, and reliability, based on error correction and detection with redundant drives.

EXERCISES

Section 9.1

1. Using the format of Figure 9.4, devise a job execution sequence for which the first-fit algorithm would require compaction before the best-fit algorithm. Sketch the fragmentation in main memory just before compaction is required for each algorithm.

2. Figure 9.10 shows how a page table in a paging system performs the same transformation of the logical address as the base register does in a multiprogramming system. The equivalent job of the bound register is not shown in the figure. **(a)** To protect other processes' memory space from unauthorized access, would a paging system require a table of bound values, one for each page, or would a single bound register suffice? Explain. **(b)** Modify Figure 9.10 to include main memory protection from other processes.

3. Suppose the page size in a paging system is 512 bytes. **(a)** If most of the files are large, that is, much greater than 512 bytes, what do you suppose is the average internal fragmentation (in bytes of unused space) for each file? Explain your reasoning. **(b)** How would your answer to part (a) change if most of the files were much smaller than 512 bytes? **(c)** How would your answer to part (b) change if you express the fragmentation in terms of the percentage of unused space instead of the number of unused bytes?

Section 9.2

4. A computer has 12-bit addresses and a main memory that is divided into 16 frames. Memory management uses demand paging. ***(a)** How many bytes is virtual memory? **(b)** How many bytes are in each page? **(c)** How many bits are in the offset of a logical and physical address? **(d)** What is the maximum number of entries in a job's page table?

5. Answer Exercise 4 for a computer with n-bit addresses and a memory divided into 2^k frames.

*6. For which pages in Figure 9.12 is the image on disk an exact replica of the page in main memory?

7. Verify the data of Figure 9.15(b), which shows Belady's anomaly, for the sequence of page references given in the text. Display the content of the frames in the format of Figure 9.13.

*8. Devise a sequence of 12 page references for which the FIFO page-replacement algorithm is better than the LRU algorithm.

9. Plot the graph of Figure 9.15(b) for the page reference sequence in Figure 9.13 using the FIFO page-replacement algorithm. On the same graph, plot the data for the LRU algorithm.

*10. If the operating system could predict the future, it could select the replacement page such that the next page fault is delayed as long as possible. Such an algorithm is called OPT, the optimum page-replacement algorithm. It is a useful theoretical algorithm because it represents the best you could possibly do. When designers measure the performance of their page-replacement algorithms, they try to get as close as possible to the performance of OPT. How many page faults does OPT produce for the sequence of Figures 9.13 and 9.16? How does that compare with FIFO and LRU?

Section 9.3

11. Suppose a disk rotates at 5,400 revolutions per minute and has each surface divided into 16 sectors. ***(a)** What is the maximum possible latency time? Under what circumstance will that occur? **(b)** What is the minimum possible latency time? Under what circumstance will that occur? **(c)** From (a) and (b), what will be the average latency time? **(d)** What is the transmission time for one block?

Section 9.4

12. ***(a)** How many data bits are required to store one of the decimal digits 0 through 9? ***(b)** How many parity bits are required to detect a single error? **(c)** Write a single-error detection code using even parity. Underline the parity bits. **(d)** What is the code distance of your code?

13. **(a)** What must the code distance be to detect five errors? **(b)** What must the code distance be to correct five errors?

14. **(a)** Which entries in Figure 9.24 represent perfect codes? **(b)** Augment the table in Figure 9.24 with additional entries to include all the perfect codes between $m = 4$ and $m = 128$. Be sure to include the overhead value. **(c)** What can you conclude about the cost of restricting the number of data bits to a power of two?

15. **(a)** How many data bits are required to store one of the decimal digits 0 through 9? **(b)** How many parity bits are required to correct a single error? **(c)** Write a single-error correction code using even parity. Underline the parity bits. **(d)** What is the code distance of your code?

16. A set of eight data bits is transmittited with the single-error correction code of Figure 9.25. For each of the received bit patterns below, state whether an error occured. If it did, correct the error.

 *(a) 1 0 0 1 1 0 1 0 1 0 0 1   **(b)** 1 1 0 1 0 0 1 1 0 0 1 0
 (c) 0 0 0 0 1 0 1 1 0 1 0 0   **(d)** 1 0 1 1 0 0 1 0 0 1 0 0

Section 9.5

17. Figure 9.28 shows a RAID system with eight physical disks. **(a)** With six physical disks, how many mirror controllers and stripe controllers would you need for level 01 and for level 10? **(b)** With $2n$ disks in general (so that $n = 4$ in Figure 9.28), how many mirror controllers and stripe controllers would you need for level 01 and for level 10?

18. **(a)** Figure 9.28 shows the RAID level 01 and RAID level 10 systems with eight physical disks. Draw the equivalent systems for level 01 and level 10 with four physical disks. **(b)** Assume that two disks go bad. The sequence BBGG means that the first and second disks are bad and the third and fourth disks are good. With this scenario, the RAID level 01 disk is good because the two bad disks are in the same first striped disk, but the RAID level 10 disk is bad because the two bad disks are in the same first mirrored disk. How many permutations of four letters with two B's and two G's are there? **(c)** Tabulate each permutation, and for each one determine whether the RAID disk is good or bad for level 01 and 10. **(d)** If two disks fail, use part (c) to determine the probability that the RAID disk fails for level 01 and 10. Which RAID system is more reliable? **(e)** With $2n$ disks in general (so that $n = 4$ in Figure 9.28), how many permutations of $2n$ letters are there with 2 B's and $2n - 2$ G's? **(f)** How many of the permutations from part (e) cause a RAID disk failure for level 01 and for level 10? **(g)** If two disks fail, use part (f) to determine the probability that the RAID disk fails for level 01 and 10. **(h)** Use part (g) to show that the probability that the RAID disk in Figure 9.28 fails is 4/7 for level 01 and 1/7 for level 10 if two disks fail.

19. You have a RAID level 4 system with eight data disks and one parity disk. **(a)** How many disk reads and disk writes must you make to write one data stripe if you do *not* make use of the old data and parity values? **(b)** How many disk reads and disk writes must you make to write one data stripe if you *do* make use of the old data and parity values?

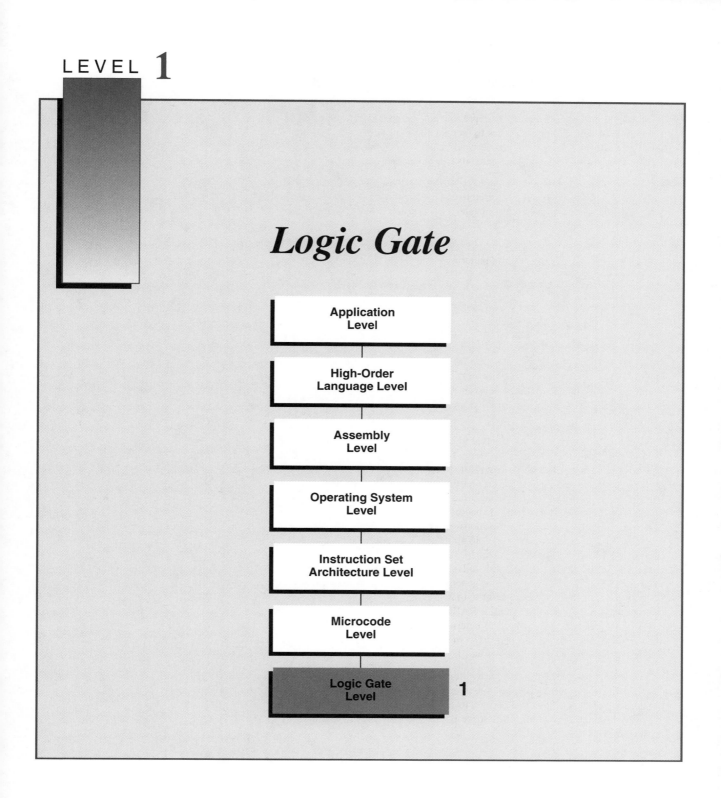

LEVEL 1

Logic Gate

Application
Level

High-Order
Language Level

Assembly
Level

Operating System
Level

Instruction Set
Architecture Level

Microcode
Level

Logic Gate
Level   1

Chapter

10

Combinational Circuits

Finally we come to the lowest level in our description of the typical computer system. Each level of abstraction hides the details that are unnecessary for the user at the next-higher level. The details at Level LG1 are hidden from the user at Level ISA3, the instruction set architecture level. Remember that the user at Level ISA3 sees a von Neumann machine whose language is machine language. The job of the designer at Level LG1 is to construct the Level ISA3 machine. These last three chapters describe the language and design principles at Level LG1 that are required to construct a von Neumann machine.

The figures in this book consistently show the microcode level between the instruction set architecture level and the logic gate level. Some designers choose to omit the microcode level in their machines and construct the Level ISA3 machine directly from Level LG1. Others choose to design their systems with a microcode level.

Omitting Level Mc2

What are the advantages and disadvantages of each design approach? The same as we encountered at Levels 7, 6, and 5. Suppose you need to design an application for a user at Level App7. Would you rather write it in C++ at Level HOL6 and compile it to a lower level or write it directly in Pep/8 assembly language at Level Asmb5? Because C++ is at a higher level of abstraction, one C++ statement can do the work of many Pep/8 statements. The C++ program would be much shorter than the equivalent Pep/8 program. It would, therefore, be easier to design and debug. But it would require a compiler for translation to a lower level. Furthermore, a good assembly language programmer can usually produce shorter, faster code than the object code from even an optimizing compiler. Though the program would execute faster, it would be difficult to design and debug; it would thus be more costly to develop.

The tradeoff at Levels 7, 6, and 5 is development cost versus execution speed. The same tradeoff applies at Levels 3, 2, and 1. Generally, systems that include Level Mc2 are simpler and less costly than those that omit it. But they usually execute more slowly than if they were built directly from Level LG1. A recent design trend is to build simple but fast von Neumann machines with small instruction sets, called *reduced instruction set computers* (RISCs). An important characteristic of a RISC machine is its omission of Level Mc2.

Two levels that are interesting but whose descriptions are not given in this book are the levels below the logic gate level, as Figure 10.1 shows. At the electronic device level (Level 0), designers connect transistors, resistors, and capacitors to make an individual logic gate at Level LG1. At the physics level (Level −1), applied physicists construct the transistors that the electrical engineer can use to construct the gates that the computer architect can use to construct the von Neumann machine. There is no level below physics, the most fundamental of all the sciences.

The languages at Levels 0 and −1 are the set of mathematical equations that model the behavior of the objects at that level. You may be familiar with some of them. At Level 0 they include Ohm's law, Kirchoff's rules, and the voltage versus current characteristics of electronic devices. At Level −1 they include Coulomb's law, Newton's laws, and some laws from quantum mechanics. At all the levels, from the calculus for relational databases at Level App7 to Newton's laws at Level −1, formal mathematics is the tool for modeling the behavior of the system.

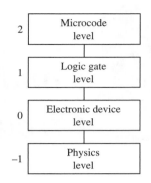

Figure **10.1**

The levels below the logic gate level.

10.1   Boolean Algebra and Logic Gates

A *circuit* is a collection of devices that are physically connected by wires. The two basic types of circuits at Level LG1 are combinational and sequential. You can visualize either type of circuit as a rectangular block called a *black box* with a fixed number of input lines and a fixed number of output lines. Figure 10.2 shows a three-input, two-output circuit.

Each line can carry a signal whose value is either 1 or 0. Electrically, a 1 signal is a small voltage, usually about 5 volts, and a 0 signal is 0 volts. The circuit is designed to detect and produce only those binary values.

You should recognize Figure 10.2 as one more manifestation of the input-processing-output structure that is present at all levels of the computer system. The circuit performs the processing that transforms the input to the output.

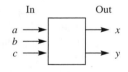

Figure **10.2**

The black box representation of a circuit.

Combinational Circuits

With a *combinational circuit*, the input determines the output. For example, in Figure 10.2 if you put in $a = 1$, $b = 0$, $c = 1$ (abbreviated $abc = 101$) today and get out $xy = 01$, then if you put in $abc = 101$ tomorrow you will get out $xy = 01$ again. Mathematically, x and y are functions of a, b, and c. That is, $x = x(a, b, c)$ and $y = y(a, b, c)$.

This behavior is not characteristic of a sequential circuit. It may be possible for you to put *abc* = 101 into a sequential circuit and get out *xy* = 01 at one moment, but *xy* = 11 a few microseconds later. Chapter 11 shows how this seemingly useless behavior comes about and how it is, in fact, indispensable for building computers.

The three most common methods for describing the behavior of a combinational circuit are

- Truth tables
- Boolean algebraic expressions
- Logic diagrams

The remainder of this section describes those representations.

a	b	c	x	y
0	0	0	0	0
0	0	1	1	0
0	1	0	0	0
0	1	1	1	1
1	0	0	0	1
1	0	1	0	0
1	1	0	0	0
1	1	1	0	0

Figure **10.3**

The truth table for a three-input, two-output combinational circuit.

Truth Tables

Of these three methods of representing a combinational circuit, truth tables are at a higher level of abstraction than algebraic expressions or logic diagrams. A truth table specifies what the combinational circuit does, not how it does it. A truth table simply lists the output for every possible combination of input values (hence the name, combinational circuit).

Example 10.1 Figure 10.3 is the truth table for a three-input, two-output combinational circuit. Because there are three inputs and each input can have one of two possible values, the table has $2^3 = 8$ entries. In general, the truth table for an *n*-input combinational circuit will have 2^n entries. ∎

Example 10.2 Another example of a combinational circuit specified by a truth table is Figure 10.4. It is a four-input circuit with 16 entries in its truth table. ∎

The black box schematic of Figure 10.2 is particularly appropriate for the truth table representation of a combinational circuit. You cannot see inside a box that is painted black. Similarly, you cannot see how a circuit produces a function that is defined by a truth table.

a	b	c	d	x	y
0	0	0	0	0	0
0	0	0	1	0	0
0	0	1	0	0	0
0	0	1	1	0	0
0	1	0	0	0	1
0	1	0	1	1	1
0	1	1	0	0	0
0	1	1	1	1	0
1	0	0	0	0	0
1	0	0	1	0	0
1	0	1	0	0	0
1	0	1	1	0	0
1	1	0	0	0	1
1	1	0	1	1	1
1	1	1	0	0	0
1	1	1	1	1	0

Figure **10.4**

The truth table for a four-input, two-output combinational circuit.

Boolean Algebra

An algebraic expression written according to the laws of boolean algebra specifies not only what a combinational circuit does, but how it does it. Boolean algebra is similar in some respects to the algebra for real numbers that you are familiar with, but it is different in other respects. The four basic operations for real algebra are addition, subtraction, multiplication, and division. Boolean algebra has three basic operations: OR (denoted +), AND (denoted ·), and complement (denoted ′). AND and OR are binary operations, and complement is a unary operation.

The 10 fundamental properties of boolean algebra are

$x + y = y + x$	$x \cdot y = y \cdot x$	commutative
$(x + y) + z = x + (y + z)$	$(x \cdot y) \cdot z = x \cdot (y \cdot z)$	associative
$x + (y \cdot z) = (x + y) \cdot (x + z)$	$x \cdot (y + z) = (x \cdot y) + (x \cdot z)$	distributive
$x + 0 = x$	$x \cdot 1 = x$	identity
$x + (x') = 1$	$x \cdot (x') = 0$	complement

Precedence	Operator
Highest	Complement
	AND
Lowest	OR

Figure 10.5

Precedence of the boolean operators.

where x, y, and z are boolean variables. As with real algebra, the notation is infix with parentheses to denote which of several operations to perform first. To simplify expressions with many parentheses, the boolean operations have the precedence structure shown in Figure 10.5. Using the precedence rules, the distributive properties are

$$x + y \cdot z = (x + y) \cdot (x + z) \qquad x \cdot (y + z) = x \cdot y + x \cdot z$$

and the complement properties are

$$x + x' = 1 \qquad x \cdot x' = 0$$

A striking difference between the properties of real algebra and boolean algebra is the distributive law. With real numbers, multiplication distributes over addition. For example,

The distributive law

$$2 \cdot (3 + 4) = 2 \cdot 3 + 2 \cdot 4$$

But addition does not distribute over multiplication. It is not true that

$$2 + 3 \cdot 4 = (2 + 3) \cdot (2 + 4)$$

In boolean algebra, however, where + represents OR and · represents AND, OR does distribute over AND.

The laws of boolean algebra have a symmetry that the laws of real algebra do not have. Each boolean property has a *dual* property. To obtain the dual expression,

Duality

- Exchange + and ·
- Exchange 1 and 0

The two forms of the distributive law are an example of dual expressions. In the distributive property

$$x + (y \cdot z) = (x + y) \cdot (x + z)$$

if you exchange the + and · operators you get

$$x \cdot (y + z) = (x \cdot y) + (x \cdot z)$$

which is the other distributive property. Each fundamental property of boolean algebra has a corresponding dual property.

The associative properties also permit simplification of expressions. Because the order in which you perform two OR operations is immaterial, you can write

The associative law

$$(x + y) + z$$

without parentheses as

$$x + y + z$$

The same is true for the AND operation.

Boolean Algebra Theorems

Because boolean algebra has a different mathematical structure from the real algebra with which you are familiar, the theorems of boolean algebra may appear unusual at first. Some theorems proved from the 10 basic properties of boolean algebra, which will be discussed next, are useful in the analysis and design of combinational circuits.

The *idempotent property* states that

$$x + x = x$$

The idempotent property

Proving this theorem requires a sequence of substitution steps, each of which is based on one of the 10 basic properties of boolean algebra:

$$x + x$$
$$= \quad \langle \text{identity} \rangle$$
$$(x + x) \cdot 1$$
$$= \quad \langle \text{complement} \rangle$$
$$(x + x) \cdot (x + x')$$
$$= \quad \langle \text{distributive} \rangle$$
$$x + (x \cdot x')$$
$$= \quad \langle \text{complement} \rangle$$
$$x + 0$$
$$= \quad \langle \text{identity} \rangle$$
$$x$$

The dual property is

$$x \cdot x = x$$

The proof of the dual theorem requires exactly the same sequence of steps, with each substitution based on the dual of the corresponding step in the original proof:

$$x \cdot x$$
$$= \quad \langle \text{identity} \rangle$$
$$(x \cdot x) + 0$$
$$= \quad \langle \text{complement} \rangle$$
$$(x \cdot x) + (x \cdot x')$$
$$= \quad \langle \text{distributive} \rangle$$
$$x \cdot (x + x')$$
$$= \quad \langle \text{complement} \rangle$$
$$x \cdot 1$$
$$= \quad \langle \text{identity} \rangle$$
$$x$$

The proofs of the idempotent properties illustrate an important application of duality in boolean algebra. Once you prove a theorem, you can assert immediately that its dual must also be true. Because each of the 10 basic properties has a dual, the corresponding proof will be identical in structure to the original proof, but with each step based on the dual of the original step. *Using duality to assert a theorem*

Here are three more useful theorems with their duals. The mathematical rule for proving theorems is that you may use any axiom or previously proved theorem in your proof. So to prove the first theorem below, you may use any of the fundamental properties or the idempotent property. To prove the second theorem, you may use any of the fundamental properties, or the idempotent property, or the first theorem, and so on. The first theorem

$$x + 1 = 1 \qquad\qquad x \cdot 0 = 0$$

The zero theorem

is called the zero theorem. 0 is the zero for the AND operator, and 1 is the "zero" for the OR operator. The second theorem

$$x + x \cdot y = x \qquad\qquad x \cdot (x + y) = x$$

The absorption property

is called the absorption property because y is absorbed into x. The third theorem

$$x \cdot y + x' \cdot z + y \cdot z = x \cdot y + x' \cdot z$$
$$(x + y) \cdot (x' + z) \cdot (y + z) = (x + y) \cdot (x' + z)$$

The consensus theorem

is called the consensus theorem. Proofs of these theorems are exercises at the end of the chapter.

Proving Complements

The complement of x is x'. To prove that some expression, y, is the complement of some other expression, z, you must show that y and z obey the same complement properties

$$y + z = 1 \qquad y \cdot z = 0$$

that x and x' obey.

An example of proving complements is *De Morgan's law*, which states that

$$(a \cdot b)' = a' + b' \qquad\qquad\qquad\qquad\qquad \textit{De Morgan's law}$$

To show that the complement of $a \cdot b$ is $a' + b'$, you must show that

$$(a \cdot b) + (a' + b') = 1 \qquad (a \cdot b) \cdot (a' + b') = 0$$

The first part of the proof is

$$(a \cdot b) + (a' + b')$$
$$= \quad \langle\text{commutative}\rangle$$
$$(a' + b') + (a \cdot b)$$
$$= \quad \langle\text{distributive}\rangle$$
$$[(a' + b') + a] \cdot [(a' + b') + b]$$
$$= \quad \langle\text{commutative and associative}\rangle$$
$$[b' + (a + a')] \cdot [a' + (b + b')]$$
$$= \quad \langle\text{complement}\rangle$$
$$[b' + 1] \cdot [a' + 1]$$
$$= \quad \langle\text{the zero theorem, } x + 1 = 1\rangle$$
$$1 \cdot 1$$
$$= \quad \langle\text{identity, } (x \cdot 1 = 1)\ [\text{x} := 1]\rangle$$
$$1$$

and the second part of the proof is

$(a \cdot b) \cdot (a' + b')$

=   ⟨distributive⟩

$(a \cdot b) \cdot a' + (a \cdot b) \cdot b'$

=   ⟨commutative and associative⟩

$b \cdot (a \cdot a') + a \cdot (b \cdot b')$

=   ⟨complement⟩

$b \cdot 0 + a \cdot 0$

=   ⟨the zero theorem, $x \cdot 0 = 0$⟩

$0 + 0$

=   ⟨identity, $(x + 0 = x)[x := 0]$⟩

0

De Morgan's second law,

$(a + b)' = a' \cdot b'$

follows immediately from duality.

De Morgan's laws generalize to more than one variable. For three variables, the laws are

$(a \cdot b \cdot c)' = a' + b' + c'$ $(a + b + c)' = a' \cdot b' \cdot c'$ *De Morgan's law for three variables*

Proofs of the general theorems for more than two variables are an exercise at the end of the chapter.

Another complement theorem is $(x')' = x$. The complement of x' is x because   *The complement of* x'
$x' + x = 1$ by the following proof

$x' + x$

=   ⟨commutative⟩

$x + x'$

=   ⟨complement⟩

1

and $x' \cdot x = 0$ by the following proof

$x' \cdot x$

=   ⟨commutative⟩

$x \cdot x'$

=   ⟨complement⟩

0

Yet another complement theorem is $1' = 0$. 1 is the complement of 0 because $1 + 0 = 1$ by the following proof   *The complement of 1*

$1 + 0$

$=$ ⟨identity, $(x + 0 = x)$ $[x := 1]$⟩

1

and $1 \cdot 0 = 0$ by the following proof

$1 \cdot 0$

$=$ ⟨commutative⟩

$0 \cdot 1$

$=$ ⟨identity, $(x \cdot 1 = x)$ $[x := 0]$⟩

0

The dual theorem, $0' = 1$, follows immediately.

Logic Diagrams

The third representation of a combinational circuit is an interconnection of logic gates. This representation corresponds most closely to the hardware because the lines that connect the gates in a logic diagram represent physical wires that connect physical devices on a circuit board or in an integrated circuit.

Each boolean operation is represented by a gate symbol, shown in Figure 10.6. The AND and OR gates have two input lines, labeled a and b. The inverter has one input line, corresponding to the fact that the complement is a unary operation. The output is x. Also shown in the figure are the corresponding boolean expression and truth table for each gate.

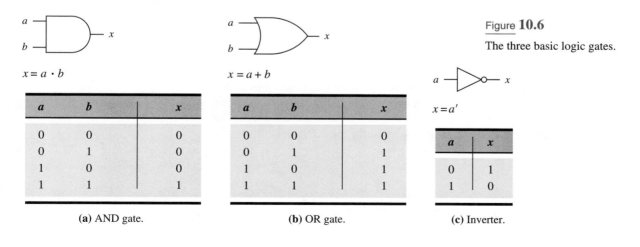

Figure **10.6**

The three basic logic gates.

$x = a \cdot b$

a	b	x
0	0	0
0	1	0
1	0	0
1	1	1

(a) AND gate.

$x = a + b$

a	b	x
0	0	0
0	1	1
1	0	1
1	1	1

(b) OR gate.

$x = a'$

a	x
0	1
1	0

(c) Inverter.

Any boolean function can be written with only the AND, OR, and complement operations. It follows that to construct any combinational circuit you only need the three basic gates of Figure 10.6. In practice, several other gates are common. Figure 10.7 shows three of them.

Figure **10.7**

Three common logic gates.

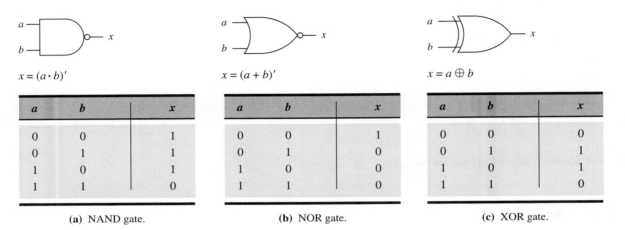

$x = (a \cdot b)'$

a	b	x
0	0	1
0	1	1
1	0	1
1	1	0

(a) NAND gate.

$x = (a + b)'$

a	b	x
0	0	1
0	1	0
1	0	0
1	1	0

(b) NOR gate.

$x = a \oplus b$

a	b	x
0	0	0
0	1	1
1	0	1
1	1	0

(c) XOR gate.

The NAND gate (Not AND) is equivalent to an AND gate followed by an inverter, as shown in Figure 10.8. Similarly, a NOR gate (Not OR) is equivalent to an OR gate followed by an inverter. Electronically it is frequently easier to build a NAND gate than to build an AND gate. In fact, an AND gate is often built as a NAND gate followed by an inverter. NOR gates are also more common than OR gates.

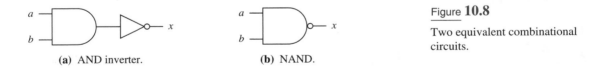

(a) AND inverter.

(b) NAND.

Figure **10.8**

Two equivalent combinational circuits.

XOR stands for *exclusive* OR in contrast to OR, which is sometimes called *inclusive* OR. The output of an OR gate is 1 if either or both of its inputs are 1. The output of an XOR gate is 1 if either of its inputs is 1 exclusive of the other input. Its output is 0 if both inputs are 1. The algebraic symbol for the XOR operation is $\oplus$. The algebraic definition of $a \oplus b$ is

$$a \oplus b = a \cdot b' + a' \cdot b$$

The precedence for the XOR operator is greater than OR but less than AND, as Figure 10.9 shows.

Example 10.3 The expression

$$a + b \oplus c \cdot d$$

fully parenthesized is $a + (b \oplus (c \cdot d))$. Expanded according to the definition of XOR, the expression becomes

$$a + b \cdot (c \cdot d)' + b' \cdot (c \cdot d)$$ ∎

Precedence	Operator
Highest	Complement
	AND
	XOR
Lowest	OR

Figure **10.9**

Precedence of the XOR operator.

The AND and OR gates are also manufactured with more than two inputs. Figure 10.10 shows a three-input AND gate and its truth table. The output of an AND gate is 1 only if all of its inputs are 1. The output of an OR gate is 0 only if all of its inputs are 0.

$x = a \cdot b \cdot c$

a	b	c	x
0	0	0	0
0	0	1	0
0	1	0	0
0	1	1	0
1	0	0	0
1	0	1	0
1	1	0	0
1	1	1	1

Figure **10.10**

The three-input AND gate.

Alternate Representations

You may have recognized the similarity of the truth tables for the AND, OR, and inverter gates and the truth tables for the AND, OR, and NOT operations in C++'s boolean expressions. The truth tables are identical, with NOT corresponding to the inverter and C++'s true and false values corresponding to boolean algebra's 1 and 0, respectively.

The mathematical structure of boolean algebra is important because it applies not only to combinational circuits, but also to statement logic. C++ uses statement logic to determine the truth of a condition contained in if and loop statements. A recent group of programming languages important in artificial intelligence makes even more extensive use of statement logic. Programs written in these languages simulate human reasoning by a technique called *logic programming*. Boolean algebra is a major component of that discipline.

Statement logic interpretation

Another interpretation of boolean algebra is a description of operations on sets. If you interpret a boolean variable as a set, the OR operation as set union, the AND operation as set intersection, the complement operation as set complement, 0 as the

Set theory interpretation

empty set, and 1 as the universal set, then all the properties and theorems of boolean algebra hold for sets.

Example 10.4   The theorem

$$x + 1 = 1$$

states that the union of the universal set with any other set is the universal set.   ■

Example 10.5   Figure 10.11 shows the set theory interpretation of an absorption property

$$x + x \cdot y = x$$

with a Venn diagram. Figure 10.11(a) shows set x. The intersection of x and y, shown in (b), is the set of elements in both x and y. The union of that set with x is shown in (c). The fact that the region in (a) is the same as the region in (c) illustrates the absorption property.   ■

Figure **10.11**

The set theory interpretation of an absorption property.

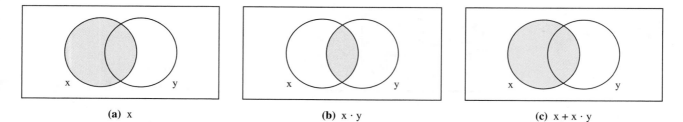

(a) x   **(b)** x · y   **(c)** x + x · y

The interpretation of boolean algebra as a description of combinational circuits and as the basis of statement logic illustrates that it is the mathematical basis of a large part of computer science. The fact that it also describes set theory shows its importance in other areas of mathematics as well.

10.2   Combinational Analysis

Every boolean expression has a corresponding logic diagram, and every logic diagram has a corresponding boolean expression. In mathematical terminology, there is a one-to-one correspondence between the two. A given truth table, however, can have several corresponding implementations. Figure 10.12 shows a truth table with several corresponding boolean expressions and logic diagrams.

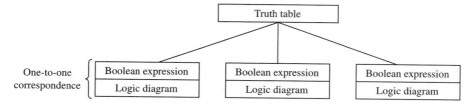

Figure **10.12**

Several implementations of a given truth table.

This section describes the correspondence among the three representations of a combinational circuit.

Boolean Expressions and Logic Diagrams

A boolean expression consists of one or more variables combined with the AND, OR, and invert operations. The number of inputs to the circuit equals the number of variables. This section and the next concentrate on circuits with one output. The last section of this chapter considers circuits with more than one output.

To draw the logic diagram from a given boolean expression, draw an AND gate for each AND operation, an OR gate for each OR operation, and an inverter for each complement operation. Connect the output of one gate to the input of another according to the expression. The output of the combinational circuit is the output of the one gate that is not connected to the input of another.

Example 10.6   Figure 10.13 shows the logic diagram corresponding to the boolean expression $a + b' \cdot c$.

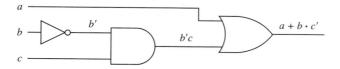

Figure **10.13**

The logic diagram for the boolean expression $a + b' \cdot c$.

From now on, we will omit the AND operator symbol and write the boolean expression as

$a + b'c$

The output of each gate is labeled with its corresponding expression.   ∎

When the expression has parentheses, you must construct the subdiagram within the parentheses first.

Example 10.7   Figure 10.14 is the logic diagram for the three-variable expression

$$((ab + bc')a)'$$

You first form ab with one AND gate, then bc' with another AND gate. The output of those two are ORed and then ANDed with a. Because the entire expression is complemented, an inverter is the last gate. ∎

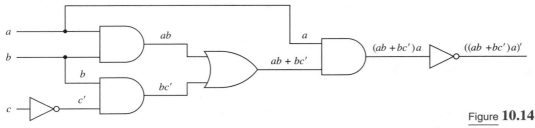

Figure **10.14**

The logic diagram for the boolean expression $((ab + bc')a)'$.

Figure 10.14 shows two junctions as small black dots where two wires are physically connected. Recall that the physical signal supplied by variable a is a voltage. When the signal from input a reaches the junction, it does not act like water in a river that encounters a fork in its path. In the river analogy, some of the water takes one path and some takes the other. In a logic diagram it does not happen that part of the signal goes to the input of one AND gate and part goes to the other gate. The full signal from a is duplicated at the inputs at both gates.

For those who know some physics, the reason for this behavior is that voltage is a measure of electric potential. The wires have low resistance, which from Ohm's law means there is negligible potential change along a wire. So, the voltage along any wires that are physically connected is constant. The full voltage signal is, therefore, available at any point, regardless of the junction. (For those who do not know some physics, this may be an incentive to learn!)

The signal from any variable can be duplicated with a junction. The complement of any variable can be produced by an inverter, which can, in turn, also be duplicated by a junction. Rather than show variable-duplicating junctions and variable inverters, they are often omitted from the logic diagram. It is assumed that any variable or its complement is available as input to any gate.

Example 10.8   Figure 10.15 shows an abbreviated version of Figure 10.14 that takes advantage of this assumption. It also recognizes that an AND gate followed by an inverter is equivalent to a NAND gate. ∎

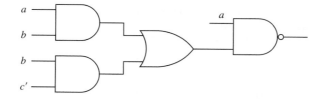

Figure **10.15**

An abbreviated version of Figure 10.14.

A disadvantage of this abbreviated diagram is that the three-input nature of the network is not as evident as it is in Figure 10.14.

Example 10.9   Figure 10.16 shows the logic diagram for the four-input boolean expression

$$(a'bc \oplus c + a + d)'$$

Note that the precedence of the exclusive OR operator is less than that of AND and greater than that of OR.   ∎

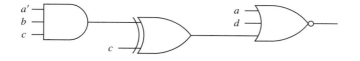

Figure **10.16**

The logic diagram for the boolean expression $(a'bc \oplus c + a + d)'$.

To write the boolean expression from a given logic diagram, simply label the output of each gate with the appropriate subexpression. If you were given the logic diagram of Figure 10.16 without the boolean expression, you would start by labeling the output of the AND gate as $a'bc$. The output of the XOR gate would be labeled $a'bc \oplus c$, which when passed through the NOR gate produces the full boolean expression.

Truth Tables and Boolean Expressions

One method for constructing a boolean expression from a truth table is to write the expression without parentheses as an OR of several AND terms. Each AND term corresponds to a 1 in the truth table.

Example 10.10   The truth table for $a \oplus b$ has two 1's. The corresponding boolean expression is

$$a \oplus b = a'b + ab'$$

If a is 0 and b is 1, the first AND term will be 1. If a is 1 and b is 0, the second AND term will be 1. In either case the OR of the two terms will be 1. Furthermore, any other combination of values for a and b will make both AND terms 0, and the boolean expression 0.   ∎

Example 10.11   Figure 10.3 shows x is 1 when $abc = 001$ and $abc = 011$; x is 0 for all other combinations of abc. A corresponding boolean expression is

$$x = a'b'c + a'bc$$

The first AND term, $a'b'c$, is 1 if and only if $abc = 001$. The second is 1 if and only if $abc = 011$. So the OR of the two terms will be 0 except under either of those conditions, duplicating the truth table.   ∎

Example 10.12   An example with four variables is the truth table for x in Figure 10.4. A corresponding expression is

$$x = a'bc'd + a'bcd + abc'd + abcd$$

which gives 1 for the four combinations of a, b, c, and d that have 1 in the truth table.   ∎

The dual technique is to write an expression as the AND of several OR terms. Each OR term corresponds to a 0 in the truth table.

Example 10.13   The expression from Figure 10.17 is

$$x = (a + b' + c')(a' + b' + c)$$

If $abc = 011$, the first OR term is 0. If $abc = 110$, the second OR term is 0. Under either of these conditions, the AND of the OR terms is 0. All other combinations of abc will make both OR terms 1 and the expression 1.   ∎

Given a boolean expression, the most straightforward way to construct the corresponding truth table is to evaluate the expression for all possible combinations of the variables.

Example 10.14   To construct the truth table for

$$x(a, b) = (a \oplus b)' + a'$$

a	b	c	x
0	0	0	1
0	0	1	1
0	1	0	1
0	1	1	0
1	0	0	1
1	0	1	1
1	1	0	0
1	1	1	1

Figure **10.17**

A three-variable truth table.

requires the evaluation of

$$x(0, 0) = (0 \oplus 0)' + 0' = 1$$
$$x(0, 1) = (0 \oplus 1)' + 0' = 1$$
$$x(1, 0) = (1 \oplus 0)' + 1' = 0$$
$$x(1, 1) = (1 \oplus 1)' + 1' = 1$$

This example requires the evaluation of all four possible combinations of the two variables a and b. ∎

If the expression contains more than two variables, sometimes it is easier to convert the boolean expression into an OR of AND terms using the properties and theorems of boolean algebra. The truth table can then be written by inspection.

Example 10.15   The expression in Figure 10.16 reduces to

$(a'bc \oplus c + a + d)'$

=   ⟨definition of $\oplus$⟩

$(a'bcc' + (a'bc)'c + a + d)'$

=   ⟨complement, $cc' = 0$, and zero theorem $x \cdot 0 = 0$⟩

$((a'bc)'c + a + d)'$

=   ⟨De Morgan⟩

$((a + b' + c')c + a + d)'$

=   ⟨distributive, complement, and identity⟩

$(ac + b'c + a + d)'$

=   ⟨absorption, $a + ac = a$⟩

$(a + b'c + d)'$

=   ⟨De Morgan⟩

$a'(b'c)'d'$

=   ⟨De Morgan⟩

$a'(b + c')d'$

=   ⟨distributive⟩

$a'bd' + a'c'd'$

a	b	c	d	x
0	0	0	0	1
0	0	0	1	0
0	0	1	0	0
0	0	1	1	0
0	1	0	0	1
0	1	0	1	0
0	1	1	0	1
0	1	1	1	0
1	0	0	0	0
1	0	0	1	0
1	0	1	0	0
1	0	1	1	0
1	1	0	0	0
1	1	0	1	0
1	1	1	0	0
1	1	1	1	0

The truth table has 16 entries. By inspection, insert a 1 where $abd = 010$ (two places) and $acd = 000$ (two places). All other entries are 0. The result is Figure 10.18. It has three 1's instead of four because one of the places where $abd = 010$ is also one of the places where $acd = 000$.

This technique saves you from evaluating the original expression 16 times. Actually, that task may not be as difficult as it first appears. With a little thought,

Figure **10.18**

The truth table for the expression in Figure 10.16.

you can reason from the original expression that when d is 1, the expression inside the parentheses must be 1, and its inverse must be 0 regardless of the values of a, b, and c. Similarly, the expression must be 0 when a is 1. That leaves you with only the four evaluations where $ad = 00$. ∎

Two-Level Circuits

The fact that every boolean expression can be transformed to an AND-OR expression has an important practical effect on the processing speed of the combinational circuit. When you change a signal at the input of a gate, the output does not respond instantly. Instead, there is a time delay during which the signal works its way through the internal electronic components of the gate. The time it takes for the output of a gate to respond to a change in its input is called the *gate delay*. Different manufacturing processes produce gates with different gate delays. To produce gates with short gate delays is more expensive, and the gates require more power to operate than gates with longer delays. A typical gate delay is 2 ns (nanoseconds), although the delay varies widely depending on the device technology.

Gate delays

   Two billionths of a second may not seem like a long time to wait for the output, but in a circuit with a long string of gates that must do its processing in a loop, the time can be significant. By way of comparison, consider the fact that the signal travels through the wires at approximately the speed of light, which is 3.0×10^8 m/s (meters per second). That is 30 cm, or about a foot, in 1 ns. In 2 ns, the time of a typical gate delay, the signal can travel through 60 cm of wire. This is such a long distance compared to the size of an integrated circuit or circuit board that the gate delay is, for all practical purposes, responsible for the limit on a network's processing speed.

Physical limits on processing speed

Example 10.16   Consider the circuit of Figure 10.16. If the gate delay is 2 ns, a change in b requires 2 ns to propagate through the AND gate, 2 ns to propagate through the XOR gate, and another 2 ns to propagate through the NOR gate. That is a total of 6 ns of propagation time. (We will ignore the propagation delay through any inverters.)

   Now consider that we used boolean algebra to write the expression for this circuit as an AND-OR expression:

$$x = (a'bc \oplus c + a + d)'$$
$$= a'bd' + a'c'd'$$

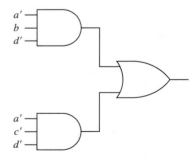

Figure **10.19**

The two-level AND-OR circuit equivalent to the circuit of Figure 10.16.

Figure 10.19 shows the corresponding circuit. It is called a two-level circuit because a change in the input requires only two gate delays to propagate to the output. ∎

Reducing the processing time from 6 ns to 4 ns is a 33% improvement in speed, which is significant. Because any boolean expression can be transformed to an AND-OR expression, which corresponds to a two-level AND-OR circuit, it follows that any function can be implemented with a combinational circuit with a processing time of two gate delays at most.

The same principle applies to the dual. It is always possible to transform a boolean expression to an OR-AND expression, which corresponds to a two-level OR-AND circuit. Such a circuit has a processing time of two gate delays at most. To obtain the boolean expression as an OR-AND expression, you can first obtain the complement as an AND-OR expression, and then use De Morgan's law.

Example 10.17   Figure 10.20 is the two-level OR-AND circuit of Figure 10.17 for the expression

$$x = (a + b' + c')(a' + b' + c)$$

Recall that each OR term corresponds to a 0 in the truth table. ∎

Example 10.18   The expression from Figure 10.13 is

$$x = a + b'c$$

To transform this expression into an OR-AND expression, first write its complement as

$$x' = (a + b'c)'$$
$$= a'(b'c)'$$
$$= a'(b + c')$$
$$= a'b + a'c'$$

which is an AND-OR expression. Now use De Morgan's law to write x as

$$x = (x')'$$
$$= (a'b + a'c')'$$
$$= (a'b)'(a'c')'$$
$$= (a + b')(a + c)$$

which is an OR-AND expression. ∎

It usually happens that a circuit with three or more levels requires fewer gates than the equivalent two-level circuit. Because a gate occupies physical space in an integrated circuit, the two-level circuit achieves its faster processing time at the expense of the extra space required for the additional gates.

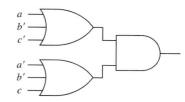

Figure **10.20**

The two-level OR-AND circuit of Figure 10.17.

This is yet another example of the space/time tradeoff in computer science. It is remarkable that the same space/time principle is manifest from software at the highest level of abstraction to hardware at the lowest level. It is truly a fundamental principle.

The fundamental space/time trade-off

The Ubiquitous NAND

The expression $(abc)'$ represents a three-input NAND gate. De Morgan's law states that

$$(abc)' = a' + b' + c'$$

You can visualize the second expression as the output of an OR gate that inverts each input before performing the OR operation. Logic diagrams occasionally render the NAND gate as an inverted input NOR, as in Figure 10.21(a).

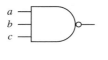

(a) A NAND gate as an inverted input OR gate.

(b) A NOR gate as an inverted input AND gate.

Figure **10.21**

Equivalent gates.

The dual concept follows from the dual expressions

$$(a + b + c)' = a'b'c'$$

A NOR gate is equivalent to an AND gate that inverts its inputs as in Figure 10.21(b).

Carrying this idea one step further to two-level circuits, consider the equivalence of

$$abc + def = [(abc)'(def)']'$$

which again follows from De Morgan's law. The first expression represents a two-level AND-OR circuit, whereas the second represents a two-level NAND-NAND circuit. Figure 10.22 shows the equivalent circuits.

Figure 10.22(a) shows an AND-OR circuit with two AND gates and one OR. You can make the equivalent circuit entirely out of NAND gates, as shown in (b). Part (c) shows the same circuit as (b) but with the last NAND drawn as an inverted-input OR. This drawing style makes it apparent that the complement following the

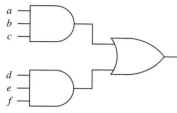
(a) An AND-OR circuit.

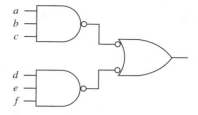
(b) The equivalent NAND-NAND circuit.

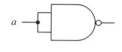
(c) The same NAND-NAND circuit as in part (b).

AND operation cancels the complement preceding the OR operation. The shape of the gate symbols becomes similar to those in the AND-OR circuit, which helps to convey the meaning of the circuit.

Not only can you replace an arbitrary AND-OR circuit entirely with NAND gates, you can also construct an inverter from a NAND gate by connecting the NAND inputs together, as shown in Figure 10.23. Because the NAND produces $(ab)'$ with input a and b, if you force $b = a$, the gate will produce $(a \cdot a)' = a'$, the complement of a.

Conceptually, you can construct any combinational circuit from only NAND gates. Furthermore, NAND gates are usually easier to manufacture than either AND or OR gates. Consequently, the NAND gate is by far the most common gate found in integrated circuits.

Of course, the same principle applies to the dual circuit. De Morgan's law for two-level circuits is

$$(a + b + c)(d + e + f) = [(a + b + c)' + (d + e + f)']'$$

which shows that an OR-AND circuit is equivalent to a NOR-NOR circuit. Figure 10.24 is the dual circuit of Figure 10.22.

The same reasoning that applies to NAND circuits also applies to NOR circuits. Any combinational circuit can be written as a two-level OR-AND circuit, which can be written as NOR-NOR. Connecting the inputs of a NOR makes an inverter. You can conceptually construct any combinational circuit with only NOR gates.

Figure **10.22**

An AND-OR circuit and its equivalent NAND-NAND circuit.

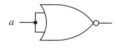

Figure **10.23**

Three equivalent circuits.

Figure **10.24**

An OR-AND circuit and its equivalent NOR-NOR circuit.

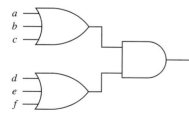
(a) An OR-AND circuit.

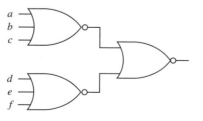
(b) The equivalent NOR-NOR circuit.

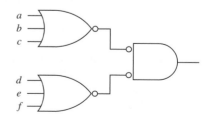
(c) The same NOR-NOR circuit as in part (b).

10.3   Combinational Design

The high speed of two-level circuits gives them an advantage over circuits with more than two levels of gates. Sometimes it is possible to reduce the number of gates in a two-level circuit and retain the processing speed of two gate delays.

Example 10.19   The boolean expression

$$x(a, b, c, d) = a'bd' + a'c'd' + a'bc'd'$$

can be simplified using the absorption property to

$$x(a, b, c, d) = a'bd' + (a'c'd') + (a'c'd')b$$
$$= a'bd' + a'c'd'$$

This expression also corresponds to a two-level circuit, but it requires only two three-input AND gates and a two-input OR gate compared to three AND gates, one of which has four inputs, and a three-input OR gate.   ∎

Minimizing the number of gates in a two-level circuit is not always straightforward with boolean algebra. This section presents a graphical method for designing two-level circuits with three or four variables that contain the minimum possible number of gates.

Canonical Expressions

The previous section shows that any boolean expression can be transformed to a two-level AND-OR expression. To minimize the two-level circuit, it is desirable to first make each AND term contain all input variables exactly once. Such an AND term is called a *minterm*. It is always possible to transform an AND-OR expression   *Minterms* into an OR of minterms.

Example 10.20   Consider the boolean expression

$$x(a, b, c) = abc + a'bc + ab$$

The first two AND terms are minterms because they contain all three variables, but the last is not. The transformation is

$$x = abc + a'bc + ab$$
$$= abc + a'bc + ab(c + c')$$
$$= abc + a'bc + abc + abc'$$
$$= abc + a'bc + abc'$$

The last expression is called a *canonical expression* because it is an OR of minterms in which no two identical minterms appear.   ∎

The definition of a canonical expression

A canonical expression is directly related to the truth table because each minterm in the expression represents a 1 in the truth table. A convenient shorthand notation for a canonical expression and its corresponding truth table is called *sigma notation*, which consists of the uppercase Greek letter sigma (Σ) followed by a list of decimal numbers that specify the rows in the truth table that contain 1's. The uppercase sigma represents the OR operation. It is understood that all the rows not listed contain 0's.

Row (dec)	a	b	c	x
0	0	0	0	0
1	0	0	1	0
2	0	1	0	0
3	0	1	1	1
4	1	0	0	0
5	1	0	1	0
6	1	1	0	1
7	1	1	1	1

Example 10.21   In Example 10.20, because the canonical expression for x has three minterms, its truth table has three 1's. Figure 10.25 shows the truth table for this function. It labels each row with the decimal number equivalent of the binary number *abc*. The corresponding sigma notation for this function is

$$x(a, b, c) = \Sigma(3, 6, 7)$$

because rows 3, 6, and 7 contain 1's.   ∎

Figure **10.25**

The truth table for a canonical expression.

The dual canonical expression is an OR-AND expression, each term of which contains all variables once, with no OR terms duplicated. The corresponding notation for this canonical expression contains the list of 0's in the truth table. The uppercase Greek letter pi (Π), which represents the AND operation, is used instead of sigma.

Example 10.22   The dual canonical expression for the previous example is

$$x(a, b, c) = (a + b + c)\,(a + b + c')\,(a + b' + c)\,(a' + b + c)\,(a' + b + c')$$

which is written in pi notation as

$$x(a, b, c) = \Pi(0, 1, 2, 4, 5)$$

because these are the five rows that contain 0's in the truth table.   ∎

Example 10.23   Using the sigma notation, x and y from Figure 10.3 are

$$x(a, b, c) = \Sigma(1, 3)$$
$$y(a, b, c) = \Sigma(3, 4)$$

Functions x and y from Figure 10.4 are

$$x(a, b, c, d) = \Sigma(5, 7, 13, 15)$$
$$y(a, b, c, d) = \Sigma(4, 5, 12, 13)$$

   ∎

Sigma and pi notation are more compact than the canonical boolean expressions or the truth tables. The remainder of this section assumes that the function to be minimized has been transformed to its unique canonical expression, or that its truth table has been given or determined.

Three-Variable Karnaugh Maps

Minimization of two-level circuits is based on the concept of distance. The *distance* between two minterms is the number of places in which they differ.   *Distance between minterms*

Example 10.24   Consider the canonical expression for this function of three variables:

$$x(a, b, c) = a'bc + abc + abc'$$

The distance between minterms $a'bc$ and abc is one, because a' and a are the only variables that differ. Variables b and c are the same in both. The distance between minterms $a'bc$ and abc' is two, because a' and c in $a'bc$ differ from a and c' in abc'.
∎

Recognizing *adjacent minterms*, that is, minterms a distance of one from each other, is key to the minimization of an AND-OR expression. Once you identify two adjacent minterms, you can factor out the common terms with the distributive property and simplify with the complement and identity properties.   *Adjacent minterms*

Example 10.25   You can minimize the expression in Example 10.24 by combining the first two minterms as follows:

$$
\begin{aligned}
x(a, b, c) &= a'bc + abc + abc' \\
&= (a' + a)bc + abc' \\
&= bc + abc'
\end{aligned}
$$

Alternatively, you can minimize by combining the second and third minterms, as they are also adjacent.

$$
\begin{aligned}
x(a, b, c) &= a'bc + abc + abc' \\
&= a'bc + ab(c + c') \\
&= a'bc + ab
\end{aligned}
$$

Either way, you have improved the circuit. The original expression is for a circuit with three three-input AND gates and one three-input OR gate. Either of the simplified expressions is for a circuit with only two AND gates, one of which has only two inputs, and an OR gate with only two inputs.   ∎

Recognizing adjacent minterms is the easy part. Sometimes it is helpful to make the expression temporarily more complicated to get a smaller final circuit. That happens when one minterm is adjacent to two other minterms. You can use the idempotent property to duplicate the minterm, then combine it with both of its adjacent minterms.

Ada Byron, Countess of Lovelace

Ada Byron was born in London on December 10, 1815. She was the daughter of the Romantic poet, Lord Byron, but never knew him, as he left her mother just a month after Ada was born. Her mother trained her in music and mathematics to counter her father's dangerous poetic tendencies.

Ada met Charles Babbage, a professor of mathematics at Cambridge, when she was 17. It was the beginning of a long relationship that produced a voluminous correspondence on a wide range of subjects including mathematics and logic. Ada married William King in 1835, with whom she had three children. King inherited a noble title, by which they became the Earl and Countess of Lovelace.

Babbage is known primarily for his foresight into the principles of construction of computing machines that were far ahead of his time. He made plans for two kinds of machines—Difference Engines to calculate mathematical tables, and the far more ambitious Analytical Engines, controlled by punched cards and capable of general-purpose computations. In the same way that logic gates process digital bits as 1's and 0's, Babbage's engines represented the value of a bit as the presence or absence of a hole punched in a card. Financial and organizational barriers prevented any of his larger engines from being built.

In the autumn of 1841, Babbage reported on his Analytical Engine at a seminar in Italy. Luigi Menabrea wrote a paper titled "A Sketch of the Analytical Engine Invented by Charles Babbage," in French, which Ada translated into English. When she showed it to Babbage, he suggested that she add her own notes.

© Crown Copyright: UK Government Art Collection.

Her notes were three times the length of the original paper, and it is for them that she is renowned.

Ada had the insight to see how to control the Analytical Engine to produce important mathematical results. An example is the computation of Bernoulli numbers, which are important in number theory and analysis. Bernoulli himself calculated the first ten numbers, and the mathematician Euler got up to the 30th one, followed by Martin Ohm, who made it to the 62nd number in 1840. All these men calculated the numbers by hand. But Ada, in the notes to Menabrea's Analytical Engine paper, wrote a program that would control the Analytical Engine to calculate the numbers automatically.

Ada Byron is regarded as the world's first programmer. She predicted that machines would be able to produce graphic images and even music. In 1979, the programming language Ada was named after her, and is still widely used. Ada died on November 27, 1852, at the young age of 37. She is buried beside the father she never knew.

Example 10.26 In Example 10.25, you can duplicate abc with the idempotent property first, then combine it with both of the remaining minterms.

$$
\begin{aligned}
x(a, b, c) &= a'bc + abc + abc' \\
&= a'bc + abc + abc + abc' \\
&= (a' + a)bc + ab(c + c') \\
&= bc + ab
\end{aligned}
$$

This is better than the result in Example 10.25, because both AND gates require only two inputs. ∎

Performing the minimization with boolean algebra is tedious and error-prone. The Karnaugh map is a tool to minimize a two-level circuit that makes it easy to spot adjacent minterms and to determine which ones need to be duplicated with the idempotent property. A *Karnaugh map* is simply a truth table arranged so that adjacent entries represent minterms that differ by one.

Karnaugh maps

Figure 10.26(a) shows the Karnaugh map for three variables. The upper left cell is for $abc = 000$. To its right is the cell for $abc = 001$. To the right of that is the cell for $abc = 011$, and then $abc = 010$. The sequence

000, 001, 011, 010

guarantees that adjacent cells differ by one. That would not be the case if the cells were in numeric order

000, 001, 010, 011

because 001 is a distance two from 010.

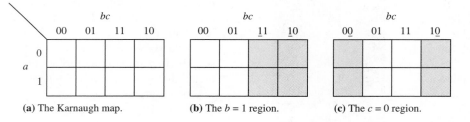

(a) The Karnaugh map.   (b) The $b = 1$ region.   (c) The $c = 0$ region.

Figure 10.26

The Karnaugh map for a function of three variables.

The top row contains entries in the truth table where $a = 0$ and the bottom row where $a = 1$. Each column gives the values for bc. For example, the first column is for $bc = 00$ and the second for $bc = 01$. The two leftmost columns are for $b = 0$, and the two rightmost columns, Figure 10.26(b), are for $b = 1$. The two outside columns, Figure 10.26(c), are for $c = 0$, and the two middle columns are for $c = 1$.

Factoring out a common term from adjacent minterms with boolean algebra corresponds to grouping adjacent cells on a Karnaugh map. After you group the cells, you write the simplified term by inspection of the region on the Karnaugh map.

The Karnaugh-map equivalent of the distributive property

Example 10.27 Figure 10.27(a) shows the Karnaugh map for the canonical expression

$$x(a, b, c) = a'bc + a'bc'$$

The 1 in the cell for $abc = 011$ is the truth table cell for the minterm $a'bc$. The 1 in the cell for $abc = 010$ is the truth table cell for the minterm $a'bc'$. Figure 10.27(b) is the same Karnaugh map with the zeros omitted for clarity. Because the two ones are adjacent, you can group them with an oval. The cells covered by the oval are in the row for $a = 0$ and the columns for $b = 1$. Therefore, they are the regions for $ab = 01$, which corresponds to the term $a'b$. So, $x(a, b, c) = a'b$. You can write down the result by inspecting of the Karnaugh map without doing the boolean algebra. ∎

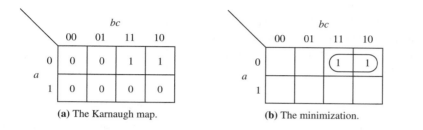

(a) The Karnaugh map.   (b) The minimization.

Figure **10.27**

The Karnaugh map for the AND-OR expression of Example 10.27.

Example 10.28 Figure 10.28(a) shows the Karnaugh map for the canonical expression

$$x(a, b, c) = ab'c' + abc'$$

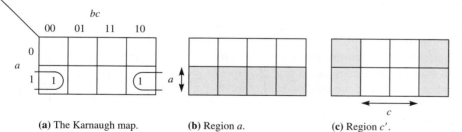

(a) The Karnaugh map.   (b) Region a.   (c) Region c'.

Figure **10.28**

The Karnaugh map for the AND-OR expression of Example 10.28.

It may appear that the $ab'c'$ cell in the lower left and the abc' cell in the lower right are not adjacent, but in fact they are. You should think of the Karnaugh map as wrapping around so that its left and right sides are adjacent, the so-called Pac-Man effect. The single oval in the figure is drawn as two open-ended half ovals to convey this property of the Karnaugh map.

The group of two cells lies in the $a = 1$ row and the $c = 0$ columns, as parts (b) and (c) of the figure show. You can imagine the two cells as the intersection of the shaded regions in (b) and (c). The region for the group is $ac = 10$. Therefore, the minimized function is $x(a, b, c) = ac'$. ∎

Duplicating a minterm with the idempotent property, so that it may be combined with two other minterms, corresponds to an overlap of two ovals in the Karnaugh map. If there are more than two minterms in the AND-OR expression, you are free to use a 1 in the truth table for more than one group.

The Karnaugh-map equivalent of the idempotent property

Example 10.29   Figure 10.29 shows the Karnaugh map for

$$x(a, b, c) = a'bc + abc + abc'$$

which is the canonical expression for Example 10.26. Part (a) shows minimization of the first and second minterms. Part (b) shows minimization of the second and third minterms. Part (c) shows that using the second term in both minimizations corresponds to an overlap of the two ovals. ∎

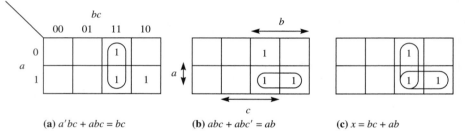

(a) $a'bc + abc = bc$ **(b)** $abc + abc' = ab$ **(c)** $x = bc + ab$

Figure **10.29**

The Karnaugh map for the AND-OR expression of Example 10.26.

When the original truth table is given in sigma notation, you can use the decimal labels of Figure 10.30 to insert 1's in the Karnaugh map.

The minimization procedure requires you to determine the best set of ovals that will cover all the 1's in the Karnaugh map. "Best" means the set that corresponds to a two-level circuit with the least number of gates and the least number of inputs per gate. The number of ovals equals the number of AND gates. The more 1's an oval covers, the smaller the number of inputs to the corresponding AND gate. It follows that you want the smallest number of ovals, with each oval as large as possible such that the ovals cover all the 1's and no 0's. It is permissible for a 1 to be covered by several ovals. The next few examples show the general strategy.

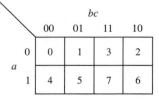

Figure **10.30**

Decimal labels for the minterms in the Karnaugh map.

Example 10.30   Figure 10.31 shows a common minimization mistake. To minimize

$$x(a, b, c) = \Sigma(0, 1, 5, 7)$$

you may be tempted to first group minterms 1 and 5 as in Figure 10.31(a). That is a bad first choice because minterm 1 is adjacent to both 0 and 5, and minterm 5 is

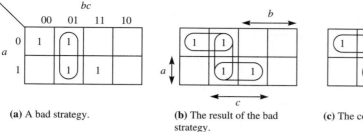

Figure **10.31**

The result of a bad first choice.

(a) A bad strategy.

(b) The result of the bad strategy.

(c) The correct minimization.

adjacent to both 1 and 7. On the other hand, minterm 0 is only adjacent to 1. To cover 0 with the largest possible oval you must group it with 1. Similarly, minterm 7 is only adjacent to 5. To cover 7 with the largest possible oval you must group it with 5.

Figure 10.31(b) shows the result of these minterm groupings. It represents the expression

$$x(a, b, c) = \Sigma(0, 1, 5, 7)$$
$$= a'b' + b'c + ac$$

which requires three two-input AND gates and a three-input OR gate. But the grouping of the first choice is not necessary. Figure 10.31(c) shows the correct minimization, which represents

$$x(a, b, c) = \Sigma(0, 1, 5, 7)$$
$$= a'b' + ac$$

This implementation requires only two two-input AND gates and a two-input OR gate. ∎

The rule of thumb that the previous example teaches us is to start a grouping with minterms that have only one nearest neighbor. Because their neighbors must be grouped with them in any event, you may be spared an unnecessary grouping of their neighbors.

Another common mistake is failing to recognize a large grouping of 1's, as Example 10.31 illustrates.

Example 10.31 Figure 10.32(a) shows the minimization of a three-variable function as

$$x(a, b, c) = \Sigma(0, 2, 4, 6, 7)$$
$$= b'c' + bc' + ab$$

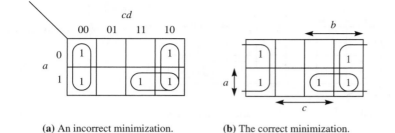

(a) An incorrect minimization.   (b) The correct minimization.

Figure **10.32**

Failing to recognize a large grouping.

which requires three two-input AND gates and one three-input OR gate. Figure 10.32(b) shows the correct minimization as

$$x(a, b, c) = c' + ab$$

which requires only one two-input AND gate and a two-input OR gate.   ∎

In a three-variable problem, a grouping of four 1's corresponds to an AND term of only one variable. Because the number of 1's in a group must correspond to an intersection of regions for a, b, and c and their complements, the number of 1's in a group must be a power of 2. For example, an oval can cover one, two, or four 1's but never three or five.

Four-Variable Karnaugh Maps

Minimization of a four-variable circuit follows the same procedure as a three-variable circuit, except that the Karnaugh map has twice as many entries. Figure 10.33(a) shows the arrangement of cells. Not only is minterm 0 adjacent to 2, and 4 adjacent to 6, but minterm 12 is adjacent to 14, and 8 to 10. Also, cells on the top row are adjacent to the corresponding cells on the bottom row. Minterm 0 is adjacent to 8, 1 to 9, 3 to 11, and 2 to 10.

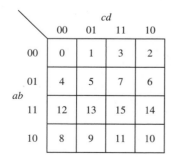

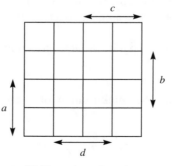

(a) Decimal labels for the minterms in the Karnaugh map.   (b) The regions where the variables are 1.

Figure **10.33**

The Karnaugh map for a function of four variables.

Each cell in a three-variable Karnaugh map has three adjacent cells. In a four-variable map, each cell has four adjacent cells. For example, the cells adjacent to minterm 10 are 2, 8, 11, and 14. Those adjacent to 4 are 0, 5, 6, and 12.

Figure 10.33(b) shows the regions of the truth table where the variables are 1. Variable a is 1 in the two bottom rows, and b is 1 in the two middle rows. Variable c is 1 in the two right columns, and d is 1 in the two middle columns.

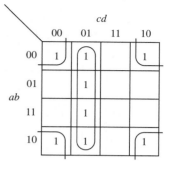

Figure 10.34

Minimizing a function of four variables.

Example 10.32   Figure 10.34 shows the minimization

$$x(a, b, c, d) = \Sigma(0, 1, 2, 5, 8, 9, 10, 13)$$
$$= c'd + b'd'$$

Note that the four corner cells can be grouped as $b'd'$. The second column of the Karnaugh map represents $c'd$. ∎

Example 10.33   Figure 10.35 shows the minimization

$$x(a, b, c, d) = \Sigma(0, 1, 2, 5, 8, 9, 10)$$
$$= a'c'd + b'c' + b'd'$$

Even though it differs from Example 10.32 by the omission of a single term, the minimization is much different.

Minterm 5 has only one adjacent 1, so it is grouped first by our rule of thumb with minterm 1. The AND term for this group is $a'c'd$, which you can determine by visualizing the intersection of the top two rows (a'), the left two columns (c'), and the middle two columns (d).

Covering minterm 9 with the largest oval requires you to group it with minterms 0, 1, and 8, not just 8. The AND term for this group is $b'c'$, which you can determine by visualizing the intersection of the top and bottom rows (b') with the left two columns (c').

The remaining uncovered 1's are minterms 2 and 10, which are grouped with 0 and 8 as before. ∎

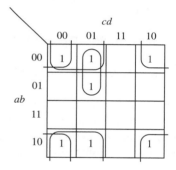

Figure 10.35

The expression of Figure 10.34 with one minterm fewer.

Example 10.34   Figure 10.36 shows that the minimization may not be unique. Two valid minimizations of this function are

$$x(a, b, c, d) = \Sigma(0, 4, 7, 8, 12, 13, 15)$$
$$= c'd' + bcd + abc'$$
$$= c'd' + bcd + abd$$

The first 1 you should group is minterm 7, because it has only one adjacent 1. Minterm 0 must be grouped with 4, 8, and 12, because there is no other possible group for it. That leaves minterm 13, which can be grouped with either 12 or 15. ∎

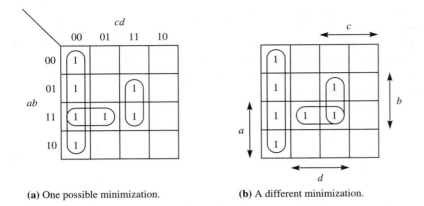

Figure **10.36**

Two different correct minimizations.

(a) One possible minimization.   **(b)** A different minimization.

Minimizing a four-variable function is not always straightforward. Sometimes you must simply experiment with several groupings in order to determine the true minimum.

Example 10.35   Figure 10.37 shows such a problem. The function is

$$\Sigma(0, 1, 2, 3, 5, 6, 7, 8, 9, 12, 13, 14)$$

Figure 10.37(a) is the result of the following reasoning. Consider minterm 12. The largest group it belongs to is the group of four corresponding to ac'. Similarly, the largest group minterm 6 belongs to is the group of four, $a'c$. Given these two groupings, you can group minterm 5 in $c'd$, minterm 0 in $a'b'$, and minterm 14 in bcd'. The expression

$$ac' + a'c + c'd + a'b' + bcd'$$

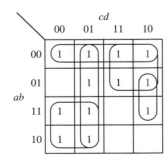
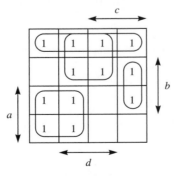

Figure **10.37**

A complicated minimization problem.

(a) A plausible but incorrect minimization.   **(b)** A correct minimization.

is plausible because none of the groupings looks redundant. You cannot remove any oval without uncovering a 1.

Given the selection of the first two groups, the remaining three groups are the best choices possible. The problem is in the selection of the second group.

Figure 10.37(b) is the result of the following reasoning. Group minterm 12 with ac' as before. Now consider minterm 14. You must group it with either 12 or 6. Because 12 is covered, group 14 with 6. Group the remaining minterms—0, 1, 2, 3, 5, 7—most efficiently, as in Figure 10.37(b). The resulting expression,

$$ac' + a'd + a'b' + bcd'$$

requires one fewer AND gate than Figure 10.37(a).

This is a tricky problem because in general you should cover a 1 with the largest possible group. That general rule does not apply in this problem, however. Once you determine the group ac', you should not place minterm 6 in the largest possible group.

Figure 10.38 shows that this solution is not unique. It begins by grouping minterm 6 in $a'c$, then minterm 14 with 12. The result is

$$a'c + b'c' + c'd + abd'$$ ∎

How do you know which minterms and groupings to consider when confronted with a complicated Karnaugh map? It simply takes practice, reasoning, and a little experimentation.

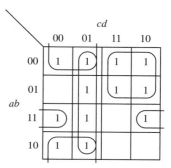

Figure **10.38**

Another correct minimization of the function of Figure 10.37.

Dual Karnaugh Maps

To minimize a function in an OR-AND expression, minimize the complement of the function in the AND-OR expression, and use De Morgan's law.

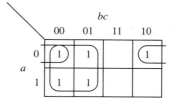

Figure **10.39**

The complement of the function in Figure 10.29.

Example 10.36   Figure 10.39 shows the minimization of the complement of the function in Figure 10.29. The original function is

$$x(a, b, c) = \Sigma(3, 6, 7)$$
$$= \Pi(0, 1, 2, 4, 5)$$

Its complement, minimized as shown in the figure, is

$$x'(a, b, c) = \Sigma(0, 1, 2, 4, 5)$$
$$= b' + a'c'$$

The original function in the minimized OR-AND expression is

$$x(a, b, c) = (x'(a, b, c))'$$
$$= (b' + a'c')'$$
$$= b(a + c)$$

which requires only two gates, compared to three with the minimized AND-OR expression,

$$x(a, b, c) = bc + ab$$ ∎

In the previous example, it pays to implement the function with a two-level NOR-NOR circuit instead of a NAND-NAND circuit. In general, you must minimize both forms to determine which requires fewer gates.

Don't-Care Conditions

Sometimes a combinational circuit is designed to process only some of the input combinations. The other combinations are not ever expected to be present in the input. These combinations are called *don't-care conditions* because you do not care what the output is if those conditions would ever appear.

Don't-care conditions give you extra flexibility in the minimization process. You can arbitrarily design the circuit to produce either 0 or 1 when a don't-care condition is present. By selectively choosing some don't-care conditions to produce 1 and others to produce 0, you can improve the minimization.

Example 10.37   Figure 10.40(a) shows minimization of

$$x(a, b, c) = \Sigma(2, 4, 6)$$
$$= bc' + ac'$$

without don't-care conditions. Now suppose that instead of requiring minterms 0 and 7 to produce 0, the problem specifies that those minterms can produce either 0 or 1. The notation for this specification is

$$x(a, b, c) = \Sigma(2, 4, 6) + d(0, 7)$$

where d preceding the minterm labels stands for a don't-care condition. Figure 10.40(b) shows × in the Karnaugh map cells for don't-care conditions.

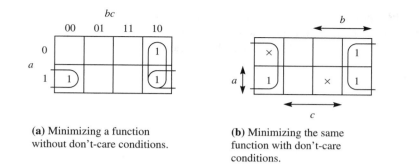

(a) Minimizing a function without don't-care conditions.

(b) Minimizing the same function with don't-care conditions.

Figure **10.40**

Don't-care conditions.

When you minimize with don't-care conditions, you are free to cover or not cover a cell with an $\times$. An $\times$ acts like a wildcard in that you can treat it as a 0 or a 1 as you like. In this problem, if you treat minterm 0 as a 1, and 7 as a 0, the minimization is

$$x(a, b, c) = \Sigma(2, 4, 6) + d(0, 7)$$
$$= \Sigma(0, 2, 4, 6)$$
$$= c'$$

The function without don't-care conditions requires two AND gates and one OR gate, whereas this function requires no AND or OR gates. ∎

10.4 Combinational Devices

This section describes some combinational devices that are commonly used in computer design. Each device can be specified as a black box with a corresponding truth table to define how the outputs depend on the inputs. Because all devices in this section are combinational, they can be implemented with two-level AND-OR circuits. Some implementations shown here trade off processing time for less space—that is, fewer gates—and have more than two levels.

Viewpoints

Several of the following devices have an input line called *enable*. The enable line acts like the on/off switch of an appliance. If the enable line is 0, the output lines are all 0's regardless of the values of the input lines. The device is turned off, or disabled. If the enable line is 1, the output lines depend on the input lines according to the function that specifies the device. The device is turned on, or enabled.

An AND gate can implement the enable property as shown in Figure 10.41(a). Line *a* is one of the outputs from the combinational circuit (not shown in the figure), which is input to the AND gate. The other input to the AND gate is the enable line.

When the enable line is 1,

$$x = a \cdot (\text{enable})$$
$$= a \cdot 1$$
$$= a$$

and the output equals the input as in Figure 10.41(b). When the enable line is 0,

$$x = a \cdot (\text{enable})$$
$$= a \cdot 0$$
$$= 0$$

regardless of the input as in Figure 10.41(c).

Implementing the enable property does not require a new "enable gate." It only requires that you adopt a different viewpoint of the familiar AND gate. You can think of input *a* as a data line and enable as a control line. The enable controls the data by either letting it pass through the gate unchanged or preventing it from passing.

Figure **10.41**

AND input as an enable.

Enable = 1	
a	*x*
0	0
1	1

Enable = 0	
a	*x*
0	0
1	0

(a) Logic diagram of enable gate.

(b) Truth table with the device turned on.

(c) Truth table with the device turned off.

Another useful gate is the *selective inverter*. For input, it has a data line and an invert line. If the invert line is 1, the output is the complement of the data line. If the invert line is 0, the data passes through to the output unchanged.

Figure 10.42(a) shows that the selective inverter is an XOR gate considered with a different viewpoint than it was previously. When the invert line is 1,

$$x = a \oplus (\text{invert})$$
$$= a' \cdot (\text{invert}) + a \cdot (\text{invert})'$$
$$= a' \cdot 1 + a \cdot 1'$$
$$= a'$$

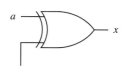

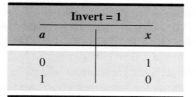

Invert = 1	
a	*x*
0	1
1	0

Invert = 0	
a	*x*
0	0
1	1

(a) Logic diagram of the selective inverter.

(b) Truth table with the inverter turned on.

(c) Truth table with the inverter turned off.

and the output equals the complement of the data input, as in Figure 10.42(b). When the invert line is 0,

Figure **10.42**

XOR input as a selective invert.

$$x = a \oplus (\text{invert})$$
$$= a' \cdot (\text{invert}) + a \cdot (\text{invert})'$$
$$= a' \cdot 0 + a \cdot 0'$$
$$= a$$

and the data passes through the gate unchanged.

Multiplexer

A *multiplexer* is a device that selects one of several data inputs to be routed to a single data output. Control lines determine the particular data input to be passed through.

Figure 10.43(a) shows the block diagram of an eight-input multiplexer. D0 to D7 are the data input lines, and S2 to S0 are the select control lines. F is the single data output line.

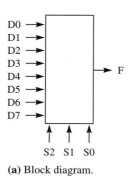

S2	S1	S0	F
0	0	0	D0
0	0	1	D1
0	1	0	D2
0	1	1	D3
1	0	0	D4
1	0	1	D5
1	1	0	D6
1	1	1	D7

Figure **10.43**

The eight-input multiplexer.

(a) Block diagram.

(b) Truth table.

Because this device has 11 inputs, a complete truth table would require 2^{11} = 2048 entries. Figure 10.43(b) shows an abbreviated truth table. The second entry shows that the output is D1 when the select lines are 001. That is, if D1 is 1, F is 1, and if D1 is 0, F is 0, regardless of the other values of D0 and D2 through D7.

Because *n* select lines can select one of 2^n data lines, the number of data inputs of a multiplexer is a power of 2. Figure 10.44 shows the implementation of a four-input multiplexer, which contains four data lines, D0 through D3, and two select lines, S1 and S0.

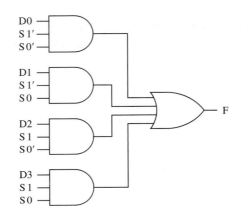

Figure **10.44**

Implementation of a four-input multiplexer.

An example of where a multiplexer might be used is in the implementation of the STr instruction in Pep/8. This instruction puts the contents of one of two registers from the CPU into memory via the bus. The CPU could do that with a two-input multiplexer that would make the selection. The select line would come from the register-r field, the inputs would come from the A and X registers, and the output would go to the bus.

Binary Decoder

A *decoder* is a device that takes a binary number as input and sets one of several data output lines to 1 and the rest to 0. The data line that is set to 1 depends on the value of the binary number that is input.

Figure 10.45(a) shows the block diagram of a 2 × 4 binary decoder. S1 S0 is the two-bit binary number input and D0 through D3 are the four outputs, one of which will be 1. Part (b) is the truth table.

S1	S0	D0	D1	D2	D3
0	0	1	0	0	0
0	1	0	1	0	0
1	0	0	0	1	0
1	1	0	0	0	1

Figure 10.45

The 2×4 binary decoder.

S1 → [ ] → D0, D1, D2, D3
S0 →

(a) Block diagram.　　　　**(b)** Truth table.

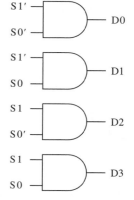

Figure 10.46

Implementation of a 2×4 binary decoder.

Because an *n*-bit number can have 2^n values, the number of data outputs of a decoder is a power of 2. Figure 10.46 shows the implementation of a 2×4 decoder. Some other possible sizes are 3×8 and 4×16.

Some decoders are designed with an enable input. Figure 10.47 is a block diagram of a 2×4 decoder with enable. When the enable line is 1, the device operates normally as in Figure 10.45(b). When the enable line is 0, all the outputs are 0. To implement a decoder with enable requires an extra input for each AND gate. The details are an exercise at the end of the chapter.

An example of where a decoder might be used is in the CPU of Pep/8. Some instructions have a three-bit addressing-aaa field that specifies one of eight addressing modes. The hardware would have eight address computation units, one for each mode, and each unit would have an enable line. The three aaa address lines would feed into a 3×8 decoder. Each output line from the decoder would enable one of the address computation units.

Demultiplexer

A multiplexer routes one of several data input values to a single output line. A *demultiplexer* does just the opposite. It routes a single input value to one of several output lines.

Figure 10.48(a) is the block diagram of a four-output demultiplexer. Part (b) is the truth table. If S1 S0 is 01, all the output lines are 0 except D1, which has the same value as the data input line.

This truth table is similar to Figure 10.45(b), the truth table for a decoder. In fact, a demultiplexer is nothing more than a decoder with enable. The data input line, D, is connected to the enable. If D is 0, the decoder is disabled, and the data output line selected by S1 S0 is 0. If D is 1, the decoder is enabled, and the data output line selected is 1. In either case, the selected output line has the same value as the data input line. This is another example of considering a combinational device from a different viewpoint to obtain a useful operation.

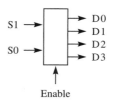

Enable

Figure 10.47

A 2×4 binary decoder with enable.

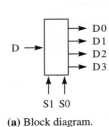

(a) Block diagram.

S1	S0	D0	D1	D2	D3
0	0	D	0	0	0
0	1	0	D	0	0
1	0	0	0	D	0
1	1	0	0	0	D

(b) Truth table.

Figure **10.48**

The four-output demultiplexer.

Adder

Consider the binary addition

$$
\begin{array}{r}
1011 \\
\text{ADD} \quad 0011 \\
\hline
C = 0 \quad 1110 \\
V = 0
\end{array}
$$

The sum of the least significant bits (LSBs) is 1 plus 1, which is 0 with a carry of 1 to the next column. To add the LSBs of two numbers requires the *half adder* of Figure 10.49(a). In the figure, A represents the LSB of the first number, and B the LSB of the second number. One output is Sum, 0 in this example, and the other is Carry, 1 in this example. Part (b) shows the truth table. The sum is identical to the XOR function and the carry is identical to the AND function. Part (c) is a straightforward implementation.

Figure **10.49**

The half adder.

A	B	Sum	Carry
0	0	0	0
0	1	1	0
1	0	1	0
1	1	0	1

(a) Block diagram.

(b) Truth table.

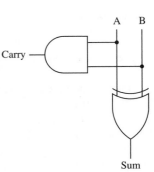

(c) Implementation.

A	B	Cin	Sum	Cout
0	0	0	0	0
0	0	1	1	0
0	1	0	1	0
0	1	1	0	1
1	0	0	1	0
1	0	1	0	1
1	1	0	0	1
1	1	1	1	1

Figure **10.50**

The full adder.

(a) Block diagram.

(b) Truth table.

To find the sum in the column next to the LSB requires a combinational circuit with three inputs: Cin, A, and B. Cin is the carry input, which comes from the carry of the LSB, and A and B are the bits from the first and second numbers. The outputs are Sum and Cout, the carry output that goes to Cin of the full adder for the next column. Figure 10.50(a) is the block diagram of the network, called a *full adder*. Figure 10.50(b) is the truth table. If the sum of the three inputs is odd, Sum is 1. If the sum of the three inputs is greater than 1, Cout is 1.

Figure 10.51 shows an implementation of the full adder that uses two half adders and an OR gate. The first half adder adds A and B. The second half adder adds the sum from the first half adder to Cin. The full adder sum is the sum from the second half adder. If either the first or second half adder has a carry, the full adder has a carry out.

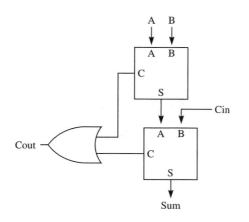

Figure **10.51**

An implementation of the full adder with two half adders.

To add the two four-bit numbers requires an eight-input circuit, shown in Figure 10.52(a). A3 A2 A1 A0 are the four bits of the first number, with A0 the LSB. B3 through B0 are the same for the second number. S3 S2 S1 S0 is the four-bit sum, with C the carry bit. An implementation of the four-bit adder can use one half adder for the LSB and three full adders, one for each of the remaining columns in the addition. That implementation is called a *ripple-carry adder* because a carry that originates from the LSB must propagate, or ripple through, the columns to the left. Figure 10.52(b) shows the implementation.

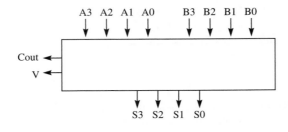

(a) Block diagram.

Figure **10.52**

The four-bit ripple-carry adder.

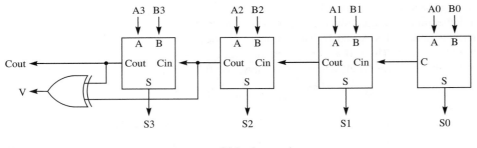

(b) Implementation.

The carry out of the ripple-carry adder is the Cout of its leftmost full adder. The carry bit indicates an overflow condition when you interpret the integer as unsigned. When you interpret the integer as signed using two's complement representation, the leftmost bit is the sign bit, and the bit next to it is the most significant bit of the magnitude. So with signed integers, the Cout signal of the penultimate full adder, S2 in this example, acts like the carry out.

The V bit indicates whether an overflow occurs when the numbers are interpreted as signed. You can only get an overflow in one of two cases.

- A and B are both positive, and the result is negative.
- A and B are both negative, and the result is positive.

The two cases for an overflow with signed integers

You cannot get an overflow by adding two integers with different signs. In the first case, A3 and B3 are both 0; there must be a carry from the penultimate full adder that makes S3 1, and Cout from the leftmost full adder is 0. In the second case, A3 and B3 are both 1, so there must be a carry out from the leftmost full adder, and there cannot be a carry out from the penultimate full adder, because S3 must be 0. In both of these cases, the carry out of the leftmost full adder is different from the carry out of the penultimate full adder. But that is precisely the XOR function. It is 1 if and only if its two inputs are different. So, the V bit is computed with the XOR gate taking its two inputs from the Cout signals of the leftmost and penultimate full adders.

The primary disadvantage of the ripple-carry adder is the time it takes the carry to ripple through all the full adders before a valid result is present in the output. Adder circuits have been extensively studied, because addition is such a basic mathematical operation. The carry-lookahead adder overcomes much of the speed disadvantage of the ripple-carry adder by incorporating a carry-lookahead unit in its design. More sophisticated adders are beyond the scope of this book.

Adder/Subtracter

To subtract B from A you could design a subtracter circuit along the same lines as the adder, but with a borrow mechanism that corresponds to the carry mechanism in addition. Rather than build a separate subtracter circuit, however, it is easier to simply negate B and add it to A. Recall the two's complement rule from Chapter 3:

NEG $x = 1 + $ NOT x

To negate a number, you invert all the bits of the number and then add 1. So, to build a circuit that will function as an adder or a subtracter, we need a way to selectively invert all the bits in B, and a way to selectively add 1 to it. Fortunately, the XOR gate comes to the rescue, because you can consider the XOR gate to be a selective inverter.

Figure 10.53 shows an adder/subtracter circuit based on this idea. Part (a) is a block diagram that differs from the block diagram of the ripple-carry adder only by the addition of a single control line labeled Sub. When Sub = 0, the circuit acts like an adder. When Sub = 1, the circuit acts like a subtracter.

Figure 10.53(b) is the implementation. With the adder circuit, you only need a half adder for the least significant bit. The adder/subtracter replaces it with a full adder. Consider the situation when Sub = 0. In that case, Cin of the least significant full adder is 0 and it acts like a half adder. Furthermore, the left input of each of the top four XOR gates is also 0, which allows the B signals to pass through them unchanged. The circuit computes the sum of A and B.

Now consider the case when Sub = 1. Because the left input of the top four XOR gates is 1, the values of all the bits in B are inverted. Furthermore, Cin of the

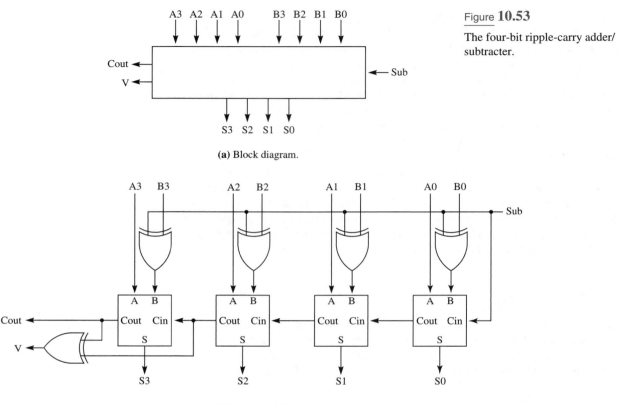

Figure **10.53**

The four-bit ripple-carry adder/subtracter.

(a) Block diagram.

(b) Implementation.

least significant full adder is 1, adding 1 to the result. Consequently the sum is the sum of A and the negation of B.

Arithmetic Logic Unit

The Pep/8 instructions that perform processing include ADDr, ANDr, and ORr. The addition is an arithmetic operation, whereas AND and OR are logical operations. The CPU typically contains a single combinational circuit called the arithmetic logic unit (ALU) that performs these computations.

Figure 10.54 shows the ALU for the Pep/8 CPU. A line with a slash represents more than one control line, with the number by the slash specifying the number of lines. The line labeled ALU represents four wires. The ALU has a total of 21 input lines—8 lines for the A input, 8 lines for the B input, 4 lines to specify the function that the ALU performs, and the Cin line. It has 12 output lines—8 lines for Result plus the 4 NZVC values corresponding to Result. The carry output line is labeled

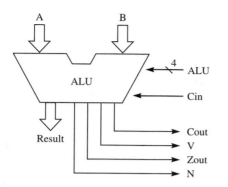

Figure **10.54**

Block diagram of the Pep/8 ALU.

Cout to distinguish it from the carry input line Cin. The zero output line is labeled Zout to distinguish it from another Z line in the CPU as described in Chapter 12.

The four ALU control lines specify which of 16 functions the ALU will perform. Figure 10.55 lists the 16 functions, most of which correspond directly to the operations available in the Pep/8 instruction set. Because the + symbol is commonly used for the logical OR operation, the arithmetic operations are spelled out as "plus" and "minus." Listed with each operation are the values of the corresponding NZVC bits.

ALU control			Status bits			
(bin)	**(dec)**	**Result**	**N**	**Zout**	**V**	**Cout**
0000	0	A	N	Z	0	0
0001	1	A plus B	N	Z	V	C
0010	2	A plus B plus Cin	N	Z	V	C
0011	3	A plus $\overline{B}$ plus 1	N	Z	V	C
0100	4	A plus $\overline{B}$ plus Cin	N	Z	V	C
0101	5	A · B	N	Z	0	0
0110	6	$\overline{A \cdot B}$	N	Z	0	0
0111	7	A + B	N	Z	0	0
1000	8	$\overline{A + B}$	N	Z	0	0
1001	9	A⊕B	N	Z	0	0
1010	10	$\overline{A}$	N	Z	0	0
1011	11	ASL A	N	Z	V	C
1100	12	ROL A	N	Z	0	C
1101	13	ASR A	N	Z	0	C
1110	14	ROR A	N	Z	0	C
1111	15	0	A<4>	A<5>	A<6>	A<7>

Figure **10.55**

The 16 functions of the Pep/8 ALU.

Figure 10.56 shows the implementation of the ALU. You can see the 21 input lines coming in from the top and the right, and the 12 output lines coming out from the bottom. The four ALU lines that come in from the right drive a 4×16 decoder. Recall that depending on the value of the ALU input, exactly one of the output lines of the decoder will be 1 and the others will all be 0. The computation unit inside the ALU performs the first 15 functions of Figure 10.55. Each of the 15 lines from the decoder into the Computation Unit enables a combinational circuit that performs the function.

Figure **10.56**

Implementation of the ALU of Figure 10.54.

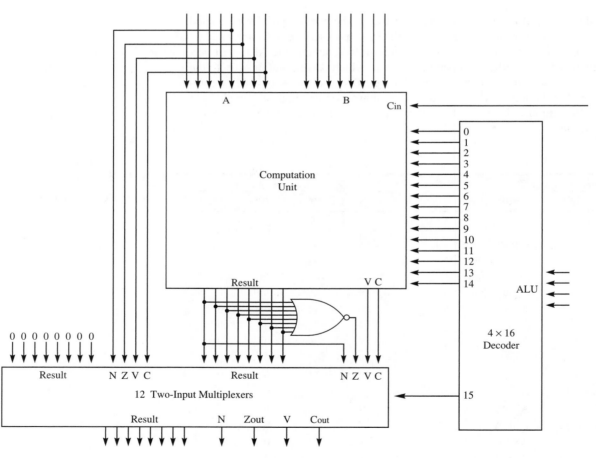

The Computation Unit has 32 input lines—8 lines for the A input, 8 lines for the B input, 1 line for Cin, and 15 lines from the decoder. It has 10 output lines— 8 lines for the result of the computation plus 1 line each for V and C. Computation of the N and Z bits is external to the Computation Unit. Figure 10.56 shows that the N bit is simply a copy of the most significant bit of Result from the Computation Unit. The Z bit is the NOR of all eight bits of Result. If all eight bits are 0, the output of the NOR gate is 1. If one or more inputs are 1, the output of the NOR gate is 0. These are precisely the conditions for which the Z bit should be set depending on the result of the computation.

Computation of the N and Z bits

The bottom box on the left is a set of 12 two-input multiplexers. The control line of each multiplexer is tied to line 15 from the decoder. The control line acts as follows:

The multiplexer of Figure 10.56

- If line 15 is 1, Result and NZVC from the left are routed to the output.
- If line 15 is 0, Result and NZVC from the right are routed to the output.

You can see how Figure 10.56 computes the last function of Figure 10.55. If the ALU input is 1111 (bin) then line 15 is 1, and Result and NZVC from the left are routed to the output of the ALU. But Figure 10.56 shows that Result from the left is tied to 0 and NZVC comes from the low nybble (half byte) of A, as required.

Figure 10.57 is an implementation of the Computation Unit of Figure 10.56. It consists of 1 A Unit, 1 Arithmetic Unit, and 10 logic units labeled logic Unit 5 through Logic Unit 14. The A Unit and the logic units are each enabled by 1 of the 15 decoder lines. If the enable line E of any unit is 0, then all bits of Result as well as V and C are 0 regardless of any other input to the unit. The Arithmetic Unit is responsible for computing Result, V, and C for the arithmetic operations that correspond to functions 1, 2, 3, and 4 in Figure 10.55. The corresponding control lines for the Arithmetic Unit are labeled d, e, f, and g, respectively. If all four of d, e, f, and g are 0, then all bits of Result as well as V and C are 0 regardless of any other input to the Arithmetic Unit.

Each output line of a Computation Unit feeds into a 12-input OR gate. The other 11 inputs to the OR gate are the corresponding lines from the other 11 Computation Units. For example, the V outputs of all 12 Computation Units feed into one OR gate. Because 11 of the Computation Units are guaranteed to be disabled, exactly 11 inputs are guaranteed to be 0 for every OR gate. The one input that is not guaranteed to be 0 is the input from the unit that is enabled. Because 0 is the identity for the OR operation

$$p \text{ OR } 0 = p$$

the output from the unit that is enabled passes through the OR gate unchanged.

Figure 10.58 is an implementation of the A Unit. It consists of eight two-input AND gates that act as enable gates for the eight bits of the A signal. Figure 10.55 specifies that V and C should be 0. Consequently, both output lines for V and C are tied to 0 in the implementation.

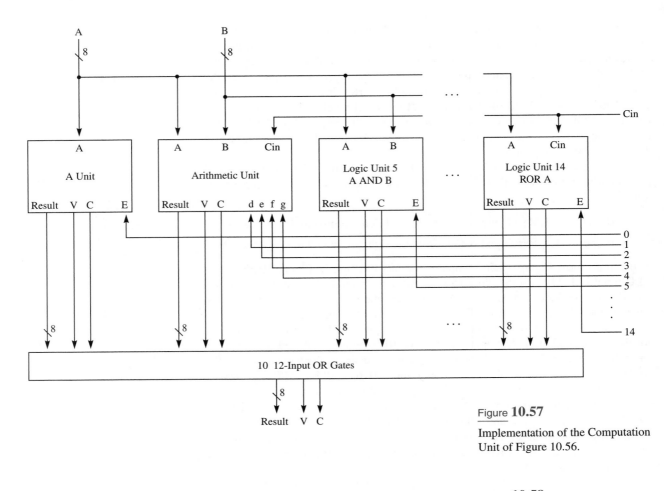

Figure **10.57**

Implementation of the Computation Unit of Figure 10.56.

Figure **10.58**

Implementation of the A Unit of Figure 10.57.

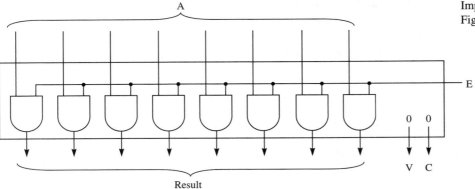

Figure 10.59 is an implementation of the Arithmetic Unit. It is an extension of the adder/subtracter circuit of Figure 10.53, modified to handle two additional cases for adding and subtracting 16-bit values with two 8-bit operations. Figure 10.60 shows how to do a 16-bit operation with two 8-bit operations. In Figure 10.60(a), you do a 16-bit add with

A plus B

on the low-order bytes of A and B, followed by

A plus B plus Cin

on the high-order bytes where Cin is the Cout of the low-order operation. In Figure 10.60(b), you do a 16-bit subtraction with

A plus $\overline{B}$ plus 1

on the low-order bytes of A and B, followed by

A plus $\overline{B}$ plus Cin

on the high-order bytes where Cin is again the Cout of the low-order operation. This last operation follows from the fact that subtracting B from A is performed in hardware by adding the two's complement of B to A. The carry out of the low-order operation is the carry out of an addition, not a subtraction. That is why the circuit adds Cin from the low-order operation instead of subtracting it.

Figure **10.59**

Implementation of the Arithmetic Unit of Figure 10.57.

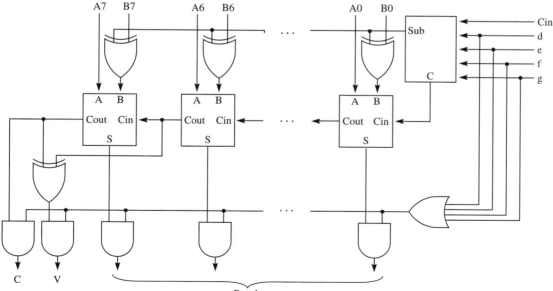

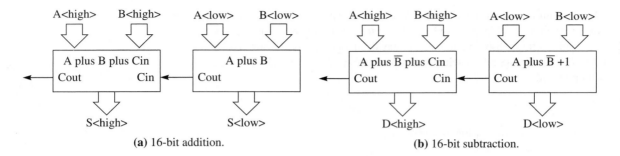

(a) 16-bit addition.   **(b)** 16-bit subtraction.

Example 10.38   Here is how the hardware subtracts $259 - 261$. As a 16-bit quantity, 259 (dec) = 0000 0001 0000 0011, so that A<high> = 0000 0001 and A<low> = 0000 0011. As a 16-bit quantity, 261 (dec) = 0000 0001 0000 0101, so that B<high> = 0000 0001 and B<low> = 0000 0101. The low-order addition is

Figure **10.60**

Using two 8-bit operations to produce a 16-bit operation.

```
           0000 0011
           1111 1010
ADD                1
C = 0   1111 1110
```

and the high-order addition is

```
           0000 0001
           1111 1110
ADD                0
C = 0   1111 1111
V = 0
```

The final difference is 1111 1111 1111 1110 (bin) = –2 (dec), as expected. The final V bit is computed from the exclusive OR of the final carry out with the penultimate carry out as follows:

$0 \oplus 0 = 0$ ∎

Example 10.39   Here is how the hardware subtracts $261 - 259$. This time, A<high> = 0000 0001, A<low> = 0000 0101, B<high> = 0000 0001, and B<low> = 0000 0011. The low-order addition is

```
           0000 0101
           1111 1100
ADD                1
C = 1   0000 0010
```

and the high-order addition is

```
          0000 0001
          1111 1110
ADD               1
C = 1   0000 0000
V = 0
```

The final difference is 0000 0000 0000 0010 (bin) = 2 (dec), as expected. The final V bit is computed from the exclusive OR of the final carry out with the penultimate carry out as follows:

$$1 \oplus 1 = 0$$ ∎

The control circuit box on the top right part of Figure 10.59 controls the function of the circuit. Figure 10.61 is its truth table. Compare the box with the Sub line that controls the adder/subtracter circuit in Figure 10.53. When Sub is 0 in the adder/subtracter, B is not inverted by the XOR gates, and the carry in of the low-order bit is 0. When Sub is 1, B is inverted, and the carry in of the low-order bit is 1. The first and third rows of Figure 10.61 duplicate these two functions. The second row of Figure 10.61 is for the high-order addition, and the last row is for the high-order subtraction.

Function	d	e	f	g	Sub	C
A plus B	1	0	0	0	0	0
A plus B plus Cin	0	1	0	0	0	Cin
A plus $\overline{\text{B}}$ plus 1	0	0	1	0	1	1
A plus $\overline{\text{B}}$ plus Cin	0	0	0	1	1	Cin

Figure 10.61

The truth table for the control circuit in Figure 10.59.

Theoretically, the Sub and C outputs of the control box are functions of d, e, f, g, and Cin. Inspection of the truth table, however, shows that Sub can be expressed as

$$\text{Sub} = f + g$$

and C can be expressed as

$$C = e \cdot \text{Cin} + g \cdot \text{Cin} + f$$

with neither depending on d.

Another requirement of the Arithmetic Unit is that if d, e, f, and g are all 0, then all the outputs must be 0 regardless of the other inputs. The output of the four-input OR gate in Figure 10.59 acts as the enable signal, which allows all 10 outputs of the unit to pass through when one of d, e, f, or g is 1.

Implementation of Logic Units 5 through 14 is left as an exercise for the student. They are straightforward to implement, because the logic operations are available as common logic gates.

Abstraction at Level LG1

Abstract data types (ADTs) are an important design tool at Level HOL6. The idea is that you should understand the behavior of an ADT by knowing what the functions and procedures that operate on the ADT do, not necessarily how they do it. Once an operation has been implemented, you can free your mind of the implementation details and concentrate on solving the problem at a higher level of abstraction.

The same principle operates at the hardware level. Each combinational device in this section has a block diagram and a truth table that describes its function. The block diagram is to hardware what an ADT is to software. It is an abstraction that specifies the input and output while hiding the implementation details.

The block diagram as an ADT

Higher levels of abstraction in the hardware are obtained by constructing devices defined by block diagrams whose implementation is an interconnection of blocks at a lower level of abstraction. Figure 10.50 is a perfect example. This full adder block is implemented with the half adder blocks in Figure 10.51.

The highest level of abstraction for the hardware is the block diagram of the Pep/8 computer we have seen repeatedly. The four blocks—input device, CPU, main memory, and output device—are connected by the bus. At a slightly lower level of abstraction you see the registers in the CPU. Each register is depicted as a block. The remaining two chapters build up successively higher levels of abstraction, culminating with the Pep/8 computer at level ISA3.

SUMMARY

In a combinational circuit, the input determines the output. Three representations of a combinational circuit are truth tables, boolean algebraic expressions, and logic diagrams. Of the three representations, truth tables are at the highest level of abstraction. They specify the function of a circuit without specifying its implementation. A truth table lists the output for all possible combinations of the input, hence the name "combinational circuit."

The three basic operations of boolean algebra are AND, OR, and NOT. The 10 fundamental properties of boolean algebra consist of five laws—commutative, associative, distributive, identity, and complement—and their duals, from which useful boolean theorems may be proved. An important theorem is De Morgan's law, which shows how to take the NOT of the AND or OR of several terms.

A boolean expression corresponds to a logic diagram, which in turn corresponds to a connection of electronic gates. Three common gates are NAND (AND followed by NOT), NOR (OR followed by NOT), and XOR (exclusive OR). Two-level circuits minimize processing time, but may require more gates than an equivalent multilevel circuit. This is another manifestation of the fundamental space/time tradeoff. Karnaugh maps help minimize the number of gates needed to implement a two-level combinational circuit.

Combinational devices include the multiplexer, the decoder, the demultiplexer, the adder, and the arithmetic logic unit (ALU). A multiplexer selects one of several data inputs to be routed to a single data output. A decoder takes a binary number as input and sets one of several data output lines to 1 and the rest to 0. A demultiplexer routes one of several data input values to a single output line, and is logically equivalent to a decoder with an enable line. A half adder adds two bits, and a full adder adds three bits, one of which is the previous carry. A subtracter works by negating the second operand and adding it to the first. An ALU performs both arithmetic and logic functions.

EXERCISES

Section 10.1

1. *(a) Prove the zero theorem $x + 1 = 1$ with boolean algebra. Give a reason for each step in your proof. Hint: Expand the 1 on the left with the complement property and then use the idempotent property. (b) Show the dual proof of part (a).

2. (a) Prove with boolean algebra the absorption property, $x + x \cdot y = x$. Give a reason for each step in your proof. (b) Show the dual proof of part (a).

3. *(a) Prove with boolean algebra the consensus theorem $x \cdot y + x' \cdot z + y \cdot z = x \cdot y + x' \cdot z$. Give a reason for each step in your proof. (b) Show the dual proof of part (a).

4. Prove De Morgan's law, $(a + b)' = a' \cdot b'$, by giving the dual of the proof in the text. Give a reason for each step in your proof.

5. (a) Prove the general form of De Morgan's law,

$$(a_1 \cdot a_2 \cdot \ldots \cdot a_n)' = a_1' + a_2' + \ldots + a_n' \quad \text{where } n \geq 2$$

from De Morgan's law for two variables using mathematical induction. (b) Show the dual proof of part (a).

6. *(a) Prove with boolean algebra that $(x + y) \cdot (x' + y) = y$. Give a reason for each step in your proof. (b) Show the dual proof of part (a).

7. (a) Prove with boolean algebra that $(x + y) + (y \cdot x') = x + y$. Give a reason for each step in your proof. (b) Show the dual proof of part (a).

8. *(a) Draw a three-input OR gate, its boolean expression, and its truth table, as in Figure 10.10. (b) Do part (a) for the three-input NAND gate. (c) Do part (a) for the three-input NOR gate.

9. For each of the following boolean properties or theorems, state the set theory interpretation:

*(a) $x + 0 = x$	(b) $x \cdot 1 = x$	(c) $x + x' = 1$	(d) $x \cdot x' = 0$
(e) $x \cdot x = x$	(f) $x + x = x$	(g) $x \cdot 0 = 0$	

10. *(a) Show the associative property for the OR operation using Venn diagrams with x, y, and z overlapping regions. Sketch the following regions to show that region (3) is the same as region (6):

(1) $(x + y)$	(2) z	(3) $(x + y) + z$
(4) x	(5) $(y + z)$	(6) $x + (y + z)$

(b) Do the dual of part (a).

11. **(a)** Show the distributive property using Venn diagrams with x, y, and z overlapping regions. Sketch the following regions to show that region (3) is the same as region (6):

   (1) x (2) $y \cdot z$ (3) $x + y \cdot z$
   (4) $(x + y)$ (5) $(x + z)$ (6) $(x + y) \cdot (x + z)$

   (b) Do the dual of part (a).

12. **(a)** Show De Morgan's law using Venn diagrams with a and b overlapping regions. Sketch the following regions to show that region (2) is the same as region (5):

   (1) $a \cdot b$ (2) $(a \cdot b)'$ (3) a' (4) b' (5) $a' + b'$

   (b) Do the dual of part (a).

13. Although a boolean variable for a combinational circuit can have only two values, 1 or 0, boolean algebra can describe a system where a variable can have one of four possible values—0, 1, A, or B. Such a system corresponds to the description of subsets of $\{a, b\}$ where $1 = \{a, b\}$ (the universal set), $A = \{a\}$, $B = \{b\}$, and $0 = \{\}$ (the empty set). The truth tables for two-input AND and OR operations have 16 entries instead of 4, and the truth table for the complement has 4 entries instead of 2. Construct the truth table for the following:

   *(a)** AND   **(b)** OR   **(c)** the complement

14. The exclusive NOR gate, written XNOR, is equivalent to an XOR followed by an inverter. ***(a)** Draw the symbol for a two-input XNOR gate. **(b)** Construct its truth table. **(c)** The XNOR is also called a comparator. Why?

Section 10.2

15. Draw the nonabbreviated logic diagram for the following boolean expressions. You may use XOR gates.

   *(a) $((a')')'$ **(b)** $(((a')')')'$
   *(c) $a'b + ab'$ **(d)** $ab + a'b'$
   (e) $ab + ab' + a'b$ **(f)** $((ab \oplus b')' + a'b)'$
   (g) $(a'bc + a)b$ **(h)** $(ab'c)'(ac)'$
   (i) $((ab)'(b'c)' + a'b'c')'$ **(j)** $(a \oplus b + b' \oplus c')'$
   (k) $(abc)' + (a'b'c')'$ **(l)** $(a + b)(a' + c)(b' + c')$
   (m) $(a \oplus b) \oplus c + ab'c$ **(n)** $(((a + b)' + c)' + d)'$
   (o) $(ab' + b'c + cd)'$ **(p)** $((a + b')(b' + c)(c + d))'$
   (q) $(((ab)'c)'d)'$ **(r)** $(((a \oplus b)' \oplus c)' \oplus d)'$

16. Draw the abbreviated logic diagram for the boolean expressions of Exercise 15. You may use XOR gates.

17. Construct the truth tables for the boolean expressions of Exercise 15.

18. Write the boolean expressions for the logic diagrams of Figure 10.62.

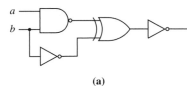

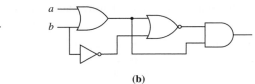

Figure 10.62

The logic diagrams for Exercise 18.

(a)

(b)

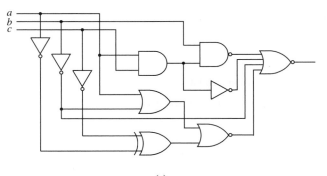

(c)

19. Write the boolean AND-OR expression for the following:

 *(a) function y in Figure 10.3
 (b) function y in Figure 10.4
 (c) function x in Figure 10.17
 (d) the NAND gate in Figure 10.7(a)
 (e) the XOR gate in Figure 10.7(c)

20. Write the boolean OR-AND expression for the following:

 (a) function y in Figure 10.3
 (b) function x in Figure 10.17
 (c) the NOR gate in Figure 10.7(b)
 (d) the XOR gate in Figure 10.7(c)

21. Use the properties and theorems of boolean algebra to reduce the following expressions to AND-OR expressions without parentheses. The expressions may not be unique. Construct the truth table, which will be unique, by inspection of your final expression.

 *(a) $(a'b + ab')'$ (b) $(ab + a'b')'$
 (c) $(ab + ab' + a'b)'$ *(d) $(ab \oplus b')' + ab$
 (e) $(a'bc + a)b$ (f) $(ab'c)'(ac)'$
 (g) $(a \oplus b) \oplus c$ (h) $a \oplus (b \oplus c)$
 (i) $(a + b)(a' + c)(b' + c')$ (j) $((a + b)' + c)'$

*22. Construct two-level circuits for the expressions of Exercise 21 using only NAND gates.

23. Use the properties and theorems of boolean algebra to reduce the following expressions to OR-AND expressions. The expressions may not be unique. Construct the truth table, which will be unique, by inspection of your final expression.

(a) $a'b + ab'$ *(b) $ab + a'b'$
(c) $ab + ab' + a'b$ (d) $((ab \oplus b')' + ab)'$
(e) $(a'bc + a)b$ (f) $(ab'c)'(ac)'$
(g) $(a \oplus b) \oplus c$ (h) $a \oplus (b \oplus c)$
(i) $((a + b)(a' + c)(b' + c'))'$ (j) $(a + b)' + c$

*24. Construct a two-level circuit for the expressions of Exercise 23 using only NOR gates.

25. Draw the logic diagram of a two-level circuit that produces the XOR function using the following:

*(a) only NAND gates   (b) only NOR gates

26. State whether each gate in Figure 10.63 is the following:

(1) an AND gate   (2) an OR gate
(3) a NAND gate   (4) a NOR gate

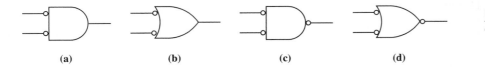

(a)   (b)   (c)   (d)

Figure **10.63**

The gates for Exercise 26.

Section 10.3

*27. Write each function of Exercise 21 with the sigma notation.

*28. Write each function of Exercise 23 with the pi notation.

29. In Figure 10.3, find the minimum AND-OR expression for the following:

*(a) $x(a, b, c)$ (b) $y(a, b, c)$

Draw the minimized two-level circuit for each expression with only NAND gates.

30. In Figure 10.3, find the minimum OR-AND expression for the following:

*(a) $x(a, b, c)$ (b) $y(a, b, c)$

Draw the minimized two-level circuit for each expression with only NOR gates.

31. Use a Karnaugh map to find the minimum AND-OR expression for $x(a, b, c)$:

*(a) $\Sigma(0, 4, 5, 7)$ (b) $\Sigma(2, 3, 4, 6, 7)$ (c) $\Sigma(0, 3, 5, 6)$
(d) $\Sigma(0, 1, 2, 3, 4, 6)$ (e) $\Sigma(1, 2, 3, 4, 5)$ (f) $\Sigma(1, 2, 3, 4, 5, 6, 7)$
(g) $\Sigma(0, 1, 2, 4, 6)$ (h) $\Sigma(1, 4, 6, 7)$ (i) $\Sigma(2, 3, 4, 5, 6)$
(j) $\Sigma(0, 2, 5)$

*32. Write each expression of Exercise 31 in pi notation, and find its minimum OR-AND expression.

33. Use a Karnaugh map to find the minimum AND-OR expression for $x(a, b, c, d)$:

    *(a) $\Sigma(2, 3, 4, 5, 10, 12, 13)$
    (b) $\Sigma(1, 5, 6, 7, 9, 12, 13, 15)$
    (c) $\Sigma(0, 1, 2, 4, 6, 8, 10)$
    (d) $\Sigma(7)$
    (e) $\Sigma(2, 4, 5, 11, 13, 15)$
    (f) $\Sigma(1, 2, 4, 5, 6, 7, 12, 15)$
    (g) $\Sigma(1, 2, 4, 5, 6, 7, 8, 11, 12, 15)$
    (h) $\Sigma(1, 7, 10, 12)$
    (i) $\Sigma(0, 2, 3, 4, 5, 6, 8, 10, 11, 13)$
    (j) $\Sigma(0, 1, 2, 3, 4, 5, 6, 10, 11, 13, 14, 15)$
    (k) $\Sigma(0, 1, 2, 3, 4, 5, 6, 7, 8, 9, 10, 11, 12, 13, 14)$

*34. Write each expression of Exercise 33 in pi notation, and find its minimum OR-AND expression.

35. Use a Karnaugh map to find the minimum AND-OR expression for $x(a, b, c)$ with don't-care conditions:

    *(a) $\Sigma(0, 6) + d(1, 3, 7)$ (b) $\Sigma(5) + d(0, 2, 4, 6)$
    (c) $\Sigma(1, 3) + d(0, 2, 4, 6)$ (d) $\Sigma(0, 5, 7) + d(3, 4)$
    (e) $\Sigma(1, 7) + d(2, 4)$ (f) $\Sigma(4, 5, 6) + d(1, 2, 3, 7)$

36. Use a Karnaugh map to find the minimum AND-OR expression for $x(a, b, c, d)$ with don't-care conditions:

    *(a) $\Sigma(5, 6) + d(2, 7, 9, 13, 14, 15)$
    (b) $\Sigma(0, 3, 14) + d(2, 4, 7, 8, 10, 11, 13, 15)$
    (c) $\Sigma(3, 4, 5, 10) + d(2, 11, 13, 15)$
    (d) $\Sigma(5, 6, 12, 15) + d(0, 4, 10, 14)$
    (e) $\Sigma(1, 6, 9, 12) + d(0, 2, 3, 4, 5, 7, 14, 15)$
    (f) $\Sigma(0, 2, 3, 4) + d(8, 9, 10, 11, 13, 14, 15)$
    (g) $\Sigma(2, 3, 10) + d(0, 4, 6, 7, 8, 9, 12, 14, 15)$

37. (a) A Karnaugh map for three variables has minterm 0 adjacent to 2, and 4 adjacent to 6. Copy Figure 10.30, cut out the Karnaugh map, and tape it in the shape of a cylinder so that adjacent minterms are physically adjacent. (b) For adjacent minterms to be physically adjacent in a four-variable Karnaugh map requires a three-dimensional *torus* (shaped like a doughnut). Construct a torus from clay or some other suitable material and inscribe or write on it the cells and their decimal labels of Figure 10.33(a). For example, the cell with 2 should be physically adjacent to the cells with 0, 3, 6, and 10.

Section 10.4

38. Using the viewpoint that one of the lines is a data line and the other is a control line, explain the operation of each of the following two-input gates:

   *(a) OR   (b) NAND
   (c) NOR   (d) XNOR

   See Exercise 14 for the definition of XNOR.

39. Draw a nonabbreviated logic diagram of an eight-input multiplexer.

*40. Construct a 16-input multiplexer from five four-input multiplexers. Draw the 16-input multiplexer as a large block with 16 data lines labeled D0 through D15 and 4 select lines labeled S3 through S0. Inside the large block, draw each 4-input multiplexer as a small block with data lines D0 through D3 and select lines S1 and S0. Show the connections to the small blocks from the outside lines and the connections between the blocks to implement the big multiplexer. Explain the operation of your circuit.

41. Do Exercise 40 with two eight-input multiplexers without enable inputs and any other gates you need. Explain the operation of your circuit.

42. *(a) Draw a nonabbreviated logic diagram of a 3 × 8 binary decoder. (b) Draw a nonabbreviated logic diagram of a 2 × 4 binary decoder with an enable input.

43. Construct a 4 × 16 binary decoder without an enable input from five 2 × 4 binary decoders with enable inputs. You may use the constant 1 as input to a device. Use the drawing guidelines of Exercise 40 to label your external and internal lines. Explain the operation of your circuit.

44. Construct a 4 × 16 binary decoder without an enable input from two 3 × 8 binary decoders with enable inputs plus any other gates you need. Use the drawing guidelines of Exercise 40 to label your external and internal lines. Explain the operation of your circuit.

45. Implement the 2 × 4 binary decoder with an enable input, as shown in Figure 10.47. Draw a nonabbreviated diagram of your circuit.

46. *(a) Draw the implementation of the full adder in Figure 10.51 showing the AND and XOR gates of the half adders. *(b) What is the maximum number of gate delays from input to output? (c) Design minimized two-level networks for Sum and Cout from the truth table of Figure 10.50(b). (d) Compute the percentage change in the number of gates and in the processing time for the design of part (c) compared to part (a). How do your results illustrate the space/time tradeoff?

47. (a) Draw the circuit of Figure 10.52 with the individual XOR, AND, and OR gates of the half adders. *(b) What is the maximum number of gate delays from input to output? Consider an XOR gate as requiring one gate delay. This problem requires some thought. Assume that all eight inputs are presented at the same time, even though the carry will ripple through the circuit.

48. Modify Figure 10.52(b) to provide two additional outputs, one for the N bit and one for the Z bit.

49. Implement a four-bit ASL shifter with select line S. The input is A3 A2 A1 A0, which represents a four-bit number with A0 the LSB and A3 the sign bit. The output is B3 B2 B1 B0 and C, the carry bit. If S is 1, the output is the ASL of the input. If S is 0, the output is the same as the input, and C is 0.

50. Do Exercise 49 for a four-bit ASR shifter.

51. The block diagram in Figure 10.64 is a three-input, two-output combinational switching circuit. If s is 0, the input a is routed directly through to x, and b is routed to y. If s is 1, they are switched with a being routed to y and b to x. Construct the circuit using only AND, OR, and inverter gates.

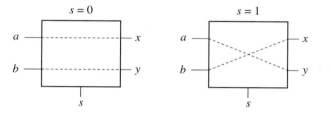

Figure **10.64**

The block diagram for Exercise 51.

52. The block diagram in Figure 10.65 is a four-input, two-output combinational switching circuit. If $s1\ s0 = 00$, the a input is broadcast to x and y. If $s1\ s0 = 01$, the b input is broadcast to x and y. If $s1\ s0 = 10$, a and b pass straight through to x and y. If $s1\ s0 = 11$, they are switched, with a being routed to y and b to x. Construct the circuit using only AND, OR, and inverter gates. (a) Use Karnaugh maps to construct the minimum AND-OR circuit. (b) Use Karnaugh maps to construct the minimum OR-AND circuit.

53. Draw the 12 two-input multiplexers of Figure 10.56. Show all the connections to the input and output lines. You may use ellipses (...) for six of the eight data lines.

54. Implement the following logic units for the Pep/8 ALU:

(a) Logic Unit 5, $A \cdot B$ (b) Logic Unit 6, $\overline{A \cdot B}$
(c) Logic Unit 7, $A + B$ (d) Logic Unit 8, $\overline{A + B}$
(e) Logic Unit 9, $A \oplus B$ (f) Logic Unit 10, $\overline{A}$
(g) Logic Unit 11, ASL A (h) Logic Unit 12, ROL A
(i) Logic Unit 13, ASR A (j) Logic Unit 14, ROR A

Figure **10.65**

55. Draw the implementation of the five-input, two-output control box of Figure 10.59.

The block diagram for Exercise 52.

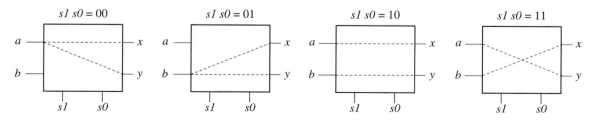

Chapter

11

Sequential Circuits

Chapter 10 discusses combinational devices, which are commonly used in computer design. As useful as these devices are, however, it is impossible to build even the smallest computers as an interconnection of combinational circuits. In all the combinational devices mentioned, the output depends only on the input. When the input changes, it is only a matter of a few gate delays before that change is reflected in the output.

The *state* of the circuit is the characteristic that distinguishes a sequential circuit from a combinational circuit. A sequential circuit can remember what state it is in. It has memory, in other words. The output of a sequential circuit depends not only on the input, but also on its state.

The distinguishing characteristic of a sequential circuit is its state.

This chapter shows how to construct the basic sequential elements and how to connect them to form useful blocks at successively higher levels of abstraction. It concludes with a description of devices that are connected to build a Pep/8 computer in the following chapter.

11.1 Latches and Clocked Flip-Flops

Sequential devices are constructed from the same gates described in Chapter 10, but with a different type of connection called *feedback*. In combinational circuits and the boolean expressions that describe them, the output of each gate goes to the input of a previously unconnected gate. A feedback connection, however, forms a loop or cycle where the output of one or more gates "feeds back" to the input of a previous gate of the circuit.

Figure 11.1 shows two simple circuits with feedback connections. Part (a) is a string of three inverters fed back to the input of the first inverter. To analyze the behavior of this circuit, suppose that point *d* has a value of 1. Because *d* is connected to *a* with the feedback loop, point *a* must also have a value of 1. One gate delay later, point *b* must have a value of 0. (Although we previously ignored the delay through an inverter for simplicity, we must take it into account with this circuit.) One more gate delay later, point *c* will have a value of 1, and after a third gate delay, *d* will have a value of 0.

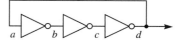

(a) An unstable circuit.

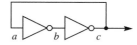

(b) A stable circuit.

Figure **11.1**

Simple feedback circuits.

The problem now is that we started our analysis assuming that point *d* has a value of 1. It will now change to 0, and three gate delays later it will become 1 again. The circuit will oscillate, with the values at each point in the circuit switching back and forth between 1 and 0 every few gate delays. A state that remains constant only for a duration of a few gate delays is called an *unstable state*.

Unstable states

In Figure 11.1(b), if you assume point *c* has a value of 1, then point *a* will be 1, *b* will be 0, and *c* will be 1, which is consistent with the first assumption. Such a state is stable. The points at all parts of the circuit will retain their values indefinitely.

Stable states

Another possible stable state is for points *c* and *a* to have a value of 0 and *b* to have a value of 1. If you construct this circuit, which state will it have? Will point *c* be 0 or 1? Like all electrical devices, gates require a source of electrical power and must be turned on to operate. If you construct the circuit of Figure 11.1(b) and turn it on, its state will be established at random. About half the time when you turn on the circuit, point *c* will be 0, and about half the time it will be 1. The circuit will remain indefinitely in the state that is established when the power is turned on.

The SR Latch

To be useful, a sequential device needs a mechanism for setting its state. Such a device is the *SR latch* of Figure 11.2. Its two inputs are S and R and its two outputs are Q and $\bar{Q}$ (pronounced *Q bar*). The feedback connections are from Q to the input of the bottom NOR and from $\bar{Q}$ to the input of the top NOR.

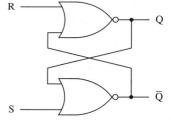

To see the possibility of a stable state, suppose S and R are both 0, and Q is also 0. The two inputs to the bottom gate are both 0, which makes $\bar{Q}$ 1. The two inputs to the top NOR are 0 (from R) and 1 (from $\bar{Q}$). Thus, the output of the top NOR is 0, which is consistent with our first assumption about Q. So the stable state is $Q\bar{Q} = 01$ when $SR = 00$.

Starting with this stable state, consider what happens if you change input S to 1. Figure 11.3 summarizes the sequence of events. T_g stands for a time interval of one gate delay, typically 2 ns.

Figure 11.2

The SR latch.

Time	S	R	Q	$\bar{Q}$	Stability
Initial	0	0	0	1	Stable
0	1	0	0	1	Unstable
T_g	1	0	0	0	Unstable
$2T_g$	1	0	1	0	Stable

Figure 11.3

Changing S to 1 in the SR latch.

At time 0, S changes to 1. That makes the two inputs to the bottom gate 1 (from S) and 0 (from Q). One gate delay later the effect of that change propagates to $\overline{Q}$, which becomes 0. Now the two inputs to the top gate are 0 (from R) and 0 (from $\overline{Q}$). After another gate delay, the output of the top gate becomes 1. Now the input to the bottom gate is 1 (from S) and 1 (from Q). That makes the output of the bottom gate 0.

The output of the bottom gate was already 0, however, so it does not change. Because a trace through the feedback connections shows consistent values, this last state is stable. The two intermediate states in Figure 11.3 are unstable because they last for only a few gate delays.

What happens if you change S back to 0? Figure 11.4 shows the sequence of events. The two inputs to the bottom gate are 0 (from S) and 1 (from Q). That makes the output of the bottom gate 0. Because it was already 0, no other changes propagate through the circuit, and the state is stable.

Figures 11.3 and 11.4 show that $\overline{Q}$ is always the complement of Q when the SR latch is in a stable state. The bar is another common notation for the complement and is equivalent to the prime notation used in Chapter 10.

Compare the first state of Figure 11.3 with the last state of Figure 11.4. In both cases the inputs are SR = 00, but in the first case the output is Q = 0 and in the second Q = 1. The output depends not only on the input, but also on the state of the latch.

Output depends on input and state.

The effect of changing S to 1 and then back to 0 was to set the state to Q = 1. If the latch begins in the state Q = 1 with SR = 00, a similar analysis shows that changing R to 1 and then back to 0 will reset the state to Q = 0. S stands for set, and R stands for reset.

An SR latch is analogous to a light switch on a wall. Changing S to 1 and back to 0 is like flipping the switch up to turn the light on. Changing R to 1 and back to 0 is like flipping the switch down. If the switch is already up and you try flipping it up, nothing changes. The switch stays up. Similarly, if Q is already 1 and you change S to 1 and back to 0, the state does not change. Q stays 1.

The normal input condition for the SR latch is SR = 00. To set or reset the latch, you change S or R to 1 and then back to 0. Normally, S and R are not 1 simultaneously. If S and R are both 1, Q and $\overline{Q}$ will both be 0, and $\overline{Q}$ will not be the complement of Q. Furthermore, if you change SR = 11 to SR = 00 simultaneously, the

The normal input condition for the SR latch

Time	S	R	Q	$\overline{Q}$	Stability
Initial	1	0	1	0	Stable
0	0	0	1	0	Stable

Figure **11.4**

Changing S back to 0 in the SR latch.

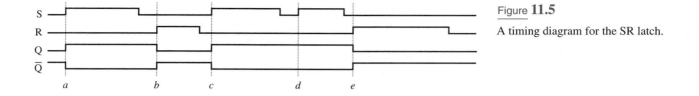

Figure **11.5**

A timing diagram for the SR latch.

state of the latch is unpredictable. About half the time it will return to $Q\bar{Q} = 01$ and half the time to $Q\bar{Q} = 10$. In practice, $SR = 11$ should not occur.

A *timing diagram* is a graphical representation of the behavior of a sequential circuit. Figure 11.5 is a timing diagram that shows the change in outputs Q and $\bar{Q}$ as inputs S and R change. The horizontal axis is time, and the vertical axis is the electrical voltage that represents 1 when it is high and 0 when it is low.

The timing diagram shows the initial state as $Q = 0$. When S goes to 1 at time a, it immediately sets Q to 1 and $\bar{Q}$ to 0. The diagram shows the transitions occurring simultaneously. As shown in our previous analysis, $\bar{Q}$ will change one gate delay after S changes, and Q will change one gate delay later than that. The timing diagram assumes that the time scale is too large to show a time interval as short as a gate delay.

When S goes back to 0, the state does not change. When R goes to 1 at time b, it resets Q to 0. When S goes to 1 again at time c, it sets Q to 1. At time d, the 0-to-1 transition of S does not change the state of the latch because Q is already 1. At all points of the diagram, $\bar{Q}$ is the inverse of Q.

Figure 11.5 also shows the transitions as instantaneous. Nothing in nature occurs in zero time. If you magnify the time scale, the transitions will show a more gradual change with a finite slope at every point. You can think of the simultaneous and instantaneous transitions in the timing diagram as a high level of abstraction that hides the details of the gate delays and gradual slopes at a lower level of abstraction.

The Clocked SR Flip-Flop

A subsystem in a computer consists of many combinational and sequential devices. Each sequential device is like an SR latch, which is in one of two states. As the machine executes its von Neumann cycle, the states of all the sequential devices change with time. To control this large collection of devices in an orderly fashion, the machine maintains a clock and requires all the devices to change their states at the same time. The clock generates a sequence of pulses, as in Figure 11.6. Ck stands for *clock pulse*.

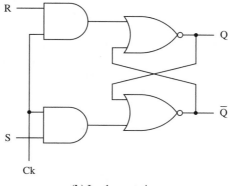

$$Ck \quad \text{———} \sqcap \text{——} \sqcap \text{——} \sqcap \text{——} \sqcap \text{——} \sqcap \text{———}$$

Figure **11.6**

A sequence of clock pulses.

Every sequential device has a Ck input in addition to its other inputs. The device is designed to respond to its inputs only during a clock pulse. The time between pulses, indicated by T in the figure, is the *period* of the clock. The shorter the period, the more frequently the devices will change their states and the faster the circuit will compute.

The clock period

Figure 11.7 is an SR latch with a clock input, called a *flip-flop*. It consists of the same pair of NOR gates with feedback that were shown in Figure 11.2. But instead of the SR inputs going directly into the NOR gates, they go through two AND gates that act as an enable. Figure 11.7(a) is the block diagram, and Figure 11.7(b) is an implementation. Notice that the convention for the block diagram has S opposite from Q at the top of the block, and the implementation has S opposite $\bar{Q}$.

During the time that Ck is low, the inputs to the NOR gates will be 0 regardless of the values of S and R. When there are inputs of 0 into the NOR gates, it means that the latch will not change its state. During the time that Ck is high, the values of S and R pass through the enable gates unchanged. The device behaves as the SR latch of Figure 11.2. The AND gates shield the NOR gates from the effect of S and R except during the time that Ck is high. Figure 11.8 is a timing diagram that shows the behavior of the device. $\bar{Q}$ is always the complement of Q and is not shown in the figure.

When S goes to 1, that change does not affect Q because the clock is still low. At time *a* when the clock goes high, Ck allows SR = 10 to pass through the AND gates and set the latch to Q = 1. A little later when the clock goes low, Ck disables

(a) Block diagram.

(b) Implementation.

Figure **11.7**

The clocked SR flip-flop.

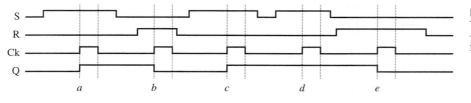

Figure **11.8**

A timing diagram of the clocked SR flip-flop.

the SR input from the latch. When R goes to 1 before time *b*, it cannot affect the state of the latch. Only at time *b*, when Ck goes high again, can R reset the latch.

It would be physically possible to let S and R make several transitions during a single time interval when the clock is high, but that does not happen in practice. The idea is to design the circuit to set up the SR input for the desired transition and wait for the next clock pulse. When the clock pulse arrives, the state may change according to the values of S and R. After the clock goes low, the circuit prepares the SR values for the next pulse.

The evenly spaced clock pulses force any change in state to occur only at evenly spaced time intervals. The S and R inputs of Figure 11.8 are identical to those of Figure 11.5, but the corresponding state changes in Q have been smoothed out by the clock. The effect of a clock is to make time (the horizontal axis of a timing diagram) digital in the same way that the electrical circuitry makes the voltage signal (vertical axis) digital. Just as a signal must be either high or low and never anything in between, a state change of a sequential device must occur at either one clock pulse or another—never between two pulses.

Digitizing the time axis

The Master–Slave SR Flip-Flop

The clocked flip-flop of Figure 11.7 is called *level sensitive* because the latch responds to Ck only when the clock is at a high level. Although the device is constrained to follow the clock as desired, it has a serious practical deficiency, illustrated in Figure 11.9.

The figure shows a possible interconnection of an SR device. It is common for the output of a sequential device to contain a feedback loop through some combinational circuit that eventually leads to the input of the same sequential device. The figure shows a three-input, two-output combinational circuit, two of whose inputs are

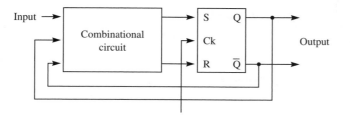

Figure **11.9**

A possible interconnection of an SR device.

feedback from the output of the SR sequential device. This feedback loop is in addition to the feedback of the NOR gates not shown in the figure within the SR block.

Consider what might happen if the SR flip-flop were level sensitive. Suppose SR is 10, Q$\overline{\text{Q}}$ is 01, and the clock is low. Because the clock disables SR from the NOR latch, S cannot set Q to 1. Now suppose the clock goes high, and after a few gate delays SR sets Q to 1.

Now imagine that the change in Q$\overline{\text{Q}}$, after propagating through the combinational circuit with the same external input, makes SR = 01. If Ck is still high, the clock will allow the value of SR to reset Q to 0 after a few more gate delays. Unfortunately, a value of 01 for Q$\overline{\text{Q}}$ will propagate through the combinational circuit again and change SR to 10.

You should recognize this situation as unstable. Every few gate delays, the feedback connection from the sequential device forces the SR flip-flop to change its state as long as the clock is high. The state may change hundreds of times while the clock is high. When the clock eventually goes low at the end of its pulse, it would be impossible to predict exactly what state the flip-flop would be in.

Possibility of an unstable state with feedback

Because feedback connections through combinational circuits are necessary for the construction of computer subsystems, we need a sequential device that is not only constrained to change its state during a clock pulse, but is also immune from further changes through the feedback connection. The device needs to be sensitive to its input for an extremely short period of time—so short that no matter how fast the feedback propagates through the combinational circuit and changes SR, that change cannot again affect the state of the flip-flop.

Two techniques for designing such devices are edge-triggered and master–slave. *Edge-triggered* flip-flops are not designed to be sensitive to their inputs when the clock is at a high level, but rather when the clock is making a transition from a low level to a high level. The implementation of an edge-triggered flip-flop is more difficult to understand than the implementation of a master–slave flip-flop and will not be considered here even though it is the more common of the two. It is enough to say that both types of flip-flops solve the same problem arising from feedback connections.

Two design solutions to the instability problem from feedback

Figure 11.10 shows an implementation of the *master–slave* SR flip-flop. Both the master and the slave are level-sensitive, clocked SR flip-flops. The $\overline{\text{Q}}$ output of the master ($\overline{\text{Q2}}$) connects to the R input of the slave (R2), and the Q output of the master (Q2) connects to the S input of the slave (S2). Ck connects to the enable of the master, and the complement of Ck connects to the enable of the slave. The block diagram of a master–slave flip-flop is identical to the block diagram of the level-sensitive flip-flop.

Operation of the master–slave circuit

Because the master is an SR flip-flop, Q2 and $\overline{\text{Q2}}$ will always be the complement of each other. Because Q2 is connected to S2 of the slave and $\overline{\text{Q2}}$ is connected to R2 of the slave, when the slave is clocked the slave will either be set or reset, depending on the state of the master. If the master is in state Q2 = 1, the master will set the slave to Q = 1 also. If the master is in state Q2 = 0, it will reset the slave to Q = 0. The reason for the master–slave terminology is that the slave obediently takes the state of the master when the slave is clocked.

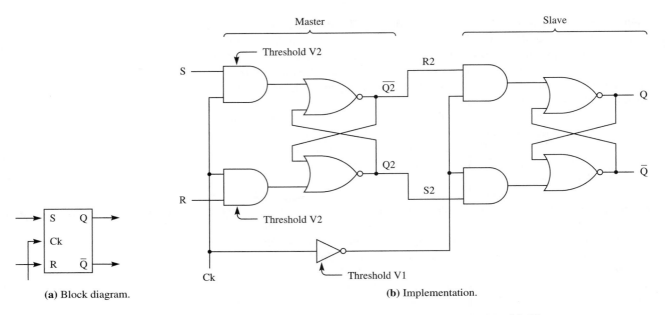

(a) Block diagram.   **(b)** Implementation.

Figure **11.10**

The master–slave SR flip-flop.

The *threshold* of a gate is the value of the input signal that causes the output to change. For the master–slave circuit to function properly, the inverter and the enable gates of the master must be designed with special threshold values. The threshold of the inverter, V1, must be less than the threshold of the master enable gates, V2.

Figure 11.11 shows V1 and V2 on a magnified timing diagram of Ck during one clock pulse. The clock does not make an instantaneous transition from a low to a high value. Instead, it gradually increases first to value V1 at time t_1, then to value V2 at time t_2 on the way to its high level. On the way down it passes through value V2 at time t_3, and then V1 at time t_4.

Before the pulse begins its upward transition, the master is disabled from the input. Regardless of the value of SR, the master will remain in its established state. The inverter ensures that the slave input is connected to the master because the slave inputs are enabled. The slave must be in the same state as the master.

As the clock signal rises and falls, passing through times t_1, t_2, t_3, and t_4, the effect of the circuit is as follows:

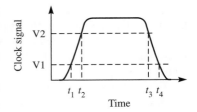

Figure **11.11**

Timing detail of a single clock pulse.

- t_1: Isolate slave from master.
- t_2: Connect master to input.
- t_3: Isolate master from input.
- t_4: Connect slave to master.

At time t_1 the signal reaches the threshold of the inverter, which makes the output of the inverter change from 1 to 0. A 0 to the enable gates of the slave shields the slave from any further effects of S2 and R2. Whatever state the slave was in at time t_1, it will remain in that state as long as Ck is above the threshold value V1.

At time t_2 the signal reaches the threshold of the master enable gates, which makes the master sensitive to the SR inputs. If SR is 10, the input will set the master to Q2 = 1. If SR is 01, the input will reset the master to Q2 = 0. If SR is 00, the master will not change its state. However, if the master does change its state, its new state will not affect the slave because the slave was isolated from the master at time t_1.

Consider how this arrangement protects the flip-flop from the feedback connection of Figure 11.9. The feedback is based on the $Q\overline{Q}$ output of the slave, which does not change as a result of the input to the master. The fact that V1 is less than V2 ensures that the slave will be isolated from the master before the master becomes sensitive to the input. Even if the gate delay through the combinational circuit were zero, the feedback would not affect the state of the slave.

When Ck makes its high-to-low transition, the clock reaches value V2 at time t_3. V2 is the threshold of the enable gates for the master, so now the master becomes insensitive to the input. Because V2 is greater than V1, the slave is still isolated from the effect of the master.

At time t_4 the clock signal becomes less than the threshold of the inverter. The output of the inverter changes from 0 to 1, connecting the slave to the master. Whatever state the master was in is forced on the slave. The slave may change its state. If there is feedback from the output of the slave to the input of the master, it will not affect the master because the master was isolated from the input at time t_3.

A rough analogy of the operation of a master–slave circuit is a decompression chamber in a spacecraft. Inside the craft, the astronauts do not need to wear spacesuits. To go for a space walk outside the craft an astronaut dons a spacesuit and approaches the decompression chamber, which has two doors that are initially closed.

The decompression chamber analogy

The astronaut opens the inner door, which connects the chamber with the craft, and steps inside the chamber. She closes the inner door, isolating the chamber from the craft, and opens the outer door, connecting the chamber with outer space. She exits the outer door, closing it behind her. At no time are both doors open at the same time. If they were, the craft would lose all its air to outer space.

Similarly, the master–slave circuit has two doors—one to isolate or connect the master to the input, and one to isolate or connect the slave to the master. At no time are both doors open, with the master connected to the input and the slave connected to the master. If they were, a feedback loop might cause an unstable state in the circuit.

Figure 11.12 is a timing diagram of the behavior of a master–slave SR flip-flop. A change occurs in Q, the state of the slave latch, at time t_4, when the slave is connected to the master. That is during the high-to-low transition of Ck.

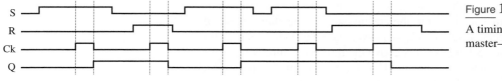

Figure **11.12**

A timing diagram of the
master–slave SR flip-flop.

Because a flip-flop is not combinational, a truth table is not sufficient to char-
acterize its behavior. Instead, flip-flops have *characteristic tables* that specify the
state of the device after one clock pulse for a given input and initial state. Figure
11.13 is the characteristic table for the SR flip-flop.

Characteristic tables

S(*t*)	R(*t*)	Q(*t*)	Q(*t* + 1)	Condition
0	0	0	0	No change
0	0	1	1	
0	1	0	0	Reset
0	1	1	0	
1	0	0	1	Set
1	0	1	1	
1	1	0	–	Not defined
1	1	1	–	

Figure **11.13**

The characteristic table for the SR
flip-flop.

S(*t*) and R(*t*) are the inputs at time *t* before a clock pulse. Q(*t*) is the state of the
flip-flop before a clock pulse, and Q(*t* + 1) is the state after the pulse. The table
shows that if SR is 00, the device does not change its state when clocked. If SR is
01, the device resets to Q = 0, and if it is 10, the device sets to Q = 1. It is impossible to predict what the state would be if SR = 11 when clocked.

The characteristic table is, in essence, a state transition table similar to Figure
7.11 for a finite state machine. An SR flip-flop is a finite state machine with two
possible states, Q = 0 and Q = 1. As with any finite state machine, its behavior can
be characterized by a state transition diagram. Figure 11.14 is the state transition
diagram for an SR flip-flop.

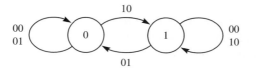

Figure **11.14**

The state transition diagram for an
SR flip-flop.

Circles denote the states of the machine with the value of Q inside the circle. Transitions are labeled with the values of SR that produce the given transition. For example, the transition from Q = 0 to Q = 1 is labeled with SR = 10.

The Basic Flip-Flops

Four flip-flops are common in computer design:

- SR   Set/reset
- JK   Set/reset/toggle
- D   Data or delay
- T   Toggle

The previous section showed how to construct the SR flip-flop. Its characteristic table defines its behavior. The other three flip-flops have their own characteristic tables that define their behaviors. Each one can be constructed from the SR flip-flop together with a few other gates. Like the SR flip-flop, the others all have Q and $\bar{Q}$ outputs. The JK flip-flop has two inputs labeled J and K in place of S and R. The D and T flip-flops each have only one input.

There is a systematic procedure to construct the other flip-flops from the SR flip-flop. The general circuit has the structure of Figure 11.9, where the Q and $\bar{Q}$ outputs of the SR flip-flop act as the Q and $\bar{Q}$ outputs of the device under construction. For the JK flip-flop, the input line of Figure 11.9 is actually two input lines, one for J and one for K. For the D flip-flop the one input line is labeled D, and for the T flip-flop it is labeled T. To design each flip-flop, you must determine the logic gates and their interconnection in the box labeled Combinational circuit.

As with any combinational circuit design, once you determine the required input and output in the form of a truth table, you can construct the minimum AND-OR circuit with the help of a Karnaugh map. So, the first step is to write down the required input and output of the box labeled Combinational circuit in Figure 11.9. A useful tool to determine the specification of the circuit is the *excitation table* of the SR flip-flop in Figure 11.15.

Contrast the excitation table with the characteristic table in Figure 11.13. The characteristic table tells you what the next state is, given the current input and the current state. But the excitation table tells you what the current input must be, given the desired transition. Here is how you build the excitation table from the characteristic table.

The first table entry is for the transition from Q = 0 to Q = 0. Two possible inputs permit this transition: SR = 00 and SR = 01. An SR value of 00 specifies the no-change condition. An SR value of 01 specifies the reset condition. Either of these conditions will cause the flip-flop to make the transition from Q = 0 to Q = 0. The $\times$ in the entry under R(t) is a don't-care value. As long as S is 0, you do not

$Q(t)$	$Q(t+1)$	$S(t)$	$R(t)$
0	0	0	$\times$
0	1	1	0
1	0	0	1
1	1	$\times$	0

Figure 11.15

The excitation table for the SR flip-flop.

care what the value of R is. The transition will be from $Q = 0$ to $Q = 0$ regardless of the value of R.

The second entry in the table is for the transition from $Q = 0$ to $Q = 1$. The only way to force this transition is to input 10 for SR, the set condition. Similarly, the third entry is for the transition from $Q = 1$ to $Q = 0$, which can occur only with a value of 01 for SR.

The last entry is for the transition from $Q = 1$ to $Q = 1$. The two possible input conditions that permit this transition are SR = 00, the no-change condition, and SR = 10, the set condition. Regardless of the value of S, if R is 0 the transition will occur. The $\times$ under $S(t)$ indicates the don't-care condition for S.

The JK Flip-Flop

The JK flip-flop resolves the undefined transition in the SR flip-flop. The J input acts like S, setting the device, and the K input acts like R, resetting the device. But when JK = 11, the condition is called the toggle condition. To toggle means to switch from one state to the other. In the toggle condition, if the initial state is 0 the final state will be 1, and if the initial state is 1 the final state will be 0. Figure 11.16 is the block diagram and the characteristic table for the JK flip-flop.

(a) Block diagram.

$J(t)$	$K(t)$	$Q(t)$	$Q(t + 1)$	Condition
0	0	0	0	No change
0	0	1	1	
0	1	0	0	Reset
0	1	1	0	
1	0	0	1	Set
1	0	1	1	
1	1	0	1	Toggle
1	1	1	0	

(b) Characteristic table.

Figure **11.16**

The JK flip-flop.

For the JK flip-flop, the box labeled Combinational circuit in Figure 11.9 has three inputs and two outputs. The inputs are J, K, and Q, which comes from the feedback connection. The outputs are S and R. So you need to design two three-input combinational circuits, one for S and one for R. First, write down the design table of Figure 11.17 with the help of the SR excitation table.

The design table tells you the inputs that are necessary for the SR flip-flop, given the transitions that the JK flip-flop must make. The first three columns list all the possible input combinations of the three inputs to the combinational circuit. It is

Q(t)	J(t)	K(t)	Q(t + 1)	S(t)	R(t)
0	0	0	0	0	×
0	0	1	0	0	×
0	1	1	1	1	0
0	1	0	1	1	0
1	0	0	1	×	0
1	0	1	0	0	1
1	1	1	0	0	1
1	1	0	1	×	0

Figure **11.17**

The design table to construct a JK flip-flop from an SR flip-flop.

a good idea to order the JK values as they will appear in the Karnaugh maps. The fourth column is the value of Q after the clock pulse. Each value of Q(t + 1) comes from the characteristic table of the JK flip-flop. For example, in the third row, JK = 11, which is the toggle condition. So the initial state Q(t) = 0 toggles to Q(t + 1) = 1. The last two columns come from the excitation table for the SR flip-flop, given Q(t) and Q(t + 1). For example, the third row has transition Q(t) Q(t + 1) = 01. The excitation table shows that SR must be 10 for that transition.

The next step is to write down the Karnaugh maps for the function. The entry in Figure 11.18(a) comes from the column labeled S(t) in the design table, and the one in (b) comes from R(t).

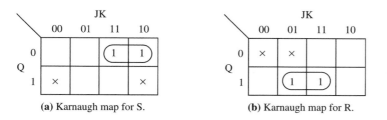

(a) Karnaugh map for S.   **(b)** Karnaugh map for R.

Figure **11.18**

The Karnaugh maps to construct a JK flip-flop from an SR flip-flop.

By inspection of the Karnaugh maps you can write the minimized AND-OR expression for S as $S = J\overline{Q}$, and for R as $R = KQ$. Figure 11.19 shows the complete design. You implement the JK flip-flop with an SR flip-flop and two two-input AND gates. You can see how the design works by considering all the possible values of JK. If JK = 00 then SR = 00 regardless of the state, and the state does not change. If JK = 11 and Q = 0, then SR = 10 and Q will change to 1. If Q = 1 initially, then SR = 01 and Q will change to 0. In both cases the state toggles, as it should for JK = 11. You should convince yourself that the circuit works correctly for JK = 01 and JK = 10 as well.

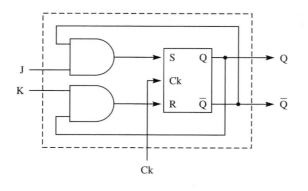

Figure **11.19**

Implementation of the JK flip-flop.

The D Flip-Flop

The D flip-flop is a data flip-flop with only one input, D, besides the clock. Figure 11.20(a) is its block diagram and (b) is its characteristic table. The table shows that $Q(t + 1)$ is independent of $Q(t)$. It depends only on the value of D at time t. The D flip-flop stores the data until the next clock pulse. Part (c) of the figure shows a timing diagram. This flip-flop is also called a delay flip-flop because on the timing diagram, the shape of Q is identical to that of D except for a time delay.

Figure **11.20**

The D flip-flop.

$D(t)$	$Q(t)$	$Q(t + 1)$	Condition
0	0	0	Delay
0	1	0	
1	0	1	Delay
1	1	1	

(a) Block diagram.   **(b)** Characteristic table.

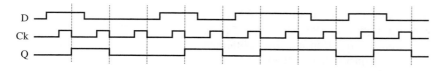

(c) A timing diagram.

Q(t)	D(t)	Q(t + 1)	S(t)	R(t)
0	0	0	0	×
0	1	1	1	0
1	1	1	×	0
1	0	0	0	1

(a) Design table.

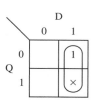

(b) Karnaugh map for S.

(c) Karnaugh map for R.

To construct a D flip-flop from an SR flip-flop, first write the design table. Because there is only one input besides Q, there are only four rows in the table as Figure 11.21(a) shows. Parts (b) and (c) show the Karnaugh maps, which contain only four cells instead of eight. Minimization of the AND-OR circuits gives $S = D$ and $R = \bar{D}$.

Figure 11.21

The design table and Karnaugh maps to construct a D flip-flop from an SR flip-flop.

Figure 11.22 is the implementation of the D flip-flop. It requires only a single inverter in addition to the SR flip-flop. This implementation has no feedback connections from Q or $\bar{Q}$ as the JK implementation does, because the next state does not depend on the current state.

Figure 11.22

Implementation of the D flip-flop.

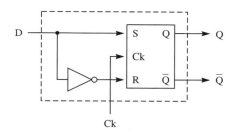

The T Flip-Flop

The T flip-flop is a toggle flip-flop. Like the D flip-flop, it has only one input, T, besides the clock. Figure 11.23(a) is the block diagram and (b) is the characteristic table. The T input acts like a control line that specifies a selective toggle. If T is 0 the flip-flop does not change its state, and if T is 1 the flip-flop toggles. Implementation of the T flip-flop is an exercise at the end of the chapter.

(a) Block diagram.

T(t)	Q(t)	Q(t + 1)	Condition
0	0	0	No change
0	1	1	
1	0	1	Toggle
1	1	0	

(b) Characteristic table.

Figure 11.23

The T flip-flop.

Excitation Tables

The preceding sections show how to construct the JK, D, and T flip-flops from the SR flip-flop and a few other gates. You can use the same systematic procedure to construct any flip-flop from any other flip-flop. It might seem pointless, for example, to construct a D flip-flop from a JK flip-flop, because you make a JK from an SR with two extra gates in the first place, and the D only requires an SR with an inverter. But the fact that you can construct any flip-flop from any other shows that all the flip-flops are equivalent in power. That is, any processing that you can do with any flip-flop you can do with any other with a few extra gates.

For example, assuming that you have, a JK flip-flop, and you want to construct a T flip-flop, you would write the design table from the characteristic table for the T and excitation table for the JK. In general, to construct flip-flop A from flip-flop B you need the characteristic table for A and the excitation table for B. Figure 11.24 shows the excitation tables for the JK, D, and T flip-flops.

You should verify the entries of each excitation table. For example, the first entry in the JK table is for the transition from Q = 0 to Q = 0. Using the same reasoning as with the SR flip-flop, the transition will occur if JK is 00 or 01; hence the don't-care condition under $K(t)$. The second table entry also has a don't-care condition. The transition from Q = 0 to Q = 1 can occur under two conditions. JK can be either 10, the set condition, or 11, the toggle condition. Both allow Q to change from 0 to 1.

11.2 Sequential Analysis and Design

A sequential circuit consists of an interconnection of gates and flip-flops. Conceptually, you can group all the gates together into a combinational circuit and all the flip-flops together in a group of *state registers*, as in Figure 11.25. This is a generalization of Figure 11.9, which contained only one state register and whose output required no additional gates from the combinational circuit.

The solid arrows in Figure 11.25 represent one or more connecting lines. The input and output lines are the external connections to the environment of the circuit. The lines from the Combinational circuit to the state registers are the input lines to SR, JK, D, or T flip-flops. The feedback lines are from the flip-flops' Q and $\overline{Q}$ outputs to the Combinational circuit. The figure assumes a common clock line (not shown) to each flip-flop in the group of state registers.

Between clock pulses, the combinational part of the circuit produces its output from the external input and the state of the circuit, that is, the states of the individual flip-flops. The amount of time it takes to produce the combinational output and the state register input depends on how many gate levels are in the circuit. The Ck period is adjusted to be long enough to allow the input to propagate through the Combinational circuit to the output before the next clock pulse. All the state regis-

Figure **11.24**

Excitation tables for the JK, D, and T flip-flops.

Q(t)	Q(t + 1)	J(t)	K(t)
0	0	0	×
0	1	1	×
1	0	×	1
1	1	×	0

(a) The JK flip-flop.

Q(t)	Q(t + 1)	D(t)
0	0	0
0	1	1
1	0	0
1	1	1

(b) The D flip-flop.

Q(t)	Q(t + 1)	T(t)
0	0	0
0	1	1
1	0	1
1	1	0

(c) The T flip-flop.

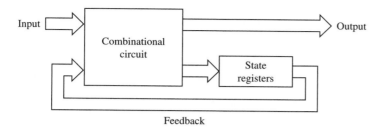

Figure **11.25**

A general sequential circuit.

ters are edge-triggered or master–slave to protect against multiple propagations through the feedback loop.

As in Figure 11.14, you can describe the behavior of a general sequential circuit with a state transition diagram or its corresponding state transition table. The difference is that Figure 11.14 is for a single device with two possible states, whereas Figure 11.25 is for n flip-flops. Because each flip-flop has two possible states, the sequential circuit has a total of 2^n states.

The difference between analysis and design at the hardware level is the same as the difference at the software level. Figure 11.26 illustrates the difference. In analysis, the input and sequential circuit are given and the output is to be determined. In design, the input and desired output are given and the sequential circuit is to be determined.

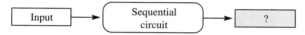

(a) Analysis—The input and sequential circuit are given. The output is to be determined.

Figure **11.26**

The difference between analysis and design.

(b) Design—The input and desired output are given. The sequential circuit is to be determined.

This section shows how to determine the output from a given sequential circuit and input stream. The general approach is to construct the analysis table from the circuit. From the analysis table you can easily determine the state transition table, the state transition diagram, and the output stream for any given input stream.

A Sequential Analysis Problem

Suppose the circuit of Figure 11.27 is given. The state registers are the two T flip-flops labeled FFA and FFB. The combinational circuit is the group of two AND

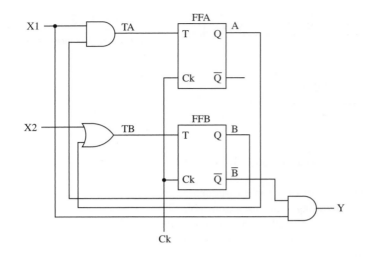

Figure **11.27**

A circuit for analysis.

gates and one OR gate. The inputs are X1 and X2, and the single output is Y. The feedback loop consists of the line from Q of FFA, labeled A, and the two lines from Q and $\overline{Q}$ of FFB, labeled B and $\overline{B}$. The input to FFA is labeled TA, and the input to FFB is labeled TB.

Because there are two flip-flops, there are four possible states,

AB = 00

AB = 01

AB = 10

AB = 11

where, for example, AB = 01 means that Q = 0 in FFA and Q = 1 in FFB. Because there are two inputs, there are four possible input combinations,

X1 X2 = 00

X1 X2 = 01

X1 X2 = 10

X1 X2 = 11

Here is the problem. You are given an initial state, AB, and an initial input, X1 X2. (a) What is the initial output? (b) What will be the next state after a clock pulse occurs? Because there are four states, and with each state there are four possible input combinations, you must answer these questions 16 times. The analysis table in Figure 11.28 provides a systematic tool to determine the answers.

A(t)	B(t)	X1(t)	X2(t)	Y(t)	TA(t)	TB(t)	A(t + 1)	B(t + 1)
0	0	0	0	0	0	0	0	0
0	0	0	1	0	0	1	0	1
0	0	1	0	1	0	0	0	0
0	0	1	1	1	0	1	0	1
0	1	0	0	0	0	0	0	1
0	1	0	1	0	0	1	0	0
0	1	1	0	0	1	0	1	1
0	1	1	1	0	1	1	1	0
1	0	0	0	0	0	1	1	1
1	0	0	1	0	0	1	1	1
1	0	1	0	1	0	1	1	1
1	0	1	1	1	0	1	1	1
1	1	0	0	0	0	1	1	0
1	1	0	1	0	0	1	1	0
1	1	1	0	0	1	1	0	0
1	1	1	1	0	1	1	0	0

Figure **11.28**

The analysis table for the circuit of Figure 11.27.

The first four columns are a list of all possible combinations of the initial state and initial input. From Figure 11.27, the boolean expressions for Y(t), TA(t), and TB(t) are

$$Y(t) = X1(t) \cdot \overline{B}(t)$$
$$TA(t) = X1(t) \cdot B(t)$$
$$TB(t) = X2(t) + A(t)$$

So, you compute the column for Y(t) as the AND of the column for X1(t) and the complement of the column for B(t). You compute the column for TA(t) as the AND of the column for X1(t) and the column for B(t). You compute the column for TB(t) as the OR of the column for X2(t) and the column for A(t). You compute the last two columns from the characteristic table for the T flip-flop, the initial state of a flip-flop, and its initial input.

Example 11.1 Consider the column for B(t + 1). In the first row, the initial state of FFB is 0 from the column for B(t). The flip-flop input is 0 from the column for

TB(*t*). From the characteristic table for the T flip-flop in Figure 11.23(b), 0 is the no-change condition. So the state remains the same, and B(*t* + 1) is 0.   ∎

Example 11.2   For the same column, consider the second row. The initial state of FFB is again 0 from the column for B(*t*). This time the flip-flop input is 1 from the column for TB(*t*). From the characteristic table for the T flip-flop, 1 is the toggle condition. So the state toggles, and B(*t* + 1) is 1.   ∎

The state transition table in Figure 11.29 is a simple rearrangement of selected columns from the analysis table. For a given initial state A(*t*) B(*t*) and a given input X1(*t*) X2(*t*), it lists the next state A(*t* + 1) B(*t* + 1) and the initial output Y(*t*). States are listed as ordered pairs. Entries in the body of the table are the next state followed by the initial output, separated by a comma.

	X1(*t*) X2(*t*)			
A(*t*) B(*t*)	**00**	**01**	**10**	**11**
00	00, 0	01, 0	00, 1	01, 1
01	01, 0	00, 0	11, 0	10, 0
10	11, 0	11, 0	11, 1	11, 1
11	10, 0	10, 0	00, 0	00, 0
	A(*t* + 1) B(*t* + 1), Y(*t*)			

Figure 11.29

The state transition table for the circuit of Figure 11.27.

It is usually easier to visualize the behavior of the circuit from its state transition diagram rather than its state transition table. Figure 11.30 is the state transition diagram constructed from the state transition table. The standard convention is to label transitions as ordered pairs of the input followed by the initial output, separated by a slash.

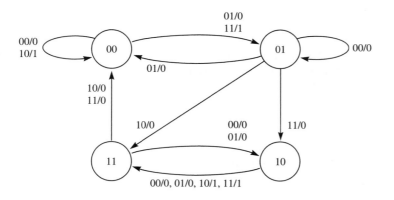

Figure 11.30

The state transition diagram for the circuit of Figure 11.27. Transitions are labeled X1(*t*) X2(*t*) / Y(*t*).

To determine the output from a given input stream, assume that you start in state AB = 11 and input the following values of X1 X2:

11, 11, 00, 10, 01

From the diagram, you will make transitions to the states

11, 00, 01, 01, 11, 10

and generate the following output

0, 1, 0, 0, 0

The analysis is similar for sequential circuits containing other flip-flops or even mixtures of different types of flip-flops. Using your knowledge of combinational circuits, you simply determine the input of each flip-flop for all possible combinations of inputs and states. Then, from the characteristic table of each flip-flop, you determine what the next state will be. In general, if there are m inputs and n flip-flops, you will need to analyze $2^m 2^n$ transitions.

Preset and Clear

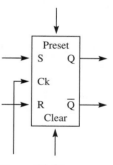

The output sequence for the previous problem assumes that the flip-flops are both in their Q = 1 state. A legitimate question is: How do the flip-flops get in their start states? In practice, most flip-flops are constructed with two additional inputs, called *preset* and *clear*. These inputs are *asynchronous*; that is, they do not depend on the clock pulse to function. Figure 11.31 shows the block diagram of an SR flip-flop with asynchronous preset and clear inputs.

In normal operation, both preset and clear lines are 0. To initialize the flip-flop to Q = 1, send preset to 1 and back to 0. To initialize the flip-flop to Q = 0, send clear to 1 and back to 0. You do not need to send a clock pulse while either input is high for it to function. Implementation of the asynchronous preset and clear is an exercise at the end of the chapter.

Figure **11.31**

The block diagram of an SR flip-flop with asynchronous preset and clear.

Sequential Design

With sequential design, the behavior of the circuit is given, frequently in the form of a state transition diagram, and the implementation of the circuit with a minimum number of gates is to be determined. Also given in the problem formulation is the type of flip-flop to be used for the state registers in the sequential circuit.

The design procedure has three steps. First, from the state transition diagram tabulate the transitions of the circuit in a design table. For each combination of initial state and input, list the initial output and the next state. Then, from the excitation tables list the necessary flip-flop input conditions to cause the transitions.

Second, transfer the entries for each flip-flop input to a Karnaugh map. It helps to prevent mistakes if you look ahead in your tabulation of the design table and list the entries in the same order as a Karnaugh map. Design the combinational part of the sequential circuit by minimizing the expressions from the Karnaugh map.

Third, draw the minimized combinational circuit. Each flip-flop input will come from a combinational circuit two gate-levels deep at most. You should recognize this procedure as a generalization of the procedure to construct the JK, D, and T flip-flops from the SR flip-flop.

A Sequential Design Problem

This example illustrates the design procedure. The problem is to implement the state transition diagram of Figure 11.32 with SR flip-flops. As in Figure 11.30, the transitions are labeled with the input values, $X1\ X2$, and the initial output, Y. The values in the state circles are the Q values of the first SR flip-flop, FFA, and the second SR flip-flop, FFB.

This machine has only three input combinations and four states, for a total of 12 transitions. The input combinations are 01, 11, and 10. Because the combination 00 is not expected to occur, you can treat it as a don't-care condition to help with the minimization.

To implement a finite state machine with eight states, you need three flip-flops. To implement a machine with five to seven states also requires three flip-flops, but some of the states are not expected to occur and can be treated as don't-care states.

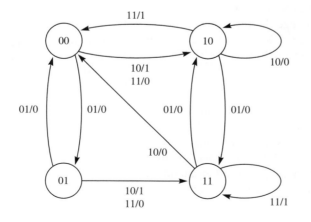

Figure **11.32**

The state transition diagram for a design problem.

Figure 11.33 is the first step in the design process. The four columns on the left are all the possible combinations of initial state and input. The middle three columns are a simple tabulation of the initial output and next state from Figure 11.32.

The four columns on the right come from the fact that there are two SR flip-flops, each with two inputs. SA is the S input of FFA, RA is the R input of FFA, and so on. The flip-flop input conditions that produce the given transition come from the excitation table for the SR flip-flop, Figure 11.15.

Figure **11.33**

The design table for the state transition diagram of Figure 11.30.

Initial state		Initial input		Initial output	Next state		Flip-flop input conditions			
							FFA		FFB	
A(t)	B(t)	X1(t)	X2(t)	Y(t)	A(t + 1)	B(t + 1)	SA(t)	RA(t)	SB(t)	RB(t)
0	0	0	1	0	0	1	0	×	1	0
0	1	0	1	0	0	0	0	×	0	1
1	1	0	1	0	1	0	×	0	0	1
1	0	0	1	0	1	1	×	0	1	0
0	0	1	1	0	1	0	1	0	0	×
0	1	1	1	0	1	1	1	0	×	0
1	1	1	1	1	1	1	×	0	×	0
1	0	1	1	1	0	0	0	1	0	×
0	0	1	0	1	1	0	1	0	0	×
0	1	1	0	1	1	1	1	0	×	0
1	1	1	0	0	0	0	0	1	0	1
1	0	1	0	0	1	0	×	0	0	×

For example, consider the first line for the transition from AB = 00 to AB = 01. The transition for FFA is from Q = 0 to Q = 0. The excitation table shows that transition is caused by a 0 for S and a don't-care condition for R. The transition for FFB is from Q = 0 to Q = 1. The excitation table shows that transition is caused by 10 for SR.

The next step is to consider that each flip-flop input is a function of four variables—the initial state, AB, and the input, X1 X2. To design the combinational circuit requires a four-variable Karnaugh map for each flip-flop input. Figure 11.34 shows the Karnaugh maps from Figure 11.33. The map for input SA, Figure 11.34(a), shows the row values for the state AB and the column values for the input X1 X2. Note that the combination X1 X2 = 00; the first column in the Karnaugh maps, is a don't-care condition.

The output, Y, is also a function of the initial state and input and requires a Karnaugh map for minimization. Shown below each Karnaugh map is the corresponding minimized expression.

Figure 11.35 is the resulting sequential circuit. Rather than show the feedback connections explicitly, the diagram is in abbreviated form.

After completing the design you might notice in Figure 11.34(c) and (d) that cell 8 of the Karnaugh map is covered and so appears to have the value 1. How can that be when Figure 11.34(a) and (b) do not have it covered and so it appears to have the value 0? How can it have the value 0 and 1 at the same time? Karnaugh maps do not show what happens in practice to the don't-care conditions. The specification of the circuit in Figure 11.32 assumes that the external input X1 X2 comes from some unknown source and that the combination X1 X2 = 00 will never occur in practice. Therefore, the combination represented by cell 8, namely A B X1 X2 = 1000 will

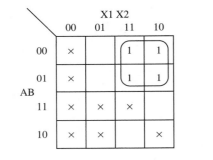

(a) SA = $\bar{A}$ X1

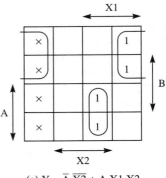

(b) RA = A B $\overline{X2}$ + A $\bar{B}$ X1 X2

(c) SB = $\bar{B}$ $\overline{X1}$

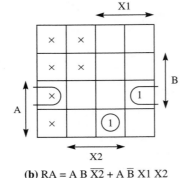

(d) RB = B $\overline{X1}$ + A $\overline{X2}$

(e) Y = $\bar{A}$ $\overline{X2}$ + A X1 X2

Figure **11.34**

The Karnaugh maps for Figure 11.33.

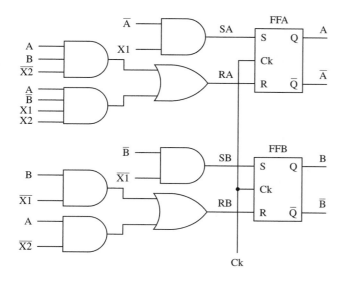

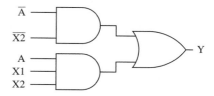

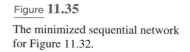

Figure **11.35**

The minimized sequential network for Figure 11.32.

never occur. You can choose to have your circuit behave any way you want for that combination, because it will never occur.

The same consideration arises if you need to design a machine with the number of states not equal to a power of two. Say you want to design a five-state machine. Two flip-flops are not enough, because they only provide four states. With three flip-flops, you have eight states possible, but only five will occur in practice. The other three can be don't-care conditions in the design. After you design such a circuit, the unused states will be inaccessible from the used states, but not necessarily vice versa. That is, there may be transitions from the unused to the used states, but such transitions will be irrelevant because they will never occur. They are analogous to dead code in a program.

The design procedure illustrated in this example has had two flip-flops and two inputs, for a total of four variables in the Karnaugh map. Four-variable maps would also be required for a design with three flip-flops and one input, or one flip-flop and three inputs. The procedure for one flip-flop and two inputs, or two flip-flops and one input, would be identical except that three-variable Karnaugh maps would suffice for the minimization.

Some sequential circuits require minimization of a combinational circuit with more than four variables. Karnaugh maps cannot conveniently handle a problem of that size. Systematic procedures exist to deal with these larger problems, of which the most common is the Quine-McCluskey method, but those are beyond the scope of this book.

11.3   Computer Subsystems

Computers are designed as a set of interconnected subsystems. Each subsystem is a black box with a well-specified interface. Sometimes the subsystem consists of an individual integrated circuit, in which case the interface is specified by the operating characteristics of the wire pins of the physical package. At a lower level of abstraction, the subsystem could be part of several subsystems within an integrated circuit. Or, at a higher level, the subsystem could be a printed circuit board made up of several integrated circuits.

However the subsystem is physically implemented, a bus connects the subsystems together. The bus could be a single wire from the output of a gate of one subsystem to the input of a gate of another subsystem. Or the bus could be a group of wires containing both data and control signals, like the bus that connects main memory to the CPU of Pep/8 shown in Figure 4.1.

Registers

A basic building block of the Level ISA3 machine is the register. You are familiar with the 16-bit registers in the Pep/8 CPU. The instruction set includes instructions to manipulate the register contents. Figure 11.36 shows a block diagram and implementation of a four-bit register.

Figure **11.36**

A four-bit register.

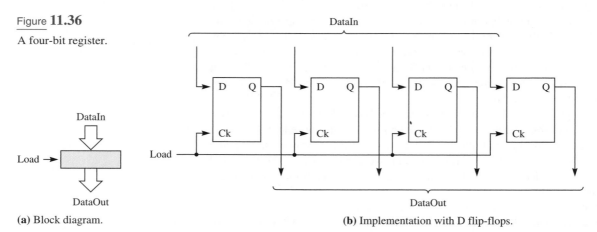

(a) Block diagram.   **(b)** Implementation with D flip-flops.

The register has four data inputs, four data outputs, and a control input that is labeled Load. The block diagram shows the four data lines as a single wide arrow. The implementation shows the data lines individually. The register is simply an array of D flip-flops. Each data input line connects to the D input of a flip-flop. Each data output line connects to the Q output of a flip-flop. The load input connects to the clock inputs of all the flip-flops. From this point on, figures that contain sequential circuits are shaded to distinguish them from combinational circuits.

The register operates by presenting the values you wish to load on the data input lines. You then clock them into the register by sending the load signal to 1 and back to 0. All four values will be loaded simultaneously into the register. If each flip-flop is a master–slave device, the output will appear when the slave is connected to the master at time t_4 of Figure 11.11.

Each D flip-flop is a bit in the register. An eight-bit register would have eight flip-flops, and a 16-bit register would have 16 flip-flops. The number of flip-flops would not affect the speed of the load operation because the load into each flip-flop occurs simultaneously. The block diagram of Figure 11.36(a) is the same regardless of the number of bits in the register.

Buses

Suppose you have two subsystems, A and B, that need to send data back and forth. The simplest way to connect them is to have two unidirectional buses—one for sending data from A to B and one from B to A. The first bus would be a group of wires, each one from the output of a gate in A to the input of a gate in B. Each wire from the second would be from the output of a gate in B to the input of a gate in A.

Unidirectional buses

One problem with this arrangement is the sheer number of wires for a wide bus. If you want to send 64 bits at a time you need two unidirectional buses, for a total of 128 wires. You can cut that number in half by using a bidirectional bus. The tradeoff is speed. With two unidirectional buses you can send information from A to B and B to A at the same time, an impossibility with a bidirectional bus. You also must pay the price of a small setup time if you need to change the direction of the data flow on the bus before sending the data.

Bidirectional buses

Figure 11.37 shows the problem that must be solved to implement a bidirectional bus. An AND gate represents the master clock-enable gate of a master–slave flip-flop

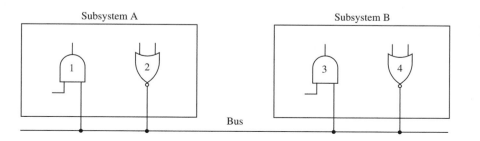

Figure **11.37**

The bidirectional bus problem.

that is part of a register. A NOR gate represents the slave Q output gate of the flip-flop of another register. To send data from A to B, the output of gate 2 must be connected to the input of gate 3. Going from B to A, the output of gate 4 must be connected to the input of gate 1. The problem is with gates 2 and 4. You can always connect the output of one gate to the input of another, but you cannot connect the output of two gates together. Suppose gate 2 wants to send a one to gate 3, but the output of gate 4 happens to be zero at the time. Their outputs are in conflict, so which one predominates?

The answer depends on the technology underlying the fabrication of the gates. With some logic gate families, you can actually connect the outputs of several gates together and if one or more gates outputs a one, the common bus will transfer a one. This kind of gate is said to have the *wired-OR property* because the signal on the bus acts like the output of an OR gate. With other families, connecting the outputs of two gates together clobbers the circuit, causing unpredictable havoc. Even with wired-OR gates, the bidirectional bus problem still exists. For example, if gate 2 wants to send a zero to gate 3, but the output of gate 4 happens to be one at the time, gate 3 would erroneously detect a one.

The wired-OR property

To make the bidirectional bus work properly, you need a way to temporarily disconnect gate 4 from the bus when gate 2 is putting data on the bus, and vice versa. A tri-state buffer can do precisely that. It has one data input, one enable control input, and one output. Figure 11.38 shows the truth table for the tri-state buffer where E is the enable control line, a is the input, and x is the output. When the device is enabled, the input passes through to the output unmodified. When it is disabled, the output is in effect disconnected from the circuit. Electrically, the output is in a high impedance state. The device is called a tri-state buffer because the output can be in one of three states—zero, one, or disconnected.

Figure 11.39 shows how the tri-state buffer solves the bidirectional bus problem. There is a tri-state buffer between the output of every gate and the bus. To send data from A to B you enable the tri-state buffers in A and disable the tri-state buffers in B, and vice versa. In order for this scheme to function properly, the subsystems must cooperate and never let their tri-state buffers be enabled simultaneously.

E	a	x
0	0	Disconnected
0	1	Disconnected
1	0	0
1	1	1

Figure **11.38**

Truth table for the tri-state buffer.

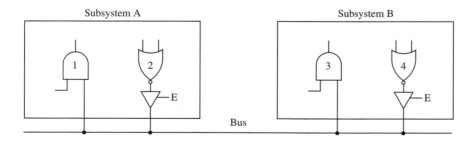

Bus

Figure **11.39**

Solution to the bidirectional bus problem with the tri-state buffer.

Memory Subsystems

Memory subsystems are constructed from several integrated circuit memory chips. Figure 11.40 shows two memory chips, each one of which stores 512 bits. Memory chips have a set of address lines labeled starting with A0, a set of data lines labeled starting with D0, and a set of control lines labeled CS, WE, and OE. The data lines have two arrowheads to indicate that they should be connected to a bidirectional bus. Part (a) shows the bits organized as a set of 64 eight-bit words. There are six address lines, because 2^6 is 64. Each possible combination of input values accesses a separate eight-bit word. Part (b) shows the same number of bits organized as a set of 512 one-bit words. There are 9 address lines because 2^9 is 512. In general, a memory chip with 2^n words has n address lines. The number of address and data lines of the chips in Figure 11.40 are unrealistically tiny to keep the examples simple. Memory chips are manufactured nowadays with hundreds of millions of bits.

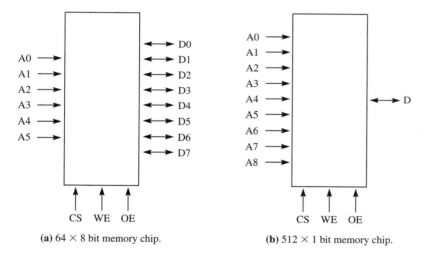

(a) 64×8 bit memory chip.   (b) 512×1 bit memory chip.

Figure **11.40**

Two integrated circuit memory chips that store 512 bits.

The control lines serve the following purpose:

- CS (chip select) to enable or select the memory chip
- WE (write enable) to write or store a memory word to the chip
- OE (output enable) to enable the output buffer to read a word from the chip

Memory chip control lines

To store a word to a chip, set the address lines to the address where the word is to be stored, set the data lines to the value that you want to store, select the chip by

Writing to a memory chip

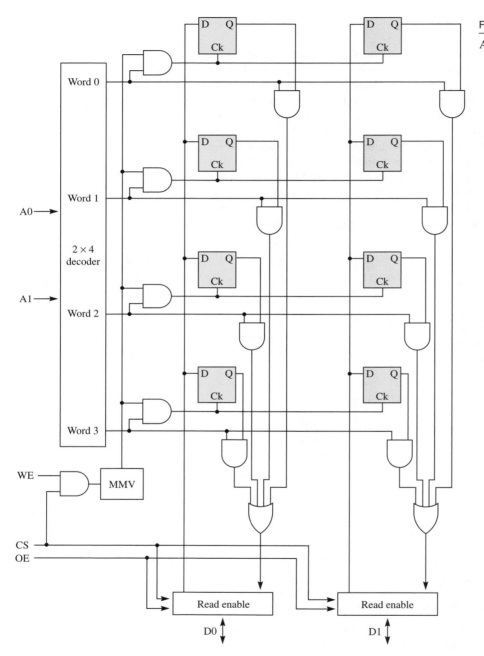

Figure **11.41**

A 4 × 2 bit memory chip.

setting CS to one, and execute the write by setting WE to one. To read a word from a chip, set the address lines to the address from which you want to read, select the chip by setting CS to one, enable the output by setting OE to one, after which the data you want to read will appear on the data lines. In practice, the control lines for most memory chips are asserted low. That is, they are normally maintained at a high voltage, representing one, and are activated by setting them to a low voltage, representing zero. This book assumes that memory chip control lines are asserted high to keep the examples simple.

Reading from a memory chip

In practice, control lines are normally asserted low

Figure 11.41 shows the implementation of a 4 × 2 bit memory chip with two address lines and two data lines. It stores four two-bit words. Each bit is a D flip-flop. The sequential devices are shaded to distinguish them from the combinational devices. The address lines drive a 2 × 4 decoder, one of whose outputs is 1 and the other three 0. The decoder output line that is 1 selects the row of D flip-flops that make up the word accessed by the chip.

The box labeled Read enable provides the interface to a bidirectional bus. Figure 11.42 shows its implementation. DR is the data read line coming from the OR gate in Figure 11.41, DW is the data write line going to the D inputs of the flip-flops, and D is the data interface to the bidirectional bus.

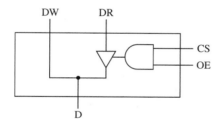

Figure **11.42**

Implementation of the box labeled Read enable in Figure 11.41.

Figure 11.43 is a truth table of the circuit. The chip is normally in one of three modes.

- CS = 0: The chip is not selected.
- CS = 1, WE = 1, OE = 0: The chip is selected for write.
- CS = 1, WE = 0, OE = 1: The chip is selected for read.

CS	OE	Operation
0	×	Disconnected
1	0	Disconnected
1	1	Connect DR to D

Figure **11.43**

Truth table for the Read enable box.

It is not permitted for WE and OE to both be 1 at the same time. The truth table and its implementation show that when CS is 0, DR is disconnected from the bidirectional bus regardless of any of the other control lines. When CS is 1 and OE is 0, DR is also disconnected. This is the write mode, in which case data is being fed from the bidirectional bus to DW. When CS is 1 and OE is 1, the tri-state buffer is enabled and data is being fed from DR to the bidirectional bus.

To see how a memory read works, consider the scenario where A1 A0 = 10, CS = 1, WE = 0, and OE = 1. The values for A1 A0 make the line labeled Word 2 out of the decoder 1, and the other word lines 0. The Word 2 line enables the AND

The memory read operation

gates connected to the Q outputs of the D flip-flops in row 2, and disables the AND gates connected to the flip-flop outputs of all the other rows. Consequently, data from the second row flows through the two OR gates into the Read enable box and onto the bidirectional bus.

A memory write works in conjunction with the box labeled MMV, which stands for monostable multivibrator, in Figure 11.41. Assuming that the D flip-flops are of the master–slave variety, to do a store requires a Ck pulse to go from low to high then high-to-low as Figure 11.11 shows. A *monostable multivibrator* is a device that provides such a pulse. Figure 11.44 shows the timing diagram of a monostable multivibrator with an initial delay. When the input line goes high it triggers a delay circuit. After a predetermined time interval, the delay circuit triggers the monostable multivibrator, which emits a clock pulse with a predetermined width. Monostable multivibrators are also known as one-shot devices because when they are activated they emit a single "one shot" pulse.

The monostable multivibrator

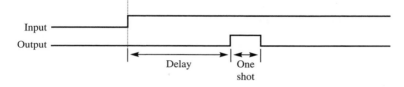

Figure 11.44

Timing diagram of a monostable multivibrator with initial delay.

To see how a memory write works, consider the scenario where A1 A0 = 10, CS = 1, WE = 1, and OE = 0. Assuming that the address lines, data lines, and control lines are all set simultaneously, the memory circuit must wait for the address signals to propagate through the decoder before clocking the data into the flip-flops. The initial delay in MMV is engineered to allow sufficient time for the outputs of the decoder to be set before clocking in the data. The Read enable circuit puts the data from the bidirectional bus on the input of all the flip-flops. However, when the MMV emits the clock pulse, three of the four AND gates to which it is connected will disable the pulse from reaching their rows. It will only reach the row of Word 2, so those are the only flip-flops that will store the data.

The memory write operation

Several types of memory chips are available on the market. The circuit model in Figure 11.41 most closely resembles what is known as *static memory* or SRAM. In practice, a master–slave D flip-flop is not the basis of bit storage, as it requires more transistors than are necessary. Many static RAM devices use a circuit that is a modification of Figure 11.1(b), a stable circuit consisting of a pair of inverters with feedback. It takes only two additional transistors to implement a mechanism for setting the state. The advantage of static RAM is speed. The disadvantage is its physical size on the chip, because several transistors are required for each bit cell.

SRAM

To overcome the size disadvantage of static memory, *dynamic memory* or DRAM uses only one transistor and one capacitor per bit cell. You store data by storing electrical charge on the capacitor. Because of the small size of the bit cells, DRAM chips have much higher storage capacities than SRAM chips. The problem with DRAM is that the charge slowly leaks off the capacitors within a few milliseconds of being fully charged. Before too much charge leaks off, the memory subsystem must read the data from the cell and charge the capacitor back up if necessary. As you would expect, the refresh operation takes time, and DRAM memory is slower than SRAM. *DRAM*

In contrast to read/write memory, *read-only memory* or ROM is designed for situations where the data to be stored never changes. The data for each bit cell can be set at the factory when the chip is manufactured, in which case the user supplies the manufacturer with the bit pattern to store. Alternatively, a *programmable* ROM or PROM chip allows the user to program the bit pattern. The process is accomplished by selectively blowing out a set of fuses embedded in the chip, and is irreversible. To overcome the irreversibility disadvantage, an *erasable* PROM or EPROM has the capability to erase the entire chip by exposing the circuit to ultraviolet radiation. EPROM chips are packaged underneath a transparent window so the circuit can be exposed to the radiation. To erase an EPROM chip you must remove it from the computer to expose it and then you must reprogram the entire chip. The *electrically erasable* PROM or EEPROM allows you to erase an individual cell with the right combination of electrical signals so that the device does not need to be removed to be reprogrammed. The circuitry to program a cell uses different voltage levels from those to read data during normal operation of the chip, and is therefore more complex to design. *ROM* *PROM* *EPROM* *EEPROM*

SRAM and DRAM are volatile. That is, when you power off the circuit you lose the data. ROM devices are nonvolatile because they retain their data without a source of external power. *Flash memory* is popular in such consumer hand-held devices as digital cameras, cell phones, and MP3 players. It is a type of EEPROM and has the advantage of retaining its data when the device is turned off. With flash memory, you can read an individual cell but you can only write an entire block of cells. Before writing the block, it must be completely erased. A flash card consists of an array of flash chips. A flash drive is the same thing, but with circuitry at the interface to make it appear to be a hard drive. It is not really a hard drive and has no moving parts. Compared to hard drives of the same size, flash drives are faster but hold much less data. An indication of how micro hard drive and flash memory technologies compete in the market, manufacturers now offer hard drives in a package whose interface makes them appear to be flash memory. You can plug them into your digital camera in place of the memory card. So now we have flash memory pretending to be a hard drive and a hard drive pretending to be a flash memory card, a testament to the practical power of abstraction. *Flash memory*

Address Decoding

A single memory chip usually does not have the capacity to provide main memory storage for an entire computer. You must combine several chips into a memory subsystem to provide adequate capacity. Most computers are byte addressable, as is Pep/8. A chip like the one in Figure 11.40(a) would be convenient for such a machine because the word size of the chip matches the cell size that the CPU addresses.

Suppose, however, that you have a set of 4×2 chips like the one in Figure 11.41 and you want to use it in Pep/8. Because the word size of the chip is 2 and the size of an addressable cell for the CPU is 8, you must group four 4×2 chips to construct a 4×8 memory module. Figure 11.45 shows the interconnections. You can see that the input and output lines of the module are identical to the input and output lines of what would be a 4×8 chip. The bits of each byte in memory are distributed over four chips. The bits of the byte at address A1 A0 = 01 are stored in the second row (Word 1) of all four chips.

Figure 11.45

Constructing a 4×8 memory module from four 4×2 memory chips.

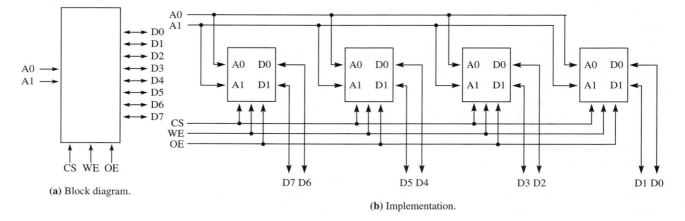

(a) Block diagram.

(b) Implementation.

Similarly, it would take eight of the chips in Figure 11.40(b) to construct a 512 $\times$ 8 memory module. For high reliability, you could use 11 of the chips for each eight-bit cell with the three extra chips used for single-error correction, as described in Section 9.4. With such an ECC system, the bits of each byte would be spread out over all 11 chips.

These examples show how to combine several $n \times m$ chips to make an $n \times k$ module where k is greater than m. In general, k must be a multiple of m. You simply hook up k/m chips with all their address and control lines in common, and assign the data lines from each chip to the lines of the module.

A different problem in constructing memory subsystems is when you have several $n \times m$ chips, m is equal to the size of the addressable cell for the CPU, and you want an $l \times m$ module where l is greater than n. In other words, if you have a set of chips whose word size is equal to the size of the addressable cell of the CPU, how do you connect them to add memory to your computer? The key is to use the chip

Lynn Conway and Carver Mead

Early computers were built with individual transistors, resistors, and capacitors. A major advance was small scale integration (SSI) where up to ten gates are fabricated on one chip. Medium scale integration (MSI) followed with up to 100 gates per chip, and then large scale integration (LSI) with up to 10,000 and very large scale integration (VLSI) with up to 100,000. Nowadays we are in the era of ultra large scale integration (ULSI) with over 10,000,000 gates per chip.

By the mid 1970s, the semiconductor industry had reached LSI. The big manufacturers produced families of LSI chips that their customers purchased and wired together to construct digital systems. Further advances in integration were thought to be beyond the reach of individuals or small firms, as such systems seemed far too complex.

Two people, however, were about to bring a sea change that shook the semiconductor industry to its roots. Lynn Conway received her master's degree in Electrical Engineering from Columbia University in 1963. After a stint at IBM Research, where she invented dynamic instruction scheduling while on the ACS-1 project, followed by work at a few other companies, she was recruited in 1973 to Xerox's exciting new Palo Alto Research Center. Carver Mead describes himself as a Caltech "lifer," having earned all his degrees there, culminating with the PhD in Electri-

cal Engineering in 1959, and teaching there for over 40 years.

Conway and Mead began collaborating in 1975. Conway was working on the Silicon Structures Project and needed to design digital circuits in a timely manner, a task that was impossibly time-consuming using the LSI chips at the time.

Together, she and Mead came up with their powerful idea—that VLSI circuit design could be computer-automated with just the right level of abstraction. They formulated their silicon design rules so that the VLSI designer would not have to deal with individual logic gates, but with black boxes at a higher level of abstraction. With low level details hidden, small design teams and even individuals could design their own custom VLSI circuits and not be restricted to the LSI chips of the day.

The reaction of the industry was extreme skepticism. Mead predicted

that custom VLSI circuits would be designed by individual organizations that need the chips then contracted out for fabrication at "silicon foundries." To promote the idea, Mead and Conway wrote their book, *Introduction to VLSI Systems* in 1979. Conway took a visiting professorship at MIT in 1978-79 and used preprint copies of the book in a course that required students to design and construct a VLSI chip in a single semester. After the success of that famous course, the book spread to over a hundred universities, whose students eventually changed the semiconductor industry forever. Silicon foundries are more than a $30 billion business today.

A few of Lynn Conway's many awards are her election as an IEEE Fellow and as a member of the National Academy of Engineering. A few of Carver Mead's are the Harry Goode Memorial Award and the National Medal of Technology.

"Listen to the technology; find out what it's telling you."

—*Carver Mead*

select line CS so that for all address requests from the CPU, no more than one chip is selected. The technique for connecting a memory chip to an address bus is called address decoding. There are two variations—full address decoding and partial address decoding.

Figure 11.46 shows the memory map for a CPU with 8 address lines capable of storing 2^8 or 256 bytes. The scenario is unrealistically small to keep the example simple. You have four chips that you need to wire into the address space of the CPU—a 64-byte RAM to install at address 0, a 32-byte RAM to install at address 64, an 8-port I/O chip to install at address 208, and a 32-byte ROM to install at address 224.

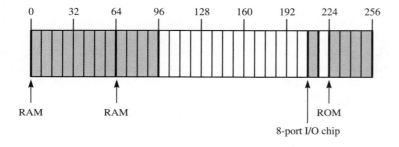

Figure **11.46**

The memory map of a 256-byte memory with eight address lines.

The 8-port I/O chip implements what is known as *memory-mapped* I/O, common in many computer systems. Computers with native I/O instructions in their instruction sets, such as Pep/8, are not required to use memory-mapped I/O. The native input and output instructions in Pep/8 are CHARI and CHARO. When you execute CHARI, the CPU takes the input from an input device not specified by the CHARI instruction and stores the byte in a memory location that depends on the operand specifier and the addressing mode. In contrast, a system with memory-mapped I/O need not have any native I/O instructions in its instruction set. Instead, the CPU's LOAD instruction does input and its STORE instruction does output. In Figure 11.46, the 8-port I/O chip maps eight I/O devices to memory addresses 208 to 215. For example, the keyboard might be mapped to address 208, the monitor to address 209, a printer to address 210, and so on. A program on a computer without memory-mapped I/O, such as Pep/8, inputs a byte from the keyboard with

Memory-mapped input/output

```
CHARI char,s
```

while a computer with memory-mapped I/O configured as in Figure 11.46 inputs a byte from the keyboard with a load instruction as

```
LDA 208,d
STA char,s
```

LOAD for memory-mapped input

Similarly, you would send a character to the printer with a store instruction as

```
LDA char,s
STA 210,d
```

For memory-mapped I/O to function, the system requires circuitry to detect when loads and stores are done to any addresses to which I/O devices are mapped. Detection of such events activates the circuitry necessary to control the I/O devices.

The RAM and ROM chips in Figure 11.46 each have 8 bidirectional data lines. The 8-port I/O chip, however, has 64 data lines. The first group of 8 would connect the keyboard to address 208. The second group would connect the monitor to address 209, and so on.

You determine how to connect the chips to the address bus with the help of the table in Figure 11.47. For each chip, write down in binary the minimum address, that is, the address of the starting byte of the chip, and the maximum address, that is, the address of the last byte of the chip. Comparing these two bit patterns, you determine the general form of the address range for which each chip is responsible. For example, the general address of the 8-port I/O chip is 1101 0xxx, which means that it is responsible for the range of addresses from 1101 0000 to 1101 0111. Each letter x can be 0 or 1. Consequently, the 8-port I/O chip must be selected when and only when the first five digits are 11010.

Device	64 × 8 RAM	32 × 8 RAM	8-port I/O	32 × 8 ROM
Minimum address	0000 0000	0100 0000	1101 0000	1110 0000
Maximum address	0011 1111	0101 1111	1101 0111	1111 1111
General address	00xx xxxx	010x xxxx	1101 0xxx	111x xxxx

Figure **11.47**

A table for address decoding the memory map of Figure 11.46.

Figure 11.48 shows the chips wired to the address bus with full address decoding. The three address lines of the 8-port I/O chip connect to the three least significant address bus lines. The most significant five address lines feed into the chip select through a pair of inverters and an AND gate. (The inverters are abbreviated in the figure and are shown as the inverted inputs to the AND gate.) You can see from the circuit that the chip select line of the 8-port I/O chip will be 1 if and only if the first six bits of the address on the bus are 11010.

To keep the figure uncluttered, it does not show the data lines of the chips. The data lines of the RAM and ROM chips all connect to an 8-bit bidirectional data bus. Also not shown are the control inputs, WE and OE, which are connected to the common WE and OE lines of the memory module.

Partial address decoding is possible if you know that your memory subsystem will never be expanded by adding more memory. A typical situation would be a small computer-controlled appliance that is not user-upgradeable. The idea is to

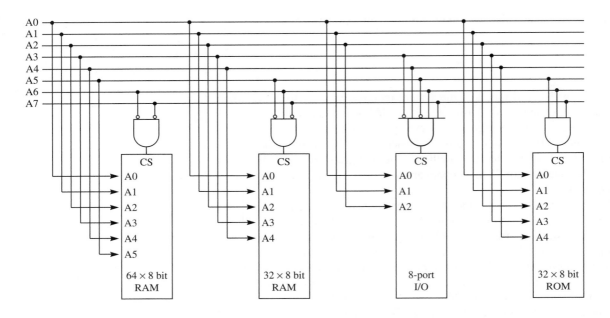

reduce the number of gates in the decoding circuits to the bare minimum needed for the system to access the devices.

Figure **11.48**

Full address decoding for the memory map of Figure 11.46.

The minimization technique is to write the general addresses of the chips, one per row, and inspect the columns. For the chips in Figure 11.47, the general addresses are

00xx xxxx, 64 × 8 bit RAM
010x xxxx, 32 × 8 bit RAM
1101 0xxx, 8-port I/O chip
111x xxxx, 32 × 8 bit ROM

Consider the first chip, and inspect the columns of the general addresses to see how you can uniquely determine the first chip with the smallest amount of information. Note that the second column, corresponding to address line A6, is 0 for the first chip and 1 for all the other chips. Therefore, you can select the first chip if A6 is 0 regardless of the value of A7.

Now consider the second chip. With full address decoding you must test three address lines—A7, A6, and A5. Can you manage by testing only two? For example, could you test A7 A5 = 00? No, because A7 A6 A5 = 000 will select the first chip, and so both chips would be selected simultaneously. Could you test A6 A5 = 10? No, because A7 A6 A5 A4 A3 = 11010 selects the 8-port I/O chip and again you would have a conflict. However, by inspection of the columns, none of the other chips have 01 as their first two bits. So you can test for A7 A6 = 01 to select the second chip.

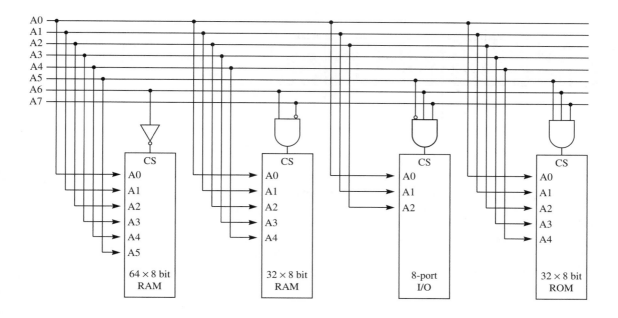

Figure **11.49**

Partial address decoding for the memory map of Figure 11.46.

Similar reasoning shows that you can select the third chip by testing A7 A6 A5 = 110 and the fourth chip by testing A7 A6 A5 = 111. Figure 11.49 shows the final result of the minimization. Compared to Figure 11.48, we have eliminated one two-input AND gate and three inverters, and decreased the number of inputs of one AND gate from three to two and of another from five to three.

The question naturally arises as to the difference in behavior between the memory modules of Figures 11.48 and 11.49. There is no difference when the CPU accesses one of the shaded regions in the memory map of Figure 11.46. With full address decoding, if the CPU accesses an address outside the shaded areas, no chip will be selected and the data on the data bus is unpredictable. However, with partial address decoding, the CPU might access a chip.

Consider the 64 × 8 bit RAM, which has a general address of 00xx xxxx, but is selected if A6 = 0. It will be selected in two cases—with an address request of 00xx xxxx and of 10xx xxxx. The first address range is by design, but the second is a side effect of partial address decoding. In effect, you have mapped one physical device into two separate regions of the address space. The CPU sees a clone of the chip at address 0 and address 128. Similar reasoning shows that the 32 × 8 bit RAM is duplicated once more at address 96, and the 8-port I/O chip at three more locations. The ROM is not duplicated, as its address decode circuitry is the same for full and partial addressing. Figure 11.50 shows the memory map with partial address decoding.

You must be careful with partial address decoding. In this example, the chips were duplicated in such a way as to completely fill the memory map with no gaps and no overlaps. If your decoding leaves gaps in the resulting map, no harm is done.

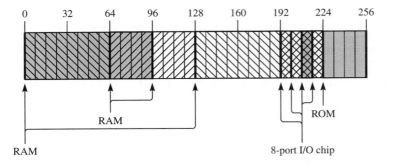

Figure **11.50**

The memory map with the partial address decoding of Figure 11.49.

If the CPU accesses a gap, then no chip is selected. If your decoding produces overlaps, however, it means that more than one chip will be selected by the CPU if it ever tries to access that region of the address space. The result could be hazardous to the system. Of course, the premise is that the CPU should never access that region, as it has no need to access a duplicated chip when it can access the original. But when is the last time you were sure there were no bugs in your program, only to discover later that there were?

A Two-Port Register Bank

The memory subsystems of the previous section all have just one set of data lines that correspond to one set of address lines. That organization is appropriate for the main memory subsystem of a computer, which normally does not reside on the same integrated circuit as the CPU. Figure 4.2 shows the registers in the Pep/8 CPU. They are organized much like a memory subsystem, but are stored in a register bank in the CPU itself. The register bank in the CPU differs from the memory organization of a memory chip in two respects:

- The data buses are unidirectional instead of bidirectional.
- There are two output ports instead of one.

Figure 11.51 shows the 32 8-bit registers, addressed from 0 to 31. The first five registers are the ones visible to the programmer at the ISA level. Each 16-bit register is divided into two 8-bit registers. That division is invisible to the machine level programmer.

The remaining registers, addressed from 11 to 31, are not visible to the machine level programmer. Registers 11 to 21 comprise a group of registers for storing temporary values. Registers 22 to 31 are read-only registers that contain fixed values. They are similar to ROM in that if you try to store to them, the value in the register will not change. Their constant values are given in hexadecimal. The read-only registers are not shaded because they are not really sequential circuits. They act more like combinational circuits because they have no states that can change.

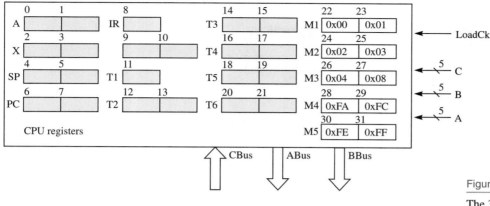

Figure **11.51**

The 32 8-bit registers in the Pep/8 CPU.

Where a main memory chip has one set of address lines and one set of bidirectional data lines, this register bank has three sets of addresses—A, B, and C—and three unidirectional data buses—ABus, BBus, and CBus. ABus and BBus are the two output ports and CBus is the input port. Each data bus is eight bits wide and each set of address lines contains five wires, capable of accessing any of the 2^5 registers. To store a value to a register, you place the address of the register on C, the data to store on the CBus, and clock the control line labeled LoadCk. The two output ports allow you to read two different registers simultaneously. You can put any address on A, any address on B, and the data from those two registers will appear simultaneously on ABus and BBus. You are allowed to put the same address on A and B, in which case the data from the one register will appear on both the ABus and the BBus.

Figure 11.52 shows the implementation of the two-port register bank. The input follows the same basic organization as a main memory chip. The five address lines from C make one decoder output line 1 and the rest 0. CBus is connected to each of the 32 registers. When you pulse the LoadCk control line, the value on CBus is clocked into one of the registers.

The two output ports consist of two 32-input multiplexers, each capable of routing an 8-bit quantity. Each of these multiplexers is a bank of eight individual 32-input multiplexers like the one in Figure 10.43. The five lines of A connect to the five select lines of all eight individual multiplexers in the first port. The first multiplexer routes the first bit from all 32 registers, the second multiplexer routes the second bit from all 32 registers, and so on.

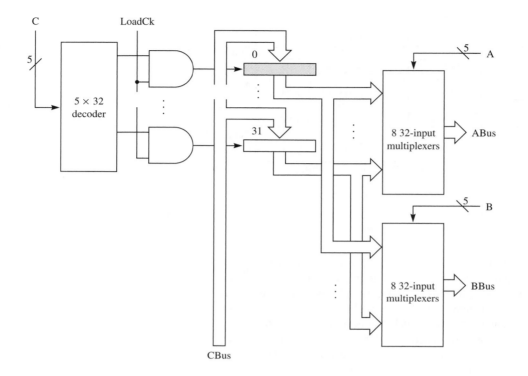

Figure **11.52**

Implementation of the two-port register bank of Figure 11.51.

SUMMARY

A sequential circuit, constructed from logic gates with feedback loops, can remember its state. The four basic sequential devices are the SR flip-flop (set, reset), the JK flip-flop, the D flip-flop (data or delay), and the T flip-flop (toggle). The S input to the SR flip-flop sets the state to 1, and the R input resets the state to 0. The input condition SR = 11 is undefined. The JK inputs correspond to SR, except that the input condition JK = 11 is defined and toggles the state. The D input transfers directly to the state. If the T input is 1, the state toggles; otherwise it remains unchanged. Each of these flip-flops may be constructed as master–slave devices to solve the instability problem that external feedback would produce.

A general sequential circuit consists of a combinational circuit whose output feeds into a set of state registers. The output from the state registers feeds back to the input of the combinational circuit. A sequential circuit can be characterized by a state transition diagram, which is a manifestation of a finite state machine. When you analyze a sequential circuit, you are given the input and the sequential circuit, and you determine the output.

When you design a sequential circuit, you are given the input and the desired output, and you determine the sequential circuit. Excitation tables aid the design process. An excitation table for a flip-flop consists of the four possible state changes of the device—0 to 0, 0 to 1, 1 to 0, and 1 to 1—and the input conditions necessary to produce the change. The design process consists of tabulating the input conditions necessary to produce the given state transition diagram, and then designing the combinational circuit to produce those input conditions.

A register is a sequence of D flip-flops. The tri-state buffer makes possible the implementation of the bidirectional bus. A memory chip is (conceptually) an array of D flip-flops with a set of address lines, data lines, and control lines. The control lines usually consist of CS for chip select, WE for write enable, and OE for output enable. Memory-mapped I/O does not require native input/output instructions in the instruction set, but relies on a LOAD instruction for input and a STORE instruction for output. Address decoding is a technique for using the CS lines to construct a memory module from a set of memory chips. Partial address decoding minimizes the number of gates in the select circuitry. The two-port register bank in the Pep/8 CPU implements the registers visible to the ISA programmer, as well as the temporary registers and constant registers that are not visible.

EXERCISES

Section 11.1

*1. Under what circumstances will a string of an arbitrary number of inverters with a feedback loop, as in Figure 11.1, produce a stable network?

2. Construct tables analogous to Figures 11.3 and 11.4 to show that changing R to 1 and back to 0 resets the SR latch to $Q = 0$ if it starts in state $Q = 1$.

3. Define the following points in Figure 11.10: (1) A is the output of the top master AND gate. (2) B is the output of the bottom master AND gate. (3) C is the output of the inverter. (4) D is the output of the top slave AND gate. (5) E is the output of the bottom slave AND gate.

Suppose $SR = 10$ and $Q = 0$ before the arrival of a clock pulse. Construct a table that shows the values of A, B, C, D, E, R2, S2, Q, and $\bar{Q}$ during each of the following intervals of Figure 11.11, assuming zero gate delay:

*(a) before t_1 *(b) between t_1 and t_2 (c) between t_2 and t_3
(d) between t_3 and t_4 (e) after t_4

4. Do Exercise 3 with $SR = 01$ and $Q = 1$ before the arrival of the clock pulse.

5. Draw the state transition diagram, as in Figure 11.14, for the following flip-flops:

(a) JK   *(b) D   (c) T

6. Draw the timing diagram of Figure 11.20(c) for the toggle flip-flop with the D input replaced by T.

7. Construct the T flip-flop from an SR flip-flop.

8. This section shows how the JK and D flip-flops can be constructed from the SR flip-flop and a few gates. In fact, any flip-flop can be constructed from any other with the help of a few gates. Construct the following flip-flops from a JK flip-flop:

*(a) D   (b) SR   (c) T

Construct the following flip-flops from a D flip-flop:

(d) SR   **(e)** JK   **(f)** T

Construct the following flip-flops from a T flip-flop:

(g) SR   **(h)** JK   **(i)** D

Section 11.2

9. *(a) Modify Figure 11.10, the implementation of the SR master–slave flip-flop, to provide an asynchronous clear input, as in Figure 11.30. When Clear is 0, the device should operate normally. When Clear is 1, both the master state, Q2, and the slave state, Q, should be forced to 0. **(b)** Modify Figure 11.10 to provide an asynchronous preset. **(c)** Modify Figure 11.10 to provide both an asynchronous clear and preset.

10. Draw the logic diagram and the state transition diagram for a sequential circuit with two JK flip-flops, FFA and FFB, and two inputs, X1 and X2, with flip-flop inputs

$$JA = X1\ B \qquad\qquad JB = X1\ \bar{A}$$
$$KA = X2 + X1\ A\ \bar{B} \qquad KB = X2 + X1\ A$$

There is no output other than the flip-flop states.

11. Draw the logic diagram and the state transition diagram for a sequential circuit with one JK flip-flop, FFA; one T flip-flop, FFB; and one input, X, with flip-flop inputs

$$J = X \oplus B \qquad\qquad T = X \oplus A$$
$$K = \bar{X}\ B$$

and output

$$Z = A\ B$$

12. Draw the logic diagram and the state transition diagram for a sequential circuit with two SR flip-flops, FFA and FFB; two inputs, X1 and X2, with flip-flop inputs

$$SA = X1 \qquad\qquad SB = \overline{X1}\ \overline{X2}\ \bar{A}$$
$$RA = \overline{X1}\ X2 \qquad RB = X1\ A + X2$$

and output

$$Z = X1\ \bar{A}$$

13. Design the sequential circuit of Figure 11.32 using the following flip-flops:

*(a) D   **(b)** T

14. Figure 11.53 is a state transition diagram for a sequential circuit with three flip-flops and one input. It counts up in binary when the input is 1 and remains in the same state when the input is 0. Design the circuit and draw the logic diagram using the following flip-flops:

(a) JK   **(b)** SR   **(c)** D   **(d)** T

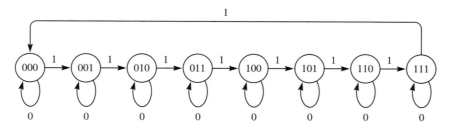

Figure **11.53**

The state transition diagram for Exercise 14.

15. Figure 11.54 is a state transition diagram for a sequential circuit with three flip-flops and one input. It counts up in binary when the input is 1 and counts down when the input is 0. Design the circuit and draw the logic diagram using the following flip-flops:

    *(a) JK   (b) SR   (c) D   (d) T

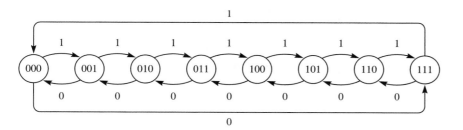

Figure **11.54**

The state transition diagram for Exercise 15.

16. Figure 11.55 is a state transition diagram for a sequential circuit with two flip-flops and two inputs. It counts up in binary when the input is 01, counts down in binary when the input is 10, and does not change state when the input is 00. An input of 11 will never occur and can be treated as a don't-care condition. Design the circuit and draw the logic diagram using the following flip-flops:

    (a) JK   (b) SR   (c) D   (d) T

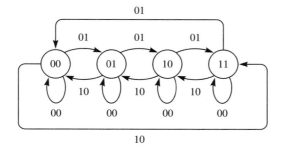

Figure **11.55**

The state transition diagram for Exercise 16.

17. A sequential circuit has six state registers and three input lines. (a) How many states does it have? (b) How many transitions from each state does it have? (c) How many total transitions does it have?

Section 11.3

18. **(a)** How many AND gates, OR gates, and inverters are in the memory chip of Figure 11.41? Include the gates in the decoder, but not in the D flip-flops. **(b)** How many of each element are in the memory chip of Figure 11.40(a)? **(c)** How many are in the memory chip of Figure 11.40(b)?

19. In practice, the chip select line of a memory chip is asserted low, and the line is labeled $\overline{CS}$ instead of CS to indicate that fact. How would Figure 11.48 change if the chip select lines on all the chips were asserted low?

20. A computer system has a 16-bit wide data bus. **(a)** If you have a box of 1K × 1 dynamic RAM chips, what is the smallest number of bytes of memory this computer can have? **(b)** Answer part (a) if the 1Kbit chips you have are configured as 256 × 4 devices.

21. You have a small CPU with a 10-bit address bus. You need to connect a 64-byte PROM, a 32-byte RAM, and a 4-port I/O chip with two address lines. Chip selects on all chips are asserted high. **(a)** Show the connection for full address decoding with the PROM at address 0, the RAM at address 384, and the PIO at address 960. (These addresses are decimal.) **(b)** Show the connection for partial address decoding with the chips at the same locations. Show the memory map with partial address decoding and ensure that no duplicate regions overlap.

22. Show how the individual multiplexers in the top port of Figure 11.52 are connected. You may use ellipses (...).

23. How many AND gates, OR gates, and inverters are in the two-port register bank of Figure 11.52? Include the gates necessary to construct the decoder and the multiplexers, but not the ones in the D flip-flops that make up the registers.

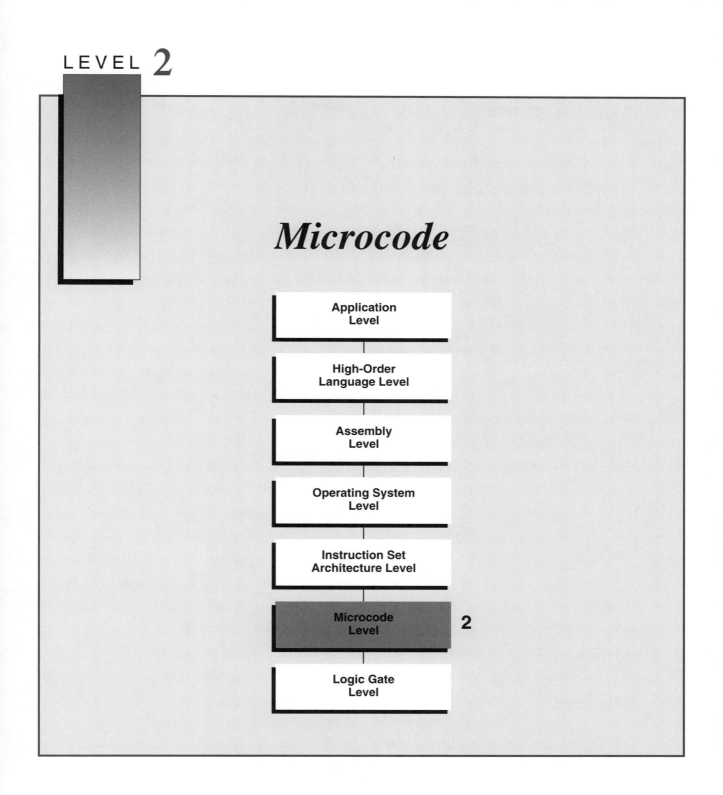

LEVEL 2

Microcode

Application
Level

High-Order
Language Level

Assembly
Level

Operating System
Level

Instruction Set
Architecture Level

Microcode
Level

2

Logic Gate
Level

Chapter

12

Computer Organization

This final chapter shows the connection between the combinational and sequential circuits at Level LG1 and the machine at Level ISA3. It describes how hardware devices can be connected to form black boxes at successively higher levels of abstraction to eventually construct the Pep/8 computer.

12.1 Constructing a Level-ISA3 Machine

Figure 12.1 is a block diagram of the Pep/8 computer. It shows the CPU divided into a data section and a control section. The data section receives data from and sends data to the main memory subsystem. The control section issues the control signals to the data section and to the other components of the computer.

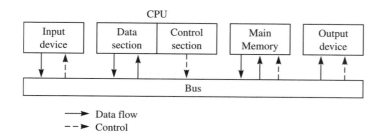

Figure **12.1**

Block diagram of the Pep/8 computer.

The Central Processing Unit

Figure 12.2 is the data section of the Pep/8 CPU. The sequential devices in the figure are shaded to distinguish them from the combinational devices. The CPU registers at the top of the figure are identical to the two-port register bank of Figure 11.51.

The control section, not shown in the figure, is to the right of the data section. The control lines coming in from the right come from the control section. There are

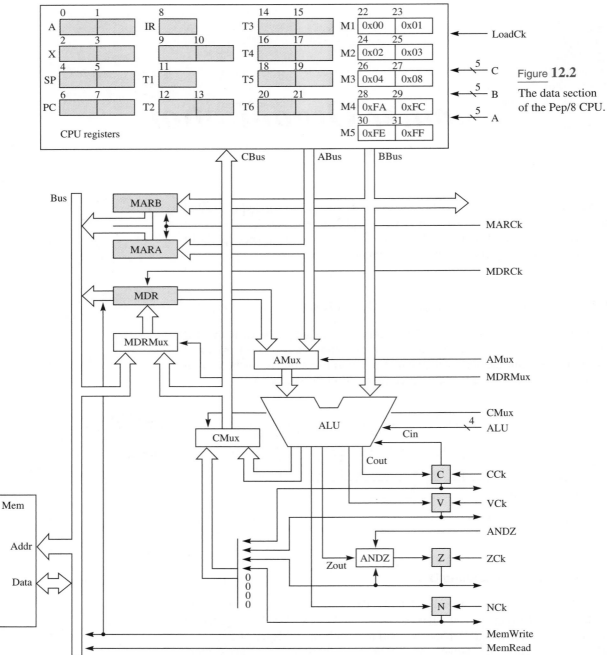

Figure **12.2**

The data section of the Pep/8 CPU.

two kinds of control signals—combinational circuit controls and clock pulses. Names of the clock pulses all end in Ck and all act to clock data into a register or flip-flop. For example, MDRCk is the clock input for the MDR. When it is pulsed, the input from the MDRMux is clocked into the MDR.

The Bus on the left of the figure is the main system bus of Figure 12.1, to which main memory and the I/O devices are attached. It consists of 8 bidirectional data lines, 16 address lines, and 2 control lines labeled MemWrite and MemRead at the bottom of the figure. Additional control lines for the input and output devices are not shown. MAR is the memory address register, divided into MARA, the high-order byte, and MARB, the low-order byte. The box labeled Mem is a 64KByte memory subsystem. The 16 address lines on the bus are unidirectional, so that the output of the MAR connects to the input of the address port of the memory subsystem over the bus. MDR is the eight-bit memory data register. Because the data bus is bidirectional, there is a set of eight tri-state buffers (not shown in the figure), between MDR and the bus, that are enabled by the MemWrite control line. The MemWrite line connects to the WE line of the memory subsystem over the main system bus. The MemRead line connects to the OE line. All the other buses in Figure 12.2 represented by the wide arrows are eight-bit data buses, including, for example, ABus, BBus, CBus, and the bus connecting the data lines of the main system bus to the box labeled MDRMux.

The main system bus

The memory address register, MAR

The memory data register, MDR

Each multiplexer—AMux, CMux, and MDRMux—is a bank of eight two-input multiplexers with their control lines connected together to form the single control line in Figure 12.2. For example, the control line labeled AMux in the figure is connected to each of the eight control lines in the bank of eight multiplexers in the block labeled AMux. A multiplexer control line routes the signal through a multiplexer as follows:

The multiplexers—AMux, CMux, and MDRMux

- 0 on a multiplexer control line routes the left input to the output.
- 1 on a multiplexer control line routes the right input to the output.

Multiplexer control signals

For example, if the MDRMux control line is 0, MDRMux routes the content of the Bus to the MDR. If the control line is 1 it routes the data from the CBus to the MDR. Similarly, if the AMux control line is 0, AMux routes the content of MDR to the left input of the ALU. Otherwise, it routes the data from the ABus to the left input of the ALU.

The block labeled ALU is the Arithmetic Logic Unit of Figure 10.54. It provides the 16 functions listed in Figure 10.55 via the four control lines labeled ALU in Figure 12.2. The status bits—N, Z, V, and C—are each one D flip-flop. For example, the box labeled C is a D flip-flop that stores the value of the carry bit. The D input to the flip-flop is the Cout signal from the ALU. The Q output of the flip-flop is at the top, into the Cin input of the ALU, and the bottom. The clock input of the flip-flop is the control signal labeled CCk. The outputs of each of the status bits feed into the low order nybble of the left bus into the CMux. The high order nybble

The status bits—N, Z, V, and C

is hard wired to four zeros. The outputs of each of the status bits are also sent to the control section.

At the ISA level, each register is 16 bits, but the internal data paths of the CPU are only 8 bits wide. To perform an operation on one 16-bit quantity requires two operations on 8-bit quantities at the LG1 level. The Z bit must be set to 1 if the 16 bits of the result are all zeros, which happens when the Zout signal from the ALU is 1 for both 8-bit operations. The combinational box labeled ANDZ facilitates the computation of the Z bit. Its output is the input of the D flip-flop for the Z bit. It has three inputs—the ANDZ input from the control section, the Zout output from the ALU, and the Q output from the D flip-flop for the Z bit. Figure 12.3 shows the truth table for the box. It operates in one of the following two modes:

- If the ANDZ control signal is 0, Zout passes directly through to the output.
- If the ANDZ control signal is 1, Zout AND Z passes to the output.

Operation of the ANDZ circuit in Figure 12.2

The Z bit is, therefore, loaded with either the Zout signal from the ALU or the Zout signal ANDed with the current value of the Z bit. Which one depends on the ANDZ signal from the control section. Implementation of the circuit is an exercise at the end of the chapter.

ANDZ	Z	Zout	Output
0	0	0	0
0	0	1	1
0	1	0	0
0	1	1	1
1	0	0	0
1	0	1	0
1	1	0	0
1	1	1	1

Figure 12.3

The truth table for the ANDZ combinational circuit in Figure 12.2.

The data flow is one big loop, starting with the 32 8-bit registers at the top, and proceeding via ABus and BBus, through AMux to the ALU, through CMux, and finally back to the bank of 32 registers via CBus. Data from main memory can be injected into the loop from the Bus, through the MDRMux to the MDR. From there, it can go through the AMux, the ALU, and the CMux to any of the CPU registers. To send the content of a CPU register to memory, you can pass it through the ALU via the ABus and AMux, through the CMux and MDRMux into the MDR. From there it can go to the memory subsystem over the Bus.

The control section has 32 control output lines and 12 input lines. The 32 output lines control the flow of data around the data section loop and specify the processing that is to occur. The 12 input lines come from the 8 lines of BBus plus

4 lines from the status bits, which the control section can test for certain conditions. Section 12.2 shows how the control section generates the proper control signals. To show how the data section works, assume for now that you can set the control lines to any desired values at any time.

The von Neumann Cycle

The heart of the Pep/8 computer is the von Neumann cycle. The data section in Figure 12.2 implements the von Neumann cycle. It really is nothing more than plumbing. In the same way that water in your house runs through the pipes controlled by various faucets and valves, signals (electrons, literally) flow through the wires of the buses controlled by various multiplexers. Along the way, the signals can flow through the ALU where they can be processed as required. This section shows the control signals necessary to implement the von Neumann cycle. It includes the implementation of some typical instructions in the Pep/8 instruction set and leaves the implementation of others as exercises at the end of the chapter.

Figure 4.31 (page 170) shows the pseudocode description of the steps necessary to execute a program at level ISA3. The do loop is the von Neumann cycle. At level LG1, the data section of the CPU operates on 8-bit quantities, even though the operand specifier part of the instruction register is a 16-bit quantity. The CPU fetches the operand specifier in two steps, the high-order byte followed by the low-order byte. The control section increments PC by 1 after fetching each byte. Figure 12.4 is a pseudocode description at level LG1 of the von Neumann execution cycle.

```
do {
```
 Fetch the instruction specifier at address in PC
 PC ← PC + 1
 Decode the instruction specifier
 `if` (*the instruction is not unary*) {
  Fetch the high-order byte of the operand specifier as specified by PC
  PC ← PC + 1
  Fetch the low-order byte of the operand specifier as specified by PC
  PC ← PC + 1
 }
 Execute the instruction fetched
```
}
```
`while` ((*the stop instruction does not execute*) && (*the instruction is legal*))

Figure **12.4**

A pseudocode description at level LG1 of the von Neumann execution cycle.

The control section sends control signals to the data section to implement the von Neumann cycle. Figure 12.5 is the control sequence to fetch the instruction specifier and to increment PC by 1. The figure does not show the method by which the control section determines whether the instruction is unary. Writing the necessary

Figure **12.5**

The control signals to fetch the
instruction specifier and increment
PC by 1.

```
// Save the status bits in T1
1. CMux=0, C=11; LoadCk

// MAR <- PC, fetch instruction specifier.
2. A=6, B=7; MARCk
3. MemRead
4. MemRead, MDRMux=0; MDRCk
5. AMux=0, ALU=0, CMux=1, C=8; LoadCk

// PC <- PC + 1, low-order byte first.
6. A=7, B=23, AMux=1, ALU=1, CMux=1, C=7; CCk, LoadCk
7. A=6, B=22, AMux=1, ALU=2, CMux=1, C=6; LoadCk

// If the instruction is not unary, fetch operand specifier
// and increment PC
...
// Restore the carry bit from T1
n. A=11, AMux=1, ALU=15; CCk

// Execute the instruction fetched
```

control signals to fetch the operand specifier if the instruction is not unary is an exercise at the end of the chapter.

Each line in Figure 12.5 is a CPU clock cycle and consists of a set of control signals that are input into the combinational devices, usually followed by a clock pulse into one or more registers. The combinational signals, denoted by the equals sign, must be set up for a long enough period of time to let the data reach the register before being clocked into the register. The combinational signals are applied concurrently, and are therefore separated from each other by a comma, which is the concurrent separator. The combinational signals are separated from the clock signals by a semicolon, which is the sequential separator, because the clock pulses are applied after the combinational signals have been set. Comments are denoted by double forward slashes ($//$).

Figure 12.6 shows the clock cycles corresponding to the lines numbered 1 through 4 in Figure 12.5. The period of a cycle T in seconds is specified by the frequency f of the system clock in Hz according to $T = 1/f$. The greater the frequency of your computer, as measured by its MHz rating, the shorter the period of one cycle, and the faster your computer will execute, all other things being equal. So, what limits the speed of the CPU? The period must be long enough to allow the signals to flow through the combinational circuits and be presented to the inputs of the registers (which are the sequential circuits) before the next clock pulse arrives. For example, at the beginning of cycle 1 of Figure 12.6 the CMux line goes to 0. Then, it takes time for the data from the left input bus to propagate through the CMux.

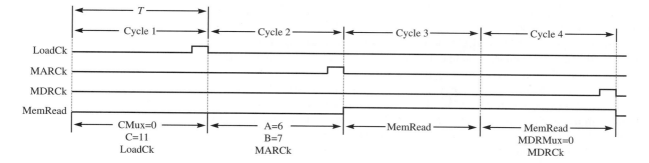

Figure **12.6**

Timing diagram of the first four
cycles of Figure 12.5.

Also, when C is set to 11 at the beginning of the cycle, it takes time for that control
signal to propagate through the decoder in Figure 11.51. The period T must be long
enough for these signals to get the data to the input of register 11 before LoadCk is
pulsed.

During the von Neumann cycle, the CPU increments the program counter, a
16-bit quantity. It adds 1 to the low-order byte of the PC and stores the C bit to use
in the high-order part of the increment. In so doing, it wipes out the C bit that may
have been set by the previous instruction. Cycle 1 in Figure 12.5 saves the status   *T1 stores the status bits.*
bits in temporary register T1. Figure 12.2 shows that the status bits feed into the left
input of the CMux. Cycle 1 routes the left input through the CMux and presents it
to the register bank. The C control signal addresses T1 (address 11 from Figure
12.2), and the LoadCk signal clocks the status bits into T1.

Cycles 2–5 fetch the instruction specifier. On cycle 2, A=6 puts register 6 on
ABus, and B=7 puts register 7 on BBus. Figure 12.2 shows registers 6 and 7 to be
the two halves of the program counter. The MARCk pulse on cycle 2 clocks PC into
the memory address register (MAR). On cycle 3, the MemRead signal initiates a   *Reading from the memory*
memory read. The address is placed on the main system bus at the end of the cycle   *subsystem*
2, so now the MemRead signal activates the OE line on the chip in the memory subsystem that is selected by the address decoding circuitry. There are so many propagation delays in the memory subsystem that it usually takes many CPU cycles
before the data is available on the main system bus. The Pep/8 computer models
this fact by requiring MemRead on two consecutive cycles after the address is
clocked into the MAR. In cycle 4, MDRMux=0 sets the MDR multiplexer line to 0,
which routes the data from the bus through the multiplexer to the input of the memory data register (MDR). The MDRCk pulse on cycle 4 clocks the instruction specifier
into the MDR.

Cycle 5 sends the instruction specifier from MDR into the instruction register,   *Sending data from the MDR to the*
IR, as follows. First, AMux=0 sets the AMux control line to 0, which routes the MDR   *register bank*
to the output of the AMux multiplexer. Next, ALU=0 sets the ALU control line to 0,
which passes the data through the ALU unchanged as specified in Figure 10.55.
CMux=1 routes the data from the ALU to the CBus. Then, C=8 sets C to 8, which
specifies the instruction register, as Figure 12.2 shows. Finally, LoadCk clocks the
content of the MDR into the instruction register.

In cycle 5, the control section must not set up the combinational signals and pulse LoadCk at the same time. It must wait for the content of MDR to propagate through the multiplexer and the ALU before it pulses LoadCk. The control section designer must count the number of gate delays through those combinational circuits to figure how long to wait before clocking the data in.

Cycles 6–7 increment PC by 1. On cycle 6, A=7 puts the low-order byte of PC on ABus, and B=23 puts constant 1 on BBus. AMux=1 selects the ABus to pass through the multiplexer. ALU=1 selects the A plus B function of the arithmetic logic unit, so the ALU adds 1 to the low-order byte of PC. CMux=1 routes the sum to the CBus, and C=7 puts the sum back into the low-order byte of PC. In the same cycle, CCk saves the carry out of the addition in the C bit. Both CCk and LoadCk must wait long enough for the data to flow through the combinational devices specified by the other control signals in cycle 6 before triggering the loads into their registers.

Incrementing PC by 1

If the original low-order byte of PC is 1111 1111 (bin), then adding 1 will cause a carry to the high-order byte. On cycle 7, A=6 puts the high-order byte of PC onto the ABus, and B=22 puts constant 0 onto the BBus. ALU=2 selects the A plus B plus Cin function for the ALU, adding the saved carry from the low-order byte to the high-order byte of PC. CMux=1 routes the result to the CBus, and C=6 directs the data on the CBus to be loaded into the high-order byte of PC, which is stored with the LoadCk pulse.

After the instruction specifier is fetched, the control section must decode the opcode, determine if the instruction is unary, and if not, fetch the operand specifier and increment the PC. Before execution of the instruction fetched, cycle n restores the C bit that was saved in cycle 1. A=11 puts register T1 on the ABus. AMux=1 sends it to the A input of the ALU. ALU=15 presents all four saved status bits to the four flip-flops, and CCk clocks the saved C bit, restoring the original value.

Restoring the C bit

It is possible to reduce the number of cycles by combining cycles 1 and 3. Cycle 1 could be eliminated, and cycle 3 (which would be renumbered to 2) could be written

Combining cycles

```
MemRead, CMux=0, C=11; LoadCk
```

While the CPU is waiting for the results from the memory read, it can be saving the status bits.

You cannot arbitrarily combine cycles in a control sequence. You must remember that a numbered line in a control sequence like Figure 12.5 represents one CPU cycle. Some cycles depend on the results from previous cycles. For example, you cannot combine cycles 4 and 5 in Figure 12.5, because cycle 5 depends on the results from cycle 4. Cycle 4 sets the content of the MDR, and cycle 5 uses the content of the MDR. Therefore, cycle 5 must happen after cycle 4.

Hardware concurrency is an important issue in computer organization. Designers are always on the alert to use hardware concurrency to improve performance. The seven-cycle sequence of Figure 12.5 would certainly not be used in a real machine, because combining cycles 1 and 3 gives a performance boost with no increase in circuitry. With a little thought, you can do even better. An exercise at the end of the chapter asks you to reduce the number of cycles from seven in Figure 12.5 to just four.

Although the details of the control section are not shown, you can imagine how it would test the instruction just fetched to determine whether it is unary. The control section would set B to 8 to put the instruction specifier on BBus, which it could then test. If the fetched instruction is not unary, the control section must fetch the operand specifier, incrementing PC accordingly. The control sequence to fetch the operand specifier and increment PC is an exercise at the end of the chapter.

After fetching an instruction, the control section tests the instruction specifier to determine which of the 39 instructions to execute. The control signals to execute the instruction depend not only on the opcode, but on the register-r field and the addressing-aaa field also. Figure 12.7 shows the relationship between the operand and the operand specifier (OprndSpec) for each addressing mode.

Addressing mode	Operand
Immediate	OprndSpec
Direct	Mem [OprndSpec]
Indirect	Mem [Mem [OprndSpec]]
Stack-relative	Mem [SP + OprndSpec]
Stack-relative deferred	Mem [Mem [SP + OprndSpec]]
Indexed	Mem [OprndSpec + X]
Stack-indexed	Mem [SP + OprndSpec + X]
Stack-indexed deferred	Mem [Mem [SP + OprndSpec] + X]

Figure **12.7**

The addressing modes for the Pep/8 computer.

A quantity in square brackets is a memory address. To execute the instruction, the control section must provide control signals to the data section to compute the memory address. For example, to execute an instruction that uses the indexed addressing mode, the control section must perform a 16-bit addition of the contents of the operand specifier (registers 9 and 10) and X (registers 2 and 3). The result of this addition is then loaded into MAR in preparation for a memory read in case of a LDr instruction or memory write in case of a STr instruction.

The control sequence to implement the first part of the von Neumann execution cycle in Figure 12.5 looks suspiciously like a program in some low-level programming language. The job of control section designers is to devise circuits that, in effect, program the data section to implement the instructions at Level ISA3, the Instruction Set Architecture level. The language at Level LG1 is a specification of the binary signals to input into the combinational circuits and the clock pulses to input into the state registers.

The next few examples show the control sequences necessary to execute some representative instructions. Each example assumes that the instruction has been fetched and PC incremented accordingly. Each statement in the program is written on a separate, numbered line and consists of a set of combinational signals to route data through a multiplexer or to select a function for the ALU, followed by one or two clock pulses to load some registers. Keep in mind that a program at this level of abstraction (Level LG1) consists of the control signals necessary to implement just one instruction at the higher level of abstraction (Level ISA3).

Implementing the Store Byte Instruction

Figure 12.8 shows the control sequence to execute the instruction

```
STBYTEA there,d
```

where there is a symbol. The RTL specification for the STBYTEr instruction is

byte Oprnd $\leftarrow$ r$\langle 8..15 \rangle$

Because the instruction specifies direct addressing, the operand is Mem [Oprnd-Spec]. That is, the operand specifier is the address in memory of the operand. The instruction stores the least significant byte of the accumulator into the memory cell at that address. The status bits are not affected.

This example, as well as those that follow, assumes that the operand specifier is already in the instruction register. That is, it assumes that the fetch, decode, and increment parts of the von Neumann execution cycle have already transpired. The programs show only the execute part of the von Neumann cycle.

```
// MAR <- OprndSpec.
1. A=9, B=10; MARCk

// MDR <- A<low>.
2. A=1, AMux=1, ALU=0, CMux=1, MDRMux=1; MDRCk

// Initiate memory write.
3. MemWrite

// Complete memory write.
4. MemWrite
```

Figure **12.8**

The control signals to implement the store byte instruction with direct addressing.

Cycle 1 transfers the operand specifier into the memory address register. A=9 puts the high-order byte of the operand specifier on the ABus, B=10 puts the low-order byte of the operand specifier on the BBus, and MARCk clocks the ABus and BBus into the MAR registers.

Cycle 2 transfers the low-order byte of the accumulator into the MDR. A=1 puts the low-order byte of the accumulator onto the ABus, AMux=1 routes it through the AMux into the ALU, ALU=0 passes it through the ALU unchanged, CMux=1 routes it onto the CBus, MDRMux=1 routes it through MDRMux to the MDR, and MDRCk latches the data into the MDR.

Cycles 3 and 4 complete the memory write, storing the data that is in the MDR to main memory at the address that is in the MAR. As with memory reads, memory writes require two consecutive cycles of the MemWrite line to give the memory subsystem time to get the data from the bus and store it.

The store instructions do not affect the status bits at the ISA level. Consequently, none of the cycles in the control sequence for LDBYTEA pulse NCk, ZCk, VCk, or CCk.

Implementing the Add Instruction

Figure 12.9 shows the control sequence to implement

```
ADDA this,i
```

The RTL specification for ADDr is

$$r \leftarrow r + Oprnd; N \leftarrow r < 0, Z \leftarrow r = 0, V \leftarrow \{overflow\}, C \leftarrow \{carry\}$$

The instruction adds the operand to register r and puts the sum in register r, in this case the accumulator. Because the instruction uses immediate addressing, the operand is the operand specifier. As usual, this example assumes that the instruction specifier has already been fetched and is in the instruction register.

Figure **12.9**

The control signals to implement the add instruction with immediate addressing.

```
// A<low> <- A<low> plus Oprnd<low>. Save carry.
1. A=1, B=10, AMux=1, ALU=1, ANDZ=0, CMux=1, C=1; ZCk, CCk, LoadCk

// A<high> <- A<high> plus Oprnd<high> plus saved carry.
2. A=0, B=9, AMux=1, ALU=2, ANDZ=1, CMux=1, C=0; NCk, ZCk, VCk, CCk, LoadCk
```

The instruction affects all four of the status bits. However, the data section of the Pep/8 CPU can only operate on 8-bit quantities, even though the accumulator holds a 16-bit value. To do the addition, the control sequence must add the low order bytes first and save the carry from the low order addition to compute the sum of the high-order bytes. It sets N to 1 if the two-byte quantity is negative when interpreted as a signed integer; otherwise, it clears N to 0. The sign bit of the most significant byte determines the value of N. It sets Z to 1 if the two-byte quantity is all zeros; otherwise, it clears Z to 0. So, unlike the N bit, the values of both the high-order and the low-order bytes determine the value of Z.

Cycle 1 adds the low-order byte of the accumulator to the low-order byte of the operand specifier. A=1 puts the low-order byte of the accumulator on the ABus, and B=10 puts the low-order byte of the operand specifier on the BBus. AMux=1 routes the ABus through the multiplexer, ALU=1 selects the A plus B function of the ALU, CMux=1 routes the sum to the CBus, C=1 directs the output of the ALU to be stored in the low-order byte of the accumulator, and LoadCk clocks it in. In the same cycle,

ANDZ=0 sends Zout through to the output of the ANDZ combinational circuit, which is presented as input to the Z one-bit register (a D flip-flop). ZCk latches the bit into the register.

Cycle 2 adds the high-order byte of the accumulator to the high-order byte of the operand specifier. A=0 puts the high-order byte of the accumulator on the ABus, and B=9 puts the high-order byte of the operand specifier on the BBus. AMux=1 routes the ABus through the multiplexer, ALU=2 selects the A plus B plus Cin function of the ALU, CMux=1 routes the sum to the CBus, C=0 directs it to be stored in the high-order byte of the accumulator, and LoadCk clocks it in. ANDZ=1 sends Zout AND Z through to the output of the ANDZ combinational circuit, which is presented as input to the Z register. ZCk latches the bit into the register. A 1 will be latched into the Z register if and only if both Zout and Z are 1. The value of Z was saved with ZCk from cycle 1, and so it contains 1 if and only if the low-order sum was all zeros. Consequently, the final value of Z is 1 if and only if all 16 bits of the sum are zeros. The other three status bits—N, V, and C—reflect the status of the high-order addition. They are saved with NCk, VCk, and CCk on cycle 2.

Implementing the Load Instruction

Figure 12.10 shows the control sequence for

LDX this,n

The RTL specification for LDr is

$$r \leftarrow Oprnd; N \leftarrow r < 0, Z \leftarrow r = 0$$

This instruction loads two bytes from main memory into the index register. Because the instruction uses indirect addressing the operand is Mem [Mem [OprndSpec]], as Figure 12.7 shows. The operand specifier is the address of the address of the operand. The control sequence must fetch a word from memory, which it uses as the address of the operand, requiring yet another fetch to get the operand.

```
// T3<high> <- Mem[OprndSpec].
1. A=9, B=10; MARCk
2. MemRead
3. MemRead, MDRMux=0; MDRCk
4. AMux=0, ALU=0, CMux=1, C=14; LoadCk

// T2 <- OprndSpec + 1.
5. A=10, B=23, AMux=1, ALU=1, CMux=1, C=13; CCk, LoadCk
6. A=9, B=22, AMux=1, ALU=2, CMux=1, C=12; LoadCk
```

Figure **12.10**

The control signals to implement the load instruction with indirect addressing.

```
// T3<low> <- Mem[T2].
7.  A=12, B=13; MARCk
8.  MemRead
9.  MemRead, MDRMux=0; MDRCk
10. AMux=0, ALU=0, CMux=1, C=15; LoadCk


// Assert: T3 contains the address of the operand.
// X<high> <- Mem[T3].
11. A=14, B=15; MARCk
12. MemRead
13. MemRead, MDRMux=0; MDRCk
14. AMux=0, ALU=0, ANDZ=0, CMux=1, C=2; NCk, ZCk, LoadCk


// T4 <- T3 + 1.
15. A=15, B=23, AMux=1, ALU=1, CMux=1, C=17; CCk, LoadCk
16. A=14, B=22, AMux=1, ALU=2, CMux=1, C=16; LoadCk


// X<low> <- Mem[T4].
17. A=16, B=17; MARCk
18. MemRead
19. MemRead, MDRMux=0; MDRCk
20. AMux=0, ALU=0, ANDZ=1, CMux=1, C=3; ZCk, LoadCk


// Restore C, assumed in T1 from Fetch.
21. A=11, AMux=1, ALU=15; CCk
```

Figure **12.10**

(Continued)

Figure 12.11 shows the effect of executing the control sequence of Figure 12.10 assuming that symbol this has the value 0x0012 and the initial values in memory are the ones shown at addresses 0012 and 26D1. Mem [0012] contains 0x26D1, which is the address of the operand. Mem [26D1] contains the operand 0x53AC, which the instruction must load into the index register. The figure shows the register addresses for each register affected by the control sequence. The first byte of the instruction register, CA, is the instruction specifier for the LDX instruction using indirect addressing.

Cycles 1–4 transfer Mem [OprndSpec] to the high-order byte of temporary register T3. On cycle 1, A=9 and B=10 put the operand specifier on the ABus and BBus, and MARCk clocks them in to the memory address register. On cycle 2, MemRead initiates a memory read, and cycle 3 completes it. Cycle 4 routes the data from MDR into the high-order byte of T3 in the usual way.

Cycles 5–6 add 1 to the operand specifier and store the result in temporary register T2. Cycle 5 adds one to the low-order byte of the operand specifier and cycle 6 takes care of a possible carry out from the low-order addition to the high-order addition.

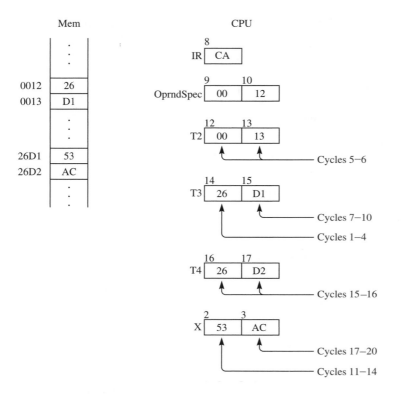

Figure **12.11**

The result of executing the control sequence of Figure 12.10.

Cycles 7–10 use the address computed in T2 to fetch the low-order byte of the address of the operand. Cycle 7 puts the content of T2 into the memory address register. Cycle 8 initiates the memory read, and cycle 9 latches the byte from memory into the MDR. Cycle 10 routes the byte from the MDR through AMux and into the low-order byte of T3.

At this point, we can assert that temporary register T3 contains the address of the operand, 0x26D1. Finally we can get the first byte of the operand and load it into the first byte of the index register. Cycles 11–14 perform that load. The RTL specification for LDr shows that the instruction affects the N and Z bits. The N bit is determined by the sign bit of the most significant byte. Consequently, cycle 14 includes the clock pulse NCk to save the N bit as the byte goes through the ALU. The Z bit depends on the value of both bytes, so cycle 14 also contains ANDZ=0 and ZCk to save the Zout signal in the Z register.

Cycles 15–16 increment the address of the first byte by one and put the result in temporary register T4. To get the second byte of the operand, cycles 17–20 put the incremented address from T4 into the memory address register. Cycle 20 finally gets the second byte into the index register. It contains ANDZ=1 so that the Z value from the low order-byte (stored in cycle 14) will be ANDed with the Zout from the high-order byte. ZCk stores the correct Z value for the 16-bit quantity that the instruction loads.

The load instruction is not supposed to affect the V or C bits. Unfortunately, the C bit was changed several times in the process of incrementing various addresses. Fortunately, the Fetch part of the von Neumann cycle saves all four status bits in temporary register T1, as cycle 1 of Figure 12.5 shows. We can assume that T1 has not been tampered with in the meantime. Cycle 21 in Figure 12.11 restores the C bit accordingly.

In the same way that performance can be improved in the fetch and increment part of the von Neumann cycle in Figure 12.5, it is possible to optimize the control sequence in Figure 12.10. An exercise at the end of the chapter asks you to reduce the number of cycles from 21 in Figure 12.10 to just 17.

Implementing the Arithmetic Shift Right Instruction

Figure 12.12 shows the control sequence to execute the unary instruction

ASRA

The RTL specification for the ASRr instruction is

$$C \leftarrow r\langle 15\rangle, r\langle 1..15\rangle \leftarrow r\langle 0..14\rangle \; ; N \leftarrow r < 0, Z \leftarrow r = 0$$

The ASRr instruction is unary, so there are no memory accesses. That makes the control sequence nice and short.

```
// Arithmetic shift right of high-order byte
1. A=0, AMux=1, ALU=13, ANDZ=0, CMux=1, C=0; NCk, ZCk, CCk, LoadCk

// Rotate right of low-order byte
2. A=1, AMux=1, ALU=14, ANDZ=1, CMux=1, C=1; ZCk, CCk, LoadCk
```

Figure 12.12

The control signals to implement the unary ASRA instruction.

Because the ALU only computes with 8-bit quantities, it must break the 16-bit shift into two 8-bit computations. Figure 12.13 shows the four shift and rotate computations that the ALU can perform. To do the arithmetic shift right, the control sequence does an arithmetic shift right of the high-order byte followed by a rotate right of the low-order byte.

In cycle 1, A=0 puts the high-order byte of the accumulator on the ABus, AMux=1 sends it to the ALU, ALU=13 selects the arithmetic shift right operation, CMux=1 and C=0 direct the result to be stored back into the accumulator, and LoadCk stores it. ANDZ=0 routes the Zout from the shift operation to the Z register and ZCk saves it. NCk saves the N bit from the high-order operation, which will be its final value. CCk saves the C bit from the high-order operation, but it will not be the final value of C.

In cycle 2, A=1 puts the low-order byte of the accumulator on the ABus, AMux=1 sends it to the ALU, ALU=14 selects the rotate right operation, CMux=1 and C=1 direct the result to be stored back into the accumulator, and LoadCk stores it. ANDZ causes

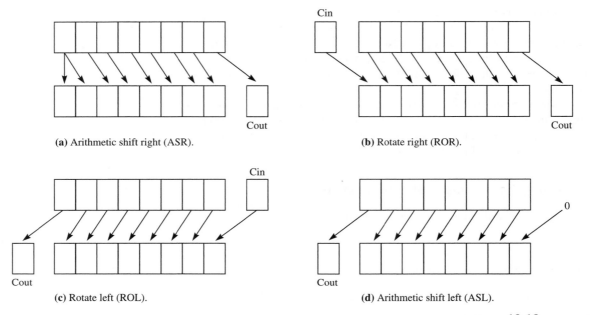

(a) Arithmetic shift right (ASR).   (b) Rotate right (ROR).

(c) Rotate left (ROL).   (d) Arithmetic shift left (ASL).

Figure 12.13

The shift and rotate operations that the Pep/8 ALU can perform.

the ANDZ combinational circuit to perform the AND operation on Zout and Z, which ZCk stores in Z as its final value. CCk stores Cout as the final value of C.

12.2   Performance Issues

From a theoretical perspective, all real von Neumann computing machines are equivalent in their computation abilities. Given a mechanism to connect an infinite amount of disk memory to a machine, it is equivalent in computing power to a Turing Machine. The only difference between what Pep/8 can compute and what the world's largest supercomputer can compute is the time it takes to perform the computation. Granted, it might take a million years for Pep/8 to compute the solution to a problem that a supercomputer could compute in a microsecond, but theoretically they can do the same things.

From a practical perspective, time matters. All other things being equal, faster is better. Although the data section in Figure 12.2 at level LG1 can implement Pep/8 at level ISA3, the question is, how fast? This section describes techniques for speeding up the computation. There are two fundamental sources of increased performance:

- The space/time tradeoff
- Parallelism

The two fundamental sources of increased performance

The space/time tradeoff comes into play by adding circuitry, which takes space on the integrated circuit, to decrease the computation time. Combining cycles in a control sequence is a form of hardware parallelism. Parallelism is also possible by reorganizing the control section so that more subsystems on the integrated circuit can operate concurrently.

The Bus Width

The most straightforward way to use the space/time tradeoff to improve performance is to increase the width of the registers and buses. Such an increase is pervasive throughout the entire integrated circuit.

For example, at the ISA3 level, Pep/8 is a 16-bit machine. That is, registers that hold data, such as the accumulator, and that hold addresses, such as the PC, are 16 bits wide. As the PC connects to the main system bus through the MAR, the address bus is 16 bits wide. All operations are on 16-bit quantities. To improve performance, you could increase the data-bus width in the data section buses—ABus, BBus, CBus, and the rest—from 8 bits to 16 bits. An increase of the data section buses from 8 bits to 16 bits would provide a dramatic increase in performance. All instructions that require processing with two cycles, one for the high-order byte and one for the low-order, would require only one cycle.

Pep/8 is a 16-bit machine.

There is a fly in the ointment, however. You would want to make MDR 16 bits wide as well, because it must be consistent with the AMux input. So, how do you access main memory? If you put 16 data lines on the main system bus, is main memory no longer byte-addressable? Another problem is how you would reorganize the registers in the register bank. Presumably all registers would be 16 bits wide. But then how would you store the instruction specifier in IR, which is a one-byte quantity?

Practically all computers nowadays are byte-addressable but have more than eight data lines in their main system bus. They work by omitting a few low-order addressing bits corresponding to the width of the data bus. Figure 12.14 shows how the scheme would work for Pep/8 with a 16-bit MDR. In part (a), which corresponds to Figure 12.2, there are 16 address lines and 8 data lines. In part (b), the MDR is 16 bits wide, the number of data lines is doubled, and address line A0 is missing.

Suppose the CPU requests the byte at 0A57 (hex), which is 0000 1010 0101 0111 (bin). The address request that goes to the memory subsystem is 0000 1010 0101 0110, where the last bit is 0 because A0 is missing. The system returns the two bytes at addresses 0A56 and 0A57. The CPU must extract the byte it wants from the two-byte word. The payoff comes when the CPU wants a two-byte word. If it requests the word at 1BD6 it can get both bytes with one access.

But now there is another fly in the ointment. Suppose the CPU wants the word at address 1BD5, which is an odd address? It would require two accesses—one from 1BD4, extracting the second byte, and one from 1BD6, extracting the first byte. You have lost the advantage of the speedup because the address of the word

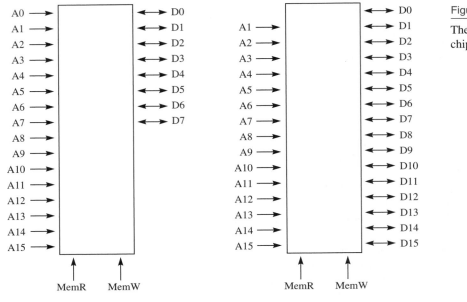

(a) The chip of Figure 12.2.   **(b)** A chip with a 16-bit data bus.

Figure **12.14**

The pinout diagram of the Pep/8 chip.

you want to fetch is not even. A more typical system would be a four-byte data bus with address lines A0 and A1 missing. A memory request of one, two, three, or four bytes, all of which fall within the four-byte boundary whose address is divisible by four, is satisfied by one memory access. This speedup advantage is so great that most assembly languages have special dot commands so the programmer can force the object code to be aligned at the address necessary to minimize the memory access time.

The memory alignment issue

You can see that increasing the bus width has a huge impact on the size of the chip. All the circuits, including the ALU, the multiplexers, and the registers, must be increased to accommodate the bus. The history of computers shows a progression toward ever wider buses and registers. Figure 12.15 shows how the Intel CPUs increased their bus widths from 4 bits to 32 bits. The 4004 was the first microprocessor on a chip. The next big step in the progression is from 32-bit machines to 64-bit machines. Although scientific workstations and servers have had 64-bit registers and buses for years, CPUs of this size are just now becoming available in desktop machines.

Chip	Date	Register width
4004	1971	4-bit
8008	1972	8-bit
8086	1978	16-bit
80386	1985	32-bit

Figure **12.15**

Historic register/bus widths.

The progression is possible only because technology advances at such a regular pace. Gordon Moore, the founder of Intel, observed in 1965 that the density of transistors in an integrated circuit had doubled every year and would continue to do so for the foreseeable future. The rate has slowed down somewhat, so that today the so-called *Moore's Law* now states that the density of transistors in an integrated circuit doubles every 18 months. This pace cannot keep up forever, because the

Moore's Law

miniaturization will eventually reach the dimensions of an atom, which cannot be subdivided. Exactly when Moore's Law will cease has been hotly debated in the past with many people predicting its demise, only to see it continue on.

The generally accepted meaning of "an n-bit computer" is that n is the number of bits in the MAR and in the CPU registers that are visible at level ISA3. Because the registers visible at level ISA3 can hold addresses, the registers are usually the same width as the MAR, so this definition is unambiguous. There is frequently confusion about this definition, especially in marketing. An n-bit computer does not necessarily have n address lines in the main system bus. Nor does it necessarily have n-bit data buses within the data section of its CPU. Nor does it necessarily have n bits in its register bank at level LG1. All these widths can be less than n. Furthermore, using the technique in Figure 12.14(b), the number of data lines in the main system bus can be greater than n.

The definition of an n-bit computer

The classic example is the IBM 360 family introduced in 1964. It was the first family of computers whose models all had the same ISA3 instruction sets and registers. It was a 32-bit machine. But, depending on the model, the data buses in the CPU were 8-bit, 16-bit, or 32-bit. Because the LG1 details are hidden from the programmer at level ISA3, all the software written and debugged on one model in the family ran unchanged on a different model. The only perceived difference between models was performance as measured by execution time. The concept was revolutionary at the time and promoted the design of computers based on levels of abstraction.

MAR width	Number of addressable bytes
8	256
16	64K
32	4G
64	17, 179, 869, 184G

Often, the new chips in a family of processors do not have the full set of address lines to match the width of the MAR. The width of the MAR places an upper limit on how many bytes of main memory the CPU can access, as Figure 12.16 shows. The big limitation on 16-bit computers was the upper limit of 64KB. When operating systems and applications needed more memory, the only alternative was to increase the width of the MAR. We are at the same kind of limit now. The big push for 64-bit computers is because multimedia applications and large databases need an address space greater than 4GB. The transition to 64-bit computers will probably be the last of its kind, however, because 64 address lines can access 16 billion GB. The increase from one generation to the next is not polynomial, but exponential. For many years, 32-bit computers had 32-bit MARs but only 24 address lines on the main memory bus. The eight high-order address bits were ignored. Users could install up to 16MB (2^{24}) on such machines, which was plenty of memory at the time. It will be the same with 64-bit computers in the future, where the number of external address lines will be less than the internal width of the MAR depending on the needs of the market.

Figure 12.16

Maximum memory limits.

Specialized Hardware Units

Another way to use the space/time tradeoff to improve the performance of a hardware system is to determine performance bottlenecks and design specialized hardware units to alleviate them. This approach is more surgical than the brute force method of increasing the bus width throughout the system. You can potentially get a significant performance increase at a fraction of the cost of increasing the bus width throughout.

Figure 12.10 is a case in point, which is the control sequence to implement LDX this,n. You probably noticed how many cycles were required to add 1 to an address because of the need to access bytes in memory at successive locations. It takes three cycles to (1) add 1 to the low-order byte of the address, (2) add a possible carry to the high-order byte, and (3) transfer the two-byte word to the MAR. Cycles 5, 6, and 7 are an example.

The problem is that the ALU is a general-purpose device designed to do many operations on eight-bit quantities. To alleviate the observed bottleneck, you need a special-purpose circuit to add 1 to a 16-bit quantity. Figure 12.17 shows one possibility. Insert a combinational circuit between the A and B buses and the MAR that includes feedback from MARA and MARB. The control line labeled MARInc works as follows:

■ MARInc = 0. ABus and BBus pass through unchanged.

■ MARInc = 1. The 16-bit sum MAR + 1 passes through.

Operation of Incrementer

Design of the Incrementer black box is an exercise at the end of the chapter. Figure 12.18 shows the control signals to implement the load instruction with indirect addressing using the address Incrementer of Figure 12.17.

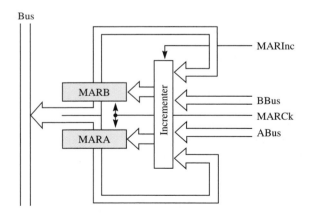

Figure **12.17**

Specialized hardware unit to increment the MAR.

```
// T3<high> <- Mem[OprndSpec].
// MAR <- OprndSpec + 1.
1. A=9, B=10, MARInc=0; MARCk
2. MemRead
3. MemRead, MDRMux=0, MARInc=1; MDRCk, MARCk
4. MemRead, AMux=0, ALU=0, CMux=1, C=14; LoadCk
```

Figure **12.18**

The control signals to implement the load instruction with indirect addressing using the address Incrementer of Figure 12.17.

```
// T3<low> <- Mem[OprndSpec + 1].
5. MemRead, MDRMux=0; MDRCk
6. AMux=0, ALU=0, CMux=1, C=15; LoadCk


// Assert: T3 contains the address of the operand.
// X<high> <- Mem[T3].
// MAR <- T3 + 1.
7. A=14, B=15, MARInc=0; MARCk
8. MemRead
9. MemRead, MDRMux=0, MARInc=1; MDRCk, MARCk
10. MemRead, AMux=0, ALU=0, ANDZ=0, CMux=1, C=2; NCk, ZCk, LoadCk


// X<low> <- Mem[T3 + 1].
11. MemRead, MDRMux=0; MDRCk
12. AMux=0, ALU=0, ANDZ=1, CMux=1, C=3; ZCk, LoadCk
```

Figure **12.18**

(Continued)

Every time you load the MAR you must remember to specify MARInc. In cycle 3, you can increment MAR at the same time MDR is loaded, as neither operation requires the same set of resources in the data section. The master–slave design ensures that the change in the MAR does not affect the address lines of the current memory read. The same reasoning goes with cycle 9. In cycles 4 and 10, you can start the next read because you have clocked the MAR in the previous cycle. An extra bonus of the address Incrementer is that the C bit is never used, and so does not need to be restored. Combining cycles in Figure 12.10 yields a total of 17 cycles. Use of the address Incrementer reduces the number of cycles from 17 to 12, a savings in time of $5/17 = 29\%$.

The address Incrementer helps minimize the number of cycles by processing an address word as a single 16-bit quantity. To make the same advance on the data side you need special-purpose hardware to access memory in 16-bit chunks as well. In the above control sequence, cycles 1 through 4 access the high-order byte of a word, and cycles 5 through 7 access the low order. If you double the number of data lines on the main system bus as in Figure 12.14(b), you can access that word with one memory read operation. To do so requires a two-byte MDR.

Furthermore, if you require that all addresses and all two-byte word operands be stored at even addresses, then you can dispense with the address Incrementer. Its only purpose is to optimize memory accesses from consecutive bytes. If both bytes are available in a single access it is no longer needed. For this scheme to work, the assembler must contain alignment dot commands to force the object code for addresses and two-byte word operands to be stored at even addresses. The requirement applies to global variables as well as locals on the run-time stack. A 32-bit computer would require storage at addresses divisible by four, and a 64-bit computer at addresses divisible by eight.

The control sequence of Figure 12.18 shows one more bottleneck that can be alleviated by modifying the paths in the data section. The only purpose of

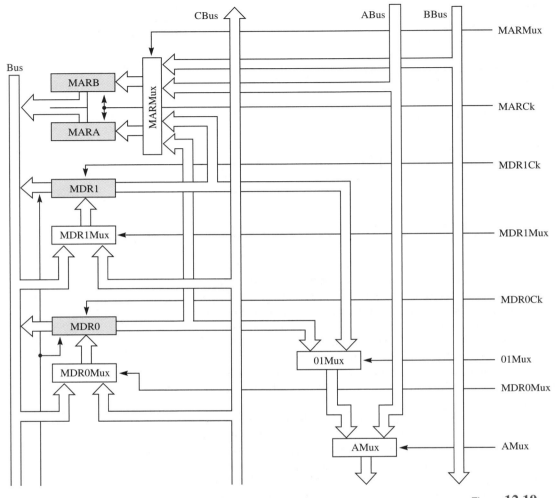

Figure **12.19**

Specialized hardware unit for the two-byte data bus of Figure 12.14(b).

temporary register T3 is to hold the address fetched from memory on its way to the MAR. If there were a 16-bit data path directly from MDR to MAR, you could save all those cycles getting the address to T3 and then back to the MAR.

In Figure 12.19, there are two MDR registers—MDR0 for holding the content of a byte at an even address, and MDR1 for holding a byte at an odd address. Each one can be loaded from the CBus through its own multiplexer. An additional multiplexer labeled 01Mux selects which MDR is injected into the main data path of the data section. As usual, a zero on the 01Mux control line routes MDR0 through the multiplexer. There is also a data path from the two-byte MDR to the two-byte MAR through the multiplexer labeled MARMux. The multiplexer control line routes the data as follows:

- 0 on MARMux routes the MDR to the MAR.

- 1 on MARMux routes ABus and BBus to the MAR.

Figure 12.20 shows the control sequence for the load instruction with indirect addressing. Unlike Figure 12.10, it assumes that both the address word and the two-byte data word are aligned. The control sequence requires eight cycles for an improvement of 53% over the original sequence with 17 cycles. The savings is greater than that with the address Incrementer, but with a much more substantial impact on the design. Adding data lines to the main system bus affects the memory subsystem and the address pinout of the CPU chip. Also, the memory alignment requirement has an impact on the assembly language programs and complicates storage on the run-time stack. Nevertheless, most CPUs today are designed with such requirements because the performance payoff is so great. Pep/8 assembly language does not have an alignment requirement to keep the programs simple.

```
// MDR <- Mem[OprndSpec].
1. A=9, B=10, MARMux=1; MARCk
2. MemRead
3. MemRead, MDR0Mux=0, MDR1Mux=0; MDR0Ck, MDR1Ck

// MAR <- MDR.
4. MARMux=0; MARCk

// MDR <- two-byte operand.
5. MemRead
6. MemRead, MDR0Mux=0, MDR1Mux=0; MDR0Ck, MDR1Ck

// X <- MDR, high-order first.
7. 01Mux=0, AMux=0, ALU=0, ANDZ=0, CMux=1, C=2; NCk, ZCk, LoadCk
8. 01Mux=1, AMux=0, ALU=0, ANDZ=1, CMux=1, C=3; ZCk, LoadCk
```

Figure **12.20**

The control signals to implement the load instruction with indirect addressing using the two-byte data bus of Figure 12.19.

Three Areas of Optimization

The ultimate performance metric of a machine is how fast it executes. Figure 12.21 shows that the time it takes to execute a program is the product of three factors. The word "instruction" in the equation means Level-ISA3 instruction.

There is a relationship between the first two factors that is not shared by the third. A decrease in the first factor usually leads to an increase in the second factor, and vice versa. That is, if you design your ISA3 machine in such a way that you decrease the number of instructions it takes to write a given program, you usually must pay the price of increasing the number of cycles it takes to execute each instruction. Conversely, if you design your ISA3 machine so that each instruction takes as few cycles as possible, you usually must make the instructions so simple that more of them are required to write a given program.

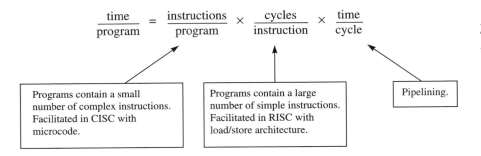

$$\frac{time}{program} = \frac{instructions}{program} \times \frac{cycles}{instruction} \times \frac{time}{cycle}$$

Programs contain a small number of complex instructions. Facilitated in CISC with microcode.

Programs contain a large number of simple instructions. Facilitated in RISC with load/store architecture.

Pipelining.

Figure **12.21**

The three components of execution time in a von Neumann machine.

The third factor in the equation is based on parallelism, and comes into play by reorganizing the control section so that more subsystems on the integrated circuit can operate concurrently. There is no tradeoff between it and either of the first two factors, however. You can introduce pipelining in the design to decrease the time per cycle, and the time per program will decrease whether you have chosen to minimize the first factor at the expense of the second, or the second at the expense of the first.

Early in the history of computing, designers concentrated on the first factor. That approach was motivated in part by the high cost of main memory. Programs needed to be as small as possible just so they could fit in the available memory. Instruction sets and addressing modes were designed to make it easy for compilers to translate from HOL6 to Asmb5. Pep/8 is an example of such a design. In this case, the motivation is for pedagogical reasons and not for reasons of limited main memory. The assembly language is designed to teach the principles of translation between levels of abstraction typical in computer systems. Those principles are easiest to learn when the translation process is straightforward.

In the early 1980s, the computing landscape had changed. Hardware was getting cheaper, and memory subsystems were getting bigger. Some designers, notably John Cocke at IBM, David Patterson at UC Berkeley, and John Hennessy at Stanford, began to promote designs based on decreasing the second factor at the expense of increasing the first. Their designs were characterized by a much smaller number of ISA3 instructions and fewer addressing modes. The moniker for their designs was Reduced Instruction Set Computers (RISC, pronounce *risk*). In contrast, the older designs began to be called Complex Instruction Set Computers (CISC, pronounced *sisk*). As there is a tradeoff between the first two factors, many people were skeptical that the net result would be a faster machine. The RISC argument is that you can extract greater parallelism, especially with pipelining, on a given integrated circuit than is possible with a CISC design.

RISC and CISC

Since the 1980s, almost all newly designed CPUs have been RISC machines. Some prominent ones are the ARM chip, which dominates the cell phone market; the MIPS chip, which is based on the Stanford design and is used in servers and Nintendo game consoles; the Sparc chip, which is based on the Berkeley design and was adopted by Sun for its servers and workstations; and the PowerPC, which is based on the IBM design and is used in IBM servers and workstations. However, there is one CISC design that continues to dominate the desktop market, namely Intel's IA-32, a direct descendent of the chips listed in Figure 12.15. Its continued dominance is due in large part to the compatibility that each chip in the family has maintained with its predecessor. It is expensive to migrate application programs and operating systems to chips with different ISA3 instructions and addressing modes. Furthermore, CISC designers were able to adopt the RISC philosophy by creating a level of abstraction with a RISC core, the details of which were hidden at a low level, that implemented the CISC machine at level ISA3.

Microcode

Figure 12.1 shows the CPU divided into a data section and a control section. Given a sequence of control signals necessary to implement an ISA3 instruction, such as the sequence in Figure 12.8 to implement the STBYTEA instruction, the problem is how to design the control section to generate that sequence of signals.

The idea behind microcode is that a sequence of control signals is, in effect, a program. Figure 12.4, which is a description of the von Neumann cycle, even looks like a C++ program. One way to design the control section is to create Mc2, the microcode level of abstraction that lies between ISA3 and LG1. Like all levels of abstraction, this level has its own language consisting of a set of microprogramming statements. The control section is its own micromachine with its own micromemory, uMem; its own microprogram counter, uPC; and its own microinstruction register, uIR. Unlike the machine at Level ISA3, the machine at Level Mc2 has only one program that is burned into uMem ROM. Once the chip is manufactured, the microprogram can never be changed. The program contains a single loop whose sole purpose is to implement the ISA3 von Neumann cycle.

Level Mc2

uMem, uPC, and uIR

Figure 12.22 shows the control section of Pep/8 implemented in microcode at Level Mc2. The data section, not shown, is to the left. It consists of the data paths of Figure 12.2 modified to accommodate the two-byte data bus of Figure 12.19. There are a total of 12 data lines coming from the data section to the control section—8 from the BBus and 4 from the status bits. There are a total of 36 control lines going to the data section.

The microprogram counter contains the address of the next microinstruction to execute. uPC is k bits wide, so that it can point to any of the 2^k instructions in uMem. A microinstruction is n bits wide, so that is the width of each cell in uMem and also the width of uIR. At Level Mc2, there is no reason to require that the width of a microinstruction be an even power of two. n can be any oddball value that you want to make it. This flexibility is due to the fact that uMem contains only instructions with no data. Because instructions and data are not co-mingled, there is no need to require the memory cell size to accommodate both.

Figure 12.23 shows the instruction format of a microinstruction. The rightmost 36 bits are the control signals to send to the data section. The remaining field

Maurice V. Wilkes

Maurice Wilkes was born in 1913 in Dudley, Staffordshire, England. He received his PhD from Cambridge University in 1936. The university established a computer laboratory the following year and appointed Wilkes to supervise the construction of a new differential analyzer. At the outbreak of World War II he left for war service, returning to the lab in 1945.

In 1946, Wilkes read von Neumann's preliminary report on the EDVAC, which described the concept of the stored-program computer controlled by the fetch-decode-increment-execute cycle. He immediately "recognized this at once as the real thing" and committed himself to building a computer based on von Neumann's principle. He attended a series of lectures in August of that year at the University of Pennsylvania and was able to meet with Herman Goldstine, von Neumann's associate, and John Mauchly and Presper Eckert. He returned to Cambridge determined to design and build the Electronic Delay Storage Automatic Computer (EDSAC).

On May 6, 1949, EDSAC, the world's first von Neumann machine, was turned on in the Cambridge lab. Wilkes's hand-written note reads, "Machine in operation for first time. Printed table of squares (0–99). Time for programme 2 mins. 35 sec."

Printing squares was a nice first demonstration for the machine, but Wilkes soon gave it more demanding tasks. Programs were input to the computer via holes punched in paper tape. Wilkes had a tape punched to program EDSAC to solve the Airy differential equation, $y'' - ty = 0$, which is used in physics to model the diffraction of light. There were about 126 lines that made up the program, and one of his first attempts was riddled with 20 errors. His quote below refers to a trip between the paper tape punching equipment and the EDSAC room. Wilkes, D. J. Wheeler, and S. Gill published *The Preparation of Programs for an Electronic Digital Computer*, the first book on programming, in 1951.

Also in 1951, Wilkes published a paper titled "The Best Way to

Design an Automated Calculating Machine" that described a new technique he dubbed microprogramming. Not only did Wilkes invent the Mc2 level of abstraction, he also built the first computer to have a microprogrammed control section. The EDSAC 2 came into operation early in 1958. The Mc2 level was the standard design for practically all commercial computers until load/store architectures became fashionable in the 1980s.

Another design innovation of EDSAC 2 was its bit-slice organization. The EDSAC machines were designed with vacuum tubes, as transistors were not yet in widespread use. To track down and replace a faulty tube was difficult and time-consuming. In much the same way that the 512×1 bit memory chip of Figure 11.40(b) is a one-bit slice of a 512-byte memory, the data section of EDSAC 2 was a series of narrow racks of tubes, each one a one-bit slice of the whole. A faulty tube could be repaired by replacing a bad rack with a good one, greatly simplifying maintenance.

Wilkes is a Distinguished Fellow of the British Computer Society, a Fellow of the Royal Society, and a Fellow of the Royal Academy of Engineering. He received the ACM Turing Award in 1967.

"I can remember the exact instant when I realized that a large part of my life from then on was going to be spent in finding mistakes in my own programs."

—*Maurice V. Wilkes*

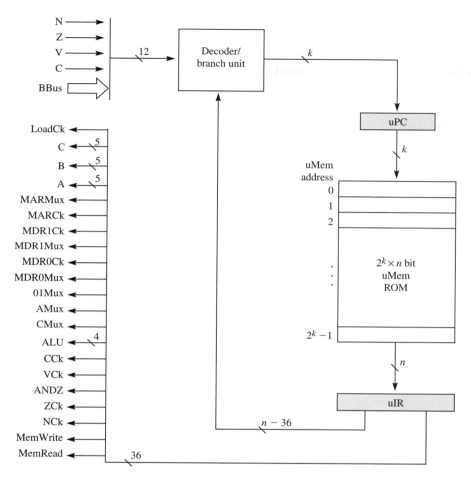

Figure **12.22**

A microcode implementation of the control section of the Pep/8 CPU.

consists of two parts—a Branch field and an Addr field. The program counter at Level ISA3 is incremented because the normal flow of control is to have the instructions stored and executed sequentially in main memory. The only deviation from this state of affairs is when PC changes due to a branch instruction. uPC at Level Mc2, however, is not incremented. Instead, every microinstruction contains within it information to compute the address of the next microinstruction. The Branch field specifies *how* to compute the address of the next microinstruction, and the Addr field contains data to be used in the computation.

For example, if the next microinstruction does not depend on any of the 12 signals from the data section, Branch will specify an unconditional branch, and Addr will be the address of the next microinstruction. In effect, every instruction is a branch instruction. To execute a set of microinstructions in sequence, you make each microinstruction an unconditional branch to the next one. The Decoder/branch

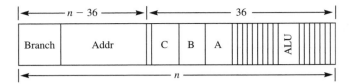

Figure **12.23**

The instruction format of a
microinstruction.

unit in Figure 12.22 is designed to pass Addr straight through to uPC when the Branch field specifies an unconditional branch, regardless of the values of the 12 lines from the data section.

An example where a conditional microbranch is necessary is the implementation of BRLT. The RTL specification of BRLT is

$$N = 1 \Rightarrow PC \leftarrow Oprnd$$

If the N bit is one, PC gets the operand. To implement BRLT, a microinstruction must check the value of the N bit, and either do nothing or branch to a sequence of microinstructions that replaces the PC with the operand. This microinstruction would contain a Branch field that specifies that the next address is computed by combining N with Addr. If N is 0, the computation will produce one address, and if N is 1 it will produce another.

In general, conditional microbranches work by computing the address of the next microinstruction from Addr and whatever signals from the data section that the condition depends on. The biggest conditional branch of all is the branch that decides which ISA3 instruction to execute—in other words, the decode part of the von Neumann cycle. The microinstruction to decode an ISA instruction would have 8 in its B field, which would put the first byte of IR on the BBus. (See Figure 12.2 for the register address of the IR.) The Branch field would specify an instruction decode, and the Decoder/branch unit would be designed to output the address of the first microinstruction in the sequence to implement that instruction.

The details of the Branch and Addr fields in a microinstruction as well as the implementation of the Decoder/branch unit are beyond the scope of this book. Although Figures 12.22 and 12.23 ignore many practical issues in the design of a microcode level, they do illustrate the essential design elements of Level Mc2.

12.3   The MIPS Machine

Pep/8 is an example of an accumulator machine, because computations always take place between an operand that could be in main memory and the accumulator or index register. For example, to perform an addition you execute ADDA, which adds the operand to the accumulator and places the result in the accumulator. Pep/8 also has a rich set of addressing modes that make it possible to translate C++ programs to Pep/8 assembly language with few instructions.

Load/Store Architectures

In contrast to an accumulator machine, a load/store machine minimizes the second factor in Figure 12.21 to reduce program execution time. The MIPS machine is a classic example of a commercially produced load/store machine. It is a 32-bit machine with 32 32-bit registers in its CPU. Figure 12.24 is a drawing to scale of the registers in the MIPS CPU compared to those in Pep/8.

Each register has a special assembler designation that begins with a dollar sign. $zero is a constant zero register similar to register 22 in Figure 12.2 but visible at Level ISA3. $v0 and $v1 are for values returned by a subroutine and $a0 through $a3 are for arguments to a subroutine, similar to the calling protocol for operator new in Section 6.5. Registers that begin with $t are temporary, not preserved across a function call, and those that begin with $s are saved registers, preserved across a function call. The $k registers are reserved for the operating system kernel. $gp is the global pointer; $sp is the stack pointer; $fp is the frame pointer; $ra is the return address.

Figure **12.24**

Comparison of MIPS and Pep/8 CPU registers.

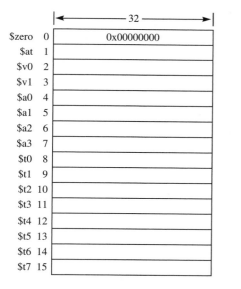

(a) MIPS registers.

(b) Pep/8 registers.

Pep/8 is a tiny machine compared to most microprocessors. Figure 12.24 shows that there are 16 times more bits in the MIPS CPU registers than the Pep/8 CPU registers. And that does not count another set of floating-point registers that MIPS has and Pep/8 does not. Even with this big mismatch in size, in two respects MIPS is simpler than Pep/8—it has fewer addressing modes, and its instructions are all the same length.

Figure 12.4 shows the von Neumann cycle for Pep/8. It is complicated by the existence of two kinds of instructions, one-byte unary and three-byte nonunary. One goal of RISC architecture is extreme simplicity to the point that each instruction might execute in a single cycle. This goal dictates that every instruction have the same length, four bytes in the case of the MIPS machine. For enhanced performance, the memory alignment issue forces the first byte of each instruction to be stored at an address evenly divisible by four. The memory chip corresponding to Figure 12.14(b) would have address lines A2 to A31 and data lines D0 to D31. Address lines A0 and A1 would be missing because instructions would be fetched in four-byte chunks. Figure 12.25 shows the von Neumann cycle for the MIPS machine. There is no if statement to determine the size of the instruction.

```
do
      Fetch the instruction at the address in PC
      PC ← PC + 4
      Decode the instruction specifier
      Execute the instruction fetched
while (true)
```

Figure **12.25**

A pseudocode description of the MIPS von Neumann execution cycle.

Figure 12.25 shows the von Neumann cycle for MIPS as an endless loop, which is more realistic than the cycle for Pep/8. Real machines have no STOP instruction because the operating system continues to execute when an application terminates.

In contrast to Pep/8, which has eight addressing modes, MIPS has the five addressing modes of Figure 12.26. The operand specifier for Pep/8 is always 16 bits, but the size of the operand specifier for MIPS depends on the addressing mode. A MIPS instruction always consists of an instruction specifier and one or more operand specifiers. Because an instruction must always be exactly four bytes, both

Addressing mode	Size of OprndSpec	Operand
Immediate	16 bits	OprndSpec
Register	5 bits	Reg [OprndSpec]
Base	5 bits and 16 bits	Mem [Reg[OprndSpec1] + OprndSpec2]
PC-relative	16 bits	Mem [(PC + 4) + OprndSpec * 4]
Pseudodirect	26 bits	Mem [(PC + 4) <0..3> : OprndSpec * 4]

Figure **12.26**

The MIPS addressing modes.

the instruction specifier and the operand specifier(s) must fit within 32 bits. It therefore follows that any operand specifier must be less than 32 bits.

Addressing modes immediate, register, and base are for accessing data. Of these three modes, only base addressing accesses main memory. The notation Reg in Figure 12.26 stands for "register" and is analogous to Mem, which stands for "memory." Because there are 32 registers in the register bank in Figure 12.24(a), and 2^5 is 32, it takes five bits to access one of them. Reg [OprndSpec] indicates the content of the register at the address specified by the operand specifier.

Addressing modes PC-relative and pseudodirect are for accessing instructions. There is no direct addressing mode. Instead, when you fetch an instruction, you always fetch it relative to the program counter. With PC-relative addressing, the 16-bit operand specifier is multiplied by four (because each instruction occupies four bytes) and then added to the incremented program counter. The result of the addition is the address in memory of the operand. With pseudodirect addressing, the colon represents concatenation. The left part of the concatenation is the first four (high-order) bits of the incremented program counter. The right part of the concatenation is the 26-bit operand specifier multiplied by four—that is, shifted left twice, giving a 28-bit quantity. The concatenation is a 32-bit address. Conditional branch instructions use PC-relative addressing, and unconditional jump instructions use pseudodirect addressing.

The Instruction Set

Figure 12.27 is a summary of some MIPS instructions. All instructions have a 6-bit opcode, although some use additional fields to further specify the action of the instruction. Operand specifiers labeled sssss and ttttt are five-bit source register fields, those labeled ddddd are five-bit destination register fields, and those labeled bbbbb are five-bit base register fields. A field of i characters is an immediate operand specifier, which is sign-extended for addition and zero-extended for AND and OR. A field of a characters is an address operand specifier, which is a sign-extended offset in an address calculation. Operand specifiers labeled hhhhh are five-bit shift amounts for the shift instructions.

The terminology and notation in this section differs slightly from the official MIPS documentation. Some terminology is altered to be consistent with the description of Pep/8. For example, Pep/8 numbers bits from left to right, but the MIPS convention is from right to left. In this text, the letter d always represents the destination register, and the letter b always represents a base register. The letter t sometimes represents the destination register in MIPS documentation.

Figure 12.28 is a comparison of the machine language format of the add instruction for MIPS and Pep/8. The MIPS add instruction does not access an operand in memory. Instead, it adds the content of two registers and puts the sum in a third. In Figure 12.28(a), rs and rt are the first and second registers of the source,

Mnemonic	Meaning	Binary instruction encoding
add	Add	0000 00ss ssst tttt dddd d000 0010 0000
addi	Add immediate	0010 00ss sssd dddd iiii iiii iiii iiii
sub	Subtract	0000 00ss ssst tttt dddd d000 0010 0010
and	Bitwise AND	0000 00ss ssst tttt dddd d000 0010 0100
andi	Bitwise AND immediate	0011 00ss sssd dddd iiii iiii iiii iiii
or	Bitwise OR	0000 00ss ssst tttt dddd d000 0010 0101
ori	Bitwise OR immediate	0011 01ss sssd dddd iiii iiii iiii iiii
sll	Shift left logical	0000 0000 000t tttt dddd dhhh hh00 0000
sra	Shift right arithmetic	0000 0000 000t tttt dddd dhhh hh00 0011
srl	Shift right logical	0000 0000 000t tttt dddd dhhh hh00 0010
lb	Load byte	1000 00bb bbbd dddd aaaa aaaa aaaa aaaa
lw	Load word	1000 11bb bbbd dddd aaaa aaaa aaaa aaaa
lui	Load upper immediate	0011 1100 000d dddd iiii iiii iiii iiii
sb	Store byte	1010 00bb bbbt tttt aaaa aaaa aaaa aaaa
sw	Store word	1010 11bb bbbt tttt aaaa aaaa aaaa aaaa
beq	Branch if equal to	0001 00ss ssst tttt aaaa aaaa aaaa aaaa
bgez	Branch if greater than or equal to zero	0000 01ss sss0 0001 aaaa aaaa aaaa aaaa
bgtz	Branch if greater than zero	0001 11ss sss0 0000 aaaa aaaa aaaa aaaa
blez	Branch if less than or equal to zero	0001 10ss sss0 0000 aaaa aaaa aaaa aaaa
bltz	Branch if less than zero	0000 01ss sss0 0000 aaaa aaaa aaaa aaaa
bne	Branch if not equal to	0001 01ss ssst tttt aaaa aaaa aaaa aaaa
j	Jump (unconditional branch)	0000 10aa aaaa aaaa aaaa aaaa aaaa aaaa

Figure **12.27**

A few instructions from the MIPS instruction set.

and rd is the destination register that gets the sum. The field named *shamt* is shift amount, which is used in the shift instructions and not applicable to the add instruction. The field named *funct* is a function field used in conjunction with the opcode field to specify the operation. This addressing mode is called register addressing for obvious reasons.

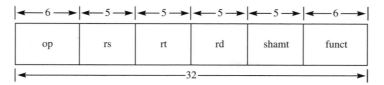

Figure **12.28**

Comparison of MIPS and Pep/8 add instruction formats.

(a) MIPS register addressing.

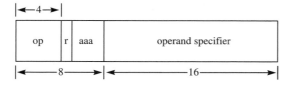

(b) Pep/8 general addressing.

The RTL specification of the add instruction is

rd ← rs + rt

The MIPS add instruction

The corresponding MIPS assembly language statement is

```
add rd,rs,rt
```

The order of the operands in assembly language is different from their order in machine language.

A key principle of load/store machines is that all computations are done on values in registers. You cannot add a value from memory to a value in a register with one instruction. You must first load the value into another register and then add the two registers together. The only instructions that access memory are the load and store instructions. In the MIPS machine, memory is byte addressable, words are 32 bits long, and word data are aligned to memory addresses divisible by four. Two instructions for accessing memory are:

- lw for load word
- sw for store word

Figure 12.29 shows the MIPS instruction format for the lw instruction. rb is called the base register and rd is the destination register.

Figure **12.29**

MIPS instruction format for load instructions with base addressing.

For the load instruction, the RTL specification is

    rd ← Mem[rb + address]   *The MIPS load instruction,* `lw`

and the corresponding MIPS assembly language statement is

`lw rd,address(rb)`

    The instruction format for the store instruction is the same as Figure 12.29 except that source register rt replaces destination register rd. See Figure 12.27. For the store instruction, the RTL specification is

    Mem[rb + address] ← rt   *The MIPS store instruction,* `sw`

and the corresponding MIPS assembly language statement is

`sw rt,address(rb)`

    The field labeled address is not an absolute address. It is an address *offset* that is added to rb, which *is* an absolute address. The rb register is 32 bits wide, but the address field is only 16 bits wide. The CPU interprets address as a signed integer, so that a load instruction can load any word within a region of $\pm 2^{15}$ or 32,768 bytes from the address in register rs.

    The Pep/8 addressing mode most similar to the addressing mode of the MIPS load and store instructions is indexed, where the operand is

    Oprnd = Mem[OprndSpec + X]   *Pep/8 indexed addressing*

A significant difference is the use of the register. In Pep/8, the register X contains the value of the index. In the MIPS machine, the register rb contains the address of the first element of the array, in other words, the base of the array. That is why register rb is called the base register and this addressing mode is called base addressing.

    In accumulator machines like Pep/8, the current value of a variable is maintained in memory. Load/store machines, however, have many registers. The compiler maintains an association of a register with a variable and does all the computations between registers. There are four situations when a variable's value must be stored in memory. First, a program might have more variables than available registers. To compute with a variable for which there is no room in the CPU, existing registers are "spilled" into main memory. Second, when you make a recursive call, local variables must be copied to the run-time stack in memory. Third, to output a value it must be copied to memory first. Fourth, array values require too much storage to be contained in registers. However, the compiler does associate a $s register with an array variable. It contains the address of the first element of the array.

Example 12.1 Suppose the C++ compiler associates $s1 with array a, $s2 with variable g, and $s3 with array b. It translates the statement

```
a[2] = g + b[3];
```

to MIPS assembly language as

```
lw $t0,12($s3)   # Register $t0 gets b[3]
add $t0,$s2,$t0  # Register $t0 gets g + b[3]
sw $t0,8($s1)    # a[2] gets g + b[3]
```

Comments begin with the # character. The load instruction has 12 for the address field, because it is accessing b[3], each word is four bytes, and $3 \times 4 = 12$. Similarly, the store instruction has 8 in the address field because of the index value in a[2]. The machine language translation of these instructions is

```
100011 10011 01000 0000000000001100
000000 10010 01000 01000 00000 100000
101011 10001 01000 0000000000001000
```

The first six bits of each instruction is the opcode. Figure 12.24 shows that $t0 is register 8 (dec) = 01000 (bin), $s3 is register 19 (dec) = 10011 (bin), $s2 is register 18 (dec) = 10010 (bin), and $s1 is register 17 (dec) = 10001 (bin). ■

The situation is a bit more complicated if you want to access the element of an array whose index is a variable. MIPS has no index register that does what the index register in Pep/8 does. Consequently, the compiler must generate code to add the index value to the address of the first element of the array to get the address of the element referenced. In Pep/8, this addition is done automatically at Level Mc2 with indexed addressing. But, the design philosophy of load/store machines is to have few addressing modes even at the expense of needing more statements in the program.

In Pep/8, words are two bytes, and so the index must be shifted left once to multiply it by two. In MIPS, words are four bytes, and so the index must be shifted left twice to multiply it by four. The MIPS instruction sll, for shift left logical, uses the shamt field in Figure 12.28(a) to specify the amount of the shift.

Example 12.2 The MIPS assembly language statement to shift the content of $s0 seven bits to the left and put the result in $t2 is

```
sll $t2,$s0,7
```

The machine language translation is

```
000000 00000 10000 01010 00111 000000
```

The first field is the opcode. The second field is not used by this instruction and is set to all zeros. The third is the rt field, which indicates $s0, register 16 (dec) = 10000. The fourth is the rd field, which indicates $t2, register 10 (dec) = 01010 (bin). The fifth is the shamt field, which indicates the shift amount. The last is the funct field used with the opcode to indicate the `sll` instruction. ■

Example 12.3   Assuming that the C++ compiler associates $s0 with variable `i`, $s1 with array `a`, and $s2 with variable `g`, it translates the statement

```
g = a[i];
```

into MIPS assembly language as follows.

```
sll $t0,$s0,2    # $t0 gets $s0 times 4
add $t0,$s1,$t0  # $t0 gets the address of a[i]
lw $s2,0($t0)    # $s2 gets a[i]
```

Note the 0 in the address field of the load instruction. ■

Like Pep/8, the MIPS machine has an immediate addressing mode. There is a special version of the add instruction with mnemonic `addi`, which stands for add immediate. Figure 12.30 shows the instruction format for immediate addressing. It has the same structure as the base addressing mode of Figure 12.29, except that the 16-bit field is used for the immediate operand instead of an address offset.

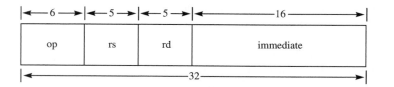

Figure **12.30**

MIPS instruction format for immediate addressing.

Example 12.4   To allocate four bytes of storage on the run-time stack, you would execute

```
addi $sp,$sp,-4  # $sp <- $sp - 4
```

where –4 is not an address but the immediate operand. The machine language translation is

```
001000 11101 11101 1111111111111100
```

where $sp is register 29. ■

You may have noticed a limitation with the `addi` instruction. The constant field is only 16 bits wide, but MIPS is a 32-bit machine. You should be able to add constants with 32-bit precision using immediate addressing. Here is another example of the load/store architecture philosophy. The primary goal is simple instructions with few addressing modes. The Pep/8 design permits instructions with different widths, that is, both unary and nonunary instructions. Figure 12.4 shows how this decision complicates the fetch part of the von Neumann cycle. The hardware must fetch the instruction specifier, then decode it to determine whether to fetch an operand specifier. This complexity is completely counter to the load/store philosophy, which demands simple instructions that can be decoded quickly. The simplicity goal demands that all instructions be the same length.

But if all instructions are 32 bits wide, how could one instruction possibly contain a 32-bit immediate constant? There would be no room in the instruction format for the opcode. Here is where decreasing the second factor in Figure 12.21 at the expense of the first factor comes into play. The solution to the problem of a 32-bit immediate constant is to require the execution of two instructions. For this job, MIPS provides `lui`, which stands for load upper immediate. It sets the high-order 16 bits of a register to the immediate operand and the low order bits to all zeros. A second instruction is required to set the low-order 16 bits, usually the OR immediate instruction `ori`.

Example 12.5 Assuming that the compiler associates register $s2 with variable g, it translates the C++ statement

```
g = 491521;
```

to MIPS assembly language as

```
lui $s2,0x0007
ori $s2,$s2,0x8001
```

The decimal number 491521 requires more than 16 bits in binary, and 491521 (dec) = 0007 8001 (hex). ∎

Pep/8 is a tiny machine compared to most microprocessors. Figure 12.24 shows that there are 16 times more bits in the MIPS CPU registers than the Pep/8 CPU registers. And that does not count another set of floating-point registers that MIPS has and Pep/8 does not. Even with this big mismatch in size, in two respects MIPS is simpler than Pep/8—it has fewer addressing modes, and its instructions are all the same length.

The most complex of the addressing modes does nothing more complicated than to add one address field of an instruction to one register. Compare that to Pep/8's most complex addressing mode, stack-indexed deferred.

Oprnd = Mem [Mem [SP + OprndSpec] + X]

Consider what the CPU must do to execute a stack-relative deferred instruction. First, it must add SP and OprndSpec. Next, it must do a memory fetch from that address. Then, it must add the quantity fetched to X. Finally, it must fetch the operand from that address. That is complex. Pep/8 is CISC.

But, what is the purpose of stack-indexed deferred? Section 6.4 shows that it is required to access an array that has been passed as a parameter, and Section 6.5 shows that it is required to access a cell in a structure that has been dynamically allocated with the new operator. Does the absence of stack-indexed deferred addressing in MIPS mean that it cannot pass arrays as parameters? Of course not. It just means that the compiler must generate more assembly language statements to compute the address of the operand. As Figure 12.21 shows, the program will contain a larger number of simple instructions.

The RISC argument is that more instructions must execute, but each instruction requires fewer cycles. Not only that, but the simpler design makes it possible to extract more parallelism from the integrated circuit, so that the net effect is a faster chip. One characteristic of load/store machines is the absence of a microcode level of abstraction. The control section for such machines is designed as a set of finite state machines directly in hardware that produce the control signals for the data section. Because you generally pay a performance price by adding a level of abstraction, eliminating a level usually results in better performance.

Cache Memories

The Pep/8 control sequence has a requirement that memory reads and writes require two cycles because of the excessive time it takes to access the memory subsystem over the main system bus. Although this requirement puts a little realism into the model, in practice the speed mismatch between main memory access time and the CPU cycle time is much more severe. Suppose it took 10 cycles instead of just two for a main memory access. You can imagine what the control sequences would look like—many cycles of MemReads. Most of the time the CPU would be waiting for memory reads, wasting cycles that could be used for making progress on the job.

But what if you could predict the future? If you knew which words from memory were going to be required by the program ahead of time, you could set up a small amount of expensive, high-speed memory right next to the CPU called a *cache*, fetch the instructions and data from main memory ahead of time, and it would be available for the data section immediately. Of course, no one can predict the future, so this scheme is impossible. Even if you could not predict the future with 100% accuracy, however, what if you could predict it with 95% accuracy? Those times your prediction was correct, the memory access time from the cache would be nearly instantaneous. If the percentage of time you were correct was high enough, the speedup would be substantial.

Cache memory

The problem is how to make the prediction. Suppose you could tap the address lines and monitor all the memory requests that a CPU makes when it executes a typical job. Would you expect to see the sequence of addresses come out at random? That is, given one address request, would you expect to see the next one close to it, or would you expect the next one to be at some random location far away?

There are two reasons you should expect to see successive memory requests close together, based on the two things stored in memory. First, the CPU must access instructions during the fetch part of the von Neumann cycle. As long as no branches execute to far-away instructions, it will be requesting from addresses that are all clumped together. Second, the CPU must access data from memory. But the assembly language programs in Chapter 6 all have their data clumped together in memory. It is true that applications and the heap are stored in low memory, and the operating system and the run-time stack are stored in high memory. But you should be able to visualize that for periods of time, the accesses will all be of bytes from the same neighborhood.

The phenomenon that memory accesses are not random is called *locality of reference*. If memory accesses were totally random, then a cache would be totally useless, because it would be impossible to predict which bytes from memory to preload. Fortunately, typical access requests exhibit two kinds of locality:

- Spatial locality—An address close to the previously requested address is likely to be requested in the near future.

- Temporal locality—The previously requested address *itself* is likely to be requested in the near future.

The two types of locality of reference

Temporal locality comes from the common use of loops in programs.

When the CPU requests a load from memory, the cache subsystem first checks to see if the data requested has already been loaded into the cache, an event called a *cache hit*. If so, it delivers the data straightaway. If not, an event called a *cache miss* occurs. The data is fetched from main memory, and the CPU must wait substantially longer for it. When the data finally arrives, it is loaded into the cache and given to the CPU. Because the data was just requested, there is a high probability that it will be requested again in the near future. Keeping it in the cache takes advantage of temporal locality. You can take advantage of spatial locality by bringing into the cache not only the data that is requested, but also a clump of data in the neighborhood of the requested byte. Even though you have brought in some bytes that have not been requested yet, you are preloading them based on a prediction of the future. The probability that they will be accessed in the near future is high because their addresses are close to the address of the previously accessed byte.

Cache hits and misses

Why not build main memory with high-speed circuits like the cache, put it where the cache is, and dispense with the cache altogether? Because high-speed memory circuits require so much more area on a chip. There is a huge size and speed difference between the fastest memory technology and the slowest. It is the classic space/time tradeoff. The more space you are willing to devote per memory cell, the faster you can make the memory operate.

Memory technology provides a range of designs between these two extremes. Corresponding to this range, three levels of cache are typical between the CPU and the main memory subsystem:

- Split L1 instruction and data cache on the CPU chip
- Unified L2 cache in the CPU package
- Unified L3 cache on the processor board

Three levels of cache in a computer system

Figure 12.31 shows the three levels. In the figure, a package is a self-contained electrical part that you can purchase separately and mount on a circuit board. Computer manufacturers typically design circuit boards, purchase packages, mount them

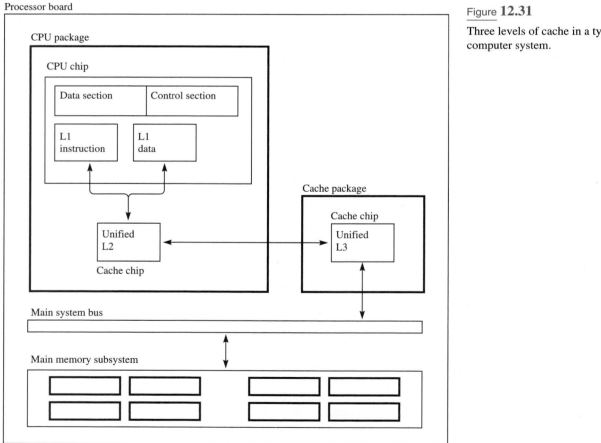

Figure **12.31**

Three levels of cache in a typical computer system.

on their boards, put the boards in a box, and sell the box as a computer. L1 cache is smaller and faster than L2 cache, which is smaller and faster than L3 cache, which is smaller and faster than the main memory subsystem. The L1 cache receives memory requests from the CPU, and passes the requests on to the L2 cache in case of a cache miss. In case of a cache miss in the L2 cache, it passes the requests on to the L3 cache. In case of a cache miss in the L3 cache, it passes the requests on to the main memory subsystem.

The L1 cache designed into the CPU integrated circuit is split between an instruction cache and a data cache. The CPU makes a distinction between an instruction fetch as part of the von Neumann cycle and a data fetch of an operand. L2 and L3 caches are known as unified caches because they store instructions and data intermixed with no distinction between them. Typical sizes are 32 to 64 KB for L1 cache. (To show how tiny Pep/8 is, its entire main memory would fit inside a typical L1 cache.) L1 cache runs at CPU speeds. L2 cache usually runs at one-half or one-quarter the speed of L1 cache and is two to four times larger. L3 is usually another factor of four slower and larger than L2. With recent advances of main system bus technology, some designs omit the L3 cache altogether because there is not enough of a speed difference between L2 and main memory to warrant the extra level.

There are two kinds of cache designs:

- Direct-mapped cache
- Set-associative cache

Two types of cache design

The simpler of the two is direct-mapped cache, an example of which is in Figure 12.32. As usual, the example is unrealistically small to help facilitate the description.

The example is for a system with 16 address lines and $2^{16} = 64$KB main memory. Memory is divided into 16-byte chunks called cache lines. On a cache miss, the system loads not only the requested byte, but also all 16 bytes of the cache line that contains the requested byte. The cache itself is a miniature memory with eight cells addressed from 0 to 7. Each cell is divided into three fields—Valid, Tag, and Data. The Data field is that part of the cache cell that holds a copy of the cache line from memory. The Valid field is a single bit that is 1 if the cache cell contains valid data from memory, and 0 if it does not.

The address field is divided into three parts—Tag, Line, and Byte. The Byte field is four bits corresponding to the fact that $2^4 = 16$, and there are 16 bytes per cache line. The line field is three bits corresponding to the fact that $2^3 = 8$, and there are eight cells in the cache. The Tag field holds the remainder of the bits in the 16-bit address, so it has $16 - 3 - 4 = 9$ bits. A cache cell holds a copy of the Tag field from the address along with the data from memory. In this example, each cache cell holds a total of $1 + 9 + 128 = 138$ bits. As there are eight cells in the cache, it holds a total of $138 \times 8 = 1104$ bits.

When the system starts up, it sets all the Valid bits in the cache to 0. The very first memory request will be a miss. The address of the cache line from memory to be loaded is simply the Tag field of the address, with the last four bits set to 0. That

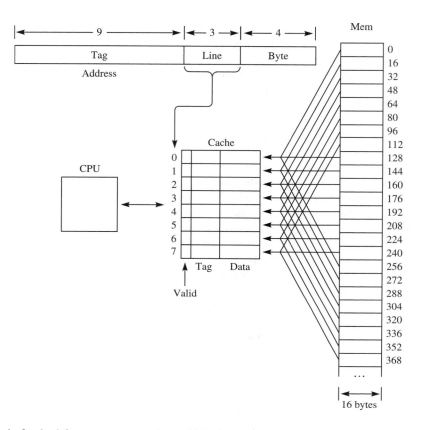

Figure **12.32**

A direct-mapped cache.

line is fetched from memory and stored in the cache cell with the valid bit set to 1 and the Tag field extracted from the address and stored as well.

If another request asks for a byte in the same line, it will be a hit. The system extracts the Line field from the address, goes to that line in the cache and determines that the Valid bit is 1 and that the Tag field of the request matches the Tag field stored in the cache cell. It extracts the byte or word from the Data part of the cache cell and gives it to the CPU without a memory read. If the Valid bit is 1 but the Tag fields do not match, it is a miss. A memory request is necessary, and the Tag and Data fields replace the old ones in the same cache cell.

Example 12.6 The CPU requests the byte at address 3519 (dec). What are the nine bits of the Tag field, what are the four bits of the Byte field, and which cell of the cache stores the data? Converting to binary and extracting the fields gives

3519 (dec) = 000011011 011 1111 (bin)

The nine bits in the Tag field are 000011011, the four bits in the Byte field are 1111, and the data is stored at address 011 (bin) = 3 (dec) in the cache. ■

Figure 12.32 shows that the blocks of memory at addresses 16, 144, 272, ..., all contend for the same cache entry at address 1. Because there are nine bits in the Tag field, there are $2^9 = 512$ blocks in memory that contend for each cache cell, which can hold only one at a time. There is a pattern of requests resulting in a high cache miss rate that arises from switching back and forth between two fixed areas of memory. An example is a program with pointers on the run-time stack at high memory in Pep/8 and the heap at low memory. A program that accesses pointers and the cells to which they point will have such an access pattern. If it happens that the pointer and the cell to which it points have the same Line field in their addresses, the miss rate will increase substantially.

Set associative caches are designed to alleviate this problem. Instead of having each cache entry hold just one cache line from memory, it can hold several. Figure 12.33(a) shows a four-way set-associative cache. It duplicates the cache of Figure 12.32 four times and allows a set of up to four blocks of memory with the same Line fields to be in the cache at any time. The access circuitry is more complex than the circuitry for a direct-mapped cache. For each read request, the hardware must check all four parts of the cache cell in parallel and route the one with the matching Line field if there is one.

Figure 12.33(b) shows the details of the read circuit. The circle with the equals sign is a comparator that outputs 1 if the inputs are equal and 0 otherwise. The bank of 128 multiplexers is simpler than usual. Four-input multiplexers usually have two select lines that must be decoded, but the four select lines of this multiplexer are already decoded. The output labeled Hit is 1 on a cache hit, in which case the output labeled Data is the data from the cache line with the same Tag field as the one in the requested address. Otherwise Hit is 0.

Another complication with set-associative caches is the decision that must be made when a cache miss occurs and all four parts of the cache cell are occupied. The question is, which of the four parts should be overwritten by the new data from memory? One technique is to use the Least Recently Used (LRU) algorithm. In a two-way, set-associative cache, only one extra bit is required per cache cell to keep track of which cell was least recently used. But in a four-way set-associative cache, it is considerably more complicated to keep track of the least recently used. You must maintain a list of four items in order of use and update the list on every cache request. One approximation to LRU for a four-way cache uses three bits. One bit specifies which group was least recently used, and the bits within each group specify which item in that group was least recently used.

Regardless of whether the cache is direct-mapped or set-associative, system designers must decide how to handle memory writes with caches. There are two possibilities with cache hits:

- Write through—Every write request updates the cache and the corresponding block in memory.
- Write back—A write request only updates the cache copy. A write to memory only happens when the cache line is replaced.

Two cache write policies with cache hits

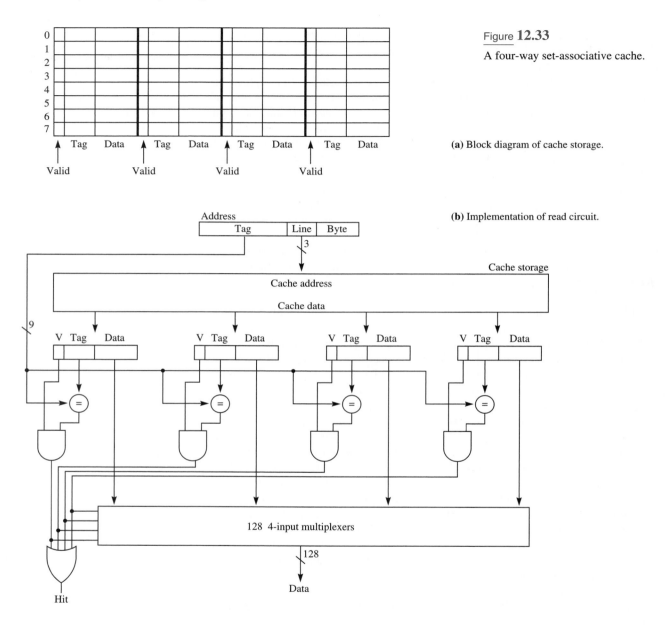

Figure 12.33

A four-way set-associative cache.

(a) Block diagram of cache storage.

(b) Implementation of read circuit.

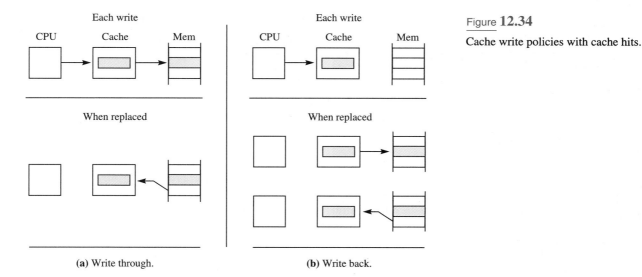

Figure **12.34**

Cache write policies with cache hits.

Figure 12.34 shows the two possibilities. Write through is the simpler design. While the system is writing to memory, the CPU can continue processing. When the cache line needs to be replaced, the value in memory is guaranteed to already have the latest update. The problem is an excessive amount of bus traffic when you get a burst of write requests. Write back minimizes the bus traffic, which could otherwise affect performance of other components wanting to use the main system bus. At any given point in time, however, memory does not have the most recent copy of the current value of the variable. Also, there is a delay when the cache line must be replaced, because memory must be updated before the new data can be loaded into the cache. By design, this event should happen rarely with a high percentage of cache hits.

Another issue to resolve with caches is what to do with a write request in conjunction with a cache miss. The policy known as write allocation brings the block from memory into the cache, possibly replacing another cache line, and then updates the cache line according to its normal cache write strategy. Without write allocation, a memory write is initiated bypassing the cache altogether. The idea here is that the CPU can continue its processing concurrently with the completion of the memory write.

Figure 12.35 shows the cache write policies without and with write allocation. Although either cache write policy with cache misses can be combined with either cache write policy with cache hits, write allocation is normally used in caches with write back for cache hits. Write through caches also tend to not use write allocation as it keeps the design simple. Parts (a) and (b) of Figures 12.34 and 12.35 thus correspond to the design choices of most caches.

The discussion of cache memories should sound familiar if you have read the discussion of virtual memory in Section 9.2. In the same way that the motivation behind virtual memory is the mismatch between the small size of main memory and

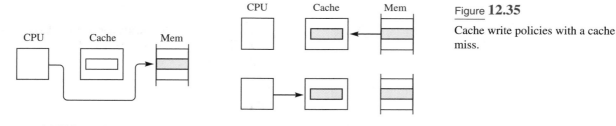

(a) Without write allocation.   **(b)** With write allocation.

Figure **12.35**
Cache write policies with a cache miss.

the size of an executable program stored on a hard drive, the motivation behind caches is the mismatch between the small size of the cache and the size of main memory. The LRU page replacement policy in a virtual memory system corresponds to the LRU replacement policy of a cache line. Cache is to main memory as main memory is to disk. In both cases, there is a *memory hierarchy* that spans two extremes of a small high-speed memory subsystem that must interface with a large low-speed memory subsystem. Design solutions in both hierarchies rely on locality of reference. It is no accident that designs in both fields have common issues and solutions. Another indication of the universality of these principles is the hash table data structure in software. In Figure 12.32, you should have recognized the mapping from main memory to cache as essentially a hash function. Set-associative caches even look like hash tables where you resolve collisions by chaining, albeit with an upper limit on the length of the chain.

Memory hierarchies

MIPS Computer Organization

Figure 12.36 shows the data section of the MIPS CPU. It has the same basic organization as the data section of Pep/8 in Figure 12.2 with an ABus and BBus that feed through the primary ALU, whose output eventually goes over the CBus to the bank of CPU registers. A significant difference in the organization is the L1 instruction and data caches in the path. As most cache memories exhibit a hit rate above 90%, we can assume that memory reads and writes operate at full CPU speed. There are no MemRead or MemWrite delays, except on those rare occasions when you get a cache miss.

Unlike Pep/8, the program counter is not one of the general registers in the register bank. The box labeled Plus4 in the figure adds 4 to the PC and routes it back to the PC through the two multiplexers PCMax and JMux. Because all instructions are exactly four bytes long, the increment part of the von Neumann cycle is simpler than that of Pep/8, and can be implemented with a specialized hardware unit without tying up the main ALU or consuming cycles. Branch instructions use PC-relative addressing where the branch address is computed by adding the 16-bit address field with sign extension to the incremented PC. The ASL2 box in the Ex section of Figure 12.36 shifts the address because the address field in the instruction does not store the two least significant bits. Those bits will always be zero because

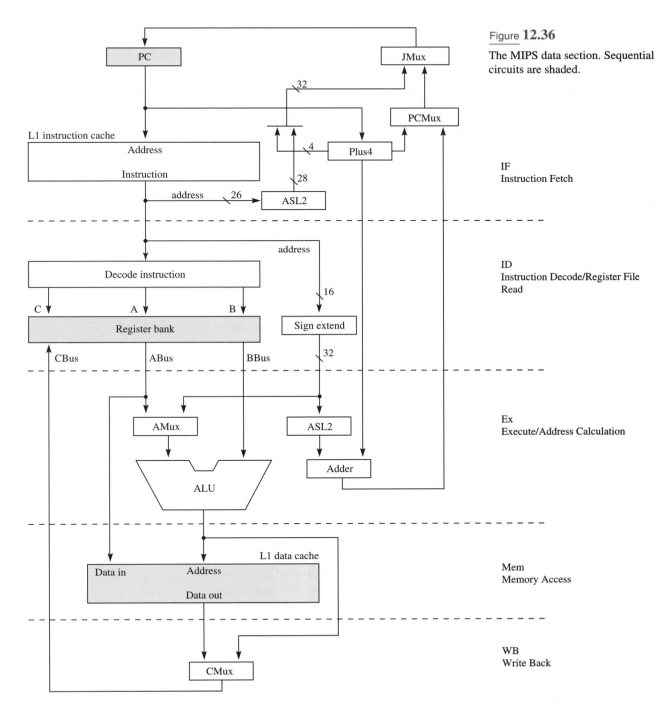

Figure **12.36**

The MIPS data section. Sequential circuits are shaded.

addresses are required to be four-byte aligned in memory. The shift by two corresponds to the multiply by four in Figure 12.26.

The jump instruction uses pseudodirect addressing. The ASL2 box in the IF section of Figure 12.36 shifts the address two places to the left with the result concatenated with the first four (high-order) bits of the incremented PC. This is the hardware implementation with special-purpose circuits of the pseudodirect addressing mode of Figure 12.26.

The CPU does not write to the instruction cache. It simply requests a read from the address specified by PC. The cache subsystem delivers the instruction from the cache immediately on a hit. On a miss, it delays the CPU and eventually reads the instruction from the L2 cache, writes it to the L1 cache, and notifies the CPU that it can continue. Because the CPU never writes to the instruction cache, it treats the cache as if it were a combinational circuit. That is why the instruction cache is not shaded.

The box labeled Register bank is a two-port bank of the 32-bit registers in Figure 12.24(a). The box labeled Decode instruction is a combinational circuit that takes as its input a 32-bit instruction. It decodes the opcode and sends the proper register address signals to A, B, and C, which are five-bit lines for addressing one of the 32 registers of Figure 12.24(a). The decode box has many control lines to the multiplexers and the ALU that are not shown in Figure 12.36.

PC is clocked on every cycle and drives the primary loop. The register bank and the data cache are not always clocked, depending on the instruction executed. There are three clocks for the three sequential circuits of Figure 12.36—PCCk for PC, LoadCk for the register bank, and DCCk for the L1 data cache.

The only purpose of the unconditional jump and conditional branch instructions is to alter the program counter. Figure 12.36 shows that all computations with PC are with specialized hardware units ASL2 to multiply PC by four and Plus4 to increment PC by four. The following examples assume the use of control lines analogous to the ones for Pep/8 in Figure 12.2, but not shown in Figure 12.36.

Example 12.7   The jump instruction uses pseudodirect addressing. Assuming the same convention for Mux control lines where 0 selects the left input and 1 selects the right input, the jump instruction requires the following control signals.

```
1. JMux=0; PCCk
```
Jump instruction

Before the cycle executes, PC has the address of the jump instruction, the 26-bit address field is presented to the ASL2 input, the first four bits of the incremented PC concatenated with the ASL2 output is presented to JMux, and the output of JMux is presented to PC. The clock pulse updates PC.   ∎

Example 12.8   The conditional branch instructions use PC-relative addressing and require the following control signals.

```
1. PCMux=1, JMux=1; PCCk
```
Branch instructions

Before the cycle executes, PC has the address of the conditional branch instruction, the 16-bit address field is presented to the ASL2 input, the ASL2 output and incremented PC are presented to the special purpose adder, the adder output is presented to PCMux, the PCMux output is presented to JMux, and the output of JMux is presented to PC. The clock pulse updates PC. ∎

The store instructions are facilitated by a clever arrangement of components in the data section. ABus provides a path from the register bank directly to the data input of the L1 data cache. Furthermore the output of the primary ALU output goes to the address lines of the data cache. Hence, the addition for the address computation of a store instruction is done by the primary ALU and not a special-purpose hardware unit. PC is updated and the data is written to the data cache simultaneously.

Example 12.9   The store word instruction sw has RTL specification

Mem [rb + address] ← rt

Because it updates PC and writes to memory, the cycle requires simultaneous clock pulses PCCk and DCCk. The control signals are

1. PCMux=0, JMux=1, A=rt, AMux=1, B=rb, ALU=A plus B; PCCk, DCCk   *Store instruction*

The PCMux=0 and JMux=1 signals simply present the incremented PC to PC. The A=rt signal puts the content of the rt source register on ABus, which is presented as data to the cache. The AMux=1 signal selects the address field of the instruction as the left input to the ALU, and the B=rb signal puts the base register on BBus as the right input to the ALU. Selecting the addition function presents the address computation on the address lines of the data cache. ∎

The register instructions use the primary ALU for their processing but do not write to memory. Therefore, the output of the ALU has a path through CMux to the register bank. As with store instructions, PC and the register bank are updated simultaneously.

Example 12.10   The add instruction add has RTL specification

rd ← rs + rt

Because it updates PC and writes to the memory bank, the cycle requires simultaneous clock pulses PCCk and LoadCk. The control signals are

1. PCMux=0, JMux=1, A=rs, AMux=0, B=rt, ALU=A plus B, CMux=0, C=rd;   *Add instruction*
PCCk, LoadCk

The PCMux=0 and JMux=1 signals present the incremented PC to PC. The A=rs signal puts the content of the rs source register on ABus, which is presented as data to the cache through AMux with the AMux=0 signal. The B=rt signal puts the base register on BBus as the right input to the ALU. Selecting the addition function presents the result on CBus through CMux with the CMux=0 signal. Signal C=rd addresses the register bank for the destination register rd.   ∎

The control signals for the load instructions are left as an exercise at the end of the chapter.

Pipelining

The instant PC changes at the beginning of a cycle, the data must propagate from it through the combinational circuits in the following order:

- IF: The instruction cache, the Plus4 adder, the shifter and multiplexers
- ID: The Decode instruction box, the Register bank, the sign extend box
- Ex: The AMux, the ASL2 shifter, the ALU, the Adder
- Mem: The data cache
- WB: The CMux, the address decoder of the Register bank.

The CPU designers must set the period of the clock long enough to allow for the data to be presented to the sequential circuits—PC, Register bank, and data cache—before clocking the data into them. Figure 12.37 shows a time line of several instructions executing, one after the other. The boxes represent the propagation time of each stage.

The situation in Figure 12.37 is analogous to a single craftsman who must build a piece of furniture. He has a shop with all the tools to do three things—cut the wood, assemble with clamps and glue, and paint. As there is only one craftsman, he builds his furniture in the same sequence, one piece of furniture after the other. With two other craftsmen there are several ways to increase the number of pieces produced per day. The other craftsmen could acquire their own tools, and all three could work concurrently, cutting the wood for three pieces at the same time, assembling the three pieces at the same time, and painting them at the same time. It is true that output per time is tripled, but at the cost of all those extra tools.

The assembly line analogy

Figure **12.37**

Instruction execution without pipelining.

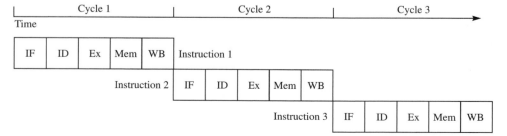

A more economical alternative is to recognize that when one person is using the clamps and glue, the tools for cutting the wood could be used for starting the next piece of furniture. Similarly, when the first piece is being painted, the second can be assembled and the wood for the first can be cut. You should recognize this organization as the basis of the factory assembly line.

The resources corresponding to the tools are the combinational circuits in the five areas listed above—instruction fetch, instruction decode/register file read, execute/address calculation, memory access, and write back. The idea of our CPU pipeline is to increase the number of cycles it takes to execute an instruction by a factor of five, but to decrease the period of each cycle by a factor of five. It might seem at first glance that there would be no net benefit. But by overlapping the execution of one instruction with the next, you get parallelism that increases the number of instructions executed per second.

To implement this idea requires a modification to the data path of Figure 12.36. The results of each stage must be saved to be used as input for the next stage. At the boundary of each of the five sections you must put a set of registers, as Figure 12.38 shows. At the end of each new shortened cycle, the data from every data path that crosses to the next stage below it gets stored in a boundary register.

You can get a perfect five-times decrease in the cycle time only if the propagation delays at each stage are exactly equal. In fact, they are not. So the new cycle time must be the propagation time of the lengthiest delay of all the shortened stages. When choosing where to put the boundary registers to implement a pipeline, a designer must strive to evenly divide the stages.

Figure 12.39 shows how pipelining works. At startup the pipeline is empty. In cycle 1, the first instruction is fetched. In cycle 2, the second instruction is fetched concurrently with the first instruction being decoded and the register bank being read. In cycle 3, the third instruction is fetched concurrently with the second instruction being decoded and the register bank being read and the first instruction executing, and so on. The speedup comes from putting more parts of the circuit to use at the same time. Pipelining is a form of parallelism. In theory, a perfect pipeline with five stages increases by 500% the number of instructions executing per second, once the pipeline is filled.

That's the good news. The bad news is that a whole host of problems can throw a monkey wrench into this rosy scenario. There are two kinds of problems, called hazards:

- Control hazards from unconditional and conditional branches
- Data hazards from data dependencies between instructions

Each of these hazards is due to an instruction that cannot complete the task at one stage in the pipeline because it needs the result of a previous instruction that has not finished executing. A hazard causes the instruction that cannot continue to stall, which creates a bubble in the pipeline that must be flushed out before peak performance can be resumed.

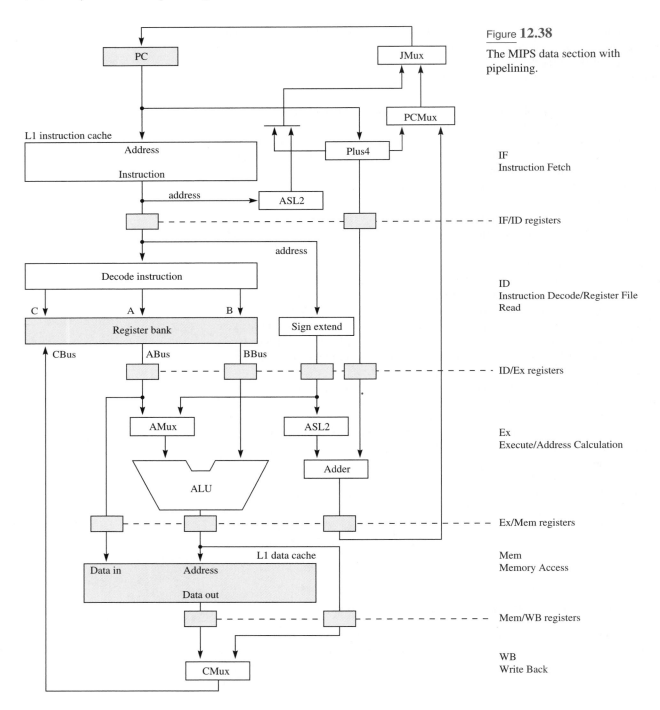

Figure **12.38**

The MIPS data section with pipelining.

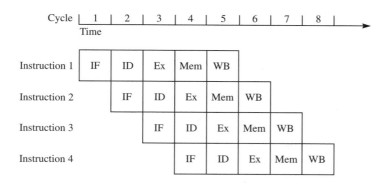

Figure **12.39**

Instruction execution with pipelining.

Figure 12.40(a) shows the execution of a pipeline from startup with no hazards. The second group of five boxes on the first line represents the sixth instruction to execute, the second on the second line represents the seventh, and so on. Starting with cycle 5, the pipeline operates at peak efficiency.

| 1 | 2 | 3 | 4 | 5 | 6 | 7 | 8 | 9 |10|11|12|13|14|15|16|17|18|19|20|21|22|23|24|25|26|

(a) No hazards.

Figure **12.40**

The effect of a hazard on a pipeline.

| 1 | 2 | 3 | 4 | 5 | 6 | 7 | 8 | 9 |10|11|12|13|14|15|16|17|18|19|20|21|22|23|24|25|26|

(b) A branch hazard.

Consider what happens when a branch instruction executes. Suppose instruction 7, which starts at cycle 7 on the second line, is a branch instruction. Assuming that the updated program counter is not available for the next instruction until the completion of this instruction, instruction 8 and every instruction after it must stall. Figure 12.40(b) shows the bubble as not shaded. The effect is as if the pipeline must start over at cycle 12. Figure 12.41 shows that branch instructions account for 15% of executing statements in a typical program on a MIPS machine. So roughly every seventh instruction must delay four cycles.

Figure **12.41**

Frequency of execution of MIPS instructions.

Instruction	Frequency
Arithmetic	50%
Load/Store	35%
Branch	15%

There are several ways to reduce the penalty of a control hazard. Figure 12.40(b) assumes that the result of the branch instruction is not available until after the write back stage. But branch instructions do not modify the register bank. So, to decrease the length of the bubble the system could eliminate the write back stage of branch instructions under the assumption that the next instruction has been delayed. The extra control hardware to do that would decrease the length of the bubble from four cycles to three.

Eliminate the write back stage of the branch instructions.

Conditional branches present another opportunity to minimize the effects of the hazard. Suppose the branch penalty is three cycles with the addition of the extra control hardware, and the computer is executing the following MIPS program:

```
beq  $s1,$s2,4
add  $s3,$s3,$s4
sub  $s5,$s5,$s6
andi $s7,$s7,15
sll  $s0,$s0,2
ori  $s3,$s3,1
```

The first instruction is a branch if equal. The address field is 4, which means a branch to the fourth instruction after the next one. Consequently, if the branch is taken, it will be to the `ori` instruction. If the branch is not taken, `add` will execute next.

Figure 12.40(b) shows a lot of wasted parallelism. While the bubble is being flushed out of the pipeline, many stages are idle. You do not know whether you should be executing `add`, `sub`, and `andi` while waiting for the results of `beq`. But you can execute them anyway assuming that the branch is not taken. If the branch is in fact not taken, you have eliminated the bubble altogether. If it is taken, you are no worse off in terms of bubble delay than you would have been if you had not started the instruction after `beq`. In that case, flush the bubble from the pipeline.

Assume conditional branches are not taken.

The problem is the circuitry required to clean up your mess if your assumption is wrong and the branch is taken. You must keep track of any instructions in the interim, before you discover whether the branch is taken, and not allow them to irreversibly modify the data cache or register bank. When you discover that the branch is not taken, you can commit to those changes.

Assuming the branch is not taken is really a crude form of predicting the future. It is like going to the race track and betting on the same horse regardless of previous outcomes. You can let history be your guide with a technique known as *dynamic branch prediction*. When a branch statement executes, keep track of whether the branch is taken or not. If it is taken, store its destination address. The next time the instruction executes, predict the same outcome. If it was taken the previous time, continue filling the pipeline with the instructions at the branch destination. If it was not, fill the pipeline with the instructions following the branch instruction.

Dynamic branch prediction

The scheme described above is called one-bit branch prediction because one bit is necessary to keep track of whether the branch was taken or not. A one-bit storage

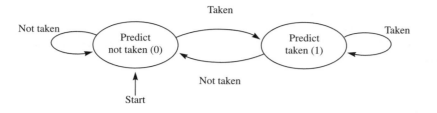

Figure **12.42**

The state transition diagram for
one-bit dynamic branch prediction.

cell defines a finite state machine with two states, corresponding to whether you predict the branch will be taken or not. Figure 12.42 shows the finite state machine.

Using the race track analogy, perhaps you should not be so quick to change the horse to bet on. Suppose the same horse you have been betting on has won three times in a row. The next time out, another horse wins. Would you really want to change your bet to the other horse based on only one result, discounting the history of previous wins? It is similar to what happens when you have a program with nested loops. Suppose the inner loop executes four times each time the outer loop executes once. The compiler translates the code for the inner loop with a conditional branch that is taken four times in a row, followed by one branch not taken to terminate the loop. Here is the sequence of branches taken and the one-bit dynamic prediction based on Figure 12.42.

```
Taken:       Y  Y  Y  Y  N  Y  Y  Y  Y  N  Y  Y  Y  Y  N  Y  Y  Y  Y  N
Prediction:  N  Y  Y  Y  Y  N  Y  Y  Y  Y  N  Y  Y  Y  Y  N  Y  Y  Y  Y
Incorrect:   x           x  x           x  x           x  x           x
```

With one-bit dynamic branch prediction, the branch of every inner loop will always be mispredicted twice for each execution of the outer loop.

To overcome this deficiency it is common to use two bits to predict the next branch. The idea is that if you have a run of branches taken and you encounter one branch not taken, you do not change your prediction right away. The criterion to change is to get two consecutive branches not taken. Figure 12.43 shows that you can be in one of four states. The two shaded states are the ones where you have a run of two consecutive identical branch types—the two previous branches either both taken or both not taken. The states not shaded are for the situation where the two previous branches were different. If you have a run of branches taken, you are in state 00. If the next branch is not taken, you go to state 01, but still predict the branch after that will be taken. A trace of the finite state machine of Figure 12.43 with the branch sequence above shows that the prediction is correct every time after the outer loop gets started.

Another technique used on deep pipelines, where the penalty would be more severe if your branch assumption is not correct, is to have duplicate pipelines with duplicate program counters, fetch circuitry, and all the rest. When you decode a branch instruction, you initiate both pipelines, filling one with instructions assuming

Build two pipelines.

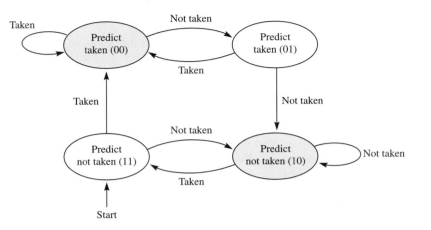

Figure **12.43**

The state transition diagram for two-bit dynamic branch prediction.

the branch is not taken and the other assuming it is. When you find out which pipeline is valid, you discard the other and continue on. This solution is quite expensive, but you have no bubbles regardless of whether the branch is taken or not.

A data hazard happens when one instruction needs the result of a previous instruction and must stall until it gets it. It is called a read-after-write (RAW) hazard. An example is the code sequence

```
add $s2,$s2,$s3  # write $s2
sub $s4,$s4,$s2  # read $s2
```

A RAW data hazard

The add instruction changes the value of $s2, which is used in the sub instruction. Figure 12.38 shows that the add instruction will update the value of $s2 at the end of the write back stage, WB. Also, the sub instruction reads from the register bank at the end of the instruction decode/register file read stage, ID. Figure 12.44(b) shows how the two instructions must overlap with the data hazard. The sub instruction's ID

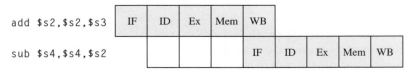

(a) Consecutive instructions without a RAW hazard.

(b) Consecutive instructions with a RAW hazard.

Figure **12.44**

The effect of a RAW data hazard on a pipeline.

stage must come after the `add` instruction's WB stage. The result is that the `sub` instruction must stall, creating a three-cycle bubble.

If there were another instruction with no hazard between `add` and `sub`, the bubble would be only two cycles long. With two hazardless instructions between them the bubble gets reduced to one cycle in length, and with three it disappears altogether. This observation brings up a possibility. If you could find some hazardless instructions nearby that needed to be executed sometime anyway, why not just execute them out of order, sticking them in between the `add` and `sub` instructions to fill up the bubble? You might object that mixing up the order in which instructions are executed will change the results of the algorithm. That is true in some cases, but not in all. If there are many arithmetic operations in a block of code, an optimizing compiler can analyze the data dependencies and rearrange the statements to reduce the bubbles in the pipeline without changing the result of the algorithm. Alternatively, a human assembly language programmer can do the same thing.

Instruction reordering

This is an example of the price to be paid for abstraction. A level of abstraction is supposed to simplify computation at one level by hiding the details at a lower level. It would certainly be simpler if the assembly language programmer or the compiler designer could generate assembly language statements in the most convenient order at Level ISA3, without knowing the details of the pipeline at Level LG1. Adding a level of abstraction always comes with a performance penalty. The question is whether the performance penalty is worth the benefits that come with the simplicity. Using the details of Level LG1 is a tradeoff of the simplicity of abstraction for performance. Another example of the same tradeoff is to design ISA3 programs taking into account the properties of the cache subsystem.

Trading off abstraction for performance

Another technique called *data forwarding* can alleviate data hazards. Figure 12.38 shows that the results of the add instruction from the ALU are clocked into an Ex/Mem boundary register at the conclusion of the Ex stage. For the add instruction, it is simply clocked into a Mem/WB boundary register at the end of the Mem stage and finally into the register bank at the end of the WB stage. If you set up a data path between the Ex/Mem register containing the result of the `add` and one of the ID/Ex registers from which `sub` would normally get the result from the register bank, then the only alignment requirement in Figure 12.44(b) is that the ID stage of `sub` follows the Ex stage of `add`. Doing so still leaves a bubble, but it is only one cycle long.

Data forwarding

A *superscalar* design exploits the idea that two instructions with no data dependencies can execute in parallel. Figure 12.45 shows two approaches. In part (a), you simply build two separate pipelines. There is one fetch unit that is fast enough to fetch more than one instruction in one cycle. It can issue up to two instructions per cycle concurrently. Scheduling is complex, because data dependencies across the two pipelines must be managed.

Superscalar machines

Figure 12.45(b) is based on the fact that the execution unit Ex is usually the weakest link in the chain, because its propagation delays are longer than those in the other stages in the pipeline. Floating-point units are particularly time consuming compared to integer processing circuits. The box labeled FP in the figure is a

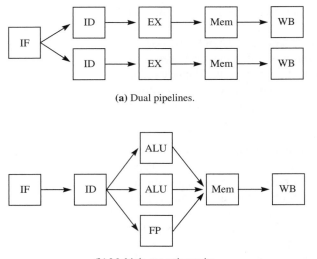

(a) Dual pipelines.

(b) Multiple execution units.

Figure **12.45**

Superscalar machines.

floating-point unit that implements IEEE 754. Each one of the execution units can be three times slower than the other stages in the pipeline. But, if their inputs and outputs are staggered in time and they work in parallel, the execution stage will not slow down the pipeline.

With superscalar machines, the instruction scheduler must consider other types of data hazards. A write after read (WAR) hazard occurs when one instruction writes to a register after the previous one reads it. An example is the following MIPS code.

```
add $s3,$s3,$s2  # read $s2
sub $s2,$s4,$s5  # write $s2
```

A WAR data hazard

In the pipelined machine of Figure 12.38, this sequence is not a hazard, because add clocks $s2 into the ID/Ex register at the end of its ID stage, and sub writes it at the end of its WB stage. A superscalar machine reorders instructions to minimize bubbles, so it might start the execution of sub before it starts add. If it does so, it must ensure that the WB stage of sub comes after the ID stage of add.

In a perfect pipeline, increasing the clock frequency by a factor of k using a pipeline with k stages increases the performance by a factor of k. What is to prevent you from carrying this design to its logical conclusion with a cycle time equal to one gate delay? All the complexities from control hazards and data hazards that reduce the performance from the ideal. There comes a point where increasing the length of the pipeline and increasing the frequency decreases performance.

But there is one more benefit to increasing the clock frequency—advertising. The megahertz rating on personal computers can be a big factor in a consumer's mind when making a decision of which computer to purchase. The *megahertz myth* says that of two machines with two different megahertz ratings, the one with more megahertz has higher performance. You can now understand why the myth is not true. Increasing the frequency by increasing the number of stages in the pipeline increases the hazard performance penalties. The question is how effective the design is in combating those penalties. Using megahertz as a measure of performance also neglects the interplay between the factors of Figure 12.21. The ultimate question is not just how many cycles per second your CPU can crank out. It is also how much useful work is done per cycle to get the program executed.

The megahertz myth

At this time in computing history, pipelining technology has hit a plateau. Although advances in clock speed still occur in commercial CPU chips, they do not do so at the same pace as before. Moore's Law continues to hold, with digital circuit engineers providing more total gates per square millimeter on the chips. But the current trend in CPU design is to use the extra circuitry to simply duplicate the entire CPU, fitting two to four CPUs called "cores" into a single package. This trend is expected to accelerate in the future. The big challenge will be for software designers to use parallel programming techniques, like those introduced in Section 8.3, to harness the power provided by these multi-core CPU chips.

Future trends

12.4 Conclusion

Pep/8 illustrates the fundamental nature of a von Neumann computer. The data section consists of combinational and sequential circuits. It is one big finite state machine. Input to the data section consists of data from main memory and control signals from the control section. Output from the data section is also sent to main memory and the control section. Each time the control section sends a clock pulse to a state register, the machine makes a transition to a different state.

In a real computer, the number of states is huge but finite. The Pep/8 data section of Figure 12.2 has 24 writable eight-bit registers and four status bits, for a total of 192 bits of storage, or 2^{192} states. With 8 inputs from the data lines on the main system bus and 32 control inputs from the control section, the number of transitions from each state is 2^{40}. The total number of transitions is 2^{192} times 2^{40}, or $2^{232} = 10^{70}$. The number of atoms in the earth is estimated to be only about 10^{50}. And Pep/8 is a tiny computer! At the most fundamental level, no matter how complex the system, computing is nothing more than executing a finite state machine with peripheral storage.

Finite state machines are the basis of all computing.

Simplifications in the Model

The Pep/8 computer illustrates the basic organizational idea behind all real von Neumann machines. Of course, many simplifications are made to keep the machine easy to understand.

One low-level detail that is different in real hardware implementations is the use of edge-triggered flip-flops throughout the integrated circuit instead of master–slave. Both kinds of flip-flop solve the feedback problem. Because the master–slave principle is easier to understand than the edge-triggered principle, that is the one that is carried throughout the presentation.

Another simplification is the interface of the CPU and main memory with the main system bus. With real computers, the timing constraints are more complex than simply putting the addresses on the bus, waiting for two cycles with MemRead asserted, and assuming that data can be clocked into MDR. A single memory access requires more than just two cycles, and there is a protocol that specifies in more detail how long the address lines must be asserted and precisely when the data must be clocked into a register on the CPU side.

Another issue with the main system bus is how it is shared among the CPU, main memory, and the peripheral devices. In practice, the CPU is not always in control of the bus. Instead, the bus has its own processor that arbitrates between competing devices when too many of them want to use the bus at the same time. An example is with *direct memory access* (DMA) in which data flows directly from a   *Direct memory access* disk over the bus to main memory not under control of the CPU. The advantage of DMA is that the CPU can spend its cycles doing useful work executing programs without diverting them to control the peripherals.

Other topics beyond the scope of this book include assembler macros, linkers, popular peripheral buses like USB and Firewire, supercomputers, and the whole field of computer networks. When you study computer networks you will find that abstraction is central. Computer systems are designed as layers of abstraction with the details of each level hidden from the level above, and Internet communication protocols are designed the same way. Each level of abstraction exists to do one thing and provides a service to the next higher level with the details of how the service provided is being hidden.

The Big Picture

Now consider the big picture from Level App7 all the way down to Level LG1. Suppose a user is entering data in a database system with an application at Level App7. She wants to enter a numerical value, so she types it and executes an Enter command. What lies behind such a seemingly innocuous action?

A C++ programmer wrote the database system, including the procedure to input the numeric value. The C++ program was compiled to assembly language, which in turn was assembled into machine language. A compiler designer wrote the compiler, and an assembler designer wrote the assembler. The compiler and assembler, being automatic translators, both contain a lexical analysis phase, a parsing phase, and a code generating phase. The lexical analysis phase is based on finite state machines.

The C++ programmer also used a finite state machine in the numeric input procedure. The compiler translated each C++ statement in that procedure to many assembly language statements. The assembler, however, translated each assembly language statement into one machine language statement. So the code to process the user's Enter command was expanded into many C++ commands, each of which was expanded into many ISA3-level commands.

Each ISA3-level command in turn was translated into the control section signals to fetch the instruction and to execute it. Each control signal is input to a multiplexer or some other combinational device, or it is a pulse to clock a value into a state register. The sequential circuits are governed by the laws of finite state machines.

Each register is an array of flip-flops, and each flip-flop is a pair of latches designed with the master–slave principle. Each latch is a pair of NOR gates with simple cross-coupled feedback connections. Each combinational part of the data section is an interconnection of only a few different types of gates. The behavior of each gate is governed by the laws of boolean algebra. Ultimately, the user's Enter command translates into electrical signals that flow through the individual gates.

The user's Enter command may be interrupted by the operating system if it is executing in a multiprogramming system. The Enter command may generate a page fault, in which case the operating system may need to execute a page replacement algorithm to determine the page to copy back to disk.

Of course, all these events happen without the user getting any hint of what is going on at the lower levels of the system. Design inefficiencies at any level can tangibly slow the processing to the extent that the user may curse the computer. Remember that the design of the entire system from Level App7 to Level LG1 is constrained by the fundamental space/time tradeoff.

The connection between one signal flowing through a single gate in some multiplexer at Level LG1 and the user executing an Enter command at Level App7 may seem remote, but it does exist. Literally millions of gates must cooperate to perform a task for the user. So many devices can be organized into a useful machine only by structuring the system into successive levels of abstraction.

Levels of abstraction

It is remarkable that each level of abstraction consists of a few simple concepts. At Level LG1, either the NAND or NOR gate is sufficient to construct any combinational circuit. There are only four basic types of flip-flops, all of which can be produced from the SR flip-flop. The simple von Neumann cycle is the controlling force at Level ISA3 behind the operation of the machine. At Level OS4, a process is a running program that can be interrupted by storing its process control block. Assembly language at Level Asmb5 is a simple one-to-one translation to machine language. A high-order language at Level HOL6 is a one-to-many translation to a lower-level language.

The concept of a finite state machine permeates the entire level structure. Finite state machines are the basis of lexical analysis for automatic translators, and they also describe sequential circuits. The process control block stores the state of a process.

Finite state machines

All sciences have simplicity and structure as their goals. In the natural sciences, the endeavor is to discover the laws of nature that explain the most phenomena with the fewest number of mathematical laws or concepts. Computer scientists have also discovered that simplicity is the key to harnessing complexity. It is possible to construct a machine as complicated as a computer only because of the simple concepts that govern its behavior at every level of abstraction.

Simplicity is the key to harnessing complexity.

SUMMARY

The central processing unit is divided into a data section and a control section. The data section has a bank of registers, some or all of which are visible to the Level-ISA3 programmer. Processing occurs in a loop, with data coming from the register bank on the ABus and BBus, through the ALU, then back to the register bank on the CBus. Data is injected into the loop from main memory via the main system bus and the memory data register at the address specified by the memory address register.

The function of the control section is to send a sequence of control signals to the data section to implement the ISA3 instruction set. The machine is controlled by the von Neumann cycle—fetch, decode, increment, execute, repeat. In a CISC machine like Pep/8, the control signals must direct the data section to fetch the operand, which may take many cycles because of complex addressing modes. A RISC machine like MIPS has few addressing modes and simple instructions so that each instruction executes with only one cycle.

Two sources of increased performance are the fundamental space/time tradeoff and parallelism. Two general ways to use the space/time tradeoff are to allocate extra hardware (space) to increase the width of the data buses, or to deploy specialized hardware units, both of which can result in a decrease in execution time.

All performance enhancements are based on three components of execution time specified by the equation

$$\frac{\text{time}}{\text{program}} = \frac{\text{instructions}}{\text{program}} \times \frac{\text{cycles}}{\text{instruction}} \times \frac{\text{time}}{\text{cycle}}$$

Accumulator machines minimize the first factor at the expense of the second. Load/store machines minimize the second factor at the expense of the first. Both organizations can use the third factor to increase performance, primarily through pipelining.

Computers with complex instructions and many addressing modes were popular early in the history of computing. They are characterized by the Mc2 level of abstraction, in which the control section has its own micromemory, microprogram counter, and microinstruction register. The microprogram of the control section produces the control sequences to implement the ISA3 instruction set. A characteristic of load/store computers is the absence of Level Mc2 because each of its simple instructions can be implemented in one cycle.

Cache memory solves the problem of the extreme mismatch between the fast speed of the CPU and the slow speed of main memory. It relies on the spatial and temporal locality of reference present in all real programs. A cache is a small high-speed memory unit that contains a copy of data from main memory likely to be accessed by the CPU.

Pipelining is analogous to an assembly line in a factory. To implement a pipeline you subdivide the cycle by putting boundary registers in the data path of the data section. The effect is to increase the number of cycles per instruction but decrease the cycle time proportionally. When the pipeline is full you execute one instruction per cycle through the parallelism inherent in the pipeline. However, control hazards and data hazards decrease the performance from the theoretical ideal. Techniques to deal with hazards include branch prediction, instruction reordering, and data forwarding. Superscalar machines duplicate pipelines or execution units for greater parallelism.

EXERCISES

Section 12.1

1. Draw the individual lines of the 8-bit bus between MDR and the main memory bus. Show the tri-state buffers and the connection to the MemWrite line.

2. Design the three-input, one-output combinational circuit ANDZ of Figure 12.2. Minimize the circuit with a Karnaugh map. Consider both AND-OR and OR-AND implementations and pick the better one.

3. The text states that you can combine cycle 1 with cycle 3 in Figure 12.5 to speed up the von Neumann cycle. Can you combine cycle 1 with cycle 2 instead? Explain.

4. The text states that you can decrease the number of cycles from seven to four in Figure 12.5. Write the control signals to fetch the instruction specifier and increment the PC by one with four cycles.

5. Write the control sequence for the von Neumann cycle to fetch the operand specifier and increment PC accordingly. Assume that the instruction specifier has already been fetched, and the control section has already determined that the instruction is nonunary.

6. The text states that you can decrease the number of cycles from 21 to 17 in Figure 12.10. Write the control signals to implement the LDX instruction with indirect addressing with 17 cycles.

7. For each of the following ISA instructions, (1) write down its RTL specification, and (2) write the control sequence to implement it. Assume that the instruction has been fetched, including the operand specifier if nonunary, and that register T1 has a copy of the status bits.

*(a)	STBYTEA there,n		(b)	STBYTEA there,s
(c)	STBYTEA there,sf		(d)	STBYTEA there,x
(e)	STBYTEA there,sx		(f)	STBYTEA there,sxf
(g)	BR there		(h)	CALL there
(i)	NOTA		(j)	NEGA
(k)	ROLA		(l)	RORA
(m)	RET4		(n)	ADDSP this,i
(o)	SUBSP this,i		(p)	SUBA this,i
(q)	ANDA this,i		(r)	ORA this,i
(s)	CPA this,i		(t)	LDBYTEA this,i
(u)	LDBYTEA this,d		(v)	MOVSPA
(w)	MOVFLGA		(x)	RETTR

8. Write the control sequence to execute the instruction DECO num,i. Assume that the instruction has been fetched. Remember that this instruction has an unimplemented opcode. You may wish to review traps in Section 8.2.

Section 12.2

*9. The text predicts that we will never need to transition from 64-bit computers to 128-bit computers because we will never need main memories bigger that 16 billion GBytes. Silicon crystals have a plane consisting of 0.5 nm square tiles, each tile containing two atoms. **(a)** Assuming that you could manufacture a memory so dense as to store one bit per atom on one plane of silicon atoms (and neglecting the interconnection issues with the wires), how long would be the side of a square chip necessary to store the maximum number of bytes addressable by a 64-bit computer? Show your calculation. **(b)** Does this calculation support the prediction? Explain.

10. Design the 33-input, 16-output address Incrementer of Figure 12.17. Draw the logic diagram using half adders to implement a ripple-carry addition for the increment. You may use ellipses (...).

11. Write the control sequence to execute each of the statements in Exercise 7 assuming the address Incrementer in Figure 12.17.

12. Assuming that you have worked Exercises 7 and 11, for each statement compute the percentage savings in the number of cycles as a result of the address Incrementer.

13. Write the control sequence to execute each of the statements in Exercise 7 assuming the two-byte MDR in Figure 12.19. Assume that all addresses and word operands are at even addresses and all byte operands are at odd addresses.

14. Assuming that you have worked Exercises 7 and 13, for each statement compute the percentage savings in the number of cycles as a result of the two-byte MDR.

15. The ASLA instruction does an arithmetic shift left of the accumulator and puts the result back in the accumulator. The RTL specification of ASLA shows that, unlike ASRA, the V bit is set to indicate an overflow when the quantity is interpreted as a signed integer. An overflow occurs if the sign of the original value differs from the sign of the shifted value. After the shift, C contains the sign of the original value, and N contains the sign of the shifted value. So, the V bit can be computed as $V = C \oplus N$. Fortunately, the XOR function is available in the Pep/8 ALU. **(a)** Write the sequence of control statements to implement ASLA. You will need to get copies of the status bits and shift them so that both copies have C and N in the position for V. You can then XOR the copies and store the Z bit. Use the fewest number of cycles possible. **(b)** You can compute V for the ASL instruction in one cycle with the right hardware. Design a specialized hardware unit that does so. **(c)** Write the control sequence to implement ASLA with your new circuit. It should take two cycles for the shift itself and one more cycle to set V. **(d)** What is the percentage decrease in the number of cycles with your new design? **(e)** Discuss the ramifications of the hardware unit on the rest of the CPU design. **(f)** Given that the hardware speeds up the computation of the V bit for only one instruction in the instruction set, do you think your hardware modification would be worth the speedup? Explain.

*16. **(a)** Suppose a C++ compiler for the MIPS machine associates $s4 with array a. $s5 with variable g, and $s6 with array b. How does it translate

```
a[4] = g + b[5];
```

into MIPS assembly language? **(b)** Write the machine language translation of the instructions in part (a).

17. **(a)** Write the MIPS assembly language statement to shift the content of register $s2 nine bits to the left and put the result in $t5. **(b)** Write the machine language translation of the instruction in (a).

18. **(a)** Suppose a C++ compiler for the MIPS machine associates $s4 with variable g, $s5 with array a, and $s6 with variable i. How does it translate

    ```
    g = a[i];
    ```

    into MIPS assembly language? **(b)** Write the machine language translation of the instructions in part (a).

19. **(a)** Suppose a C++ compiler for the MIPS machine associates $s4 with variable g, $s5 with array a, and $s6 with variable i. How does it translate

    ```
    a[i] = g;
    ```

    into MIPS assembly language? **(b)** Write the machine language translation of the instructions in part (a).

20. **(a)** Suppose a C++ compiler for the MIPS machine associates $s4 with variable g, $s5 with array a, and $s6 with variable i. How does it translate

    ```
    g = a[i+3];
    ```

    into MIPS assembly language? **(b)** Write the machine language translation of the instructions in part (a).

21. **(a)** Suppose a C++ compiler for the MIPS machine associates $s5 with array a and $s6 with variable i. How does it translate

    ```
    a[i] = a[i+1];
    ```

    into MIPS assembly language? **(b)** Write the machine language translation of the instructions in part (a).

22. **(a)** Write the MIPS assembly language statement to allocate 12 bytes of storage on the run-time stack. **(b)** Write the machine language translation of the instruction in part (a).

23. Suppose a C++ compiler for the MIPS machine associates $s5 with variable g. How does it translate

    ```
    g = 529371;
    ```

    into MIPS assembly language? **(b)** Write the machine language translation of the instructions in part (a).

24. The CPU requests the byte at address 4675 (dec) with the cache of Figure 12.32. **(a)** What are the nine bits of the tag field? **(b)** What are the four bits of the byte field? **(c)** Which cell of the cache stored the data?

25. A CPU can address 16 MBytes of main memory. It has a direct-mapped cache in which it stores 256 8-byte cache lines. **(a)** How many bits are required for a memory address? **(b)** How many bits are required for the byte field of the address? **(c)** How many bits are required for the line field of the address? **(d)** How many bits are required for the tag field of the address? **(e)** How many bits are required for the data field of each cache entry? **(f)**

How many bits total are required for all the fields of one cache entry? **(g)** How many bits total are required for the entire cache?

26. The CPU of Exercise 25 has a two-way set-associative cache, again with 256 8-byte cache lines. How many bits are required for each cache entry?

27. In Figure 12.33, **(a)** draw the implementation of a comparator, the circle with the equals sign. (*Hint:* Consider the truth table of an XOR followed by an inverter, sometimes called an XNOR gate.) **(b)** Draw the implementation of the 32 four-input multiplexers. You may use ellipses (...) in both parts of the exercise.

28. A direct-mapped cache is at one extreme of cache designs, with set-associative caches in the middle. At the opposite extreme is the *fully-associative cache* where there is in essence only one entry in the cache of Figure 12.32, and the line field of the address has zero bits. That is, it is missing altogether, and an address consists of only the tag field and the byte field. **(a)** In Figure 12.33, instead of having 8 cache cells, each with 4 lines, you could use the same number of bits with 1 cache cell having 32 lines. Would this design increase the cache hit percentage over that in Figure 12.33? Explain. **(b)** How many comparitors in the read circuit would be required for the cache of part (a)?   *Fully-associative caches*

29. Suppose a CPU can address 1 MByte of main memory. It has a fully-associative cache (see Exercise 28) with 16 32-byte cache lines. **(a)** How many bits are required for a memory address? **(b)** How many bits are required for the byte field of the address? **(c)** How many bits are required for the tag field of the address? **(d)** How many bits are required for the data field of each cache entry? **(e)** How many bits total are required for the entire cache?

30. **(a)** What is the RTL specification for the lw instruction? **(b)** For Figure 12.36, write the control signals to execute the lw instruction.

31. In Figure 12.38, **(a)** how many bits are in each of the two IF/ID boundary registers? **(b)** How many bits are in each of the four ID/Ex boundary registers? **(c)** How many bits are in each of the three Ex/Mem boundary registers? **(d)** How many bits are in each of the two Mem/WB boundary registers?

32. For Figure 12.40(b), place a checkmark for each circuit that is idle in each of the cycles in the table below, and list the total number of circuits that are idle for each cycle.

Cycle	7	8	9	10	11	12	13	14	15	16
IF										
ID										
Ex										
Mem										
WB										
Number idle										

33. Suppose the five-stage pipeline of Figure 12.40(a) executes a branch 15% of the time, each branch causing the next instruction that executes to stall until the completion of the branch, as in Figure 12.40(b). **(a)** What is the percentage increase in the number of cycles over the ideal pipeline with no bubbles? **(b)** Suppose an n stage pipeline executes a branch x% of the time, each branch causing the next instruction that executes to stall until the completion of the branch. What is the percentage increase in the number of cycles over the ideal pipeline with no bubbles?

34. The text states that you can eliminate the write back stage of an unconditional branch under the assumption that the next instruction has been delayed. **(a)** Draw cycles 7 through 16 of Figure 12.40(b) with that design. **(b)** Complete the table of Exercise 32 with that design.

35. **(a)** In Figure 12.42 for one-bit dynamic branch prediction, what pattern of Taken outcomes will produce the maximum percentage of incorrect predictions? What is the maximum percentage? **(b)** In Figure 12.43 for two-bit dynamic branch prediction, what pattern of Taken outcomes will produce the maximum percentage of incorrect predictions? What is the maximum percentage?

36. Construct the one-input finite state machine of Figure 12.43 to implement two-bit dynamic branch prediction. Minimize your circuit with a Karnaugh map. **(a)** Use two SR flip-flops. **(b)** Use two JK flip-flops. **(c)** Use two D flip-flops. **(d)** Use two T flip-flops.

Pep/8 Architecture

This appendix summarizes the architecture of the Pep/8 computer.

Figure **A.1**

The hexadecimal conversion chart.

	0	1	2	3	4	5	6	7	8	9	A	B	C	D	E	F
0_	0	1	2	3	4	5	6	7	8	9	10	11	12	13	14	15
1_	16	17	18	19	20	21	22	23	24	25	26	27	28	29	30	31
2_	32	33	34	35	36	37	38	39	40	41	42	43	44	45	46	47
3_	48	49	50	51	52	53	54	55	56	57	58	59	60	61	62	63
4_	64	65	66	67	68	69	70	71	72	73	74	75	76	77	78	79
5_	80	81	82	83	84	85	86	87	88	89	90	91	92	93	94	95
6_	96	97	98	99	100	101	102	103	104	105	106	107	108	109	110	111
7_	112	113	114	115	116	117	118	119	120	121	122	123	124	125	126	127
8_	128	129	130	131	132	133	134	135	136	137	138	139	140	141	142	143
9_	144	145	146	147	148	149	150	151	152	153	154	155	156	157	158	159
A_	160	161	162	163	164	165	166	167	168	169	170	171	172	173	174	175
B_	176	177	178	179	180	181	182	183	184	185	186	187	188	189	190	191
C_	192	193	194	195	196	197	198	199	200	201	202	203	204	205	206	207
D_	208	209	210	211	212	213	214	215	216	217	218	219	220	221	222	223
E_	224	225	226	227	228	229	230	231	232	233	234	235	236	237	238	239
F_	240	241	242	243	244	245	246	247	248	249	250	251	252	253	254	255

Hexadecimal	Binary	Hexadecimal	Binary	Hexadecimal	Binary	Hexadecimal	Binary
0	0000	4	0100	8	1000	C	1100
1	0001	5	0101	9	1001	D	1101
2	0010	6	0110	A	1010	E	1110
3	0011	7	0111	B	1011	F	1111

Figure **A.2**

The relationship between hexadecimal and binary.

Char	Bin	Hex	Char	Bin	Hex	Char	Bin	Hex	Char	Bin	Hex
NUL	000 0000	00	SP	010 0000	20	@	100 0000	40	`	110 0000	60
SOH	000 0001	01	!	010 0001	21	A	100 0001	41	a	110 0001	61
STX	000 0010	02	"	010 0010	22	B	100 0010	42	b	110 0010	62
ETX	000 0011	03	#	010 0011	23	C	100 0011	43	c	110 0011	63
EOT	000 0100	04	$	010 0100	24	D	100 0100	44	d	110 0100	64
ENQ	000 0101	05	%	010 0101	25	E	100 0101	45	e	110 0101	65
ACK	000 0110	06	&	010 0110	26	F	100 0110	46	f	110 0110	66
BEL	000 0111	07	'	010 0111	27	G	100 0111	47	g	110 0111	67
BS	000 1000	08	(	010 1000	28	H	100 1000	48	h	110 1000	68
HT	000 1001	09	)	010 1001	29	I	100 1001	49	i	110 1001	69
LF	000 1010	0A	*	010 1010	2A	J	100 1010	4A	j	110 1010	6A
VT	000 1011	0B	+	010 1011	2B	K	100 1011	4B	k	110 1011	6B
FF	000 1100	0C	,	010 1100	2C	L	100 1100	4C	l	110 1100	6C
CR	000 1101	0D	-	010 1101	2D	M	100 1101	4D	m	110 1101	6D
SO	000 1110	0E	.	010 1110	2E	N	100 1110	4E	n	110 1110	6E
SI	000 1111	0F	/	010 1111	2F	O	100 1111	4F	o	110 1111	6F
DLE	001 0000	10	0	011 0000	30	P	101 0000	50	p	111 0000	70
DC1	001 0001	11	1	011 0001	31	Q	101 0001	51	q	111 0001	71
DC2	001 0010	12	2	011 0010	32	R	101 0010	52	r	111 0010	72
DC3	001 0011	13	3	011 0011	33	S	101 0011	53	s	111 0011	73
DC4	001 0100	14	4	011 0100	34	T	101 0100	54	t	111 0100	74
NAK	001 0101	15	5	011 0101	35	U	101 0101	55	u	111 0101	75
SYN	001 0110	16	6	011 0110	36	V	101 0110	56	v	111 0110	76
ETB	001 0111	17	7	011 0111	37	W	101 0111	57	w	111 0111	77
CAN	001 1000	18	8	011 1000	38	X	101 1000	58	x	111 1000	78
EM	001 1001	19	9	011 1001	39	Y	101 1001	59	y	111 1001	79
SUB	001 1010	1A	:	011 1010	3A	Z	101 1010	5A	z	111 1010	7A
ESC	001 1011	1B	;	011 1011	3B	[	101 1011	5B	{	111 1011	7B
FS	001 1100	1C	<	011 1100	3C	\	101 1100	5C			111 1100	7C
GS	001 1101	1D	=	011 1101	3D	]	101 1101	5D	}	111 1101	7D
RS	001 1110	1E	>	011 1110	3E	^	101 1110	5E	~	111 1110	7E
US	001 1111	1F	?	011 1111	3F	_	101 1111	5F	DEL	111 1111	7F

Abbreviations for Control Characters

NUL	null, or all zeros	FF	form feed	CAN	cancel
SOH	start of heading	CR	carriage return	EM	end of medium
STX	start of text	SO	shift out	SUB	substitute
ETX	end of text	SI	shift in	ESC	escape
EOT	end of transmission	DLE	data link escape	FS	file separator
ENQ	enquiry	DC1	device control 1	GS	group separator
ACK	acknowledge	DC2	device control 2	RS	record separator
BEL	bell	DC3	device control 3	US	unit separator
BS	backspace	DC4	device control 4	SP	space
HT	horizontal tabulation	NAK	negative acknowledge	DEL	delete
LF	line feed	SYN	synchronous idle		
VT	vertical tabulation	ETB	end of transmission block		

Figure A.3

The American Standard Code for Information Interchange (ASCII).

Central processing unit (CPU)

The central processing unit of the Pep/8 computer.

(a) The two parts of a nonunary instruction.

(b) A unary instruction.

The Pep/8 instruction format.

aaa	Addressing mode
000	Immediate
001	Direct
010	Indirect
011	Stack-relative
100	Stack-relative deferred
101	Indexed
110	Stack-indexed
111	Stack-indexed deferred

(a) The addressing-aaa field.

a	Addressing mode
0	Immediate
1	Indexed

(b) The addressing-a field.

r	Register
0	Accumulator, A
1	Index register, X

(c) The register-r field.

Figure **A.6**

The Pep/8 instruction specifier fields.

Addressing Mode	aaa	Letters	Operand
Immediate	000	i	OprndSpec
Direct	001	d	Mem [OprndSpec]
Indirect	010	n	Mem [Mem [OprndSpec]]
Stack-relative	011	s	Mem [SP + OprndSpec]
Stack-relative deferred	100	sf	Mem [Mem [SP + OprndSpec]]
Indexed	101	x	Mem [OprndSpec + X]
Stack-indexed	110	sx	Mem [SP + OprndSpec + X]
Stack-indexed deferred	111	sxf	Mem [Mem [SP + OprndSpec] + X]

Figure **A.7**

The Pep/8 addressing modes.

Instruction Specifier	Mnemonic	Instruction	Addressing Modes	Status Bits
0000 0000	STOP	Stop execution	U	
0000 0001	RETTR	Return from trap	U	
0000 0010	MOVSPA	Move SP to A	U	
0000 0011	MOVFLGA	Move NZVC flags to A	U	
0000 010a	BR	Branch unconditional	i, x	
0000 011a	BRLE	Branch if less than or equal to	i, x	
0000 100a	BRLT	Branch if less than	i, x	
0000 101a	BREQ	Branch if equal to	i, x	
0000 110a	BRNE	Branch if not equal to	i, x	
0000 111a	BRGE	Branch if greater than or equal to	i, x	
0001 000a	BRGT	Branch if greater than	i, x	
0001 001a	BRV	Branch if V	i, x	
0001 010a	BRC	Branch if C	i, x	
0001 011a	CALL	Call subroutine	i, x	
0001 100r	NOTr	Bitwise invert r	U	NZ
0001 101r	NEGr	Negate r	U	NZV
0001 110r	ASLr	Arithmetic shift left r	U	NZVC
0001 111r	ASRr	Arithmetic shift right r	U	NZC
0010 000r	ROLr	Rotate left r	U	C
0010 001r	RORr	Rotate right r	U	C
0010 01nn	NOPn	Unary no operation trap	U	
0010 1aaa	NOP	Nonunary no operation trap	i	
0011 0aaa	DECI	Decimal input trap	d, n, s, sf, x, sx, sxf	NZV
0011 1aaa	DECO	Decimal output trap	i, d, n, s, sf, x, sx, sxf	
0100 0aaa	STRO	String output trap	d, n, sf	
0100 1aaa	CHARI	Character input	d, n, s, sf, x, sx, sxf	
0101 0aaa	CHARO	Character output	i, d, n, s, sf, x, sx, sxf	
0101 1nnn	RETn	Return from call with n local bytes	U	
0110 0aaa	ADDSP	Add to stack pointer (SP)	i, d, n, s, sf, x, sx, sxf	NZVC
0110 1aaa	SUBSP	Subtract from stack pointer (SP)	i, d, n, s, sf, x, sx, sxf	NZVC
0111 raaa	ADDr	Add to r	i, d, n, s, sf, x, sx, sxf	NZVC
1000 raaa	SUBr	Subtract from r	i, d, n, s, sf, x, sx, sxf	NZVC
1001 raaa	ANDr	Bitwise AND to r	i, d, n, s, sf, x, sx, sxf	NZ
1010 raaa	ORr	Bitwise OR to r	i, d, n, s, sf, x, sx, sxf	NZ
1011 raaa	CPr	Compare r	i, d, n, s, sf, x, sx, sxf	NZVC
1100 raaa	LDr	Load r from memory	i, d, n, s, sf, x, sx, sxf	NZ
1101 raaa	LDBYTEr	Load byte from memory	i, d, n, s, sf, x, sx, sxf	NZ
1110 raaa	STr	Store r to memory	d, n, s, sf, x, sx, sxf	
1111 raaa	STBYTEr	Store byte r to memory	d, n, s, sf, x, sx, sxf	

Figure **A.8**

The Pep/8 instruction set.

.ADDRSS	the address of a symbol
.ASCII	a string of ASCII bytes
.BLOCK	a block of bytes
.BURN	initiate ROM burn
.BYTE	a byte value
.END	the sentinel for the assembler
.EQUATE	equate a symbol to a constant value
.WORD	a word value

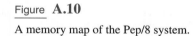

Figure **14.9**

The eight pseudo-ops of Pep/8 assembly language.

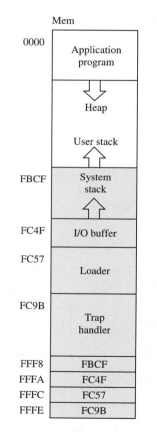

Figure **A.10**

A memory map of the Pep/8 system.

Mnemonic	Register transfer language specification
STOP	Stop execution
RETTR	$NZVC \leftarrow Mem[SP] \langle 4..7 \rangle$; $A \leftarrow Mem[SP + 1]$; $X \leftarrow Mem[SP + 3]$; $PC \leftarrow Mem[SP + 5]$; $SP \leftarrow Mem[SP + 7]$
MOVSPA	$A \leftarrow SP$
MOVFLAGA	$A \langle 0..11 \rangle \leftarrow 0$, $A \langle 12..15 \rangle \leftarrow NZVC$
BR	$PC \leftarrow Oprnd$
BRLE	$N = 1 \vee Z = 1 \Rightarrow PC \leftarrow Oprnd$
BRLT	$N = 1 \Rightarrow PC \leftarrow Oprnd$
BREQ	$Z = 1 \Rightarrow PC \leftarrow Oprnd$
BRNE	$Z = 0 \Rightarrow PC \leftarrow Oprnd$
BRGE	$N = 0 \Rightarrow PC \leftarrow Oprnd$
BRGT	$N = 0 \wedge Z = 0 \Rightarrow PC \leftarrow Oprnd$
BRV	$V = 1 \Rightarrow PC \leftarrow Oprnd$
BRC	$C = 1 \Rightarrow PC \leftarrow Oprnd$
CALL	$SP \leftarrow SP - 2$; $Mem[SP] \leftarrow PC$; $PC \leftarrow Oprnd$
NOTr	$r \leftarrow \neg r$; $N \leftarrow r < 0$, $Z \leftarrow r = 0$
NEGr	$r \leftarrow -r$; $N \leftarrow r < 0$, $Z \leftarrow r = 0$, $V \leftarrow \{overflow\}$
ASLr	$C \leftarrow r\langle 0 \rangle$, $r\langle 0..14 \rangle \leftarrow r\langle 1..15 \rangle$, $r\langle 15 \rangle \leftarrow 0$; $N \leftarrow r < 0$, $Z \leftarrow r = 0$, $V \leftarrow \{overflow\}$
ASRr	$C \leftarrow r\langle 15 \rangle$, $r\langle 1..15 \rangle \leftarrow r\langle 0..14 \rangle$; $N \leftarrow r < 0$, $Z \leftarrow r = 0$
ROLr	$C \leftarrow r\langle 0 \rangle$, $r\langle 0..14 \rangle \leftarrow r\langle 1..15 \rangle$, $r\langle 15 \rangle \leftarrow C$
RORr	$C \leftarrow r\langle 15 \rangle$, $r\langle 1..15 \rangle \leftarrow r\langle 0..14 \rangle$, $r\langle 0 \rangle \leftarrow C$
NOPn	Trap: Unary no operation
NOP	Trap: Nonunary no operation
DECI	Trap: $Oprnd \leftarrow \{decimal\ input\}$
DECO	Trap: $\{decimal\ output\} \leftarrow Oprnd$
STRO	Trap: $\{string\ output\} \leftarrow Oprnd$
CHARI	byte $Oprnd \leftarrow \{character\ input\}$
CHARO	$\{character\ output\} \leftarrow$ byte $Oprnd$
RETn	$SP \leftarrow SP + n$; $PC \leftarrow Mem[SP]$; $SP \leftarrow SP + 2$
ADDSP	$SP \leftarrow SP + Oprnd$; $N \leftarrow SP < 0$, $Z \leftarrow SP = 0$, $V \leftarrow \{overflow\}$, $C \leftarrow \{carry\}$
SUBSP	$SP \leftarrow SP - Oprnd$; $N \leftarrow SP < 0$, $Z \leftarrow SP = 0$, $V \leftarrow \{overflow\}$, $C \leftarrow \{carry\}$

Figure **A.11**

RTL specification of Pep/8 instructions.

Mnemonic	Register transfer language specification
ADDr	$r \leftarrow r + \text{Oprnd}$; $N \leftarrow r < 0$, $Z \leftarrow r = 0$, $V \leftarrow \{\textit{overflow}\}$, $C \leftarrow \{\textit{carry}\}$
SUBr	$r \leftarrow r - \text{Oprnd}$; $N \leftarrow r < 0$, $Z \leftarrow r = 0$, $V \leftarrow \{\textit{overflow}\}$, $C \leftarrow \{\textit{carry}\}$
ANDr	$r \leftarrow r \wedge \text{Oprnd}$; $N \leftarrow r < 0$, $Z \leftarrow r = 0$
ORr	$r \leftarrow r \vee \text{Oprnd}$; $N \leftarrow r < 0$, $Z \leftarrow r = 0$
CPr	$T \leftarrow r - \text{Oprnd}$; $N \leftarrow T < 0$, $Z \leftarrow T = 0$, $V \leftarrow \{\textit{overflow}\}$, $C \leftarrow \{\textit{carry}\}$
LDr	$r \leftarrow \text{Oprnd}$; $N \leftarrow r < 0$, $Z \leftarrow r = 0$
LDBYTEr	$r\langle 8..15\rangle \leftarrow \text{byte Oprnd}$; $N \leftarrow r < 0$, $Z \leftarrow r = 0$
STr	$\text{Oprnd} \leftarrow r$
STBYTEr	$\text{byte Oprnd} \leftarrow r\langle 8..15\rangle$
Trap	$T \leftarrow \text{Mem[FFFA]}$; $\text{Mem}[T-1] \leftarrow IR$; $\text{Mem}[T-3] \leftarrow SP$;
	$\text{Mem}[T-5] \leftarrow PC$; $\text{Mem}[T-7] \leftarrow X$; $\text{Mem}[T-9] \leftarrow A$;
	$\text{Mem}[T-10]\langle 4..7\rangle \leftarrow NZVC$; $SP \leftarrow T-10$; $PC \leftarrow \text{Mem[FFFE]}$

Figure **A.11**

(Continued)

```
SP := Mem [FFFA]
PC := Mem [FFFC]
```

Figure **A.12**

The load option.

```
SP  := Mem [FFF8]
PC  := 0000
```

Figure **A.13**

The execute option.

Solutions to Selected Exercises

Chapter 1

2. **(a)** 11,110, not counting Khan

3. **(a)**

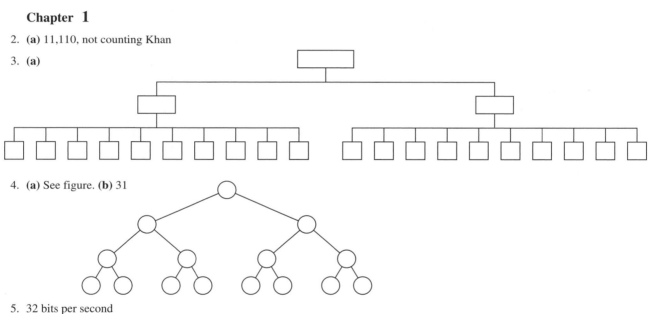

4. **(a)** See figure. **(b)** 31

5. 32 bits per second

9. **(a)** 153,600 **(b)** 19,200 bytes, which is about 19.2 Kbytes

12. **(a)** 18.5 hours

16. Temp 5

F.Name	F.Major	F.State
Ron	Math	OR

Temp 6

S.Name	S.Class	S.Major	S.State
Beth	Soph	Hist	TX
Allison	Soph	Math	AZ

17. **(a)**

```
select Sor where S.Name = Beth giving Temp
project Temp over S.State giving Result
```

Chapter 2

1. **(a)** Four times

2. **(a)** Called seven times. Maximum of four stack frames. Calling order:

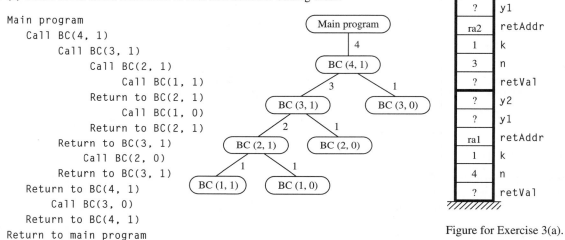

```
Main program
    Call BC(4, 1)
        Call BC(3, 1)
            Call BC(2, 1)
                Call BC(1, 1)
            Return to BC(2, 1)
                Call BC(1, 0)
            Return to BC(2, 1)
        Return to BC(3, 1)
            Call BC(2, 0)
        Return to BC(3, 1)
    Return to BC(4, 1)
        Call BC(3, 0)
    Return to BC(4, 1)
Return to main program
```

1	y2
1	y1
ra2	retAddr
1	k
2	n
2	retVal
?	y2
?	y1
ra2	retAddr
1	k
3	n
?	retVal
?	y2
?	y1
ra1	retAddr
1	k
4	n
?	retVal

Figure for Exercise 3(a).

3. **(a)** See figure in margin.

Chapter 3

1. **(a)**	**(b)**	**(c)**	**(d)**
267	2102	10101	2433
270	2110	10110	2434
271	2111	10111	2440
272	2112	11000	2441
273	2120	11001	2442
274	2121	11010	2443
275	2122	11011	2444
276	2200	11100	3000
277	2201	11101	3001
300	2202	11110	3002
301	2210	11111	3003

3. **(a)** 18 **(b)** 6 **(c)** 11 **(d)** 8 **(e)** 31 **(f)** 85

5. **(a)** 11001 **(b)** 10000 **(c)** 1 **(d)** 1110 **(e)** 101 **(f)** 101001

7. **(a)** 00 to 11 (bin) and 0 to 3 (dec) **(b)** 000 to 111 (bin) and 0 to 7 (dec)

8. **(a)** C = 0, 111 0100 **(b)** C = 1, 001 0000 **(c)** C = 1, 111 1110 **(d)** C = 1, 000 0000

12. **(a)** $7 \times 8^4 + 0 \times 8^3 + 1 \times 8^2 + 4 \times 8^1 + 6 \times 8^0$

13. **(a)** $2 \times 10^2 + 9 \times 10^0 + 4 \times 10^{-1} + 5 \times 10^{-2} + 8 \times 10^{-3}$

15. **(a)** 011 0001 **(b)** 110 0101 **(c)** 000 0000 **(d)** 100 0000 **(e)** 111 1111 **(f)** 111 1110

17. **(a)** 29 **(b)** −43 **(c)** −4 **(d)** 1 **(e)** −64 **(f)** −63

19. **(a)** N = 0, Z = 0, V = 0, C = 0, 011 1001 **(b)** N = 0, Z = 0, V = 0, C = 1, 000 0110
    (c) N = 0, Z = 0, V = 1, C = 1, 001 1011 **(d)** N = 1, Z = 0, V = 0, C = 1, 101 0110
    (e) N = 1, Z = 0, V = 1, C = 0, 100 0001 **(f)** N = 1, Z = 0, V = 0, C = 0, 111 0100

21. **(a)** From 10 to 01 in binary or −2 to 1 in decimal **(b)** From 100 to 011 in binary or −4 to 3 in decimal

22. **(a)** N = 0, Z = 0, 010 1000 **(b)** N = 0, Z = 0, 000 0101 **(c)** N = 1, Z = 0, 110 1110
    (d) N = 1, Z = 0, 101 1111 **(e)** N = 0, Z = 0, 100 0110 **(f)** N = 0, Z = 0, 101 1010
    (g) 101 0100 **(h)** 001 0101

24. ASL operation:

    (a) 24 (dec) = 001 1000 (bin), ASL 001 1000 = 011 0000 (bin) = 48 (dec),
    N = 0, Z = 0, V = 0, C = 0
    (b) 37 (dec) = 010 0101 (bin), ASL 010 0101 = 100 1010 (bin) = −54 (dec),
    N = 1, Z = 0, V = 1, C = 0
    (c) −26 (dec) = 110 0110 (bin), ASL 110 0110 = 100 1100 (bin) = −52 (dec),
    N = 1, Z = 0, V = 0, C = 1
    (d) 1 (dec) = 000 0001 (bin), ASL 000 0001 = 000 0010 (bin) = 2 (dec), N = 0, Z = 0,
    V = 0, C = 0
    (e) 0 (dec) = 0000 0000 (bin), ASL 000 0000 = 000 0000 (bin) = 0 (dec),
    N = 0, Z = 1, V = 0, C = 0
    (f) −1 (dec) = 111 1111 (bin), ASL 111 1111 = 111 1110 (bin) = −2 (dec),
    N = 1, Z = 0, V = 0, C = 1

    ASR operation:

    (a) 24 (dec) = 001 1000 (bin), ASR 001 1000 = 000 1100 (bin) = 12 (dec), N = 0,
    Z = 0, C = 0
    (b) 37 (dec) = 010 0101 (bin), ASR 010 0101 = 001 0010 (bin) = 18 (dec), N = 0,
    Z = 0, C = 1
    (c) −26 (dec) = 110 0110 (bin), ASR 110 0110 = 111 0011 (bin) = −13 (dec),
    N = 1, Z = 0, C = 0
    (d) 1 (dec) = 000 0001 (bin), ASR 000 0001 = 000 0000 (bin) = 0 (dec), N = 0,
    Z = 1, C = 1
    (e) 0 (dec) = 0000 0000 (bin), ASR 000 0000 = 000 0000 (bin) = 0 (dec), N = 0,
    Z = 1, C = 0
    (f) −1 (dec) = 111 1111 (bin), ASR 111 1111 = 111 1111 (bin) = −1 (dec), N = 1,
    Z = 0, C = 1

27. **(a)** 101 1011, C = 0 **(b)** 101, 1010, C = 0
    (c) 101 0110, C = 1 **(d)** 001 0110, C = 1

30. **(a)** 3AB7, 3AB8, 3AB9, 3ABA, 3ABB, 3ABC

31. **(a)** 11,615 (dec)

32. **(a)** 68CF

34. **(a)** -35 **(b)** 47 **(c)** -64

36. **(a)** 65 (hex) **(b)** 3F (hex) **(c)** 7F (hex)

38. Have a nice day!

40. 101 0000   110 0001   111 10001   010 0000   010 0100   011 0000

    010 1110   011 1001   011 0010

43. **(a)** An octal digit represents three bits.

44. **(a)** 6.640625   **(b)** 0.046875   **(c)** 1.0

46. **(a)** 1101.00101   **(b)** 0.0000101   **(c)** 0.10011001100...

50. **(a)** 1 110 1001

51. **(a)** 0.90625

52. **(a)** 41D8 D000

53. **(a)** $64.0 = 1.0 \times 2^6$

Chapter 4

1. **(a)** 65,536 bytes **(b)** 32,768 words **(c)** 524,288 bits **(d)** 92 bits **(e)** 5699 times bigger

3. **For instruction 7AF82C**   **For instruction D623D0**

   (a) opcode = 0111   **(a)** opcode = 1101

   (b) It adds to register r   **(b)** It loads a byte from memory to register r

   (c) r = 1   **(c)** r = 0

   (d) The index register, X   **(d)** The accumulator, A

   (e) aaa = 010   **(e)** aaa = 110

   (f) Indirect   **(f)** Stack-indexed

   (g) OprndSpec = F82C   **(g)** OprndSpec = 23D0

5.

	A	X	Mem[0A3F]	Mem[0A41]
Original content	19AC	FE20	FF00	103D
(a) C1 = Load accumulator	FF00	FE20	FF00	103D
(b) D1 = Load byte accumulator	19FF	FE20	FF00	103D
(c) D9 = Load byte index register	19AC	FE10	FF00	103D
(d) F1 = Store byte accumulator	19AC	FE20	FF00	AC3D
(e) E9 = Store index register	19AC	FE20	FE20	103D
(f) 89 = Subtract index register	19AC	EDE3	FF00	103D
(g) 81 = Subtract accumulator	1AAC	FE20	FF00	103D
(h) A1 = OR accumulator	FFAC	FE20	FF00	103D
(i) 19 = Invert index register	19AC	01DF	FF00	103D

7. Joy

9. **(a)** M

Chapter 5

1. **(a)** `ORX 0xEF2A, n` **(b)** `MOVSPA` **(c)** `LDBYTEA 0x003D, sxf`

3. **(a)** 1C **(b)** 4B000F **(c)** 0C01E6

5. **(a)** 42 65 61 72 00 **(b)** F8 **(c)** 0316

7. `mug`

10. -57
    72
    Hi

12. **(a)** Object code is 38 00 6D 50 00 0A 38 6D 6D 50 00 0A 50 00 26 00
    Output
    109
    28013
    &

13. `here` has value 0003. `there` has value 0005. Object code is 04 00 05 00 09 39 00
    03 00

15. `this` has value 0000. The output is Q. The output comes from 51 (hex) = Q (ASCII),
    where 51 is the first byte of the object code.

18. The compiler uses its symbol table to store the type of each variable. It consults the
    symbol table whenever it encounters an expression or assignment statement to verify
    that the types are compatible.

Chapter 6

3. Because the current value of i will be in the accumulator regardless of whether control
   came from the STA at 0009 or from the BR at the bottom of the loop. Before the BR at the
   bottom of the loop, the accumulator was used to increment i, thus its current value will
   still be in the accumulator when CPA executes.

6.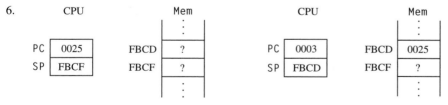

8. The branch address is calculated as

   Oprnd = Mem[OprndSpec + X]
         = Mem[0013 + 8]
         = Mem[001B]
         = 4100

   You cannot tell from the program listing what bits are at 4100, but assuming that they
   are all 0's, the von Neumann cycle blindly interprets the 00 at address 4100 as the STOP
   instruction.

Chapter 7

1. The fundamental question of computer science is, What can be automated?

3. **(a)**

```
<identifier> ⇒ <identifier> <digit>
            ⇒ <identifier> 3
            ⇒ <identifier> <digit> 3
            ⇒ <identifier> 2  3
            ⇒ <identifier> <digit> 2  3
            ⇒ <identifier> 1  2  3
            ⇒ <identifier> <digit> 1  2  3
            ⇒ <identifier> c  1  2  3
            ⇒ <identifier> <letter> c  1  2  3
            ⇒ <identifier> b  c  1  2  3
            ⇒ <letter> b  c  1  2  3
            ⇒ a  b  c  1  2  3
```

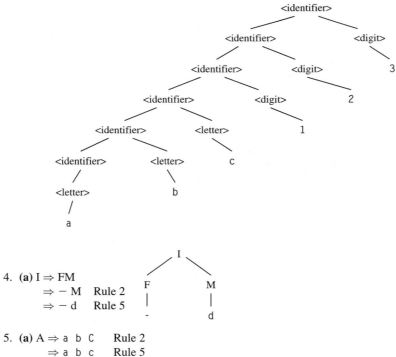

4. **(a)** $I \Rightarrow FM$
   $ \Rightarrow - M$ Rule 2
   $ \Rightarrow - d$ Rule 5

5. **(a)** $A \Rightarrow a \ b \ C$ Rule 2
   $ \Rightarrow a \ b \ c$ Rule 5

6. **(a)** It can be derived as follows:

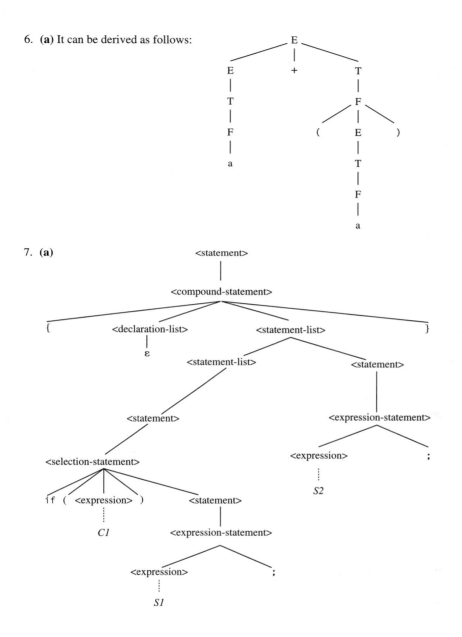

7. **(a)**

8. **(a)**

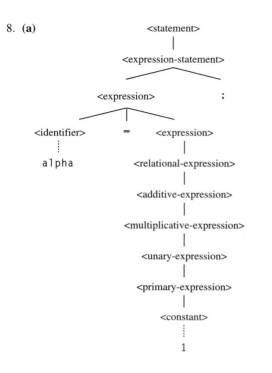

11. **(a)** The machine is deterministic. There are no inaccessible states.

13. **(a)**

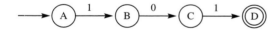

Chapter 8

2. **(a)** 0036 (hex), which is the ASCII code for 6 in the 27th byte, 6C **(b)** 0036 **(c)** 0360

4. **(a)** 0031, the instruction specifier of the interrupted instruction **(b)** 0006 (hex)

5. **(a)** 0039, the instruction specifier of the interrupted instruction **(b)** 0007 (hex)

6. **(a)** 0041, the instruction specifier of the interrupted instruction **(b)** 0008 (hex)

7. **(a)** The instruction changes the accumulator from 0033, the ASCII value of 3, to 0003 by masking the left nybble. **(b)** 0007, the numeric value of the second character in 37 **(c)** 0000, the value of init, the start state

8. Hint: The first character input is the ASCII hyphen character.

9. **(a)** 0025 (hex), which is 37 (dec) **(b)** 0025, not negated because it was already nonnegative **(c)** The CALL from FF78 is for writing the 100's place. The accumulator still contains 0025, which is 37 (dec) because 37 mod 100 is 37.

10. Hint: −2068 (dec) = F7EC (hex), which is 0814 (hex) when you take its two's complement.

11. **(a)** 0012, the address of the first byte of the string to output **(b)** 0054, the ASCII value of the letter T

12. **(a)** 0008, the address of the next instruction after DECI **(b)** 0006, the address of the operand specifier of DECI **(c)** 0003, the address of the operand of DECI

18. **(a)** The algorithm no longer guarantees mutual exclusion. Suppose P1 and P2 are both in their remainder sections with enter1 and enter2 both false. P1 could execute its while loop test and be interrupted, after which P2 could execute its while loop test. They could then assign their respective Enter variables to true and enter their critical sections simultaneously.

20. **(a)** S = 0, and there are no blocked processes.

22. **(a)** The algorithm guarantees mutual exclusion. If you remove the t semaphore altogether you get the algorithm of Program 8.5, which guarantees mutual exclusion, regardless of any other code present in the algorithm.

24. **(a)** Mutual exclusion is no longer guaranteed. Can you find a trace that allows P1 and P2 to enter their critical sections simultaneously? Deadlock, however, cannot occur.

25. **(a)** Contains a deadlock cycle:

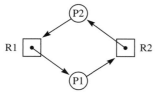

(b) Does not contain a cycle, and therefore does not have a deadlock:

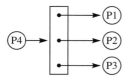

Chapter 9

2. **(a)** A single bound register would suffice since only one process at a time can execute. If a user process tries to access a memory location outside its logical address space, the hardware must interrupt the access before the page table because there is no such page in main memory. Can you show this modification to Figure 9.9? How many bound values must the operating system keep track of: one for each process, one for each page in the page table, or one for each main memory frame?

4. **(a)** 2^{12}, or 4,098, bytes.

6. Those that have a dirty bit value of N, namely, the ones in frames 2, 5, and 6

8. The start of one page reference sequence for a job that has three frames allocated is 1, 2, 3, 1, 4, 2, ..., which has four faults for FIFO and five for LRU. Can you complete the sequence in such a way that FIFO is better in this special case?

10. It produces five faults compared to seven for FIFO and six for LRU. You should trace the algorithm to verify this figure.

11. **(a)** Hint: The worst case occurs when the start of the block has just rotated past the read/write head when the head has reached the track. Hence, it is time for the disk to make one complete revolution. You can calculate it from the RPM number.

12. **(a)** Four data bits **(b)** One parity bit

16. **(a)** An error occurred at position 2. The corrected code word is 1101 1010 1001.

Chapter 10

1. **(a)**
$$\begin{aligned}
x + 1 &= x + (x + x') && \langle\text{complement}\rangle \\
&= (x + x) + x' && \langle\text{associative}\rangle \\
&= x + x' && \langle\text{idempotent}\rangle \\
&= 1 && \langle\text{complement}\rangle
\end{aligned}$$

4. To show that the complement of $a + b$ is $a'b'$ you must show that

$$(a + b) \cdot (a' \cdot b') = 0 \quad \text{and} \quad (a + b) + (a' \cdot b') = 1$$

The first part of the proof is

$$\begin{aligned}
(a + b) \cdot (a' \cdot b') &= [(a' \cdot b') \cdot a] + [(a' \cdot b') \cdot b] && \langle\text{commutative}\rangle \\
&= [(a' \cdot a) \cdot b'] + [a' \cdot (b \cdot b')] && \langle\text{commutative, associative}\rangle \\
&= [0 \cdot b'] + [a' \cdot 0] && \langle\text{complement}\rangle \\
&= 0 && \langle\text{identity}\rangle
\end{aligned}$$

6. **(a)** Hint:

$$\begin{aligned}
(x + y) \cdot (x' + y) &= (y + x) \cdot (y + x') && \langle\text{commutative}\rangle \\
&= y + (x \cdot x') && \langle\text{distributive}\rangle \\
&\ \ \text{etc.}
\end{aligned}$$

8. **(a)**

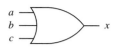

$x = a + b + c$

a	b	c	x
0	0	0	0
0	0	1	1
0	1	0	1
0	1	1	1
1	0	0	1
1	0	1	1
1	1	0	1
1	1	1	1

9. **(a)** The union of any set with the empty set is the set itself.

10. **(a)**

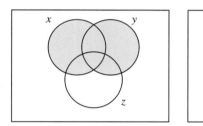

(1) $(x + y)$

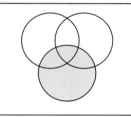

(2) z

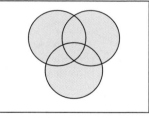

(3) $(x + y) + z$

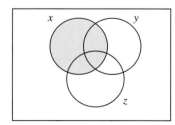

(4) x

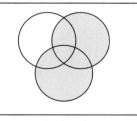

(5) $(y + z)$

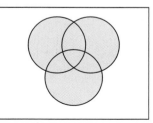

(6) $x + (y + z)$

13. **(a)**

x	*y*	*x* AND *y*
0	0	0
0	A	0
0	B	0
0	1	0
A	0	0
A	A	A
A	B	0
A	1	A
B	0	0
B	A	0
B	B	B
B	1	B
1	0	0
1	A	A
1	B	B
1	1	1

14. **(a)**

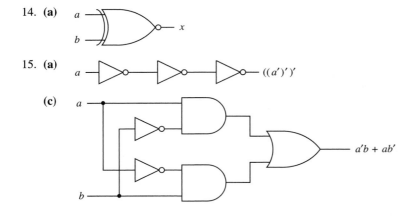

15. **(a)**

(c)

19. **(a)** $y(a, b, c) = a'bc + ab'c'$

20. **(a)** $y(a, b, c) = (a + b + c)(a + b + c')(a + b' + c)(a' + b + c')(a' + b' + c)$
$(a' + b' + c')$

21. **(a)** $ab + a'b'$ **(d)** $a'b + ab$

a	b	20(a)	20(d)
0	0	1	0
0	1	0	1
1	0	0	0
1	1	1	1

22. **(a)**   **(d)**

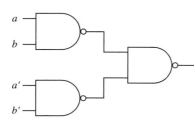
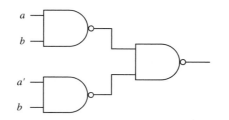

23. **(b)** $(a' + b)(a + b')$

a	b	
0	0	1
0	1	0
1	0	0
1	1	1

24. **(b)**

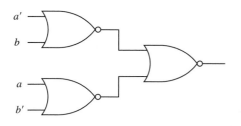

25. **(a)**

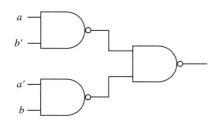

27. **(a)** $\Sigma(0, 3)$ **(d)** $\Sigma(1, 3)$

28. **(b)** $\Pi(1, 2)$

29. **(a)** $x = a'c$

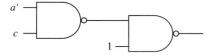

30. **(a)** $x = (a')(c)$

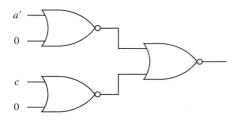

31. **(a)** $x(a, b, c) = ac + b'c'$

32. **(a)** $x(a, b, c) = \Pi(1, 2, 3, 6) = (a + c')(b' + c)$

33. **(a)** $x(a, b, c, d) = bc' + a'b'c + b'cd'$

34. **(a)** $\Pi(0, 1, 6, 7, 8, 9, 11, 14, 15),\ x(a, b, c, d) = (b + c)(b' + c')(a' + c' + d')$ or
    $x(a, b, c, d) = (b + c)(b' + c')(a' + b + d')$

35. **(a)** $x(a, b, c) = a'b' + ab$

36. **(a)** $x(a, b, c, d) = bc + bd$

38. **(a)** The control line acts as an enable that passes the data through unchanged when it is 0. When the control line is 1, it disables the output, which is set to 1, regardless of the data input.

40.

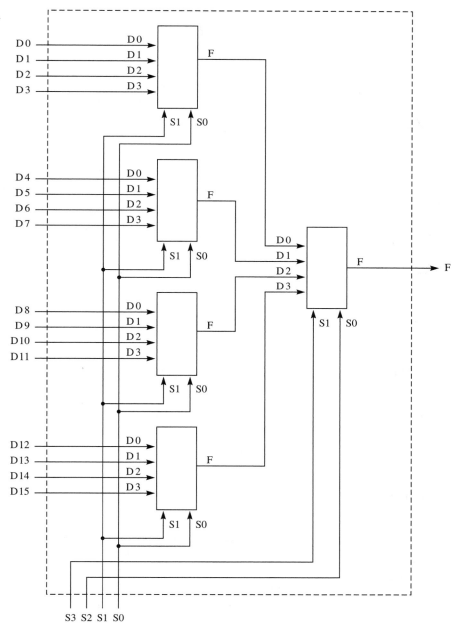

42. **(a)**

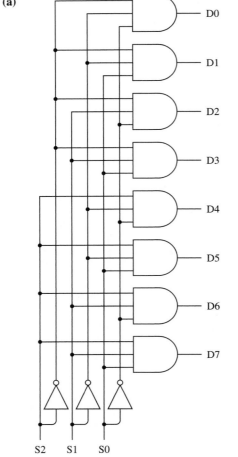

46. **(a)**

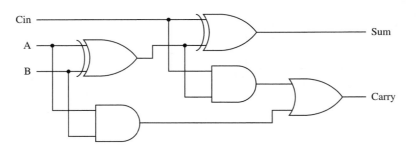

(b) Maximum of three gate delays

47. **(b)** Hint: If you look at Figure 10.52 and use the fact that a full adder has three gate delays and a half adder has one gate delay, you might conclude that the total gate delay is 10. However, it is less than that.

Chapter 11

1. The network will be stable if there is an even number of inverters.

3.

	A	B	C	D	E	R2	S2	Q	$\overline{Q}$
(a)	0	0	1	1	0	1	0	0	1
(b)	0	0	0	0	0	1	0	0	1

5. **(b)**

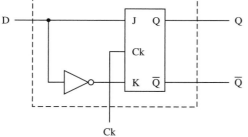

8. **(a)**

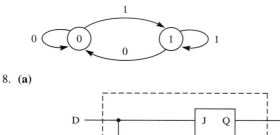

9. **(a)** Hint: To force the master and slave to 0, the Clear input should (1) force the slave to be connected to the master regardless of the output of the inverter, and (2) force the master to the $Q = 0$ state. To implement (2), consider the possibility of adding a third input line to one of the master NOR gates and/or a third input line to one of the master AND gates.

13. **(a)** $DA = A\,\overline{X}1 + \overline{A}\,X1 + A\,B\,\overline{X}2 + B\,X1\,X2$
$\quad DB = \overline{B}\,\overline{X}1 + B\,X1\,X2 + \overline{A}\,B\,X1$
$\quad\; Y = \overline{A}\,X2 + A\,X1\,X2$

15. **(a)** $JA = \overline{B}\,\overline{C}\,\overline{X} + B\,C\,X \qquad KA = \overline{B}\,\overline{C}\,\overline{X} + B\,C\,X$
$\quad\;\; JB = \overline{C}\,\overline{X} + C\,X \qquad\qquad KB = \overline{C}\,\overline{X} + C\,X$
$\quad\;\; JC = 1 \qquad\qquad\qquad\quad KC = 1$

Chapter 12

7. **(a)**

```
// STBYTEA there,n
// RTL: byte Oprnd <- r<8..15>
// Oprnd = Mem[Mem[OprndSpec]]

// T3<high> <- Mem[OprndSpec]
1. A=9, B=10; MARCk
2. MemRead
3. MemRead, MDRMux=0; MDRCk
4. AMux=0, ALU=0, CMux=1, C=14; LoadCk

// T2 <- OprndSpec + 1
5. A=10, B=23, AMux=1, ALU=1, CMux=1, C=13; CCk, LoadCk
6. A=9, B=22, AMux=1, ALU=2, CMux=1, C=12; LoadCk

// T3<low> <- Mem[T2]
7. A=12, B=13; MARCk
8. MemRead
9. MemRead, MDRMux=0; MDRCk
10. AMux=0, ALU=0, CMux=1, C=15; LoadCk

// Mem[T3] <- A<low>, restore C in T1 from Fetch
11. A=14, B=15; MARCk
12. A=1, AMux=1, ALU=0, CMux=1, MDRMux=1; MDRCk
13. MemWrite
14. MemWrite, A=11, AMux=1, ALU=15; CCk
```

You can combine cycles in the above solution to get an implementation with only 12 cycles as follows:

```
// T3<high> <- Mem[OprndSpec], T2 <- OprndSpec + 1
1. A=9, B=10; MARCk
2. MemRead, A=10, B=23, AMux=1, ALU=1, CMux=1, C=13; CCk, LoadCk
3. MemRead, MDRMux=0, A=9, B=22, AMux=1, ALU=2, CMux=1, C=12;
   MDRCk, LoadCk
4. AMux=0, ALU=0, CMux=1, C=14; LoadCk

// T3<low> <- Mem[T2]
5. A=12, B=13; MARCk
6. MemRead
7. MemRead, MDRMux=0; MDRCk
8. AMux=0, ALU=0, CMux=1, C=15; LoadCk

// Mem[T3] <- A<low>, restore C in T1 from Fetch
9. A=14, B=15; MARCk
10. A=1, AMux=1, ALU=0, CMux=1, MDRMux=1; MDRCk
11. MemWrite
12. MemWrite, A=11, AMux=1, ALU=15; CCk
```

9. Hint: **(a)** Using 16 billion GBytes equal to $16 \times 10^9 \times 10^9$ bytes, the chip would be 4×4 meters square, but you must show your calculation. **(b)** Yes, but you must explain.

16. **(a)**
```
lw $t0,20($s6)  # Register $t0 gets b[5]
add $t0,$s5,$t0 # Register $t0 gets g + b[5]
sw $t0,16($s4)  # a[2] gets g + b[5]
```

(b)
```
100011 10110 01000 0000000000010100
000000 10101 01000 01000 00000 100000
101011 10100 01000 0000000000010000
```

Index

A

Absorption property, *See* Boolean algebra
Abstraction, 3–10
    definition of, 3
    in computer systems, 8–10, 300, 657
Add instruction, Pep/8, 160–161
add instruction, MIPS, 629, 645–646
ADDA instruction, Pep/8, 198–200, 607–608, 624
Adder, 528–531
    full, 529
    half, 528
    ripple-carry, 530–531
Adder/subtracter, 531–532
Addition
    signed, 97–99, 537–539
    unsigned, 95–96
    16-bit with two 8-bit, 538–539
Address decoding, 582–588
Addressing modes, MIPS, 626
    base, 627, 630, 645
    immediate, 627, 632–633
    PC-relative, 627, 644–645
    pseudodirect, 627, 644
    register, 627, 629, 645–646
Addressing modes, Pep/8, 154–156, 192, 285, 605
    direct, 157–158, 606–607
    immediate, 202–203, 607–608
    indexed, 287–288, 299–300, 630
    indirect, 305–306, 608–611
    stack-indexed, 290–291
    stack-indexed deferred, 295–297, 318–319
    stack-relative, 238–241
    stack-relative deferred, 276–277, 309
    trap assertion, 401–403
    trap operand computation, 403–406
.ADDRSS pseudo-op, 194, 299
ADDSP instruction, 238
Aiken, Howard H., 89
Alphabet, 332, 335
Algorithm, 17
ALU, 532–540
American Standard Code for Information Interchange,
    See ASCII
Analysis vs. design
    hardware, 565
    software, 20–22
AND gate, 497–499
AND operator, 107–108
AND-OR circuit, 506–509
And instruction, 162–163
App7, 8–10
Arithmetic Logic Unit, *See* ALU
Arithmetic shift left, *See* ASL
Arithmetic shift right, *See* ASR
Arrays, *See also* Parameters
    in C++, 46–47
    called by reference in C++, 61
    global, 285–288
    local, 288–291
    MIPS, 631–632
ASCII, 115–117
.ASCII pseudo-op, 194, 195–196, 215–217
ASL operation, 109–111
ASLr instruction, 224–226

Asmb5, 8–10
ASR operation, 109–111
ASRr instruction, 224–226, 611–612
Assembler, 196–197
    cross, 201–202
    resident, 201–202
    using Pep/8, 200–201
Assignment operator, 38
Assignment statement, 218–221, 228
Associative law, *See* Boolean algebra
Asynchronous interrupts, 420–421
Atanasoff, John V., 90, 225

B

Backun Naur Form, *See* BNF
Base conversions
    floating point and decimal, 118–127
    hexadecimal and decimal, 113–115
    signed integer and decimal, 101–104
    unsigned integer and decimal, 93–94
Base register, *See* Register
BCD, 134
Belady's anomaly, 463–464
Best-fit algorithm, 453–454
Binary coded decimal, *See* BCD
Binary decoder, 526–527
Bit, 90
.BLOCK pseudo-op, 194, 197–198
BNF, 344
Bohm, Corrado, 257
Boolean algebra, 491–497
    absorption property, 494
    associative law, 493
    axioms, 492
    complements, 496–497
    consensus theorem, 494
    De Morgan's law, 495–496
    distributive law, 492
    duality, 492
    idempotent property, 493–494
    zero theorem, 494
Boolean expressions
    and logic diagrams, 501–503
    and truth tables, 503–506

Boolean operators, 42
Boolean types, 281–284
Bound register, *See* Register
BR instruction, 203–206
BRC instruction, 244
BREQ instruction, 244
BRGE instruction, 244
BRGT instruction, 244
BRLE instruction, 244
BRLT instruction, 244
BRNE instruction, 244
BRV instruction, 244
.BURN pseudo-op, 194, 392–393
Bus, 11, 575–576
    width, 613–615
Byron, Ada, 513
Byte, 13
.BYTE pseudo-op, 194, 198–200

C

C bit, 96, 105, 150–151, 532, 533, 599
C++
    compiler, 33–34, 214–218
    compiler, optimizing, 246–247
    machine independence, 34
    memory model, 35–36
    memory model, heap, 303
Cache memories, 634–642
    direct-mapped, 637–638
    fully-associative, Exercise 12.28, 662
    locality of reference, 635
    MIPS, 642–644
    set–associative, 639–642
    write policies, 639–642
CALL instruction, 260–263
Call-by-reference parameters, *See* Parameters
Call-by-value parameters, *See* Parameters
Canonical expressions, 510–511
Carry bit, *See* C bit
Central processing unit (CPU), 11, 16–17
    MIPS, 642–646
    Pep/8, 150–151, 597–601
Character input/output instructions, 166–168
Character representation, 115–118

Characteristic tables, 558
 for D flip-flop, 562
 for JK flip-flop, 560
 for SR flip-flop, 558
 for T flip-flop, 563
CHARI instruction, 197–198, 218–221
CHARO instruction, 195–196
Church, Alonzo, 353
cin statement, 218–221
CISC, 620
Clear flip-flop line, 569
Clocked SR flip-flop, 552–554
Closure of an alphabet, 333
Code generator, 331, 368–381
Codd, Edgar, 23
Combinational circuit, 490–491
Compiler, *See* C++
Complements, *See* Boolean algebra
Concatenation, 333
Concurrent processes, 424–425
Consensus theorem, *See* Boolean algebra
Constants, 226–228
Context sensitive grammar, 338–339, 346
Conversion between bases, *See* Base conversions
Conway, Lynn, 583
Corbató, Fernando J., 434
cout statement, 215–221
CPr instruction, 247–249
Critical section, 426–427

D
D flip-flop, 562–563
Data forwarding, *See* Pipelining
Database systems, 22–27
Deadlocks, 435–437
DECI instruction, 194, 203–206, 218–221, 396,
 408–414
DECO instruction, 194, 203–206, 396, 414–417
Decoder, *See* Binary decoder
delete operator, 35, 74
De Morgan's law, *See* Boolean algebra
Demultiplexer, 527–528
Denormalized numbers, 125
Derivations in a grammar, 336

Deterministic FSM, See Finite state machines
Dijkstra, Edsger W., 257–259
Direct addressing, *See* Addressing modes
Direct memory access, 656
Disassemblers, 209–211
Disk drives, 465–466
Distributive law, *See* Boolean algebra
Division
 integer vs. floating point, 40–41
do loop, 45–46, 250–252
Don't care condition, *See* Karnaugh maps
DRAM, 581
Duality, *See* Boolean algebra
Dynamic branch prediction, *See* Pipelining
Dynamic memory allocation, 74–80

E
Eckert, J. Presper, 90, 225
Edge-triggered flip-flops, 555
EEPROM, 581
Empty string, 333
Empty transitions, 349–351
Enable lines, 523–525
.END pseudo-op, 194, 195–196
ENIAC computer, 90
EPROM, 581
.EQUATE pseudo-op, 194, 226–228, 243
Error-correcting codes, 472–476
Error-detecting codes, 470–472
Excess representations, 120–121
Excitation tables, 559
 for D flip-flop, 564
 for JK flip-flop, 564
 for SR flip-flop, 559
 for T flip-flop, 564
Exclusive OR, *See* XOR

F
FIFO page-replacement algorithm, 462–464
Finite state machines, 332, 346–360, 655, 657
 deterministic, 348, 351
 direct code, 357–360
 implementation of, 355–357

Finite state machines *(continued)*
　　empty transitions in, 349–351
　　nondeterministic, 348–349
　　simplified, 347–348
　　table-lookup implementation of, 355–357
First-fit algorithm, 454
Flash memory, 581
Floating point representation, 118–130
`for` loop, 46–47, 252–253
FORTRAN, 256, 259
Format trace tags, *See* Trace tags
Full adder, *See* Adder
Functions, *See also* parameters
　　call mechanism, 35, 263, 265, 269
　　prototype, 72
　　void, 48–50, 260–267

G

Gate delay, 506
Global variables, *See* Variables
Goto controversy,
Grammars, 332, 335–346
　　context sensitive, 338–339, 346
　　for C++ identifiers, 336–337
　　for C++ language, 341–346
　　for expressions, 340–341
　　for signed integers, 337–338
　　four parts of, 335

H

Half adder, *See* Adder
Hamming distance, 471
Hardware, 10–17
Hazard, *See* Pipelining
Heap, *See* C++ memory model
Hexadecimal representation, 112–115
Hidden bit, 121–122
HOL6, 8–10

I

Idempotent property, *See* Boolean algebra
Identity element, 333
IEEE 754 floating point, 127–130
`if` statement, 41–43, 245–246, 247–249
Immediate addressing, *See* Addressing modes

Indexed addressing, *See* Addressing modes
Indirect addressing, *See* Addressing modes
Instruction reordering, *See* Pipelining
Instruction set
　　MIPS, 627–628
　　Pep/8 at ISA3, 155
　　Pep/8 at Asmb5, 193
Instruction specifier, 154–156
Integer
　　conversions, *See* Base conversions
　　range for signed, 99–101
　　range for unsigned, 94–95
　　signed binary representation, 97–99
　　unsigned binary representation, 91–92
Invert instruction, 164
Inverter, 497–499
ISA3, 8–10

J

Jacopini, Giuseppe, 257
JK flip-flop, 560–562
`join` operator, 25–26

K

Kahan, William V., 128
Karnaugh maps, 512–523
　　don't care conditions, 522–523
　　dual, 521–522
　　four-variable, 518–521
　　three-variable, 512–518
Kemeny, John, 353
Kleene, Stephen, 353

L

Language, 333–334
Latency, 466
`LDr` instruction, 198–200, 608–611
LG1, 8–10
Linked data structures, 77–80, 314–318
Load byte instruction, 165–166
Load instruction, 158–159
Loaders, 392–395
　　relocatable, 449
Local variables, *See* Variables

Logic diagrams, 497–499, 501
    and boolean expressions, 501–503
Logical address, 449–450, 458
LRU page-replacement algorithm, 464
lui instruction, MIPS, 633
lw instruction, MIPS, 629–630

M

Machine vectors, 182–183
main(), 37
MAR, 599
Mark I computer, 89
Master-slave SR flip-flop, 554–559
Matisse, Henri, 4–5
Mauchly, John W., 90, 225
Mc2, 8–10, 621–624
MDR, 599
Mead, Carver, 583
Megahertz myth, 655
Memory, 16
    alignment, 613–614
    hierarchies, 642
    main, of Pep/8, 151–153, 392
    map of Pep/8, 182
    random access, 181
    read-only, 181–182
    subsystems, 577–581
Memory model, *See* C++ memory model
Microcode, 621–624
Minterm, 510, 512
MIPS, 624–634, 642–655
Mnemonics 192–194
Monostable multivibrator, 580
Moore's Law, 614
MOVSPA instruction, 280–281
Multiple token recognizers, 351–354, 361–368
Multiplexer, 525–526
Multiplication algorithm
    iterative, Problem 6.24, 324–325
    recursive, Problem 6.18, 323
Multiprocessing, 423, 425
Multiprogramming, 421, 425
    fixed-partition, 448–451
    variable-partition, 452–454
Mutual exclusion, 427–435

N

N bit, 106, 150–151, 533, 599
NaN, 124
NAND gate, 498
NAND-NAND circuit, 508–509
NEG operation, 98–99
Negate instruction, 164–165
Negative bit, *See* N bit
new operator, 35, 74–75, 300–306
Nondeterministic FSM, *See* Finite state machines
NOP instruction, 194, 396, 406–407
NOPn instruction, 194, 396, 406–407
NOR-NOR circuit, 509
NOR gate, 498
NOT operation, 98–99
Nybble, 394–395

O

Octal, 92
One shot device, *See* Monostable multivibrator
Ones' complement, 98
Opcode, 154
    unimplemented, 194
Operand specifier, 154–156
Operating system, 19–20, 391
    Pep/8, 182–183, 392–419
Optimization
    compiler, *See* C++
    hardware, 619–621
OR-AND circuit, 507–509
OR gate, 497–499
OR operator, 107–108
Or instruction, 162–163
ORA instruction, 198–200
ori instruction, MIPS, 633
Overflow bit, *See* V bit

P

Paging, 455–457
Parallelism, 612–613
Parameters
    arrays, 291–297
    call-by-reference, 51–55, 273–277, 277–281
    call-by-value, 48–51, 263–269
Parity bit, 470

Parser, 331, 381–382
Parsing problem, 339–340
PCB, 397, 421–423
Perfect code, 475
Peterson's algorithm, 429–431
Pipelining, 646–655
    control hazards, 650
    dynamic branch prediction, 650–652
    data forwarding, 653
    hazards, 647
    instruction reordering, 653–654
    RAW data hazard, 652–653
    superscalar machines, 653–654
    WAR data hazard, 654
Pointers, 74–76
    assignment rule, 75
    global, 300–306
    local, 306–309
    zero as a special value, 78
Pop operation, 35
Preset flip-flop line, 569
Process, 397
    concurrent, 419–437
Process control block, See PCB
Productions in a grammar, 336
Program, 18
    analysis vs. design, 21
    self-modifying, 177–179
project operator, 25–26
PROM, 581
Push operation, 35

Q
Queue of PCBs, 420–423

R
Rabin, Michael O., 353
RAID storage systems, 476–483
    Level 0: Nonredundant striped, 477–478
    Level 1: Mirrored, 478
    Levels 01 and 10: Striped and mirrored, 478–480
    Level 2: Memory-style ECC, 480–481
    Level 3: Bit-interleaved parity, 481–482

    Level 4: Block-interleaved parity, 482–483
    Level 5: Block-interleaved distributed parity, 483
RAM, 181–182, 577–580
RAW data hazard, See Pipelining
Recursion, 55–74
    cost of, 73–74
    and mathematical induction, 60
    mutual, 72–73
Reduced Instruction Set Computer, See RISC
Register
    base and bound, 450
    implementation of, 574–575
    MIPS, 625
    Pep/8, 150–151
    two-port bank for Pep/8, 588–590
Register transfer language, 108–109
Regular expressions, 332
Relational operators, 41
Resource allocation graph, 435–437
RETn instruction, 260–263
RETTR instruction, 397–398
RISC, 489–490, 620
Ritchie, Dennis M., 460
ROL operation, 111–112
ROLr instruction, 224–226
ROM, 181–182, 581
ROR operation, 111–112
RORr instruction, 224–226
Rotate left operation, See ROL
Rotate right operation, See ROR
Run-time stack, 35, 238–241

S
Scott, Dana, 353
Seek time, 466
select operator, 25–26
Semantics, 331
Semaphore, 431–435
Set, bit-mapped representation, 402
Set interpretation of boolean algebra, 500
Sign bit, 97
sll instruction, MIPS, 631–632
Software, 17–22

Space/time tradeoff, 612–613
    combinational circuits, 508, 523
    Exercise 10.46, 546
Spaghetti code, 253–256
Specialized hardware units
    Exercise 12.15, 660
    MIPS, 642, 644,
    Pep/8, 615–619
Spin locks, 431
SR latch, 550–552
SRAM, 580
Stable state, *See* State
Stack, 35
Stack-indexed addressing, *See* Addressing modes
Stack-indexed deferred addressing, *See* Addressing modes
Stack-relative addressing, *See* Addressing modes
Stack-relative deferred addressing, *See* Addressing modes
State, 549–550
State transition diagram, 346–347
    for SR flip-flop, 558
State transition table, 347
STBYTEA instruction, 198–200, 606–607
Stop instruction, 158
STOP instruction, 195–196, 216
Store byte instruction, 165–166
Store instruction, 159–160
STRO instruction, 194, 206–207, 215–217, 396, 417–419
Stroustrup, Bjarne, 70
Structured programming theorem, 257
Structures, 76–77, 310–314
SUBSP instruction, 238
Subtract instruction, 161–162
Subtracter, *See* Adder/subtracter
Subtraction, binary, 537–539
Superscalar machines, *See* Pipelining
Supervisor call, 420
sw instruction, MIPS, 630, 645
switch statement, 43–44, 297–300
Symbol trace tags, *See* Trace tags
Symbol tracer, 223
Symbols, 211–213, 217–218
Syntax, 331
Syntax tree, 341

T
T flip-flop, 563
Thompson, Ken, 460
Time out, 420
Timing diagram
    of clocked SR flip-flop
    of master-slave SR flip-flop
    of SR latch, 552
    of von Neumann cycle, 603
Token, 351
Trace tags, 223
    format, 223, 243, 288
    symbol, 243
Transmission time, 466
Trap handlers
    DECI, 408–414
    DECO, 414–417
    NOP, 406–407
    NOPn, 406–407
    STRO, 417–419
Traps, 396–419
    mechanism, 396–397
Tri-state buffer, 576, 579
Truth table, 491, 501
    and boolean expressions, 503–506
Turing, Alan, xxvii, 353
Two-level circuits, 506–508
Two's complement binary representation, 97–106
    range, 99–101
Type compatibility, 221–222

U
Unicode, 118
Unimplemented opcode, *See* Opcode
Uniprogramming, 448
Unstable state, *See* State
USB flash drive, 14

V
V bit, 105–106, 150–151, 532, 533, 599
Variables, *See also* C++ memory model
    attributes of, 36
    global, 36–39, 218–221, 263–267, 273–277
    local, 39–41, 241–243, 267–272, 277–281

Virtual memory, 458–459
von Neumann bugs, 174–175
von Neumann execution cycle
    MIPS, 626
    Pep/8 at level ISA3, 168–170, 205, 262–263
    Pep/8 at level LG1, 601–604

W
WAR data hazard, *See* Pipelining
Watson, Thomas J., 89, 225
while loop, 44–45, 249–250
Wilkes, Maurice V., 622

.WORD pseudo-op, 194, 198–200
Working set, 458

X
XOR gate, 498
XOR operator, 107–108, 283–284

Z
Z bit, 106, 150–151, 533, 599
Zero bit, *See* Z bit
Zero theorem, *See* Boolean algebra
Zuse, Konrad, 225